# A COMMENTARY

ON THE

GREEK TEXT OF THE EPISTLE OF PAUL

TO

THE GALATIANS

# A COMMENTARY

ON THE

# GREEK TEXT OF THE EPISTLE OF PAUL

TO

# THE EPHESIANS

JOHN EADIE, D.D., LL.D.

EDITED BY REV. W. YOUNG, M.A., GLASGOW

Eugene, Oregon

Wipf and Stock Publishers
199 West 8th Avenue, Suite 3
Eugene, Oregon 97401

A Commentary on the Greek Text of the Epistle of Paul to the Ephesians
By Eadie, John
ISBN: 1-57910-161-5
Publication date 10/5/1998

# PREFACE

THE object of this Commentary is the same as that stated in the prefaces to my previous volumes on Ephesians, Colossians, and Philippians. Nor do its form and style greatly vary from those earlier Works. Only it is humbly hoped, that longer and closer familiarity with the apostle's modes of thought and utterance may have conferred growing qualification to expound him. The one aim has been to ascertain the meaning through a careful analysis of the words. Grammatical and lexical investigation have in no way been spared, and neither labour nor time has been grudged in the momentous and responsible work of illustrating an epistle which contains so vivid an outline of evangelical truth. To find the sense has been my first step, and the next has been to unfold it with some degree of lucid and harmonious fulness. How far my purpose has been realized, the reader must judge; but, like every one who undertakes such a task, I am sadly conscious of falling far short of my own ideal. While I am not sensible of being warped by any theological system, as little am I aware of any deviation from recognised evangelical truth. One may differ in the interpretation of special words and phrases, and still hold the great articles of the Christian creed. I have gone over every clause with careful and conscientious effort to arrive at its sense, and without the smallest desire to find a meaning for it that may not jar with my theology. For "Theology," as Luther said, "is nothing else than a grammar and lexicon applied to the words of the Holy Spirit." I am well aware that scholastic theology has done no small damage to biblical interpretation, as may be seen in so many of the proof-texts attached to Confessions of Faith. The divine words of Scripture are "spirit and life," and have an inherent vitality, while the truth wedged into a system has often become as a mummy swathed up in numerous folds of polemical dialectics.

Several features of this epistle render its exposition somewhat difficult. In some sections, as in the address to Peter, the apostle's theology is but the expression of his own experience; brief digressions and interjected thoughts are often occurring; longer deviations are also met with before he works round more or less gradually to the main theme. The epistle is not like a dissertation, in which the personality of the author is merged; it is not his, but himself—his words welling up freshly from his heart as it was filled by varying emotions of surprise, disappointment, anger, sorrow, and hope. So, what he thought and felt was immediately written down before its freshness had faded; vindication suddenly passes into dogma, and dogma is humanized by intermingled appeals and warnings, —the rapid interchange of I, We, Thou, Ye, They, so lighting up the illustration that it glistens like the changing hues of a dove's neck. The entire letter, too, is pervaded by more than wonted fervour; the crisis being very perilous, his whole nature was moved to meet it, so as to deliver his beloved converts from its snares. One result is, that in his anxiety and haste, thought occasionally jostles thought; another idea presses upon him before the one under hand is brought to a formal conclusion; his faculty of mental association being so suggestive and fertile, that it pressed all around it into his service. These peculiarities show that the letter is an intensely human composition—the words of an earnest man writing in the fulness of his soul to other men, and naturally throwing himself on their affection; while there lies behind, in conscious combination, that divine authority which conferred upon him the apostleship in connection with the appearance and voice of the Saviour, and that divine training which opened up to him those sudden and perfect intuitions which he terms Revelation. The contents and circumstances of the epistle endeared it to Luther, for it fitted in wondrously to his similar experiences and trials, and he was wont to call it, as if in conjugal fondness, his Katherine von Bora. One may also cordially indorse the eulogy of Bunyan: "I prefer this book of Martin Luther's (except the Bible) before all the books that I have ever seen, as most fit for a wounded conscience." For the epistle unveils the relation of a sinner to the law which condemns him, and from which, therefore, he cannot hope for acceptance, and it opens up the great doctrine of justification by faith, which modern spiritualism either ignores or explains away. Its explicit theology is, that through faith one enjoys pardon and has the Spirit conferred upon him, so that he is free from legal yoke; while his life is characterized by a sanctified activity and self-denial, for grace is not in conflict with such obedience, but is rather the spring of it—death to the law being life to God. It is also a forewarning to all time of the danger of modifying the freeness and fulness of the gospel, and of allowing works or any element of mere ritual to be mixed up with the atoning death of the Son of God, as if to give it adaptation or perfection.

Any one writing on Galatians must acknowledge his obligation to the German exegets, Meyer, De Wette, Wieseler, and the others who are referred to in the last chapter of the Introduction. Nor can he forget to thank, among others at home, Bishop Ellicott, Dean Alford, and Prof. Lightfoot, for their learned and excellent labours. Each of these English commentaries has its distinctive merits; and my hope is, that this volume, while it has much in common with them, will be found to possess also an individual character and value, the result of unwearied and independent investigation. Ellicott is distinguished by close and uniform adherence to grammatical canon, without much expansion into exegesis; Alford, from the fact that his exposition extends to the whole New Testament, is of necessity brief and somewhat selective in his remarks; while Lightfoot himself says, that "in his explanatory notes such interpretations only are discussed as seemed at all events possibly right, or are generally received, or possess some historical interest;" and his collateral discussions occupy longer space than the proper exposition. I have endeavoured, on the other hand, to unite grammatical accuracy with some fulness of exegesis, giving, where it seemed necessary, a synopsis of discordant views, and showing their insufficiency, one-sidedness, ungrammatical basis, or want of harmony with the context; treating a doctrine historically, or throwing it into such a form as may remove objection; noticing now and then the views and arguments of Prof. Jowett; and, as a new feature in this volume, interspersing several separate Essays on important topics. Authorities have not been unduly heaped together; in the majority of cases, only the more prominent or representative names have been introduced. The text is for the most part, but not always, the seventh edition of Tischendorf, to whom we are indebted for the Codex Sinaiticus ℵ, and for his recent and exact edition of the Vatican Codex of the New Testament.

My thanks are due to Mr. John Cross, student of Balliol College, Oxford, for looking over the sheets as they passed through the press.

And now, as an earnest and honest attempt to discover the mind of the Spirit in His own blessed word, I humbly dedicate this volume to the Church of Christ.

JOHN EADIE

6 THORNVILLE TERRACE, HILLHEAD,
  GLASGOW, 1st January 1869.

# CONTENTS

Some of the longer illustrations and separate discussions referred to in the Preface are noted in the following brief Table of Contents:—

|  | PAGE |
|---|---|
| Abraham—in him, with him, | 238-240 |
| Accursed, | 26 |
| Adoption, | 298 |
| All things to all men, | 32-33 |
| Allegory, | 359-363 |
| Antagonism, inner, | 409-412 |
| Brothers of our Lord, neither step-brethren nor cousins—patristic and modern theories reviewed (a Dissertation), | 57-100 |
| Christ's self-oblation not a mere Jewish image, as Jowett affirms, | 12 |
| Clementines, | 199-200 |
| Cut off which trouble you—meaning of the phrase, | 397-400 |
| Druidism, | xxxiv-xxxix |
| Dying to the law—living to God, | 181-186 |
| Elements, | 295 |
| Faith, life by, | 244-246 |
| Fault, overtaken in, | 431-433 |
| Flesh, works of, | 415-420 |
| Four hundred years, | 259-261 |
| Galatia province—its history, | xiii |
|     Population of, Keltic in blood, | xx |
|     Introduction of the gospel into, | xxviii |
|     Epistle to—contents of, | xxxix |
|     „ genuineness of, | xlvii |
|     „ commentators on, | lxii |
| Hagar—Mount Sinai: allegory, | 364-368 |
| Harmony of Paul with the other apostles, | 123-135 |
| Israel of God, | 470 |
| James—brother; relationship discussed, | 57-100 |
| James, certain from, at Antioch, | 397 |
| Jowett on atonement, reviewed, | 12, 192-194 |
| Judaism, exclusiveness of, | 131 |

# CONTENTS

| | PAGE |
|---|---|
| Justification by faith, . . . . . | 166, 229-235 |
| Law, meaning of, . . . . . . | 163-164 |
| Law as instrument of death to itself, . . . . | 182 |
| Law 430 years after the promise, . . . . | 259 |
| Law, uses of, etc., . . . . . . | 262-269 |
| Law, not under—meaning of, . . . . . | 412-415 |
| Law a pædagogue, . . . . . . | 279-284 |
| Love the fulfilment of the law, . . . . | 402-406 |
| Letters, large, used by the apostle, . . . . | 454-459 |
| Mediator not of one—God is one, . . . . | 267-275 |
| Names of the Saviour—meaning and varying use, . . | 169-170 |
| Paganism, religious truth underlying, . . . . | 312 |
| Paul and Peter at Antioch—long correspondence between Jerome and Augustine on the subject (a Dissertation), . . | 198-213 |
| Putting on Christ, . . . . . . . | 286-287 |
| Revelation, its nature, . . . . . . . | 45 |
| Righteousness, . . . . . . . | 227-236 |
| Sarah, Jerusalem above, . . . . . . | 368-369 |
| Seasons, sacred—condemnation of keeping them, no argument against Christian Sabbath-keeping, . . . | 313-317 |
| Seed—harvest, . . . . . . . . | 444-448 |
| Seeds—Seed, . . . . . . . . | 256-258 |
| Sinners, found to be—meaning of the phrase, . . . | 176-177 |
| Son, minor, servant—Roman law, . . . . | 290-296 |
| Spirit, fruit of, . . . . . . . | 421-426 |
| Thorn in the flesh, the apostle's infirmity in Galatia (a Dissertation), . . . . . . . | 329-345 |
| Visits of the apostle to Galatia, . . . . | xxviii-xxxi |
| Visits of the apostle to Jerusalem (a Dissertation), . . | 133-145 |

# GREEK WORDS AND PHRASES

| | PAGE |
|---|---|
| Ἀββᾶ ὁ πατήρ, | 303 |
| Ἀδελφὸς τοῦ Κυρίου, | 57–100 |
| Αἰών, | 14 |
| Ἀκοή, | 220 |
| Ἁμαρτιῶν with ἀντὶ, περὶ, ὑπέρ, | 10 |
| Ἀνάθεμα, | 26–28 |
| Ἀπόστολος, | 95 |
| Ἀσέλγεια, | 416 |
| Βασκαίνω, | 215 |
| Διά, | 102, 320–325 |
| Διαθήκη, | 453 |
| Δικαιοσύνη, δικαιόω, | 229–235 |
| Δωρεάν, | 196 |
| Ἐγκράτεια, | 424 |
| Εἷς, ἑνός, | 269–274 |
| Ἐνδύομαι, | 286 |
| Ἔργα νόμου, | 163 |
| Ἐριθεία, | 418 |
| Ἕτερος, | 22 |
| Ζῆλος, | 417 |
| Ζῆν, ζωή, | 185–190 |
| Θυμός, | 417 |
| Κλίμα, | 53 |
| Λογίζομαι εἰς, | 228–229 |
| Μετατίθεσθαι, | 19 |
| Μυκτηρίζω, | 445 |
| Νόμος, | 163–164, 262–269 |
| Οἰκεῖος, | 453 |
| Οὐδὲ γάρ, | 35 |
| Παιδαγωγός, | 282 |
| Παράδοσις, | 41 |
| Πηλίκος, | 455 |
| Πίστις, | 244–246 |

|  | PAGE |
|---|---|
| Πρόσωπον λαμβάνειν, . . . . | 120 |
| Πρωτότοκος, . . . . . | 60 |
| Σκόλοψ, . . . . . | 335 |
| Σπέρμα, . . . . | 255–258 |
| Στίγμα, . . . . . | 472 |
| Στοιχεῖα, . . . . . | 295 |
| Στῦλος, *fig.* . . . . . | 126 |
| Σύν, ἐν, . . . . | 238–240 |
| Χρηστότης, . . . . . | 423 |

# THE LITERATURE OF THE EPISTLE

―o―

I —EPHESUS, AND THE PLANTING OF A CHRISTIAN CHURCH IN IT

EPHESUS, constituted the capital of proconsular Asia[1] in B.C. 129, had been the scene of successful labour on the part of the apostle. On his first and hurried visit to it, during his second missionary tour, his earnest efforts among his countrymen made such an impression and created such a spirit of inquiry, that they besought him to prolong his sojourn. Acts xviii. 19-21. But the pressing obligation of a religious vow compelled his departure, and he "sailed from Ephesus" under the promise of a speedy return, but left behind him Priscilla and Aquila, with whom the Alexandrian Apollos was soon associated. On his second visit, during his third missionary circuit, he stayed for at least two years and three months, or three years, as he himself names the term in his parting address at Miletus. Acts xx. 31. The apostle felt that Ephesus was a centre of vast influence—a key to the western provinces of Asia Minor. In writing from this city to the church at Corinth, when he speaks of his resolution to remain in it, he gives as his reason—" for a great door and effectual is opened unto me." 1 Cor xvi. 9. The gospel seems to have spread with rapidity, not only among the native citizens of Ephesus, but among the numerous strangers who landed on the quays of the Panormus and crowded its streets. It was the highway into Asia from Rome; its ships traded with the ports of Greece, Egypt, and the Levant;[2] and the Ionian cities poured their inquisitive population into it at its great annual festival in honour of Diana. Ephesus had been visited

[1] *Linquantur Phrygii—ad claras Asiæ volemus urbes.* Catullus, *Epig.* xlvi.
[2] Strabo, xiv. vol. iii. ed. Kramer, Berlin, 1848; Cellarius, *Notitiæ,* ii. 80.

by many illustrious men, and on very different errands. It had passed through many vicissitudes in earlier times, and had through its own capricious vacillations been pillaged by the armies of rival conquerors in succession ; but it was now to experience a greater revolution, for no blood was spilt, and at the hands of a mightier hero, for truth was his only weapon. Cicero is profuse in his compliments to the Ephesians for the welcome which they gave him as he landed at their harbour on his progress to his government of Cilicia (*Ep. ad Att.* v. 13); but the Christian herald met with no such ovation when he entered their city. So truculent and unscrupulous was the opposition which he at last encountered, that he tersely styles it "fighting with wild beasts at Ephesus," and a tumultuous and violent outrage which endangered his life hastened his ultimate departure. Scipio, on the eve of the battle of Pharsalia, had threatened to take possession of the vast sums hoarded up in the temple of Diana, and Mark Antony had exacted a nine years' tax in a two years' payment;[1] but Paul and his colleagues were declared on high authority "not to be robbers of churches:" for their object was to give and not to extort, yea, as he affirms, to circulate among the Gentiles "the unsearchable riches of Christ." The Ephesians had prided themselves in Alexander, a philosopher and mathematician, and they fondly surnamed him the "Light;" but his teaching had left the city in such spiritual gloom, that the apostle was obliged to say to them—"ye were sometimes darkness ; " and himself was the first unshaded luminary that rose on the benighted province. The poet Hipponax was born at Ephesus, but his caustic style led men to call him ὁ πικρός, "the bitter," and one of his envenomed sayings was, "There are two happy days in a man's life, the one when he gets his wife, and the other when he buries her." How unlike the genial soul of him of Tarsus, whose spirit so often dissolved in tears, and who has in "the well-couched words" of this epistle honoured, hallowed, and blessed the nuptial bond ! The famed painter Parrhasius, another boast of the Ionian capital, has indeed

---

[1] Article "Ephesus," Smith's *Dictionary of Greek and Roman Geography;* Perry, *De Rebus Ephesiorum*, Göttingen, 1837 ; or the full and interesting work of Guhl—*Ephesiaca:* Scripsit Ernestus Guhl, Phil. Dr. Berolini, 1843 ; Smith's *Dictionary of the Bible,* Art. "Ephesus."

received the high praises of Pliny (*Hist. Nat.* 35, 9) and Quintilian, for his works suggested "certain canons of proportion," and he has been hailed as a lawgiver in his art; but his voluptuous and self-indulgent habits were only equalled by his proverbial arrogance and conceit, for he claimed to be the recipient of Divine communications. *Institut.* xii. 10. On the other hand, the apostle possessed a genuine revelation from on high—no dim and dreary impressions, but lofty, glorious, and distinct intuitions; nay, his writings contain the germs of ethics and legislation for the world: but all the while he rated himself so low, that his self-denial was on a level with his humility, for he styles himself, in his letter to the townsmen of Parrhasius, "less than the least of all saints."

During his abode at Ephesus, the apostle prosecuted his work with peculiar skill and tact. The heathen forms of worship were not vulgarly attacked and abused, but the truth in Jesus was earnestly and successfully demonstrated and carried to many hearts; so that when the triumph of the gospel was so soon felt in the diminished sale of silver shrines, the preachers of a spiritual creed were formally absolved from the political crime of being "blasphemers of the goddess." The toil of the preacher was incessant. He taught "publicly and from house to house." Acts xx. 20. He went forth "bearing precious seed, weeping;" for "day and night" he warned them "with tears." Acts xx. 31. What ardour, earnestness, and intense aspiration; what a profound agitation of regrets and longings stirred him when "with many tears" he testified "both to the Jews and also to the Greeks repentance toward God and faith toward our Lord Jesus Christ"! By his assiduous labours the apostle founded and built up a large and prosperous church. The fierce and prolonged opposition which he encountered from "many adversaries" (1 Cor. xvi. 9), and the trials which befell him through "the lying in wait of the Jews" (Acts xx. 19), grieved, but did not alarm, his dauntless heart. The school of Tyrannus[1] became the scene of daily instruction and argument, and amidst the bitter railing and maledictions of the Jews, the masses of the heathen

---

[1] For various opinions about Tyrannus, see Witsius, *Meletemeta Leidensia*, § viii. 8; Suidas, *sub voce;* Neander, *Pflanzung*, i. 359; Vitringa, *de Vet. Synag.* p. 137.

population were reached, excited, and brought within the circle of evangelical influence. During this interval the new religion was also carried through the province, the outlying hamlets were visited, and the Ionian towns along the banks of the Cayster, over the defiles of Mount Tmolus, and up the valley of the Mæander, felt the power of the gospel; the rest of the "seven churches" were planted or watered, and "all they which dwelt in Asia heard the word of the Lord Jesus." Demetrius excited the alarm of his guild by the constrained admission—"Moreover, ye see and hear that not alone at Ephesus, but almost throughout all Asia—σχεδὸν πάσης τῆς 'Ασίας—this Paul hath persuaded and turned away much people." Acts xix. 26.

The eloquence of the apostle was powerfully aided at this crisis by his miracles—δυνάμεις οὐ τὰς τυχούσας. Surprising results sprang from the slightest contact with the wonder-worker; diseases fled at the approach of light articles of dress as the symbols or conductors of Divine power; and the evil spirits, formally acknowledging his supremacy, quailed before him, and were ejected from the possessed. These miracles, as has been well remarked, were of a kind calculated to suppress and bring into contempt the magical pretensions for which Ephesus was so famous. None of the Ephesian arts were employed. No charm was needed; no mystic scroll or engraven hieroglyph; there was no repetition of uncouth syllables, no elaborate initiation into any occult and intricate science by means of expensive books; but shawls and aprons—σουδάρια ἢ σιμικίνθια—were the easy and expeditious vehicles of healing agency. The superstitious "characters"—'Εφέσια γράμματα, so famous as popular amulets in the Eastern world, and which the Megalobyzi (Hesychius, *sub voce*) and Melissæ, the priests and priestesses of Artemis, had so carefully patronized—were shown by the contrast to be the most useless and stupid empiricism. Some wandering Jewish exorcists—a class which was common among the "dispersion"—attempted an imitation of one of the miracles, and used the name of Jesus as a charm. But the demoniac regarded such arrogant quackery as an insult, and took immediate vengeance on the impostors. This sudden and signal defeat of the seven sons of Sceva produced a deep and general sensation among the Jews and Greeks, and "the name of the Lord Jesus was magnified." Nay more, the followers of magic felt themselves so utterly exposed and outdone, that they "confessed and showed their deeds." They were forced to bow to a higher power, and acknowledge that their "curious arts "—τὰ περίεργα—were mere pretence and delusion. Books containing the description of the secret power and application of such a talisman, must have been eagerly sought and highly prized. Those who possessed them now felt their entire worthlessness, and, convinced of the inutility and sin of studying them or even keeping them, gathered them and burnt them "before all men."—an open act of homage to the new and mighty power which Christianity had established among them. The smoke and flame of those rolls were a sacrificial desecration to Artemis—worse and more alarming than the previous burning of her temple by the madman Herostratus. The numerous and costly books were then reckoned up in price, and their aggregate value was found to be above two thousand pounds sterling—ἀργυρίου μυριάδας πέντε. The sacred historian, after recording so decided a triumph, adds with hearty emphasis—" so mightily grew the word of God and prevailed." Acts xix. 20.

But "no small stir "—τάραχος οὐκ ὀλίγος—was made by the progress of Christianity and its victorious hostility to magic and idolatry. The temple of Diana or the oriental Artemis had long been regarded as one of the wonders of the world. The city claimed the title of νεωκόρος, a title which, meaning originally "temple-sweeper," was regarded at length as the highest honour, and often engraved on the current coinage. Guhl, p. 124; Conybeare and Howson, vol. ii. p. 76. The town-clerk artfully introduced the mention of this dignity into the commencement of his speech, for though all the Ionic Hellenes claimed an interest in the temple, and it was often named ὁ τῆς Ἀσίας ναός, yet Ephesus enjoyed the special function of being the guardian or sacristan of the edifice. The Ephesians were quite fanatical in their admiration and wardenship of the magnificent Ionic colonnades.[1] The quarries of Mount Prion had supplied the marble; the

---

[1] The asylum afforded by the temple—*impunitas asyla statuendi*—led to great abuses—interfering with the regular course of justice; and in the reign of

art and wealth of Ephesian citizens and the jewellery of Ephesian ladies had been plentifully contributed for its adornment; its hundred and twenty-seven graceful columns, some of them richly carved and coloured, were each the gift of a king; its doors, ceiling, and staircase were formed respectively of cypress, cedar, and vine-wood; it had an altar by Praxiteles and a picture by Apelles; and in its coffers reposed no little of the opulence of Western Asia. Thus Xenophon deposited in it the tithe—$\tau\grave{\eta}\nu$ $\delta\epsilon\kappa\acute{a}\tau\eta\nu$—which had been set apart at Athens from the sale of slaves at Cerasus. *Anab.* v. 34. A many-breasted idol of wood,[1] rude as an African fetich, was worshipped in its shrine, in some portion of which a meteoric stone may have been inserted, the token of its being "the image that fell from Jupiter"—$\tau o\hat{v}$ $\delta\iota o\pi\epsilon\tau o\hat{v}\varsigma$.[2] Still further, a flourishing trade was carried on in the manufacture of silver shrines—$\nu a o\acute{\iota}$—or models of a portion of the temple. These are often referred to by ancient writers, and as few strangers seem to have left Ephesus without such a memorial of their visit, this artistic " business brought no small gain to the craftsmen." But the spread of Christianity was fast destroying such gross and material superstition and idolatry, for one of its first lessons was, as Demetrius rightly declared—"they be no gods which are made with hands." The shrewd craftsman summoned together his brethren of the same occupation—$\tau\epsilon\chi\nu\hat{\iota}\tau a\iota$, $\dot{\epsilon}\rho\gamma\acute{a}\tau a\iota$—laid the matter before them, represented the certain ruin of their manufacture, and the speedy extinction of the worship of Diana of Ephesus. The trade was seized with a panic, and raised the uproarious shout—" Great is Diana of the Ephesians!" "The whole city was filled with confusion." A mob was gathered and seemed on the eve of effecting what Demetrius contemplated, the expulsion or assassination of the apostle and his coadjutors by lawless violence, so that no one could be singled out or punished for the outrage. It would seem, too, that this tumult took place at that season of the year—the month of May,

---

Tiberius that city was heard by its delegates—*legati*—before the Roman senate in defence of the sacredness of the edifice. —Tacitus, *Annal.* iii, 60.

[1] Πολύμαστον—*multimammiam*, Jerome, *Procem. in Ep. ad Ephes.*

[2] Creuzer, *Symbolik*, ii. 113; Euripides, *Iphig. in Taur.* 977; Ovid, *Fasti*, iii. 72; Dionys. Halicar. ii. 71.

sacred to Diana, the period of the Pan-Ionic games—when a vast concourse of strangers had crowded into Ephesus, so that the masses were the more easily alarmed and collected. The *émeute* was so sudden, that "the most part knew not wherefore they had come together." As usual on such occasions in the Greek cities, the rush was to the theatre, to receive information of the cause and character of the outbreak. (*Theatrum ubi consultare mos est.* Tacitus, *Hist.* ii. 80.) Two of Paul's companions were seized by the crowd, and the apostle, who had escaped, would himself have very willingly gone in—εἰς τὸν δῆμον—and faced the angry and clamorous rabble, if the disciples, seconded by some of the Asiarchs or presidents of the games, who befriended him, had not prevented him. A Jew named Alexander, probably the "coppersmith," and, as a Jew, well known to be an opponent of idolatry, strove to address the meeting—ἀπολογεῖσθαι τῷ δήμῳ—probably to vindicate his own race, who had been long settled in Ephesus, from being the cause of the disturbance, and to cast all the blame upon the Christians. But his appearance was the signal for renewed clamour, and for two hours the theatre resounded with the fanatical yell—"Great is Diana of the Ephesians." The town-clerk or recorder—γραμματεύς—a magistrate of high standing and multifarious and responsible functions in these cities, had the dexterity to pacify and dismiss the rioters, first, by an ingenious admixture of flattery, and then by sound legal advice, telling them that the law was open, that the great Ephesian assize was going on—ἀγοραῖοι ἄγονται—and that all charges might be formally determined before the sitting tribunal—"and there are deputies—καὶ ἀνθύπατοί εἰσιν; while other matters might be determined—ἐν τῷ ἐννόμῳ ἐκκλησίᾳ—in the lawful assembly." Such a scene could not fail to excite more inquiry into the principles of the new religion, and bring more converts within its pale. The Divine traveller immediately afterwards left the city. After visiting Greece, he sailed for Jerusalem, and touching at Miletus, he sent for the presbyters of the Ephesian church, and delivered to them the solemn parting charge recorded in Acts xx. 18-35.

[1] Conybeare and Howson, vol. ii. pp. 80, 81.

## II — TITLE AND DESTINATION OF THE EPISTLE

It can surely be no matter of wonder that the apostle should afterwards correspond with a community which had such an origin and history as the church of Christ in Ephesus.[1] We cannot sympathize with Conybeare in his remark, that it "is a mysterious dispensation of Providence" that Paul's epistle to the metropolitan church at Ephesus "should not have been preserved to us."[2] For we believe that it has been preserved, and that we have it rightly named in the present canon of the New Testament. And such is the general testimony of the early church.

Great stress cannot be laid on the evidence of Ignatius. In the twelfth chapter of his own epistle to the Ephesians, according to the longer reading, there is no distinct reference to the Pauline epistle, though there is a high probability of it; but there is an allusion to the apostle, and an intimation that ἐν πάσῃ ἐπιστολῇ—"in the whole epistle," he makes mention of them. But in the briefer form of the Ignatian composition —that found in a Syriac version—the entire chapter, with the one before and after it, is left out, and, according to the high authority of Bunsen[3] and Cureton,[4] they are all three decidedly spurious. Yet even in the Syriac version the diction is taken, to a great extent, from the canonical book. It abounds in such resemblances, that one cannot help thinking that Ignatius, writing to Ephesus, thought it an appropriate beauty to enrich his letter with numerous forms of thought, style, and imagery, from that epistle which an inspired correspondent had once sent to the church in the same city. According to one recension, we have allusions to Eph. i. 1 in cap. ix., and to iv. 4 in cap. vi.

Irenæus, in the second century, has numerous references to the epistle, and prefaces a quotation from Eph. v. 30 by these words—καθὼς ὁ μακάριος Παῦλός φησιν, ἐν τῇ πρὸς Ἐφεσίους ἐπιστολῇ—"as the blessed Paul says in his epistle to the

---

[1] Gude, *Comment. de Eccles. Ephes. Statu*, Leips. 1732.
[2] Conybeare and Howson, vol. ii. p. 404, note.
[3] *Ignatius von Antiochien und Seine Zeit*, p. 23, Hamburg, 1847.
[4] *Corpus Ignatianum*, etc., by William Cureton, M.A., F.R.S., London, 1849.

Ephesians." Again, quoting Eph. i. 7, ii. 13-15, he begins by affirming—*quomodo apostolus Ephesiis dicit;* and similarly does he characterize Eph. i. 13—*in epistola quæ ad Ephesios est, dicens.* Again, referring to v. 13, he says, τοῦτο δὲ καὶ ὁ Παῦλος λέγει. *Adversus Hæres.*, lib. v. pp. 104, 718, 734, 756.

Nor is the testimony of Clement of Alexandria, later in the same century, less decisive; for, in the fourth book of his *Stromata,* quoting Eph. v. 21, he says—διὸ καὶ ἐν τῇ πρὸς Ἐφεσίους γράφει; and in his *Pædagogue* he introduces a citation from Eph. iv. 13, 14, by a similar formula—Ἐφεσίοις γραφῶν. *Opera,* pp. 499, 88, Colon. 1688. His numerous other allusions refer it plainly to the Apostle Paul.

In the next century we find Origen, in his book against Celsus, referring to the Epistle to the Ephesians, as first in order, and then to the Epistles to the Colossians, Thessalonians, Philippians, and Romans, and speaking of all these compositions as the words of Paul—τοὺς Παύλου λόγους. *Contra Celsum,* lib. iii. p. 122, ed. Spencer, Cantabrigiæ, 1677. Again, in his tract *On Prayer,* he expressly refers to a statement—ἐν τῇ πρὸς Ἐφεσίους.

The witness of Tertullian is in perfect agreement. For example, in his book *De Monogamia,* cap. v., he says—*Dicit apostolus, ad Ephesios scribens,* quoting Eph. i. 10. Again, in the thirty-sixth chapter of his *De Præscriptionibus,* his appeal is in the following terms—*Age jam, qui voles curiositatem melius exercere in negotio salutis tuæ, percurre ecclesias apostolicas, apud quas ipsæ adhuc cathedræ apostolorum suis locis præsident, apud quas ipsæ authenticæ litteræ eorum recitantur . . . si potes in Asiam tendere, habes Ephesum.* Lastly, in lib. iv. cap. 5 of his work against Marcion, we find him saying—*Videamus, quid legant Philippenses, Thessalonicenses, Ephesii.* *Opera,* vol. i. p. 767, vol. ii. pp. 33, 165, ed. Oehler, 1854.

Cyprian, in the next age, is no less lucid; for, in the seventh chapter of the third book of his *Testimonies,* he uses this language—*Paulus apostolus ad Ephesios;* quoting iv. 30, 31, and in his seventy-fifth epistle he records his opinion thus —*sed et Paulus apostolus hoc idem adhuc apertius et clarius manifestans ad Ephesios scribit et dicit, Christus dilexit ecclesiam;* v. 25. *Opera,* pp. 280 and 133, ed. Paris, 1836.

Such is the verdict of the ancient church. But though its

testimony is so decisive, it is not unanimous. Still, this diversity of opinion only confirms the evidence of the vast majority. In consequence, however, of this exception, the question whether the common title to this epistle be the correct one, has been matter of prolonged controversy, and a variety of opinion still exists among expositors and critics. Apart from the evidence already adduced, the settlement of the question depends, to a great extent, on the idea formed of the genuineness of the words ἐν Ἐφέσῳ in the first verse. The old versions are unanimous in their favour, and among existing MSS. only three throw any doubt upon them. "But what are these among so many?" In Codex 67, they have been deleted by some later correctionist. In Codex B they stand on the margin, as an apparent supplement of the discovered omission by the original copyist, according to Hug;[1] but according to Tischendorf, on whose critical acumen and experience we place a higher confidence, they are an evident emendation from a second and subsequent hand.[2] In the Codex Sinaiticus yet unpublished, they are absent, but supplied in like manner by a later hand.[3]

Origen, as quoted in Cramer's *Catena*, says—ἐπὶ μόνων Ἐφεσίων εὕρομεν κείμενον, τὸ "τοῖς ἁγίοις τοῖς οὖσι·" καὶ ζητοῦμεν εἰ μὴ παρέλκει προσκείμενον τὸ "τοῖς ἁγίοις τοῖς οὖσι," τί δύναται σημαίνειν. ὅρα οὖν εἰ μὴ ὥσπερ ἐν τῇ Ἐξόδῳ ὄνομα φησιν ἑαυτοῦ ὁ χρηματίζων Μωσεῖ τὸ ὤν, οὕτως οἱ μετέχοντες τοῦ ὄντος, γίνονται ὄντες, καλούμενοι οἱονεὶ ἐκ τοῦ

---

[1] "Juxta tantum in margine a prima manu, pari elegantia et assiduitate ac reliqua pars operis . . . sed charactere paullo exiliori."—*De Antiq. Cod. Vat. Commentatio*, 1810.

[2] "Manu alte a posteriore in margine ista suppleta sunt."—*Novum Test. in loc.* seventh ed. Also more fully in *Studien und Kritiken*, 1846, p. 133.

[3] Tischendorf says—"Multi sunt qui codicem post ipsum scriptorem attigerunt. Alii certos tantum libros, alii totum codicem vel certe pleraque recensuerunt, rursus alii non tam recensendo textui quam supplementis quibusdam studuerunt, ut Ammonii Eusebiique numeris addendis. Qua de re accuratiora in Prolegomenis dabimus. Is qui h. l. εν εφεσω supplevit, item ad finem evang. Lucæ και ανιφιρ. ως τον ουρανον, totum N. T. recensuit. Sæculo vixisse videtur sexto exeunte vel septimo atque in numero correctorum eorum qui imprimis in censum veniunt quartum locum occupat. In brevi adnotatione critica textui paginarum duodeviginti addita nobis dicitur corr. Ex re enim esse visum est ut correctores et ætate et scriptura et indole cognati uno eodemque numero comprehendantur, nec nisi ubi certo distingui possunt singulatim indicentur." *Notitia Editionis Codicis Bibliorum Sinaitici*, page 19, Lipsiæ, 1860.

μὴ εἶναι εἰς τὸ εἶναι· "ἐξελέξατο γὰρ ὁ Θεὸς τὰ μὴ ὄντα," φησὶν ὁ αὐτὸς Παῦλος, "ἵνα τὰ ὄντα καταργήσῃ."—" We found the phrase 'to the saints that are,' occurring only in the case of the Ephesians, and we inquire what its meaning may be. Observe then whether, as He who revealed His name to Moses in Exodus calls His name I AM, so they who are partakers of the I am, are those who be, being called out of non-existence into existence—for God, as Paul himself says, chose the things that are not that He might destroy the things that are." This, however, must be compared with the references in Origen previously given by us.

The declaration of Basil of Cappadocia, not unlike that of Origen, has often been quoted and discussed. The object of Basil is to show that the Son of God cannot be said to be ἐξ οὐκ ὄντων, because He is ὄντως ὤν; for while the Gentiles who know Him not are called οὐκ ὄντα, His own people are expressly named οἱ ὄντες. The following is his proof from Scripture, and he must have been sadly in lack of argument when he could resort to it:[1] Ἀλλὰ καὶ τοῖς Ἐφεσίοις ἐπιστέλλων ὡς γνησίως ἡνωμένοις τῷ ὄντι δι' ἐπιγνώσεως, ὄντας αὐτοὺς ἰδιαζόντως ὠνόμασεν, εἰπών· τοῖς ἁγίοις τοῖς οὖσι καὶ πιστοῖς ἐν Χριστῷ Ἰησοῦ· οὕτω γὰρ καὶ οἱ πρὸ ἡμῶν παραδεδώκασι, καὶ ἡμεῖς ἐν τοῖς παλαιοῖς τῶν ἀντιγράφων εὑρήκαμεν. "But also writing to the Ephesians, as being truly united by knowledge to Him WHO IS ; he called them in a special sense THOSE WHO ARE, saying, To the saints τοῖς οὖσι, WHO ARE, and the faithful in Christ Jesus. For thus those before us have transmitted it, and we have found it in the ancient copies." No little refinement and subtlety have been employed in the analysis of these words. It does not much concern the critical fact which Basil states, whether, with L'Enfant, Wolf, and Lardner, we understand him as basing his argument on the article τοῖς; or whether, with Wiggers, we regard him as discovering his mystical exegesis in the participle οὖσιν; or whether, with Michaelis and Koppe, we hold that τοῖς οὖσι is the phrase on which the absurd emphasis is placed. The fact is plain, that in ancient MSS. handed down from previous centuries, he had found the first verse without the words ἐν Ἐφέσῳ, and thus—τοῖς οὖσι

[1] *Contra Eunomium*, lib. ii. cap. 19 ; *Opera*, ed. Garnier, tom. i. pp. 254, 255.

καὶ πιστοῖς. Had the phrase ἐν Ἐφέσῳ occurred in the clause, Basil's ingenuity could have found neither impulse nor pabulum; and there is no proof that it ever stood in the verse in any other position than that occupied by it in the majority of Codices. Saints, says the father, are there called οἱ ὄντες—they who are—that is, persons in actual possession of spiritual existence; and they receive this appellation after Him WHO IS—ὁ ὤν—the Being of pure and underived essence. The omission of the words ἐν Ἐφέσῳ could only warrant such a phantasy, for otherwise the statement might have been founded as well on the initial verses of the Epistles to Rome or Philippi. The sum of Basil's statement is, that in the early copies which he had consulted, ἐν Ἐφέσῳ was wanting; but the inference is, that the words existed in the copies then in common circulation, nay, that the father himself looked upon the epistle as inscribed to the church in Ephesus. At the same time, Basil does not state how many old copies he saw, nor in what countries they originated, nor what was their general character for accuracy. The corroborative assertion that he himself had seen them, would seem to indicate that they were neither numerous nor of easy access. He does not appeal to the received and ordinary reading of the verse, but prides himself on a various reading which he had discovered in ancient copies, and which does not seem to have been commonly known, and he finally interposes his own personal inspection and veracity as the only vouchers of his declaration.

The statement of Jerome is not dissimilar. In his Commentary on Eph. i. 1, he says — *Quidam curiosius quam necesse est, putant ex eo, quod Moysi dictum sit: Hæc dices filiis Israel, qui est misit me, etiam eos, qui Ephesi sunt, sancti et fideles essentiæ vocabulo nuncupatos, ut ab eo qui est, hi qui sunt appellentur. Alii vero simpliciter non ad eos qui sunt, sed qui Ephesi sancti et fideles sunt, scriptum arbitrantur. Opera*, ed. Vallarsius, tom. vii. p. 543. "Some, with an excessive refinement, think from what was said to Moses— 'These words shalt thou say to the children of Israel, HE WHO IS, has sent me'—that the saints and faithful at Ephesus are addressed by a term descriptive of essence, as if from him WHO IS, they had been named THEY WHO ARE. Others, indeed, suppose that the epistle was written not simply to those WHO

ARE, but to those WHO ARE AT EPHESUS, saints and faithful." The language of Jerome does not warrant, so explicitly as that of Basil, the supposition that he found any copies wanting the words, in Ephesus. At the same time, it is a strange misapprehension of Böttger (*Beiträge*, etc. iii. p. 37) and Olshausen to imagine, that Jerome did not himself adopt the common reading, when he expressly delivers his opinion in the very quotation. One would almost think, with Meyer, that Jerome speaks of persons who gave οὖσι a pregnant sense, though it stood in connection with ἐν 'Εφέσῳ; but the origination of such an exegesis in this verse only, and in none others of identical phraseology, surpasses our comprehension for its absurdity and caprice. Probably Jerome records the mere fact or existence of such an interpretation, though he might not have seen, and certainly does not mention, any MSS. on whose peculiar omission it might have been founded. He would, in all likelihood, have pointed out the origin of the quaint exegesis from the absence of the local designation, if he had known it; and the apparent *curiositas* of the explanation lay in the fact, that τοῖς οὖσιν had an evident and natural connection with ἐν 'Εφέσῳ. Such a hypothesis appears to be warranted by the order in which he arranges the words in his Latin version—*qui Ephesi sunt sancti et fideles*—as if in order to give countenance to the alleged interpretation, the words ἐν 'Εφέσῳ had, in construing the sentence, been dislodged from their proper position. The probability is, however, that Jerome refers to the passage from Origen already quoted; for in his preface he says—*Illud quoque in prefatione commoneo ut sciatis Origenem tria volumina in hanc epistolam conscripsisse, quem et nos ex parte sequuti sumus.*

The general unanimity of the ancient church is also seen in the peculiar and offensive prominence which was given to Marcion's fabrication. This heresiarch, among his other interpolations, altered the title of the epistle, and addressed it to the Laodiceans—πρὸς Λαοδικέας. One of the most acute and vigorous of the ancient fathers thus describes and brands the forgery—*Prætereo hic et de aliâ epistolâ quam nos ad* Ephesios *præscriptam habemus, hæretici vero ad* Laodicenos. . . . *Ecclesiæ quidem veritate epistolam istam ad Ephesios habemus emissam, non ad Laodicenos: sed Marcion ei* titulum *aliquando interpolare gestiit, quasi et in isto diligentissimus explorator. Nihil autem de titulis interest, cum ad omnes apostolus scripserit, dum ad quosdam*—" I pass by in this place another epistle in our possession addressed to the Ephesians, but the heretics have inscribed it to the Laodiceans. . . . According to the true testimony of the church, we hold this epistle to have been sent to the Ephesians. But Marcion sometimes had a strong itching to change the title, as if in that matter he had been a very diligent inquirer. The question about titles is of no great moment, since the apostle wrote to all when he wrote to some." *Advers. Marcion,* lib. v. cap. 11, 17; *Opera,* ed. Oehler, vol. ii. pp. 309, 323. We think it a strained inference on the part of Meyer, that Tertullian did not read ἐν Ἐφέσῳ in his copies, since in such a case he would have appealed not to the testimony of the church, but to the words of the sacred text. But the testimony of the church and the testimony of the text were really identical, for it was only on the text as preserved by the church that her testimony could be intelligently based. By "title" in the preceding extract we understand, in accordance with Tertullian's *usus loquendi,* the superscription prefixed to the epistle, not the address contained in ver. 1. But if Marcion changed the extra-textual title, consistency must soon have obliged him also to alter the reading of the salutation, and change ἐν Ἐφέσῳ into ἐν Λαοδικείᾳ. Tertullian, then, means to say, that Marcion in his critical tamperings had interfered with the constant and universal title of this epistle, and that he did this as the avowed result of minute inquiry and antiquarian research (*quasi diligentissimus explorator*). We know not on what his judgment was founded. He may have found the epistle in circulation at Laodicea, or, as Pamelius conjectures in his notes on Tertullian, it was the interpretation he attached to Col. iv. 16—" And when this epistle is read among you, cause that it be read also in the church of the Laodiceans; and that ye likewise read the epistle from Laodicea." Marcion's view was not only in contradiction of the whole church, but his other literary misdemeanours throw a suspicion at once on the motives of his procedure, and on the sobriety and trustworthiness of his judgment.

The result of the whole inquiry is, that in some ancient

copies the words ἐν ’Εφέσῳ did not exist, and that some theologians built a doctrine upon the words of the clause as read with the omission; that the omission was not justified by the current MSS. in the third and fourth centuries; that the judgment of the ancient church, with such slight exceptions, regarded the epistle as inscribed to the Ephesians; and that one noted heretic imagined that the current title should be changed, and the inspired letter inscribed to the Laodiceans.

It seems strange indeed that this last opinion should have been adopted by any succeeding writers. Yet we find that several critics hold the view that the epistle was meant for the church at Laodicea, among whom are Grotius, Mill, du Pin, Wall, Archbishop Wake, the younger Vitringa,[1] Venema, Crellius, Wetstein, Pierce, Benson, Whiston, Paley,[2] Greswell,[3] Huth,[4] Holzhausen, Räbiger,[5] and Constable.[6] The only plausible argument for the theory is, that there are no personal references or salutations in the epistle—a circumstance supposed to be scarcely compatible with the idea of its being sent to Ephesus, a city in which Paul had lived and laboured, but quite in harmony with the notion of an epistle to the church in Laodicea, in which the apostle is supposed to have been a stranger. But such a hypothesis cannot set aside the all but unanimous voice of Christian antiquity. And how came it that out of all copies Laodicea has dropt, and that it is found in no early MS. or version, and that no ancient critic but Marcion ever dreamed of exchanging the local terms? Again, if Col. iv. 16 be appealed to in the phrase "the Epistle from Laodicea," then if that is to be identified with the present Ephesian letter, it must have been written long prior to the epistle to Colosse—a conjecture at variance with many internal proofs and allusions; for the so-called epistle to Ephesus and that to Colosse were composed about the same period, and despatched by the same trusty messenger, Tychicus. And how should the apostle command the Colossian church to

---

[1] *Dissertatio de genuino titulo epistolæ D. P. quæ vulgo inscribitur ad Ephesios*, pp. 247–379. Franequeræ, 1731.
[2] *Horæ Paulinæ*, c. vi.
[3] *Dissertations upon a Harmony of the Gospels*, vol. iv. pp. 208, 217, sec.
[4] *Epistola ex Laodicea in encyclica ad Ephesios asservata*. Erlang. 1751.
[5] *De Christologia Paulina*, p. 47. Vratislaviæ, 1852.
[6] *Essays Critical and Theological*, p. 77. London, 1852.

salute in his name the brethren of Laodicea, if the Laodiceans had received such a communication by the very same messenger who carried the letter to Colosse, and who was charged to give them all minute particulars as to the apostle's welfare and thus comfort their hearts?

It is also to be borne in mind, that Marcion does not fully bear out this theory usually traced to him; for according to Epiphanius, while he had some parts, μέρη, of an epistle to the Laodiceans, he put into his canon as the seventh of Paul's epistles that to the Ephesians—ἑβδόμη πρὸς 'Εφεσίους. *Hæres.*, xlii. cap. 9, p. 310, ed. Petavius; Paris, 1662. Whatever may be meant, in Col. iv. 16, by the epistle from Laodicea, it is plain that it cannot, as Stier supposes, be the epistle before us; and plainer still, that it cannot be the brief and tasteless forgery which now passes under the name of an Epistle to the Laodiceans.

Another hypothesis which has received a very large support is, that the epistle is an encyclical letter—a species of inspired circular not meant for any special church, but for a variety of connected communities. The idea was originated by Usher, in his *Annales Veteris et Novi Testamenti*, under the year 64 A.D.—*Ubi notandum, in antiquis nonnullis codicibus (ut ex Basilii libro ii. adversùs Eunomium, et Hieronymi in hunc Apostoli locum commentario, apparet) generatim inscriptam fuisse hanc epistolam* τοῖς ἁγίοις, τοῖς οὖσι, καὶ πιστοῖς ἐν Χριστῷ 'Ιησοῦ, *vel (ut in litterarum encyclicarum descriptione fieri solebat)* sanctis qui sunt . . . . *et fidelibus in Christo Jesu, ac si Ephesum primò, ut præcipuam Asiæ metropolim, missa ea fuisset; transmittenda inde ad reliquas (intersertis singularum nominibus) ejusdem provinciæ ecclesias: ad quarum aliquas, quas Paulus ipse nunquam viderat, illa ipsius verba potissimùm spectaverint.* His idea has been followed by a whole host of scholars and critics, by Garnier in his note to the place cited in Basil,[1] by Ziegler,[2] Hänlein,[3] Justi,[4] and Schmid, by such writers of "Introductions" as Michaelis,

[1] The treatises by the most of these authors are well known: some of them may be noted.
[2] In *Henke's Magazin*, iv. 2, p. 225.
[3] *Commentat. de lectoribus, quibus epistola Pauli quæ ad Ephesios missa traditur, vere scripta esse videatur.* Erlang. 1797.
[4] *Vermischte Behandlungen*, vol. ii. p. 81.

Eichhorn, Bertholdt, Credner, Schneckenburger, Hug, Feilmoser, Cellerier, Guerike, Horne, Böttger, Schott, and Neudecker, also by Neander, Hemsen, Schrader, Lünemann, Anger,[1] Wiggers, Conybeare, and Burton, and by the commentators Bengel, Harless, Boehmer, Zachariae, Rückert, Matthies, Olshausen, Baumgarten-Crusius, Bloomfield, Meier, Macknight, Stier, and Bisping. These authors agree generally that Ephesus was not the exclusive recipient of the epistle, and the majority of them incline, in the face of all evidence, to hold the words ἐν ’Εφέσῳ as a spurious interpolation. Others, such as Beza, Turner, Harless, Boehmer, Schott, Lünemann,[2] Wiggers,[3] Schrader, Ellicott, Schaff,[4] and Hodge, reject this line of proof, and build their argument on another foundation—believing that Ephesus received the epistle, but that some daughter-churches in the immediate vicinity were associated with it. To such an opinion there is less objection, though, while it seems to solve some difficulties, it suggests others. The advocates of the encyclical character of the epistle are not agreed among themselves. Many suppose that the apostle left a blank space—τοῖς οὖσιν . . . καὶ πιστοῖς, and that the name of the intended place was filled in either by Paul himself in the several copies ere they were despatched, or by Tychicus as opportunity prompted, or that copies were transcribed in Ephesus with the proper address inserted in each. Each of these hypotheses is shaped to serve an end—to explain why so many Codices have ἐν ’Εφέσῳ, and none ἐν Λαοδικείᾳ. There are some who believe that no blank room was originally left at all, but that the sentence is in itself complete. With such an extraordinary view, the meaning differs according as οὖσιν is joined to the preceding ἁγίοις or the following πιστοῖς. Meier and Credner join οὖσιν to πιστοῖς, and render *den Heiligen, die auch getreu sind*—" the saints who are also faithful," an interpretation which cannot be sustained. See under i. 1, pp. 3, 4. Credner propounds a worse view, and regards πιστοῖς as signifying genuine Pauline Christians. Schnecken-

---

[1] *Über den Laodicenerbrief,* Leipz. 1843, replied to in Zeller's *Theol. Jahrbuch* for 1844, p. 199.

[2] *De epistolæ quam Paulus ad Ephesios dedisse perhibetur authentia, primis lectoribus, argumento summo ac consilio.* Götting. 1842.

[3] *Studien und Kritiken,* 1841-42, p. 423.

[4] *History of the Apostolic Church,* vol. ii. p. 380. Edinburgh, 1854.

burger and Matthies connect οὖσιν with ἁγίοις, the latter giving a sense—*welche da sind*—which Bengel had already advanced — *qui præsto sunt* — that is, as he explains it, in the places which Tychicus was under commission to visit. Schneckenburger renders to the saints who are really so— *den Heiligen die es in der That sind.* Gresswell holds a similar view; but the numerous so-called similar Greek formulæ which he adduces are not in point. Now the usual exordiums of the apostle are fatal to these hypotheses, for in them not only is the place of destination named, even though, as in the case of Galatia, it include a province or circuit of churches, but the participle is simply used along with the local name and without pregnant emphasis.

How the words ἐν 'Εφέσῳ came to be dropt out of the text, as Basil affirms, we know not. Perhaps some early copyist, seeing the general nature of the epistle, left out the formula, to give it the aspect of universal applicability. Or, the churches "in Asia" claiming an interest in the apostle and his letters might have copies without the special local designation; or, as Wieseler suggests, the tendency of the second century to take away personal reference out of the New Testament, may have led to the omission, just as the words ἐν 'Ρώμῃ are left out in several MSS. of the Epistle to the Romans, i. 7.

External evidence is thus wholly against the notion that either Laodicea by itself, or Ephesus with a noted cluster of sister communities, was the designed and formal recipient of this epistle. Nor is the result of internal proof more in favour of such hypotheses. It is argued that the apostle sends no greetings to Ephesus—a very strange omission, as he had laboured there three years, and must have known personally the majority of the members of the church. But the argument is two-edged, for Paul's long years of labour at Ephesus must have made him acquainted with so many Christian people there, that their very number may have prevented him from sending any salutation. A roll far longer than the epistle itself might have been filled, and yet the list would have by no means been exhausted. Omissions might have given offence, and Tychicus, who was from the same province, seems to have been charged with all such private business. In churches where the apostles knew only a few prominent individuals, they are greeted, as in Philippi, Colosse, Rome, and Corinth. It is also objected that an air of distance pervades the epistle, and that it indicates nothing of that familiarity which the previous three years' residence must certainly have induced. This idea is no novelty. Theodoret, in the preface to his *Exposition*, refers to some who were led to suppose from such language that Paul wrote this letter before he had visited the Ephesians at all. Euthalius[1] and the author of the Synopsis of sacred Scripture found in the works of Athanasius,[2] express a similar opinion. To such statements, either in their simple or more exaggerated form, we certainly demur, as the proofs adduced in their behalf do by no means sustain them. The expression in i. 15 has been usually fixed on—"Wherefore I also, after I heard of your faith in the Lord Jesus, and love unto all the saints." But this statement is no proof that Paul was a stranger. It rather indicates the reverse, as may be seen by consulting our comment on the place. Dr. Davidson and others instance the similar use of ἀκούσας in the letter to Philemon, so that the inference based on the use of the term in Ephesians cannot be justified. The same remarks apply to other passages commonly adduced to prove the encyclical nature of the Ephesian epistle. In iii. 2 the apostle says— εἴγε ἠκούσατε, rendered by some—"if ye have heard of the dispensation of grace committed to me for you." But the phraseology does not express doubt. Constable maintains that εἴγε everywhere has the idea of doubt attached to it. *Essays*, p. 90. But the statement is unguarded, as the particle puts the matter in a hypothetical shape, and by its use and position takes for granted the truth of what is stated or assumed. Klotz-Devarius, ii. p. 308. Constable also refers to the commendation given to Tychicus, vi. 21, as if that implied that he was a stranger. But Tychicus might be of Asia, and yet not of Ephesus—while the eulogy pronounced upon him is a species of warrant, that whatever he said about the apostle and his private affairs to them might be absolutely credited; for he was intimate with the apostle—"beloved"—and he was trusty. On the other hand, there are not a few distinct

---

[1] Zacagnii, *Collectanea Monumentorum Vet. Eccles.* etc. p. 524. Paris, 1698.
[2] Athanasius, *Opera*, tom. iii. p. 191, ed. Benedict. Paris, 1698.

intimations of the writer's personal knowledge of those whom he addressed. He writes to them as persons whom he knew as sealed with the Spirit, as exhibiting the possession of faith and love—the Gentile portion of them as one with the believing Jews—as so well acquainted with him that they were prone to faint at his sufferings, as having enjoyed distinct and plenary instruction, and as taking such a deep interest in his personal affairs, that they would be comforted by the appearance of Tychicus. And these statements are also direct language, pointedly addressed to one community, and not vaguely to an assemblage of churches, unless they were regarded as one with it. In short, the letter is intended for advanced Christians; and such surely were those, so many of whom had for so long a period enjoyed instruction from the apostle's own lips. Some years had elapsed since he had been at Ephesus, and perhaps on that account personal reminiscences were not inserted into the communication. "Nothing," as Dr. Davidson says, " is more unjust than to restrict the apostle of the Gentiles, in his writings, to one unvarying method." The opinion of Wetstein, Lünemann, and de Wette, that this epistle is written to Gentile converts, while the church at Ephesus was composed principally of Jews, is not according to the facts of the history, nor according to the language of the epistle. It is true that the first members of that church were Jews, and that the twelve converted disciples of John seem to have formed its nucleus. But was not Paul forced to leave the synagogue? and what raised the ferment about the falling off in the sale of shrines? Still we cannot accede to some commentators and Dr. Davidson, that when Paul, in the first chapter, uses ἡμεῖς he means himself and the Jewish converts; but when he employs ὑμεῖς, the Gentile disciples are alone intended. There is no hint that such is the case; and is it solely for the Gentile Christians that the magnificent prayer in the first chapter is presented? There is nothing so distinctive about " we " as to confine it to Jews, or about " ye " as to restrict it to heathens, save where, as in ii. 11, the apostle marks the limitation himself.

Timothy indeed is mentioned in the salutation to the Colossians, but not in that to the Ephesians. But this fact affords no argument against us; for no matter in what form the solution is offered, whether Timothy be supposed to have been absent from Rome, or to have been in Ephesus, or to have been a stranger at the time to the Ephesian church—no matter which hypothesis is adopted, the absence of the name does not prove the encyclical character of the epistle. There may be many reasons unknown to us why Timothy's name was left out. If Timothy came to Ephesus soon after the arrival of the epistle, Tychicus might have private information to communicate about him, or have a letter from himself. So that as his personal teaching was so soon to be enjoyed, this epistle emanates solely from the great apostle.

We are therefore brought to the conclusion that the epistle was really meant for and originally entituled to the church at Ephesus. The strong external evidence is not weakened by internal proof or statement; the seal and the superscription are not contradicted by the contents. Such was the opinion of the ancient church as a body, as seen in its MSS., quotations, commentaries, and all its versions; of the mediæval church; and in more modern times of the commentators Calvin, Bucer, Wolf, Estius, Crocius, Piscator, Cocceius, Witsius, Zanchius, Bodius, Rollock, Aretius, Van Til, Röell, Quandt, Fergusson, Dickson, Chandler, Whitby, Lardner, and more recently of Cramer, Morus, Meyer, Davidson, Stuart,[1] Alexander,[2] Rinck,[3] Wurm,[4] Wieseler,[5] Alford, Newland, and Wordsworth.

### III —GENUINENESS OF THE EPISTLE

The proofs that the Apostle Paul wrote this letter are stronger still than those which vouch for the correctness of its present title. It may be doubted, with Meyer, whether at least the first of the two citations usually adduced from the twelfth chapter of Polycarp's letter to the Philippians be one

[1] Notes to Fosdick's English Translation of Hug's *Introduction*, p. 757, Andover, 1836.
[2] In Kitto's *Cyclopædia*, art. Epistle to the Ephesians.
[3] *Studien und Kritiken*, 1849, p. 946—under the title *Kann der Epheserbrief an die Gemeinde zu Ephesus gerichtet seyn?* von W. Fr. Rinck, Pfarrer zu Grenzbach in Badischen Oberlande.
[4] *Tübin. Streitschriften*, 1833, p. 97.
[5] *Chronologie des Apost. Zeitalt.* p. 442, etc.

from this epistle, since it may be regarded as taken from the Old Testament; and perhaps the formula introducing both is more usually employed in reference to the Old Testament than the New. *Patres Apostolici*, ed. Jacobson, vol. ii. p. 487. In the first chapter of the same letter there is a quotation from Eph. ii. 8, 9—ὅτι χάριτί ἐστε σεσωσμένοι, οὐκ ἐξ ἔργων. *Id.* vol. ii. p. 466. Besides the authorities already given, we might refer to Origen, who, in his Commentary on John, says —Πῶς ὁ Παῦλος φησί που, καὶ ἤμεθα τέκνα φύσει ὀργῆς. Again, in his Commentary on Matthew, he refers to Eph. v. 32, under the same heading—ὡς Παῦλος φησίν. *Commentaria*, ed. Huet. vol. i. p. 497, ii. p. 315. From Polycarp downwards, through the succession of patristic correspondents, apologists, and commentators, the evidence is unanimous, and even Marcion did not secede from this catholic unity, nor apparently did the Valentinians. Irenæus, *Adv. Hæres.* § i. 8, 5. The heretics, as well as the orthodox, agreed in acknowledging the Pauline authorship. The quotations already adduced in reference to the title, are, at the same time, a sample of the overwhelming evidence. But de Wette, Usteri, Baur, and Schwegler, have risen up against this confronting host of authorities, and cast suspicion on the Pauline origin. Ewald, too, in his *die Sendschreiben des Apostels Paulus*, etc., omits the Epistle to the Ephesians, and regards the salutations in the last chapter of Romans as a fragment of an epistle sent to Ephesus. Not that there is any external fact in their favour; nor that any ancient writer falters in his belief, or hints that any of his predecessors or contemporaries had the least hesitation. Nay, the evidence may be traced back to the first link: for the Apostle John lived long at Ephesus, and there Polycarp must have learned from him that Paul was the author; while Irenæus, who is so decided in his testimony, enjoyed the tuition of Polycarp. And what shall we say of the additional witness of Ignatius and Origen, of Clement and Tertullian, Basil and Cyprian ? But these German critics have a test of their own, and they apply it at once, not to the external history or chain of proof, but to the contents of the epistle. So thoroughly do they believe themselves imbued with the spirit and idiom of the inspired writer, that they can feel at once, and by an infallible sense, whether any composition ascribed to him be genuine or spurious. They may not be able to detail the reasons of their critical feeling, but they rely with calm self-possession on their æsthetical instincts.

De Wette adduces against the genuineness of this epistle, its dependency (*Abhängigkeit*) on that to the Colossians—a thing, he says, without example, except in the case of the First Epistle to Timothy, which is also spurious. This epistle is only a mere "verbose expansion"—*wortreiche Erweiterung*—of that to the Colossians, and besides there are against it the employment of unusual words, phrases, parentheses, digressions, and pleonasms, and an indefinite un-Pauline colour and complexion, both in doctrine and diction. *Einleit. in N. T.* § 146. Take a sample of the resemblances from the first chapters of both epistles:—

### EPHESIANS

i. 4.—εἶναι ἡμᾶς ἁγίους καὶ ἀμώμους κατενώπιον αὐτοῦ.

i. 7.—Ἐν ᾧ ἔχομεν τὴν ἀπολύτρωσιν διὰ τοῦ αἵματος αὐτοῦ, τὴν ἄφεσιν τῶν παραπτωμάτων.

i. 10.— Εἰς οἰκονομίαν τοῦ πληρώματος τῶν καιρῶν, ἀνακεφαλαιώσασθαι τὰ πάντα ἐν τῷ Χριστῷ, τὰ ἐν τοῖς οὐρανοῖς καὶ τὰ ἐπὶ γῆς, ἐν αὐτῷ.

i. 21.— Ὑπεράνω πάσης ἀρχῆς καὶ ἐξουσίας καὶ δυνάμεως καὶ κυριότητος καὶ παντὸς ὀνόματος ὀνομαζομένου οὐ μόνον ἐν τῷ αἰῶνι τούτῳ ἀλλὰ καὶ ἐν τῷ μέλλοντι.

### COLOSSIANS

i. 22.—Παραστῆσαι ὑμᾶς ἁγίους καὶ ἀμώμους καὶ ἀνεγκλήτους κατενώπιον αὐτοῦ.

i. 14.—Ἐν ᾧ ἔχομεν τὴν ἀπολύτρωσιν, τὴν ἄφεσιν τῶν ἁμαρτιῶν.

i. 20.—Καὶ δι' αὐτοῦ ἀποκαταλλάξαι τὰ πάντα εἰς αὐτόν, εἰρηνοποιήσας διὰ τοῦ αἵματος τοῦ σταυροῦ αὐτοῦ, δι' αὐτοῦ, εἴτε τὰ ἐπὶ τῆς γῆς εἴτε τὰ ἐν τοῖς οὐρανοῖς.

i. 16-18—Ὅτι ἐν αὐτῷ ἐκτίσθη τὰ πάντα τὰ ἐν τοῖς οὐρανοῖς καὶ τὰ ἐπὶ τῆς γῆς, τὰ ὁρατὰ καὶ τὰ ἀόρατα, εἴτε θρόνοι εἴτε κυριότητες εἴτε ἀρχαὶ εἴτε ἐξουσίαι. τὰ πάντα δι' αὐτοῦ καὶ εἰς αὐτὸν ἔκτισται. [17]Καὶ αὐτός ἐστιν πρὸ πάντων καὶ τὰ πάντα ἐν αὐτῷ συνέστηκεν. [18]Καὶ αὐτός ἐστιν ἡ κεφαλὴ τοῦ σώματος, τῆς ἐκκλησίας· ὅς ἐστιν ἀρχή, πρωτότοκος ἐκ τῶν νεκρῶν, ἵνα γένηται ἐν πᾶσιν αὐτὸς πρωτεύων.

These resemblances are not so strong as to warrant the idea of imitation. The thought and connection are different in both epistles. Thus in Eph. i. 4 perfection is presented as the end or ideal of the eternal choice; but in Col. i. 22 it is held out as the result of Christ's death. The forgiveness of sins in Eph. i. 7 is introduced differently from Col. i. 14, though in both places it is in natural connection with Christ; in the first as a sequence of predestination, but in the second as an element of redemption, and as introductory to a description of the Redeemer's person. The references to the final effects of Christ's death, in the two epistles, are also different, both in introduction and aspect; it is recapitulation in Eph. i. 10, and reconciliation in Col. i. 20. In Eph. i. 21 the apostle pictures Christ's official exaltation over all the heavenly hosts, but in Col. i. 16, 18 he represents Christ as Creator, and therefore Head or Governor by essential and personal right. In both epistles Christ is κεφαλή, and the church is σῶμα; but the accompanying illustration is different.

Other similar terms are selected by de Wette—πλήρωμα, Eph. i. 23, Col. i. 19, ii. 9; μυστήριον, Eph. i. 9, Col. i. 26; καὶ ὑμᾶς ὄντας, Eph. ii. 1, Col. i. 13. Then come such phrases as περιτομὴ χειροποίητος, Eph. ii. 11 — περιτομὴ ἀχειροποίητος, Col. ii. 11; ἀπηλλοτριωμένοι, Eph. ii. 12 and Col. i. 21; ἐν δόγμασιν, Eph. ii. 15, and in Col. ii. 14; ἀποκαταλλάξαι, Eph. ii. 16 and Col. i. 20. These resemblances, like the previous ones, are however in connections so different that they are proofs of originality, and not of imitation.

De Wette finds many other parallels, both in the thoughts of the general sections, and also in particular phrases; those in Ephesians being moulded from those in Colossians. Thus the paragraph, iii. 1–21, is said to be from Col. i. 24–29, and the practical section, Eph. iv. 17–vi. 20, is alleged to be from Col. iii. 5–iv. 4. Still these and many other similarities adduced by the objector are by no means close; some of them are not even striking parallels, and they have no tame or servile air about them. The passages in Ephesians are as bold, free, and natural, as they are in Colossians. There is nothing about them betraying imitation; nothing like a cautious or artistic selection of Pauline phrases, and setting them anew, as if to disguise the theft and trick out a spurious letter. Even Baur, who denies the Pauline authority of both epistles, admits that both may have had the same author. *Paulus*, p. 455—*Dass der Epheserbrief in einem secundären Verhältniss zum Colosserbrief steht, geht aus allem klar hervor, ob er aber viel später geschreiben ist und einen andern zum Verfasser hat kann bezweifelt werden. Sollten nicht beide Briefe zusammen als Brüderpaar in die Welt ausgegangen seyn?* Besides, as Meyer has remarked, so far from Ephesians being a verbose expansion of Colossians, as de Wette asserts, it shows in several places a brevity of allusion where there is fuller statement in Colossians. Compare Eph. i. 15, 17—Col. i. 3–6; Eph. iv. 32—Col. iii. 12–14. The apostle's use of the quotation from the 68th Psalm, in iv. 8, is brought against him by de Wette, and, if so, what then shall we say of Rom. x. 6 and x. 18? The quotation in v. 14 is said by de Wette to be from an unbiblical writing, and therefore unapostolic in manner; but it is rather a free quotation from Isa. lx. 1, and is not without parallel even in the Gospels. Matt. ii. 15, 23. Objections are also taken to the demonology, ii. 2, vi. 12, that it is exceptional; and to the characteristic epithets or clauses connected with the name of God, that they are singular, as in i. 17, iii. 9, 15, etc. Other peculiarities, as the prohibition of stealing and the comparison of Christ to a bridegroom, are brought forward for the same end. We may reply that not only are such representations apostolic, but that they are also Pauline, for in other Pauline writings, in some form or other, they find a place. The Epistle to the Ephesians has certainly no system of dogmas or circle of allusions peculiar to itself. It does in some points resemble that to the Colossians—but surely if two letters are written by the same person, about the same period, and upon kindred subjects, similarity of diction will inevitably occur. It would be the merest affectation to seek to avoid it, nor do the strictest notions of inspiration forbid it. The mind insensibly vibrates under the influence of former themes, and the earlier language unconsciously intrudes itself. And if the topics, though generally similar, are specifically different, we expect in the style generic resemblances, but specific variations. De Wette edited the correspondence of Luther, but he has not rejected any letter, which, written in the same month with a previous one upon some similar themes, is not unlike it in spirit and phrase. Such a phenomenon occurs in this epistle, for many of its verses contain diction somewhat similar to correspondent passages in Colossians. It is like that to the Colossians, and yet unlike it—not with the tawdry and dull similarity of imitation, disguised by the artful sprinkling of a few discrepancies; but it has that likeness which springs from unity of contemporaneous origin and theme, and that difference which results, at the same time, from living independent thought. And if it do contain un-Pauline thoughts and diction, how came it to be received? how was the forgery not detected? The reasoning against its genuineness seems to be on this wise.—It is so like Colossians that it cannot be an original document; but it is also so unlike other Pauline letters, that it cannot be ascribed to Paul. The statement neutralizes itself. If usual words prove it an imitation, what do the unusual words prove? Does not rather the natural combination of the so-called usual and unusual phrases mark it as a document akin to the other production, and having a purpose, at the same time, peculiar to itself? Every original composition on a distinct topic presents those very characteristics and affinities. But the whole is Pauline in spirit and form. As in the other acknowledged writings of Paul, so you have here the same easy connection of thought, by means of a series of participles—the same delight in compound terms, especially formed with ὑπέρ, and in words that border on pleonasm—the same tendency to go off at a word, and strike into a parenthesis—the same recurrence of γάρ and ὅτι introducing a reason, and of ἵνα pointing to a high and final cause—the same culmination of an argument, in the triumphant insertion of οὐ μόνον and μᾶλλον δέ—the same favourite formula of a conclusion or deduction in ἄρα οὖν—the same fondness for abstract terms, with the accumulation of exhaustive epithets—the same familiar appeal to the Old Testament, and striking illustrations drawn from it—the same occasional recurrence to personal authority and inspired warrant, in a mighty and irresistible ἐγώ or φημί —the same irregular and inconsequent syntax, as if thought jostled thought—the same rich and distinctive terminology that calls the gospel μυστήριον, and prefixes πλοῦτος to so many of its blessings; that includes δικαιοσύνη, πίστις, κλῆσις, καταλλαγή, and ζωή among its distinctive doctrines; that places υἱοθεσία, οἰκοδομή, ἀνακαίνωσις, and προσαγωγή among its choicest privileges; that gives Jesus the undivided honour of σωτήρ, κεφαλή, κύριος, and κριτής; and in its ethics opposes πνεῦμα to σάρξ, finds its standard in νόμος, its power in ἀγάπη, and its reward in ἐλπίς with its rich and eternal κληρονομία. The style and theology of Paul are the same here as elsewhere; and we are struck with the same lofty genius and fervid eloquence; the same elevated and self-denying temperament; the same throbbings of a noble and yearning heart; the same masses of thought, luminous and many-tinted, like the cloud which glows under the reflected splendours of the setting sun; the same vigorous mental grasp which, amidst numerous digressions, is ever easily connecting truths with first principles—all these, the results of a master mind into which nature and grace had poured in royal profusion their rarest and richest endowments.

If, therefore, there be generic sameness in the two epistles to Ephesus and Colosse, it is only in keeping; but if there be specific difference, it is only additional resemblance. If there should be thirty-eight ἅπαξ λεγόμενα in this epistle, there are forty in the first two chapters of Colossians, above a hundred in Romans, and no less than two hundred and thirty in the 1st Epistle to the Corinthians. (See our Introduction to Colossians.) The writer does use some peculiar terms, but why not? Might there not be many reasons in the modes of thought and speech peculiar to Ephesus, and perfectly familiar to the apostle, that led him to use in this epistle such words and phrases as ἐν τοῖς ἐπουρανίοις, i. 3, 20, ii. 6, iii. 10, vi. 12; τὰ πνευματικά, vi. 12; διάβολος, iv. 27, vi. 11; κοσμοκράτωρ, vi. 12; σωτήριον, vi. 16; οἰκονομία, i. 10, iii. 2, 9; μυστήριον, v. 32; πλήρωμα, i. 23; εὐλογία, i. 3; αἰών, ii. 2; περιποίησις, i. 14; ἀφθαρσία, vi. 24; μανθάνειν, iv. 20; φωτίζειν, iii. 9; πληροῦσθαι ἐν, v. 18; and εἰς, iii. 19; βασιλεία τοῦ Θεοῦ καὶ Χριστοῦ, v. 5; τὸ θέλημα τοῦ κυρίου, v. 17. The forms of construction excepted against are without any difficulty, such as ἵνα with the optative, i. 17, iii. 16; ἴστε γινώσκοντες, v. 5; and ἵνα φοβῆται, v. 33. Nor is there any stronger proof of spuriousness in the want of the article in the instances adduced by the objector. Any forger who had studied the apostle's style, could easily have avoided such little singularities. In fine, what de Wette calls pleonasms (*Breite und Pleonasmus*), as in i. 19, vi. 10, are clauses where each word has its distinctive meaning; various relations and aspects of one great idea being set out in their connection or development. And if the epistle be a forgery, it is a base one, for the author of it distinctly and frequently personates the apostle —" I Paul "—" I Paul, the prisoner of Jesus Christ," etc. Indeed, the imitation is so good, that de Wette ascribes it to the first century, and to a pupil of the apostle's. We can scarcely suppose that an imposition so gross could be associated with a genius so lofty as that which has composed such a letter. Nor can we imagine that the Ephesian church would not detect the plagiarism. This "discerning of spirits" was one of their special gifts, for the keen and honest exercise of which the Saviour eulogizes them when he says: "Thou hast tried them which say they are apostles and are not, but hast found them liars." Rev. ii. 2.

There is, as we have said, that natural difference of style which arises from difference of subject and situation, in itself a proof of Pauline authorship. But we deny that there is any inferiority, such as de Wette complains of, or any of that verbosity, tedious and imperfect illustration, or superfluity of terms which are adduced by him as objections. The style betokens fulness of thought and a rich mind. There is order without system, reasoning without technical argument, progress without syllogistic landmarks, the connection free and pliant as in a familiar letter—all converging on one great end, and yet with a definite aim in the several parts. The immediate terms are clear and precise, and yet the thoughts are superposed—

"With many a winding bout
In linked sweetness long-drawn out."

Each surge may be gauged, but the advancing tide is beyond measurement.

Therefore the attack of de Wette, faintly responded to by Usteri in his preface to his *Paulin. Lehrbegriff*, is wholly unwarranted. It is based upon critical caprice, and upon a restless subjectivity which gives its mere tastes the authority of argument. Though so often self-deceived and exposed, it still deludes itself with a consciousness of immense superiority, as if in possession of a second and subtle inspiration. We place in opposition to de Wette's opinion the following testimonies:—

Chrysostom, no mean judge of a Greek style, says in his preface to his Commentary, that as Ephesus was a place of intellectual eminence—ταῦτα δὲ ἡμῖν οὐχ ἁπλῶς εἴρηται, ἀλλ' ὥστε δεῖξαι, ὅτι πολλῆς ἔδει τῷ Παύλῳ σπουδῆς πρὸς ἐκείνους γράφοντι. Λέγεται δὲ καὶ τὰ βαθύτερα τῶν νοημάτων αὐτοῖς ἐμπιστεῦσαι ἅτε ἤδη κατηχημένοις. Ἔστι δὲ νοημάτων μεστὴ ἡ ἐπιστολὴ ὑψηλῶν καὶ δογμάτων . . . καὶ ὑψηλῶν σφόδρα γέμει τῶν νοημάτων καὶ ὑπερόγκων. Ἃ γὰρ μηδαμοῦ σχεδὸν ἐφθέγξατο ταῦτα ἐνταῦθα δηλοῖ. "Paul would necessarily take great pains and trouble in writing to the Christians there. He is said to have intrusted them with his profoundest conceptions, as they had been already so highly instructed, and the epistle is full of lofty conceptions and doctrines," etc. Jerome says in his preface—*Nunc ad Ephesios transeundum est, mediam apostoli epistolam, ut ordine ita et sensibus. Mediam autem dico, non quo primas sequens, extremis major sit, sed quomodo cor animalis in medio est, ut ex hoc intelligatis quantis difficultatibus, et quam profundis quæstionibus involuta sit.* Erasmus testifies—*Idem in hac epistola Pauli fervor, eadem profunditas, idem omnino spiritus ac pectus.* Passing Luther and others, we refer to Witsius, who adds in his *Meletemata Leidensia* (p. 192), in higher phraseology—*Ita vero universam religionis Christianæ summam divina hac epistola exponit, ut exuberantem quandam non sermonis tantum Evangelici παρρησίαν, sed et Spiritus Sancti vim et sensum, et charitatis Christianæ flammam quandam ex electo illo pectore emicantem, et lucis divinæ fulgorem quendam admirabilem inde elucentem, et fontem aquæ vivæ inde scaturientem, aut ebullientem potius, animadvertere liceat: idque tantâ copia, ut superabundans illa cordis plenitudo, ipsa animi sensa intimosque conceptus, conceptus autem verba prolata, verba denique priora quæque subsequentia, premant, urgeant, obruant.* Grotius, too, no enthusiast, thus describes it—*Rerum sublimitatem adæquans verbis sublimioribus quam ulla unquam habuit lingua humana.* "In this," says Coleridge, "the divinest composition of man, is every doctrine of Christianity, first, those doctrines peculiar to Christianity, and secondly, those precepts common to it with natural religion." *Table Talk*, p. 82: London, 1851. Similar testimonies might be taken from Eichhorn's *Einleitung*, and from the prefaces of several of the commentators.

The attack upon the genuineness of this epistle (or rather both epistles, for Colossians is set aside as well as Ephesians) by the Tübingen school of criticism is of a different nature. Their idea is, that the epistle is a composition of the second century, and that it had its origin in the Valentinian Gnosticism. Baur,[1] the Coryphæus of the party, has openly maintained the extraordinary hypothesis. Schwegler,[2] Zeller, and Schneckenburger have gone beyond their master in extravagance; while Bruno Bauer[3] has surpassed them all in anti-Pauline bitterness and absurdity.

This hypothesis has its origin in the leading error of the Tübingen school, viz., that the original type of Christianity was nothing more than Ebionitism, and that its expansion by the apostle of the Gentiles was in direct antagonism to Peter, James, and the rest of the apostolical college. In proof, it is maintained that John, in speaking of only twelve apostles, in the Apocalypse, xxi. 14, excludes Paul from the sacred number, and that he praises these very Ephesians for having sifted and rejected his claims, when he says: "Thou hast tried them which say they are apostles, and are not, but hast found them liars." It is surely needless to dwell on the refutation of such an uncritical statement. An excellent reply to the whole delusion will be found in a recent work of Lechler, *Das Apostolische und Nachapostolische Zeitalter*, etc., 2nd ed. Stuttgart, 1857.

In fact, the entire theory is a huge anachronism. The Gnosticism of the second century was not wholly unchristian either in idea or nomenclature, but it took from Scripture whatever in thought or expression suited its specious theosophy, and borrowed such materials to a large extent from the epistles of the New Testament.[4] Such a procedure may be plainly proved. The same process has been repeated in various forms, and in more recent times in Germany itself. The inference is not, as the critics hold, that the Epistles to Colosse and

---

[1] *Der Apostel Paulus, sein Leben und Wirken*, etc., p. 420, etc., Stuttgart, 1845; or his *Kritische Miscellen zum Epheserbrief*, in *Zeller's Theolog. Jahrb.* 1844, p. 378. Baur died in December 1860.

[2] *Das Nachapostolische Zeitalter*, etc. ii. 325, 326. Tübingen, 1846, *passim*.

[3] *Kritik der Paulinischen Briefe*, iii. p. 101. Berlin, 1852.

[4] *De Origine Ep. ad Coloss. et Eph. a criticis Tubingensibus e Gnosi Valentiniana deducta*. Scripsit Albertus Kloepper, Theol. Lic. Gryphiæ, 1853.

Ephesus are the product of Gnosticism in array against Ebionitism, but only that the Gnostic sophists gilded their speculations with biblical phraseology. As well, were it not for the long interval of centuries, might we infer that the pantheism of Strauss originated no little of the language of the Apostle John, rather than was copied from it; or that the Book of Mormon was the source of the original Scripture, and not, as it is, a clumsy and recent caricature. We may well ask—How could a document so distinctly Gnostic be accepted by the church, which was ever in conflict with Gnosticism?

Baur and his followers hold that this epistle is a Gnostic effusion, because of its exalted views of the person and reign of Christ, its allusions to various ranks in the heavenly hierarchy, its repeated employment of the term πλήρωμα and its allied verb, and its doctrine of the re-capitulation of all things in Christ, as if such teaching and even diction were not common in Paul's acknowledged epistles addressed to European churches.[1] Thus the Christology is offensive to Baur, Eph. i. 20, though the idea is found in 1 Cor. xv. 24. Why should not the apostle develop his ideas more fully on some points, in addressing churches in a region where errors on the same point might soon intrude? What connection have Gnostic æons—shadowy and impalpable emanations from the Bythos or from one another—with those thrones and dominions, principalities and powers, over which Christ Jesus presides as Governor. Nay, the Gnostics distinguished Christ and Jesus as æons; the former having, in fact, sent the latter as Saviour. The theosophic speculations of the Valentinians are applied by Baur to the term πλήρωμα, in a way that is wholly unwarranted by its occurrence in both epistles. In this epistle the term is applied to time, as marked out by God, and so fulfilled or filled up; to the church as filled by Christ, and to God as denoting His spiritually perfect nature; and to Christ in the phrase, "the stature of the fulness of Christ." But in such phrases there is no allusion to any metaphysical notion of the Absolute, either to what contains it or what is contained in it. Most certainly in the nuptial illustrations, v. 25, etc., there is no reference to male and female æons, or to the Suzygies of the Valentinian system—such as that of

[1] Räbiger, *De Christologia Paulina contra Baurium.* Vratislaviæ, 1852.

the λόγος with ζωή from whom were generated ἄνθρωπος and ἐκκλησία, as if the relation of Christ to His church were a similar relation—absolute essence realizing and developing itself in a concrete Being, as the wife is the complement of the man—κατὰ συζυγίαν. One may indeed wonder how Baur could dream that in iii. 10—" that now unto the principalities and powers in the heavenly places might be made known by the church the manifold wisdom of God "—was contained the Gnostic idea of the æon σοφία struggling to be united with βυθός, and her final return to the πλήρωμα through the συζυγία between Christ and His ἐκκλησία. Or who besides Baur could imagine that in the phrases—κατὰ τὸν αἰῶνα τοῦ κόσμου τούτου; εἰς πάσας τὰς γενεὰς τοῦ αἰῶνος τῶν αἰώνων; πρόθεσις τῶν αἰώνων—there is a reference to the relation which the Gnostic æons sustained to God, as the primal extra-temporal unity of time individualizing Himself in them as periods, or to their relation to another in sexual union and development? Nay more, in the phrases—" as is now revealed unto His holy apostles and prophets—ye are built upon the foundation of the apostles and prophets"—the quick eye of Baur discovers traces of Montanism—because in it prophets had a high and honoured place as the organs of divine communication. So that in his opinion the man who wrote those phrases must have lived at a period when so-called prophets enjoyed apostolic honour, and thus unconsciously betrays himself and the lateness of his time. As if in Acts, Romans, and 1st Corinthians there were no allusion to this class of men, or as if all those documents too had a post-apostolic origin! And then Baur would require to tell us how two systems so opposed as Montanism and Gnosticism could thus coalesce in the same epistle. The epithet ἅγιος applied to the apostles and prophets, betrays, according to de Wette also, a late origin, and the writer manifests his lateness by his anxiety to identify himself and exalt himself—as an apostle, a prisoner for the Gentiles—a minister, less than the least of all saints —and ambassador in chains. What is this objection but dictating to the apostle how he shall write when an old man in a prison, what amount of personal reference shall go into his letters, or how large or small shall be the subjective elements in his communication to any particular community, and through it to all churches and for all time? The expression—"less than the least of all saints"—is in no way inconsistent with such an exalted assertion as—"by revelation he made known unto me the mystery;" for this refers to official function, and that only to personal emotion. A more decided contrast is found in 1 Cor. xv. 9—"the least of the apostles, that am not meet to be called an apostle;" and 2 Cor. xi. 5—"I was not a whit behind the very chiefest apostles." Surely, then, the resemblance which the subsequent Gnosticism bears to these doctrines in its theosophy and angelology, is a proof that it borrowed the shadowy likeness, but no proof that out of it were manufactured the apostolic documents. In fine, the whole scheme has been overwhelmed with confusion; for it has been proved by citations from Hippolytus,[1] that some books of the New Testament are quoted by him more than half a century before these Tübingen critics dated or allowed of their existence.

## IV—RELATIONSHIP OF THE EPISTLES TO EPHESUS AND COLOSSE

The letters of the apostle are the fervent outburst of pastoral zeal and attachment, written without reserve and in unaffected simplicity. Sentiments come warm from the heart without the shaping out, pruning, and punctilious arrangement of a formal discourse. There is such a fresh and familiar transcription of feeling, and so much of conversational frankness and vivacity, that the reader associates the image of the writer with every paragraph, and his ear seems to catch and recognize the very tones of oral address. These impressions must have been deepened by the thought that the letter came from "such an one as Paul the aged," often a sufferer, and now a prisoner. If he could not speak, he wrote; if he could not see them in person, he despatched to them those silent messengers of love. Is it then any matter of amazement that one letter should resemble another, or that two written about the same time should have so much in common, and each at the same time so much that is

[1] Bunsen's *Hippolytus*, vol. i. Pref. London, 1852.

peculiar? The close relationship between the epistles to Colosse and Ephesus must strike every reader, and the question has been raised, which of them is the earlier production. The answer is one very much of critical taste, and therefore different decisions have been given. A great host of names, which the reader will find in Davidson's *Introduction*, are in favour of the letter to Ephesus; but others, and these including Meyer, Harless, Wieseler, and Olshausen, declare for that to Colosse.

Neander says—*Und daraus erhellt auch, dass er den Brief an die Colosser zuerst unter diesen beiden geschreiben hat; denn in demselben zeigen sich uns diese Gedanken in ihrer ursprünglichen Entstehung und Beziehung, wie sie durch den Gegensatz gegen jene in diesem Briefe von ihm bekämpfte Sekte hervorgerufen wurden.* Geschichte der Pflanzung, etc., vol. i. p. 524, 4th ed. That is—" In the epistle to the Colossians the apostle's thoughts exhibit themselves in their original form and connection, as they were called forth by his opposition to the sect (of Judaizing Gnostics) whose sentiments and practices he combats in that epistle." Little stress can be laid on such an argument, for whenever the mind assumes an agonistic attitude, its thoughts have always more vigour and specialty, more pith and keenness, than when in calmness and peace it discusses any ordinary and impersonal topic. Harless and Wiggers have fixed upon Eph. vi. 21, compared with Col. iv. 8. In Colossians the apostle says of Tychicus, "Whom I have sent unto you that he might know your estate." But in Ephesians he adds—καί, "that ye also may know my affairs, and what I am doing, Tychicus, a beloved brother, shall make known to you all things." In using the word "also," the apostle seems to refer to what he had said to the Colossians. Naturally he first says to the Colossians, "that ye may know," but in a second letter to the Ephesians, "that ye also may know." This hypothesis takes for granted that the Ephesians would know what was contained in the letter to Colosse, or at least that Tychicus would inform them of its existence, and of its reference to himself as the bearer of personal and private tidings of the apostle. The καί, however, may refer not to the Colossians, but to the apostle himself—as Alford puts it—"I have been going at length into the matters concerning you, so if you also on your part wish to know my matters," etc. The argument from καί, therefore, cannot be conclusively relied on. On the other hand, it is contended by Hug and others, that the absence of Timothy's name in the beginning of the Epistle to the Ephesians is a strong proof in favour of its priority. Various solutions have been given; one probability is, that Timothy was absent on some important embassy. These critics suppose that he had not by this time come to Rome, but did arrive ere Paul composed the Epistle to Colosse. This circumstance is too precarious for an argument to be founded upon it.

Efforts have been also made to demonstrate the priority of the Epistle to the Ephesians, from its containing no expression of any hopes of deliverance, and no reference to the success of the gospel, whereas these occur in the Epistle to the Philippians, written about the same time. But neither in Colossians are there any such intimations, and in the letter to Philemon, which Onesimus carried to him, as both he and Tychicus carried theirs to the Colossians, he says, generally—"I trust that through your prayers I shall be given unto you." The question can scarce be solved on such data. It may be tried by another criterion. Supposing Paul to be in imprisonment, which of these two churches would he most probably write to, which of them stood most in need of an epistle, which of them was in circumstances most likely to attract the immediate attention of the prisoner—that of Ephesus or that of Colosse? Lardner has virtually laid down such a test. There might be many considerations inducing the apostle to write to the Ephesians soon after his arrival at Rome. Ephesus was a place of great importance and traffic, and in it Paul had stayed longer than in any other city, except Antioch. Here also he had wrought many and special miracles, and had enjoyed great success in his preaching. He had on a previous occasion determined to sail by Ephesus, and when he came to Miletus "he sent to Ephesus and called the elders of the church." These things may have induced him to write first to Ephesus on his coming to Rome, and having liberty of correspondence. But we might thus reply to these statements. The Ephesian church had preserved its faith unsullied, for no reproof or warning is contained in the epistle. They stood in no immediate need of apostolic correspondence. No difficulty pressed them, for none is solved. No heresy had crept in among them, for none is refuted. But Colosse was threatened by a false system, which would corrupt the simplicity of the gospel, which had in it the elements of discord and ruin, but which had a peculiar charm for the contemplative inhabitants of Phrygia, so prone to mysticism, and therefore would be the more seductive to the church of Colosse, and the more calculated to work havoc among its members. This being known to the apostle, such a jeopardy being set before him, would he not at once write to Colosse, expose the false system, warn against it, and exhort the adherents of Christianity to a stedfast profession? Would he not feel an immediate necessity for his interference, would not the case appear to his mind more urgent, and having more claim on his labour than the church of Ephesus, where, truth was yet kept pure, and the fire on the altar ascended with a steady brilliancy? Thus, of such an argument as that of Lardner no advantage can be taken. Still, balancing probabilities in a matter where facts cannot be fully ascertained, we may incline to the opinion that the earlier epistle is that to the Colossians.

The following table will point out the similarities between the two epistles:—

| Eph. i. 1, | with Col. i. 1. | Eph. iv. 15, | with Col. ii. 19. |
|---|---|---|---|
| — i. 2, | — — i. 2. | — iv. 19, | — — iii. 1, 5. |
| — i. 3, | — — i. 3. | — iv. 22, | — — iii. 8. |
| — i. 7, | — — i. 14. | — iv. 25, | — — iii. 8. |
| — i. 10, | — — i. 20. | — iv. 29, | — — iii. 8; iv. 6. |
| — i. 15–17, | — — i. 3, 4. | — iv. 31, | — — iii. 8. |
| — i. 18, | — — i. 27. | — iv. 32, | — — iii. 12. |
| — i. 21, | — — i. 16. | — v. 3, | — — iii. 5. |
| — i. 22, | — — i. 18. | — v. 4, | — — iii. 8. |
| — ii. 1, 12, | — — i. 21. | — v. 5, | — — iii. 5. |
| — ii. 5, | — — ii. 13. | — v. 6, | — — iii. 6. |
| — ii. 15, | — — ii. 14. | — v. 15, | — — iv. 5. |
| — ii. 16, | — — i. 20. | — v. 19, | — — iii. 16. |
| — iii. 1, | — — i. 24. | — v. 21, | — — iii. 18. |
| — iii. 2, | — — i. 25. | — v. 25, | — — iii. 19. |
| — iii. 3, | — — i. 26. | — vi. 1, | — — iii. 20. |
| — iii. 7, | — — i. 23, 25. | — vi. 4, | — — iii. 21. |
| — iii. 8, | — — i. 27. | — vi. 5, | — — iii. 22. |
| — iv. 1, | — — i. 10. | — vi. 9, | — — iv. 1. |
| — iv. 2, | — — iii. 12. | — vi. 18, | — — iv. 2. |
| — iv. 3, | — — iii. 14. | — vi. 21, | — — iv. 7. |

Not a few of these similarities are but accidental, and those which really deserve the name are corroborative proofs of genuineness.

## V—PLACE AND DATE OF ITS COMPOSITION

The usual opinion has been that the epistle was written in Rome. Some of the later German critics, however, have concluded that Cæsarea was the place of composition. Schulz in the *Studien und Kritiken*, 1829, p. 612, first broached this hypothesis, and he has been followed by Schneckenburger, Böttger, Reuss,[1] Wiggers, and even by Schott, Thiersch,[2] and Meyer.

We find that Paul when in Cæsarea was subjected to very rigorous confinement. His own countrymen were bigoted and violent, and only his friends might come and minister unto him. Intercourse with other churches seems to have been entirely prohibited. On the other hand, in Rome the watch and ward, unstimulated by Jewish malice, were not so strict. The apostle might preach, and labour to some extent in his spiritual vocation. Again, Onesimus was with the apostle, a fugitive slave who would rather run and hide himself in the crowds of Rome, than flee to Cæsarea where he might be more easily detected. Aristarchus and Luke were at Rome too, but there is no proof of their being with Paul at Cæsarea. Besides, we have mention of the palace and "Cæsar's household." We cannot be brought to believe by all Böttger's reasoning, that such an expression might apply to Herod's royal dwelling in Cæsarea. Surely Herod's house could never receive the lofty appellation of Cæsar's. Antiquity, with the probability of fact, supports the notion that Rome was the place where the epistle was composed. Those who contend for Cæsarea lay stress on the distance of Asia Minor from Rome, and on the omission of the name of Onesimus in the Epistle to the Ephesians, as if, setting out from Cæsarea, the bearer of the letter would arrive at Colosse first, and Onesimus delivering himself up to his master, would not proceed with Tychicus onward to Ephesus. But there were peculiar

---
[1] *Geschichte d. Heil. Schrift. Novi Testamenti*, § 114.
[2] *Die Kirche in der Apostolischen Zeitalter*, etc., p. 17. Frankfurt, 1852.

reasons for commending Onesimus to the Colossian church. His flight and conversion would make him notorious and suspected. Besides, as Paul says, he was one of themselves, and if he touched at Ephesus first, he needed no formal introduction, being in the society of Tychicus. Emphasis is laid on the phrase πρὸς ὥραν, "for a season," as if it signified "soon," and referred to the period elapsing between the flight of the slave and his reaching Paul, as if such brevity would be realized more likely at Cæsarea than Rome. But, as has been answered, the phrase qualifies ἐχωρίσθη, and denotes that his separation from his master was only temporary. On the whole, the argument preponderates in favour of Rome as the place whence this epistle was despatched, and probably about the year 62.[1] From the metropolis of the world, where luxury was added to ambition, and licentiousness bathed in blood, an obscure and imprisoned foreigner composes this sublime treatise, on a subject beyond the mental range of the wisest of Western sages, and dictates a brief system of ethics, which in purity, fulness, and symmetry eclipses the boasted "Morals" of Seneca, and the more laboured and rhetorical disquisitions of Cicero.

VI—OBJECT AND CONTENTS OF THE EPISTLE

The design of the apostle in writing to the Ephesian church was not polemical. In Colossians, theosophic error is pointedly and firmly refuted; but in Ephesians, principles are laid down which might prove a barrier to its introduction. The apostle indeed, in his farewell address at Miletus, had a sad presentiment of coming danger. Acts xx. 29, 30—"For I know this, that after my departure shall grievous wolves enter in among you, not sparing the flock. Also of your own selves shall men arise, speaking perverse things, to draw away disciples after them." But the epistle has no distinct allusion to such spiritual mischief and disturbance. In 2nd Timothy, too, the heresy of Hymenæus and Philetus is referred to, while Phygellus and Hermogenes are said to have deserted the

[1] Graul, *De Sententia scripsisse Paulum suas ad Ephes. Coloss. Philem. Epistolas, in Cæsareensi Captivitate.* Lipsiæ, 1836.

apostle at Rome. In the apocalyptic missive addressed to Ephesus as the first of the seven churches, no error is specified; but the grave and general charge is one of spiritual declension. The epistle before us may therefore be regarded as prophylactic more than corrective in its nature. What the immediate occasion was, we know not; possibly it was gratifying intelligence from Ephesus. It seems as if the heart of the apostle, fatigued aud dispirited with the polemical argument and warning to the Colossians, enjoyed a cordial relief and satisfaction in pouring out its inmost thoughts on the higher relations and transcendental doctrines of the gospel. The epistle may be thus divided :—

I. The salutation, i. 1, 2. II. A general description of Divine blessing enjoyed by the church in its source, means, purpose, and final result, wound up with a prayer for further spiritual gifts, and a richer and more penetrating Christian experience, and concluding with an expanded view of the original condition and present honours and privileges of the Ephesian church, i. 3–23, and ii. 1–11. III. A record of that marked change in spiritual position which the Gentile believers now possessed, ending with an account of the writer's selection to and qualification for the apostolate of heathendom, a fact so considered as to keep them from being dispirited, and to lead him to pray for enlarged spiritual benefactions on his absent sympathizers, ii. 12–22, and iii. 1–21. IV. A chapter on the unity of the church in its foundation and doctrine, a unity undisturbed by diversity of gifts, iv. 1–17. V. Special injunctions variously enjoined, and bearing upon ordinary life, iv. 17–32, v. 1–33, vi. 1–10. VI. The image of a spiritual warfare, mission of Tychicus, and valedictory blessing, vi. 11–24. The paragraphs of this epistle could be sent to no church partially enlightened, and but recently emerged from heathendom. The church at Ephesus was, however, able to appreciate its exalted views. And therefore are those rich primary truths presented to it, tracing back all to the Father's eternal and benignant will as the one origin; to the Son's mediation and blood as the one channel, union with Him being the one sphere; and to the Spirit's abiding work and influence as the one inner power; while the grand end of the provision of salvation and the organization and blessing of the church is His own glory in all the elements of its fulness. The purpose of the apostle seems to be—to refresh the consciousness of the church by the retrospect which he gives of their past state and God's past sovereign mercy, and by the prospect which he sets out of spiritual development crowned with perfection in Him in whom all things are re-gathered—as well as by the vivid and continual appeal to present grace and blessing which edges all the paragraphs.

Whatever emotions the church of Ephesus felt on receiving such a communication, the effects produced were not permanent. Though warned by its Lord, it did not return to its "first love," but gradually languished and died. The candlestick was at length removed out of his place, and Mahometan gloom overspread the city. The spot has also become one of external desolation. The sea has retired from the harbour, and left behind it a pestilential morass. Fragments of columns, arches, and porticos are strewn about, and the wreck and rubbish of the great temple can scarcely be distinguished. The brood of the partridge nestles on the site of the theatre, the streets are ploughed by the Ottoman serf, and the heights of Coressus are only visited by wandering flocks of goats. The best of the ruins—columns of green jasper—were transplanted by Justinian to Constantinople, to adorn the dome of the great church of Sancta Sophia, and some are said to have been carried into Italy. A straggling village of the name of Ayasaluk, or Asalook, is the wretched representative of the great commercial metropolis of Ionia. While thousands in every portion of Christendom read this epistle with delight, there is no one now to read it in the place to which it was originally addressed. Truly the threatened blight has fallen on Ephesus.[1]

### VII —WORKS ON THE EPISTLE

The principal writers on the literature of the epistle have already been mentioned in the course of the previous pages. Several ancient expositions of the epistle have been lost; for Jerome makes mention of one by Origen, of another by Apol-

---

[1] On the present state of Ephesus, the travels of Ainsworth and Fellowes, and the work of Arundel *On the Seven Churches*, may be read with advantage.

linaris of Laodicea, and of a third by Didymus of Alexandria. Among the Fathers we have the twenty-four homilies of Chrysostom, and the commentaries of his followers Theodoret, Œcumenius, and Theophylact. We have often referred to these, and to others in Cramer's *Catena*, as presenting the earliest specimens of Greek commentary. The commentaries of Jerome, Pelagius, and Ambrosiaster[1] belong to the Latin church. Exposition was not the work of mediæval times, though we have found some good notes in Anselm, Thomas Aquinas, and Peter Lombard, and in the Postills of Nicolas de Lyra of the fourteenth century. The expositors of the Reformation period follow: Erasmus, Calvin, Beza, Musculus, Bucer, and Bullinger; somewhat later among the Catholics, Estius and a-Lapide; and among the Protestants, Zanchius, Calovius, Calixtus, Crocius, Cocceius, Piscator, Hunnius, Tarnovius, Aretius, Jaspis, Hyperius, Schmid, Röell, and Wolf— all of whom have written more or less fully on the Epistle to the Ephesians. Wetstein and Grotius follow, in another era, with several of the writers in the *Critici Sacri*. In England there appeared "*An Entire Commentary upon the whole Epistle to the Ephesians*, wherein the text is learnedly and powerfully opened, etc.—preached by Paul Bayne, sometime preacher of God's Word at St. Andrew's, Cambridge;" London, 1643: and "*An Exposition of the First and part of the Second Chapter of the Epistle to the Ephesians*, by Thomas Goodwin, D.D., sometime President of Magdalen College in Oxford," was published in London in 1681. In Scotland we have the Latin folio of Principal Boyd (Bodius), published at London in 1652; the Latin duodecimo of Principal Rollock, reprinted at Geneva, 1593; the *Expositio Analytica* of Dickson (Professor of Theology in the University of Glasgow) on this and the other Epistles, published at Glasgow, 1645, and dedicated to the Marquis of Argyle, because his Grace had urged that the Professor should devote some portion of his course to biblical exegesis. Fergusson of Kilwinning also sent out a *Brief Exposition of the Epistles of Paul to the Galatians and Ephesians*, at Edinburgh, 1659. The Com-

---

[1] An unknown writer, so called to distinguish him from Ambrose, to whom his Commentaries were long ascribed, and with whose works they are still bound up. Many suppose him to have been Hilary the deacon.

mentaries of the Socinian Crellius and Slichtingius are contained in the *Fratres Poloni*. We have also the eloquent French work of Du Bosc on a portion of the epistle, and a similar and smaller *Méditation* by Gauthey, published in 1852. Lardner mentions an exposition by a Dutch minister of Rotterdam, Peter Dinant, of which a flattering review appeared in the *Bibliotheca Bremensis*, 1721. He opposed both the theory of Grotius and Usher. We pass over the various editors of the New Testament, such as Slade, Burton, Trollope, Valpy, Grinfield, and Bloomfield; and the numerous annotators and collectors of illustrations, such as Elsner, Kypke, Krebs, Knatchbull, Loesner, Küttner, Raphelius, Palairet, Bos, Heinsius, Alberti, Keuchenius, Dougtæus, and Cameron, pronounced by Bishop Hall, the most learned man that Scotland ever produced. We have not space to characterize Hammond, Chandler, Whitby, Callander, Locke, Doddridge, A. Clarke, Macknight, Peile, and Barnes, and the more popular works on this epistle by Lathrop, M'Ghee, Evans, Eastbourne, and Pridham. We hasten to specify the recent German commentaries. From that prolific nation of scholars and critics we have not only such works as those of Morus, Flatt, Koppe, Rosenmüller, von Gerlach, Kähler, and others, but we have the following formal and specific expositions on this epistle. Simply mentioning the comments of Spener (1730), of Baumgarten (Halle, 1767), of Schutz (Leipzig, 1778), of Müller (Heidelberg, 1793), and of Krause (Leipzig, 1789), we refer especially to the following : Cramer, *neue Uebersetzung des Briefes an die Epheser nebst einer Auslegung desselben.* Kiel, 1782. Holzhausen, *der Brief des Apostels Paulus an die Epheser übersetzt und erklärt.* Hannover, 1833. Rückert, *der Brief Pauli an die Epheser erläutert und vertheidigt.* Leipzig, 1834. Matthies, *Erklärung des Briefes Pauli an die Epheser.* Greifsvald, 1834. Meier, *Commentar über den Brief Pauli an die Epheser.* Berlin, 1834. Harless, *Commentar über den Brief Pauli an die Epheser.* Erlangen, 2nd ed. 1860. Olshausen, *Biblischer Commentar*, vol. iv. Königsberg, 1840. Meyer, *Kritisch exegetischer Commentar über das N. T.; Achte Abtheilung Kritisch Exegetisches Handbuch über den Brief an die Epheser.* Göttingen, 1859. De Wette, *Exegetisches Handbuch zum N. T.* vol. ii. Leipzig,

1843. Passavant, *Versuch einer praktischen Auslegung des Briefes Pauli an die Epheser.* Basel, 1836. *Catenæ in Sancti Pauli Epist. in Gal. Ephesios*, etc., ed. Cramer. Oxon. 1842. *Commentar über den Brief Pauli an die Epheser*, von L. F. O. Baumgarten-Crusius, ed. Kimmel and Schauer. Jena, 1847. Stier, *Auslegung des Briefes an die Epheser.* Berlin, 1848.[1] Bisping, *Erklärung der Briefe an die Epheser, Philipper*, etc. Münster, 1855. To these must be added the following recent English and American writers:— Turner, *The Epistle to the Ephesians in Greek and English.* New York, 1856. Alford, *Greek Testament*, vol. iii. London, 1856. Hodge, *A Commentary on the Epistle to the Ephesians.* New York, 1856. Ellicott, *A Critical and Grammatical Commentary on St. Paul's Epistle to the Ephesians*, 2d ed. London, 1859. Wordsworth, *Greek Testament*, part iii. London, 1859. Newland, *A New Catena on St. Paul's Epistles—a Practical and Exegetical Commentary on the Epistle of St. Paul to the Ephesians.* Oxford and London, 1860.

NOTE

In the following pages, when Buttmann, Matthiæ, Kühner, Madvig, Krüger, Bernhardy, Schmalfeld, Scheuerlein, Donaldson, Jelf, Winer, Rost, Alt, Stuart, Green, and Trollope are simply quoted, the reference is to their respective Greek grammars; and when Suidas, Hesychius, Passow (ed. Rost Palm, etc.), Robinson, Pape, Wilke, Wahl, Bretschneider, Liddell and Scott, are named, the reference is to their respective lexicons. If Hartung be found without any addition, we mean his *Lehre von den Partikeln der Griechischen Sprache*, 2 vols. Erlangen, 1832. The majority of the other names are those of the commentators or philologists enumerated in the previous chapter, or authors whose works are specified. The references to Tischendorf's New Testament are to the seventh edition.

[1] In Tholuck's *Anzeiger* for 1838 occurs a series of reviews of the commentaries of Matthies, Meier, Rückert, Holzhausen, and Harless, written, we believe, by Prof. Baumgarten, late of Rostock.

# COMMENTARY ON EPHESIANS

## CHAPTER I

THE first paragraph of the epistle introduces, according to ancient usage, the name and title or office of the writer, and concludes with a salutation to the persons addressed, and for whom the communication is intended.[1]

(Ver. 1.) Παῦλος, ἀπόστολος Χριστοῦ Ἰησοῦ.—" Paul, an apostle of Christ Jesus." The signification of the term ἀπόστολος will be found under chap. iv. 11. While the genitive Χριστοῦ Ἰησοῦ is that of possession, and not of ablation, yet naturally, and from its historical significance, it indicates the source, dignity, and functions of the apostolical commission, Acts xxvii. 23. Though, as Harless suggests, the idea of authorization often depends on some following clause, yet the genitive apparently includes it—the idea of authority being involved in such possession. This formal mention of his official relation to Jesus Christ is designed to certify the truth and claims of the following chapters. On similar occasions he sometimes designates himself by a term which has in it an allusion to the special labours which his apostleship involved, for he calls himself "a servant of Jesus Christ," Rom. i. 1; Phil. i. 1; Tit. i. 1. See under Col. i. 1; and especially under Phil. i. 1:—

διὰ θελήματος Θεοῦ—" by the will of God." The preposition διά points out the efficient cause. The apostle is fond of recurring to the truth expressed in this clause, 1 and 2 Cor. i. 1; Col. i. 1; 2 Tim. i. 1. Sometimes the idea is varied, as κατ' ἐπιταγὴν Θεοῦ, in 1 Tim. i. 1; and to give it intensity other adjuncts are occasionally employed, such as κλητός in

[1] Ἀρχαῖον ἔθος τὸ ἐπιστολαῖς προστιθέναι τὸ χαίρειν.—Suidas.

Rom. i. 1; 1 Cor. i. 1. The notion of Alford, hinted at by Bengel in his reference to vers. 5, 9, 11, that the phrase may have been suggested "by the great subject of which he is about to treat," is not sustained by analogous instances. It is added by the apostle generally, as the source and the seal of his office, and not inserted as an anticipative thought, prompted by the truth on which his mind was revolving. For his was no daring or impious arrogation of the name and honours of the apostolate; and that "will" according to which Paul became an apostle, had signally and suddenly evinced its origin and power. The great and extraordinary fact of his conversion involved in it both a qualification for the apostleship and a consecration to it—εἰς οὓς ἐγώ σε ἀποστέλλω, Acts xxvi. 17; 1 Cor. ix. 1, xv. 8. It was by no deferred or circuitous process that he came at length to learn and believe that God had ordained him as an apostle; but his convictions upon this point were based from the first on his own startled and instructive experience, which, among other elements of self-assurance, included in it the memory of that blinding splendour which enveloped him as he approached Damascus on an errand of cruelty and blood; of the tenderness and majesty of that voice which at once reached and subdued his heart; of the surprising agony which seized and held him till Ananias brought him spiritual relief; and of the subsequent theological tuition which he enjoyed in no earthly school. Gal. i. 11, 12; 1 Tim. i. 11–13. So that writing to the churches of Galatia, where his apostleship had been underrated if not denied, he says, with peculiar edge and precision, "Paul, an apostle, not of men, neither by man, but by Christ Jesus and God the Father." Gal. i. 1. This epistle is addressed—

τοῖς ἁγίοις τοῖς οὖσιν ἐν 'Εφέσῳ—" to the saints that are in Ephesus." "Ἅγιος, as a characteristic appellation of the Christian church, occurs first in Acts ix. 13. The word, rarely used by the Attic writers, who employ the kindred adjective ἁγνός, is allied to ἄζομαι and ἄγαμαι, and signifies one devoted or set apart to God. Porson, *Adversaria*, p. 139; Buttmann, *Lexilogus, sub voce*. This radical meaning is clearly seen in the related ἁγιάζω, in such passages as Matt. xxiii. 17; John x. 36, xvii. 17. It is not, however, to classic usage that we are to trace the special meaning of ἅγιος in the New Testament, but to its employment in the Septuagint as the Greek representative of the Hebrew קדש, Deut. xxxiii. 3. This notion of consecration is not, as Robinson seems to intimate, founded on holiness; for persons or things became holy in being set apart to God, and, from this association of ideas, holiness was ascribed to the tabernacle, with its furniture, its worshippers, and its periods of service. The idea of inner sanctity contained in the expressive epithet originates, therefore, in the primary sense of unreserved and exclusive devotement to Jehovah. Nor, on the other hand, can we accede to the opinion of Locke and Harless, that the word has no reference in itself to internal character, for consecration to God not only implied that the best of its kind was both claimed by Him and given to Him, but it also demanded that the hallowed gift be kept free from sacrilegious stain and debasement. So that, by the natural operation of this conservative element, holiness, in the common theological sense of the term, springs from consecration, and the "saints" do acquire personal and internal holiness from their near relation to God; the consciousness of their consecration having an invincible tendency to deepen and sustain spiritual purity within them. When Harless says that the notion of holiness which cannot be disjoined from a Christian ἅγιος, is not got from the word, but from our knowledge of the essence of that Christian community to which such a ἅγιος belongs, he seems to confound source and result; for one may reply that it is the ἅγιοι who, as such, originate the character of the Christian community, and not it which gives a character to them. The appellation ἅγιοι thus exhibits the Christian church in its normal aspect—a community of men self-devoted to God and His service. Nor does it ever seem to lose this meaning, even when used as a general epithet or in a local sense, as in Acts ix. 32, xxvi. 10; Rom. xv. 25. The words τοῖς οὖσιν ἐν Ἐφέσῳ, which simply indicate locality, have been already analyzed in the Prolegomena. The saints are further characterized—

καὶ πιστοῖς ἐν Χριστῷ Ἰησοῦ—" and believers in Christ Jesus." These words contain an additional element of description, and the two clauses mark out the same society in two special characteristics. But the meaning of πιστός in this connection must first be determined. There are two classes of interpreters:—1. Such as give the adjective the sense of *fidelis*, "faithful," in the modern acceptation of the English term—that is, true to their profession. Such is the view of Grotius, Rosenmüller, Meier, and Stier. But were such a sense adopted, we must suppose the apostle either to make a distinction between two classes of persons who were or had been members of the Ephesian church, or to affirm that all of them were trusty—were, in his judgment, persons of genuine and of untainted integrity. Did he then suppose that all the professed ἅγιοι were faithful? Or among the ἅγιοι did he distinguish and compliment such of them as were blessed with fidelity? The word in itself is not very determinate, though generally in New Testament usage πιστός in the sense of faithful—*fidelis*—is accompanied by an accusative with ἐπί, or a dative with ἐν, in reference to things over which trust has been exercised, and by the dative when the person is referred to toward whom the faithfulness is cherished. The idea of "faithful to Christ" would have required but the simple dative, as in Heb. iii. 2. We have indeed the phrase in 1 Cor. iv. 17—ἀγαπητὸν καὶ πιστὸν ἐν κυρίῳ, but there the formula, "in the Lord," qualifies both adjectives. 2. Some give the term its active sense of "believers," faithful, in its original and old English meaning, faith-full—full of faith—πιστός being equivalent to πιστεύων, save that the adjective points to condition rather than act. Many old interpreters, such as Röell, Cocceius, Vatablus, Crellius, and Calovius, with the majority of modern interpreters, take the word in this signification. For a like use of the word in classical writers —a use common to similar verbal adjectives—see Kühner, § 409, 3. The term πιστός has often this meaning, and is so rendered in our version, John xx. 27; Acts x. 45, xvi. 1; 2 Cor. vi. 15; 1 Tim. iv. 3, 10, 12, v. 16, vi. 2. It should have been so translated in other places, as Gal. iii. 9; Acts xvi. 15; Tit. i. 6. The Syriac version also renders it by the participle ܡܗܝܡܢܐ—believing. Hesychius defines it by εὐπειθής. The phrase is thus a second and appropriate epithet, more distinctive than the preceding, while the article is not repeated. It is a weak supposition of Morus and

Macknight, that these words were added merely for the sake of distinction, because the epithet "saints" had but the simple force of a common title in the apostolical letters. Neither do we conceive that the full force and meaning are brought out, if with some, as Beza, Bodius, a-Lapide, Calovius, and Vorstius, we take the καί as epexegetical, and reduce the clause into a mere explanation of the preceding title, as if it stood thus—" To the saints in Ephesus, to wit, the believers in Christ Jesus." For the salient point of their profession was faith in Christ Jesus, belief in the man Jesus as the Messiah, the anointed Saviour, the commissioned and successful deliverer of the world from all the penal effects of the fall. It was its faith specifically and definitely in Christ Jesus that distinguished the church in Ephesus from the fane of Artemis and the synagogue of the sons of Abraham. Πιστός[1] is here followed by ἐν referring to the object in which faith terminates and reposes; εἰς is sometimes employed, but ἐν is found with the noun in this chapter, ver. 15; Gal. iii. 26; Col. i. 4; see also Mark i. 15. The same usage is found in the Septuagint, Ps. lxxviii. 22, Jer. xii. 6, based perhaps on the Hebrew formula "הֶאֱמִין בְּ." Though the verbal adjective be used here in its active sense, it may therefore be followed by this preposition. If, when εἰς is employed, faith is usually represented as going out and leaning on its object, and if ἐπί expresses the additional idea of the trustworthiness of him whom we credit, then ἐν in the formula before us gives prominence to the notion of placid exercise, especially as ἐν is not so closely attached to the adjective as it would be to the verb or participle if it followed either of them. Fritzsche, *Comment in Marc.*, p. 25. The faith of the Ephesian converts rested in Jesus, in calm and per-

---

[1] The disputed signification of this word affords a peculiar and curious instance of the hazard of extreme opinions. H. Stephens had affirmed in his *Thesaurus* that πιστός is never used in an active sense, and never seems to signify one *qui fidem habet,* aut etiam *qui credulus est.* N. Fuller in his *Miscellanea Sacra,* lib. i. ch. 19, maintains, in opposition to the great lexicographer, that whenever the term is applied to a Christian man—*pro homine Christiano seu pio usurpatur,* it invariably denotes a believer, *qui credit* aut *fidem adhibet Deo.* The usage of the New Testament in at least nineteen places, shows that it has this latter or active sense; still, in some clauses, even when applied to Christians, it seems to bear the sense of *fidelis*—1 Tim. i. 12; 2 Tim. ii. 2; Col. iv. 9; 1 Pet. v. 12; Rev. ii. 10. Among the Greek Fathers, the word is used in both senses, as the examples adduced by Suicer, *sub voce,* abundantly testify.

manent repose. It was not a mere extended dependence placed on Him, but it had convinced itself of His power and love, of His sympathy and merits; it not only knew the strength of His arm, it had also penetrated and felt the throbbing tenderness of His heart—it was therefore *in* Him. There might have been agitation, anxiety, and terrible perturbation of spirit when the claims of Christ were first presented and brought into sharp conflict with previous convictions and traditionary prepossessions; but the turmoil had subsided into quiescent and immoveable confidence in the Son of God.

But does ἐν Χριστῷ ᾽Ιησοῦ simply qualify πιστοῖς? or does it not also qualify ἁγίοις? Storr renders it—*Qui Christo sacri sunt et in eum credunt.* (*Opuscula*, ii. 121.) The phrase "saints in Christ Jesus" occurs in Phil. i. 1, and the meaning is apparent—saints in spiritual fellowship with Christ. In Col. i. 2 we have "saints and believing brethren in Christ," where the words in question may not only qualify "saints," but also describe the essence and circle of the spiritual brotherhood. But we are inclined, with Jerome, Meyer, de Wette, and Ellicott, in opposition to Harless, Meier, and Baumgarten-Crusius, to restrict the words ἐν Χριστῷ ᾽Ιησοῦ to πιστοῖς. The previous epithet is complete without such an addition, but this second one is not so distinctive without the supplement. The intervention of the words τοῖς οὖσιν ἐν ᾽Εφέσῳ separates the two phrases, and seems to mark them as independent appellations. But though grammatically they may be separate names of the same Christian community, they are essentially and theologically connected. "Nemo fidelis," says Calvin, "nisi qui sanctus; et nemo rursum sanctus, nisi qui fidelis." The more powerful and pervading such faith is, the more the whole inner nature is brought under its controlling and assimilating influence; the more deeply and vividly it realizes Christ in authority, example, and proprietary interest in "the church which He has purchased with His own blood," then the more cordial, entire, and unreserved will be the consecration.

(Ver. 2.) Χάρις ὑμῖν καὶ εἰρήνη—"Grace to you and peace." The apostolical salutation is cordial and comprehensive. "Claudius Lysias to the most excellent governor, greeting"—Paul to the Ephesians, "grace and peace." It is far more expressive than the ὑγιαίνειν, χαίρειν, or εὖ πράττειν of the ancient classic formula. The same or similar phraseology occurs in the beginning of most of the epistles. Χάρις, allied to χαίρειν and the Latin *gratia*, signifies favour, and, especially in the New Testament, divine favour — that goodwill on God's part which not only provides and applies salvation, but blesses, cheers, and assists believers. As a wish expressed for the Ephesian church, it does not denote mercy in its general aspect, but that many-sided favour that comes in the form of hope to saints in despondency, of joy to them in sorrow, of patience to them in suffering, of victory to them under assault, and of final triumph to them in the hour of death. And so the apostle calls it χάριν εἰς εὔκαιρον βοήθειαν—grace in order to well-timed assistance. Heb. iv. 16.

Εἰρήνη — Peace, is the Greek equivalent of the Hebrew שָׁלוֹם—a term of familiar and beautiful significance. It includes every blessing—being and wellbeing. It was the formula of ordinary courtesy at meeting and parting. "Peace I leave with you," said our Lord; but the term was no symbol of cold and formal politeness—"not as the world giveth, give I unto you." John xiv. 27. The word in this connection denotes that form of spiritual blessing which keeps the heart in a state of happy repose. It is therefore but another phase, or rather it is the result, of the previous χάρις. Stier distinguishes these two blessings, as if they corresponded to the previous epithets ἁγίοις καὶ πιστοῖς, grace being appropriate to the "saints," as the first basis of their sanctification; and peace to the "faithful," as the last aim or effect of their confidence in God. But "grace and peace" are often employed in salutations where the two epithets of saints and believers in Christ Jesus do not occur, so that it would be an excess of refinement either to introduce such a distinction in this place, or to say, with the same author, that the two expressions foreshadow the dualism of the epistle—first, the grace of God toward the church, and then its faith toward Him. Nor can we, as Jerome hints, ascribe grace to the Father and peace to the Son as their separate and respective sources. A conscious possession of the divine favour can alone create and sustain mental tranquillity. To use an impressive figure of Scripture, the unsanctified heart resembles "the troubled sea," in constant uproar and agitation—dark, muddy, and tempestuous; but the storm subsides, for a voice of power has cried, " Peace, be still," and there is " a great calm:" the lowering clouds are dispelled, and the azure sky smiles on its own reflection in the bosom of the quiet and glassy deep. The favour of God and the felt enjoyment of it, the apostle wishes to the members of the Ephesian church in this salutation ; yea, grace and peace— ἀπὸ Θεοῦ πατρὸς ἡμῶν καὶ Κυρίου 'Ιησοῦ Χριστοῦ—"from God our Father and the Lord Jesus Christ." The source of these spiritual blessings is now stated. Erasmus, Morus, and some Socinian interpreters, would understand the connection as if κυρίου were governed by πατρός, and not by ἀπό— "From God our Father, the Father, too, of our Lord Jesus Christ." This interpretation would sever Jesus from the bestowment of these blessings, as, in such an exegesis, they are supposed to descend from God, who is our Father, and who is at the same time designated as Christ's Father. This construction is wholly unwarranted. Father and Son are both specified as the sources of grace and peace. Grace and peace are not earth-born blessings ; they descend from heaven, from God on His glorious throne, whose high prerogative it is to send down those special influences; and from Christ at His right hand, who has provided these blessed gifts by His sufferings and death—who died to secure, and is exalted to bestow them, and whose constant living sympathy with His people enables Him to appreciate their wants, and prompts Him out of His own fulness to supply them. God is described as our Father—ἡμῶν. Our sonship will be illustrated under ver. 5. The universal Governor being the parent of believers, who have a common fatherhood in Him, grace and peace are viewed as *paternal* gifts.

The Saviour is characterized as Lord Jesus Christ; "Lord," Master, or Proprietor. Ὁ κύριος is often applied to Jesus in the Pauline writings. It corresponds to the theocratic intimations of a king—a great king—to preside over the spiritual Sion. Ps. cx. 1. Gabler, in his *New Theological Journal*, iv. p. 11, has affirmed, that in the New Testament κύριος, without the article, refers to God, and that ὁ κύριος is the uniform appellation of Christ—a distinction which cannot be maintained, as may be seen by a reference to Rom. xv. 11; 1 Cor. x. 26; Heb. viii. 2; for in all those passages the reference is to God, and yet the article is prefixed. Winer, § 19, 1. Like Θεός in many places, it is often used without the article when it refers to Christ. In about two hundred and twenty instances in the writings of Paul, κύριος denotes the Saviour, and in about a hundred instances it is joined to His other names, as in the phrase before us. Perhaps in not more than three places, which are not quotations or based on quotations, does Paul apply κύριος to God.[1] It was a familiar and favourite designation—the exalted Jesus is "Lord of all"—"He has made Him both Lord and Christ." He has won this Lordship by His blood. Phil. ii. 8, 11. "He has been exalted," that every tongue should salute Him as Lord. 1 Cor. xii. 3. While the title may belong to Him as Creator and Preserver, it is especially given Him as the enthroned God-man, for His sceptre controls the universe. The range of that Lordship has infinitude for its extent, and eternity for its duration. The term, as Suicer quaintly remarks, refers not to οὐσία, but to ἐξουσία. And as He is Head of the Church, and "Head over all things to the Church"—its Proprietor, Organizer, Governor, Guardian, Blesser, and Judge—whose law it obeys, whose ordinances it hallows, whose spirit it cherishes, whose truth it conserves, and whose welcome to glory it anticipates and prepares for; therefore may He, sustaining such a relation to His spiritual kingdom, be so often and so fondly named as Lord. The apostle invokes upon the Ephesians grace and peace from the Lord Jesus Christ, whose supreme administration was designed to secure, and does actually confer, those *lordly* gifts.

The mention of spiritual blessing fills the susceptible mind of the apostle with ardent gratitude, and incites him to praise. In his writings argument often rises into doxology—logic swells into lyrics. The Divine Source of these glorious gifts, He who gives them so richly and so constantly, is worthy of rapturous homage. They who get all must surely adore Him who gives all. With the third verse begins a sentence which terminates only at the end of the 14th verse, a sentence which enumerates the various and multiplied grounds of praise. These are:—holiness as the result and purpose of God's eternal

---

[1] Stuart's Essay, *Biblical Repository*, vol. iv.

choice—adoption with its fruits, springing from the good,
pleasure of His will with the profuse bestowment of grace—all
tracing themselves to the Father: pardon of sin by the blood
of Christ—the summation of all things in Him—the interest
of believers in Him—these in special connection with the
Son : and the united privilege of hearing, and trusting, and
being sealed, with their possession of the Earnest of future
felicity—a sphere of blessing specially belonging to the Holy
Ghost. Such are the leading ideas of a magnificent anthem
—not bound together in philosophical precision, but each
suggesting the other by a law of powerful association. The
one truth instinctively gives birth to the other, and the connection is indicated chiefly by a series of participles.

(Ver. 3.) Εὐλογητὸς ὁ Θεὸς καὶ πατὴρ τοῦ Κυρίου ἡμῶν
Ἰησοῦ Χριστοῦ—" Blessed be the God and Father of our
Lord Jesus Christ." The verb is usually omitted. The
adjective in the doxology is placed before the substantive,
because being used as a predicate, and representing an
abstract quality, the emphasis lies on it. Such is the invariable
usage in the Old Testament—not God is blessed, but, from
the position of the words—Blessed be God, בָּרוּךְ יְהוָה. At least
thirty times does the formula occur. Ps. lxviii. 19, in the
Septuagint being a mistranslation or doubled version of the
Hebrew, is only an apparent exception, and the phrase,
Rom. ix. 5, we do not regard as a doxology. In all the passages
quoted by Ellicott after Fritzsche—Rom. ix. 5, as if they
were exceptions to this rule, it is εὐλογημένος and not
εὐλογητός which is employed, and there is a shade of difference
between the participle and the adjective—for while in the
Septuagint εὐλογημένος is applied to God, εὐλογητός is never
applied to man. Thus in 1 Kings x. 9, 2 Chron. ix. 8, which
are parallel passages—γένοιτο being employed in the first
instance, and ἔστω in the second; and in Job i. 21, Ps. cxii. 2,
in both of which ὄνομα κυρίου with εἴη occurs, the verbs, as
might be expected, are followed immediately by their nomi-
natives. Εὐλογητός in the New Testament is applied only
to God—His is perpetual and unchanging blessedness, perpetual and unchanging claim on the homage of His creatures.
Εὐλογημένος is used of such as are blessed of God, and on
whom blessing is invoked from Him. Matt. xxi. 9 ; Luke i. 28.

But the blessedness we ascribe to God comes from no foreign source; it is already in Himself, an innate and joyous possession. Paul's epistles usually begin with a similar ascription of praise (2 Cor. i. 3). But in many cases—the majority of cases—he does not utter a formal ascription: he expresses the fact in such phrases as "I thank," "We thank," "We are bound to thank"—"God."

One would think that there is little dubiety in a formula so plain; for Θεός and πατήρ are in apposition, and both govern the following genitive—Blessed be the God of, and the Father of, our Lord Jesus Christ. The Divine Being is both God and Father of our Lord Jesus Christ. Yet there are many who sever the two nouns—disjoining Θεός from κυρίου—and so render it, Blessed be God, who is the Father of our Lord Jesus Christ. Theodoret, the Peschito, Whitby, and Bodius, with Harless, Meyer, Holzhausen, Baumgarten-Crusius, Bisping, and Ellicott, are in favour of this opinion. But Jerome, Theophylact, Koppe, Michaelis, Rückert, Stier, Olshausen, and Alford, adhere to the former view, which we are disposed to adopt. The words of themselves would bear either construction, though Olshausen remarks that, to bring out the first opinion, the Greek should run εὐλογητὸς Θεὸς ὁ πατήρ. Theodoret capriciously inserts the adjective ἡμῶν in his note upon Θεός. He represents the apostle as showing—δηλῶν, ὡς ἡμῶν μέν ἐστι Θεός, τοῦ δὲ κυρίου ἡμῶν πατήρ, as if Paul meant to describe the Divine Being as our God and Christ's Father. To say with Meyer that only πατήρ requires a genitive and not Θεός, is mere assertion. The statement of Harless, too, that τε should have been inserted before καί, if Θεός governed κυρίου, appears to us to be wholly groundless, nor do the investigations of Hartung, to which he refers, at all sustain him. *Lehre von den Partikeln der Griech. Sprache*, vol. i. 125. Compare 1 Pet. ii. 25. Had the article occurred before πατήρ, this particle might have been necessary; but its omission shows that the relation of Θεός and πατήρ is one of peculiar unity. Distinct and independent prominence is not assigned to each term. Winer, § 19, 3, note. Nor is there any impropriety of thought in joining Θεός with κυρίου—the God of our Lord Jesus Christ. Θεὸς μέν, says Theophylact, ὡς σαρκωθέντος, πατὴρ δὲ ὡς θεοῦ λόγου. The diction of the Greek Father, in the last clause, is not strictly correct, for the correlative terms are Father, Son, πατήρ, υἱός: God, Word, Θεός, λόγος. "The God of our Lord Jesus Christ" is a phrase which occurs also in the 17th verse of this chapter. On the cross, in the depth of His agony, the mysterious complaint of Jesus expressed the same relationship, "My God, my God." "I ascend," said He to Mary, "to my God and your God." Rev. iii. 12. The phrase is therefore one of scriptural use. As man, Jesus owned Himself to be the servant of God. God's commission He came to execute, God's law He obeyed, and God's will was His constant Guide. As a pious and perfect man He served God, prayed to God, and trusted in God. And God, as God, stands in no distant relation to Christ—He is also His Father. The two characters are blended—"God and Father."—See under ver. 17. Sonship cannot indeed imply on Christ's part posteriority of existence or derivation of essence, for such a notion is plainly inconsistent with His supreme Divinity. The name seems to mark identity of nature and prerogative, with infinite, eternal, unchanging, and reciprocal love.[1] Since this God and Father of our Lord Jesus Christ sent Him into the world, prescribed His service of suffering and death, and accepted it as a complete atonement, it is therefore His prerogative to dispense the blessings so secured—

ὁ εὐλογήσας ἡμᾶς—"who blessed us"—"us," not the apostle simply, as Koppe supposes from the contrast of ὑμεῖς in ver. 14. The persons blessed are the apostle and the members of that church addressed by him—he and they were alike recipients of divine favour. The εὐλογήσας stands in ideal contrast to the εὐλογητός—God blessed us, and we bless God; but His blessing of us is one of deed, our blessing of Him is only in word. He makes us blessed, we pronounce Him blessed. He confers on us wellbeing, we ascribe to Him wellbeing. Ours is *benedicere*, His is *benefacere*. The participle here, as in many places, has virtually a causal significance. Kühner, § 667, *a*. We bless Him because He has blessed us. As the word expresses that divine beneficence which excites our gratitude,

---

[1] For a spirited view of the doctrine of the Θιάνθρωπος in the hymnology of the early Church, the reader may consult Dorner, *die Lehre von der Person Christi*, second edition, vol. i. p. 294. See also Thomasius, *Christi Persona*, etc., § 41 (1857).

it must in a doxology have its widest significance. The enraptured mind selects in such a case the most powerful and intense term, to express its sense of the divine generosity. As Fergusson in his own Doric says, "The apostle does not propound the causes of salvation warshly, and in a cauldrife manner:"—

ἐν πάσῃ εὐλογίᾳ πνευματικῇ—" with all spiritual blessing." Ἐν is used in an instrumental sense, and similar phraseology in reference to God occurs in Tob. viii. 15, Jas. iii. 9. εὐλογία is not verbal wish expressed, but actual blessing conferred. The reader will notice the peculiar collocation of the three allied terms, εὐ-λογητός-λογήσας-λογίᾳ, a repetition not uncommon in the Hebrew Scriptures, and found occasionally among the Greek classics.

The blessings are designated as spiritual, but in what sense?
1. Chrysostom, Grotius, Aretius, Holzhausen, and Macknight suppose that the apostle intends a special and marked contrast between the spiritual blessings of the new dispensation, and the *material and temporal* blessings of the old economy. Temporal blessings, indeed, were of frequent promise in the Mosaic dispensation—dew of heaven, fatness of the earth, abundance of corn, wine, and oil, peace, longevity, and a flourishing household. It is true that such gifts are not now bestowed as the immediate fruits of Christ's mediation, though, at the same time, godliness has "the promise of the life that now is." But mere worldly blessings have sunk into their subordinate place. When the sun rises, the stars that sparkled during night are eclipsed by the flood of superior brilliance and disappear, though they still keep their places; so the blessings of this world may now be conferred, and may now be enjoyed by believers, but under the new dispensation their lustre is altogether dimmed and absorbed by those spiritual gifts which are its profuse and distinctive endowments. If there be any reference to the temporal blessings of the Jewish covenant, it can only, as Calvin says, be "tacita antithesis."
2. Others regard the adjective as referring to the mind or soul of man, such as Erasmus, Estius, Flatt, Wahl, and Wilke; while Koppe, Rückert, and Baumgarten-Crusius express a doubtful acquiescence in this opinion. This interpretation yields a good meaning, inasmuch as these gifts are adapted to

our inner or higher nature, and it is upon our *spirit* that the Holy Ghost operates. But this is not the ruling sense of the epithet in the New Testament. It is, indeed, in a generic sense opposed to σαρκικός in 1 Cor. ix. 11, and in Rom. xv. 27; while in 1 Cor. xv. 44–46 it is employed in contrast with ψυχικός—the one term descriptive of an animal body, and the other of a body elevated above animal functions and organization, with which believers shall be clothed at the last day. Similar usage obtains in Eph. vi. 12; 1 Pet. ii. 5; 1 Cor. x. 3, 4. 3. But in all other passages where, as in this clause, the word is used to qualify Christian men, or Christian blessings, its ruling reference is plainly to the Holy Spirit. Thus—spiritual gifts, Rom. i. 11; a special endowment of the Spirit, 1 Cor. xii. 1, xiv. 1, etc.; spiritual men, that is, men enjoying in an eminent degree the Spirit, 1 Cor. ii. 15, xiv. 37; and also in Gal. vi. 1; Rom. vii. 14; Eph. v. 19; Col. iii. 16; and in 1 Cor. ii. 13, "spiritual" means produced by or belonging to the Holy Spirit. Therefore the prevailing usage of the New Testament warrants us in saying, that these blessings are termed spiritual from their connection with the Holy Spirit. In this opinion we have the authority of the old Syriac version, which reads ܕܪܘܚ—"of the Spirit;" and the concurrence of Cocceius, Harless, de Wette, Olshausen, Meier, Meyer, and Stier. The Pauline *usus loquendi* is decidedly in its favour.

Πάσῃ—"All." The circle is complete. No needed blessing is wanted—nothing that God has promised, or Christ has secured, or that is indispensable to the symmetry and perfection of the Christian character. And those blessings are all in the hand of the Spirit. Christianity is the dispensation of the Spirit, and as its graces are inwrought by Him, they are all named "spiritual" after Him.

It certainly narrows and weakens the doxology to confine those "blessings" wholly or chiefly to the charismata, or extraordinary gifts of the primitive Church, as Wells and Whitby do. Those gifts were brilliant manifestations of divine power, but they have long since passed away, and are therefore inferior to the permanent graces—faith, hope, and love. They were not given to all, like the ordinary donations of the Holy Ghost. Theodoret, with juster appreciation, long ago said, that in addition to such endowments, ἔδωκε τὴν ἐλπίδα τῆς ἀναστάσεως, τὰς τῆς ἀθανασίας ἐπαγγελίας, τὴν ὑπόσχεσιν τῆς βασιλείας τῶν οὐρανῶν, τὸ τῆς υἱοθεσίας ἀξίωμα —" the blessings referred to here are, the hope of the resurrection, the promises of immortality, the kingdom of heaven in reversion, and the dignity of adoption." The blessings are stated by the apostle in the subsequent verses, and neither gifts, tongues, nor prophecy occupy a place in the succinct and glowing enumeration :—

ἐν τοῖς ἐπουρανίοις ἐν Χριστῷ—" in the heavenly places, in Christ"—a peculiar idiom, the meaning of which has been greatly disputed. What shall be supplied — πράγμασι or τόποις, things or places ? The translation, " In heavenly things," is supported by Chrysostom, Theodoret, Œcumenius, Luther, Baumgarten-Crusius, Holzhausen, Matthies, and Meier. This view makes the phrase a more definite characterization of the spiritual blessings. But the construction is against it, for the insertion of τοῖς seems to show that it is neither a mere prolonged specification, nor, as in Homberg's view, a mere parallel definition to ἐν πάσῃ εὐλογίᾳ. The sentence, with such an explanation, even though the article should be supposed to designate a class, appears confused and weakened with somewhat of tautology. Nor can we suppose, with Van Til, that there is simply a designed contrast to the terrestrial blessings of the Old Testament. The other supplement, τόποις, appears preferable, and such is the opinion of the Syriac translator—who renders it simply ܒܫܡܝܐ, in heaven—of Jerome, Drusius, Beza, Bengel, Rückert, Harless, Olshausen, de Wette, Meyer, Stier, and Bisping. The phrase occurs four times besides—i. 20 ; ii. 6 ; iii. 10 ; vi. 12. In all these places in this one epistle, the idea of locality is expressly implied, and there is no reason why this clause should be an exception. Harless remarks that the adjective, as ἐπί would suggest, has in the Pauline writings a local signification.

But among such as hold this view there are some differences of opinion. Jerome, Beza, Bodius, and Rückert would connect the phrase directly with εὐλογήσας; but the position of the words forbids the exegesis, and the participle must in such a case be taken with a proleptic or future signification. Beza alternates between two interpretations. According to his double view, men may be said to be blessed "in heaven," either because God the Blesser is in heaven, or because the blessings received are those which are characteristic of heaven —such blessings as are enjoyed by its blessed inhabitants. Calvin, Grotius, and Koppe argue that the term points out the special designation of the spiritual blessings; that they are to be enjoyed in heaven. Grotius says these spiritual blessings place us in heaven—"*spe et jure.*" The sweeping view of Calovius comprehends all these interpretations; the spiritual blessings are ἐν τοῖς ἐπουρανίοις—*ratione et originis, qualitatis, et finis.*[1] The opinion of Slichtingius, Zanchius, and Olshausen is almost identical. The latter calls it "the spiritual blessing which is in heaven, and so carries in it a heavenly nature."[2]

We have seen that the idea of locality is distinctly implied in the phrase ἐν τοῖς ἐπουρανίοις. Olshausen is in error when he says that "heavenly places" in Paul's writings signify heaven absolutely, for the phrase sometimes refers to a lower and nearer spiritual sphere of it; "He hath raised us up, and made us sit together with Christ in the heavenly places." Our session with Christ is surely a present elevation—an honour and happiness even now enjoyed. "We wrestle against principalities, against powers—against spiritual wickedness in heavenly places," vi. 12. These dark spirits are not in heaven, for they are exiles from it, and our struggle with them is in the present life. There are, therefore, beyond a doubt, "heavenly places" on earth. Now the gospel, or the Mediatorial reign, is "the kingdom of heaven." That kingdom or reign of God is "in us," or among us. Heaven is brought near to man through Christ Jesus. Those spiritual blessings conferred on us create heaven within us, and the scenes of Divine benefaction are "heavenly places;" for wherever the

---

[1] While we heartily admire the enterprise of M. Pacho and Archdeacon Tattam, and the critical erudition of Mr. Cureton in reference to the literary remains of Ignatius, we may be allowed to refer in a matter of philology to two of his so-called epistles. Mention is made of τὰ ἐπουράνια καὶ ἡ δόξη τῶν ἀγγίλων, the heavenly regions and the glory of the angels. *Ep. ad Smyrn.* vi. and also *Ep. ad Trall.*—τὰ ἐπουράνια καὶ τὰς τοποθισίας τὰς ἀγγελικάς—where τοποθισία stands in apposition to τὰ ἐπουράνια.

[2] "Der geistliche Segen welcher in Himmel ist, also auch himmlische Natur an sich trägt."

light and love of God's presence are to be enjoyed, there is heaven. If such blessings are the one Spirit's inworking,— that Spirit who in God's name "takes of the things that are Christ's and shows them unto us,"—then His influence diffuses the atmosphere of heaven around us. "Our country is in heaven," and we enjoy its immunities and prerogatives on earth. We would not vaguely say, with Ernesti, Teller, and Schutze, that the expression simply means the church. True, in the church men are blessed, but the scenes of blessing here depicted represent the church in a special and glorious aspect, as a spot so like heaven, and so replete with the Spirit in the possession and enjoyment of His gifts—so filled with Christ and united to Him—so much of His love pervading it, and so much of His glory resting upon it, that it may be called τὰ ἐπουράνια. The phrase may have been suggested, as Stier observes, by the region of Old Testament blessing—Canaan being given to the chosen people of God as the God of Abraham.

The words ἐν Χριστῷ might be viewed as connected with τὰ ἐπουράνια, and their position at the end of the verse might warrant such an exegesis. Christ at once creates and includes heaven. But they are better connected with the preceding participle, and in that connection they do not signify, as Chrysostom and Luther suppose, "through Christ" as an external cause of blessing, but "in Him." Castalio supposing ἐν to be superfluous, affectedly renders—*in rebus Christi cœlestibus*, and Schoettgen erroneously takes the noun for the *dativus commodi*—*in laudem Christi*. The words are reserved to the last with special emphasis. The apostle writes of blessing— spiritual blessing—all spiritual blessing—all spiritual blessing in the heavenly places; but adds at length the one sphere in which they are enjoyed—in Christ—in living union with the personal Redeemer. God blesses us: if the question be, When? the aorist solves it; if it be, With what sort of gifts? the ready answer is, "With all spiritual blessings"—ἐν; and if it be, Where? the response is, "In the heavenly places"—ἐν; and if it be, How? the last words show it, "in Christ"—ἐν, the one preposition being used thrice, to point out varied but allied relations. If Christians are blessed, and so blessed with unsparing liberality and universal benefaction in Christ through the Spirit's influence upon them; and if the scenes of such transcendent enjoyment may be named without exaggeration "heavenly places"—may they not deeply and loudly bless the God and Father of our Lord Jesus Christ? And so the triune operation of the triune God is introduced: the Father who blesses—the Son, in whom those blessings are conferred—and the Spirit, by whose inner work they are enjoyed, and from whom they receive their distinctive epithet.

(Ver. 4.) Καθὼς ἐξελέξατο ἡμᾶς ἐν αὐτῷ—" According as He chose us in Him." The adverb καθώς defines the connection of this verse with the preceding. That connection is modal rather than causal; καθώς, like καθότι, may signify sometimes "because," but the cause specified involves the idea of manner. Καθώς, in classic Greek καθά, is the later form (Phrynichus, ed. Lobeck, p. 426), and denotes, as its composition indicates, "according as." These spiritual blessings are conferred on us, not merely because God chose us, but they are given to us in perfect harmony with His eternal purpose. Their number, variety, adaptation, and fulness, with the shape and the mode of their bestowment, are all in exact unison with God's pre-temporal and gracious resolution; they are given after the model of that pure and eternal archetype which was formed in the Divine mind—

ἐξελέξατο.—1 Cor. i. 27. The action belongs wholly to the past, as the aorist indicates. Krüger, § 53, 5, 1; Scheuerlein, § 32, 2. The idea involved in this word lay at the basis of the old theocracy, and it also pervades the New Testament. The Greek term corresponds to the Hebrew בָּחַר of the Old Testament, which is applied so often to God's selection of Abraham's seed to be His peculiar people. Deut. iv. 37, vii. 6, 7; Isa. xli. 8; Ps. xxxiii. 12, xlvii. 4, etc. Usteri, *Paulin. Lehrbegriff*, p. 271. The verb before us, with its cognate forms, is used frequently to indicate the origin of that peculiar relation which believers sustain to God, and it also assigns the reason of that distinction which subsists between them and the world around them. Whatever the precise nature of this choice may be, the general doctrine is, that the change of relation is not of man's achievement, but of God's, and the aorist points to it as past; that man does not unite himself to God, but that God unites man to Himself, for there is no attractive power in man's heart to collect and gather in upon it those spiritual blessings. But there is not merely this palpable right of initiation on the part of God; there is also the prerogative of sovereign bestowment, as is indicated by the composition of the verb and by the following pronoun, ἡμᾶς—"us"—we have; others want. The apostle speaks of himself and his fellow-saints at Ephesus. If God had not chosen them, they would never have chosen God.

Hofmann (*Schriftb.* p. 223, etc., 2nd ed. 1857) denies that the verb contains the idea of choice in its theological use. Admitting that it does mean to "choose," as in Josh. viii. 3, and to prefer, as in Gen. xiii. 11, Luke x. 42, he abjures in this place all notion of selection—they are chosen not out of others, but chosen for a certain end—*für etwas*. The supposition is ingenious, but it is contrary to the meaning of the compound verb, even in the passages selected by him, as Ex. xviii. 25, Acts vi. 5, in which there is formal selection expressed—judges out of the people by Moses; deacons out from the membership of the early church. The phrase οἱ ἐκλεκτοὶ ἄγγελοι in 1 Tim. v. 21, may, for aught we know, have a meaning quite in harmony with the literal signification, or ἐκλεκτός may bear a secondary sense, based on its primary meaning, such as Hofmann finds in Luke xxiii. 35, and according to a certain reading, in Luke ix. 35. But while there is a high destiny set before us, there is a choice of those who are to enjoy it, and this choice in itself, and plainly implying a contrast, the apostle describes by ἐξελέξατο. On the other hand, Ebrard—*Christliche Dogmatik*, § 560, vol. ii. p. 65, 1851—denies that the end of election, considered as individual eternal happiness, is contained in the verb; for election, according to him, signifies not the choice of individuals, but of a multitude out of the profane world into the church, so that ἐκλεκτός is synonymous with ἅγιος. Election to external privilege is true, but it does not exhaust the purpose: for it would be stopping at the means without realizing the end. Besides, the choice of a multitude is simply the choice of each individual composing it. That multitude may be regarded as a unity by God, but to Him it is a unity of definite elements or members. On the divine side, the elect, whatever their number, are a unity, and are so described—πᾶν ὃ δέδωκέ μοι, John vi. 39; πᾶν ὃ δέδωκας αὐτῷ, John xvii. 2—a totality viewed by Omniscience as one; but on the human side, the elect are the whole company of believers, but thus individualized—πᾶς ὁ θεωρῶν τὸν υἱὸν καὶ πιστεύων—John vi. 40 :—

Ἐν αὐτῷ—" in Him," for such is the genuine reading, not ἑαυτῷ, or *in ipso*, as the Vulgate has it and some commentators take it; nor "to Himself," as the Ethiopic renders it. The reference is to Christ, but the nature of that reference has been disputed. Chrysostom says, "He by whom He has blessed us, is the same as He by whom He has chosen us;" but afterwards he interprets the words before us thus—διὰ τῆς εἰς αὐτὸν πίστεως, and he capriciously ascribes the elective act to Christ. Many, as a-Lapide, Estius, Bullinger, and Flatt, translate virtually, "on account of Christ." But the apostolical idea is more definite and profound. Ἐν αὐτῷ seems to point out the position of the ἡμᾶς. Believers were looked upon as being in Christ their federal Head, when they were elected. To the prescient eye of God the entire church was embodied in Jesus—was looked upon as "in Him." The church that was to be appeared to the mind of Him who fills eternity, as already in being, and that ideal being was in Christ. It is true that God Himself is in Christ, and in Christ purposes and performs all that pertains to man's redemption; but the thought here is not that God in Christ has chosen us, but that when He elected us, we were regarded as being in Christ our representative—like as the human race was in Adam, or the Jewish nation in Abraham. We were chosen—

πρὸ καταβολῆς κόσμου,—" before the foundation of the world."—Similar phraseology occurs in Matt. xiii. 35; John xvii. 24; 1 Pet. i. 20. The more usual Pauline expressions are — πρὸ τῶν αἰώνων, 1 Cor. ii. 7; πρὸ χρόνων αἰωνίων, 2 Tim. i. 9. Καταβολή is also used in the same sense in the classics, and by Philo. Lœsner, *Observat.* p. 338; Passow, *sub voce*. Chrysostom, alluding to the composition of the noun κατα-βολή, says fancifully,—" Beautiful is that word, as if he were pointing to the world cast down from a great height—yes, vast and indescribable is the height of God, so wide the distance between Creator and creature."[1] The phrase itself declares that this election is no

---

[1] Καὶ καλῶς καταβολὴν εἶπεν, ὡς ἀπό τινος ὕψους καταβιβλημένον μεγάλου αὐτόν δεικνύς, καὶ γὰρ μέγα καὶ ἄφατον τὸ ὕψος τοῦ Θιοῦ, οὐ τῷ τοπῷ, ἀλλὰ τῷ ἀνακεχωρηκότι

act of time, for time dates from the creation. Prior to the commencement of time were we chosen in Christ. The generic idea, therefore, is what Olshausen calls *Zeitlosigkeit, Timelessness,* implying of course absolute eternity. The choice is eternal, and it realizes itself or takes effect in that actual separation by which the elect, οἱ ἐκλεκτοί, are brought out of the world into the church, and so become κλητοὶ, ἅγιοι, καὶ πιστοί. Before that world which was to be lost in sin and misery was founded, its guilt and helplessness were present to the mind of God, and His gracious purposes toward it were formed. The prospect of its fall coexisted eternally with the design of its recovery by Christ—

εἶναι ἡμᾶς ἁγίους καὶ ἀμώμους κατενώπιον αὐτοῦ—" in order that we should be holy, and without blame before Him." Εἶναι is the infinitive of design—" that we should be." Winer, § 44, 1; Col. i. 22. The two adjectives express the same idea, with a slight shade of variation. Deut. vii. 6, xiv. 2. The first is inner consecration to God, or holy principle—the positive aspect; the latter refers to its result, the life governed by such a power must be blameless and without reprehension—the negative aspect, as Alford and Ellicott term it. Tittmann, *Synonym,* p. 21. The pulsation of a holy heart leads to a stainless life, and that is the avowed purpose of our election.

That the words describe a moral condition is affirmed rightly by Chrysostom, Theophylact, Calvin, Matthies, Meier, Stier, Baumgarten-Crusius, and de Wette. Some, however, such as Koppe, Meyer, von Gerlach, Bisping, and Harless, refer the phrase to that perfect justifying righteousness of believers to which the apostle alludes in Rom. iii. 21, 22, v. 1, etc., viii. 1, etc.; 1 Cor. vi. 11. But the terms found here are different from those used by the apostle in the places quoted, where men are said to be justified, or fully acquitted from guilt, by their interest in the righteousness of Christ. On the other hand, the eternal purpose not only pardons, but also sanctifies, absolves in order to renew, and purifies in order to bestow perfection. It is the uniform teaching of Paul, that

τῆς φύσεως. It is marvellous that Adam Clarke should find any allusion in the phrase to "the commencement of the religious system of the Jews," and that Barrington should render it, "Before the foundation of the Jewish state."

holiness is the end of our election, our calling, our pardon and acceptance. The phrase, "holy and without blame," is never once applied to our complete justification before God; and, indeed, men are not regarded by God as innocent or sinless, for the fact of their sin remains unaltered; but they are treated as righteous—they are absolved from the penal consequences of their apostasy. It is no objection to our interpretation, which gives the words a moral, and not a legal or forensic signification, that men are not perfect in the present state. We would not say apologetically, with Calixtus—*Quantum fieri potest, per Dei ipsius gratiam et carnis nostræ infirmitatem*. We can admit no modification; for though the purpose begins to take effect here, it is not fully wrought out here, and we would not identify incipient operation with final perfection. The proper view, then, is that perfection is secured for us—that complete restoration to our first purity is provided for us—that He who chose us before time began, and when we were not, saw in us the full and final accomplishment of His gracious purpose. When He elected us—He beheld realized in us His own ideal of restored and redeemed humanity.—See under chap. v. 27. Men are chosen in Christ, in order to be holy and without blame. 1 Thess. iv. 7; Tit. ii. 14. Jerome says, *Hoc est, qui sancti et immaculati ante non fuimus, ut postea essemus*. The father vindicates this view, and refutes such objections as Porphyry was wont to advance, by putting the plain question, "Why, if there be no sovereignty, have Britain and the Irish tribes not known Moses and the prophets?" These facts are as appalling as any doctrine, and the fact must be overturned ere the doctrine can be impugned. The last lesson deduced by Jerome is, *Concede Deo potentiam sui*.

κατενώπιον αὐτοῦ—"before Him," לְפָנָיו. No good end is gained by reading αὑτοῦ, with Harless and Scholz, as the subject is remote. The meaning is, indeed, before Himself, that is, before God. Winer, § 22, 5; note from Bremi; Kühner, § 628. As the middle form of ἐξελέξατο indicates, they were chosen by God for Himself, and they are to be holy and blameless before Him. The reference to God is undoubted, and the phrase denotes the reality or genuineness of the holy and blameless state. God accounts it so. The "elect" are not esteemed righteous "merely before men," as Theophylact explains. Their piety is not a brilliant hypocrisy. It is regarded as genuine, "before Him" whose glance at once detects and frowns upon the spurious, however plausible the disguise in which it may wrap itself. Such is another or second ground of praise.

The reader may pardon a few digressive illustrations of the momentous doctrine of this verse. It would be a narrow and superficial view of these words to imagine that they are meant to level Jewish pride, and that they describe simply the choice of the Gentiles to religious privilege. The purpose of the election is, that its object should be holy, an end that cannot fail, for they are in Christ; in Him ideally when they were chosen, and also every man in his own order in Him actually, personally, and voluntarily, by faith. Yet the sovereign love of God is strikingly manifested, even in the bestowment of external advantage. Ephesus enjoyed what many a city in Asia Minor wanted. The motive that took Paul to Ephesus, and the wind that sped the bark which carried him, were alike of God's creation. It was not because God chanced to look down from His high throne, and saw the Ephesians bowing so superstitiously before the shrine of Diana, that His heart was moved, and He resolved in His mercy to give them the gospel. Nor was it because its citizens had a deeper relish for virtue and peace than the masses of population around them, that He sent among them the grace of His Spirit. "He is of one mind, and who can turn Him?" Every purpose is eternal, and awaits an evolution in the fulness of the time which is neither antedated nor postponed.

And the same difficulties are involved in this choice to external blessing, as are found in the election of men to personal salvation. The whole procedure lies in the domain of pure sovereignty, and there can therefore be no partiality where none have any claim. The choice of Abraham is the great fact which explains and gives name to the doctrine. Why then should the race of Shem be selected, to the exclusion of Ham and Japheth? Why of all the families in Shem should that of Terah be chosen? and why of all the members of Terah's house should the individual Abraham be marked out, and set apart by God to be the father of a new race? As well impugn the fact as attempt to upset the doctrine. Providence presents similar views of the divine procedure. One is born in Europe with a fair face, and becomes enlightened and happy; another is born in Africa with a sable countenance, and is doomed to slavery and wretchedness. One has his birth from Christian parents, and is trained in virtue from his earlier years; another has but a heritage of shame from his father, and the shadow of the gallows looms over his cradle. One is an heir of genius; another, with some malformation of brain, is an idiot. Some, under the enjoyment of Christian privilege, live and die unimpressed; others, with but scanty opportunities, believe, and grow eminent in piety. Does not more seem really to be done by God externally for the conversion of some who live and die in impenitence, than for many who believe and are saved? And yet the divine prescience and predestination are not incompatible with human responsibility. Man is free, perfectly free, for his moral nature is never strained or violated. We protest, as warmly as Sir William Hamilton, against any form of Calvinism which affirms "that man has no will, agency, or moral personality of his own."[1] Foreknowledge, which is only another phase of electing love, no more changes the nature of a future incident, than afterknowledge can affect a historical fact. God's grace fits men for heaven, but men by unbelief prepare themselves for hell. It is not man's non-election, but his continued sin, that leads to His eternal ruin. Nor is action impeded by the certainty of the divine foreknowledge. He who believes that God has appointed the hour of his death, is not fettered by such a faith in the earnest use of every means to prolong his life. And God does not act arbitrarily or capriciously. He has the best of reasons for His procedure, though He does not choose to disclose them to us. Sovereignty is but another name for highest and benignest equity. As Hooker says, "They err who think that of the will of God to do this or that, there is no reason but His will." *Eccles. Pol.*, lib. i. chap. ii. 3. The question of the number of the saved is no element of the doctrine we are illustrating. There have, alas! been

---

[1] *Discussions on Philosophy, Literature, etc.*, p. 600. Edin. 1852.

men, *Calvino Calviniores*, who have rashly, heartlessly, and unscripturally spoken of the ἐκλεκτοί as a few—a small minority. God forbid. There are many reasons and hints in Scripture leading us to the very opposite conclusion. But, in fine, this is the practical lesson; Christians have no grounds for self-felicitation in their possession of holiness and hope, as if with their own hand they had inscribed their names in the Book of Life. Their possession of "all spiritual blessing in the heavenly places" is not self-originated. Its one author is God, and He hath conferred it in harmony with His own eternal purpose regarding them. His is all the work, and His is all the glory. And therefore the apostle rejoices in this eternal election. It is cause of deep and prolonged thankfulness, not of gloom, distrust, or perplexity. The very eternity of design clothes the plan of salvation with a peculiar nobleness. It has its origin in an eternity behind us. The world was created to be the theatre of redemption. Kindness, the result of momentary impulse, has not and cannot have such claim to gratitude as a beneficence which is the fruit of a matured and predetermined arrangement. The grace which springs from eternal choice must command the deepest homage of our nature, as in this doxology—Εὐλογητὸς ὁ Θεὸς—καθὼς ἐξελέξατο.

The eternity of the plan suggests another thought, which we may mention without assuming a polemical aspect, or entering into the intricacies of the supra- and sub-lapsarian controversies. It is this—salvation is an original thought and resolution. It is no novel expedient struck out in the fertility of divine ingenuity, after God's first purpose in regard to man had failed through man's apostasy. It is no afterthought, but the embodiment of a design which, foreseeing our ruin, had made preparation for it. Neander, indeed, says the object of the apostle in this place is to show that Christianity was not inferior to Judaism as a new dispensation, but was in truth the more ancient and original, presupposed even by Judaism itself. The election in Christ preceded the election of the Jewish nation in their ancestors. *Geschichte der Pflanzung*, etc., ii. 443. But to represent this as the main object of the apostle is to dethrone the principal idea, and to exalt a mere inferential lesson into its place.

Before proceeding to the words ἐν ἀγάπῃ, we may remark, that the theory which makes foreseen holiness the ground of our election, and not its design, is clearly contrary to the apostolical statement; chosen—in order that we should be holy. So Augustine says that God chose us not *quia futuri eramus, sed ut essemus sancti et immaculati.* There is no room for the conditional interjection of Grotius, *Si et homines faciant, quod debent.* The dilemma of those who base predestination upon prescience is:[1] if God foresaw this faith and holiness, then those qualities were either self-created, or were to be bestowed by Himself; if the former, the grace of God is denied; and if the latter, the question turns upon itself —What prompted God to give them the faith and holiness which He foresaw they should possess? The doctrine so clearly taught in this verse was held in its leading element by the ancient church—by the Roman Clement, Ignatius, Hermas, Justin Martyr, and Irenæus, before Augustine worked it into a system, and Jerome armed himself on its behalf. It is foreign to our purpose to review the theory of Augustine, the revival of it by Gottschalk, or its reassertion by Calvin and Janssen; nor can we criticise the assault made upon it by Pelagius, or describe the keen antagonism of Calixtus and Julian, followed up in later times by Arminius, Episcopius, Limborch, and Tomline. Suffice it to say, that many who imagine that they have explained away a difficulty by denying one phase of the doctrine, have only achieved the feat of shifting that difficulty into another position. The various modifications of what we reckon the truth contained in the apostolical statement, do not relieve us of the mystery, which belongs as well to simple Theism as to the evangelical system.[2]

[1] The Chevalier Ramsay and Dr. Adam Clarke deny that God knows the free actions of moral agents before they take place.

[2] That prince of thinkers, the late Sir William Hamilton, says of the "Philosophy of the Conditioned"—"It is here shown to be as irrational as irreligious, on the ground of human understanding, to deny, either, on the one hand, the foreknowledge, predestination, and free grace of God, or, on the other, the free will of man; that we should believe both, and both in unison, though unable to comprehend even either apart. This philosophy proclaims with *St. Augustine,* and Augustine in his maturest writings: 'If there be not free grace in God, how can He save the world? and if there be not free will in man, how can the world by God be judged?' (*Ad Valentinum,* Epist. 214.) Or, as the same doctrine is perhaps expressed even better by *St. Bernard:* 'Abolish free

Dr. Whately has, with characteristic candour, admitted that the difficulty which relates to the character and moral government of God, presses as hard on the Arminian as the Calvinist, and Sir James Mackintosh has shown, with his usual luminous and dispassionate power, how dangerous it is to reason as to the moral consequences which the opponents of this and similar doctrines may impute to them.[1] In short, whether this doctrine be identified with Pagan stoicism or Mahometan fatalism, and be rudely set aside, and the world placed under the inspection of an inert omniscience; or whether it be modified as to its end, and that be declared to be privilege, and not holiness; or as to its foundation, and that be alleged to be not gratuitous and irrespective choice, but foreseen merit and goodness; or as to its subjects, and they be affirmed to be not individuals, but communities; or as to its result, and it be reckoned contingent, and not absolute; or whether the idea of election be diluted into mere preferential choice: whichever of these theories be adopted,—and they have been advocated in some of these aspects not only by some of the early Fathers,[2] but by Archbishops Bramhall,[3] Sancroft,[4] King,[5] Lawrence,[6] Sumner,[7] and Whately,[8] and by Milton,[9] Molina,[10] will, and there is nothing to be saved; abolish free grace, and there is nothing wherewithal to save.' (*De Gratiâ et Libero Arbitrio*, c. i.—*Discussions*, etc., p. 598.)"

[1] *Miscellaneous Works*, p. 139.

[2] Origen, *Philoc.* cap. xxv.; Justin Martyr, *Dial. cum Tryph.* § 141; Clem. Alex. *Strom.* vi. See also Wiggers, *Versuch einer pragmatischen Darstellung des Augustinismus und Pelagianismus.* Berlin, 1821.

[3] Controversy with Hobbes on Liberty and Necessity. *Works*, tome iii. Dublin, 1677.

[4] *Für Prædestinatus, etc.*, a satire which Lord Macaulay justly styles "a hideous caricature."—*History of England*, vol. ii. p. 389, 8th ed.

[5] Sermon on Predestination, preached before the Irish House of Lords in 1719 —usually annexed to his well-known treatise, *On the Origin of Evil*, and reprinted with notes by Dr. Whately in 1821.

[6] Bampton Lecture, *On the Articles of the Church of England improperly considered Calvinistical.* 1826.

[7] Archbishop of Canterbury, *Apostolical Preaching Considered.* 1826.

[8] *Essays on Some Difficulties in the Writings of St. Paul*, p. 91.

[9] In his treatise *De Doctrinâ Christianâ*, printed first in 1825, by Dr. Sumner, now Bishop of Winchester.

[10] A Spanish Jesuit of the University of Evora in Portugal, who, in his advocacy of semipelagian views, first gave currency to the term *scientia media*, in his treatise *Liberi arbitrii concordia cum gratiæ donis, Divina præscientia, providentia, prædestinatione, et reprobatione.* Lisbon, 1588.

Faber,[1] Nitzsch,[2] Hase,[3] Lange,[4] Copleston,[5] Chandler, Locke, Watson,[6] and many others,—such hypotheses leave the central difficulty still unsolved, and throw us back on the unconditioned and undivided sovereignty of Him "of whom, to whom, and through whom are all things,"—all whose plans and purposes wrought out in the church, and designed to promote His glory, have been conceived in the vast and incomprehensible solitudes of His own eternity. I can only say, in conclusion, with the martyr Ridley, when he wrote on this high theme to Bradford—"In these matters I am so fearful, that I dare not speak further; yea, almost none otherwise than the text does, as it were, lead me by the hand."

The position of the words ἐν ἀγάπῃ will so far determine their meaning, but that position it is difficult to assign. Much may be said on either side. 1. If the words are kept, as in the Textus Receptus, at the end of the fourth verse, then some would join them to ἐξελέξατο, and others to the adjectives immediately preceding them. That ἐν ἀγάπῃ at the end of the verse should refer to ἐξελέξατο at the beginning, is highly improbable. The construction would be so awkward, that we wonder how Œcumenius, Flacius, Olearius, Bucer, and Flatt could have adopted it. The entire verse would intervene

---

[1] *On the Primitive Doctrine of Election.* London, 1842.

[2] *System der Christl. Lehre,* § 141, 5th Auflage. 1844.

[3] *Hutterus Redivivus,* § 91, 6th Auflage. Leipzig, 1845.

[4] *Von der freien und Allgemeinen Gnade Gottes.* Elberfeld, 1831. Written against Booth's *Reign of Grace.* See Payne's *Lectures on Divine Sovereignty,* p. 69.

[5] *An Inquiry into the Doctrine of Necessity and Predestination.* 1821.

[6] *Institutes of Theology,* vol. iii. See for opposing arguments the systems of Hill, Dick, Woods, Chalmers, Wardlaw, and Finney, and of Mastricht, Turretine, Stapfer, and Pictet. See Reuss, *Histoire de la Théologie Chrét., etc.,* vol. ii. 132, Strasbourg 1852. Schmidt's *Dogmatik,* part iii. § 30, Dritte Auflage, Frankfort 1853. Messner, *die Lehre der Apostel, etc.,* p. 252. See also *Treatise on the Augustinian Doctrine of Predestination,* by J. B. Mozley, B.D., Oxford. In this volume, with no little argument, he elaborates the theory that where our conceptions are indistinct, contradictory propositions may be accepted as equally true—such contradictory propositions as God's predestination and man's free will. But surely we cannot affirm them to be contradictory unless we fully comprehend them, and though they may appear contradictory when viewed under human aspects and conditions, we dare not transfer such contradictions to the domain of theology, for the whole question, as Mansel says, "transcends the limits of human thought." Bampton Lecture, p. 412, 2nd ed.

between a reference to the act of election and the motive which is supposed to prompt to it. 2. Others, such as the Vulgate and Coptic, Ambrosiaster, Erasmus, Luther, Beza, Calvin, Grotius, Matthies, Meier, Baumgarten-Crusius, and Alford, join the words to the adjectives ἅγιοι καὶ ἄμωμοι, as if love were represented as the consummation of Christian virtue. The doctrine itself is a glorious truth—all the Christian graces at length disappear in love, as the flower is lost in the fruit. Those who refer the adjectives to justifying righteousness—*justitia imputata*—object to this view that it is not Pauline, but that ἐν πίστει would be the words employed. 3. Though we are not hampered by such a false exegesis, we prefer to join ἐν ἀγάπῃ to the following verse, and for these reasons :— Where ἅγιος is used along with ἄμωμος, as in Eph. v. 27, and even in Col. i. 22, where a third epithet, ἀνέγκλητος, is also employed, there is no such supplementary phrase as ἐν ἀγάπῃ. Alford tries to get rid of this objection by saying that ἐν ἀγάπῃ refers not to the epithets alone, but to the entire last clause. Yet the plea does not avail him, for his exegesis really makes ἐν ἀγάπῃ a qualification of the two adjectives. Olshausen appeals to other passages, but the reference cannot be sustained; for in Jude 24 the additional phrase ἐν ἀγαλλιάσει qualifies not ἄμωμος, but the entire preceding clause—the presentation of the saved to God. When synonymous epithets are used, a qualifying formula is sometimes added, as in ἀμέμπτους, 1 Thess. iii. 13, but blameless in what? the adjective is proleptic, and ἐν ἁγιωσύνῃ is added. Koch, *Comment.* p. 272. The words ἐν εἰρήνῃ occur also in 2 Pet. iii. 14, in the same clause with ἀμώμητος, but they belong not, as Olshausen supposes, to the adjective; they rather qualify the verb εὑρεθῆναι— "found in peace." If ἐν ἀγάπῃ belonged to the preceding adjectives, we should expect it to follow them immediately; but the words κατενώπιον αὐτοῦ intervene. The construction is not against the Pauline style and usage, as may be seen, chap. iii. 18, vi. 18, in which places the emphasis is laid on the preceding phrase. Nor has Alford's other argument more force in it—that the verbs and participles in this paragraph precede these qualifying clauses: for we demur to the correctness of the statement. 1. We interpret the 8th verse differently, and make ἐν πάσῃ σοφίᾳ καὶ φρονήσει qualify the following γνωρίσας. 2. The other qualifying clauses following the verbs and participles in this paragraph are of a different nature from this, four of them being introduced by κατά— referring to rule or measurement, and not to motive in itself or its elements. 3. It is more natural, besides, to join the words to the following verse, where adoption is spoken of; for the only source of it is the love of God, and it forms no objection to this view that ἐν ἀγάπῃ precedes the participle. Love is implied in predestination. *Di*-lectio præsupponitur *E*-lectioni, says Thomas Aquinas. And lastly, the spirit of the paragraph is God's dealing towards man in its great and gracious features; and not precisely or definitely the features or elements of man's perfection as secured by Him. The minuter specifications belong to God—His eternal purpose and His realization of it.

The union of ἐν ἀγάπῃ with προορίσας is sanctioned by the old Syriac version, by the fathers Chrysostom, Theophylact, Theodoret, and Jerome; by Zanchius, Crocius, Bengel, Koppe, Storr, Rückert, Harless, de Wette, Olshausen, Holzhausen, Stier, Turner, and Ellicott; and by the editors Griesbach, Scholz, Lachmann, and Tischendorf.

(Ver. 5.) Ἐν ἀγάπῃ προορίσας ἡμᾶς εἰς υἱοθεσίαν Ἰησοῦ Χριστοῦ εἰς αὐτόν — "In love having predestinated us for the adoption of children by Jesus Christ to Himself." Still another or third ground of praise. Ἐν ἀγάπῃ, φησί, προορίσας, says Chrysostom, and Jerome renders *in charitate prædestinans*. Saints enjoy the privilege and heritage of adoption. The source of this blessing is love, and that love, unrestrained and self-originated, has developed its power and attachment—"according to the good pleasure of His will." This verse is, to some extent, only a different phase of the truth contained in the preceding one. The idea of adoption was a favourite one with the apostle—Rom. viii. 14, 15, 19, 23, ix. 4; 2 Cor. vi. 18; Gal. iii. 7, 26, iv. 5, 6, 7; Heb. ii. 10, xii. 5-8, etc. In the Old Testament, piety is denominated by the filial relationship "sons of God." Gen. vi. 2. The theocratic connection of Israel with God is also pictured by the same tender tie. Ex. iv. 22; Jer. iii. 19; Hos. i. 10. Υἱοθεσία—θετὸν υἱὸν ποιεῖσθαι—conveys a similar idea, with this distinction, that the sonship is not a natural but a constituted relationship, for the θετός was quite distinct from the γνήσιος. The idea here is not merely that of sonship, as Usteri imagines, but sonship acquired by adoption. *Paulin. Lehrbegriff*, p. 194. Whatever blessings were implied or shadowed out in the Israelitish adoption, belong now to Christians. For they possess a likeness to their Father in the lustrous lineaments of His moral character, and they have the enjoyment of His special love, the privilege of near and familiar access, the wholesome and necessary discipline withheld from the bastard or foundling—Heb. xii. 8 —and a rich provision at the same time out of His glorious fulness, for they have an inheritance, as is told in ver. 11. God and all that God is, God and all that God has, is their boundless and eternal possession—1 Cor. iii. 21-23—to be enjoyed in that home whose material glories are only surpassed by its spiritual splendours. Adoption is, therefore, a combined subjective view of the cardinal blessings of justification and sanctification.

Προορίσας—The signification of the verb is, "to mark out beforehand," and it is the act of God. We were marked out for adoption—πρό; not before others, but before time. The πρό does not of itself express this, but the spirit of the context would lead to this conclusion. The general idea is the same as that involved in ἐξελέξατο, though there is a specific distinction. The end preappointed—πρό, is implied in the one; the mass out of which choice is made—ἐκ, is glanced at by the other. In the first case, the Divine mind is supposed to look *forward* to the glorious destiny to which believers are set apart; in the second case, it looks *down* upon the undeserving stock out of which it chose them. Προορίσας may indicate an action prior to ἐξελέξατο—" Having foreappointed us to the adoption of children, He chose us in Christ Jesus." Donaldson, § 574; Winer, § 45, 1. Homberg—*Parerga*, p. 286—thus paraphrases, *Postquam nos prædestinavit adoptandos, elegit etiam nos, ut simus sancti.* But as the action both of verb and participle belongs to God, we would rather take the participle as synchronous with the verb. Bernhardy, p. 383. For though the order of the Divine decrees is a subject too high for us, as we can neither grasp infinitude nor span eternity, yet we may say that there is oneness and not succession of thought in God's mind, simultaneous idea and not consecutive arrangement. See Martensen's *Christliche Dogmatik*, §§ 207, 208, 209; Kiel, 1855. The doctrine taught is, that our reception of the blessings, prerogatives, and prospects implied in adoption, is not of our own merit, but is wholly of God. The returning prodigal does not win his way back into the paternal mansion. This purpose to accept us existed ere the fact of our apostasy had manifested itself, and being without epoch of origin, it comes not within the limits of chronology. It pre-existed time. It is strange to find the German psychology attempting to revive out of these words Origen's dream of the pre-existence of souls. Surely it forgets that He whose mind comprises beginning and end, "calls things that are not, as though they were."

διὰ 'Ιησοῦ Χριστοῦ—not simply for Christ's sake, but by means of His mediation, since but for Him the family had never been constituted. God's Son is the "first-born" of the vast household, and fraternal relation to Him is filial relation to God.

εἰς αὐτόν—"to Himself." It matters not much whether the reading be αὑτόν or αὐτόν. The former, coming so closely after διὰ I. X., is certainly preferable, while the latter reading has at least the merit of settling the reference. Griesbach, Knapp, and Scholz, following Beza, Stephens, and Mill, have αὑτόν. Other editors, such as Erasmus, Wetstein, Lachmann, and Tischendorf, prefer αὐτόν, and they are supported by Harless, Olshausen, and Meyer. The reference of the word, however, is plainly to God. Τὸ δὲ εἰς αὐτὸν, τὸν πατέρα λέγει—Theodoret. Some, indeed, refer the pronoun to Christ. The scholastic interpreters, Anselm and Thomas Aquinas, did this, and they have been followed by Vorstius, Bullinger, a-Lapide, and Goodwin, who, however, as his manner is, combines both the views; "the Holy Ghost," he adds, "intended both." But these expositors are more or less paraphrastic and wide of the truth. Others, referring it to God, give it the signification of a dative, such as Calvin, Beza, and Calixtus, and join the words with προορίσας, and find in the formula this idea, that the cause of our adoption lies only in God, that predestination is not caused by any motive or power foreign to Himself—*extra seipsum*. But this exegesis is a capricious and unwarranted construction of εἰς with its accusative. Others, again, take it as a *dativus commodi* for ἑαυτῷ, as Grotius, Koppe, Holzhausen, and Meier: "God has made us His own children," a meaning which does not bring out the full force of the word. Not very different is the explanation of Rückert, who makes it equivalent to αὑτοῦ in the genitive —"He has predestined us to His own adoption." The apostle does not use the preposition where a simple dative or genitive would have sufficed. Others, retaining the undoubted meaning of the accusative, would render it in various ways. Piscator translates—*Ad gloriam gratiæ suæ*. Theophylact, with Œcumenius, explains, τὴν εἰς αὐτὸν ἀνάγουσαν—adoption leading to Him. Olshausen's notion is not dissimilar. De Wette renders simply *für ihn;* that is, for Him whose glory is the ultimate end of the great work of redemption. Theodore of Mopsuestia thus expounds it, ἵνα αὐτοῦ υἱοὶ λεγοίμεθά τε καὶ χρηματίζωμεν. Something of the truth lies in all those modes of explanation, with the exception of the view of Calvin, and those who think with him. Εἰς occurs twice in the verse, first pointing out the nearer object of προορίσας, and then the relation of the spiritual adoption to God. In such a case as the last, εἰς indicates a relation different from the simple dative, and one often found in the theology of the apostle. Winer, § 49, a, c (δ), § 31, 5. Adoption has its medium in Christ: but it has its ultimate enjoyment and blessing in God. Himself is our Father— HIS household we enter—HIS welcome we are saluted with —HIS name and dignity we wear—HIS image we possess— HIS discipline we receive—and HIS home, secured and prepared for us, we hope for ever to dwell in. To HIMSELF we are adopted. The origin of this privilege and distinction is the Divine love. That love was not originated by us, nor is it an essential feeling on the part of God, for it has been exercised—

κατὰ τὴν εὐδοκίαν τοῦ θελήματος αὐτοῦ—" according to the good pleasure of His will." Κατά, as usual, denotes rule or measure. Winer, § 49, d (a). Εὐδοκία, according to Jerome a word coined by the Seventy, *rebus novis nova verba fingentes*, has two meanings; that of will—it seems good to me— *voluntas liberrima*—" mere good pleasure;" and that of benevolence or goodwill. The former meaning is held by Chrysostom (τὸ σφοδρὸν θέλημα), by Grotius, Calvin, Flatt, Rückert, de Wette, Ellicott, and Stier, with the Vulgate and Syriac. The notion of "goodwill," or benignant purpose, is advocated by Drusius, Beza, Bodius, Röell, Harless, Olshausen, and Baumgarten-Crusius. Such is its prevailing acceptation in the Septuagint, as representing the Hebrew רָצוֹן. The translators gave this rendering on purpose and with discrimination, for when רָצוֹן signifies will or decree, as it sometimes does, they render it by θέλημα. Compare Ps. xix. 15, li. 19, lxxxix. 18, cv. 4, with Esth. i. 8; Ps. xxix. 5, xl. 8; Dan. viii. 4, xi. 3, 16, etc. The Seventy render the proper name תִּרְצָה (Delight), Cant. vi. 4, by εὐδοκία, Symmachus by εὐδοκητή. In the New Testament the meaning is not different. Luke ii. 14; Rom. x. 1; Phil. i. 15, ii. 13. Matt. xi. 26, and the parallel passage, Luke x. 21, may admit of the other meaning, and yet, as Harless suggests, the context, with its verb ἠγαλλιάσατο, seems to support the more common signification. Fritzsche, *ad Rom.* ii. 369, *note.* Ellicott virtually gives up his decision, by admitting that "goodness is necessarily involved;" and the philological and contextual arguments of Hodge for the first view are utterly inconclusive. We agree with de Wette that the reference in εὐδοκία is to be sought, not in the προωρισμένοι, but in προορίσας; but it defines His will as being something more than a mere decree resting on sovereignty, and there is on this account all the more reason why praise is due, for the clause is still connected with εὐλογητός. Œcumenius well defines it, ἡ ἐπ' εὐεργεσίᾳ βούλησις. Theodoret says, that the Sacred Scripture understands by εὐδοκία,—τὸ ἀγαθὸν τοῦ Θ. θέλημα. The θέλημα—not an Attic term (Phrynichus, ed. Lobeck, p. 7)—in itself simple purpose, has in it an element of εὐδοκία. Benignity characterizes His unbiassed will.

And the proof of this statement is plain to a demonstration. For though adoption among men usually results from childlessness, and because no son has a seat on their hearth, they bring home the orphaned wanderer, no motive of this kind has place with God. His heart rejoices over myriads of His unfallen progeny, and His glory would not have been unseen, nor His praises unsung, though this fallen world had sunk into endless and hopeless perdition. Again, while men adopt a child not merely because they like it, but because they think it likeable in features or in temper, there was nothing in us to excite God's love, nay there was everything to quench it in such a ruined and self-ruined creature. So plain is it, that if God love and adopt us, that love has no assignable reason save "the good pleasure of His will." In endeavouring to show that the occurrence of κατὰ τὴν εὐδοκίαν after ἐν ἀγάπῃ is no tautology, Olshausen says, that ἀγάπη refers to the proper essence of God, and that εὐδοκία brings out the prominent benevolence of the individual act of His will. The opinion of Harless is similar, that ἀγάπη is the general emotion, and that its special expression as the result of will is contained in εὐδοκία. Perhaps the apostle's meaning is, that while adoption is the correlative fruit of love, purpose, special and benign, has its peculiar and appropriate sphere of action in predestination—προορίσας—κατά. There is "*will*," for if God love sinners so as to make them sons, it is not because His nature necessitates it, but because He wills it. Yet this will clothes itself, not in bare decree, but "*in good pleasure*," and such good pleasure is seen deepening into love in their actual inbringing. The idea of this clause is therefore quite different from that of the last clause of v. 11.

(Ver. 6.) *Εἰς ἔπαινον δόξης τῆς χάριτος αὐτοῦ*—"To the praise of the glory of His grace." Εἰς occurs thrice in the sentence—first pointing out the object of predestination—then, in immediate sequence, marking the connection of the adopted with God—and now designating the final end of the process—relations objective, personal, and teleological, different indeed, yet closely united. Δόξης has not the article, being defined by the following genitive, which with its pronoun is that of possession. Winer, § 19, 2, *b*;[1] Madvig, § 10, 2. This verse describes not the mere result, but the final purpose, of God's προορισμός. The proximate end is man's salvation, but the ultimate purpose is God's own glory, the manifestation of His moral excellence. 2 Cor. i. 20; Phil. i. 11, ii. 11. It was natural in an ascription of praise to introduce this idea, the apostle's offering of praise—εὐλογητὸς ὁ Θεός—being at that moment a realization of this very purpose, and therefore

[1] See Moulton's Winer, p. 155, note 6.

acceptable to Him. Some critical editors read αὐτοῦ, but without valid reason.

The reduction of the phrase to a Hebraism is a feeble exegesis. That reduction has been attempted in two ways. Some, like Grotius and Estius, resolve it into εἰς ἔπαινον ἔνδοξον —to the glorious praise of His grace. Others, as Beza, Koppe, Winer, Holzhausen, and Meier, construe it as χάρις ἔνδοξος. But it is not generally His glorious grace, but this one special element of that grace which is to be praised. Winer, § 30, 3, 1; Bernhardy, p. 53. Χάρις is favour, Divine favour, proving that man has not only no merit, but that, in spite of demerit, he is saved and blessed by God. (See under chap. ii. 5–8.) Its glory is its fulness, freeness, and condescension. It shrinks from no sacrifice, averts itself from no species or amount of guilt, enriches its objects with the choicest favours, and confers upon them the noblest honours. It has effected what it purposed—stooping to the depths, it has raised us to the heights of filial dignity. Still further: this grace, with its characteristic glory, is a property in God's nature which could never have been displayed but for the introduction of sin, and God's design to save sinners. This, then, was His great and ultimate end, that the glory of His grace should be seen and praised, that this element of His character should be exhibited in its peculiar splendour, for without it all conceptions of the Divine nature must have been limited and unworthy. And as this grace lay in His heart, and as its exhibition springs from choice, and not from essential obligation, it is praised by the church, which receives it, and by the universe, which admires it. Therefore to reveal Himself fully, to display His full-orbed glory, was an end worthy of God.[1] The idea of Stier, that the words have a subjective reference, is far-fetched, as if the apostle had said that we are predestined to be ourselves the praise of His glory. All that is good in this interpretation is really comprised in the view already given.

ἐν ᾗ, or ἧς ἐχαρίτωσεν ἡμᾶς.—The former reading has in its favour D, E, F, G, K, L. The Vulgate and Syriac cannot be adduced as decided authorities, as they have often charac-

---

[1] No one who has read, can forget, the magnificent tract of Jonathan Edwards—*God's Chief End in Creation.* Works, i. p. 41; ed. 1806, London.

teristic modes of translation in such places. For ἧς we have the two old MSS. A and B, and Chrysostom's first quotation of the clause. Authorities are pretty nearly balanced, and editors and critics are therefore divided—Tischendorf and Ellicott being for the first, Lachmann and Alford for the second—but the meaning is not affected whichever reading be adopted. While ἐν ᾗ is well supported, ἧς would seem to be quite in harmony with Pauline usage, and is the more difficult of the two readings, tempting a copyist on that account to alter it. It stands so by attraction, Bernhardy, p. 299; Winer, § 24, 1; Eph. iv. 1; 2 Cor. i. 4; see also under ver. 8. Two classes of meanings have been assigned to the verb:—

1. That of Chrysostom, and the Greek fathers, who usually follow him, Theodoret, Theophylact, and Œcumenius; also of many of the Catholic interpreters, and of Beza, Luther, Calvin, Piscator, Olshausen, Holzhausen, Passavant, and the English version. The verb is supposed by them to refer to the personal or subjective result of grace, which is to give men acceptance with God—*gratos et acceptos reddidit.* Men filled with *gratia* are *gratiosi* in the eye of God. Luther renders *angenehm gemacht,* as in our version, "made accepted." Chrysostom's philological argument is, the apostle does not say ἧς ἐχαρίσατο ἀλλ' ἐχαρίτωσεν ἡμᾶς, that is, the apostle does not say, "which He has graciously given," but "with which He has made us gracious." He further explains the term by καὶ ἐπεράστους ἐποίησεν—"He has made us objects of His love;" and He employs this striking and beautiful figure—"It is as if one were to take a leper, wasted with malady and disease, with age, destitution, and hunger, and were to change him all at once into a lovely youth, surpassing all men in beauty, shedding a bright lustre from his cheeks, and eclipsing the solar beam with the glances of his eyes, and then were to set him in the flower of his age and clothe him in purple, and with a diadem, and all the vestments of royalty. Thus has God arrayed and adorned our soul, and made it an object of beauty, delight, and love." But the notion conveyed in this figure appears to us to be foreign to the meaning of the term. The word occurs, indeed, with a similar meaning in the Septuagint, Sirach xviii. 17,

where ἀνὴρ κεχαριτωμένος is a man full of grace and blandness; and the same book, ix. 8, according to Codex A and Clement's quotation, has the same participle, as if it were synonymous with εὔμορφος—comely, well-shaped. *Opera*, p. 257; Coloniæ, 1688. Such a sense, however, is not in harmony with the formation of the verb or the usage of the New Testament. Yet Möhler, in his *Symbolik*, § 13, 14, uses the clause as an argument for the *justitia inhærens* of the Romish Church.

2. The verb χαριτόω, a word of the later Greek, signifies, according to the analogy of its formation—to grace, to bestow grace upon. So some of the older commentators, as Cocceius, Röell, and most modern ones. Verbs in όω signify to give action or existence to the thing or quality specified by the correlate noun, have what Kühner appropriately calls *eine factitive Bedeutung*, § 368. Thus, πυρόω — I set on fire, θανατόω—I put to death, that is, I give action to πῦρ and θάνατος. Buttmann, § 119. Χαριτόω will thus indicate the communication or bestowment of the χάρις. The grace spoken of is God's, and that grace is liberally conferred upon us. To maintain the alliteration it may be rendered, The grace with which He graced us, or the favour with which He favoured us. The Vulgate has *gratificavit*, and the Syriac ܐܫܦܥ—which He has poured out. Χάρις has an objective meaning here, as it usually has in the Pauline writings, and κεχαριτωμένη, applied to the Virgin (Luke i. 28, Valcknaer, *ap. Luc.* i. 28), signifies favoured of God, the selected recipient of His peculiar grace. Test. xii. Patr. p. 698. The use of a noun with its correlate verb is not uncommon. Eph. i. 3, 19, 20; ii. 4; iv. 1; Donaldson, § 466; Winer, § 24, 1. The spirit of the declaration is—To the praise of the glory of His grace, which He so liberally conferred upon us—the aorist referring to past indefinite time and not to present condition. The liberal bestowment of that grace is its crown and glory. It was with no stinted hand that God gave it, as the following context abundantly shows. This glory of grace which is to be lauded is not its innate and inoperative greatness, but its communicated amount. The financial prosperity of a people is not in useless and treasured bullion, but the coined metal in actual circulation. The value is not in the jewel as it

lies in the depth of the mine, in the midst of unconscious darkness, but as it is cut, polished, and sparkling in the royal diadem. So it is not grace as a latent attribute, but grace in profuse donation, and effecting its high and holy purpose; it is not grace gazed at in God's heart, but grace felt in ours, felt in rich variety and continuous reception—it is "the grace with which He graced us," that is to be praised for its glory. And it is poured out—

ἐν τῷ ἠγαπημένῳ—"in the Beloved." Some MSS., such as D$^t$, E, F, G, add υἱῷ αὐτοῦ, an evident gloss followed by the Vulgate and Latin fathers. The Syriac adds the pronoun, in his Beloved—ܒܚܒܝܒܗ. The reference is undoubtedly to Christ. Matt. iii. 17, xvii. 5; John iii. 16; 1 John iv. 9, 10, 11; or Col. i. 13—ὁ υἱὸς τῆς ἀγάπης αὐτοῦ. Jesus is the object of the Father's love—eternal, boundless, and immutable; and "in Him" as the one living sphere, not for His sake only, men are enriched with grace. But what suggested such an epithet here? 1. The apostle had said, "In love having predestinated us to the adoption of children." We, as adopted children, are indeed loved, but there is another, the Son, the own beloved Son. It was not, therefore, affection craving indulgence, or eager for an object on which to expend itself, that led to our adoption. There was no void in His bosom, the loved One lay in it. 2. The mediatorial representative of fallen humanity is the object of special affection on the part of God, and in Him men are also loved by God. Bengel suggests that the χάρις we enjoy is different from this ἀγάπη. Still the apostle affirms that we share in love as well as grace. 3. The following verse tells us that redemption comes to us διὰ τοῦ αἵματος—by His blood, for the Beloved One is the sacrifice. What love, therefore, on the Father's part to deliver Him up—what praise to the glory of His grace—and what claim has Jesus to be the loved One also of His church, when His self-sacrificing love for them has proved and sustained its fervour in the agonies of a violent and vicarious death! For the next thought is—

(Ver. 7.) Ἐν ᾧ ἔχομεν τὴν ἀπολύτρωσιν διὰ τοῦ αἵματος αὐτοῦ—"In whom we have redemption by his His blood." The apostle now specifies some fruits of that grace—illustrates ἐχαρίτωσεν. From a recital of past acts of God toward us, he comes now to our present blessing. Redemption stands out to his mind as the deliverance—so unique in its nature and so well known, that it has the article prefixed. It is enshrined in solitary eminence. The idea fills the Old Testament, for the blessing which the Levitical ritual embodied and symbolized was redemption—deliverance from evil by means of sacrifice. Lev. i. 4, 9; iv. 26; xvii. 11. Blood was the medium of expiation and of exemption from penalty. Umbreit, *Der Brief an die Römer ausgelegt*, p. 261: Gotha, 1856. Ἀπολύτρωσις, as its origin intimates, signifies deliverance by the payment of a price or ransom—λύτρον. It has been said that the idea of ransom is sometimes dropped, and that the word denotes merely rescue. We question this, at least in the New Testament; certainly not in Rom. viii. 23, for the redemption of the body is, equally with that of the soul, the result of Christ's ransom-work. Even in Heb. xi. 35, and in Luke xxi. 28, we might say that the notion of ransom is not altogether sunk, though it be of secondary moment; in the one case it is apostasy, in the other the destruction of the Jewish state, which is the ideal price. We have the simple noun in Luke i. 68, ii. 38, Heb. ix. 12; and λυτροῦν in Luke xxiv. 21, Tit. ii. 14. The human race need deliverance, and they cannot, either by price or by conquest, effect their own liberation, for the penal evil which sin has entailed upon them fetters and subdues them. But redemption is not an immediate act of sovereign prerogative; it is represented as the result of a process which involved and necessitated the death of Christ. The means of deliverance, or the price paid, was the blood of Christ—διὰ τοῦ αἵματος αὐτοῦ; as in Acts xx. 28, where we have περιεποιήσατο, and 1 Cor. vi. 20, where we have, under a different aspect, ἠγοράσθητε, and similarly in Gal. iii. 13. Blood is the material of expiation. The death of Jesus was one of blood, for it was a violent death; and that blood—the blood of a sinless man, on whom the Divine law had no claim, and could have none—was poured out as a vicarious offering.[1] The atonement was indispensable to remission of

[1] "Quand donc vous entendez ici parler de son sang, ne vous représentez ni celui de la Circoncision, quand le couteau de la Loi lui en fît perdre quelques gouttes, huit jours après sa naissance; ni celui de son agonie, quand l'excès du trouble

sin—it was τὸ λύτρον—the price of infinite value. Matt. xx. 28, xxvi. 28; Mark x. 45; Heb. ix. 22. The law of God must be maintained in its purity ere guilty man can be pardoned. The universal Governor glorifies His law, and by the same act enables Himself to forgive its transgressors. The *nexus* we may not be able to discover fully, but we believe, in opposition to the view of Schleiermacher, Coleridge, and others, that the death of Christ has governmental relations, has an influence on our salvation totally different in nature and sphere of operation, from its subjective power in subduing the heart by the love which it presents, and the thrilling motives which it brings to bear upon it. See Reuss, *Hist. de la Théologie Chrétienne au Siècle Apostolique*, tome ii. p. 182.

ἐν ᾧ—"in whom;" not as Koppe, Flatt, and others would have it, "on account of whom." The διά points to the instrumental connection which the death of Christ has with our redemption, but ἐν to the method in which that redemption becomes ours. Rom. iii. 24. Διά regards the means of provision, ἐν the mode of reception—in Christ the Beloved, in loving, confiding union with Him as the one sphere—a thought vitally pervading the paragraph and the entire epistle. For how can we have safety if we are out of the Saviour? Rom. viii. 1, 33.

The apostle places the forgiveness of sins in apposition with redemption, not as its only element, but as a blessing immediate, characteristic, and prominent—

τὴν ἄφεσιν τῶν παραπτωμάτων—"the forgiveness of sins." Col. i. 14. Παράπτωμα—falling aside, offence, differs from ἁμαρτία, not exactly, as Jerome affirms, that the first term means the lapse toward sin, and the second the completed act in itself, for παράπτωμα is expressly applied by Paul in Rom. x. 15, etc., to the first sin of the first man—that offence of which ἁμαρτία, or a sinful state, is the sad and universal result. The word, therefore, signifies here that series and succession of individual sinful acts with which every man is chargeable, or the actual and numerous results and manifesta-

qu'il ressentoit en son esprit, lui en fît suër des grumeaux dans le jardin des Olives ; ni celui de sa flagellation, quand les verges des soldats lui en tirerent des ruisseaux dans le Prétoire. C'est celui de sa mort même."—*Sermons sur l'Epître de St. Paul aux Ephesiens*, par feu M. Du Bosc, tome i. p. 277. 1699.

tions of our sinful condition. Ἄφεσις—sometimes standing by itself, but generally with ἁμαρτιῶν—is release from something which binds, from the chain which fetters—Luke iv. 19 —or the debt or tribute which oppresses. Esth. ii. 18. It frees from the ὀφείλημα—from debt, as at the year of jubilee. Lev. xxv. 31, xxvii. 24. It is, therefore, the remission of that which is due to us on account of offences, so that our liability to punishment is cancelled. It is surely wrong in Alford to make ἄφεσιν coextensive with ἀπολύτρωσιν. In the New Testament the noun does not signify "all riddance from the practice and consequences of our transgression," but definitely and specially remission of the penalty. Mark iii. 29; Acts ii. 38 (the gift of the Spirit there succeeding that of forgiveness); Acts xiii. 38, 39, xxvi. 18; Heb. x. 18. But ἀπολύτρωσις is much wider, being not only man's deliverance from all evil—from sin, Satan, and death—but his entrance into all the good which a redeeming God has provided—peace, joy, and life—a title to heaven and preparation for it. The ἄφεσις of this verse is not, therefore, "equipollent" with ἀπολύτρωσις, but the following paragraph is; for the ἀπολύτρωσις contains the series of blessings described in it, and among them forgiveness of sins has a first and prominent place. Ἄφεσις differs from πάρεσις (Rom. iii. 25), for the latter is prætermission, not remission; the suspension of the penalty, or the forbearing to inflict it, but not its entire abrogation. Fritzsche, *Ad Rom.*, vol. i. p. 199; Trench *On Synon.*, § 33. But the blessing here is remission. And it is full, all past sin being blotted out, and provision being made that future guilt shall also be remitted. Permanent dwelling in Christ (ἐν ᾧ) secures continued forgiveness. That forgiveness also is free, because it is the result of His sacrifice —διὰ αἵματος; and it is irreversible, since it is God that justifies, and who shall impeach His equity? or shall He revoke His own sentence of absolution?

And the apostle says, ἔχομεν—in the present time; not like εὐλογήσας, ἐξελέξατο, προορίσας, ἐχαρίτωσεν—descriptive of past acts of God. The meaning is not—We have got it, and now possess it as a distinct and perfect blessing, but we are getting it—are in continuous possession of it. We are ever needing, and so are *ever having it*, for we are still "in Him," and the merit of His blood is unexhausted. Forgiveness is not a blessing complete at any point of time in our human existence, and therefore we are still receiving it. See under Col. i. 14.

But those παραπτώματα are many and wanton—not only numerous, but provoking, so that forgiveness, to reach us, must be patient and ample, and the apostle characterizes its measure as being—

κατὰ τὸ πλοῦτος τῆς χάριτος αὐτοῦ—"according to the riches of His grace." With Rückert, Lachmann, and Tischendorf, on the authority of A, B, D†, F, G, we prefer the neuter τὸ πλοῦτος, a form which occurs, according to the best MSS., in Eph. ii. 7, iii. 8, 16; Phil. iv. 19; Col. i. 27, ii. 2; Winer, § 9, 2, 2. Πλοῦτος is what Paley calls one of the "cant" words of the apostle, that is, one of the favourite terms which he often introduces—"riches of goodness," "riches of glory," "riches of full assurance," "riches of wisdom," etc. It serves no purpose to resolve the formula into a Hebraism, so that it might be rendered "His rich grace," or "His gracious riches," for the genitive is that of possession connected with its pronoun. Winer, § 30, 3, 1. The classic Greeks use a similar construction of two substantives. The αὐτοῦ evidently refers to God, and some MSS. read αὑτοῦ. Χάρις—see under ii. 8. The spirit of the clause may be thus illustrated:—The favour of man toward offenders is soon exhausted, and according to its penury, it soon wearies of forgiving. But God's grace has unbounded liberality. Much is expended; many sinners of all lands, ages, and crimes are pardoned, fully pardoned, often pardoned, and frankly pardoned, but infinite wealth of grace remains behind. It is also to be remarked, that χάρις and αἷμα are really not opposed. Atonement is not in antagonism with grace. For the opulence of His grace is seen not only in its innumerable forms and varieties of operation among men, but also in the unasked and unmerited provision of such an atonement, so perfect and glorious in its relation to God and man, as the blood of the "Beloved One."

(Ver. 8.) Ἧς ἐπερίσσευσεν εἰς ἡμᾶς.—"Which He has made to abound toward us." Ἧς is the result of attraction. If it stand for ἥν, then the verb will have a transitive signification—"Which He hath made, or caused to abound." But if ἧς stand for the dative, as Calvin, Camerarius, and Schmid suppose, the meaning is that of our version—" In which He has abounded toward us." Winer, § 24, 1. But the New Testament affords no example of such an attraction, though this be the usual signification of the verb. The Vulgate, taking it for a nominative, falsely reads *quæ superabundavit in nobis;* and Piscator's exegesis is wholly arbitrary, *copiose se effudit.* It is, however, natural to suppose that there is no change in the ruling nominative. Attraction seldom takes place except when the relative should stand in the accusative (Kühner, § 787, Anmerk 4; Jelf, § 822), so that, with the more modern interpreters, we take ἧς as the substitute of the accusative, and prefer the transitive sense of the verb. Such a Hiphil signification belongs to the word in 1 Thess. iii. 12; 2 Cor. iv. 15, ix. 8. The relative does not denote the mode of abundance, but the matter of it. It has been suggested— Ellicott, p. 164—that, as *verba faciendi*, like περισσεύω, may have an appended accusative elicited from the verb, "make an abundance of," so the principle of attraction need not be applied to ἧς. Beza gives it, *qua redundavit.* The riches of His grace are not given us in pinched exactness, or limited and scanty measurement —where sin abounds, grace superabounds, Rom. v. 20. God knows that He cannot exhaust the wealth of His grace, and therefore He lavishes it with unstinted generosity upon us. Theophylact explains the clause thus: ἀφθόνως ἐξέχεεν—" He hath poured it upon us unsparingly." And the apostle, having spoken of forgiveness as an immediate blessing, adds—

ἐν πάσῃ σοφίᾳ καὶ φρονήσει—" in all wisdom and prudence." The preliminary question refers to the position of this clause. Should it be joined to the preceding ἐπερίσσευσεν, or does it belong to the following verse, and qualify the participle γνωρίσας? If it stand in connection with the foregoing verb, it may be variously interpreted. Four forms of exegesis have been proposed:—

1. Calvin, Balduin, and Beza understand the phrase as a general name for the gospel, and their meaning is, that the vocation of men, by the perfectly wise plan of the gospel, is to be ascribed to grace as really as is their election.

2. Others understand it as referring to the gifts of wisdom

and prudence which accompany the reception of divine forgiveness. So Aretius, Calixtus, Wolf, Bengel, Morus, Flatt, Meyer, Meier, Matthies, Bisping, Baumgarten-Crusius, and virtually Harless—"According to the riches of His grace, which He made to abound toward us, *along with* the gifts of wisdom and prudence." Or as Ellicott says—"It may mark out the sphere and element in which the περίσσευσεν is evinced and realized." But the clause so interpreted may be either logically connected with ἐπερίσσευσεν or γνωρίσας, and may mean either "He hath abounded toward us," and one proof and result of such abundance is the bestowment of these graces; or He hath made us wise and prudent, because He hath made known to us the mystery of His will. Thus Œcumenius, who joins the words with the following verse—σοφοὺς καὶ φρονίμους ποιήσας οὕτως ἐγνώρισεν τὸ μυστήριον. If we preferred this exegesis, we should adopt the latter modification, which some of these critics also espouse, namely, that the wisdom and prudence are neither the proof nor the sphere of grace abounding toward us, but are the effects of God's disclosure of the mystery of His will.

3. Some, again, refer the words to God, as if they were descriptive of the manner in which He has caused His grace to abound toward us. God in all wisdom and prudence has made all grace to abound toward us. So Castalio, Rückert, de Wette, Grotius (in one of his explanations), Baumgarten-Crusius, and Alford—a connection which Ellicott stigmatizes "as in the highest degree unsatisfactory."

4. The opinion of Olshausen, endorsed by Stier, is quite arbitrary and peculiar—"that we should walk in all wisdom and prudence;" a paraphrase which would indicate an unwonted and fatal elasticity in the apostle's diction.

We propose to join the words with the participle, γνωρίσας —"Having in all wisdom and prudence made known to us the mystery of His will." The construction is similar to that vindicated in ver. 5, with regard to ἐν ἀγάπῃ, and is not unusual in the Pauline writings. The idea is homogeneous, if the words are thus connected. Wisdom and prudence have no natural connection with the abounding of grace. Grace in its wealth or profusion does not suggest the notions of wisdom and prudence. The two circles of thought are not concentric in any of the hypotheses we have referred to. For if the words " in all wisdom and prudence " be referred to God, as descriptive of His mode of operation, they are scarcely in harmony with the leading idea of the verse; at least there would be a want of consecutive unity. For it is not so much His wisdom as His love, not so much His intelligence as His generosity, which marks and glorifies the method of His procedure. The same remarks equally apply to the theory which looks upon the clause in dispute as a formal description of the scheme of the gospel.

Nor, if the words be referred to gifts of "wisdom and prudence," conferred along with grace, or be regarded as the sphere of its operation, is the harmony any better preserved. Wisdom and prudence are not the ideas you would expect to find in such a connection. But, on the other hand, " wisdom and prudence " are *essentially* connected with the disclosure of a mystery. A mystery is not to be flung abroad without due discrimination. The revealer of it wisely selects his audience, and prudently chooses the proper time, place, and method for his disclosure. To make it known to minds not prepared to receive it, to flash it upon his attendants in full force and without previous and gradual training, might defeat the very purpose which the initiator has in view. The qualities referred to are therefore indispensable requisites to the publication of a mystery.

An objection, however, is stated against this exegesis by Harless, and the objection is also adopted by Meyer, Matthies, and Olshausen. Harless boldly affirms that $\phi\rho\acute{o}\nu\eta\sigma\iota\varsigma$ cannot be predicted of God. It is true that this intellectual quality is not ascribed to God in the New Testament, the word occurring only in another place. But in the Septuagint, on which the linguistic usage of the New Testament is based, it is applied to God as Creator (Prov. iii. 19), and in a similar passage, Jer. x. 12; and the Divine attribute of wisdom personified in Prov. viii. 14, exclaims, $\dot{\epsilon}\mu\grave{\eta}$ $\phi\rho\acute{o}\nu\eta\sigma\iota\varsigma$—"intelligence is mine." Why should $\phi\rho\acute{o}\nu\eta\sigma\iota\varsigma$ be less applicable than $\gamma\nu\hat{\omega}\sigma\iota\varsigma$ to God ? Prudence, indeed, in its common acceptation, can scarcely be ascribed to the Omniscient. Still, if God in any action displays those qualities which in a man might be called prudence, then such a property may be ascribed to him in perfect analogy with the common anthropomorphism of Scripture. But φρόνησις may not signify prudence in its usual acceptation. It is the action of the φρήν or mind. Wisdom is often ascribed to God, and φρόνησις is the action of His wise mind—its intuitive formation of purposes and resolutions in His infinite wisdom. To refer φρόνησις always to practical discretion, as Estius, Bengel, and Krebs do, is unwarranted. Σοφία is not simply and always *scientia theoretica*, nor φρόνησις *scientia practica*. The words are so explained, indeed, by Cicero—φρόνησις, *quæ est rerum expetendarum fugiendarumque scientia. De Offic.* i. 43. In the passages adduced by Krebs[1] and Loesner[2] from Josephus and Philo, the word does not certainly bear out Cicero's definition, but in some of them rather signifies insight, or perspicacity. In the classics it often denotes that practical wisdom which is indispensable to civil government. The term occurs only in another place in the New Testament, Luke i. 17, where it is rendered "the wisdom of the just," and where it certainly does not refer to prudence. It stands in the Septuagint as the representative of no less than nine different Hebrew words. That it is referred to God in the Seventy, shows that it may be predicated of Him in the New Testament. Σοφία is the attribute of wisdom, and φρόνησις is its special aspect, or the sphere of operation in which it developes itself. Thus, in Prov. x. 23, ἡ δὲ σοφία ἀνδρὶ τίκτει φρόνησιν. Compare also in Septuagint 1 Kings iv. 29 ; Dan. ii. 21 ; Joseph. *Antiq.* ii. 5, 7, viii. 7, 5. It is not so much the result of wisdom, as a peculiar phase of its action. Intellectual action under the guidance of σοφία is φρόνησις—intelligence. Beza's view is not very different from this. The word, therefore, may signify in this clause that sagacity which an initiator manifests in the disclosure of a mystery—a quality which, after the manner of men, is ascribed to God.

It is objected, again, that the adjective πάσῃ, added to σοφ. καὶ φρόν., forbids the application of the terms to God. Meyer admits that φρόνησις may be applied to God, but denies that πᾶσα φρόνησις can be so applied. We can say of God, Harless remarks, "in Him is all wisdom, but not He has done

[1] *Observationes in Novum Test. e Fl. Josepho*, p. 325.
[2] *Observationes in Novum Test. e Philone Alexandrino*, p. 338.

this or that in all wisdom." Olshausen homologates the statement, his argument being, that God possesses all attributes absolutely. De Wette, who, however, joins the words to the preceding clause, but applies them to God, answers, that the Divine wisdom, in reaching its end by every serviceable means, appears not as absolute, but only as relative, and he explains the clause, *in aller dazu dienlicher Weisheit und Einsicht*. But what hinders that the word should be rendered "in all," which though it may be literally "every kind," yet virtually signifies highest, or absolute wisdom and discretion? Harless again withstands this, and says, *es bezeichnet nie die Intension sondern nur die Extension*. Let the following examples suffice for our purpose:—Matt. xxviii. 18, πᾶσα ἐξουσία—all power—absolute power; Acts v. 23, the prison was shut, ἐν · πάσῃ ἀσφαλείᾳ—"with all safety," in their opinion, with absolute security; 1 Tim. i. 15, πάσης ἀποδοχῆς ἄξιος—worthy of all or of absolute credit and welcome; and in many other places. Nor is this sense unknown to the classics: πάντ' ἐπιστήμης—absolute knowledge;[1] πᾶσα ἀνάγκη—utmost or absolute necessity;[2] ἐς πᾶν κακοῦ—into extreme distress;[3] εἰς πάντα κίνδυνον—into extreme danger;[4] εἰς πᾶσαν ἀπορίαν—to the utmost embarrassment.[5] So that in πᾶς the idea of intension is at least inferentially bound up with that of extension. Such appear to us sufficient reasons for connecting the words with γνωρίσας, and regarding them as qualifying it, or defining the method in which the mystery has been disclosed.

But among those who connect the words with γνωρίσας, there are some forms of interpretation adopted which may be noticed and set aside. The first is that of Chrysostom, who, in one of his expositions, refers the "wisdom and prudence" to the mystery, as if they were descriptive of its qualities: τοῦτο γὰρ ἐστι τὸ μυστήριον τὸ πάσης σοφίας τε γέμον καὶ φρονήσεως—"for this mystery is marked by its fulness of wisdom and prudence." He is followed by Koppe, who, as is common with him, suggests this metaphrase: τὸ μυστήριον σοφώτατον καὶ φρονιμώτατον. These interpretations are not

---

[1] Sophocles, *Antig.* 721.  [2] Plato, *Phædr.* 235.
[3] Herod. vii. 118; ix. 118.  [4] Xenophon, *Cyr.* vii. 2, 22.
[5] Polybius, iii. 77, 4. See also Pape and Passow in their respective Lexicons.

warranted by the syntax. Reverting, then, to the view we have already stated, we are of opinion that the words qualify γνωρίσας. For this purpose there is no need that they be placed after it. The participle is at the same time intimately connected with the verb ἐπερίσσευσεν. It contains one of the elements of the χάρις, which God has made to abound. His having made known of His goodwill this higher aspect of Christ's work, is ascribed to that grace which, in this way and for this purpose, He hath caused to abound towards us. It is also one of the elements of ἀπολύτρωσις, and one of the fruits of that death which secured it. This connection is approved by Chrysostom, Theodoret, Jerome, Homberg, Baumgarten-Crusius, Koppe, Semler, and Holzhausen, by the editors Griesbach and Scholz, and by Conybeare. The verses are left undivided by Lachmann and Tischendorf.

(Ver. 9.) Γνωρίσας ἡμῖν τὸ μυστήριον τοῦ θελήματος αὐτοῦ —"Having in all wisdom and prudence made known to us the mystery of His will." Γνωρίσας stands to ἐπερίσσευσεν much in the same way as προορίσας did to ἐξελέξατο. Bernhardy, p. 383. And so in iii. 10, when the apostle speaks of God unveiling a great mystery, he adds that by such a disclosure His "manifold wisdom" is made known to the principalities and powers. The essential idea of μυστήριον, whatever may be the application, is, something into the knowledge of which one must be initiated, ere he comprehend it. In such a passage as this, it is not something unknowable, but something unknown till fitting disclosure has been made of it; something long hid, but at length discovered to us by God, and therefore a matter of pure revelation. The mystery itself is unfolded in the following verse. It is not the gospel or salvation generally, but a special purpose of God in reference to His universe. And it is called the mystery of "His will" —τοῦ θελήματος—the genitive being either subjective, because it has its origin in His own inscrutable purpose; or rather, the genitive being that of object, because His will is its theme—

κατὰ τὴν εὐδοκίαν αὐτοῦ—" according to His good pleasure." Εὐδοκία has been already explained under ver. 5. Though the mystery be His will, yet in His benevolent regards He has disclosed it. We preferred in the previous edition joining the phrase with the following clause and verse, but the similar use of κατά and its model clause in ver. 5 induces us, with Meyer, Rückert, and Olshausen, to connect it with γνωρίσας:— ἣν προέθετο ἐν αὑτῷ—"which He purposed in Himself." The verb occurs only in two other places, Rom. i. 13, iii. 25—and there may be here a quasi-temporal sense in πρo. The meaning implied in the reflexive form αὑτῷ, which Hahn rightly prints in opposition to Tischendorf and Lachmann, is correct. Luther and Bengel refer it to Christ, but the recurrence of the proper name in the next clause forbids such a reference in the pronoun here. The purpose takes effect in Christ, but it is conceived in God's own heart. "In Himself" He formed this design, for He is surrounded by no co-ordinate wisdom—"With whom took He counsel?" This and the next verse are intimately connected. Some, such as Bengel, suppose the verb ἀνακεφαλαιώσασθαι to be connected with γνωρίσας, and others unite it with προέθετο, but it stands out as the object to which the whole previous verse points, and of which it is an explanation.

(Ver. 10.) Εἰς οἰκονομίαν τοῦ πληρώματος τῶν καιρῶν— "In reference to the dispensation of the fulness of the times." Winer, § 49, a, c (δ). The article is absent before οἰκονομίαν, as the term is so well defined by the following genitives. Winer, § 19, 2, b. Εἰς does not signify "until," as Bullinger, Erasmus, Calvin, Estius, Bucer, Zanchius, and Grotius have supposed; as if the sense were—that the mystery had been kept concealed until this dispensation was introduced. This gives an emphasis and intensity of meaning to προέθετο, which the word cannot well bear. Nor can εἰς be rightly taken for ἐν, as is done by Jerome, Pelagius, Anselm, Beza, Piscator, and the Vulgate, for the meaning would be vague and diluted. Εἰς is "in reference to." Οἰκονομία signifies house-arrangement, or dispensation, and is rendered by Theophylact, διοίκησις, κατάστασις. The word in the New Testament occurs in Luke xvi. 2, 3, 4, in the general sense of stewardship, either the administration itself or the office, and the corresponding noun, οἰκονόμος, is found in the same chapter, and in Rom. xvi. 23. Schweigh. *Lex. Polyb.* p. 403. Οἰκονομία is also used with special reference to the gospel, and sometimes describes it as an arrangement or dispensation under charge of the apostles as its "stewards." 1 Cor. iv. 1, 2, ix. 17; Eph. iii. 2; Col. i. 25; Tit. i. 7; 1 Pet. iv. 10. Luther, led away by this idea, and by the "dispensatio" of the Vulgate, refers the term to preaching, and to the disclosure of the mystery—*dass es geprediget würde*. The noun does not signify specifically and of itself, the dispensation of grace, though the context leaves us in no doubt that such is the allusion here; but it characterizes it as an arrangement organized and secured in all its parts. Eph. iii. 2, 9; 1 Tim. i. 4. It is not made up of a series of disconnected truths and events, but it is a compact and symmetrical system of perfect harmony in all its reciprocal bearings and adaptations. The adjustment is exact, so that each truth shines and is shone upon; each fact is a cause and a consequent, is like a link in a chain, which holds and is held. It is a plan of infinite wisdom, where nothing is out of place, or happens either within or beyond its time.

And the scheme is characterized as being τοῦ πληρώματος τῶν καιρῶν—the genitive having its characterizing sense. Scheuerlein, § 16, 3. Into the sense of πλήρωμα we shall inquire at some length under the last verse of this chapter. The phrase marks the period of the dispensation. It cannot be the genitive of object—*administratio eorum quæ restant temporum*, as Storr supposes, taking πλήρωμα in an active sense; nor can we say with Koppe, that there is any reference to *extrema tempora*—the last day; nor with Baumgarten-Crusius, that the time specified is the remaining duration of the world. Harless gives, perhaps too narrowly, an exegetical sense to the words, as if they explained what was meant by the economy, to wit, a period when the mystery might be safely revealed—making the genitive that of identity. Nor can we suppose, with Stier, that these "times are parallel to the economy, and of equal duration," that they comprehend *die ganze Zeitdauer dieser Anstalt*—"for it developes and completes itself through adjusted times and periods." This view is adopted and eulogized by Alford. It seems to us, however, to be putting more into the words than of themselves they will bear. The genitive καιρῶν presents a temporal idea, and πληρώματος may be that of characterization. Winer, § 30, 2; or as in Jude, κρίσις μεγάλης ἡμέρας. It is an economy characterized by the fulness of the times—that is, introduced at the fulness of the times. The passages adduced by Alford are not at all analogous, for they have different contextual relations, and all of them want the element of thought contained in πλήρωμα. True, there are under the gospel καιροὶ ἐθνῶν, Luke xvi. 24; καιροὶ ἀναψύξεως, Acts iii. 19; καιροῖς ἰδίοις, 1 Tim. ii. 6—each of these phrases having a special and absolute reference. But πλήρωμα is relative, and implies a period which gradually, and in course of ages, has become filled up; and as the coming of Christ was preceded both by expectancy and preparation—so we have τὰ τέλη τῶν αἰώνων (1 Cor. x. 11), ἐπ' ἐσχάτων τῶν ἡμερῶν (Heb. i. 1), in the New Testament; and again and again in the Old Testament, "the latter days"—"days to come:" therefore the phrase here may define the economy by its marked temporal characteristic, as being full-timed and right-timed. Our view may be thus expressed: The time prior to the dispensation is at length filled up, for we take πλήρωμα in its passive sense. The πλήρωμα is regarded as a vast receptacle into which centuries and millenniums had been falling, but it was now filled. Thus, Herodotus iii. 22, ζώης πλήρωμα μακρότατον —the longest fulness of life—the sense of the clause being, The longest period for a person to live is eighty years. Schott, in *Ep. ad Galatas*, chap. iv. 4, p. 488; Winer, *ibid.*; Mark i. 15; Luke xxi. 24; John vii. 8; Gal. iv. 4; also in Septuagint, Gen. xxv. 24, xxix. 21; Dan. x. 3. It is not τοῦ χρόνου, as in Gal. iv. 4—in which past time is regarded as a unity—but τῶν καιρῶν, time being imaged under successive periods.[1] Theodoret has somewhat vaguely—τὸν ὁρισθέντα παρὰ τοῦ Θεοῦ καιρόν. This is one aspect, and that of Calovius—*dispensatio propria plenitudini temporis*—is another aspect, both of which seem to be comprehended in the phrase. The economy commenced at a period which implies that the times destined to precede it were filled up. Two ideas seem to be contained. 1. It marks God's time—the time prearranged and set apart by Him; a time which can neither be anticipated nor delayed. 2. It specifies the best time in the world's history for the occurrence to take place. Being God's

---

[1] The noun καιρός is allied to κείρω, and is often a synonym of μέτρον.—Donaldson's *New Cratylus*, § 191.

time, it must be the best time. The epoch is marked by God in His own calendar, and years roll on till their complement is numbered, while the opportuneness of the period in the world's annals proves and ratifies divine wisdom and foresight. That fulness of the time in which the economy was founded, is the *precise* period, for the Lord has appointed it; and the *best* period, for the age was ripe for the event. We cannot, however, with Usteri, place the entire emphasis of the phrase on this latter idea. *Paulin. Lehrbegriff*, p. 81. The Grecian arms extended the Hellenic tongue, and prepared the nations for receiving the oracles of the New Testament in a language so rich and so exact, so powerful in description and delicate in shades of expression. Roman ambition had also welded the various states of the civilised world into one mighty kingdom, so that the heralds of the cross might not be impeded in their progress by the jealousy of rival states, but might move freely on their mission under the protection of one general sovereignty. Awakened longing had been created over the East, and in the West the old superstitions had lost their hold on thinking minds.[1] The apostle utters this thought virtually in 1 Cor. i. 21. The world was allowed full time to discover by prolonged experiment the insufficiency of its own wisdom to instruct and save it. It was sighing deeply for deliverance, and in the maturity of this crisis there suddenly appeared in Judæa "the Desire of all nations." The Hebrew seer who looked forward to it, regarded it as the "latter day" or "last time;" the nations who were forewarned of it were in fevered anticipation of its advent, for it was to them, as Cappell says, *complementum prophetarum*, and, as Beza paraphrases, "*tempus tam diu expectatum.*" But we, "on whom the ends of the world have come," look back upon it, and feel it to be a period which took its rise after the former cycles had fulfilled their course, and all preparations for it had been duly completed. We do not deny to Alford that what characterized the introduction of the economy characterizes all its epochs, and that this may be implied in the remarkable phrase. But in the third chapter

---

[1] Der Kreislauf, in welchem sich die Bestimmung und Idee der Heidenthums, und Judenthums vollendete, musste erst sein Ziel erreicht haben.—Usteri, *Paulin. Lehrbegriff*, p. 85.

the apostle unfolds a portion of the mystery, and as if in reference to this phrase, he says of it—" Which in other ages was not made known to the sons of men;" to wit, it was first revealed in the fulness of the times. The mystery of this full-timed dispensation is now described—

ἀνακεφαλαιώσασθαι τὰ πάντα ἐν τῷ Χριστῷ—" to gather together all things in Christ." The infinitive does not need the article, being explanatory in its nature. Winer, § 44, 2; Madvig, § 144. The signification of the verb has been variously understood. 1. Some give it the sense of renew, as Suidas in his Lexicon. Theodoret explains it by μεταβάλλειν, and refers to this change—τῶν ἀνθρώπων ἡ φύσις ἀνίσταται καὶ τὴν ἀφθαρσίαν ἐνδύεται. Tertullian renders it—*ad initium reciprocare*—(*De Monogam.* 5), and the Syriac and Vulgate correspond. And this was a general opinion in the ancient church. Augustine, *Enchiridion*, 62; *Op.* vol. vi. p. 377, ed. 1837. The Gothic has *aftra usfulljan*, again to fill up. It would, however, be difficult to vindicate such an exposition on philological grounds. 2. It has been supposed to signify to collect again under one head—κεφάλαιον, or κεφαλή. Such is the general critical opinion of Chrysostom, Œcumenius, Theophylact, Erasmus, H. Stephens, Piscator, Calovius, Bengel, Matthies, Meier, de Wette, Olshausen, and Stier. "What," asks Chrysostom, "is the meaning of the word ἀνακεφ.? It is, to knit together, συνάψαι. It has another signification—To set over one and all the same Head, Christ, according to the flesh —μίαν κεφαλὴν ἐπιθεῖναι." Beza insists against this meaning, that the word comes from κεφάλαιον, not from κεφαλή. Besides, the Headship of Christ is not formally introduced till the 22nd verse. The meaning of ἀνα in composition must not be overlooked. Though it have only a faint signification, as compound words abound in the later age of a language, it does not quite lose that significance. It signifies here, apparently, "again"—as if there now existed, under the God-man as Redeemer, that state of things which had, prior to the introduction of evil, originally existed under the Logos, the Creator and Governor. 3. The word is supposed to signify, as in our version, "to gather together in one;" so Beza, Meyer, Baumgarten-Crusius, Harless, and others. Rom. xiii. 9. The summing up of the data, *rerum repetitio et congregatio*, was called, as Quintilian avers, ἀνακεφαλαίωσις. *De Instit. Orator.* vi. 1. The simple verb is found with such a meaning in Thucydides, vi. 91, viii. 53; and compounded with σύν it occurs in Polybius iii. 3, 1. Xen. *Cyr.* viii. 1, 15. Such a summation appears to Grotius and Hammond under the figure of the reunion of a dispersed army, but Jerome and Cameron view it as the addition of arithmetical sums. This third meaning is the most natural—there is a re-collection of all things in Christ as Centre, and the immediate relation of this re-gathering to God Himself is expressed by the middle voice. The objects of this re-union are—

τὰ ἐν τοῖς οὐρανοῖς καὶ τὰ ἐπὶ τῆς γῆς—"the things in heaven and the things on earth." This is a mode of expression designed to be general, as the employment of the neuter indicates. Some few MSS. supply the particle τέ after the τά of the first clause, and B, D, E, L, read ἐπί for ἐν in the same clause, a reading which cannot be sustained. Critical opinions on the meaning of the phrase are very varied. According to Morus, it denotes God and man; according to Schoettgen, Baumgarten-Crusius, Ernesti, Macknight, Schleusner, and Koppe—Jews and Gentiles; according to Beza, Piscator, Bodius, Rollock, Moldenhauer, Flatt, and Peile—the spirits of good men, especially under the Old Testament and the present church; and according to the great majority, the phrase signifies the union of spirits in heaven, angels or otherwise, with men on earth. So the Scholium preserved by Matthiae—ἀνακεφαλαίωσιν καλεῖ—τὴν εἰς μίαν κεφαλὴν ἕνωσιν, ὡς τῶν ἀγγέλων διὰ Χριστοῦ τοῖς ἀνθρώποις συναφθέντων. With these interpretations we agree, so far as they contain truth. But they have the truth in fragments, like broken pieces of a mirror. We take the τὰ πάντα here to be co-equal in extent of meaning with the phrase, Col. i. 16, "By Him were all things created that are in heaven, and that are in earth, visible and invisible, whether they be thrones, or dominions, or principalities, or powers; all things were created by Him and for Him." These τὰ πάντα are said in ver. 20 to be reconciled to Him. See under Col. i. 20. The phrase "things in heaven" denotes the higher and more distant spheres of creation, and these, along with "things on earth," may comprehend the universe—τὰ πάντα including, according to Meyer, all things and beings, while Harless gives the words the general sense of the universe. So do von Gerlach, Olshausen, and Stier. The neuter has a generalizing meaning. Winer, § 27, 5; Poppo, Thucydides, i. 104. It cannot be supposed to be used for the masculine, as no masculine is implied in the verse. Hodge limits τὰ πάντα to the church in heaven and earth—because, he says, the union effected is by the redemption of Christ. This "union," as he names it, is indeed a result of redemption; but the gathering together described here is a consequence above and beyond human salvation—a consequence connected with it, but held out apart from it as a mystery disclosed according to His good pleasure. The sense is weakened altogether by the notion of Turner, that the infinitive may express a divine intention which may yet be thwarted. The idea seems then to be that heaven and earth are now united under one government. Christ as Creator was rightfully the Governor of all things, and till the introduction of sin, that government was one and undivided. But rebellion produced disorder, the unity of the kingdom was broken. Earth was morally severed from heaven, and from the worlds which retained their pristine integrity. But Jesus has effected a blessed change, for an amnesty has been proclaimed to earth. Man is reconciled to God, and all who bear God's image are reconciled to man. Angels are "ministering spirits" to him, and all holy intelligences delight in him. Not only has harmony been restored to the universe, and the rupture occasioned by sin repaired, but beings still in rebellion are placed under Christ's control, as well as the unconscious elements and spheres of nature. This summation is seen in the form of government; Jesus is universal Regent. Not only do angels and the unfallen universe worship the same Governor with the redeemed, but all things and beings are under the same administration. The anthem to God and the Lamb begins with saints, is taken up by angels, and re-echoed by the wide creation. Rev. v. 9, 14.

The death of Jesus is described in this paragraph both in its primary and ultimate results. First, by it "we have redemption—the forgiveness of sins." And, secondly, by the same event, the universe is gathered together in Christ. The language, by its very terms, denotes far more than the union of the church in Him. Now the revelation of this great truth, as to the ultimate effect of Christ's mediation, is called a "mystery." Man could not have discovered it—the knowledge of it was not essential to his salvation. But it has been disclosed with peculiar wisdom and delicacy. It was not revealed in former times, when it could not have been appreciated; nay, it was not published till the means of it were visibly realized, till Jesus died and rose again, and on the right hand of God assumed this harmonizing presidency.

Since the days of Origen, the advocates of the doctrine of universal restoration have sought a proof-text in this passage. But restoration is not predicated—it is simply re-summation. Unredeemed humanity, though doomed to everlasting punishment, and fallen spirits for whom everlasting fire is prepared, may be comprised in this summation—subjugated even against their will. But the punishment of the impenitent affects not the unity of Christ's government. Evil has lost its power of creating disorder, for it is punished, confined, and held as a very feeble thing in the grasp of the Almighty Avenger. In fine, it is going beyond the record to deduce from this passage a proof of the doctrine of the confirmation of angels by the death of Christ—*ut perpetuum statum retineant*. Such are the words of Calvin. Were such a doctrine contained or clearly revealed in Scripture, we might imagine that the new relation of angels to Christ the Mediator might exercise such an influence over them as to preclude the possibility of their apostasy; or that their pure and susceptible spirits were so deeply struck with the malignity of sin as exhibited in the blood of the Son of God, that the sensation and recoil produced by the awful spectacle for ever operate as an infallible preservative.

And this *re-capitulation* of all things is declared a second time to be in Christ—$\dot{\epsilon}\nu$ $a\dot{v}\tau\hat{\omega}$—a solemn and emphatic re-assertion, Kühner, § 632. His mediative work has secured it, and His mediatorial person is the one centre of the universe. As the stone dropped into the lake creates those widening and concentric circles, which ultimately reach the farthest shore, so the deed done on Calvary has sent its undulations through the distant spheres and realms of God's great empire.

But ἐν αὐτῷ is the connecting link also with the following verse. Kühner, § 632. See also Col. i. 19, 20.

(Ver. 11.) 'Εν ᾧ καὶ ἐκληρώθημεν. For ἐκληρώθημεν some read ἐκλήθημεν, supported by A, D, E, F, G, and the *vetus Itala*. Lachmann, following Griesbach, prefers the latter; but Tischendorf rightly advocates the former reading, on what we reckon preponderant authority. Still is the connection marked as usual, "in Christ," and by the ever-recurring formula ἐν ᾧ. 'Εκληρώθημεν has its foundation in the usage of the Old Testament, in the theocratic inheritance—נַחֲלָה, as in Deut. iv. 20, and in numerous other places. The κλῆρος, κληρονόμος, and κληρονομία are also familiar epithets in the apostolical writings. The inheritance was the characteristic blessing of the theocratic charter, and it associated itself with all the popular religious feelings and hopes. The ideas which some attach to the term, but which refer not to this source and idiom, are therefore to be rejected. 1. The notion of Koppe, and of the lexicographers Wahl, Bretschneider, and Wilke, is peculiar. According to them, it denotes simply to obtain, and the object obtained is, or, "it has kindly happened to us," that we should be to the praise of His glory. The passages selected by Elsner (*Observ. Sacræ*, p. 204) out of Ælian and Alciphron, are foreign to the purpose, for the verb is there regularly construed with the accusative of the object, and it is not from classic usage that the apostolic term has been taken. 2. Nor is another common interpretation much better supported, according to which the verb signifies to "obtain by lot"—the opinion of Chrysostom and his Greek imitators, and of the Vulgate, Augustine, Ambrosiaster, Aquinas, Erasmus, Estius, and a - Lapide. Chrysostom explains the word thus—κλήρου γενομένου ἡμᾶς ἐξελέξατο. Still this explanation does not come up to our idea of the Pauline κλῆρος, which refers not to the manner of our getting the possession, but to the possession itself—not to the lot, but to the allotment. 3. Bengel, Flatt, Holzhausen, Bisping, de Wette, and Stier take it, that we have become the κλῆρος— the peculiar people of God. This, no doubt, yields a good sense. The Jews are also called by this name—the noun, however, being employed as the epithet, and not the verb as affirming the condition. Besides, the κλῆρος in Col.

i. 12, and in ver. 18, is not our subjective condition, as this exegesis implies, but our objective possession in which we participate, and in the hope of which we now rejoice. 4. So that with Valla, with Luther, Calvin, and Beza among the reformers, and with Wolf, Rosenmüller, Harless, Matthies, Meyer, Scholz, and Meier, we take the passive verb to signify "we have been brought into possession"—*zum Erbtheil gekommen*—as Luther has it. In whom we have been enfeoffed, in whom we have had it allotted to us. Deut. iv. 20, ix. 29, xxxii. 9. The verb may certainly bear this meaning; κληρόω —"I assign an inheritance to some one;" in the passive —"I have an inheritance assigned to me," as verbs which in the active govern the genitive or dative of a person have it as a nominative in the passive. Winer, § 39; Bernhardy, p. 341; Rom. iii. 2; Gal. ii. 7, iv. 20. We see no force in Stier's objection that such a meaning should be followed by εἰς τὸ ἔχειν ἡμᾶς, whereas it is followed by εἰς τὸ εἶναι ἡμᾶς, for the inheritance is got that the inheritors may *be*, in the mode of their introduction to it and their enjoyment of it, to the praise of His glory. The καί might, if connected with the unexpressed pronoun, signify "indeed;" but it may be better to connect it with the verb—"in whom we have also obtained an inheritance." Hartung, Kap. ii. 7; Devarius-Klotz, p. 636; Matthiae, § 620. That which is spiritual and imperishable is not, like money, the symbol of wealth, but it is something which one feels to be his own—an inheritance. It is not exhausted with the using, and it comes to us not as a hereditary possession. "Corruption runs in the blood, grace does not." It is God's gift to the believers in Christ, conferred on them in harmony with His own eternal purpose. The nominative to the verb, indicated by "we," does not refer specially to Jewish Christians in this verse, as even Harless supposes; far less does it denote the apostles, or ministers of religion, as Barnes imagines. The writer, under the term "we," simply speaks primarily of himself and the saints and faithful in the Ephesian church, as being—

προορισθέντες κατὰ πρόθεσιν τοῦ τὰ πάντα ἐνεργοῦντος κατὰ τὴν βουλὴν τοῦ θελήματος αὐτοῦ—"being predestinated according to the purpose of Him who worketh all things after the counsel of His will." The general significance of these terms has been already given under previous verses. βουλή and θέλημα are here connected—"the counsel of His will." The correspondent verbs, βούλομαι and ἐθέλω, are distinguished by Buttmann thus: the latter is the more general expression, containing the idea that the purpose formed lies within the power of the person who formed it (*Lexilogus*, p. 35); while Tittmann adds, that θέλημα is an expression of will, but βουλή has in it the further idea of propension or inclination. *De Synon.* p. 124. But the distinction is vague. The words occur with marked distinction in 1 Sam. xviii.; for in ver. 22, θέλει ἐν signifies "he has pleasure in;" while in ver. 25, βούλεται ἐν denotes desire consequent upon a previous resolution. Compare also 2 Sam. xxiv. 3; 1 Chron. xxviii. 4. Θέλημα, therefore, is will, the result of desire—*voluntas;* βουλή is counsel, the result of a formal decision—*propositum.* Donaldson's *New Cratylus*, §§ 463, 464. Here βουλή is the ratified expression of will—the decision to which His will has come. The Divine mind is not in a state of indifference, it has exercised θέλημα—will; and that will is not a lethargic *velleity*, for it has formed a defined purpose, βουλή, which it determines to carry out. His desire and His decrees are not at variance, but every resolution embodies His unthwarted pleasure. This divine fore-resolve is universal in its sweep—"He worketh *all* things after the counsel of His own will." The plan of the universe lies in the omniscient mind, and all events are in harmony with it. Power in unison with infinite wisdom and independent and undeviating purpose, is seen alike whether He create a seraph or form a gnat —fashion a world or round a grain of sand—prescribe the orbit of a planet or the gyration of an atom. The extinction of a world and the fall of a sparrow are equally the result of a free pre-arrangement. Our "inheritance" in Christ springs not from merit, nor is it an accidental gift bestowed from casual motive or in fortuitous circumstances, but it comes from God's fore-appointment, conceived in the same independence and sovereignty which guide and control the universe.

(Ver. 12.) Εἰς τὸ εἶναι ἡμᾶς εἰς ἔπαινον δόξης αὐτοῦ, τοὺς προηλπικότας ἐν τῷ Χριστῷ — "That we should be to the praise of His glory—we who have before hoped in Christ." The critical opinions on this verse, and on its connection with the preceding one, are very contradictory. Meyer and Ellicott join it to ἐκληρώθημεν — "we have been brought into the inheritance, in order that we should be to the praise of His glory." Others, as Calovius, Flatt, and Harless, take εἰς ἔπ. as the final cause of the predestination, and read thus, "that we who first trusted in Christ should be to the praise of His glory." Harless would render—*die wir vorher bestimmt waren u.s.w., diejenigen zu seyn zum Ruhme seiner Herrlichkeit, die schon vorher auf Christus hofften*—thus making this forehope the blessing to which they were predestinated. But the blessings to which men are predestinated are not pre-Messianic, but actual Christian blessings. Besides, such a construction is needlessly involved, and in verses 5 and 14 the blessings which believers enjoy are specified, and the phrase "to the praise of His glory" follows as a general conclusion. Εἰς ἔπαινον τῆς δόξης is therefore not the proximate purpose, but the ultimate result.

The main struggle has been to determine who are meant by the ἡμᾶς τοὺς προηλπικότας. Koppe, followed by Holzhausen, understands the apostle to use the style royal, and to mean himself. The majority of commentators suppose the words to denote the believing Jews, so called, in the opinion of Beza, Grotius, Estius, Bodius, Bengel, Flatt, Olshausen, and Stier, because their faith in Christ preceded in point of time that of the Gentiles. This exegesis admits of various modifications. The hope of the Jews in Christ preceded that of the Gentiles, either, as Harless imagines, because they had heard of Him earlier; or, as Rosenmüller, Meyer, Olshausen, Chandler, and others affirm, because they possessed the Old Testament prophecies, and so had the hope of Him before He came into the world. But it may be replied, that this sudden change of meaning in ἡμεῖς, so different from all the preceding verses, is a gratuitous assumption; for the "we" and the "us" in the preceding context denote the community of believers with whom the apostle identifies himself, and why should he so sharply and abruptly contract the signification, and confine it to himself and his believing countrymen? There is no hint that such particularization is intended, and there is nothing to point out the Jews as its object. Were this the idea, that the Christian

Jews were distinguished from the Gentiles by the forehope of a Messiah, as the great object of their nation's anticipations and desires, then we might have expected that the phrase would have been προηλπικότες εἰς τὸν Χριστόν. Nor do we apprehend that there is anything in the participle to limit its meaning to the Hebrew portion of the church. The πρό may not signify before or earlier in comparison with others, but, as de Wette maintains, it may simply mean "already"— prior to the time at which the apostle writes. Many confirmatory examples occur: Eph. iii. 3, καθὼς προέγραψα—as I have already written; Col. i. 5, ἐλπίδα ἣν προηκούσατε— the hope of which ye have already heard; Acts xxvi. 5, προγινώσκοντες—who have already known; Gal. v. 21, ἃ προλέγω—which I have already told you; Rom. iii. 25, τῶν προγεγονότων ἁμαρτημάτων — of sins already committed; 1 Thess. ii. 2, ἀλλὰ προπαθόντες — but having already suffered; and so in many other cases. The preposition indeed has often a more distinctive meaning, but there is thus no necessity caused by the words of the clause to refer it to Jews. The use of ὑμεῖς in the following verse might be said to be a direct transition, natural in writing a letter, when the composer of it passes from general to more special allusions and circumstances. The verb ἐλπίζω also is used in reference to the Gentiles, Matt. xii. 21, Rom. xv. 12; and it might here denote that species of trust which gives the mind a firm persuasion that all promises and expectations shall be fully realized. But while these difficulties stand in the way, still, on a careful review of the passage, we are rather inclined from the pointed nature of the context to refer the ἡμᾶς to believing Jews. The participle may certainly bear the meaning of having hoped beforehand—that is, before the object of that hope appeared; or it may mean before in comparison with others, Acts xx. 13. Thus the ὑμεῖς of the following verse forms a sharp contrast to the expressed ἡμᾶς and the τοὺς προηλπικότας, which is a limiting predication, with emphasis upon it, as indicated by its position and by the specifying article. Donaldson, § 492. So understood, the claim describes the privilege of believing Jews in contrast with Gentiles. Lightfoot *on Luke*, ii. 34. The article τῆς before δόξης is omitted by many MSS., and is justly cancelled by Tischendorf and Lachmann. The clause itself has been explained under ver. 6.

(Ver. 13.) *Ἐν ᾧ καὶ ὑμεῖς.* This clause is variously construed. Morus harshly renders *ἐν ᾧ*—"therefore," making it to correspond to the Hebrew בַּאֲשֶׁר. Meyer, Peile, and Alford supply the verb of existence—"in whom are ye." But this appears tame in contrast with the other significant verbs of the paragraph. Far better, if a verb is to be supplied to the clause at all, either to take *ἠλπίκατε,* with Beza, Calvin, and Estius; or *ἐκληρώθητε,* with Zanchius, a-Lapide, Bodius, Koppe, Meier, Harless, and Olshausen. But the clause presents only one compacted sentence—"In whom also ye, having heard the word of truth, the gospel of your salvation; in whom (I repeat) ye, having believed, were sealed." *Ἐν ᾧ καὶ ὑμεῖς* refers to the verb *ἐσφραγίσθητε*—in Christ ye too have been sealed; and the second *ἐν ᾧ καί* resumes and intensifies the declaration, for it refers to Christ, as Harless, Olshausen, and Stier rightly think, and not—as Piscator, Grotius, and Rosenmüller affirm—to *λόγος,* or—as Castalio, Calvin, Beza, and Meyer aver—to *εὐαγγέλιον.* The apostle, in assuring the Gentile converts that their interest in Christ, though more recent, was not less secure than that of believing Jews, first of all turns to their initial privilege as having heard the gospel, and then he cannot but refer to their faith; and this second reference, so important, suspends the construction for a moment. The apostle describes their privilege—

*ἀκούσαντες τὸν λόγον τῆς ἀληθείας*—"having heard the word of the truth." The aorist has its proper meaning, though rendered "having heard," and points to the period when their privilege commenced. The genitive is that of contents or substance. Scheuerlein, § 12, 1. This clause describes the revealed system of mercy. That word has truth, absolute truth, for its essence. There is no occasion to suppose any allusion to the types of the Old Testament, with Chrysostom, or to the lying vanities and ambiguous oracles of Heathendom, with Baumgarten-Crusius and a-Lapide. The idea was familiar to the mind of Paul, Rom. i. 18; ii. 8; Col. i. 5—*ἡ ἀλήθεια*; 2 Thess. ii. 12. This special truth is adapted to man's spiritual state. It is a truth that there is a

God, but the truth that this God is the Saviour; a truth that God is benevolent, but the truth that grace is in His heart toward sinners; a truth that there is a future world, but the truth that heaven is the home of the redeemed. The gospel is wholly truth, and that very truth which is indispensable to a guilty world. And it comes as a word, by special oral revelation, for it is not gleaned and gathered: there is a kind and faithful oracle.

It is further characterized as τὸ εὐαγγέλιον τῆς σωτηρίας ὑμῶν—" the gospel of your salvation." But what is the precise form of the genitive? We cannot regard it, with Harless, as merely a peculiar form of apposition; nor can we make it, with other critics, the gospel which secures your salvation. Rom. i. 16. For the occurrence of ἀκούσαντες, as explaining their relation to the gospel, would suggest the explanation—the gospel which reveals salvation, because it contains it. Bernhardy, p. 161; Winer, § 30, 2, b. The gospel is good news, and that good news is our salvation— the best of all news to a sinful and dying world. Salvation makes *safe* from all the elements of that penalty which their sin brought down upon transgressors, and possession to the inheritance of the highest good—the enjoyment of the Divine favour, and the possession of the Divine image. This truthful and cheering revelation they had heard, and that at two several periods, from the lips of the apostle himself. Having heard the gospel, they believed it: "Faith cometh by hearing." They heard so as that they believed, for they had heard with candour, docility, and attention. While others might criticise the terms of the message, or scoff at it, they believed it, they took it for what it professed to be. They gave it credit, received its statements as truths, and felt its blessings to be realities.

ἐν ᾧ καὶ πιστεύσαντες—" in whom also having believed." The pronoun has Χριστός for its antecedent, and it is in close connection with the verb. The verb πιστεύω is found with ἐν in Mark i. 15, but not in the writings of the apostle. The aorist marks a time antecedent to the following verb. They not only heard, but they also believed the word of truth.

ἐσφραγίσθητε τῷ Πνεύματι τῆς ἐπαγγελίας τῷ ἁγίῳ—" ye were sealed with the Holy Spirit of promise." The dative is that of instrument, and the position of τῷ ἁγίῳ gives a signal solemnity to the epithet. This Divine Being is termed Πνεῦμα, not on account of His essence, since the whole Godhead is Spirit, but because of His relation to the universe as its Life, and to the believing soul as its Quickener. And He is the HOLY Spirit, not as if the sanctity of His character were more brilliant than that of Father and Son, but because of His economic function as the Sanctifier. The genitive ἐπαγγελίας is supposed by Chrysostom, Calvin, Beza, and the early church, to have an active sense, and to mean the Spirit who confirms the promise. Better is the idea which makes the genitive denote quality, as in the Syriac version—the Spirit which was promised. The genitive is almost that of ablation, as Theophylact in his first explanation gives it—ὅτι ἐξ ἐπαγγελίας ἐδόθη. The Spirit is a prominent and pervading promise in the Old Testament. Isa. xxxii. 15, xliv. 3; Ezek. xxxvi. 27, xxxix. 29; Joel ii. 28; Zech. xii. 10. The Spirit was also the leading promise which Christ left to His disciples, as recorded in John, referred to in Acts i. 4–8, and in Gal. iii. 14. See Luke xxiv. 49. The fact is, that up to the period of our Lord's ascension, the Spirit stood to the church in the relation and attitude of a promised gift. John vii. 39. "Holy Ghost was not yet" in plenary possession and enjoyment, "because Jesus was not yet glorified." The same truth was taught by the apostle at Ephesus. Acts xix. 2. Paul said to certain disciples there who had been baptized into John's baptism, "Did ye receive the Holy Ghost when ye believed? And they said unto him, We did not so much as hear whether there be any Holy Ghost." Surely such ignorance referred not to the person of the Holy Ghost, for these men were Jews; but the reply seems to be, "We did not hear whether His promised outpouring has been vouchsafed." And when they were rebaptized, the blessing came upon them. To a church where such a scene occurred, where men had waited for the Spirit, and felt that His descent did not follow John's baptism—for it was the prerogative of the Messiah to baptize with the Holy Ghost—no wonder that Paul designates this Divine Agent by the name of the Spirit of promise. And though the church now possess Him, still, in reference to enlarged operation and reviving energy, He is the Spirit of promise. By this Spirit they were sealed. 2 Cor. i. 22. The sealing followed the believing, and is not coincident with it, as Harless argues. This sealing is a peculiar work of the Spirit. 2 Tim. ii. 19. Various ideas may be contained in the general figure. It seems to have, in fact, both an objective and a subjective reference. There are the seal, the sealer, and the sealed. The Holy Ghost is the seal, God the sealer. Σφραγὶς βασιλικὴ εἰκών ἐστι [1]—the Divine image in the possession of the Spirit is impressed on the heart, and the conscious enjoyment of it assures the believer of perfection and glory—Rom. viii. 16—or, as Theodore of Mopsuestia says, τὴν βεβαίωσιν ἐδέξασθε. He who seals feels a special interest in what is so sealed—it is marked out as His: "The Lord knoweth them that are His." He recognizes His own image. So Chrysostom—καθάπερ γὰρ εἴ τις τοὺς λαχόντας αὑτῷ δήλους ποιήσειεν, just as if one were to make manifest such as have fallen to his lot. The notion of Theophylact is similar. But the idea that the sealing proves our security to others, or is meant to do so, is foreign to the meaning. That seal unbroken remains a token of safety. Rev. vii. 3. Whatever bears God's image will be safely carried home to His bosom. The sealed ones feel the assurance of this within themselves. That there may be an allusion in the phrase to the miraculous gifts of the early ages, is not to be entirely denied, though certainly all who possessed those charismata were not converted men. Baptism was named "a seal" in early times, σφραγίς—signaculum. Greg. Naz. Or. xl. De Bapt.; Tertull. Apol. xxi. The reason of the name is obvious, but there is no allusion to it here. Augusti, Handb. der Christ. Archæologie, vol. ii. p. 315, 16.

(Ver. 14.) Ὅς ἐστιν ἀρραβὼν τῆς κληρονομίας ἡμῶν— "Who is the earnest of our inheritance." The reading ὅ is found in A, B, F, G, L, but appears to be a correction. The relative does not agree with its antecedent in gender, not that, as Bloomfield imagines, such a change is any argument in favour of the personality of the πνεῦμα, for it only assumes the gender of the following definitive predicate. So Mark

[1] Polyænus, p. 763.

xv. 16; Gal. iii. 16; 1 Tim. iii. 13, etc. Winer, § 24, 3; Kühner, § 786, 3; Madvig, § 98. From not perceiving this idiom, some refer to Christ as the antecedent. Ἀῤῥαβών—earnest, is but the Oriental עֲרָבוֹן in Greek letters. 2 Cor. i. 22, v. 5. The earnest is not, properly speaking, a mere pledge, *pignus*, as the Vulgate has it. The pledge is restored when the contract has been performed, but the earnest is a portion of the purchase money. Isidore, lib. v. 25; Gaius, iii. 139; Suicer, *sub voce*. The master gives the servant a small coin when the paction is agreed on, and this *handgelt*, or earnest, πρόδομα, as Hesychius defines it, is the token that the whole sum stipulated for will be given when the term of service expires. The earnest is not withdrawn, but is supplemented at the appointed period, for it is only, as Chrysostom explains it, μέρος τοῦ παντός. Irenæus also says—" *Quod et pignus dixit Apostolus, hoc est partem ejus honoris qui a Deo nobis promissus est, in epistola quæ ad Ephesios est.*"—*Adv. Hæres.* lib. v. cap. 11. The inheritance, κληρονομία, is that glorious blessing which awaits us, which is in reserve for us, and held by Christ in our name—that inheritance in which we have been enfeoffed (ver. 11), and which belonged to the υἱοθεσία; and ἡμῶν is resumed, for it belonged alike to believing Jew and Gentile.

The enjoyment of the earnest is a proof that the soul has been brought by faith into union with God. It has said to the Lord, "Thou art my Lord." This covenant of "God's peace" is ratified by the earnest given. The earnest is less than the future inheritance, a mere fraction of it—*ex decem solidis centum solidorum millia*, as Jerome illustrates. The work of God's Spirit is never to be undervalued, yet it is only a small thing in relation to future blessedness. That knowledge which the Spirit implants is but limited—the dawn, faint in itself, and struggling with the gloom of departing night, compared to the broad effulgence of mid-day. The holiness He creates is still imperfect, and is surrounded and often oppressed with remaining infirmities in "this body of death," and the happiness He infuses is often like gleams of sunshine on a "dark and cloudy day," faint, few, and evanescent. But the earnest, though it differ in degree, is the same in kind with the prospective inheritance. The earnest is not withdrawn, nor a totally new circle of possessions substituted. Heaven is but an addition to present enjoyments. Knowledge in heaven is but a development of what is enjoyed on earth; its holiness is but the purity of time elevated and perfected; and its happiness is no new fountain opened in the sanctified bosom, but only the expansion and refinement of those susceptibilities which were first awakened on earth by confidence in the Divine Redeemer. The "earnest," in short, is the "inheritance" in miniature, and it is also a pledge that the inheritance shall be ultimately and fully enjoyed. God will not resile from His promise, the Spirit conferred will perfect the enterprise. To give believers a foretasting, and then withhold the full enjoyment, would be a fearful torture. The prelibation will be followed by the banquet. As an earnest of the inheritance, the Holy Ghost is its pledge and foretaste, giving to believers the incipient experience of what it is, and imparting the blissful assurance of its ultimate and undisturbed possession. And all this—

εἰς ἀπολύτρωσιν τῆς περιποιήσεως, εἰς ἔπαινον τῆς δόξης αὐτοῦ—"till the redemption of the purchased possession, to the praise of His glory." "The expression is idiomatic and somewhat difficult." 1. Some suppose περιποίησις to mean *salus, conservatio*, deliverance and life. The allied verb sometimes signifies in the Septuagint "to save alive," and so Whitby renders the phrase "the redemption of life," and Bretschneider, *redemptio qua vitæ æternæ servamur*. Wetstein, Bengel, and Bos have virtually the same explanation. Holzhausen justifies this criticism at some length, and resolves the clause εἰς ἀπολ. καὶ περιποίησιν. 2. Others take the noun in the sense of possession. In 2 Chron. xiv. 13, the noun seems to signify "a remnant preserved," καὶ ἔπεσον Αἰθίοπες ὥστε μὴ εἶναι ἐν αὐτοῖς περιποίησιν. 3. Some connect the two substantives as cause and effect. Luther renders *zu unserer Erlösung, dass wir sein Eigenthum würden*—to our redemption, that we should be His possession. In this view Luther was preceded by Theodoret and Pelagius, and has been followed by Homberg and von Gerlach. Bucer has *redemptio qua contingat certa vitæ possessio*. But with an active sense the noun, as may be seen under ver. 7, is followed by a genitive. 4. Vatablus, Koppe, and Wahl give the noun a participial rendering—the redemption which has been secured or purchased for us. Koppe also gives it another turn, "which we have already possessed," in allusion to ver. 7. 5. Others change this aspect, and give it this rendering, *ad obtinendam redemptionem*. Beza translates, *dum in libertatem vindicemur*—a rendering which would require the words to be reversed. 6. Another party, H. Stephanus, Bugenhagen, Calovius, and Matthies, preceded by Ambrosiaster and Augustine, who seem to have understood it in the same sense, take the word in the general sense of possession—*hæreditas acquisita*. But the inheritance needs not to be redeemed; the redemption certainly applies to us, and not to the blessedness prepared for us. 7. The verb denotes to acquire for oneself: Gen. xxxvi. 6, xxxi. 18; Prov. vii. 4; Isa. xliii. 21, λαός μου ὃν περιεποιησάμην; Acts xx. 28, ἐκκλησία, ἣν περιεποιήσατο διὰ τοῦ αἵματος τοῦ ἰδίου; 1 Tim. iii. 13, βαθμὸν ἑαυτοῖς καλὸν περιποιοῦνται. Similar instances occur in the Apocrypha, and the same meaning is found in the classics. Didymus defines it, περιπ. γὰρ κατ' ἐξαίρετον ἐν περιουσίᾳ καὶ κτήματι λελογισμένον, that is περιπ., which is emphatically reckoned as portion of our substance and possession. Theophylact explains the words by the same terms, and Œcumenius defines it by itself, περιπ. ἡμᾶς καλεῖ διὰ τὸ περιποιήσασθαι ἡμᾶς τὸν θεόν.[1] In this way the noun is used in 1 Thess. v. 9, εἰς περιπ. σωτηρίας; 2 Thess. ii. 14, εἰς περιπ. δόξης; Heb. x. 39, εἰς περιπ. ψυχῆς. In all these cases there is the idea of acquisition for oneself, and the noun followed by a genitive has an active significance, which it cannot have here, and Meyer's connection with αὐτοῦ is strained. The idea of life, vitality, or safety, found in the term so often when it stands in the Old Testament as the representative of חיה, and on which some exegetes lay such stress, is evidently a secondary use. The central idea is to preserve for oneself, and as life is the most valuable of possessions, so the word was employed κατ' ἐξοχήν—to preserve it. The great majority of critics understand περιποίησις in the abstract—the possession, *i.e.* the people pos-

---

[1] Such a meaning belongs to the verb in the Greek classics. Οἱ ἐπελθόντες περιποίησαν τὸ χωρίον. Thucyd. 3, 102. Τὰς ψυχὰς περιποιήσασθι. Xenoph. *Cyrop.* 4, 4. 3. Ἡ δὲ τύχη καὶ ὁ δαίμων περιποίησι. Herodian, 8, 8. 12. See the Lexicons of Passow, Pape, and Liddell and Scott, *sub voce.*

sessed—περιποιηθέντες. As a collective noun to denote a body of people, περιτομή is employed in Phil. iii. 3, and so ἐκλογή stands in Rom. xi. 7 for οἱ ἐκλεκτοί. The word thus corresponds to the Hebrew סְגֻלָּה, often rendered by a similar term—περιούσιος. Compare Ex. xix. 5; Deut. vii. 6, xiv. 2, xxvi. 18; Isa. xliii. 21; or Mal. iii. 17, ἔσονταί μοι εἰς περιποίησιν. The περιποίησις in the Old Testament refers not to any possession held by the people, but to the people themselves held in possession by God. Titus ii. 14; and λαὸς εἰς περιποίησιν, 1 Pet. ii. 9. The collective people of God are His περιποίησις—the body of the faithful whom He has taken to be His κλῆρος. They are His by the blood paid for their ransom. Οἵτινες, says Theophylact, ἐσμὲν περιποίησις καὶ κλῆσις καὶ περιουσία θεοῦ. And the redemption which is here referred to, is their complete and final deliverance from all evil. The people who form the "possession" become God's by redemption, and shall fully realize themselves as God's when that redemption shall be completed.

Olshausen, Meyer, and Stier understand εἰς to denote the final cause—" for the redemption of the purchased possession." Still in this case "for" would have virtually a subtemporal sense. De Wette and Rückert render it "until;" iv. 30. Whether the words be joined with ἐσφραγίσθητε or with the immediately preceding clause, it matters not, for the meaning is much the same. The sealing and earnest are alike intermediate, and point to a future result—εἰς implying a future purpose and period, when both shall be superseded. The earnest is enjoyed up till the inheritance be received, when it is absorbed in its fulness. The idea is common in the Old Testament, as showing the relation which the ancient Israel bore to God as His "inheritance"—His, and His by a special tie, for He had redeemed them out of Egypt. Triune divine operation is again developed;—the Father seals believers, and His glory is the last end; in the Son are they sealed, and their redemption is His work; while the Spirit—" which proceedeth" from the Father, and is sent by the Son—is the Seal and the Earnest.

And this ἀπολύτρωσις is our absolute redemption, as Chrysostom terms it. Wilke understands by ἀπολύτρωσις— the liberation of the minor on his majority, comparing this passage with one somewhat similar in Galatians. But ἀπολύ-τρωσις seems, in the apostle's idea of it, to be a long process, including not a single and solitary blessing, but a complete series of spiritual gifts, beginning with the pardon of sin, and stretching on to the ultimate bestowment of perfection and felicity, for it rescues and blesses our entire humanity. In Jesus "we are having redemption;" and pardon, enlightenment, and inheritance, with the Spirit as the signet and the earnest, are but its present elements, given us partially and by instalments in the meanwhile: for though it begin when sin is forgiven, yet it terminates only when we are put in possession of that totality of blessing which our Lord's obedience and death have secured. Rom. viii. 23; 1 Cor. i. 30. "We have redemption" so soon as we believe; we are ever having it so long as we are on earth; and when Jesus comes again to finish the economy of grace, we shall have it in its full and final completion. Thus the redemption in ver. 7 is incipient, and in ver. 14 is final—the first and last stages of the same ἀπολύτρωσις.

And all issues εἰς ἔπαινον τῆς δόξης αὐτοῦ—"to the praise of His glory"—His grace having now done its work. As in verses 5th and 6th, εἰς with the proximate end is followed by εἰς with the ultimate purpose. The περιποίησις—"the LORD'S OWN," "the Holy Catholic Church" in heaven, praises Him with rapturous emotion, for His glory is seen and felt in every blessing and hope, and this perpetual and universal consciousness of redemption is ever jubilant in its anthems and halleluiahs. See under ver. 6.

The period of redemption expires with the παρουσία. No more is redemption to be offered, for the human race has run its cycle; and no more is it to be partially enjoyed, for the redeemed are to be clothed with perfection: so that the period of perfection in blessing harmonizes with that of perfection in numbers. As long as the process of redemption is incomplete, the collection of recipients is incomplete too. The church receives its complement in extent at the very same epoch at which it is crowned with fulness of purity and blessedness. "May it please Thee of Thy gracious goodness shortly to accomplish the number of Thy elect, and to hasten Thy kingdom," is an appropriate petition on the part of all saints.

(Ver. 15.) This verse begins a new section. After praise comes prayer. The apostle having given thanks to God for the Ephesian converts, offers a fervent and comprehensive prayer on their behalf, that they may enjoy a deeper insight, so as to know the hope of His calling, the riches of His future glory, and His transcendent vivifying and exalting power, as seen in the resurrection and glorification of Christ.

Διὰ τοῦτο—" Wherefore," not, as Grotius says, and in which saying he is joined by Rückert and Matthies, "because we are bound to thank God for benefits," for the words have a wider retrospective connection than merely with the last clause of the preceding paragraph. Nor, on the other hand, is it natural, with Chrysostom, Œcumenius, and Harless, to give them a reference to the whole previous section. It is better, with Theophylact and Meyer, to join them to the 13th and 14th verses. For in these verses the apostle turns to the believing Ephesians, and, directly addressing them, describes briefly the process of their salvation, and then, and for that reason, prays for them. The prayer is not for "us," but for "you," and for you, because ye heard and believed, and were sealed.

Κἀγώ, rendered "I also." But such a translation suggests the idea of others, tacitly and mentally alluded to, besides the apostle. Who then can be referred to in the word "also"? Is it, "Others thank God for you, so do I"? or is it, "Ye thank God yourselves, I do it also for you"? thus, as Meyer says, (*zusammenwirkt*)—he co-operates with them. These suppositions seem foreign to the context, since there is no allusion to any others beside the writer, nor is there any reference to the Ephesians as praying or giving thanks for themselves. Καί may be merely continuative, as it often is in the New Testament; it may merely mark transition to another topic; or it may indicate the transition from the second person to the first. Stuart, § 185. Κἀγώ[1] may signify "indeed," *quidem;* or it may have the first of those meanings in the Pauline diction. Compare Acts xxvi. 29; Rom. iii. 7; 1 Cor. vii. 8, 40, x. 33, xi. 1; 2 Cor. xi. 16; Gal. iv. 12; Phil. ii. 19; 1 Thess. iii. 5. The word would thus mean

---

[1] Buttmann pronounces it to be an error to write κἀγώ with iota subscribed, § 29, n. 2; Jelf, § 14.

"Wherefore I indeed"—the apostle who first preached to you, and who has never ceased to yearn over you—ἀκούσας τὴν καθ' ὑμᾶς πίστιν ἐν τῷ Κυρίῳ Ἰησοῦ—"having heard of your faith in the Lord Jesus." It is wrong to argue from this expression, with Olshausen and de Wette, that the apostle had no personal knowledge of the persons whom he addressed. This was an early surmise, for it is referred to by Theodoret. Some, says he, have supposed that the apostle wrote to the Ephesians, ὡς μηδέπω θεασάμενος αὐτούς.[1] As we have seen in the Introduction, those who wish to regard this epistle as a circular letter, lay stress on the same term. But some years had elapsed since the apostle had visited Ephesus, and seen the Ephesian church, and might he not therefore refer to reports of their Christian stedfastness which had reached him? Nay, his use of the aorist may signify that such intelligence had been repeatedly brought to him. Kühner, § 442, 1; Buttmann, § 137, 8, Obs. 5. But this frequentive sense, however, is denied to aorists in the New Testament. Winer, § 40, 5, b, 1.[2] The verb παύομαι, connected with this aorist, is in the present tense, as if the apostle meant to say, that such tidings from Ephesus were so satisfactory, that he could not cease to thank God for them. His thanksgiving was never allowed to flag, for it sprang from information as to the state of the church in Ephesus, and especially of what the apostle emphatically names—

τὴν καθ' ὑμᾶς πίστιν. The expression is peculiar. Winer, § 22, 7, renders it *fidem quæ ad vos pertinet*, but in such a version the phrase expresses no other than the common form of the pronoun—ὑμετέρα πίστις. Harless and Rückert trans-

[1] The criticism of Hammond upon ἀκούσας is ingenious, but not satisfactory. He renders it here *cum sciverim*, for ἀκούω, he adds, often signifies to know or to understand. Gen. xi. 7, xlii. 23; 1 Cor. xiv. 2. He that speaketh in an unknown tongue speaketh not to man—οὐδεὶς γὰρ ἀκούει—for no one understands him. The use of the verb is similarly idiomatic in the other places cited. It signifies, to hear so as to understand. These phrases refer, however, to personal conference, where difference of language rendered conversation unintelligible. But in this clause it refers to reports by third parties, and therefore cannot be so used. The idiom is one easily understood, for it occurs in many similar phrases. Thus, to hear prayer is to comply with the request; to hear one in danger, is to help him. With us in Scotland the order is inverted. One says to his friend, "Speak for a moment," which means, "Hear me speak for a moment."

[2] See Moulton's *Winer*, p. 347, n. 2.

late, *den Glauben bei euch*—"the faith which is among you;" Rückert holding that a species of local meaning is implied in the idiom, and Harless maintaining that if the adjective pronoun had been used, the subjective view of their faith would have been given—faith as theirs; whereas by this idiom, their faith in its objective aspect is depicted—faith as it exists among them. Though this mode of expressing relation came to be common in later Greek, as Meyer has shown, still we are inclined to think that there was something emphatic in the form. Bernhardy, p. 241. Acts xvii. 28, τινες τῶν καθ' ὑμᾶς ποιητῶν—"certain of the poets among you"—some of your poets, not ours — not Jewish or Christian bards, but Greek ones, whom ye claim and recognize as your national minstrels. Acts xviii. 15, the Roman proconsul says, "If it be a question of your law," νόμου τοῦ καθ' ὑμᾶς—your law; the law that obtains among you, not the Roman law—your Jewish law, to which you cling, and the possession and observance of which mark and characterize you as a people. So in Acts xxvi. 3—τῶν κατὰ Ἰουδαίους ἐθῶν—customs among Jews — specially Jewish; the very thing under discussion, and spoken of by one who had been educated at Rome. The ordinary phrase, ἡ πίστις ὑμῶν, is used seventeen times, and this form seems to denote not simply possession, as the genitive ὑμῶν or pronoun ὑμετέρα would imply, but also characteristic possession. It is that faith which not only is among you, but which you claim and recognize as your peculiar possession—that faith which gave them the appellation of πιστοί in the first verse, and which is said in ver. 13 to have secured for them the sealing influences of the Holy Spirit. At all events, the instance adduced by Ellicott and Alford as against us, is not parallel. The phrase "your law," John viii. 17, τῷ νόμῳ τῷ ὑμετέρῳ, is not parallel to Acts xviii. 15, for the first was spoken by a Jew to Jews—it was His law as well as theirs (Gal. iv. 4); but not so in the case of the Roman deputy in Achaia. It seems foreign to the phrase to bring out of it, as Alford does after Stier, "the possibility of some not having this faith." He had named them πιστοί already, and will κατά with the partitive meaning imply that some might not have this faith? That faith reposed—

ἐν τῷ κυρίῳ Ἰησοῦ. The usage and meaning of κύριος are

fully referred to under ver. 2. Such a characteristic faith was in Christ. Winzer[1] indeed proposes to connect ὑμᾶς with this clause—*fidem, quæ, vobis Domino Jesu veluti insitis, inest.* The position of the words excludes such a connection. Their faith lay immoveable in Jesus, and the same idea, expressed by ἐν, is very frequent in the preceding verses. See under ver. 1. Πίστις followed by ἐν is not common; yet εἰς, πρός, ἐπί occur often in such connection in the Septuagint; Ps. lxxviii. 22; Jer. xii. 6; Gal. iii. 26; Col. i. 4; 1 Tim. i. 14, iii. 13; 2 Tim. i. 13, iii. 15. See under the first verse. The πίστις, so well defined by καθ' ὑμᾶς, and so closely allied to κύριος, needs not the article after it, and the want of the article indicates the unity of conception. The article is similarly omitted in Gal. iii. 26, and in Col. i. 4; Winer, § 20, 2. That faith wrought by love—

καὶ τὴν ἀγάπην τὴν εἰς πάντας τοὺς ἁγίους—"and your love to all the saints." Some MSS. such as A, B, etc., omit τὴν ἀγάπην, and Lachmann, true to his critical principles, leaves them out in his edition. But the omission is an evident blunder. The Syriac version, older than any of these MSS., has the words, and without them no sense could be made of the verse. Chrysostom also reads the words, and says that the apostle always knits and combines faith and love, a glorious pair—θαυμαστήν τινα ξυνωρίδα:—

ἅγιος is explained under ver. 1. Faith and love are often associated by the apostle. Col. i. 4; Philem. 5; 1 Thess. i. 3. The article is repeated after ἀγάπην, because the relation expressed by εἰς is not so intimate as that denoted by ἐν, because it has not the well-understood foundation of πίστις, and it may also signalize the difference of allusion—ἀγάπη, not to Christ, but—τὴν εἰς πάντας τοὺς ἁγίους. This conception, therefore, has not the unity of the preceding: it is love, but love further defined by a special object—"to all the saints." It is not philanthropy—love of man as man—but the love of the brethren, yea, "*all*" the brethren—"the household of faith." Community of faith begets community of feeling, and this brother-love is an instinctive emotion, as well as an earnest obligation. In that spiritual temple which the Spirit is rearing in the sanctified bosom, faith and love are the

[1] *Commentatio in Eph.* cap. i. v. 19. *Pfingstprogramm*, Leipzig, 1836.

Jachin and Boaz, the twin pillars that grace and support the structure.

(Ver. 16.) Οὐ παύομαι εὐχαριστῶν ὑπὲρ ὑμῶν—"I cease not giving thanks for you." Ὑπέρ is thus used, v. 20; 1 Tim. ii. 1. Εὐχαριστεῖν, in the sense of "to give thanks," belongs to the later Greek, for, prior to the age of Polybius, it signified to please or to gratify. Phryn. ed. Lobeck, p. 18. Instead of a participle the infinitive is sometimes employed, but there is a difference of meaning. The participle expresses an action which already exists, and this form of construction prevails in the New Testament. "As one giving thanks for you I cease not." The infinitive εὐχαριστεῖν would mean, "I cease not from a supposed period to give thanks." Winer, § 45, 4; Stuart, § 167; Scheuerlein, § 45, 5; Hermann, *Ad Viger.* p. 771; Bernhardy, p. 477.[1] The Gothic version of Ulphilas has preserved the peculiar point of the expression—"unsveibands aviliudo,"—*non-cessans gratias dico.* The apostle, though he had visited them, does not felicitate himself on his pastoral success among them, but gives thanks on this account to God, for His grace had changed them, and had sustained them in their Christian profession.

μνείαν ὑμῶν ποιούμενος ἐπὶ τῶν προσευχῶν μου—"making mention of you in my prayers." Rom. i. 9; Phil. i. 3; 1 Thess. i. 2, 3. Some MSS., as A, B, and D, omit ὑμῶν, and it is rejected by Lachmann; but there is no good reason for its exclusion, for it may have been omitted because of the previous ὑμῶν so close upon it, for A and B have the same omission in 1 Thess. i. 2. F and G place the pronoun after the participle. The terms εὐχαριστῶν and μνείαν ποιούμενος are not to be identified. The apostle gave thanks, and his thanks ended in prayer. As he blessed God for what they had enjoyed, he implored that they should enjoy more. He *thanked* for their faith and hope, and he *prayed* as he glanced into the future. And he made special mention of the Ephesian church; ποιούμενος in the middle voice implying—"for himself"—ἐπὶ τῶν προσευχῶν μου. The preposition has a temporal meaning with a sub-local reference. Bernhardy, p.

---

[1] Kühner occupies no less than seven sections in enumerating and defining the different classes of verbs which are followed by a participle rather than an infinitive (§ 657-664).

246; Winer, § 47, g, d; Stallbaum's *Plato, de Rep.* p. 460. He did it as his usual work and pleasure, and perhaps the language implies that he made formal mention of them whenever and wherever he prayed. He yearned over them as his children in Christ, and he bore their names on his heart before the Lord in fervent, repeated, and effectual intercession.

(Ver. 17.) "Ἵνα ὁ Θεὸς τοῦ Κυρίου ἡμῶν Ἰησοῦ Χριστοῦ δῴη—"That the God of our Lord Jesus Christ would give." Making mention of you in my prayers, offering this prayer for you, that the God, etc. His prayer for them had this special petition—that. "Ἵνα is thus used with the optative, and that telically to denote the object of desire, the blessing wished for. Bernhardy, p. 407. We see no reason to agree with Harless, Olshausen, Winer, Robinson, Rückert, and others, in denying the proper telic use of ἵνα in such a connection, or after verbs of entreaty. Ellicott also gives it a sub-final meaning—the purport of the prayer being blended with the purpose. Winer, § 41, b, 1. On the other hand, to deny with Fritzsche the ecbatic sense of ἵνα, is an extreme quite opposed to many passages of the New Testament, and as wrong as to give it too often this softened meaning. Harless says, that the optative is here used for distinctness, because a verb expressing desire is omitted. But the final cause of entreaty is—"in order that" something may be given. The object of the apostle's prayer was, that God would give the Ephesians the spirit of wisdom. He prayed for this end—this final purpose was present to his mind; he prayed with this avowed intent—ἵνα. Ellicott's statement is after all but a truism: if a man tell you to what end he prays, he surely tells you the substance of his prayers. Disclosure of the purpose must express the purport, and ἵνα, pointing out the first, also of necessity introduces the last. But the ἵνα in such an idiom contains in itself the idea of previous desire, and the optative is used, not as if there were any doubt in the apostle's mind that his prayer might not be granted, or as if the answer might be only a probable result, but that God's giving the object prayed for would be the hoped-for realization of the intention which he had, when he began to offer the petitions which he was still continuing. Jelf, § 807, γ; Devarius-Klotz, p. 622. Had the wish that God would confer blessing begun merely when the apostle wrote the words, had the whole aim of the prayer been regarded as future to that point of time, the subjunctive would have been used. $\Delta ῴη$ is a later form for δοίη. Phrynichus, ed. Lobeck, pp. 345, 346 ; Sturz, *De dialecto Alexandrino*, p. 52. Lachmann, however, reads δώῃ in the Ionic subjunctive form, but without sufficient ground. The Divine Being to whom Paul presented intercessory prayer for the Ephesians, is referred to under two peculiar and unusual epithets—

Ὁ Θεὸς τοῦ Κυρίου ἡμῶν Ἰησοῦ Χριστοῦ—" The God of our Lord Jesus Christ." He is elsewhere called the God and Father of our Lord Jesus Christ, but only in this place, simply, " the God of our Lord Jesus Christ." The language has needlessly startled many commentators, and obliged them to make defence against Arian critics. Suicer, *sub voce*. The dangerous liberties taken with the words in the capricious use of hyperbaton and parenthesis by Menochius, Vatablus, Estius, and a-Lapide, do not gain the end which they were intended to serve. It is with some of them—" the Father of our Lord Jesus Christ, the God of glory," or " the God (of our Lord Jesus Christ the Father) of glory." The criticism of Theodoret is more rational, though not strictly correct, for he thus distinguishes the two divine appellations in reference to Christ, —Θεὸν μὲν ὡς ἀνθρώπου, πατέρα δὲ ὡς Θεοῦ. The reader will find an explanation of the phrase under the first clause of the 3rd verse. The exposition of Harless is somewhat loose. His explanation is—the God by whom Christ was sent to earth, from whom He received attestation in word and deed, and to whom He at length returned. But more special ideas are included—1. To be His God is to be the object of His worship—my God is the divinity whom I adore. As a man Jesus worshipped God, often prayed to Him, often consulted Him, enjoyed His presence, and complained on the cross of His desertion, saying—" My God, my God." 2. The language implies that God blessed Him—my God is He who blesses me. Gen. xxviii. 21. He prepared for Him His body, sustained His physical life, bestowed upon Him the Spirit, protected Him from danger, " gave His angels charge concerning Him," raised Him from the dead, and exalted Him to glory. 1 Cor. xi. 3, xv. 27 ; 1 Pet. i. 21. Especially, as

Harless intimates, did He as Messiah come from God and do the will of God, and He is now enjoying the reward of God. Possessed Himself of supreme divinity, He subordinated Himself to God, in order by such an economy to work out the glorious design of man's salvation. The immanent distinctions of the one Godhead are illustrated in their nature and necessity from the scheme of redemption. And the reason why Paul refers to God in this relation to Jesus is, that having sent His Son and qualified and commissioned Him, having accepted from Him that atonement of infinite value, and having in proof of this acceptance raised Him to His own right hand, it is now His divine function and prerogative to award the blessings of the mediatorial reign to humble and believing suppliants.

At the same time we cannot fully acquiesce in many interpretations of the Nicene Creed, even as illustrated by Petavius,[1] and adopted by such acute defenders as Cudworth[2] and Bull.[3] To admit the divinity of the Son, and yet to deny Him to be αὐτόθεος as well as the Father, seems to us really to modify and impugn the Saviour's Godhead by a self-contradictory assertion. We cannot but regard self-existence as essential to divinity. Bishop Bull says, however—"*Pater solus naturam illam a se habet.*" The Creed of Nice declares, "We believe in our Lord Jesus Christ, the Son of God, the only-begotten of the Father, that is, of the Essence of the Father, God of God, Light of Light, very God of very God, begotten, not made, of one Essence with the Father." These sentiments have been the faith of the church in every age, but they have been in many instances explained by unjustifiable imagery and language, often taken in the earlier centuries from the Platonic ontology, and drawn in later times from material sources. The arguments against what is called the eternal sonship, by Röell, Drew, Moses Stuart, Adam Clarke, and others, are, with all their show of argument, without foundation in Scripture, for a sonship in the Divine nature appears to be plainly taught and implied in it. But a sonship which affirms the Divine nature of the Son to be derived from the Father, makes that Son only δεύτερος Θεός—a secondary Deity. Not only is the Son ὁμοούσιος τῷ πατρί—of the same essence

---

[1] *De Trinitate*, i. 5. [2] *Intellectual System*, vol. ii. 406, ed. 1845, London. [3] *Defensio Fidei Nicænæ.* Works, vol. v. ed. 1827, Oxford.

with the Father, but He is also αὐτόθεος—God in and from Himself. Sonship appears to refer not to essence, but to existence—not to being in itself, but to being in its relations, and does not characterize nature so much as personality. But such difference of position is not inequality of essence, and when rightly understood will be found as remote from the calumnious imputation of Tritheism, as from the heresy of Modalism or Sabellianism.[1]

ὁ Πατὴρ τῆς δόξης—"the Father of glory"—is a unique phrase, having no real parallel in Scripture. It has some resemblance to the following phrases—"King of glory" in Ps. xxiv. 7; "Lord of glory," 1 Cor. ii. 8; "God of glory," Ps. xxix. 3, quoted in Acts vii. 2; Πατὴρ τῶν φώτων, Jas. i. 17; ὁ Πατὴρ τῶν οἰκτιρμῶν, 2 Cor. i. 3; and χερουβὶμ δόξης, Heb. ix. 5. Δόξης is the genitive of characterizing quality. Winer, § 30, 2. The notion of Theodoret is, that δόξα signifies the Divine nature of Christ, and many of the Fathers held a similar view. Athanasius remarks on this passage, that the apostle distinguishes the economy—καὶ δόξαν μὲν τὸν μονογενῆ καλεῖ, referring to the phrase in John i. 14, "the glory of the only-begotten of the Father"—an idea also repeated by Alford. Theophylact quotes Gregory of Nazianzus as giving the same view—καὶ Θεὸν καὶ Πατέρα; Χριστοῦ μὲν ἤγουν τοῦ ἀνθρωπίνου, Θεὸν· τῆς δὲ δόξης, ἤγουν τῆς θεότητος, Πατέρα. Cyril also (De Adoratione, lib. xi.), Jerome, and Bengel adopt the same hypothesis. Suicer, Thesaurus, i. 944, 5. These views are strained and moulded by polemical feelings, and the use of δόξα in reference to Jesus in other parts of the New Testament will not warrant such a meaning here. While this special and personal application is without ground on the one hand, it is a vague and pointless exegesis on the other, which resolves the phrase into Πατὴρ ἔνδοξος. De Wette

---

[1] See also Schleiermacher, der Christl. Glaube, § 170-190; Twesten, Vorlesungen über die Dogmatik, § 41; Hase, Hutterus Redivivus, § 72; Treffry, On the Eternal Sonship of Christ, London, 1839. It is a pity that so many non-biblical terms have been found necessary in the treatment of this awful subject, but sad and fatal errors seem to have made the coinage of them indispensable. One is disposed to say of them with Calvin—"Utinam quidem sepulta essent, constaret modo hæc inter omnes fides, Patrem et Filium et Spiritum esse unum Deum: nec tamen aut Filium esse Patrem, aut Spiritum Filium, sed proprietate quadam esse distinctos."—Institutio Christ. Religionis, vol. i. p. 89, ed. Berolini, 1834.

renders—The Father with whom glory is ever present; referring to the last clause of ver. 18—the glory of the inheritance. Others find in πατήρ the sense of origination—source of glory—*auctor, fons*. So Erasmus, Fesselius,[1] a-Lapide, Grotius, and Olshausen, though with varying applications of the general exegesis. This explanation is at least admissible. Did we, with some, regard δόξα as the immanent or essential glory of God, it would be impossible. Such glory is coeval with the Divine nature, the Essence and Effulgence are coeternal. Or did we, with others, regard δόξα as meaning glorious gifts conferred upon us, then such a notion would not be in harmony with the context. That Πατήρ may signify originator is plain, though Harless expressly denies it. What is Πατὴρ τῶν πνευμάτων but their Creator? (Heb. xii. 9); or Πατὴρ τῶν φώτων (Jas. i. 17) but their Producer? or Πατὴρ τῶν οἰκτιρμῶν (2 Cor. i. 3) but their Originator? Harless refers the δόξα very much to the epithets of the following verses, while Stier and Alford virtually maintain an allusion to the God-man, in whom God's glory is revealed, by whom it dwells in humanity, and in whom all His people are glorified. On the other hand, and more in harmony with the course of thought, δόξα appears to us to be that glory so often already referred to, and throwing its radiance over this paragraph. Men are elected, predestinated, sanctified, and adopted—εἰς ἔπαινον δόξης; enlightened, enfeoffed in an inheritance according to eternal purpose—εἰς ἔπαινον δόξης αὐτοῦ; and they hear, believe, are sealed, and enjoy the earnest of the Spirit—εἰς ἔπαινον τῆς δόξης αὐτοῦ. The three preceding paragraphs are thus each wound up with a declaration of the final result and purpose—the glory of God. And now, when the apostle refers to God, what more natural than to ascribe to Him that glory which is His own chief end, and His own prime harvest in man's redemption? Here stand, as repeated and leading ideas, ver. 6, δόξης—ver. 12, δόξης—ver. 14, δόξης; so that in ver. 17 He is saluted with the title, Πατὴρ τῆς δόξης. This glory is not His essential glory as Jehovah, but the glory which He has gathered for Himself as the God of our Lord Jesus Christ. The clause is in close union with the preceding one. This Saviour-God, the God of our Lord Jesus Christ, is in this

---

[1] *Adversaria Sacra*, i. 350.

very character the possessor and thus the exhibiter of glory. It is then wholly—πρὸς τὸ προκείμενον, as Œcumenius says, that such a title as this is given to God, that is, because of the contextual allusions, but not simply because the gifts prayed for are manifestations of this glory, as Olshausen supposes; nor merely, as Cocceius and Meyer argue, because He will do that in answer to prayer which serves to promote His own glory.

The gift prayed for is—that He would give "you"—ὑμῖν —πνεῦμα σοφίας καὶ ἀποκαλύψεως ἐν ἐπιγνώσει αὐτοῦ—" the Spirit of wisdom and revelation in the knowledge of Him." Though πνεῦμα wants the article, there is no reason, with Middleton, Chandler, Crellius, and Locke, to deny its reference to the Holy Spirit, and to make it signify "a wise disposition," for the word came to be regarded very much as a proper name.[1] Thus, Matt. xii. 28, ἐν πνεύματι Θεοῦ—" by the Spirit of God;" Rom. i. 4, κατὰ πνεῦμα ἁγιωσύνης; 1 Pet. i. 2, ἐν ἁγιασμῷ πνεύματος; and in Mark i. 8; Luke i. 15, 35, 41, 67. The reference in these cases is plainly to the Holy Spirit, in some peculiar phases and manifestations of His divine influence. The canon of Middleton is not borne out by usage. *On Greek Art.*, pp. 125, 126. The genitives are not wholly those of possession, but perhaps also of character. Rom. viii. 2, 15; 2 Cor. iv. 13; 2 Tim. i. 7. The Ephesians had possessed the Spirit as an earnest and seal, and now the apostle implores His influence in other modes of it to descend upon them. This "revelation" is His mode of operation, and the enlightened eye is the fruit of His presence. Indeed, Chrysostom and Theodoret use σοφία πνευματική—spiritual wisdom—in explanation of πνεῦμα σοφίας, but Chrysostom distinctly acknowledges the influence of the Spirit. Theophylact plainly specifies the gift of the Divine Spirit, "That He may supply you with spiritual gifts, so that by the Spirit you may be enlightened—ὥστε διὰ τοῦ πνεύματος φωτισθῆναι." The Reformers supposed that the Spirit of grace and revelation is taken for the grace itself, as Calvin explains—*spiritus sapientiæ et revelationis pro ipsa gratia capitur*. We prefer a clear and formal reference to the Holy Spirit—the gift of God

[1] Compare Gersdorf, *Beiträge zur Sprach-Characteristik der Schriftsteller des neuen Test.*, Kap. iv.

through Christ. Σοφία and ἀποκάλυψις are intimately joined, but not, as Meyer thinks, by the union of a general and special idea. Nor can we, with Olshausen, refer the words to the ancient charismata, and make ἀποκάλυψις mean the capacity for receiving revelation, or for being a prophet. These supernatural endowments cannot be alluded to, because the apostle prays for the bestowment of wisdom and revelation to enable the Ephesians to know those blessings in the knowledge of which every Christian is interested, and which all Christians through all time receive in a greater or less degree from the Holy Ghost.

The Ephesians had already enjoyed spiritual blessings, and they had been sealed by the Holy Spirit. Now the apostle prays that they may enjoy Him as a Spirit of wisdom and revelation. Σοφία is wisdom, higher intelligence, rising at length into the "riches of the full assurance of understanding." It is connected with ἀποκάλυψις, for the Spirit of wisdom is the Spirit of revelation, and by such revelation that wisdom is imparted. The oracles of the New Testament had not then been collected, and therefore truth in its higher aspects might be imparted or extraordinarily revealed by the Holy Ghost. Such generally is the view also of Harless, σοφία, however, being, according to him, the subjective condition, and ἀποκάλυψις the objective medium. The clause is no hendiadys. It resembles Rom. i. 5, "This grace and apostleship," that is, grace, and the form in which the grace was given—that of the apostolate; Rom. xi. 29, "The gifts and calling of God," that is, the gifts and the medium of their conferment—the Divine calling. Here we have the gift of wisdom along with the mode of its bestowment—revelation. We cannot say, with Ellicott, that σοφία is the general and ἀποκάλυψις the more special gift, for the last term carries in it the notion of mode as well as result—insight communicated so as to impart wisdom. Nor can we see how it is illogical to mention the gift, and then refer to the vehicle of its bestowment.

And still all spiritual truth is His revelation. The Bible is His gift, and it is only when the prayerful study of the Bible is blessed by spiritual influence that wisdom is acquired. Solemn invocation of the Holy Spirit must precede, and His presence accompany, all faithful interpretation of the word of God. As we contemplate the holiness and veracity of its Author, the grace and truth of all His statements, and the benevolent purpose of His revelation, the heart will be softened into that pure sensibility which the Holy Ghost delights in, as of old the strains of music in the schools of the prophets soothed and prepared the rapt spirit of the seer for the illapse of his supernatural visitant. Earthly passions and turbulent emotions must be repressed, for the "dew" descends not amidst the storm; the conflicting sensations of a false and ungodly heart forbid His presence, as the "dove" alights not amidst the tossings of the earthquake. The serenity resulting from "that peace which passeth all understanding," not only draws down the Spirit of God, not only imparts a freer scope to the intellectual powers, a purer atmosphere to the spiritual vision, and a new relish to the pursuits of biblical study, but also refines and strengthens those faculties which unite in discovering, perceiving, and feeling the truths and beauties of inspiration.

ἐν ἐπιγνώσει αὐτοῦ. The αὐτοῦ refers to God, and not to Christ, as Calvin, Beza, Bodius, Calovius, Flatt, and Baumgarten suppose. 'Ἐν does not signify εἰς—in reference to, or in order to, as Jerome, Anselm, Luther, a-Lapide, Grotius, Bengel, and von Gerlach erroneously argue. The spirit of this exegesis may be seen in the note of Piscator—" *Ut eum in dies magis magisque cognoscatis.*" Such an unusual meaning is unnecessary. The versions, " through " the knowledge of God, as Rollock renders, or " along with " it, as Hodge makes it, are foreign to the context. Tyndale cuts the knot by translating —"That he myght geve vnto you the Sprete of wisdom, and open to you the knowledge of him silfe." Meyer, Harless, and Matthies suppose that ἐν marks out the sphere of operation —*die Geistige Thätigkeits-Sphäre*. Connecting the words especially with ἀποκαλύψεως, we suppose them, while they formally denote the sphere, virtually to indicate the material of the revelation. In the last view they are taken by Homberg, Rückert, and Stier. If the knowledge of God be the sphere in which the Spirit of revelation operates, it is that He may deepen or widen it—in our possession of it. In what aspect is the Spirit prayed for? It is as a Spirit of wisdom. How is this wisdom communicated by Him? By revelation. What is the central sphere, and the characteristic type, of this revelation? It is the knowledge of God, not *agnitio*, as the Vulgate has it, and Beza and Bodius expound it, but *cognitio*— not the acknowledgment, but the knowledge of God. The knowledge of God stands out objectively to us as the first and best of the sciences; and when the Spirit imparts it, and gives the mind a subjective or experimental acquaintance with it, that mind has genuine wisdom.[1] Ἐπίγνωσις Θεοῦ is the science, and σοφία is the result induced by the Spirit of revelation. The preposition ἐπί, in ἐπί-γνωσις, contains probably the idea of the "*additional*" as the image of intensive. Such a preposition sometimes loses its full original force in composition, but it would be wrong to say with Olshausen, that here such a meaning is wholly obliterated. Tittmann, *De Synonymis*, etc., p. 217; Wilke, *Appendix*, p. 560. Ἐπίγνωσις is not ascribed to God in the New Testament, neither could it with propriety. His knowledge admits of no improvement either in accuracy or extent. Phavorinus defines the term ἡ μετὰ τὴν πρώτην γνῶσιν τοῦ πράγματος κατὰ δύναμιν παντελὴς κατανόησις. The simple verb and its compound are used with beautiful distinction in 1 Cor. xiii. 12, ἄρτι γινώσκω ἐκ μέρους, τότε δὲ ἐπιγνώσομαι. That knowledge of God in which the Spirit of revelation works, and which He thereby imparts, is a fuller and juster comprehension of the Divine Being than they had already enjoyed. The subsequent verses show that this additional knowledge of God concerns not the works of His creation, which is but the "time vesture" of the Eternal, but the grace and the purposes of His heart, His possession and exhibition of love and power, His rich array of blessings which are kept in reserve for His people, and that peculiar influence which He exercises over them in giving them spiritual and permanent vitality. Harless says that ἐπίγνωσις signifies the knowledge of experience, because

[1] Stier quotes a remark "*sehr naiv*" from one of Francke's *Fast-Sermons*, illustrating at once the spirit of the good old man's peculiar pietism, as well as his opinion of the godless and Christless teaching beginning to prevail in the colleges of Germany: "The apostle does not say he wished that a university should be founded in the city of Ephesus, to which should be appointed a host of professors by whom the people should be made wise. O no: he implored the Spirit of wisdom."

δύναμις stands as its object. This view, however, is defective, for δύναμις is not the only object—there is also the "inheritance," which is future, and therefore so far *external* to believers.

Some, however, join the clause with the following verse —" In the knowledge of Him the eyes of your heart being enlightened." Thus construe Chrysostom, Theophylact, Zachariae, Olshausen, Lachmann, and Hahn. Such a construction is warped and unnatural. Olshausen's reason is connected with his notion that σοφία and ἀποκάλυψις are charismata or extraordinary gifts, and could not be followed up and explained by such a phrase as the " knowledge of God." But the verb φωτίζω is nowhere accompanied by ἐν; in Rev. xviii. 1 it is followed by ἐκ. The Syriac renders, " And would enlighten the eyes of your hearts to know what is," etc.

(Ver. 18.) Πεφωτισμένους τοὺς ὀφθαλμοὺς τῆς καρδίας ὑμῶν—" The eyes of your heart having been enlightened; " that is, by the gifts or process just described. Καρδίας is now generally preferred to διανοίας, as it has preponderant authority, such as MSS. A, B, D, E, F, G, etc., with the Syriac, Coptic, and Vulgate, etc. Thus, too, Clemens Romanus— οἱ ὀφθαλμοὶ τῆς καρδίας. *Ep. ad Corinth.* § 36. Various forms of construction have been proposed. 1. Some understand the clause to be the accusative governed by δῴη. The words are so taken by Zanchius, Matthies, Rückert, Meier, Harless, Olshausen, de Wette, Stier, and Turner. This construction, however, seems awkward. Bengel remarks that the presence of the article before ὀφθαλμούς is against such a construction. For the eyes were, not precisely a portion of the gift, but only the enlightenment of them ; whereas, according to this construction, if τοὺς ὀφθαλμούς be governed by δῴη, both the eyes and their illumination would be described as alike the Divine donation. This, however, is not the apostle's meaning. The eyes of the heart needed both a quicker perception and a purer medium in order to distinguish those glorious objects which were presented to them. The words, as placed by the apostle, are different from a prayer for "enlightened eyes ; " and the clause is not parallel with those of the preceding verse, but describes the result. 2. Πεφωτισμένους may be supposed to agree by anticipation with the following ὑμᾶς —" that you, enlightened as to the eyes of your heart." 3. Ellicott takes it as a lax construction of the participle πεφωτισμένους referring to ὑμῖν, with τοὺς ὀφθαλμούς as the accusative of limiting reference. But in a broken construction the participle usually reverts to the nominative. See Buttmann, *Gram. der Neutest. Sprach.* § 145, 4. 6. 7. The clause may be a species of accusative absolute—"the eyes of your heart having been enlightened," and it expresses the result of the gift of the "Spirit of wisdom and revelation in the knowledge of Him." Such is the view of Beza, Grotius, Bengel, Küttner, and Koppe. Kühner, § 682; Bernhardy, p. 133. But we cannot adopt the hint of Heinsius, that the participle has εἶναι understood, and that the formula is then equivalent to φωτίζεσθαι. *Exercit. Sac.* p. 459. The "heart" belongs to the "inner man," is the organ of perception as well as of emotion; the centre of spiritual as it is physically of animal life. Delitzsch, *System der Bibl. Psychol.* § 12; Beck, *Umriss der Bib. Seelenlehre*, § 26. The verb φωτίζω, used in such a relation, has a deep ethical meaning. Light and life seem to be associated in it—as, on the other hand, darkness and death are in Hebrew modes of conception. Thus Ps. xiii. 3, xxxvi. 9; John i. 4, viii. 12. The light that falls upon the eyes of the heart is the light of spiritual life—there being appreciation as well as perception, experience along with apprehension. Suicer, *sub voce* φῶς. Matt. xiii. 15; Mark vi. 52; John xii. 40.[1] The figure is common too among classical writers. If the spirit of wisdom and revelation in the knowledge of God be conferred, then the scales fall from the moral vision, and the cloudy haze that hovers around it melts away. It is as if a man were taken during night to a lofty eminence shrouded in vapour and darkness, but morning breaks, the sun rises, the mist disparts, rolls into curling wreaths and disappears, and the bright landscape unfolds itself. Such is the result, and the design, is that they may obtain a view of three special truths. And first—

εἰς τὸ εἰδέναι ὑμᾶς, τίς ἐστιν ἡ ἐλπὶς τῆς κλήσεως αὐτοῦ— "that ye may know what is the hope of His calling"—the

[1] Olshausen's virtual denial of any reference in the phrase to the perceptive faculty, is contrary to the passages quoted. See also his *Opuscula*, p. 159.

infinitive of aim with εἰς and the article, Winer, § 44, 6; and the genitive being that of origin or possession—the hope associated with or the hope springing out of His calling. Κλῆσις is a favourite Pauline word. It describes Christian privilege in its inner power and source, for the "calling" is that Divine summons or invitation to men which ensures compliance with itself. The term seems to havè originated in the historical fact of Abraham's call, and the fact gives name and illustration to the spiritual doctrine. It is His calling—man's calling is often slighted, but God's is "effectual calling." The κλῆσις is the incipient realization of the ἐκλογή. Calovius and Goodwin take ἐλπίς wrongly as the ground of hope. Zanchius, Calovius, Flatt, Meyer, Harless, and Baumgarten-Crusius maintain it to be the subjective hope which His calling creates, but the reference seems rather to be to the object of that hope—the inheritance of the following clause. Ἐλπίς is τὸ ἐλπιζόμενον—*res sperata,* in the opinion of Meier, Olshausen, and Stier; but of course the knowledge of the thing hoped for sustains the emotion of hope, so that the two ideas are closely allied. The apostle seems to refer rather to what the hope embraces, than either to its basis or to its character. Col. i. 5; Tit. ii. 13. It needs no special grace to know the emotion of hope within us; it can be gauged in its depth, and analyzed in its character; but it does need special enlightenment to comprehend in their reality and glory what are the objects hoped for in connection with God's calling. We give τίς its ordinary meaning, "what"—not making it mean *qualis vel cujusnam naturæ,* with Harless; nor *quanta, ποταπή,* with Baumgarten-Crusius and Stier. That it may occasionally bear such a sense we deny not; but the simple signification is enough in the clause before us, though indeed it involves the others. What, then, is the hope of His calling? Abraham's calling had hope, and not immediate possession attached to it, for not he, but his seed, were to inherit in future years. Salvation is partially enjoyed by "the called" on earth, but much of it is in reserve for them in heaven. Therefore all that lies over for us creates hope, and this rich reversion is here connected, not with our election—the reality of which prior to our calling we knew not—but with the calling itself, and the conscious response of the heart to the influence of the truth and the Spirit. The apostle also specifies a second design—

καὶ τίς ὁ πλοῦτος τῆς δόξης τῆς κληρονομίας αὐτοῦ ἐν τοῖς ἁγίοις—" and what the wealth of the glory of His inheritance among the saints." The καί is omitted by some MSS., such as A, B, D¹, K̄, G, and by Lachmann; but it is found in D³, E, K, L, and is rightly retained by Tischendorf. The repetition of καί in the next verse might have led to its omission. Τίς is repeated to bring out the emphatic thought. "The riches of the glory of His inheritance" is a phrase to be resolved neither, with some, into the rich glory of the inheritance, nor the riches of the glorious inheritance. The words represent, as they stand, distinct but connected ideas. It was the riches of His grace in ver. 7—the norm according to which blessing is enjoyed now; here it is the riches of glory to be enjoyed in the future, the genitives being those of possession. Κληρονομία has been already explained under ver. 11, in connection with the verb ἐκληρώθημεν.

The phrase ἐν τοῖς ἁγίοις is attended with some difficulty. 1. Winer and others insert the verb ἐστι, and suppose it to signify "which is in the possession of the saints." The strain of the context forbids the exegesis—it is future, and not present blessing, which the apostle refers to. 2. It is taken by Homberg and Calovius in the neuter gender as a local epithet—"in the holy places." Such an idea is not found in the epistles, and is not of Pauline usage. 3. Others assume the meaning of "for,"—"prepared for the saints," such as Vatablus, Bullinger, and Baumgarten; but this gives an unwarranted meaning to the preposition ἐν. 4. Stier understands the words with special reference to his own interpretation of ver. 11, which he renders—"in whom we have become God's inheritance"—so that God's inheritance is the saints; and as they form it, it possesses a peculiar glory. But the inheritance, as we understand it, is something external to the saints—something yet to be fully enjoyed by them, and of which in the interval the Holy Spirit is declared to be the earnest. 5. The better opinion, then, is, with Rückert, Harless, Winzer, Meier, Olshausen, Ellicott, and Alford, to take ἐν in the sense of "among,"—"among the saints." Job xlii. 15. Of Job's daughter it is said, their father gave them κληρονομίαν ἐν τοῖς ἀδελφοῖς—" among their brethren." So Acts xx. 32, κληρονομίαν ἐν τοῖς ἡγιασμένοις —"inheritance among the sanctified." Also Acts xxvi. 18. Perhaps the full formula may be seen in Num. xviii. 23, ἐν μέσῳ υἱῶν Ἰσραὴλ κληρονομίαν. There seems no need to supply ἐστιν, as is done by Ellicott after Meyer—nor does the article need to be repeated. Ἅγιος has been explained under the first verse, and means here, those possessed of completed holiness, or as Cameron—τοὺς τετελειωμένους. *Myrothecium*, p. 248. The inheritance is meant for the possession of the saints. It is their common property. And the consecrated ones are not merely, as Baumgarten-Crusius says, those of the former dispensation who first were called "holy," though saints alone enjoy the gift. It is "His," and they are His. The possession of holiness is the prerequisite for heaven. Such a character is in harmony with the pursuits, enjoyments, and scenes of the celestial world. Saints have now the incipient heritage, but not in its full fruition. It is not here presented to us as a rich blessing of Christ's present kingdom; but it is the blessing in prospect. The two clauses are thus nearly related. The prayer is, that the Ephesians might first know the reality of the future blessing; and, secondly, might comprehend its character. What, then, are the riches of its glory? There is the "glory" of the inheritance itself, and that glory is not a mere gilding—glitter without value; for there are also "the riches" of the glory. There is glory, for the inheritance in its subjective aspect is the perfection of the "saints." But there are also "riches of glory," for that perfection is complete in the sweep and circle of its enjoyments, and is not restricted to one portion of our nature—the mind being filled with truth, and the heart ruled in all its pulsations by undivided love. There is "glory," in that the inheritance is God's, and they who receive it shall hold fellowship with Him; but there are in addition "riches of glory," inasmuch as this fellowship is uninterrupted, the harmony of thought and emotion never disturbed, and the face of God never eclipsed, but shedding a new lustre on the image of Himself reflected in every bosom. There is "glory," in that the inheritance yields satisfaction, for a perfect spirit in perfect communion with God must be a happy spirit; but there are likewise "riches of glory," since that blessedness is unchanging, has no pause and no end; all, both in scene and society, being in unison with it, while it excites the purest susceptibilities, and occupies the noblest powers of our nature, giving us eternity for our lifetime and infinitude for our home.

The third thing which the apostle wished them to know, was the nature of that power which God had exerted upon them in their conversion. The calling of God had glorious hopes attached to it or rising out of it. The wealthy inheritance lay before them, and the apostle wished them to know how or by what spiritual change they had been brought into these peculiar privileges, and how they were to be sustained till their hopes were realized. Not only had they been the objects of God's affection, as is told them in the first paragraph—but also, and especially, of God's power. Infinite love prompted into operation omnipotent strength. And that power is exercised in a certain normal direction, for it works on believers as it wrought in Christ, and, as the apostle shows in the second chapter, it does to them what it did to their great Prototype. The same kind of power manifested in the resurrection and glorification of Jesus, is exhibited in the quickening of sinners from death. The 20th verse of this chapter is illustrated by the 6th of the following chapter, and all between is a virtual digression, or suspension of the principal idea in the analogy. The power which the apostle wishes them to comprehend was the power which quickened Jesus, and had in like manner quickened them; which raised Jesus, and had in the same way raised them; which had elevated Jesus to God's right hand in the heavenly places, and had also raised them with Christ, and made them sit with Christ in the heavenly places. Such is the general idea. He says—

(Ver. 19.) Καὶ τί τὸ ὑπερβάλλον μέγεθος τῆς δυνάμεως αὐτοῦ εἰς ἡμᾶς τοὺς πιστεύοντας—" And what is the exceeding greatness of His power to us-ward who believe." 2 Cor. xiii. 4. The apostle writes τίς . . . τίς . . . τί—repeating the adjective in his emphatic and distinct enumeration. Εἰς ἡμᾶς—" in the direction of us "—is most naturally connected with δυνάμεως, and not with an understood ἐστι—power exercised upon us believers. Winer, § 49, c, δ. The greatness of that power is not to be measured; it is "exceeding," for it stretches beyond the compass of human calculation. It is the power of giving life to the dead in trespasses and sins— a prerogative alone of Him who is "Life." Compounds with ὑπέρ are great favourites with the apostle, and this word is used by him alone. Speaking of those who are to enjoy the future glorious inheritance, he calls them absolutely οἱ ἅγιοι, but those on whom rests this power in the meantime are only οἱ πιστεύοντες; and while in recording his prayer he naturally says "you," he now as naturally includes himself—ἡμᾶς.

The connection of this with the following clause is important—κατὰ τὴν ἐνέργειαν. Some join the words with the immediately preceding πιστεύοντας—an exegesis followed by Chrysostom, Meier, Matthies, and Hodge. On the other hand, the words are joined to δυνάμεως by Œcumenius, in one of his explanations, by Calvin, Olshausen, Meyer, Alford, Ellicott, and Stier. The last appears to be preferable. It is indeed true, that in consequence of God's mighty power men believe. See under Col. ii. 12. But the adoption of such a meaning, advocated also by Crellius, Griesbach,[1] and Junkheim, would be almost tantamount to making the apostle say—that they might know the greatness of His power on them who believe in virtue of His power. Some of the older divines adopted this view as a mode of defence against Arminian or Pelagian views of human ability, and as a proof of the necessity and the invincibility of Divine grace. But κατά rarely signifies "in virtue of," and even then the idea of conformity is implied. Certainly the weak faith of man is not in conformity with the mighty power of God. Nor can κατά point out the object of faith in such a construction as this, and it never occurs with πιστεύω to denote the cause of faith. Besides, and especially, it is not to show either the origin or measure of faith that the apostle writes, but to illustrate the power of God in them who already believe. Κατά, therefore, signifies "after the model of." It points out how the power to us-ward operates; κατά—after the model of that power which operated in Christ.

[1] *Opuscula*, ii. 9; *Brevis Commentatio in Ephes.* i. 19.

It weakens the point of the apostle's argument to take the clause followed by κατά merely as an amplification, as Chrysostom, Calvin, Calixtus, Estius, Grotius, Meier, and Winzer have done. It is not the apostle's design to illustrate the mere ὑπερβάλλον—the mere vastness of the power, but to define its nature and mode of operation. Nor can we agree with Harless, after Ambrosiaster, Bucer, and Zanchius, in making this clause and those which follow it belong equally to the ἐλπίς and κληρονομία, and in regarding the paragraph as a general illustration of the nature of the hope, and the wealth and glory of the inheritance. Thus Ambrosiaster:— *Exemplum salutis credentium et gloriæ in resurrectione Salvatoris consistere profitetur, ut ex ea cognoscant fideles quid eis promissum est.* This explanation is too vague, for ἐνέργεια and the allied words are connected with δύναμις naturally, but not with the hopes or the inheritance. The exegesis of Harless would imply, that the blessings described in the paragraph are future blessings, whereas, as himself virtually admits, they are blessings already enjoyed by Christians (ii. 6). Ellicott errs in the same way when he says, that the reference is "*primarily* to the power of God, which shall *hereafter* quicken us even as it did Christ." What he calls primary the context places as secondary, for it is present power which is causing itself to be felt on present believers. The order of thought is not, the hope—then the inheritance—and then the power which shall confer it; but, the hope—the inheritance —and the power which sustains and prepares us for its possession. Meyer's notion is similar to Ellicott's.

Nor does κατά, as in the opinion of Koppe and Holzhausen, signify mere similitude. For if the resurrection of Jesus be the normal exhibition of Divine power, the implication is, that other similar exhibitions are pledged to Christ's people. That power has operated, κατά—after the model of that energy which God wrought in Christ. Œcumenius has the right idea to some extent when he compares the two acts—τὸ ἀναστῆναι ἡμᾶς τοῦ ψυχικοῦ θανάτου καὶ τὸ ἀναστῆναι τοῦ σωματικοῦ τὸν Χριστόν. The objection of Matthies that, had the apostle meant to show the correspondence between the power exerted on us and that on Christ in His resurrection, he would have said ἐν ὑμῖν, as he has said ἐν τῷ Χριστῷ, is without foundation, because the power put forth on Christ was an act long past and perfect, whereas the power put forth on believers is of present and continuous operation, and a stream of that divine influence is ever coming—εἰς ἡμᾶς τοὺς πιστεύοντας. This use of the article and participle, instead of a simple adjective, is emphatic in its nature. The participial meaning is brought into prominence—"on us who are believing," on us in the act or condition of exercising faith. Nor is the objection of de Wette more consistent. It is illogical, he affirms, to speak of applying a norm or scale to exceeding greatness. But the apostle does not use a scale to mete out and measure the exceeding greatness of God's power, he merely presents a striking example to enable us to know something of its mode of operation. The sacred writer illustrates his meaning by the presentation of a fact, and that meaning will be best brought out after we have examined the phraseology. For God puts forth that power—

κατὰ τὴν ἐνέργειαν τοῦ κράτους τῆς ἰσχύος αὐτοῦ—"according to the working of the force of His might." To suppose that the apostle used these three terms without distinction, and for no other purpose than to give intensity of idea by the mere accumulation of synonyms, would indeed be a slovenly exegesis. Nor is it better to reduce the phrase to a Hebraism, connecting τοῦ κράτους, as Peile proposes, with ἐνέργειαν, as if it were equivalent to τὴν κρατοῦσαν; or, on the other hand, resolving it either into κράτος ἰσχυρόν, or ἰσχὺς κρατερά, as is recommended by Koppe and the lexicographers Bretschneider, Robinson, and Wahl. Ἰσχύς, connected with ἴσχω, another form of ἔχω, is—power in possession, ability, or latent power, strength which one has, but which he may or may not put forth. Mark xii. 30; Luke x. 27; 2 Pet. ii. 11. Κράτος, from κράς, the head, is that power excited into action — might. Luke i. 51; Acts xix. 20; Heb. ii. 14. Ἰσχύς, viewed or evinced in relation to result, is κράτος. Hence it is used with the verb ποιεῖν. The words occur together, Eph. vi. 10; Isa. xl. 26; Dan. iv. 27; Sophocles, *Phil.* 594. Ἐνέργεια, as its composition implies, is power in actual operation. Ἰσχύς, to take a familiar illustration, is the power lodged in the arm, κράτος is that arm stretched out or uplifted with conscious aim, while ἐνέργεια is the same arm at actual work, accomplishing the designed result. Calvin compares them thus : ἰσχύς—*radix* ; κράτος—*arbor* ; ἐνέργεια —*fructus*. The connection of words similarly allied is not uncommon. Lobeck, *Paralipomena*, Diss. viii. § 13, p. 534. The language is meant to exalt our ideas of Divine power. That might exercised upon believers is not only great, but exceeding great, and therefore the apostle pauses to describe it slowly and analytically; first in actual operation—ἐνέργεια; then he looks beyond that working and sees the motive power —κράτος; and still beneath this he discerns the original unexhausted might—ἰσχύς. The use of so many terms arises from a desire to survey the power of God in all its phases; for the spectacle is so magnificent, that the apostle lingers to admire and contemplate it. Epithet is not heaped on epithet at random, but for a specific object. The mental emotion of the writer is anxious to embody itself in words, and, after all its efforts, it laments the poverty of exhausted language. The apostle now specifies one mode of operation—

(Ver. 20.) Ἣν ἐνήργησεν ἐν τῷ Χριστῷ, ἐγείρας αὐτὸν ἐκ νεκρῶν—" Which He wrought in Christ, having raised Him from the dead"—in Christ our Head and Representative, ἐν denoting the substratum, or ground, or range, as Winer calls it, on or in which the action takes effect, § 48, a, 3. The use of a verb with its correlate noun has been noticed already, chap. i. 3, 6. In such cases there is some intensification of meaning. Bernhardy, p. 106. The participle is contemporaneous with the verb. That manifestation of power is now described in its results, to wit, in the resurrection and glorification of Christ. He raised Him from the dead. It was the work of the Father —having sent His Son, and having received the atonement from Him—to demonstrate its perfection, and His own acceptance of it, by calling Jesus from the grave.

In the meantime, we may briefly illustrate this third section of the apostle's prayer—" that ye may know the exceeding greatness of His power to us-ward who believe, according to the working of the might of His power which He wrought in Christ, when He raised Him from the dead." Our general view has been already indicated. The specimen and pledge of that power displayed in quickening us, is Christ's resurrection. Now, 1. It is transcendent power — ὑπερβάλλον μέγεθος. The body of Jesus was not only lifeless, but its organization had been partially destroyed. The spear had pierced the pericardium, and blood and water—blood fast resolving itself into *serum* and *crassamentum*, issued immediately from the gash. To restore the organization and to give life, not as the result of convalescence, but immediate and perfect life, was a sublime act of omnipotence. To vivify a dead heart is not less wonderful, and the life originally given is the life restored. But created effort is unequal to the enterprise. The vision of Ezekiel is on this point full of meaning. The valley lay before the mind's eye of the prophet, full of bones, dry and bleached, not only without muscle and integument, but the very form of the skeleton had disappeared. Its vertebræ and limbs had been separated, and the mass was lying in confusion. The seer uttered the oracle of life, and at once there was a shaking—the various pieces and organs came together — "bone to his bone." The osseous framework was restored in its integrity, nay, sinew and flesh came upon it, and "the skin covered them above." But there was no breath in them. The organization was complete, but the vital power—the direct gift of God—was absent. The prophet invoked the "breath of Jehovah." It descended and enveloped the host, and at the first throb of their heart they started to their feet, "an exceeding great army." The restoration of spiritual life to the dead soul results immediately from the working of the might of His power. Conviction, impression, penitence, and reformation, may be to some extent produced by human prophesying; but life comes as God's own gift—a Divine operation of the power of His might, analogous to the act of our Lord's resurrection.

2. It is power already experienced by believers—power— εἰς—"to us-ward." They had felt it in prior time. It is not some mighty influence to be enjoyed by them in some future scene of being, or, as Chandler and others suppose, at the resurrection. "You *did He quicken,*" raise up, and enthrone with Christ.

3. It is resurrectionary power—power displayed in restoring life, for it has its glorious prototype in the resurrection of Jesus. Divine power restored physical life to Jesus, and that same power restored spiritual life to those who "were dead

in trespasses and sins." The context shows plainly that this is the meaning of the reference, for the subject is resumed at ver. 5 of the succeeding chapter. There was spiritual life once in man—in his great progenitor; but it left him and he died; and the great purpose of the gospel is to unite him to God, and to give back to him, through union with "Christ our life," this life which he originally enjoyed. See chap. ii. 5, 6.

4. The resurrection of Jesus is in this respect not merely a specimen or illustration—it is also a pledge. Some regard it as a mere comparison. Morus defines κατά merely—*simili modo*. Koppe says the power in us is *non minor*—" not less" than that in Christ; and Grotius looks upon it as a proof of God's ability—*quod factum apparet, id iterum fieri potest*. Chrysostom, on the first verse of the next chapter, says—ὅτι τοῦ νεκροὺς ἀνιστᾶν τὸ ψυχὴν νενεκρωμένην ἰάσασθαι πολλῷ μεῖζόν ἐστι—" to heal a dead soul is a far greater thing than to raise the dead." But when God raised His Son—the representative of redeemed humanity—the deed itself was not only an illustration of the mode, but also a pledge of the fact, that all His constituents should be quickened, and should have this higher life restored to them. For the man Jesus died, that men who were dead might live, and the revivification of His dead body was at once a proof that the enterprise had been accomplished, and a pledge that all united to Him should live in spirit, and live at length like Himself in an entire and glorified humanity. The nobler life of soul, and the reunion of that quickened spirit with a spiritualized body, are covenanted blessings. Olshausen makes the general resurrection of believers from the dead the prinicipal reference of the passage. But this, as we have seen, is a mistaken view. Still, as this new life cannot be fully matured in the present body, for its powers are cramped and its enjoyments curtailed, so it follows that a frame suited to it will be prepared for it, in which all its faculties and susceptibilities will be completely and for ever developed and perfected. Present spiritual life and future resurrection are therefore both involved. He raised Him—

καὶ ἐκάθισεν ἐν δεξιᾷ αὐτοῦ ἐν τοῖς ἐπουρανίοις—" and He set Him at His own right hand in the heavenly places."

Lachmann reads καθίσας, after A, B, and some other MSS., but the common reading is the best sustained, and the other has the plausibility of an emendation, like the reading ἐνήργηκεν in the previous clause. This recurrence to the aorist forms, therefore, an anacolouthon or inconsequent construction. These anacoloutha only occur when the mind, in its fervour and hurry, overlooks the formal nexus of grammatical arrangement, or when the writer wishes to lay emphasis on special ideas or turns of thought. Winer, § 63, 2, b. The transition is sometimes marked by δέ. In similar cases it appears as if the writer wished to indicate a change in the train of illustration, his immediate purpose being served. John v. 44—λαμβάνοντες—καὶ οὐ ζητεῖτε; 2 John 2—τὴν μένουσαν —καὶ ἔσται. So in the present passage. The sense is complete—ἐγείρας αὐτὸν ἐκ νεκρῶν; the principal, essential, and prominent idea illustrative of Divine power is brought out. But, changing the construction as if to indicate this, the apostle adds, not καὶ καθίσας, but ἐκάθισεν—his mind fondly carrying out the associated truths. The chief object of the apostle is to show the nature of that power which God has exercised upon believers. It is power which operates after the model of that which He wrought in Christ. Power was manifested in Christ's resurrection, visibly and impressively, but not in the same form in His glorification. Might is seen in the one and honour in the other. In the sixth verse of the following chapter the principal thought is that of revivification or spiritual resurrection, though the other idea of glorification is also annexed; but it is still a minor idea, for though we are spiritually brought into a new life as really as Christ was physically quickened, yet we are not ἐν τοῖς ἐπουρανίοις, in the very same sense as Christ personally is, but only as being in Him—members of the body of which He is the ever-living and glorified Head.

The verb ἐκάθισεν has a hiphil signification, and like some other verbs of pregnant meaning, seems here as if to contain its object in itself. It is not therefore followed by a formal accusative. So the corresponding Hebrew verb, לְהֹשִׁיב, wants the personal pronoun as its accusative in 1 Sam. ii. 8.

ἐν δεξιᾷ αὐτοῦ—" at His own right hand." Mark xvi. 19 Heb. viii. 1, x. 12, xii. 2. The language refers us to Ps. cx.

ἐν τοῖς ἐπουρανίοις. The phrase has been explained under ver. 3. Lachmann reads—ἐν τοῖς οὐρανοῖς, without any eminent authority. We cannot say with Matthies, and Hunnius quoted and approved by Harless, that the expression has a special reference to things and not to places, and denotes the *status cœlestis*. For the idea of place does not necessarily imply local and limited conceptions of the Divine essence. Our Master taught us to pray, " Our Father which art in heaven." The distressed mind instinctively looks *upward* to the throne of God. The phrase τὰ ἐπουράνια does not signify heaven in its special and ordinary sense, but the heavenly provinces. In the highest province Jesus is at the right hand of God, and in the lowest province of the same region the church is located, as we have seen under i. 3, and shall see again under ii. 5, 6.

Jesus was not only raised from the dead, but placed at the Father's " right hand." Three ideas, at least, are included in the formula, as explained in Scripture. 1. It is the place of honour. Jesus is above all created dignities, whatever their position and rank. Ver. 21.

2. It is the place of power. He sits " on the right hand of power." Matt. xxvi. 64. " All things are under His feet." He wields a sceptre of universal sovereignty. Ver. 22.

3. It is the place of happiness—happiness possessed, and happiness communicated. " At Thy right hand there are pleasures for evermore." Ps. xvi. 11. The crowned Jesus possesses all the joy which was once set before Him. But His humanity, though glorified, is not deified—is not endowed with any of the essential attributes of divinity. Whatever the other results of the ἕνωσις καθ' ὑπόστασιν, or the *communicatio idiomatum*, may be, we believe that the inferior nature of Jesus remains a distinct, perfect, and unmixed humanity. The Θεάνθρωπος is in heaven, was seen in heaven, " from whence we look for Him," and the saints are to be caught up to meet their Lord in the air.[1] Augustine says well (*Ep.* 57)

---

[1] In the *Formula Concordiæ*, ii. 8, *De Persona Christi*, ubiquity is without hesitation claimed for Christ's humanity—" *Ut videlicet etiam secundum illam suam assumtam naturam, et cum eâ præsens esse possit, et quidem præsens sit, ubicunque velit.*"—*Die symbolischen Bücher der evangelisch-lutherischen Kirche*, ed. Müller, Stuttgart, 1848, p. 674 et seq. Hase, *Hutterus Redivivus*, § 105. Schmidt, *Dogmatik der Evang.-Luth. Kirche*, p. 243, etc.

—*Cavendum est, ne ita divinitatem adstruamus hominis, ut veritatem corporis auferamus.*

(Ver. 21.) Ὑπεράνω πάσης ἀρχῆς καὶ ἐξουσίας καὶ δυνάμεως καὶ κυριότητος—" Far above all principality, and power, and might, and lordship." The clauses to the end of the chapter explain and illustrate, as we have now hinted, the session at the right hand of God. These various appellations are used as the abstract for the concrete, as if for sweeping significance. The highest position in creation is yet beneath Christ. Some of the beings that occupy those stations have specific and appropriate names, but not only above these, but above every conceivable office and being, Jesus is immeasurably exalted. There is no exception; He has no equal and no superior, not simply among those with whose titles we are so far acquainted, but in the wide universe there is no name so high as His, and among all its spheres, there is no renown that matches His. These principalities stand around and beneath the throne, but Jesus sits at its right hand. It is a strange whim of Schoettgen, on the one hand, to refer these names to the Jewish hierarchy, and of van Til, on the other hand, to regard them as descriptive of heathen dignities.

To attempt to define these terms would serve little purpose, and those definitions given by the pseudo-Dionysius, and others even of the more sober and intelligent Greek fathers, are but truisms. For example: ἀρχαί are defined by Dionysius—ὡς ἐκείνην τὴν ἀρχὴν ἀναφαίνουσαι; δυνάμεις are pronounced by Theodoret—ὡς πληροῦν τὰ κελευόμενα δυνάμενοι; and the κυριότητες are stated by Phavorinus to be—δυνάμεις ἅγιαι λειτουργικαὶ κυρίου. The first two of these four terms are used of human magistracy, Tit. iii. 1; in this epistle, of the hostile powers of darkness, vi. 12; of the celestial hierarchy, in iii. 10; and they are spoken of as distinct from angels, in Rom. viii. 38, and 1 Pet. iii. 22. Jesus is described as at the right hand of the Father—ἐν τοῖς ἐπουρανίοις, and perhaps the beings referred to under these four designations are the loftiest and most dignified in heaven. To restrict the word solely to angels, with Meyer, or good angels, with Ellicott, might be too narrow; and it would be too vague, with Erasmus, Zachariae, Rosenmüller, and Olshausen, to refer it to any kind of dignity or honour. These dignities and honours are at least heavenly in their position, and belong, though perhaps not exclusively, to the creatures who, from their office, are termed angels. To say that He who is at the right hand is raised above human dignitaries, would be pointless and meaningless; and to affirm that He occupies a station superior to any on which a fiend may sit in lurid majesty, would not be a fitting illustration of His exalted merit and proportionate reward. Yet both are really included. Human princedoms and hellish potentates must hold a position beneath the powers and principalities of heaven, above which the Son of God is so loftily exalted.

What the distinction of the words among themselves is, and what degrees of celestial heraldry they describe, it is impossible for us to define. We are obliged to say, with Chrysostom, that the names are to us ἄσημα καὶ οὐ γνωριζόμενα; and, with Augustine—*dicant, qui possunt, si tamen possunt probare quod dicunt; ego me ista ignorare confiteor.* Hofmann denies that the words indicate any gradations of angelic rank, but only indicate the manifoldness of which their relation to God and to the world is capable. This may be true so far, but the relation so held may indicate of itself the rank of him who holds it. *Schriftb.* vol. i. p. 347. The four terms form neither climax nor anticlimax; the two first of them here are the two last in Col. i. 16, and the last term here, κυριότητες, stands second in the twin epistle. The first and last have special reference to government, princedom, or lordship, and the intervening two may refer more to prerogative and command. And they may be thus connected: Whoever possesses the ἀρχή enjoys and displays ἐξουσία; and whoever is invested with the δύναμις, wields it in his appointed κυριότης. Speculations on the angelic world, its number, rank, and gradations, were frequent in the earlier centuries. Basil and Gregory of Nazianzus set the example, but the pseudo-Dionysius mustered the whole angelic band under his review, and arranged them in trinary divisions:—

I. Θρόνοι, Χερουβίμ, Σεραφίμ.
II. Κυριότητες, Ἐξουσίαι, Δυνάμεις.
III. Ἀρχαί, Ἀρχάγγελοι, Ἄγγελοι.[1]

[1] *Enchiridion*, cap. 58.

The Jewish theology also held that there were different ranks of angels, and amused itself with many fantastic reveries as to their power and position.[1] All that we know is, that there is foundation for the main idea—that there is no dull and sating uniformity among the inhabitants of heaven—that order and freedom are not inconsistent with gradation of rank —that there are glory and a higher glory—power and a nobler power—rank and a loftier rank, to be witnessed in the mighty scale.[2] As there are orbs of dazzling radiance amidst the paler and humbler stars of the sky, so there are bright and majestic chieftains among the hosts of God, nearer God in position, and liker God in majesty, possessing and reflecting more of the Divine splendour, than their lustrous brethren around them. But above all Jesus is enthroned—the highest position in the universe is His. The seraph who adores and burns nearest the eternal throne is only *proximus Huic*—

"*Longo sed proximus intervallo.*"

ὑπεράνω—"over above;" not reigning over, as Bengel has it, but simply in a position high above them. The majority of cases where the word is used in the Septuagint would seem to show that it may intensify the idea of the simple ἄνω. We cannot agree with Ellicott's denial of this. It is true that compounds are numerous in Alexandrian Greek, and cease from use to have all their force; yet in the Septuagint the passages referred to and others, from the spirit of them or the suggested contrast to the position of the observer, point to a full sense of the compound term. Deut. xxvi. 19, xxviii. 1; Ezek. i. 25, x. 19, xi. 22.

The second clause expands and rivets the idea of the first, and corresponds, as Stier well remarks, to the οὔτε τις κτίσις ἑτέρα, in Rom. viii. 39. For the apostle subjoins—

καὶ παντὸς ὀνόματος ὀνομαζομένου—"and every name that is named." Καί introduces a final and comprehensive assertion, "and in a word" (Ellicott)—*et omnino*. Fritzsche on Matt., p. 786. Erasmus, Calvin, Grotius, Estius, Meier, and

---

[1] *Hierarchia Cœlestis*, cap. vi.
[2] Eisenmenger, *Entdecktes Judenthum*, ii. p. 374; Boehmer, *Isagoge in Ep. ad Col.* p. 292; Petavius, *Dogmata Theol.* tom. iii. p. 101; Twesten, *Dogmatik*, vol. ii. p. 305.

Bloomfield, take ὄνομα here as a name or title of honour, referring to Phil. ii. 9; John xii. 28; Acts iv. 12; 2 Tim. ii. 19; and to the verb in Rom. xv. 20. To this we see no great objection, especially in such a context. But as the following participle has its usual meaning, ὄνομα may be taken in its common signification—an exegesis certainly preferable to that of Morus, Harless, and Rückert, who qualify it by its position, and make it denote every name of such a kind as those just rehearsed. To show the height of Christ's exaltation, the apostle affirms that He sits above all

"Thrones, dominations, princedoms, kingdoms, powers;"

but to enlarge the sweep of his statement he now adds—and also above every name of being or of rank that the universe contains. Bodius, Meyer, and de Wette say—πᾶν ὄνομα is simply for πᾶν; Beza renders—*quicquid existit*. Œcumenius makes it equivalent to πᾶν ῥητὸν καὶ ὀνομαστόν—which is preferable.

οὐ μόνον ἐν τῷ αἰῶνι τούτῳ, ἀλλὰ καὶ ἐν τῷ μέλλοντι— "not only in this world, but also in that which is to come." This clause does not belong to the preceding ἐκάθισεν, as Calvin, Beza, Bodius, Koppe, Holzhausen, Küttner, and Burton suppose; for they regard it as expressing the permanency of Christ's dominion. The intervening sentences show that this exegesis is unfounded, and that the words must be construed with ὀνομαζομένου—"every name named, not only in this world, but also in that which is to come." What, then, is meant by αἰὼν οὗτος and αἰὼν μέλλων? The phrase cannot have its Jewish acceptation—the period before Messiah and the period of Messiah, as Cocceius and others hold. The plain meaning is—the present life and the life to come,[1] with the attached idea of the region where each life is respectively spent—earth and heaven, but without any marked ethical reference. "The future," as Olshausen remarks, "is in the phrase opposed to the present." Over all the beings we can name now, or shall ever be able to name, Jesus is exalted— over all that God has brought, or will bring, into existence. Whether, as Chrysostom, Theodoret, and Bengel suppose from this verse, we shall have our knowledge of the celestial

[1] *Vide* Koppe, *Excursus* I.; Witsius, *Miscellanea Sacra*, vol. i. 618.

powers extended, is a question which it does not directly solve. Lest, however, there should be any imagined exception to Christ's supremacy, or any possible limitation of it—any power or principality anywhere left uncompared or out of view, the apostle says, Jesus is exalted not only above such of them as men now and on earth are in the habit of familiarly naming, but also above every name of existence or rank in every sphere and section of the universe. *Nihil est*, says Calvin, *tam sublime aut excellens quocunque nomine censeatur, quod non subjectum sit Christi majestati.* There seems to be no immediate polemical reference in this extraordinary paragraph. Not only is there exaltation, but there is also authority—

(Ver. 22.) Καὶ πάντα ὑπέταξεν ὑπὸ τοὺς πόδας αὐτοῦ— "And put all things under His feet." The allusion is clearly to the language of the 8th Psalm. In the 110th Psalm the enemies of Messiah are specially referred to, and their subjugation is pictured out by their being declared to be His footstool. The allusion is not, however, in this clause, to enemies defeated and humbled, as Grotius, Rosenmüller, Holzhausen, and Olshausen, to some extent, suppose. The apostle is describing the authority of the Saviour by this peculiar figure. It is no repetition of the idea in the preceding verse. That exhibits His honour, but this proclaims His imperial prerogative. Heb. ii. 8. The πάντα not only contains what has been specified, but leaves nothing excluded. The brow once crowned with thorns now wears the diadem of universal sovereignty; and that hand, once nailed to the cross, now holds in it the sceptre of unlimited dominion. He who lay in the tomb has ascended the throne of unbounded empire. Jesus, the brother-man, is Lord of all: He has had all things put under His feet—the true apotheosis of humanity. This quotation from the Psalms Theodoret names τὴν προφητικὴν μαρτυρίαν, for this old Hebrew ode plainly refers to man's original dignity and supremacy—to the race viewed in unfallen Adam (Gen. i. 26–28); but it also, as interpreted in Heb. ii. 6, 7, as plainly refers to the Second Adam, or to humanity restored and elevated in Him—in Christ as its Representative and Crown.

καὶ αὐτὸν ἔδωκε κεφαλὴν ὑπὲρ πάντα τῇ ἐκκλησίᾳ—" and gave Him to be Head over all things to the church." There is no reason for changing the ordinary meaning of ἔδωκε, and rendering it "appointed"—ἔθηκε—as is suggested by Calvin, Beza, Harless, Meier, and Olshausen. In chap. iv. 11 we have the same verb. His occupancy of this exalted position is a Divine benefaction to the church; His appointment is the result of love, which gives with wise and willing generosity. Nay more, and with emphasis—καὶ αὐτὸν ἔδωκε—" and Him He gave." The natural meaning of ἔδωκε is thus sustained by the prefixing of the pronoun, and it governs the dative, ἐκκλησίᾳ, after it. This repetition of the pronoun intensifies the idea, and its position in this clause is emphatic—" and Him, so exalted and invested, so rich in glory and power— even Him and none other, has He given as Head."

The most difficult phrase is κεφαλὴν ὑπὲρ πάντα. The Vulgate merely evades the difficulty by its translation—*supra omnem ecclesiam*. The Syriac rendering is preferable:— " Him who is over all hath He given to be Head," transposing the order of the words, a rendering followed by Chrysostom— τὸν ὄντα ὑπὲρ πάντα Χριστόν; and the same idea is adopted by Erasmus, Camerarius, Estius, and a-Lapide. The position of the words shows that ὑπὲρ πάντα qualifies κεφαλήν. But in what sense? Not—

1. In the vague sense of " special." Ἐπὶ πᾶσι—in " preference to all," as it is explained by Bodius and Baumgarten. Bodius thus paraphrases—*Super omnia, nempe cœtera superius enumerata, hoc est, præ aliis omnibus creaturis.* Nor—

2. In the general sense of " Supreme Head," as is advocated by Beza, Rückert, Meier, Baumgarten-Crusius, Olshausen, Conybeare, Bisping, and de Wette. This exegesis gives ὑπέρ the sense of " above," as the highest head is the Head above all other heads. Koppe resolves it by ὑπερέχουσα πάντων—" overtopping all;" but no comparison of this nature seems to be in the apostle's mind. Olshausen says, the apostles and prophets were also in a certain sense heads of the church, while Christ was—κεφαλὴ ὑπὲρ πάντα. But the πάντα has no such implied contrast in itself, and it naturally turns our attention to the previous verses, where the principalities and powers are not only pronounced to be inferior to Christ, but are affirmed to be under His special jurisdiction.

3. The words may mean—" He gave Him as Head over

all things to the church," or "He gave Him who is Head over all things to be Head to the church." The former of these renderings is expressed by Harless, Alford, and Ellicott in his second edition, the latter by Stier and Meyer. The difference is not very material. Meyer supposes that by a figure of speech called Brachyology, a second κεφαλή is understood. Matthiae, § 634; Kühner, § 852; Jelf, § 893. But there is no need of this shift—and the first exegesis is preferable (Madvig, § 24, a); the noun being a species of what Donaldson calls "tertiary predicates"—§ 489. *New Cratylus*, § 302. Christ is already declared by the apostle to be above all in position and power, ὑπὲρ πάντα; but besides, He is by the Father's gift κεφαλή to the church. The πάντα are not connected with Him as their κεφαλή, their relation to Him being merely denoted by ὑπέρ; but the church claims Him as its Head, yea, claims as its Head Him who is over all. Were the ὑπέρ to be taken in the active sense of superintendence, the genitive would be employed, as Harless intimates; but it denotes here, above or beyond all in honour and prerogative, for ὑπέρ in the New Testament with the accusative, has always this tropical meaning. Matt. x. 24; Luke xvi. 8; Acts xxvi. 13; Phil. ii. 9; Philem. 16. The signification, therefore, is—This glorious Being, above all angelic essences, and having the universe at His feet, is, by Divine generosity, Head to the church, for the πάντα refers not to members of the church, as Jerome and Wahl argue and as Harless favours, but to things beyond the church, being equivalent to πάντα in the preceding clauses; nor is the word to be restricted to good angels, as Theophylact and Œcumenius seem to suppose.

The noun ἐκκλησία is the name of the holy and believing community under the New Testament. Its meaning is obvious —the one company—קָהָל, who have been called or summoned together to salvation. The church here spoken of is specially the church on earth, which stands in need of protection, though the church in heaven be equally related to Jesus, and equally enjoy the blessings of His Headship. Jerome, Nösselt, Koppe, and Rosenmüller extend it to all good beings—an extension not warranted by the name or the context. The dative is not, as de Wette takes it, a *dativus commodi*, nor is it connected with the κεφαλήν immediately preceding as its complement, but it belongs naturally to the verb ἔδωκεν. The relation of Christ to the church is not that of austere government, or lofty and distant patronage. He is not to it merely ὑπὲρ πάντα— a glorious being to contemplate and worship, but He is its Head, in a near, tender, necessary, and indissoluble relation. And that Head is at the same time "Head over all." His intelligence, His love, and His power, therefore, secure to the church that the πάντα will "work together for good." Under His "over all" Headship, everything that happens benefits His people — discoveries in science, inventions in art, and revolutions in government—all that is prosperous and all that is adverse. The history of the church is a proof extending through eighteen centuries; a proof so often tested, and by such opposite processes, as to gather irresistible strength with its age; a proof varied, ramified, prolonged, and unique, that the exalted Jesus is Head over all things to the church. And the idea contained in this appellation is carried out to its correlative complement in the following verse, and in these remarkable words—

(Ver. 23.) "Ητις ἐστὶν τὸ σῶμα αὐτοῦ—" which indeed is His body." "Ητις—*welche ja*, as it is rendered by de Wette. Kühner, § 781, 4, 5. Of this meaning of ὅστις there are many examples in the New Testament, though it has also other significations. "Head over all things to the church, which in truth is His body." The mode of expression is not uncommon. Chap. ii. 16, iv. 4, 12, 16, v. 23, 30; 1 Cor. xii. 15; Col. i. 18, 24, ii. 19, iii. 15, etc. Head and body are correlative, and are organically connected. The body is no dull lump of clay, no loose coherence of hostile particles; but bone, nerve, and vessel give it distinctive form, proportion, and adaptation. The church is not a fortuitous collection of believers, but a society, shaped, prepared, and life-endowed, to correspond to its Head. The Head is one, and though the corporeal members are many, yet all is marked out and "curiously wrought" with symmetry and grace to serve the one design; there being organization, and not merely juxtaposition. There is first a connection of life: if the head be dissevered, the body dies. The life of the church springs from its union to Christ by the Spirit, and if any member or community be separated from Christ, it dies. There is also a connection of mind: the purposes of the head are wrought out by the corporeal organs —the tongue that speaks, or the foot that moves. The church should have no purpose but Christ's glory, and no work but the performance of His commands. There is at the same time a connection of power: the organs have no faculty of self-motion, but move as they are directed by the governing principle within. The corpse lies stiff and motionless. Energy to do good, to move forward in spiritual contest and victory, and to exhibit aggressive influence against evil, is all derived from union with Christ. There is, in fine, a connection of sympathy. The pain or disorder of the smallest nerve or fibre vibrates to the Head, and there it is felt. Jesus has not only cognizance of us, but He has a fellow-feeling with us in all our infirmities and trials. And the members of the body are at the same time reciprocally connected, and placed in living affinity, so that mutual sympathy, unity of action, co-operation, and support are anticipated and provided for. No organ is superfluous, and none can defy or challenge its fellow. Similar fulness and adjustment reign in the church. See under iv. 15, 16. Not only is the church His body, but also—

τὸ πλήρωμα τοῦ τὰ πάντα ἐν πᾶσι πληρουμένου—" the fulness of Him that filleth all in all."

1. The term πλήρωμα is in apposition to σῶμα, and is not governed by ἔδωκε, as is the strange view of Homberg, Castalio, and Erasmus, who says—τὸ πλήρωμα videtur accusandi casu legendum, ut referatur ad Christum. Meier holds a similar view, making the words ἥτις ἐστὶ τὸ σῶμα αὐτοῦ a parenthesis, and supposing that πλήρωμα stands in apposition to αὐτόν. This arrangement not only does violence to the natural and obvious syntax, but, as Olshausen well observes, God cannot make Christ to be the πλήρωμα, for Christ possesses the fulness of the Godhead, not through an act of the Father's will, but by the necessity of His nature. Bengel regards πλήρωμα as neither referring to the church, nor as governed by ἔδωκε. It stands, in his opinion, as a species of accusative absolute, like μαρτύριον in 1 Tim. ii. 6, and forms an epiphonema—a *quod erat demonstrandum*. The violence resorted to in such an exegesis is not less objectionable than that seen in the opposite opinion of Storr, who imagines that

it signifies that "which is in God abundantly," and that it is employed as a species of nominative in apposition to ὁ Θεὸς πλούσιος, ii. 4.

2. Many understand the noun in the general sense of multitude—*copia, cœtus numerosus*, making πλήρωμα equivalent to πλῆθος. Such is the view which Storr calls probable, and it is that of Wetstein, Koppe, Küttner, Wahl, and even Fritzsche.[1] Hesychius and Phavorinus define πλήρωμα by πλῆθος, and Schoettgen renders, *Multitudo cui Christus prœest*. This notion is plainly unwarranted by the philology of the term. Πλῆθος has always a reference to abundance, but such an idea is only secondary in πλήρωμα—fulness being merely a relative term, in application either to a basket (Mark viii. 20), or to the globe (Ps. xxiv. 1), and its quantity is determined by the subject. What meaning in such a case would be borne by the homogeneous πληρουμένου? Besides, the idea of unity in σῶμα would ill correspond with that of multiplicity given to πλήρωμα. Cameron and Bos render πλήρωμα "the full body," *plenitudo illa quæ est in corpore*—a meaning which the simple word cannot bear, and which is borrowed from iv. 16, where other terms are joined with the substantives.

3. Some refer the use of the term to the familiar employment of the שְׁכִינָה [2]—the divine glory, or visible manifestation of God, which some, such as Harless, identify with πλήρωμα. But the church cannot stand in such a relation to God—the Shechinah is the highest personal manifestation of His own infinite fulness, the glory of which is reflected by the church, as shone the face of Moses when even a few straggling rays of the divine radiance fell upon it.

4. Allied to this last view is the more general one of those who regard the πλήρωμα in the light of a temple in which the glory of God resides, and who refer it in this sense to the church. Michaelis and Bretschneider espouse this notion, the latter of whom paraphrases πλήρωμα—*quasi templum, in quo habitat, quod occupat et regit, ut anima corpus*. The idea of Harless, found originally in Hackspann, is very similar. "As," says he, "the apostle employs the same term to denote the church, which he uses to represent the richness of that glory

---
[1] *Comment. in Rom.* vol. ii. 469.
[2] Buxtorf, *Lex. Talmud.* 2394; Wagenseil, *Sota*, p. 83.

which dwells in God and Christ, and emanates from them, so the church may be called 'the fulness of Christ,' not because it is the glory which dwells in Him, but because it is the glory which He makes to dwell in her as in everything else. It is the glory not of One, who without it suffers want, but of One who fills all—*das All*—in all places—'The whole earth is full of His glory.' In fact, 'the church' is the glory of Christ, because He is united to it alone as the head with its body." This is also the view of von Gerlach : "the church is His fulness—*seine Herrlichkeit*, that is, His glory. All His Divine perfections are manifest in it. It is His visible appearance upon the earth." This exegesis, however, gives the word a peculiar conventional meaning, not warranted by its derivation, but drawn from expressions in Colossians which have no affinity with the place under review; and such a sense, moreover, is so recondite and technical, that we can scarce suppose the apostle to give it to the word without previous warning or peculiar hint and allusion. No traces of hostility to Gnosticism and its technical κένωμα and πλήρωμα are found in the context, and there is no ground for such a conjecture on the part of Trollope, Burton, and Conybeare. The fulness of the Godhead dwells in Christ—σωματικῶς, says the apostle in a letter which formally opposes a false philosophy. Col. ii. 9. Here he says, on the other hand, the church is Christ's body, His fulness. Passing by those forms of interpretation which are not supported either by analogy or by the nature of the context, we proceed to such as have higher ground of probability.

The grammatical theory in the case of verbal nouns is, that those ending in μός embody the intransitive notion of the verb, while those in σις have an active, and those in μα have a passive sense, or express the result of the transitive idea contained in the verb. Kühner, § 370. The theory, however, is often modified by usage. According to it—and in this case it is verified by many examples—πλήρωμα will be equivalent to τὸ πεπληρωμένον—the thing filled, just as πρᾶγμα is τὸ πεπραγμένον—the thing done; or the word may be taken in an abstract sense, as κλάσμα—not the thing broken, but the fragment itself. Thus the meaning may pass to that by which the effect is produced, and this is virtually the so-called active sense of such nouns; not, as Alford observes, "an active sense properly at all, but a logical transference from the effect to that which exemplifies the effect." In fact, those aspects of active and passive meanings depend on the view assumed—whether one thinks first of the container, and then of the contained, or the reverse. Thus, Ps. xxiv. 1; 1 Cor. x. 26, ἡ γῆ καὶ τὸ πλήρωμα αὐτῆς— "the earth and its fulness." So the noun is used of the inhabitants of a city, as its complement of population; of the manning of a ship; the armed crew in the Trojan horse; and the animals in Noah's ark.[1] In such examples the idea is scarcely that of complement, but rather the city, ark, and ship are represented as in a state of fulness. What they contain is not regarded as filling them up—πλήρωσις, but they are looked upon simply as being already filled up.

The great question has been, whether πλήρωμα has an active or a passive sense. Critics are divided. Harless[2] affirms, with Bähr, that the word is used only in an active sense, while Baumgarten-Crusius[3] as stoutly maintains on the other side, that the noun occurs with only a passive signification. The truth seems to lie between the two extremes. The word sometimes occurs in the so-called active sense, denoting that which fills up (Matt. ix. 16), where πλήρωμα is equivalent to ἐπίβλημα—the piece of new cloth designed to fill up the rent. Mark ii. 21. But it is often used in a passive sense to denote fulness—the state of fulness: Mark viii. 20, Πόσων σπυρίδων πληρώματα—"the fulnesses of how many baskets"—"how many filled baskets of fragments?" So Rom. xiii. 10, πλήρωμα νόμου—"fulfilment or full obedience of the law." The idea of amplitude is sometimes involved, as Rom. xv. 29, ἐν πληρώματι εὐλογίας—"in the fulness of the blessing;" and in Rom. xi. 25, πλήρωμα τῶν ἐθνῶν—"the fulness of the Gentiles," where it is opposed to ἀπὸ μέρους, and in the 12th verse is contrasted with ἥττημα. As applied to time (Gal.

[1] Robinson, Passow, Liddell and Scott, *sub voce.*
[2] "Ich betrachte es nun mit Bähr als ein unzweifelhaftes Resultat der geführten Untersuchung, dass es im N. T. nur im activen Sinne gebraucht werde," etc., p. 122.
[3] "Gewiss aber hat πλήρωμα auch in N. T., wie in dem gesammten Sprachgebrauche durchaus passive Bedeutung, nur den Schein activer Bedeutung nimmt es," etc., p. 50.

iv. 4; Eph. i. 10), it signifies that the time prior to the appointed epoch is regarded as filled up, and therefore full. See under i. 10.

1. An active signification, however, is preferred by Chrysostom, Œcumenius, Ambrosiaster, Theophylact, Anselm, Thomas Aquinas, Calvin,[1] Beza,[2] Rollock, Zanchius, Hammond, Crocius, Zegerus, Calovius, Estius, Bodius, Passavant, Richter, von Gerlach, Bisping, and Hofmann. The words of Chrysostom are—"The head is in a manner filled up by the body, because the body is composed of all its parts, and needs every one of them. It is by all indeed that His body is filled up. Then the head is filled up, then is the body made perfect, where we all together are knit to one another and united."[3] The notion involved in this exegesis, which is also beautifully illustrated by Du Bosc in his French sermons on this epistle, is the following: The church is His body; without that body the head feels itself incomplete—the body is its complement. The idea is a striking, but a fallacious one. It is not in accordance with the prevailing usage of πλήρωμα in the New Testament, and it stretches the figure to an undue extent. Besides, where πλήρωμα has such an active sense, it is followed by the genitive of what it fills up, as πληρώματα κλασμάτων. How, then, would it read here—the filling up of Him who fills all in all? But if He fill all in all already, what addition can be made to this infinitude? Or, if the participle be passive—the filling up of Him who is filled as to all in all; then, if He be already filled, no other supplement is required. We are not warranted to use language as to the person of Christ, as if either absolute or relative imperfection marked it. According to this hypothesis also, that

---

[1] "Hic vero," says Calvin, "summus honor est Ecclesiæ, quod se Filius Dei quodammodo imperfectum reputat, nisi nobis sit conjunctus."

[2] Beza says: "Complementum sive supplementum. Is enim est Christi amor ut quum omnia omnibus ad plenum præstet, tamen sese veluti mancum et membris mutilum caput existimet, nisi ecclesiam habeat sibi instar corporis adjunctam."

[3] Πλήρωμα φησί, τουτέστιν, οἷον κεφαλὴ πληροῦται παρὰ τοῦ σώματος· διὰ γὰρ πάντων μερῶν τὸ σῶμα συνέστηκε καὶ ἑνὸς ἑκάστου χρῄζει. Ὅρα πῶς αὐτὸν κοινῇ πάντων χρῄζοντα εἰσάγει. Ἂν γὰρ μὴ ὦμεν πολλοὶ καὶ ὁ μὲν χεὶρ, ὁ δὲ πούς, ὁ δὲ ἄλλο τι μέρος, οὐ πληροῦται ὅλον τὸ σῶμα. Διὰ πάντων οὖν πληροῦται τὸ σῶμα αὐτοῦ. Τότε πληροῦται ἡ κεφαλὴ, τότε τέλειον σῶμα γίνεται ὅταν ὁμοῦ πάντες ὦμεν συνημμένοι καὶ συγκεκολλημένοι.

mystical body will be gradually growing, and will not be complete until the second coming. Moreover, in other parts of the New Testament, the word, when used in a religious sense, expresses not any fulness which passes from us to Christ, but, as we shall see in the next paragraph, that fulness which passes from Christ to us. We need scarcely allude to the view of Rückert, that πλήρωμα is the means by which the πληροῦν is to be realized, or by which Christ fulfils all things —the means of His fulfilling the great destiny which has devolved upon Him of restoring the world to God. But τὰ πάντα cannot be restricted to the Divine plan of that redemption, which the church is Christ's means of working out, neither can πλήρωμα signify means of fulfilment, nor does the verse contain any hint of universal restoration. Bitterly does Stier say, "We venture to wish in truth and in love, that such an interpreter might learn to read the writing ere he interpret it."

2. The word, we apprehend, is rightly taken in a passive sense—that which is filled up. This is the view of Theodoret,[1] Cocceius, Grotius, Röell, Wolf, Flatt, Cramer, Olshausen, Baumgarten-Crusius, Matthies, de Wette, Meyer, Holzhausen, Stier, Alford, and Ellicott. This exegesis is certainly more in unison with the formation, and general use of the term in the New Testament, and with the present context. So πλήρωμα is employed, Lucian, *Rerum Hist.* ii. 37, Ἀπὸ δύο πληρωμάτων ἐμάχοντο—they fought from two filled vessels ; and so, 38—πέντε γὰρ εἶχον πληρώματα—the ship being named πλήρωμα from its full equipment. So the church is named πλήρωμα, or fulness, because it holds or contains the fulness of Christ. It is the filled-up receptacle of spiritual blessing, from Him, and thus it is His πλήρωμα, for He ascended—ἵνα πληρώσῃ τὰ πάντα. Again, Col. ii. 10—καί ἐστε ἐν αὐτῷ πεπληρωμένοι—"in Him dwells all the fulness of the Godhead bodily, and in Him ye are filled,"—ye have become His πλήρωμα or fulness. John i. 16—"Of His fulness have all we received, and so we become His fulness." Believers are

---

[1] Theodoret thus explains it—ἐκκλησίαν. . . προσηγόρευσε τοῦ μὲν Χριστοῦ σῶμα, τοῦ δὲ Πατρὸς πλήρωμα· ἐπλήρωσε γὰρ αὐτὴν παντοδαπῶν χαρισμάτων, καὶ οἰκεῖ ἐν αὐτῇ, καὶ ἐμπεριπατεῖ κατὰ προφητικὴν φωνήν. This interpretation is wrong in one particular, but it rightly explains πλήρωμα.

filled with all the fulness of God—that fulness which dwells in Him, iii. 19.

The τοῦ which follows πλήρωμα I refer to Jesus; not to God, as do Theodoret, Koppe, Winer, Wetstein, Meier, Alford, Turner, and Stier. It is Jesus, the Head, who is spoken of; the church is His body, and the next clause stands in apposition—" which is also His fulness "—
τὰ πάντα ἐν πᾶσιν πληρουμένου. Τά is not found in the Textus Receptus, but on the testimony of A, B, D, E, F, G, J, K—the majority of minuscules, etc., and the Greek fathers, it is rightly received into the text.[1] Many take πληρουμένου as a passive, such as Chrysostom, Jerome,[2] Anselm, Wetstein, Winer, and Holzhausen. So the Vulgate reads *adimpletur*. Estius has a similar explanation, and also Bisping, who finds it a proof-text for the dogma of the merit of the saints. The exegesis of these critics almost necessitated such a view of the participle. The idea of Beza, adopted by Dickson, is better, viz., that the phrase is added to show that Jesus does not stand in need of this supplement—*ut qui efficiat omnia in omnibus reverâ*. If the participle be taken as a passive form, the words τὰ πάντα ἐν πᾶσι present a solecistic difficulty, and we are therefore inclined, with the majority of interpreters, to regard the participle as of the middle voice. Winer, § 38, 6.[3] Similar usage occurs in Xenophon,[4] Plato,[5] and Pollux.[6] The force of the middle voice is—" who fills for himself," all in all. The Gothic version has *usfulljandins*—" filling ; " and the Syriac also has the active. Holzhausen capriciously makes the phrase equivalent to *das Ewige*—the Eternal, that is, Christ carries in Himself the fulness of eternal blessings. Both nouns—πάντα and πᾶσι—seem to be neuter, and are therefore to be taken in their broadest significance—" who fills the universe with all blessings." In Col. i. 16, τὰ πάντα is used as the appellation of the universe which the Son of God has created. 1 Cor. viii. 6 ; Eph. iii. 9. It narrows the sense of the idiom to give πᾶσι a masculine

---

[1] Reiche, *Comment. Criticus in N. T.*, vol. ii. p. 144 ; Gottingæ, 1859.
[2] "Sicut adimpletur imperator, si quotidie ejus augeatur exercitus, et fiant novæ provinciæ, et populorum multitudo succrescat, ita et Christus in eo quod sibi credunt omnia—ipse adimpletur in omnibus."
[3] Moulton, p. 323.   [4] *Hellen*. 6, 2, 14.   [5] *Gorg*. 493.   [6] *Onomast*. 164-175.

signification, and confine it, with Grotius, Matthies, and Stier, to members of the church—His body; or, with Michaelis, to give it the sense of—"in all places;" or, with Harless and de Wette, to translate it—"in different ways and forms;" or, with Cramer, to interpret it as meaning, that religious blessings are no longer nationally restricted, but may be enjoyed by all! The preposition is instrumental, v. 18. Winer, § 48, a, 3, d. The true meaning is—"in all things," as Fritzsche rightly maintains. *Comment. in Rom.* xi. 12. The idiom occurs, 1 Cor. xv. 28; 2 Cor. xi. 6; 1 Tim. iii. 11; Tit. ii. 9. Macknight, preceded by Whitby, takes πάντα as a masculine—"who fills all his members with all blessings." But why should the adjective dwindle in meaning? Why should τὰ πάντα be less comprehensive here than the repeated indefinite πάντα of the preceding verse? On the one hand the verse speaks nothing for the ubiquity of Christ's body, nor does it bear such a reference to Gnostic philosophy and nomenclature as betokens a post-apostolical origin, as Baur conjectures. Ebrard, *Christ. Dogmatik*, ii. p. 139; Martensen, *ibid.* § 176, etc. But see also Thomasius, *Christi Person und Werk*, vol. ii. § 45; Schmid, *Die Dogmatik der Evang. Luth. Kirche*, §§ 31, 32, 33.

The church, then, is the πλήρωμα—the glorious receptacle of such spiritual blessings. And as these are bestowed in no scanty or shrivelled dimensions—for the church is filled, so loaded and enriched, that it becomes fulness itself—and as that fulness is so vitally connected with its origin, it is lovingly and truly named "the fulness of Christ." The storehouse, "filled with the finest of the wheat," is the farmer's fulness. The blessings which constitute this fulness, and warrant such a name to the church—for they fill it to overflowing, "good measure, pressed down, shaken together, and running over"—are those detailed in the previous verses of the chapter. "All spiritual blessings," the Divine purpose realizing itself in perfect holiness; filial character and prerogative; redemption rooting itself in the pardon of sin; grace exhibited richly and without reserve; the sealing and earnest of the Spirit till the inheritance be fully enjoyed—the results of the apostle's prayer—Divine illumination; the knowledge and hope of future blessedness, and of the depth and vastness of that Divine power by which the new life is given and sustained, union to Jesus as the Body with the Head, the source of vitality and protection—all these benefactions, conferred upon the church and enjoyed by it, constitute it a filled church, and being so filled by Christ, it is aptly and emphatically called—HIS FULNESS.

And the exalted goodness of the Mediator is not confined to filling the church. His benign influence extends through the universe—τὰ πάντα, as gathered together in Him. As all ranks of unfallen beings are beneath Him, they receive their means of happiness from Him; and as all things are beneath His feet, they share in the results of His Mediatorial reign. The Head of the church is at the same time Lord of the universe. While He fills the church fully with those blessings which have been won for it and are adapted to it, He also fills the universe with all such gifts as are appropriate to its welfare—gifts which it is now His exalted prerogative to bestow.

## CHAPTER II

THE apostle resumes the thought which he had broken off in ver. 20. He wished the Ephesian saints to know what was the exceeding greatness of God's power toward those who believe—a species of power exemplified and pledged in the resurrection of Jesus. That power, he virtually intimates, you have experienced, for he who gave life to Jesus gave life to you, when you were dead in trespasses and sins.

(Ver. 1.) Καὶ ὑμᾶς ὄντας νεκροὺς τοῖς παραπτώμασι καὶ ταῖς ἁμαρτίαις—"And you being dead in trespasses and sins." We do not connect the words grammatically with ver. 20, and we hold it to be a loose interpretation which Calvin, Hyperius, Bloomfield, and Peile express, when they say that this verse is a special exemplification of the general act of Divine grace expressed in the last clause of the former chapter. The connection, as we have stated it, is more precise and definite, for it is the resumption of a previous train of thought. The verb which governs ὑμᾶς is not ὑπέταξεν, nor ἐπλήρωσε mentally supplied, nor the πληρουμένου of the preceding verse, as is supposed by Calovius, Cramer, Koppe, Rosenmüller, and Chandler, for "filling" and death are not homogeneous ideas. The governing verb is συνεζωοποίησε in ver. 5, as Jerome and Œcumenius rightly affirm, though the former blames Paul for a loose construction there—*conjunctionem vero causalem arbitramur, aut ab indoctis scriptoribus additam, et vitium inolevisse paulatim, aut ab ipso Paulo, qui erat imperitus sermone sed non scientia, superflue usurpatam.* The thought is again interrupted between vers. 1 and 4, as it had been between the previous ver. 20 and ver. 1 of this chapter. The apostle's mind was eminently suggestive, influenced by powerful laws of mental association, and prone to interpolate subsidiary ideas—but he resumes by δέ in ver. 4. Bengel, Lachmann, and Harless separate the two chapters only by a comma, but the sense is complete at the termination of the first chapter, and the καί—giving emphasis, however, to the following ὑμᾶς—continues the discourse, signifying not "even," but simply "and."

The MSS. B, D, E, F, G, etc., the Syriac, Coptic, Arabic, and Latin versions, with Jerome, Theodoret, and Ambrosiaster, place ὑμῶν at the end of the verse. Lachmann has received it into the text, so has Tischendorf in his seventh edition, with Hahn and Meyer. A has ἑαυτῶν, showing emendation at work. It is long since attempts were made to show a distinction between παραπτώματα and ἁμαρτίαι. Augustine, in his twentieth question on Leviticus, says—*Potest etiam videri illud esse delictum, quod imprudenter, illud peccatum quod ab sciente committitur.* Jerome says that the former is—*quasi initia peccatorum,* and the latter—*cum quid opere consummatum pervenit ad finem.* These definitions are visionary and unsupported. On the other hand, Olshausen regards παραπτώματα as denoting sinful actions, and ἁμαρτίαι as indicating more the sinful movements of the soul in inclinations and words. Meier, again, supposes the words to be synonymous, but yet to be distinguished—*wie Handlung und Zustand*—as action and condition. The opinion of Baumgarten-Crusius is akin. Bengel imagines that the first term had an emphatic reference to Jewish, and the last term to Gentile transgressions—an opinion in which Stier virtually concurs; while Matthies characterizes παραπτώματα as spiritual errors and obscurations, and ἁμαρτίαι as moral sins and faults. Tittmann says that the first substantive refers to sin as if rashly committed, and is therefore a milder term than ἁμαρτίαι, which denotes a willing act. *De Synonymis,* etc., p. 45. Lastly, Harless gives it as his view, that παράπτωμα denotes the concrete lapse—the act, while the term ἁμαρτίαι, as the forcible plural of an abstract noun, signifies the manifestations of sin, without distinguishing whether it be in word, deed, or any other form. Crocius, Calovius, Flatt, Meyer, and Rückert regard the two words as synonymous. (Παράπτωμα has been explained under i. 7.) Perhaps while the first term refers to violations of God's law as separate and repeated acts, the last, as de Wette supposes, may represent all kinds of sin, all forms and developments of a sinful nature.

Thus παραπτώματα, under the image of "falling," may carry an allusion to the desires of the flesh, open, gross, and palpable, while ἁμαρτίαι, under the image "missing the mark," may designate more the desires of the mind, sins of thought and idea, of purpose and inclination. Müller, *Lehre von der Sünde*, vol. i. p. 118; Buttmann, *Lexil.* p. 79, ed. Fishlake; Fritsche, *in Rom.* v. 12. The two words in close connection must denote sin of every species, form, and manifestation, of intent as well as act, of resolve as well as execution, of inner meditation as well as outer result. In Ps. xix. 13, 14, there is apparently a contrast between the terms—the last being the stronger term—παραπτώματα τίς συνήσει, and then καθαρισθήσομαι ἀπὸ ἁμαρτίας μεγάλης. The article before each of the nouns has, according to Olshausen and Stier, this force—Sins, "which you are conscious of having committed." We prefer this emphasis—Sins, which are well known to have characterized your unconverted state.

In the corresponding passage in Col. ii. 13, ἐν precedes the substantives, and denotes the state or condition of death. Compare also, for the use and omission of ἐν in a similar clause, Eph. ii. 15 with Col. ii. 14. Though that preposition be wanting here, the meaning, in our apprehension, is not very different, as indeed is indicated by the phraseology of ver. 2—"in which ye walked." The "trespasses and sins" do not merely indicate the cause of death, as Zanchius, Meier, Ellicott, and Harless maintain, but they are descriptive also of the state of death. They represent not simply the instrument, but at the same time the condition of death. The dative may signify sphere. Winer, 31, 6; Donaldson, § 456. The very illustration used by Alford, "sick in a fever," represents a condition, while it points to a cause. Sin has killed men, and they remain in that dead state, which is a criminal one—ἔγκλημα ἔχει, as adds Chrysostom. Quite foreign to the meaning of the context is the opinion of Cajetan and Barrington, who would render the phrase neither dead *by* nor dead *in* trespasses and sins, but dead *to* trespasses and sins. Appeals to clauses and modes of expression in the Epistle to the Romans are out of place here, the object of illustration being so different in the two epistles. Such a sense, moreover, would not harmonize with the vivification described in ver. 5.

The participle ὄντας points to their previous state—that state in which they were when God quickened them—and is repeated emphatically in ver. 5. The adjective νεκρός is usually and rightly taken in a spiritual sense. 1. But Meyer contends for a physical sense, as if it were equivalent to *certo morituri*, and Bretschneider vaguely renders it by *morti obnoxii*. This exegesis not only does violence to the terms, but it is plainly contradicted by the past tense of the verb—συνεζωοποίησε. The life was in the meantime enjoyed, and the death was already past. (The reader may consult what is said under i. 19.) Meyer's opinion is modified in his last edition, and he speaks now of eternal death—*der ewige Tod*. But this is not the apostle's meaning, for he refers to a past, not a future death. 2. Some, such as Koppe and Rosenmüller, give the words a mere figurative meaning; wretched, miserable—*miseri, infelices*. Such an idea is indeed involved in the word, but the exegesis does not express the full meaning, does not exhaust the term. The term, it is true, was often employed both by the rabbinical[1] and classical writers[2] in a sense similar to its use before us. But the biblical phrase is more expressive than the מֵתִים of the Jewish doctors, or the satirical epithets of Pythagorean or Platonic preceptors.[3] Without putting any polemical pressure on the phrase, we may regard it as spiritual death, not liability to death, but actual death—νέκρωσις ψυχική, as Theophylact terms it. The epithet implies: 1. Previous life, for death is but the cessation of life. The Spirit of life fled from Adam's disobedient heart, and it died in being severed from God. 2. It implies insensibility. The dead, which are as insusceptible as

---

[1] Talmud, *Berachoth*, 3 ; Levi Gerson, *Comment. in Pentat.* p. 192; Schoettgen, *Horæ Hebraicæ*, 1 Tim. v. 6 ; Pocock, *Porta Mosis*, p. 185.

[2] Clemens Alexandrinus, *Strom.* lib. v.; Arrian, *Diss.* 43 ; Epictet. Anton. 4, 41.

[3] Raphelius, *Annotat. Philol.* p. 469. Clement of Alexandria remarks, that in the barbaric philosophy, apostates were called dead νεκροὺς καλοῦσι τοὺς ἐκπεσόντας τῶν δογμάτων—*Strom.* v. p. 574. Jamblichus (*De Vita Pythag.* xxxiv.) says, that for rejected apostates a cenotaph was built by their former fellow-pupils. Origen, *Contra Celsum*, lib. iii. See also Brucker, *Dissertat. Exeget. in loc.* in the *Tempe Helvetica*, ii. 58.

their kindred clay, can be neither wooed nor won back to existence. The beauties of holiness do not attract man in his spiritual insensibility, nor do the miseries of hell deter him. God's love, Christ's sufferings, earnest conjurations by all that is tender and by all that is terrible, do not affect him. Alas! there are myriads of examples. 3. It implies inability. The corpse cannot raise itself from the tomb and come back to the scenes and society of the living world. The peal of the last trump alone can start it from its dark and dreamless sleep. Inability characterizes fallen man. Νεκροί, says Photius, ὅσον πρὸς ἐνέργειαν ἀγαθοῦ τινος. And this is not natural but moral inability, such inability as not only is no palliation, but even forms the very aggravation of his crime. He cannot, simply because he will not, and therefore he is justly responsible. Such being man's natural state, the apostle characterizes it by one awful and terrific appellation—"being dead in trespasses and sins."

(Ver. 2.) Ἐν αἷς ποτὲ περιεπατήσατε—"In which ye once walked." This use of the verb originated in the similar employment of the Hebrew הָלַךְ, especially in its hithpahel conjugation, in which it denotes "course of life." The αἷς agrees in gender with the nearest antecedent—ἁμαρτίαις, but refers, at the same time, to both substantives. Kühner, § 786, 2; Matthiae, § 441, 2, c. The ἐν marks out the sphere or walk which they usually and continually trod, for in this sleep of death there is a strange somnambulism. Col. iii. 7. The figure in περιπατεῖν has been supposed to disappear and leave only the general sense of *vivere*, as Fritzsche maintains on Rom. xiii. 13, yet the idea of something more than mere existence seems to be preserved. It is life, not in itself, but in its manifestations. Thus living and walking are placed in logical connection—πνεύματι περιπατεῖτε is different plainly from ζῶμεν πνεύματι. Gal. v. 16, 25. Though there was spiritual death, there was yet activity in a circuit of sin, for physical incapacity and intellectual energy were not impaired. Yea, "the dead," unconscious of their spiritual mortality, often place up, as their motto of a lower life—"*Dum vivimus vivamus.*"[1] But this sad period of death-walking was past— ποτέ. Their previous conduct is next described as being—

[1] "*Mori vero in peccatis, est peccatis vivere.*"—Rollock, *in loc.*

κατὰ τὸν αἰῶνα τοῦ κόσμου τούτου—"according to the course of this world"—κατά, as usual, expressing conformity. Semler, Beausobre, Brucker, Michaelis, and Baur (*Paulus*, p. 433) take the αἰών as a Gnostic term, and as all but identical with the Being described in the following clauses—the evil genius of the world. Such a sense is non-biblical and very unlikely, yea rather, impossible. Others, such as Estius, Koppe, and Flatt, regard αἰών and κόσμος as synonymous, and understand the phrase as a species of pleonasm. The translation of the Syriac is alliterative—ܥܠܡܐ ܕܥܠܡܐ ܗܢܐ,—"the worldliness of this world," or the "secularity of this seculum." But the αἰών defines some quality, element, or character of the κόσμος. It is a rash and useless disturbance of the phraseology which Rückert on the one hand suggests—κατὰ τὸν αἰῶνα τοῦτον τοῦ κοσμοῦ; or which is proposed by Bretschneider on the other—ὁ κόσμος τοῦ αἰῶνος τούτου, meaning—*homines pravi, ut nunc sunt*. Αἰών sometimes signifies in the New Testament—"this or the present time"—certain aspects underlying it. Gal. i. 4. Anselm and Beza would render it simply—"the men of the present generation;" but in the connection before us it seems to denote *mores, vivendi ratio*—not simply, however, external manifestations of character, but, as Harless argues, the inner principle which regulates it—*Weltleben in geistiger, ethischer Beziehung*—"world-life in a spiritual, ethical relation." It is its "course," viewed not so much as composed of a series of superficial manifestations, but in the moving principles which give it shape and distinction. It is, in short, nearly tantamount to what is called in popular modern phrase, "the spirit of the age"—τὴν παροῦσαν ζωήν, as Theodoret explains it. The word has not essentially, and in itself, a bad sense, though the context plainly and frequently gives it one. Κόσμος, especially as here, and followed by οὗτος, means the world as fallen away from God—unholy and opposed to God. John xii. 31, xviii. 36; 1 Cor. i. 20, iii. 19, v. 10; Gal. iv. 3. None of the terms has a bad meaning in or by itself; nor does the apostle here add any epithet to point out their wickedness. But this use of the simple words shows his opinion of the world, and he condemns it by his simple mention of it, while the demonstrative οὗτος confines the special reference to the time then current. The meaning therefore is, that the Ephesians, in the period of their irregeneracy, had lived, not generally like other men of unholy heart, but specifically like the contemporaneous world around them, and in the practice of such vices and follies as gave hue and character to their own era. They did not pursue indulgences fashionable at a former epoch, but now obsolete and forgotten. Theirs were not the idolatries and impurities of other centuries. No; they lived as the age on all sides of them lived—in its popular and universal errors and delusions; they walked in entire conformity to the reigning sins of the times.

The world and the church are now tacitly brought into contrast as antagonistic societies; and as the church has its own exalted and glorious Head, so the world is under the control of an active and powerful master, thus characterized—

Κατὰ τὸν ἄρχοντα τῆς ἐξουσίας τοῦ ἀέρος—" According to the prince of the power of the air "—κατά being emphatically repeated. The prince of darkness is not only called ἄρχων, but ὁ θεὸς τοῦ αἰῶνος τούτου, 2 Cor. iv. 4; and his ἐξουσία is mentioned Acts xxvi. 18. Again, he is styled ὁ ἄρχων τοῦ κόσμου τούτου. John xii. 31, xiv. 30, xvi. 11. His principality is spoiled, Col. ii. 15, and Jesus came to destroy his works. 1 John iii. 8. Believers are freed from his power. 1 John v. 18; Col. i. 13. The language here is unusual, and therefore difficult of apprehension, and the modes of explanation are numerous, as might be expected.

Flatt is inclined to take ἐξουσίας in apposition with ἄρχοντα —*qui est princeps*, or, as Clarius and Rosenmüller render it— *princeps potentissimus*. There is no occasion to resort to this syntactic violence. Ἐξουσία does not seem to signify simply " might," as Chrysostom, Jerome, Theodoret, and Theophylact hold; but it is rather a term describing the empire of spirits over whom Satan presides—spirits, so called, either as possessed of *power*, as Rückert and Harless think, or rather, because they collectively form the principality of Satan, as Zanchius and Baumgarten-Crusius imagine—a meaning which nouns similarly formed, as δουλεία, συμμαχία, frequently have. Bernhardy, p. 47. Such passages as Luke xxii. 53 and Col. i. 13 show that the opinion which joins both views is justified by biblical usage.

'Ἀήρ does not denote that which the ἐξουσία commands or controls, as Erasmus, Beza, Flacius, and Piscator suppose, but it points out the seat or place of dominion; not, however, in the sense of Robinson, von Gerlach, Barnes, and Doddridge. Holzhausen propounds the novel interpretation, that the apostle understands by the "power of the air"—*die heidnische Götterwelt*, "the heathen world of gods." That ἀήρ of itself should signify darkness, is an opinion which cannot be sustained. Heinsius,[1] Estius, Storr, Flatt, Matthies, Bisping, and Hodge identify the term with σκότος, in ver. 12 of the 6th chapter, or in Col. i. 13. The passages adduced from the ancient writers, such as Homer,[2] Hesiod, and Plutarch, in support of this rendering, can scarcely be appealed to for the usage of the term in the days of the apostle. The word in a feminine form signified fog or haze, and is derived from ἄω, ἄημι—"I breathe or blow," and is used in opposition to αἰθήρ—"the clear upper air;" and it has been conjectured that the original meaning of the term may have suggested its use to the apostle in the clause before us.

But more specially, 1. Some of the Greek fathers take the genitive as a noun of quality—"prince of the aërial powers"—ἀσώματοι δυνάμεις. Thus Chrysostom—Τοῦτο πάλιν φησὶ ὅτι τὸν ὑπουράνιον ἔχει τόπον, καὶ πνεύματα πάλιν ἀέρια αἱ ἀσώματοι δυνάμεις εἰσὶν αὐτοῦ ἐνεργοῦντος—"Again he says this, that Satan possesses the sub-celestial places, and again, that the bodiless powers are aërial spirits under his operation." Œcumenius quaintly reasons of this mysterious ἄρχων, "that his ἀρχή is under heaven, and not above it; and if under heaven, it must be either on earth or in the air. Being a spirit, it is in the air, for they have an aërial nature." With more exactness, Cajetan describes this host as having *subtile corpus nostris sensibus ignotum, corpus simplex ac incorruptibile*. Ignatius, in his Epistle to the Ephesians, refers also to the ἀερίων πνευμάτων. The opinion of Harless is much the same as that of Olshausen—"These evil powers are certainly not earthly, and as certainly they are not heavenly," and they are therefore named by an epithet which defines neither the one nor the other quality. This is substantially the interpretation

---

[1] *Exercitat. sac.* p. 459.
[2] Damm, *Lexicon, sub voce;* Buttmann, *Lexilogus, ibid.*

of Œcumenius, of Hahn, and of Hofmann, *Schriftb.* p. 455. The interpretation of Moses Stuart is virtually identical,[1] and the notion of Stier is not altogether different, but it is somewhat mystically expressed. The view of a-Lapide and Calixtus, that those "aërial" imps could and did raise storms and hurricanes, is as puerile on the one side, as that of Calvin and Beza is vaguely figurative on the other—that man is in as great and constant danger from those fiends, as if they actually inhabited the air. Thomas Aquinas and Erasmus take "air" by a metonymy as meaning earth and air together, or the earth surrounded by the air—an opinion connected with the reading of F, G—ἀέρος τούτου—and of the Vulgate, *aëris hujus*. Others, not satisfied with these fanciful opinions, give the epithet "aërial" a figurative signification. So Rieger alleges, that the power of these evil spirits resembles that of the atmosphere—swift, mighty, and invisible. Cocceius also takes the term metaphorically, as if it described that darkness, blindness, and danger on "slippery places," which Satan inflicts on wicked men. Bucer says indeed, that the apostle describes the air as the habitation of fallen and wicked spirits—*ex peculiari revelatione*. But, 2. There are others who argue, that the apostle borrowed the notion either from the Pythagorean or Gnostic demonology. Wetstein affirms—*Paulus ita loquitur, ex principiis philosophiæ Pythagoreæ, quibus illi ad quos scribit imbuti erant*. The Pythagorean philosophy, it is true, had opinions not unlike that supposed to be expressed by the apostle. Plutarch says —ὕπαιθρον ἀέρα καὶ τὸν ὑπουράνιον ὄντα καὶ θεῶν καὶ δαιμόνων μεστόν.[2] Diogenes Laertius records, that according to Pythagoras, the air was full of spirits—πάντα τὸν ἀέρα ψυχῶν ἔμπλεον. Apuleius, Maximus Tyrius, Manilius, Chalcidius, and others, make similar avowals, as may be found at length in the quotations adduced by Wetstein, Elsner,[3] and Dougtæus.[4] The same sentiments are also found in Philo, in his treatises *De Gigantibus*[5] and *De Plantatione*.[6] Nay,

---

[1] *Bibliotheca Sacra*, 1843, p. 140; Maimonides, *Moreh Nevochim*, iii. c. 51; Buxtorf, *Lexic. Talmud*, sub voce מטטרן.

[2] *Quæst. Rom.* i. p. 274, also in his *De Iside et Osiride*, p. 361.
[3] *Observat.* p. 206. [4] *Analecta*, p. 127.
[5] *Opera*, cura Pfeiffer, ii. p. 359. [6] Do. iii. p. 93.

Augustine held that the demons were penally confined to the air—*damnatum ad aërem tanquam ad carcerem. Comment. on Ps.* cxliii. And Boyd (Bodius), as if dreaming of a Scottish fairy-land, thinks that the devil got the principality of the air from its connection with us, who live partly on earth and partly in air, and that his relation to sinful man is seen in his union with that element which is so essential to human life. But is it at all likely that the inspired apostle gave currency to the tenets of a vain philosophy—to the dreams and delusions of fantastic speculation? Besides, there is no polemical tendency in this epistle, and there was no motive to such doctrinal accommodation. Gnosticism is always refuted, not flattered, by the apostle of the Gentiles. 3. Others, again, such as Meyer and Conybeare, suppose that the language of the rabbinical schools is here employed. Harless has carefully shown the falsity of such a hypothesis. A passage in Rabbi Bechai, *in Penta.* p. 90, has been often quoted, but the Rabbi says—"The demons which excite dreams dwell in the air, but those which tempt to evil inhabit the depths of the sea," whereas these *submarine* fiends are the very class which the apostle terms the principality of the *air*.[1] Some of the other quotations adduced from the same sources are based upon the idea that angels are furnished with wings, with which, of course, they flutter in the atmosphere, as they approach, or leave, or hasten through our world. *Sciendum*, says the Munus Novum, as quoted by Drusius, *a terrâ usque ad expansum omnia plena esse turmis et præfectis, omnesque stare et volitare in aëre.* These notions are so puerile, that the apostle could not for a moment have made them the basis of his language.[2] The other six places in which ἀήρ occurs throw no light on this passage, as it is there used in its ordinary physical acceptation.

In none of these various opinions can we fully acquiesce. That the physical atmosphere is in any sense the abode of demons, or is in any way allied to their essential nature, appears to us to be a strange statement.[3] When fiends move from place to place, they need not make the atmosphere the

---

[1] Eisenmenger, *Entdecktes Juden.* p. 437.
[2] Bartolocci, i. p. 320. *Testament.* xii. *Patr.* p. 729.
[3] But see Cudworth, *Intellectual System*, vol. ii. p. 664, ed. Lond. 1845.

chief medium of transition, for many of the subtler fluids of nature are not restricted to such a conductor, but penetrate the harder forms of matter as an ordinary pathway. There is certainly no scriptural hint that demons are either compelled to confinement in the air as a prison, or that they have chosen it as a congenial abode, either in harmony with their own nature, or as a spot adapted to ambush and attack upon men, into whose spirit they may creep with as much secrecy and subtlety as a poisonous miasma steals into their lungs during their necessary and unguarded respiration. We think, therefore, that the ἀήρ and κόσμος must correspond in relation. Just as there is an atmosphere round the physical globe, so an ἀήρ envelopes this κόσμος. Now, the κόσμος is a spiritual world—the region of sinful desires—the sphere in which live and move all the ungodly. We often use similar phraseology when we say "the gay world," "the musical world," "the literary world," or "the religious world;" and each of these expressive phrases is easily understood. So the κόσμος of the New Testament is opposed to God, for it hates Christianity; the believer does not belong to it, for it is crucified to him and he to it. That same world may be an ideal sphere, comprehending all that is sinful in thought and pursuit—a region on the actual physical globe, but without geographical boundary—all that out-field which lies beyond the living church of Christ. And, like the material globe, this world of death-walkers has its own atmosphere, corresponding to it in character—an atmosphere in which it breathes and moves. All that animates it, gives it community of sentiment, contributes to sustain its life in death, and enables it to breathe and be, may be termed its atmosphere. Such an air or atmosphere belting a death-world, whose inhabitants are νεκροὶ τοῖς παραπτώμασι καὶ ταῖς ἁμαρτίαις, is really Satan's seat. His chosen abode is the dark nebulous zone which canopies such a region of spiritual mortality, close upon its inhabitants, ever near and ever active, unseen and yet real, unfelt and yet mighty, giving to the κόσμος that "form and pressure"—that αἰών—which the apostle here describes as its characteristic element. If this interpretation be reckoned too ingenious—and interpretations are generally false in proportion to their ingenuity—then we can only say, that either the apostle used current language which did not convey error, as Satan is called Beelzebub without reference to the meaning of the term—"Lord of flies;" or that he meant to convey the idea of what Ellicott calls "near propinquity," for air is nigh the earth; or that he embodies in the clause some allusions which he may have more fully explained during his abode at Ephesus.

In their trespasses and sins they walked—κατά—"according to" the prince of the power of the air. This preposition used in reference to a person, as here, signifies "according to the will," or "conformably to the example." This dark princedom is further identified as—

τοῦ πνεύματος τοῦ νῦν ἐνεργοῦντος ἐν τοῖς υἱοῖς τῆς ἀπειθείας —"of the spirit which now worketh in the children of disobedience." The connection with the preceding clause is somewhat difficult of explanation. Flatt supposes it, though it is in the genitive, to be in apposition to the accusative ἄρχοντα. So, apparently, Ambrosiaster, who has the translation—*spiritum*. Bullinger cuts the knot by rendering—*qui est spiritus*, and so Luther by his—*nämlich nach dem Geist*. Others, as Piscator, Crocius, Rückert, and de Wette, suppose a deviation from the right construction in the use of the genitive for the accusative. Some, again, take πνεύματος in a collective sense, as Vatablus, Grotius, Estius, and Holzhausen. Governed by ἄρχοντα, the meaning would then be—"the prince of that spirit-world," the members of which work in the children of disobedience. Winer, § 67, 3. Meier and Ellicott take πνεύματος as governed by ἄρχοντα, and they understand by πνεῦμα that spirit or disposition which reigns in worldly and ungodly men, of which Satan may be considered the master. Meyer, adopting the same construction, defines πνεῦμα as a principle emanating from Satan as its lord, and working in men. Harless, Olshausen, Matthies, and Stier take the word in apposition with ἐξουσίας, and governed by ἄρχοντα, and suppose it to mean that influence which Satan exercises over the disobedient; or, as Harless names it—*wirksame teuflische Versuchung*—"actual devilish temptation;" or, as Stier characterizes it—*eine verfinsternde tödtende Inspiration*—"a darkening and killing inspiration." But how does this view harmonize with the phraseology? Surely an influence, or principle, or inspiration is not exactly in unison with ἄρχων. We cannot well say—prince of an influence or disposition. We would therefore take πνεύματος in apposition with ἐξουσίας, but refer it to the essential nature of the ἐξουσία. It is a *spiritual* kingdom which the devil governs, an empire of *spirits* over which he presides. And the singular is used with emphasis. The entire objective ἐξουσία, no matter what are its numbers and varied ranks, acts as one spirit on the children of disobedience, is thought of as one spirit, in perfect unity of operation and purpose with its malignant ἄρχων. Nay, the prince and all his powers are so combined, so identified in essence and aim, that to a terrified and enslaved world they stand out as one πνεῦμα. In Luke iv. 33 occurs the phrase—πνεῦμα δαιμονίου ἀκαθάρτου. This "spirit" is in its subjective form called τὸ πνεῦμα τοῦ κόσμου. 1 Cor. ii. 12. And it is a busy spirit-world —τοῦ νῦν ἐνεργοῦντος.

'Απείθεια is not specially unbelief of the gospel, as Luther, Bengel, Scholz, and Harless suppose, but disobedience, as the Syriac renders it. It characterizes the world not as in direct antagonism to the gospel, but as it is by nature—hostile to the will and government of God, and daringly and wantonly violating that law which is written in their hearts. Deut. ix. 23, 24; Heb. iv. 6. The phrase υἱοὶ τῆς ἀπειθείας is a species of Hebraism, and is found v. 6; Col. iii. 6, etc. Compare Rom. ii. 16, and Fritzsche's remarks on it. The idiom shows the close relation and dependence of the two substantives. As its "children," they have their inner being and its sustenance from "disobedience;" or, as Winer says, they are "those in whom disobedience has become a predominant and second nature," § 34, 3, *b*, 2. The adverb νῦν denotes "at the present time" —the spirit which at the present moment is working in the disobedient. Meier, not Meyer as Olshausen quotes, gives the adverb this peculiar but faulty reference—"The spirit which yet reigns, though the gospel be powerfully counter-working it;" and Olshausen as baselessly supposes it to mark that the working of the devil is restricted, in contrast to the eternal working of the Holy Ghost. The νῦν appears to stand in contrast to the ποτέ—"Ye, the readers of this epistle, were *once* in such a condition, and those whom you left behind when you became the children of God, are in the same condition *still*." There is, accordingly, no reason to render the word *nunc maxime*, as if, as Stier argues, there was more than usual energy on the part of Satan. As little ground have Rückert and Holzhausen to suppose, that the clause denotes some extraordinary manifestation of evil influence. The verse is but a vivid description of the usual condition of the unconverted and disobedient world. The world and the church are thus marked in distinct and telling contrast. The church has its head—κεφαλή; the world has its—ἄρχων. That Head is a man, allied by blood to the community over which He presides; that other prince is an unembodied spirit—an alien as well as a usurper. The one so blesses the church that it becomes His "fulness," the other sheds darkness and distress all around Him. The one has His Spirit dwelling in the church, leading it to holiness; the other, himself the darkest, most malignant, and unlovely being in the universe, exercises a subtile and debasing influence over the minds of his vassals, who are "children of disobedience." Matt. xiii. 38; John viii. 44; Acts xxvi. 18; 2 Cor. iv. 4. The apostle honestly describes their former spiritual state, for he adds—including himself—συντάττει καὶ ἑαυτόν—as Theodoret says—

(Ver. 3.) Ἐν οἷς καὶ ἡμεῖς πάντες ἀνεστράφημέν ποτε ἐν— "Among whom also we all had our conversation once in . . ." The οἷς does not refer to παραπτώμασι, as is supposed by the paraphrase of the Syriac version, and as is imagined by Jerome, Estius, Cocceius, Koppe, Baumgarten, and Stier; but it agrees with υἱοῖς, as is argued by de Wette, Baumgarten-Crusius, Meyer, Harless, Meier, Matthies, and Rückert. The first ἐν refers to persons, "among whom" as a portion of them; and the second, in immediate connection with the verb, to things. It appears altogether too refined to suppose, with Stier, that in ver. 2, and in connection with the ἁμαρτίαι of ver. 1, the apostle refers to the heathen world, and that in this verse, and in connection with παράπτωμα, he characterizes the Jewish world. Least of all can the change from "you" to "we" vindicate such a meaning. We wait till the apostle, in a subsequent verse, makes the distinction himself. The ἡμεῖς πάντες is—we all, Jew and Gentile alike. See also Rom. iv. 16, viii. 32; 1 Cor. xii. 13; 2 Cor. iii. 18. There is not in this section such a characteristic definition of sins, as should warrant us to refer the one verse to Jews, and the other to Gentiles. We cannot accede to such a view, though it is advocated by Harless and Olshausen, and almost all the modern commentators, with the exception of de Wette; advocated, too, in former times by no less names than Pelagius and Calvin, Zanchius and Grotius, Clarius and Bengel. As much ground is there for Hammond's strange idea, that the Christians of Rome are here described. Nor is there in the verse any feature of criminality, such as should lead us to say that the apostle classes himself among these sinners, simply, as some would have it, by a common figure of speech. There is nothing here of which the apostle does not accuse himself in other places. 1 Tim. i. 13. ἀνεστράφημέν ποτε. 2 Cor. i. 12; Gal. i. 13; 1 Tim. iii. 15. This has much the same meaning with the similar terms of the preceding verse, perhaps with the additional idea of greater attachment to the scene or haunt; *speciosius quam ambulare,* says Bengel. All we—all of us—Jew and Gentile, were once so distinguished. For we walked—

ἐν ταῖς ἐπιθυμίαις τῆς σαρκὸς ἡμῶν—"in the lusts of our flesh." This clause marks out the sphere of activity. Σάρξ signifies man's fallen and corrupted nature, in its antagonism to the Spirit of God, and it probably has received such a name because of its servitude to what is material and sensuous. Not that we at all espouse the notion that sin has no other origin than sensuousness, or that it is but the predominance of sensuous impulse over the intellect and will. This theory, befriended in some of its aspects by Kant and Schleiermacher, has been overthrown with able argument by Müller; and the reply of de Wette, who had also adopted it, is a failure as a defence. But though σάρξ, in apostolic language, include the will, and have a meaning which neither σῶμα nor κρέας has, the question still recurs, How has our whole nature come to be represented by a term which truly and properly denotes only one part of it? Delitzsch, *Bib. Psychologie,* p. 325. Σάρξ does sometimes stand in opposition to the human πνεῦμα, as 1 Cor. v. 5, Col. ii. 5; but in such places its meaning is restricted by the antithesis. Gen. vi. 3. If what properly signifies a portion of our nature come to signify the whole of it under a certain aspect, there must be some connection. What is material, as σάρξ naturally is, may represent what is external and so far unspiritual; while what is non-spiritual is sinful, as being opposed to the Spirit of God. See Ebrard, *Christliche Dogmatik*, § 323, vol. i. p. 463; Messner, *Die Lehre der Apostel*, p. 207. Ἐπιθυμία in such a connection, has a stigma upon it, for it represents desires or appetites which are irregular and sinful — such inclinations as are formed and pursued by unregenerate humanity. The spiritual life is dead, and therefore the σάρξ is unchecked in all its impulses and desires. And the apostle adds—

ποιοῦντες τὰ θελήματα τῆς σαρκὸς καὶ τῶν διανοιῶν— "doing the desires of the flesh and of the thoughts." The principal differences of interpretation respect the word διανοιῶν, which has a good sense in the classics. The exegesis of the Greek fathers is too vague. Chrysostom sums up the meaning by saying — τουτέστιν, οὐδὲν πνευματικὸν φρονοῦντες. Stier denies that by σαρκός and διανοιῶν different species of sin are indicated, but adds that the last term refers to reasons or arguments—*denkerei*—which check or guide the flesh in its sinful propensities. The view of Bengel is coincident. This interpretation does not bring out the distinction between the two terms—a distinction which the article before each seems to intimate. The exegesis of Flatt is his usual hendiadys: "flesh and thoughts" stands for fleshly thoughts; or, as Crellius also latinizes it—*cogitationes carnales*. Some understand by the terms "depraved fancies," as Hase; others, like Olshausen, "sinful thoughts, which have no sensual lust for their basis;" and others, like Harless, "unresolute, shifting thoughts, which determine the will." Rückert and Meier make it "immoral thoughts." Διάνοιαι in the plural is found only here, and in the singular it stands often in the Septuagint for the Hebrew לֵב. In the plural, as if for διανοήματα, it apparently denotes thoughts or sentiments, ideal fancies and resolves. See Num. xv. 39; Isa. lv. 9. Σάρξ in the first clause may signify humanity as it is fallen and debased by sin; while here the meaning is more defined and restricted to our fleshly nature. The general "conversation" of disobedient men may be said to be "in the lusts of the flesh," but when their positive activity is described—ποιοῦντες, and when these ἐπιθυμίαι become actually θελήματα—when inclinations become resolves, a distinction at once arises, and sins of a grosser are marked out from those of a more spiritual nature. Such is the view of Jerome. The "desires of the flesh" are those grosser gratifications of appetite which are palpable and easily recognized; and the "desires of the thoughts," those mental trespasses which may or may not be connected with sensuous indulgences. Matt. xv. 19; Luke xi. 17. Our Lord has exposed such "thoughts" as violations of the Divine law. The σάρξ is one, all its appetences are like; but the word διάνοιαι is plural, for it describes what is complex and multiform. See σοφίαι, Aristoph. *Ranæ*, v. 688; and *Sapientiæ*, Cicero, *Tusc.* ii. 18. Thought follows thought, as the shadows flit across the field on a cloudy summer day. Men may scorn intemperance as a degrading vice, and shun it, and yet cherish within them pride high as Lucifer's, and wrath foul and fierce as Tophet. Under the single head of σάρξ (Gal. v. 19, 20) the apostle includes both classes of sins—"hatred, variance, emulation, wrath, strife, seditions, heresies," as well as "adultery, fornication, murder, drunkenness, and revellings." The historian Polybius describes men sinning, as many of them, διὰ τὴν ἀλογιστίαν—from want of thought, as διὰ τὴν φύσιν, by nature. Lib. xvii. cap. viii. *apud Raphel*. But there is an awful and additional clause— καὶ ἦμεν τέκνα φύσει ὀργῆς — " and we were by nature children of wrath." This common reading is retained by Tischendorf, followed by Rückert. Lachmann, however, after A, D, E, F, G, J, has φύσει τέκνα ὀργῆς. But there appears no good ground for departing from the order of the Textus Receptus, the changed order wearing the aspect of an emendation. Ὀργή is not simply "punishment," but that just indignation which embodies itself in punishment. The word is often so used in the New Testament. Τέκνα ὀργῆς resembles the previous υἱοὶ τῆς ἀπειθείας, but implying, as Alford says, "closer relation." That phrase does not denote, liable to disobedience, but involved in it; and therefore τέκνα ὀργῆς does not signify—liable to wrath, but actually under it. Thus, Deut. xxv. 2, בִּן הַכּוֹת—a son of stripes—not liable to be scourged, but actually scourged. The idiom, then, does not mean "worthy of wrath," as the Greek fathers, when they render it ὀργῆς ἄξιοι, and as Grotius, Koppe, Baumgarten, and others have understood it; but it describes a present and actual condition. The awful wrath of God is upon sinners, for sin is so contrary to His nature and law, that His pure anger is kindled against it. Nor is this ὀργή to be explained away after the example of the early Fathers,[1] as if it were simply chastisement, κόλασις—not judicial infliction, but benignant castigation; for as Alford well says—then the phrase would, from its nature, imply that they had been "actually punished." 'Οργή is God's holy anger against sin, which leads Him justly to punish it. Rom. i. 18. But God's manifestation of wrath is not inconsistent with His manifestation of love; for, to repeat the oft-quoted words of Lactantius—*Si Deus non irascitur impiis et injustis, nec pios justosque diligit.*

The apostle says further, τέκνα φύσει—" children by nature;" the dative, as Madvig says, defining " the side, aspect, regard, or property on and in which the predicate shows itself," § 40. See also Phrynichus, ed. Lobeck, p. 688; Kühner, 585, Anmerk 1. Φύσις—" nature "—in such an idiom, signifies what is essential as opposed to what is accidental, what is innate in contrast with what is acquired; as Harless puts the antithesis—*das Gewordene im Gegensatz zum Gemachten.* This is its general sense, whatever its specific application. Thus —φαρμάκου φύσις[2] is the nature of a drug, its colour, growth, and potency. Φύσις τοῦ Αἰγύπτου[3] is the nature of the land of Egypt—a phrase referring to no artificial peculiarity, but to results which follow from its physical conformation. It stands opposed to νόμος or ἀνάγκη, as marking what is spontaneous, in contrast to what is enjoined or is inevitable. Thus Plato, *De Leg.* lib. x.—Some say that the gods are οὐ φύσει ἀλλὰ τισὶ νόμοις. Again, the noun is often used in the dative, or in the accusative with κατά or παρά in descriptions of condition or action, and then its signification is still the same: φύσει τυφλός—" blind by nature," not by disease;[4] τὸν φύσει δοῦλον—" the slave by nature," that is, from birth, and not by subjugation;[5] οἱ φύσει πολέμιοι—" warriors by nature," by constitutional tendency, and not by force of circumstances.[6] And so in such phrases as, κατὰ φύσιν—" agreeably to nature," not simply to education or habit; παρὰ φύσιν—contrary not

---

[1] Suicer, *Thesaurus, sub voce.*
[2] *Odyss.* x. 303.
[3] Herodot. ii. 5.
[4] Aristot. *Nicomach.* iii. 7.
[5] *Dio Chrysost.* xv. p. 239.
[6] Ælian, *Var. Hist.* iii. 22.

to mere conventional propriety, but to general or ordinary instinctive development; thus—ὁ κατὰ φύσιν υἱός—"the natural," not the adopted "son." The usage is similar in the Hellenistic writers. Wisdom vii. 20, φύσεις ζώων—"the natures of animals," not the habits induced by training. Φύσει πάντες εἰσὶν φίλαυτοι—"all are by nature," not by training, "self-lovers."[1] Φύσει πονηρὸς ὤν.—"being evil by nature,"[2] and not simply by education. So also in the same author—of the constitutional clemency of the Pharisees—φύσει ἐπιεικῶς ἔχουσιν.[3] Likewise in Philo, εἰρηναῖοι φύσει —"peaceful by nature," not from compulsion;[4] and in many other places, some of which have been collected by Loesner. The usage of the New Testament is not different. Save in Jas. iii. 7 and 2 Pet. i. 4, where the word has a signification peculiar to these passages, the meaning is the same with that which we have traced through classical and Hellenistic literature. If the term characterize the branches of a tree, those which it produces are contrasted with such as are engrafted (Rom. xi. 21-24); if it describe action or character, it marks its harmony with or its opposition to instinctive feeling or sense of obligation (Rom. i. 26, ii. 14; 1 Cor. xi. 14); if it point out nationality, it is that of descent or blood. Rom. ii. 27; Gal. ii. 15. See Fritzsche on the references to Romans. And when the apostle (Gal. iv. 8) speaks of idols as being φύσει "not Gods," he means that idols become objects of worship from no inherent claim or quality, but simply by "art and man's device." And so "we are children of wrath," not accidentally, not by a fortuitous combination of circumstances, not even by individual sin and actual transgression, but "by nature"—by an exposure which preceded personal disobedience, and was not first created by it; an exposure which is inherent, hereditary, and common to all the race by the very condition of its present existence, for they are "so born" children of wrath. For φύσις does not refer to developed character, but to its hidden and instinctive sources. We are therefore not atomically, but organically children of wrath; not each simply by personal guilt, but the entire race as a whole; not on account of nature, but by

---

[1] Joseph. *Antiq.* iii. 8, 1.  
[2] *Ibid.* xi. 2, 2.  
[3] *Ibid.* xiii. 10, 6.  
[4] *De Confusione Ling. C.*

nature. Wholly contrary, therefore, to usage and philology is the translation of the Syriac ܐܝܟ ܡܠܐ—*plene;* that of Theophylact, Œcumenius, and Cyril, ἀληθῶς or γνησίως—" really" or " truly ; " that of Julian, *prorsus*, and that even of Suidas —" a constant and very bad disposition and long and evil habits "—ἀλλὰ τὴν ἔμμονον καὶ κακίστην διάθεσιν καὶ χρονίαν καὶ πονηρὰν συνήθειαν, for on the contrary, φύσις and συνήθεια are placed by the Greek ethical writers in contrast. Harless adduces apt quotations from Plutarch and Aristotle. Pelagius, as may be expected, thus guards his exegesis—*Nos paternæ traditionis consuetudo possederat, ut omnes ad damnationem nasci* VIDEREMUR. Erasmus, Bengel, Koppe, Morus, Flatt, de Wette, Reiche, and others, take the word as descriptive of the state of the Ephesian converts prior to their conversion, or, as Bengel phrases it—*citra gratiam Dei in Christo*. But, as Meyer observes, the *status naturalis* is depicted in the whole description, and not merely by φύσει. Such an interpretation is also unsatisfactory, for it leaves untouched the real meaning of the word under dispute. That the term may signify that second nature which springs from habit, we deny not. *Natura* had such a sense among the Latins[1]—*quod consuetudo in naturam vertit*—but in many places where it may bear this meaning, it still implies that the habit is in accordance with original inclination, that the disposition or character has its origin in innate tendencies and impulses. When Le Clerc[2] says that the word, when applied to a nation, signifies *indoles gentis*, he only begs the question; for that *indoles* or φύσις in the quotations adduced by him, and by Wetstein and Koppe, from Isocrates, the so-called Demetrius Phalereus, Polyænus, Jamblichus, Cicero, and Sallust, is not something adventitious, but constitutional—an element of character which, though matured by discipline, sprang originally from connate peculiarities. The same may be said of Meyer's interpretation—*durch Entwickelung natürlicher Disposition*— " through the development of natural disposition ; " for if that disposition was natural, its very germs must have been in us at our birth, and what is that but innate depravity? And yet he argues that φύσις cannot refer to original sin, because

---

[1] Quintilian, i. 2; Sallust, *Jugurtha*, 87 ; Freund, *Latein. Wörterbuch, sub voce*.
[2] *Ars Critica*, Londini, 1698, p. 194.

the church doctrine on that subject is not the doctrine of Paul, and one reason why Koppe will not take even the interpretation of Le Clerc is, that it necessarily leads to the doctrine of original sin. Grotius, Meyer, de Wette, and Usteri (*Paulin. Lehrbegriff*, p. 30) object that the word cannot refer to original depravity, because it is only of actual sin that the apostle speaks in the preceding clauses. So little has Grotius gone into the spirit of the passage, that he says—that it cannot refer to original sin, as the preceding verses show, in which vices are described from which many of the ancients were free —*a quibus multi veterum fuere immunes*. Usteri is disposed to cancel φύσει altogether, and Reiche (*Comment. Criticus*, 1859) dilutes it to a *habitus naturalis connatus quasi*, p. 147. See also Episcopius, *Instit.* ii. 5, 2 ; Limborch, *Theolog. Christ.* iii. 4, 17, p. 193 ; Amstelædami, 1686. We may reply with Olshausen, that in this clause actual sins are naturally pointed out in their ultimate foundation—" in the inborn sinfulness of each individual by his connection with Adam." Besides, the apostle means to say that by natural condition, as well as by actual personal guilt, men are children of wrath. Had he written καὶ ὄντες, as following out of the idea of ποιοῦντες, there might have been a plea against our view of innate depravity—"fulfilling the desires of the flesh and of the mind, and being, or so being, children of wrath." But the apostle says, καὶ ἦμεν—" and we were," at a point of time prior to that indicated in ποιοῦντες. This exegesis is also supported by the following clause—

ὡς καὶ οἱ λοιποί—" as also are the rest of mankind ; " not Gentiles simply, nor the remainder of the unbelieving Jews, as is held by Stier and Bisping. Turner apparently imputes our exegesis, which is simply and plainly grammatical, to want of candour and to a desire to support a "preconceived doctrinal theory."

Having described the character of unregenerate men, the apostle adverts to their previous condition. We and the entire human family are by nature children of wrath, even as Crellius himself is obliged to paraphrase it—*velut hæreditario jure*. Those who hold that ἡμεῖς refers to the Jews injure their interpretation, and Harless and Olshausen unnecessarily suppose that the apostle contrasts the natural state of the

Jews with their condition as the called of God, though they do not, like Hofmann, join φύσει to ὀργῆς, as if the allusion were to the Jews, and the meaning were—objects of God's love as the children of Abraham, but of His anger as children of Adam. *Schriftb.* i. p. 564. Thus Estius opposes *filii naturâ* to *filii adoptione ;* and Holzhausen's idea is—that they were children of wrath "which rises from the ungodly natural life." To get such a meaning the article must be repeated, as Harless says—τῆς φύσει ὀργῆς; or as Meyer, τῆς τῇ φύσει, or, ἐκ τῆς φύσεως ὀργῆς. We do not imagine, with many commentators, that φύσει stands in contrast with χάριτι. The former denotes a condition, and cannot well be contrasted with an act or operation of God. Death by or in sin, walk in lust, vassalage to Satan, indulgence of the disorderly appetites of a corrupted nature, and the fulfilling of the desires of the flesh and of the mind—these form a visible and complex unity of crime, palpable and terrific. But that is not all; there is something deeper still; even by nature, and prior to actual transgression, we were "the children of wrath." The apostle had just referred to the σάρξ—feeble and depraved humanity, and knowing that "that which is *born* of the flesh is flesh," and that the taint and corruption are thus hereditary, he adds, "and we were by nature," through our very birth, "children of wrath;" that is, we have not become so by any process of development. Thus also Müller (*Die Lehre von der Sünde*, ii. p. 378) says—"that they, that is, Christians, from among the Jews as well as others, had been objects of Divine punitive justice"—*nach ihrer natürlichen angebornen Beschaffenheit Gegenstände ;* and Lechler also calls man's natural condition—*eine angeborne Zorneskindschaft d. h. eine angeborne Verderbniss der Menschennatur. Das Apost. und das nachap. Zeitalter*, etc., p. 107. Barnes and Stuart[1] deny, indeed, that the use of this term can prove what is usually called the doctrine of original sin. It is true that the apostle does not speak of Adam and his sin, nor does he describe the germs and incipient workings of depravity. It is not a formal theological assertion, for φύσει is unemphatic in position; but what is more convincing, it is an incidental allusion —as if no proof were needed of the awful truth. How and

[1] *Biblical Repository*, 2nd ser. vol. ii. 38.

when sin commences is not the present question. Still the term surely means, that in consequence of some element of relation or character, an element *inborn* and not *infused*, men are exposed to the Divine wrath. The clause does not, as these critics hold, simply mean that men in an unconverted state are obnoxious to punishment, but that men, apart from all that is extrinsic and accidental, all that time or circumstance may create or modify, are "children of wrath." As Calvin says—*Hoc uno verbo quasi fulmine totus homo quantusquantus est prosternitur.* It would be, at the same time, wholly contrary to Scripture and reason to maintain, with Flacius, that sin is a part of the very essence and substance of our nature. The language of this clause does not imply it. Sin is a foreign element — *an accident* — whatever be the depth of human depravity.

It belongs not to the province of interpretation to enter into any illustration of the doctrine expressed or implied in the clause under review. The origin of evil is an inscrutable mystery, and has afforded matter of subtle speculation from Plato down to Kant and Schelling, while, in the interval, Aquinas bent his keen vision upon the problem, and felt his gaze dazzled and blunted. Ideas of the actual nature of sin naturally modify our conceptions of its moral character, as may be seen in the theories which have been entertained from those of Manichæan dualism and mystic pre-existence,[1] to those of privation,[2] sensuousness,[3] antagonism,[4] impreventibility,[5] and the subtle distinction between formal and real liberty developed in the hypothesis of Müller.[6] While admitting the scriptural account of the introduction of sin, many have shaped their views of it from the connection in which they place it in reference to Divine foreknowledge, and so have sprung up the Supralapsarian and Sublapsarian hypotheses.

[1] Müller, *Die Christliche Lehre von der Sünde*, vol. ii. p. 495, 3rd ed. See also Beecher's *Conflict of Ages*.
[2] Leibnitz, *Essais de Théodicée sur la Bonté de Dieu*, etc., pp. 85, 86, 288. Amsterdam, 1726.
[3] De Wette, *Christliche Sittenlehre*, § 10, and *Studien und Kritiken*, 1849; Rothe, *Ethik*, vol. i. pp. 98, 99; Schleiermacher, *Der Christliche Glaube*, § 66.
[4] Lactantius, *Instit. Divin.* lib. ii. cap. 8; 9; Hegel, *Philosophie des Rechts*, § 139.
[5] *The Mystery, or Evil and God.* By John Young, LL.D. London, 1856.
[6] Müller, vol. ii. pp. 6-48.

Attempts to form a perfect scheme of Theodicy, or a full vindication of the Divinity, have occupied many other minds than that of Leibnitz. The relation of the race to its Progenitor has been viewed in various lights, and analogies physical, political, and metaphysical, with theories of Creationism and Traducianism, have been employed in illustration, from the days of Augustine and Pelagius[1] to those of Erasmus and Luther, Calvin and Arminius, Taylor and President Edwards. Questions about the origin of evil, transmission of depravity, imputation of guilt, federal or representative position on the part of Adam, and physical and spiritual death as elements of the curse, have given rise to long and laboured argumentation, because men have looked at them from very different standpoints, and have been influenced in their treatment of the problem by their philosophical conceptions of the Divine character, the nature of sin, and that moral freedom and power which belong to responsible humanity. The *modus* may be and is among "the deep things of God," but the *res* is palpable; for experience confirms the Divine testimony that we are by nature "children of wrath," *per generationem*, not *per imitationem*.

(Ver. 4.) Ὁ δὲ Θεὸς, πλούσιος ὢν ἐν ἐλέει—"But God, being rich in mercy." The apostle resumes the thought started in ver. 1. The δέ not only intimates this, but shows also that the thought about to be expressed is in contrast with that which occupies the immediately preceding verses. The fact of God's mercy succeeds a description of man's guilt and misery, and the transition from the one to the other is indicated by the particle δέ. Hartung, vol. i. p. 173; Jelf, § 767. Jerome rashly condemns the use of δέ; but Bodius stigmatizes the patristic critic as judging—*nimis profecto audacter et hypercritice*. Ἔλεος signifies "mercy," and is a term stronger and more practical than οἰκτιρμός. It is not mere emotion, but emotion creating actual assistance—sympathy leading to succour. The participle ὤν does not seem to have here a causal significance, as such an idea is expressed by the following διά. And in this mercy God is rich. It has no scanty foothold in His bosom, for it fills it. Though mercy has been expended by God for six millenniums, and myriads of myriads

[1] Wiggers, *August. und Pelag.* Kap. 20; Nitzsch, § 105, 107.

have been partakers of it, it is still an unexhausted mine of wealth—

διὰ τὴν πολλὴν ἀγάπην αὐτοῦ, ἣν ἠγάπησεν ἡμᾶς—" on account of His great love with which He loved us." The former clause describes the general source of blessing; this marks out a direct and special manifestation, and is in immediate connection with the following verb. On the use of a verb with its cognate noun carrying with it an intensity of meaning, the reader may turn to i. 3, 6, 20; Winer, § 32, 2; Kühner, § 547. The ἡμᾶς are Paul and his contemporary believers, and, of course, all possessing similar faith. That love is πολλή—great indeed; for a great God is its possessor, and great sinners are its objects. The adjective probably marks the quality of intensity; indeed, while its generic meaning remains, its specific allusion depends upon its adjuncts. The idea of frequency may thus be included, as it seems to be in some uses of the word [1]—number being its radical meaning. Πολλὴ ἀγάπη, therefore, is love, the intensity of which has been shown in the fervour and frequency of its developments. See under i. 5. And what can be higher proof than this—

(Ver. 5.) Καὶ ὄντας ἡμᾶς νεκροὺς τοῖς παραπτώμασιν—" Us being even dead in trespasses." The καί does more than mark the connection. It does not, however, signify "also," as Meier supposes—" us, too, along with you;" nor, as Flatt, Rückert, Matthies, and Holzhausen think, does it merely show the connection of the ὑμᾶς of ver. 1 with this ἡμᾶς of ver. 5. Nor does it mean "yet," "although," as Koppe takes it. In this view, to give any good sense, it must be joined to the preceding verb—" He loved us, even though we were dead in sins." But such a construction destroys the unity of meaning. With Meyer and Harless, we prefer joining the καί to the participle ὄντας, and making it signify "indeed," or when we "were truly" dead in sins. Hartung, vol. i. p. 132. See chap. i. 11, 15.

συνεζωοποίησεν τῷ Χριστῷ — " quickened together with Christ." Some MSS. and texts have the preposition ἐν before τῷ Χριστῷ, but for this there is no authority, as the dative is governed by the συν- in composition with the verb.

[1] Passow, Pape, Lex. sub voce.

The σύν is repeated before the dative in Col. ii. 13. The entire passage, and the aorist form of the three verbs, show that this vivification is a past, and not a future blessing. It is a life enjoyed already, not one merely secured to us by our ideal resurrection with Christ. The remark of Jerome is foreign to the purpose, that the aorist is used with reference to the Divine prescience—*id quod futurum est, quasi factum esse jam dixerit.* We have already exhibited the validity of our objection under i. 19. Theodoret's interpretation is out of place,—ἐκείνου γὰρ ἀναστάντος, καὶ ἡμεῖς ἐλπίζομεν ἀναστήσεσθαι. Meyer's view has been already rejected under the 1st verse of this chapter; for as the death there described is not a physical death to come upon us, but a death already experienced, so this is not a physical resurrection to be enjoyed at some distant epoch, but one in which, even now, we who were dead have participated. Therefore, with the majority of interpreters, we hold that it is spiritual life to which the apostle refers. The exegesis of Harless, found also in the old Scottish commentator Dickson, though it be cleverly maintained, is too refined, and is not in accordance with the literal and sincere appeal of the apostle to present Christian experience, for in his opinion, life, resurrection, and glorification, are said to be ours, not because we actually enjoy them, but because Jesus has experienced them, and they are ours in Him, or ours because they are His. Olshausen advocates a similar view, though not so broadly. Slichtingius and Crellius suppose that the verb refers to the *jus*, not the *ipsum factum;* and it is of necessity the theory of all who, like Rollock and Bodius, maintain that the resurrection and enthronement described are specially connected with the body and its final ascension and blessedness. The interpretation of Chrysostom—εἰ γὰρ ἡ ἀπαρχὴ ζῇ, καὶ ἡμεῖς—"if the first-fruits live, so do we," does not wholly bring out the meaning. Theophylact's exposition, which is shared in by Augustine and Erasmus, is more acute. God raised up Christ, ἐκεῖνον ἐνεργείᾳ—Him in fact, but us δυνάμει νῦν—potentially now, but afterwards in fact also. Harless compares the language with that in Rom. viii. 30, which Meyer also quotes, where the verbs are all aorists, and where the last verb refers to future but certain glory. But the apostle in that verse describes, by the aorists, God's normal method of procedure viewed as from the past—the call, justification, and glorification being contained in a past predestination, and regarded as coincident with it. The apostle is not appealing to the Roman Christians, and saying, "God has called and glorified you;" he is only describing God's general and invariable method of procedure in man's salvation. But here he speaks to the Ephesian converts, and tells them that God quickened them, raised them up, and gave them a seat with Jesus. He is not unfolding principles of divine government; but analyzing human experience, and verifying that analysis by an appeal to living consciousness. Were no more intended by the words than Harless imagines, then they would be quite as true of Christians still unborn as they were of Ephesian believers at that time in existence, since all who shall believe to the end of time were spiritually comprised in the risen Saviour. Nay more, the sentiment would be true of men in an unconverted state who were afterwards to believe. But here the apostle speaks of union with Jesus not only as a realized fact, but of its blessed and personal results. The death was a personal state, and the life corresponds in character. It is not a theoretic abstraction, but as really an individual blessing as the death was an individual curse. The life and resurrection spoken of are now possessed, and their connection with Christ seems to be of the following nature. When God quickened and raised Christ, this process, as we have seen, was the example and pledge of our spiritual vivification. When He was raised physically, all His people were *ideally* raised in Him; and in consequence of this connection with Him, they are, through faith, *actually* quickened and raised, i. 19, 20. The object of the apostle, however, is not merely to affirm that spiritual life and resurrection have been secured by such a connection with Jesus, but that, having been so provided, they are also really possessed. The writer tells the Ephesians that they had been dead, and he assures them that life in connection with Christ had been given them, and not merely through Christ potentially secured for them, and reserved for a full but future enjoyment. The verb συνεκάθισεν, on which Olshausen and Harless lay stress as supporting their view, does not, as we shall see, at all support their exegesis. In a word, the apostle appears to intimate not only that the mediatorial person of Jesus had a peculiar and all-comprehending relation to His whole people, so that, as Olshausen says, "Christ is the real type for every form of life among them," but that the Ephesian believers possessed really and now these blessings, which had their origin and symbol in Jesus, the Saviour and Representative. And therefore the notion of Beza and Bloomfield, that συν- in the verb glances at a union of Jew and Gentile, is as wide of the truth on the one side, as is on the other the opinion that it means "after the example of"—the opinion of Anselm, Marloratus, Koppe, Grotius, a-Lapide, and Rosenmüller. See on κατά in i. 19. Calvin limits the possession too much to objective happiness and glory laid up for us in Christ. The language of Crocius is better—*nos excitatos esse in Christo, ut in capite membra; idque non potentia, non spe, sed actu et re ipsa.*

Now, the life given corresponds in nature to the death suffered. It is therefore spiritual life, such as is needed for man's dead spirit. The soul restored to the divine favour lives again, and its new pulsations are vigorous and healthful. As every form of life is full of conscious enjoyment, this too has its higher gladness; truth, peace, thankfulness, and hope swelling the bosom, while it displays its vital powers in sanctified activity: for all its functions are the gift of the Vivifier, and they are dedicated to His service. That life may be feeble at first, but "the sincere milk of the word" is imbibed, and the expected maturity is at length reached. Its first moment may not indeed be registered in the consciousness, as it may be awakened within us by a varying process, in harmony with the quickness or the slowness of mental perception, and the dulness or the delicacy of the moral temperament. The sun rises in our latitude preceded by a long twilight, which gradually brightens into morning; but within the tropics he ascends at once above the horizon with sudden and exuberant glory. (For an illustration of God's power in giving this life, the reader may consult under verses 19 and 20 of the previous chapter.) Then follows the interjected thought—

χάριτί ἐστε σεσωσμένοι—" by grace have ye been saved." The δέ or γάρ found in some MSS. is a clumsy addition, and οὗ, the genitive of the relative pronoun, occurring in D†, E, F, G (οὗ τῇ χάριτι, or οὗ χάριτι), and plainly followed by the Vulgate and Ambrosiaster, is rejected alike by Lachmann and Tischendorf. The grace referred to is that of God, not of Christ—as Beza supposes. The thought is suddenly and briefly thrown in, as it rose to the apostle's mind, for it is a natural suggestion; and so powerfully did it fill and move his soul, that he suddenly writes it, but continues the illustration, and then fondly returns to it in ver. 8. This mental association shows how closely Paul connected life with safety—how mercy and love, uniting us to Christ, and vivifying us with Him, are elements of this grace, and how this union with Jesus and the life springing from it are identical with salvation. But he proceeds—

(Ver. 6.) Καὶ συνήγειρεν—" And raised us up with." The meaning of συν- is of course the same as in the preceding συνεζωοποίησε. Believers are not only quickened, but they are also raised up; they not only receive life, but they experience a resurrection. The dead, on being quickened, do not lie in their graves; they come forth, cast from them the cerements of mortality, and re-enter the haunts of living humanity. Jesus rose on being vivified, and left His sepulchre with the grave-clothes in it. His people enjoy the activities as well as the elements of vitality, for they are raised out of the spiritual death-world, and are not found "the living among the dead." It is a violation of the harmony of sense to understand the first verb of spiritual life, and the second of physical resurrection, or the hope of it, as do Menochius, Bodius, Estius, and Grotius. Still more—

καὶ συνεκάθισεν—"and seated us together with." This verb is to be understood in a spiritual sense as well as the two preceding ones. It is the spirit which is quickened, raised, and co-enthroned with Christ. And the place of honour and dignity is—

ἐν τοῖς ἐπουρανίοις ἐν Χριστῷ Ἰησοῦ—"in the heavenly places in Christ Jesus." This idiom has been already considered both under ver. 3 and ver. 20 of the 1st chapter. It does not denote heaven proper, but is the ideal locality of the church on the earth, as "the kingdom of heaven"— above the world in its sphere of occupation and enjoyment.

The addition of ἐν Χριστῷ Ἰησοῦ occurs also i. 3; and in both places the epithet τὰ ἐπουράνια points out the exalted position of the church. Union to Christ brings us into them. His glory is their bright canopy, and His presence diffuses joy and hope. The ἐν before Χριστῷ Ἰησοῦ has perplexed commentators, for συν- is also in composition with the verb, and would have been supposed to govern these nouns, had not ἐν been expressed. But ἐν again, as frequently in the previous portion of the epistle, defines the sphere, and refers to the three aorists—so anxious is the apostle to show that union to Christ is the one source of spiritual honour and enjoyment. This spiritual enthronement with Jesus is not more difficult to comprehend than our "royal priesthood." The loose interpretations of it by Koppe and Rosenmüller rob it of its point and beauty. Nor is the mere "arousing of the heavenly consciousness" all that is meant, as Olshausen supposes. Indeed, Rückert, Meier, Matthies, and Conybeare are nearer the truth. Our view is simply as follows—Our life, resurrection, and enthronement follow one another, as in the actual history of the great Prototype. But this "sitting with Jesus" is as spiritual as the life, and it indicates the calmness and dignity of the new existence. The quickened soul is not merely made aware that in Christ, as containing it and all similar souls, it is enlivened, and raised up, and elevated, but along with this it enjoys individually a conscious life, resurrection, and session with Jesus. It feels these blessings in itself, and through its union with Him. It lives, and it is conscious of this life; it has been raised, and it is aware of its change of spiritual position. It is more than Augustine allows—*Nondum in nobis, sed jam in Illo*—for it feels itself in the meantime sitting with Jesus, not solely because of its relation to Him in His representative character, but because of its own joyous and personal possession of royal elevation, purity, and honour. "He hath made us kings." Rev. i. 6. What is more peculiar to the spirit in this series of present and beatific gifts, shall at length be shared in by the entire humanity. The body shall be quickened, raised, and glorified, and the redeemed man shall, in the fulness of his nature, enjoy the happiness of heaven. The divine purpose is—

(Ver. 7.) *Ἵνα ἐνδείξηται ἐν τοῖς αἰῶσιν τοῖς ἐπερχομένοις*— " In order that He might show forth in the ages which are coming "—*ἵνα* indicating design. The meaning of this verse depends on the sense attached to the last word. Harless, Meyer, Olshausen, de Wette, and Bisping, take them as descriptive of the future world. Thus Theophylact also—*Νῦν μὲν γὰρ πολλοὶ ἀπιστοῦσιν, ἐν δὲ τῷ μέλλοντι αἰῶνι πάντες γνώσονται τί ἡμῖν ἐχαρίσατο, ὁρῶντες ἐν ἀφάτῳ δόξῃ τοὺς ἁγίους*; the idea being that the blessings of life, resurrection, and elevation with Christ now bestowed upon believers, may be hidden in the meantime, but that in the kingdom of glory they shall be seen in their peculiar lustre and pre-eminence. Thus Wycliffe also—"in the worldlis above comying." But the language of this verse is too full and peculiar to have only in it this general thought. Why should the greatness of the grace that quickened and elevated such sinners as these Ephesians, not be displayed till the realms of glory be reached? Or might not God intend in their salvation at that early age to show to coming ages, as vicious as they, what were the riches of His grace? The verb *ἐνδείξηται*, which in the New Testament is always used in the middle voice, means to show for oneself—for His own glory. Jelf, § 363, 1. Still, the language of the verse suggests the idea of sample or specimen. Paul, who classes himself with the Ephesians in the *ἡμᾶς*, makes this use of his own conversion. 1 Tim. i. 16. The peculiar plural phrase *αἰῶνες*, with the participle *ἐπερχόμενοι*, denotes " coming or impending ages." Luke xxi. 26, 37; Jas. v. 1. The *αἰών* is an age or period of time, and these *αἰῶνες* form a series of such ages, which were to commence immediately. These ages began at the period of the apostle's writing, and are still rolling on till the second advent. The salvation of such men as these Ephesians at that early period of Christianity, was intended by God to stand out as a choice monument to succeeding generations of " the exceeding riches of His grace "—

*τὸ ὑπερβάλλον πλοῦτος τῆς χάριτος αὐτοῦ*. The neuter form is preferred by Tischendorf and Lachmann on the authority of A, B, D¹, F, G. Gersdorf, *Beiträge*, p. 282; Winer, § 9, 2, note 2. The participle *ὑπερβάλλον* has been already explained i. 19. The conversion of the Ephesians was a manifestation of the grace of God—of its riches, of its overflowing riches. That was not restricted grace—grace to a few, or grace to the more deserving, or grace to the milder forms of apostasy. No; it has proved its wealth in the salvation of such sinners as are delineated in the melancholy picture of the preceding verses. Nay, it is couched—

ἐν χρηστότητι ἐφ' ἡμᾶς ἐν Χριστῷ 'Ιησοῦ—"in kindness toward us in Christ Jesus." Four terms are already employed by the apostle to exhibit the source of salvation—ἔλεος, ἀγάπη, χάρις, χρηστότης—conveying the same blessed truth in different aspects. The first respects our misery; the second defines the co-essential form of this—ἔλεος; the third characterizes its free outgoing, and the last points to its palpable and experienced embodiment. Trench, *Syn.* p. 192. Winer suggests that ἐφ' ἡμᾶς is connected with ὑπερβάλλον, § 20, 2, *b*. But the structure of the sentence forbids altogether such a connection, and the construction proposed by Homberg and Koppe is as violent—τῆς χάριτος καὶ χρηστότητος, supplying ὄντας also to the phrase ἐν Χριστῷ 'Ιησοῦ. The noun χρηστότης may be followed itself by ἐπί, as in Rom. xi. 22, or as when the adjective occurs, Luke vi. 35. We do not understand, with Olshausen, that ἐν χρηστότητι is a closer definition of the more general χάρις. Nor is there any need of a metonymy, and of taking the term to denote a benefit or the result of a kindness. This kindness is true generosity, for it contains saving grace. It is not common providential kindness, but special "kindness in Christ Jesus," no article being inserted to show the closeness of the connection, and the preposition ἐν again, as so often before, marking Christ Jesus as the only sphere of blessing. See under i. 16. There is an evident alliteration in χάρις, χρηστότης, Χριστός. The kindness of God in Christ Jesus is a phrase expressive of the *manner* in which grace operates. His grace is *in* His goodness. Grace may be shown among men in a very ungracious way, but God's grace clothes itself in kindness, as well in the time as in the mode of its bestowment. What kindness in sending His grace so early to Ephesus, and in converting such men as now formed its church! O, He is so kind in giving grace, and such grace, to so many men, and of such spiritual demerit and degradation; so kind as not only to forgive sin, but even to forget it (Heb. viii. 12); so kind, in short, as not only by His grace to quicken us, but in the riches of His grace to raise us up, and in its exceeding riches to enthrone us in the heavenly places in Christ! And all the grace in this kindness shown in the first century is a lesson even to the nineteenth century. What God did then, He can do now and will do now; and one reason why He did it then was, to teach the men of the present age His ability and desire to repeat in them the same blessed process of salvation and life.

(Ver. 8.) Τῇ γὰρ χάριτί ἐστε σεσωσμένοι διὰ τῆς πίστεως— "For by grace ye have been saved, through your faith." The particle γάρ explains why the apostle has said that the exceeding riches of God's grace are shown forth in man's salvation, and glances back to the interjectional clause at the end of ver. 5. Salvation must display grace, for it is wholly of grace. The dative χάριτι, on which from its position the emphasis lies, expresses the source of our salvation, and the genitive πίστεως with διά denotes its subjective means or instrument. Salvation is of grace by faith—the one being the efficient, the other the modal cause; the former the origin, the latter the method, of its operation. The grace of God which exists without us, takes its place as an active principle within us, being introduced into the heart and kept there by the connecting or conducting instrumentality of faith.

χάρις—"favour," is opposed to necessity on the part of God, and to merit on the part of man. God was under no obligation to save man, for His law might have taken its natural course, and the penalty menaced and deserved might have been fully inflicted. Grace springs from His sovereign will, not from His essential nature. It is not an attribute which must always manifest itself, but a prerogative that may either be exercised or held in abeyance. Salvation is an abnormal process, and "grace is no more grace" if it is of necessary exhibition. Grace is also opposed to merit on man's part. Had he any title, salvation would be "of debt." The two following verses are meant to state and prove that salvation is not and cannot be of human merit. In short, the human race had no plea with God, but God's justice had a high and holy claim on them. The conditions of the first economy had been violated, and the guilty transgressor had only to anticipate the infliction of the penalty which he had so wantonly incurred. The failure of the first covenant did not either naturally or necessarily lead to a new experiment. While man had no right to expect, God was under no necessity to provide salvation. It is "by grace."[1]

But this grace does not operate immediately and universally. Its medium is faith — διὰ τῆς πίστεως. The two nouns "grace" and "faith" have each the article, as they express ideas which are at once familiar, distinctive, and monadic in their nature; the article before χάριτι, referring us at the same time to the anarthrous term at the close of the fifth verse, and that before πίστεως, giving it a subjective reference, is best rendered, as Alford says, by a possessive. Lachmann, after B, D¹, F, G, omits the second article, but the majority of MSS. are in its favour. It is the uniform doctrine of the New Testament, that no man is saved against his will; and his desire to be saved is proved by his belief of the Divine testimony. Salvation by grace is not arbitrarily attached to faith by the mere sovereign dictate of the Most High, for man's willing acceptance of salvation is essential to his possession of it, and the operation of faith is just the sinner's appreciation of the Divine mercy, and his acquiescence in the goodness and wisdom of the plan of recovery, followed by a cordial appropriation of its needed and adapted blessings, or, as Augustine tersely and quaintly phrases it— *Qui creavit te sine te, non salvabit te sine te.* Justification by faith alone, is simply pardon enjoyed on the one condition of taking it.

And thus "ye have been saved;" not—ye will be finally saved; not—ye are brought into a state in which salvation is possible, or put into a condition in which you might "work and win" for yourselves, but—ye are actually saved. The words denote a present state, and not merely "an established process." Green's *Gram. of New Test.* 317. Thus Tyndale translates—"By grace ye are made safe thorowe faith." The

---

[1] This generic meaning of the word is the true one here, and it is not to be regarded specially and technically as in the scholastic theology, and divided into *gratia præveniens, operans, co-operans;* the first having for its object *homo convertendus;* the second, *homo, qui convertitur;* and the third, *homo conversus sed sanctificandus.*

context shows the truth of this interpretation, and that the verb denotes a terminated action. If men have been spiritually dead, and if they now enjoy spiritual life, then surely they are saved. So soon as a man is out of danger, he is safe or "saved." Salvation is a present blessing, though it may not be fully realized. The man who has escaped from the wreck, and has been taken into the lifeboat, is from that moment a saved man. Even though he scarce feel his safety or be relieved from his tremor, he is still a saved man; yea, though the angry winds may howl around him, and though hours may elapse ere he set his feet on the firm land. The apostle adds more precisely and fully—

καὶ τοῦτο οὐκ ἐξ ὑμῶν—" and that not of yourselves "—ἐκ, as it often does, referring to source or cause. Winer, § 47, b. The pronoun τοῦτο does not grammatically agree with πίστεως, the nearest preceding noun, and this discrepancy has originated various interpretations. The words καὶ τοῦτο are rendered "and indeed" by Wahl, Rückert, and Matthies. This emphatic sense belongs to the word in certain connections. Rom. xiii. 11; 1 Cor. vi. 6; Phil. i. 28. The plural is also similarly used. 1 Cor. vi. 8; Heb. xi. 12; Matthiae, § 470, 6. The meaning of the idiom may here be—"Ay, and this" is not of yourselves. But what is the point of reference?

Many refer it directly to πίστις—"And this faith is not of yourselves." Such is the interpretation of the fathers Chrysostom, Theodoret, and Jerome. Chrysostom says—οὐδὲ ἡ πίστις ἐξ ἡμῶν, εἰ γὰρ οὐκ ἦλθεν, εἰ γὰρ μὴ ἐκάλεσε, πῶς ἠδυνάμεθα πιστεῦσαι. Jerome thus explains—*Et hæc ipsa fides non est ex vobis, sed ex eo qui vocavit vos.* The same view is taken by Erasmus, Beza, Crocius, Cocceius, Grotius, Estius, Bengel, Meier, Baumgarten-Crusius, Bisping, and Hodge. Bloomfield says that "all the Calvinistic commentators hold this view," and yet Calvin himself was an exception. There are several objections to this, not as a point of doctrine, but of exegesis. 1. If the apostle meant to refer to faith—πίστις, why change the gender? why not write καὶ αὕτη? To say, with some, that faith is viewed in the abstract as τὸ πιστεύειν, does not, as we shall see, relieve us of the difficulty. 2. Granting that καὶ τοῦτο is an idiomatic expression, and that its gender is not to be strictly taken into account, still

the question recurs, What is the precise reference of δῶρον?
3. Again, πίστις does not seem to be the immediate reference, as the following verse indicates. You may say—" And this faith is not of yourselves: it is God's gift;" but you cannot say—" And this faith is not of yourselves, but it is God's gift; not of works, lest any man should boast." You would thus be obliged, without any cause, to change the reference in ver. 9, for you may declare that salvation is not of works, but cannot with propriety say that faith is not of works. The phrase οὐκ ἐξ ἔργων must have salvation, and not faith, as its reference. The words from καὶ τοῦτο to the end of the verse may be read parenthetically—" By grace are ye saved, through faith (and that not of yourselves: it is the gift of God), not of works;" that is, " By grace ye are saved, through faith," " not of works." Even with this understanding of the paragraph, the difficulty still remains, and the idea of such a parenthesis cannot be well entertained, for the ἐξ ὑμῶν corresponds to the ἐξ ἔργων. Baumgarten-Crusius argues that the allusion is to πίστις, because the word δῶρον proves that the reference must be to something internal—auf Innerliches. But is not salvation as internal as faith? So that we adopt the opinion of Calvin, Zachariae, Rückert, Harless, Matthies, Meyer, Scholz, de Wette, Stier, Alford, and Ellicott, who make καὶ τοῦτο refer to ἐστε σεσωσμένοι—" and this state of safety is not of yourselves." This exegesis is presented in a modified form by Theophylact, Zanchius, Holzhausen, Chandler, and Macknight, who refer καὶ τοῦτο to the entire clause— " this salvation by faith is not of yourselves." Theophylact says—οὐ τὴν πίστιν λέγει δῶρον Θεοῦ, ἀλλὰ τὸ διὰ πίστεως σωθῆναι, τοῦτο δῶρον ἐστι Θεοῦ. But some of the difficulties of the first method of interpretation attach to this. The καὶ τοῦτο refers to the idea contained in the verb, and presents that idea in an abstract form. At the same time, as Ellicott shrewdly remarks, " the clause καὶ τοῦτο, etc., was suggested by the mention of the subjective medium—πίστις, which might be thought to imply some independent action on the part of the subject." This condition of safety is not of yourselves—is not of your own origination or procurement, though it be of your reception. It did not spring from you, nor did you suggest it to God; but—

Θεοῦ τὸ δῶρον—" God's is the gift." God's gift is the gift —the genitive Θεοῦ being the emphatic predicate in opposition to ὑμῶν. Bernhardy, p. 315. Lachmann and Harless place this clause in a parenthesis. The only objection against the general view of the passage which we have taken is, that it is somewhat tautological. The apostle says—" By grace ye are saved," and then—" It is the gift of God;" the same idea being virtually repeated. True so far, but the insertion of the contrasted οὐκ ἐξ ὑμῶν suggested the repetition. And there is really no tautology. In chap. iii. 7 occur the words—κατὰ τὴν δωρεὰν τῆς χάριτος τοῦ Θεοῦ; χάρις being the thing given, and δωρεάν pointing out its mode of bestowment. Men are saved by grace—τῇ χάριτι; and that salvation which has its origin in grace is not won from God, nor is it wrung from Him; "His is the gift." Look at salvation in its origin—it is "by grace." Look at it in its reception—it is "through faith." Look at it in its manner of conferment—it is a "gift." For faith, though an indispensable instrument, does not merit salvation as a reward; and grace operating only through faith, does not suit itself to congruous worth, nor single it out as its sole recipient. Salvation, in its broadest sense, is God's gift. While, then, καὶ τοῦτο seems to refer to the idea contained in the participle only, it would seem that in Θεοῦ τὸ δῶρον there is allusion to the entire clause—God's is the whole gift. The complex idea of the verse is compressed into this brief ejaculation. The three clauses, as Meyer has remarked, form a species of asyndeton—that is, the connecting particles are omitted, and the style acquires greater liveliness and force. Dissen, *Exc.* ii. *ad Pind.* p. 273; Stallbaum, *Plato—Crit.* p. 144.

Griesbach places in a parenthesis the entire clause from καὶ τοῦτο to ἐξ ἔργων, connecting the words ἵνα μή τις καυχήσηται with διὰ τῆς πίστεως, but the words οὐκ ἐξ ἔργων have an immediate connection with the ἵνα—a connection which cannot be set aside. Matthies again joins οὐκ ἐξ ἔργων to the foregoing clause—" and that not of yourselves; the gift of God is not of works." Such an arrangement is artificial and inexact. The apostle now presents the truth in a negative contrast—

(Ver. 9.) Οὐκ ἐξ ἔργων—" Not of works "—the explanation

of οὐκ ἐξ ὑμῶν. The apostle uses διά with the article before πιστεως in the previous verse, but here ἐξ without the article before ἔργων—the former referring to the subjective instrument, or *causa apprehendens*; the latter to the source, and excluding works of every kind and character. 'Εκ again refers to source or cause. Schweighaüser, *Lex. Herodot.* p. 192. Salvation is by grace, and therefore not of us; it is through faith, and therefore not of works; it is God's gift, and therefore not of man's origination. Such works belong not to fallen and condemned humanity. It has not, and by no possibility can it have any of them, for it has failed to render prescribed obedience; and though it should now or from this time be perfect in action, such conformity could only suffice for present acceptance. How, then, shall it atone for former delinquencies? The first duty of a sinner is faith, and what merit can there be where there is no confidence in God? "Without faith it is impossible to please Him." The theory that represents God as having for Christ's sake lowered the terms of His law so as to accept of sincere endeavours for perfect obedience, is surely inconsistent in its commixture of merit and grace. For if God dispense with the claims of His law now, why not for ever—if to one point, why not altogether —if to one class of creatures, why not to all? On such a theory, the moral bonds of the universe would be dissolved. The distinction made by Thomas Aquinas between *meritum ex congruo* and *meritum ex condigno*, was too subtle to be popularly apprehended, and it did not arrest the Pelagian tendencies of the mediaeval church.

ἵνα μή τις καυχήσηται—"lest any one should boast." According to the just view of Rückert, Harless, Meyer, and Stier, the conjunction marks design, or is telic; according to others, such as Koppe, Flatt, Holzhausen, Macknight, Chandler, and Bloomfield, it indicates result—"so as that no one may boast." So also Theophylact—τὸ γὰρ ἵνα, οὐκ αἰτιολογικόν ἐστι, ἀλλ' ἐκ τῆς ἀποβάσεως τοῦ πράγματος; that is, the ἵνα is not causal, but eventual in its meaning. Koppe suggests as an alternative to give the words an imperative sense—"Not of works: beware then of boasting." Stier proposes that the ἵνα be viewed from a human standpoint, and as indicative of the writer's own purpose; as if the apostle had said—"Not of works, I repeat it, lest any one should boast." This exegesis is certainly original, as its author has indeed mentioned; but it is as certainly unnatural and far-fetched. Macknight has argued that ἵνα cannot have its telic force, for it would represent God as appointing our salvation to be by faith, merely to prevent men's boasting, "which certainly is an end unworthy of God in so great an affair;" but this is not a full view of the matter, for the apostle does not characterize the prevention of boasting as God's only end, but as one of His purposes. For what would boasting imply? Would it not imply fancied merit, independence of God, and that self-deification which is the very essence of sin? A pure and perfect creature has nothing to boast of; for what has he that he has not received? "Now, if thou didst receive it, why dost thou glory, as if thou hadst not received it?" When God purposes to preclude boasting, or even the possibility of it, He resolves to effect His design in this one way, by filling the mind with such emotions as shall infallibly banish it. He furnishes the redeemed spirit with humility and gratitude—such humility as ever induces man to confess his emptiness, and such gratitude as ever impels him to ascribe every blessing to the one source of Divine generosity. We see no reason, therefore, to withhold from ἵνα its natural and primary sense, especially as in the mind and theology of the apostle, event is so often viewed in unison with its source, and result is traced to its original design, in the Divine idea and motive. And truly boasting is effectually stopped. For if man be guilty, and being unable to win a pardon, simply receive it; if, being dead, he get life only as a Divine endowment; if favour, and nothing but favour, have originated his safety, and the only possible act on his part be that of reception; if what he has be but a gift to him in his weak and meritless state—then surely nothing can be further from him than boasting, for he will glorify God for all. 1 Cor. i. 29–31. Ambrosiaster truly remarks—*hæc superbia omni peccato nocentior omni genere est elationis insanior*. And further, salvation cannot be of ourselves or of works—

(Ver. 10.) Αὐτοῦ γάρ ἐσμεν ποίημα—"For we are His workmanship." The γάρ has its common meaning. It renders the reason for the statement in the two previous verses.

It does not signifiy "yet," as Macknight has it. Others carelessly overlook it altogether. Nor can we accede to the opinion of Theophylact, Photius, and Bloomfield, that this verse is introduced to prevent misconception, as if the meaning were —"Salvation is not of works," yet do them we must, "for we are His workmanship." This notion does not tally with the simple reasoning of the apostle, and helps itself out by an unwarranted assumption. Rückert and Meier join this verse in thought to the last clause of the preceding one—" No man who works can boast, for the man himself is God's workmanship." But the apostle has affirmed that salvation is not of works, so that such works are not supposed to exist at all; and therefore there is no ground for boasting. Nor can we, with Harless, view the verse as connected simply with the phrase—Θεοῦ τὸ δῶρον. We regard it, with Meyer, as designed to prove and illustrate the great truth of the 9th verse, that salvation is not of works. "By grace ye are saved, through faith, and that not of yourselves—not of works, for we are His workmanship." Hooker, vol. ii. 601; Oxford, 1841.

But the terms may be first explained. The apostle changes from the second to the first person without any other apparent reason than the varied momentary impulse one yields to in writing a letter. The noun ποίημα, as the following clause shows, plainly refers to the spiritual re-formation of believers, and it is as plainly contrary to the course of thought to give it a physical reference, as did Gregory of Nazianzus, Tertullian, Basil, Photius, and Jerome. The same opinion, modified by including also the notion of spiritual creation, is followed by Pelagius, Erasmus, Bullinger, Rückert, and Matthies. The process of workmanship is next pointed out—

κτισθέντες ἐν Χριστῷ Ἰησοῦ—" created in Christ Jesus." This added phrase explains and bounds the meaning of ποίημα. The reference here is to the καινὴ κτίσις (2 Cor. v. 17; Gal. vi. 15), and the form of expression carries us back to many portions of the Hebrew prophets, and to the use of בָּרָא in Ps. li. 10, and in Ps. cii. 18 (Schoettgen, *Horæ Hebraicæ*, i. p. 328). See also verse 15 of this chapter. Chrysostom adds, with peculiar and appropriate emphasis—ἐκ τοῦ μὴ ὄντος, εἰς τὸ εἶναι παρήχθημεν. Again is it ἐν Χριστῷ Ἰησοῦ, for Christ Jesus is ever the sphere of creation, or, through their vital union with Him, men are formed anew, and the spiritual change that passes over them has its best emblem and most expressive name in the physical creation, when out of chaos sprang light, harmony, beauty, and life. The object of this spiritual creation in Christ is declared to be—

ἐπὶ ἔργοις ἀγαθοῖς—" in order to," or "for good works." This meaning of ἐπί may be seen in Gal. v. 13 ; 1 Thess. iv. 7. Winer, § 48, c; Kühner, § 612, 3, c; Phrynichus, ed. Lobeck, p. 474. Palairet, in his *Observat. Sac. in loc.*, has given several good examples of ἐπί with such a sense. Our entire renovation, while it is of God in its origin, and in Christ as its medium, has good works for its object.

Now, as already intimated, we understand this verse as a proof that salvation is not of works. For, 1. The statement that salvation is of works involves an anachronism. Works, in order to procure salvation, must precede it, but the good works described by the apostle come after it, for they only appear after a man is in Christ, believes and lives. 2. The statement that salvation is of works involves the fallacy of mistaking the effect for the cause. Good works are not the cause of salvation ; they are only the result of it. Salvation causes them; they do not cause it. This workmanship of God—this creation in Christ Jesus—is their true source, implying a previous salvation. Thus runs the well-known confessional formula—*Bona opera non præcedunt justificandum, sed sequuntur justificatum.* The law says—" Do this and live ; " but the gospel says—" Live and do this." 3. And even such good works can have in them no saving merit, for we are His workmanship. *Talia non nos efficimus,* says Bugenhagen, *sed Spiritus Dei in nobis ;* or, as Augustine puts it—*ipso in nobis et per nos operante, merita tua nusquam jactes, quia et ipsa tua merita Dei dona sunt.* Comment. in Ps. cxliv. The power and the desire to perform good works are alike from God, for they are only fruits and manifestations of Divine grace in man ; and as they are not self-produced, they cannot entitle us to reward. Such, we apprehend, is the apostle's argument. Salvation is not ἐξ ἔργων ; yet it is ἐπὶ ἔργοις ἀγαθοῖς—" in order to good works "—the fruits of salvation and acceptance with God, proofs of holy obedience, tokens of the possession of Christ's image, elements of the imitation of

Christ's example, and the indices of that holiness which adorns the new creation, and "without which no man can see the Lord." Peter Lombard says well—*Sola bona opera dicenda sunt, quæ fiunt per dilectionem Dei.* But there can be no productive love of God where there is no faith in His Son, and where that faith does exist, salvation is already possessed. The disputes on this point at the period of the Reformation were truly lamentable; Solifidians and Synergists battled with mischievous fury: Major arguing that salvation was dependent on good works, and Amsdorf reprobating them as prejudicial to it; while Agricola maintained the Antinomian absurdity, that the law itself was abolished, and no longer claimed obedience from believers. And these "good" works are no novelty nor accident—

οἷς προητοίμασεν ὁ Θεός, ἵνα ἐν αὐτοῖς περιπατήσωμεν— "which God before prepared that we should walk in them." The interpretation of this sentence depends upon the opinion formed as to the regimen of the pronoun οἷς.

1. Some, taking the word as a dative, render—"To which God hath afore ordained us, in order that we should walk in them." Such is the view of Luther, Semler, Zachariae, Morus, Flatt, Meier, Bretschneider, and virtually of Fritzsche,[1] Alt,[2] and Wahl. But the omission of the pronoun ἡμᾶς is fatal to this opinion. The idea, too, which in such a connection is here expressed by a dative, is usually expressed by the accusative with εἰς. Rom. ix. 23; 2 Tim. ii. 21; Rev. ix. 7.

2. Valla, Erasmus, Er. Schmidt, and Rückert give οἷς a personal reference, as if it stood for ὅσοις ἡμῶν—"among whom God before prepared us."—But the antecedent ἡμεῖς is too remote, and the οἷς appears to agree in gender with ἐν αὐτοῖς.

3. Bengel, Koppe, Rosenmüller, and Baumgarten-Crusius take the phrase as a kind of Hebraism, or as a special idiom, in which, along with the relative pronoun, there is also repeated the personal pronoun and the preposition—אֲשֶׁר בָּם—ἐν οἷς ἵνα περιπατήσωμεν ἐν αὐτοῖς, προητοίμασεν ὁ Θεός. But this exegesis is about as intricate as the original clause.

4. The large body of interpreters take the οἷς for ἅ by attraction. Winer, § 24, 1. This opinion is simple, the

[1] *Comment.* in Matt. iii. 12.   [2] *Gram. Ling. Græc. N. T.* p. 229.

change of case by attraction is common, and a similar use of ἵνα is found in John v. 36. So the Vulgate—*Quæ præparavit.*

5. Acting upon a hint of Bengel's, Stier suggests that the verb may be taken in a neuter or intransitive sense, as the simple verb thus occurs in 2 Chron. i. 4, and in Luke ix. 52. Could this exegesis be fully justified, we should be inclined to adopt it—" For which God has made previous preparation, that we should walk in them." The fourth opinion supposes the preparation to belong to the works also, but in a more direct form—the works being prepared for our performance of them. In this last view, the preparation refers more to the persons—preparation to enable them to walk in the works. The fourth interpretation is the best grammatically, and the meaning of the phrase, "which God has before prepared," seems to be—"in order that we should walk in those works," they have been prescribed, defined, and adapted to us.

It is wrong to ignore the προ in προητοίμασεν, as is done by Flatt and Baumgarten-Crusius. Wisdom ix. 8 ; Philo, *De Opif.* § 25. Nor can we, with Augustine, de Wette, and Harless, give the verb the same meaning as προορίζειν, or assign it, with Koppe and Rosenmüller, the sense of *velle*, or *jubere;* Harless saying that it is used of things as the verb last referred to is used of persons, but without sufficient proof ; and Olshausen supposing that the two verbs differ thus—that προετοιμάζειν refers to a working of the Divine eternal will which is occupied more with details. Perhaps the difference is more accurately brought out in this way :—προορίζειν marks appointment or destination, in which the end is primarily kept in view, while in προετοιμάζειν the means by which the end is secured are specially regarded as of Divine arrangement, the προ referring to a period anterior to that implied in κτισθέντες. We could not walk in these works unless they had been prepared for us. And, therefore, by prearranging the works in their sphere, character, and suitability, and also by preordaining the law which commands, the inducement or appliances which impel, and the creation in Christ which qualifies and empowers us, God hath shown it to be His purpose that " we should walk in them." Tersely does Bengel say, *ambularemus, non salvaremur aut viveremus.* These good works, though they do not secure salvation, are by God's eternal purpose essentially connected with it, and are not a mere offshoot accidentally united to it. Nor are they only joined to it correctionally, as if to counteract the abuses of the doctrine that it is not of works. The figure in the verb περιπατήσωμεν is a Hebraism occurring also in ver. 2. See under it. Tit. ii. 14, iii. 8. Though in such works there be no merit, yet faith shows its genuineness by them. In direct antagonism to the Pauline theology is the strange remark of Whitby—" that these works of righteousness God hath prepared us to walk in, are conditions requisite to make faith saving." The same view in substance has been elaborately maintained by Bishop Bull in his *Harmonia Apostolica*. Works, vol. iii. ed. Oxford, 1827. Nor is the expression less unphilosophical. Works cannot impart any element to faith, as they are not of the same nature with it. The saving power of faith consists in its acceptance and continued possession of God's salvation. Works only prove that the faith we have is a saving faith. And while Christians are to abound in works, such works are merely demonstrative, not in any sense supplemental in their nature. Καὶ ἐκτίσθης οὐκ ἵνα ἀργῆς, ἀλλ' ἵνα ἐργαζῃ (Theophylact). But the Council of Trent—*Sess.* vi. cap. 16—declares "that the Lord's goodness to all men is so great that He will have the things which are His own gifts to be their merits"—*ut eorum velit esse merita quæ sunt ipsius dona*. See Hare, *Mission of the Comforter*, i. 359.

(Ver. 11.) The second part of the epistle now commences, in a strain of animated address to the Gentile portion of the church of Christ in Ephesus, bidding them remember what they had been, and realize what by the mediation of Christ they had now become—

Διὸ μνημονεύετε—" Wherefore remember." The reference has a further aspect than to the preceding verse—διό commencing the paragraph, as in Rom. ii. 1, and in this epistle, iii. 13, iv. 25; though in some other places it winds up a paragraph, as in 2 Cor. xii. 10; Gal. iv. 31. These things being so, and such being the blessings now enjoyed by them, lest any feeling of self-satisfaction should spring up within them, they were not to forget their previous state and character. This exercise of memory would deepen their humility, elevate their ideas of Divine grace, and incite them to ardent and continued thankfulness. The apostle honestly refers them to their previous Gentilism. Remember—

ὅτι ποτὲ ὑμεῖς τὰ ἔθνη ἐν σαρκὶ—"that ye, once Gentiles in the flesh." Ὄντες is understood by some, and ἦτε by others; but of such a supplement there is no absolute need—the construction being repeated emphatically afterwards. The article τά before ἔθνη signifies a class, and it is omitted before ἐν σαρκί to indicate the closeness of idea. Ἔθνη—גוים—has a special meaning attached to it. Not only were they foreigners, but they were ignorant and irreligious. Matt. xviii. 17. If ἔθνη simply signified non-Israelites, then they were so still, for Christianity does not obliterate difference of race; but the word denotes men without religious privilege, and in this sense they were ποτέ—once—heathen. But their ethnical state no longer existed. Some render ἐν σαρκί—"by natural descent," as Bucer, Grotius, Estius, Stolz, and Kistmacher. This meaning is a good one, but the last clause of the verse points to a more distinct contrast. Ambrosiaster, Zanchius, Crocius, Wolf, and Holzhausen take the term in its theological sense, as if it signified corrupted nature; but κατὰ σάρκα would have been in that case the more appropriate idiom. Jerome supposes the phrase to stand in opposition to an implied ἐν πνεύματι. But the verse itself decides the meaning, as Drusius, Calvin, Beza, Rollock, Bengel, Rückert, Harless, Olshausen, Meyer, de Wette, and Stier rightly suppose. Natural Israel was so—ἐν σαρκί; the Gentiles were also so—ἐν σαρκί. Col. ii. 13. Both phrases have, therefore, the same meaning, and denote neither physical descent nor corrupted nature, but simply and literally "*in flesh.*" The absence of the "seal" in their flesh proved them to be Gentiles, as the presence of it showed the Jews to be the seed of Abraham. If ἐν σαρκί denoted natural descent, then the fact of it could not be changed. Heathens, and born so, they must be so still, but they had ceased to be heathen on their introduction into the kingdom of God. The world beyond them, whose flesh had been unmarked, was on that account looked down upon by the Jews, and characterized as τὰ ἔθνη. The apostle now explains his meaning more fully—

οἱ λεγόμενοι Ἀκροβυστία—"who are called the Uncircumcision." The noun ἀκροβυστία is, according to Fritzsche (on Rom. ii. 26), an Alexandrian corruption for ἀκροποσθία. This term has all the force of a proper name, and no article precedes it. Middleton, *Greek Art.* p. 43. It was, on the part of the Jews, the collective designation of the heathen world, and it sigmatized it as beyond the pale of religious privilege. Gen. xxxiv. 14; Lev. xix. 23; Judg. xiv. 3; 1 Sam. xiv. 6; Isa. lii. 1; Ezek. xxviii. 10. And the Gentiles were so named—עָרֵל—

ὑπὸ τῆς λεγομένης Περιτομῆς—"by the so-called Circumcision"—this last also a collective epithet. This was the national distinction on which the Jews flattered themselves. Other Abrahamic tribes, indeed, were circumcised, but the special promise was—"In Isaac shall thy seed be called." The next words—ἐν σαρκὶ χειροποιήτου—"hand-made in the flesh," as a tertiary predicate, do not belong to λεγομένης. "In the flesh made by hands" was no portion of their boasted name, but the phrase is added by the apostle, and the Syriac rightly renders it—ܘܐܝܬܝܗ̇ ܥܒܕ ܐܝܕܝ̈ܐ ܒܒܣܪ—"and it is a work of the hands in the flesh." He cannot, as Harless and Olshausen remark, be supposed to undervalue the right of circumcision, for it was *signum sanctitatis.* Indeed, his object in the next verses is to show, that the deplorable condition of the Gentiles was owing to their want of such blessings as were enjoyed by the chosen seed. Still, the apostle, by the words now referred to, seems to intimate that in itself the rite is nothing—that it is only a symbol of purity, a mere chirurgical process, which did not and could not secure for them eternal life. Rom. ii. 28, 29; Gal. v. 6; Philip. iii. 3; Col. ii. 11, iii. 11. The word is used in a good sense in Acts x. 45, xi. 2; Rom. xv. 8; Gal. ii. 7, 8, 9; Col. iv. 11; Tit. i. 10. The apostle alludes mentally to the "true circumcision" made without hands, which is not "outward in the flesh," and which alone is of genuine and permanent value. Remember—

(Ver. 12.) *Ὅτι ἦτε τῷ καιρῷ ἐκείνῳ χωρὶς Χριστοῦ*—"That at that same time ye were without Christ." The preposition ἐν is of doubtful authority, and is rejected by Lachmann and Tischendorf. Kühner, § 569; Winer, § 31, 9, *b.* External authority, such as that of A, B, D[1], F, G, is against it, though the Pauline usage, as found in Rom. iii. 26, xi. 5, 1 Cor. xi. 23, 2 Cor. viii. 13, etc., seems to be in its favour. The reference in the phrase—"at that time," is to the period of previous Gentilism. The conjunction ὅτι resumes the thought with which the preceding verse started, and τῷ καιρῷ points back to ποτέ. The verb ἦτε, as de Wette suggests, and as Lachmann points, may be connected with the participle ἀπηλλοτριωμένοι—" that at that time, being without Christ, ye were excluded from theocratic privileges." Ellicott and Alford call this construction harsh, and make ἐν Χριστῷ a predicate. We will not contend for the construction, but we do not see such harshness in it. In this syntactic arrangement, χωρὶς Χριστοῦ would give the reason why they were aliens from the Hebrew commonwealth. Χωρὶς Χριστοῦ corresponds to ἐν Χριστῷ Ἰησοῦ in ver. 13.[1] But in what sense was the Gentile world without Christ? According to Anselm, Calovius, Flatt, and Baumgarten-Crusius, the phrase means—"without the knowledge of Christ." Olshausen, Matthies, and Rückert connect with the words the idea of the actual manifestation and energy of the Son of God, who dwelt among the ancient people prior to His incarnation. Koppe, Meyer, and Meier give this thought prominence in their interpretation—" without any connection with Christ,"—an exegesis, in an enlarged form, adopted by Stier. De Wette rightly gives it—"without the promise of Christ," and in this he has followed Calvin, Bucer, Bullinger, and Grotius. Harless takes it as a phrase concentrating in its two words the fuller exposition of itself given in the remaining clauses of the verse. Now it is to be borne in mind, that the apostle's object is to describe the wretched state of Gentilism, especially in contrast with Hebrew theocratic privilege. The Jewish nation had Christ in some sense in which the Gentiles had Him not. It

---

[1] According to Tittmann (*De Synon.* p. 94), ἄνευ Χριστοῦ would be only—Christ was not with you; but χωρὶς Χριστοῦ is—ye were far from Christ, χωρίς referring to the subject as separate from the object. Not to contradict this refinement, we might add that ἄνευ, allied to *in, un, ohne*, might, in a general sense, signify privation; but χωρίς marks that privation as caused by separation. The Gentiles are viewed as being not merely without Him, but far away from Him. Their relation to Him is marked by a great interval—χωρίς. But, as Ellicott says, "this distinction must be applied with caution, when it is remembered that χωρίς is used forty times in the New Testament, and ἄνευ only three times."

had the Messiah—not Jesus indeed—but the Christ in promise. He was the great subject—the one glowing, pervading promise of their inspired oracles. But the Gentiles were "without Christ." No such hopes or promises were made known to them. No such predictions were given to them, so that they were in contrast to the chosen seed—"without Christ." The rites, blessings, commonwealth, and covenants of old Israel had their origin in this promise of Messiah. On the other hand, the Gentiles being without Messiah, were of necessity destitute of such theocratic blessings and institutions. Such seems to be the contrast intended by the apostle. In this verse he says—χωρὶς Χριστοῦ, as Χριστός was the official designation embalmed in promise; but he says in ver. 13— ἐν Χριστῷ 'Ιησοῦ, for the Messiah had appeared and had actually become Jesus.

ἀπηλλοτριωμένοι τῆς πολιτείας τοῦ 'Ισραήλ—" being aliens from the commonwealth of Israel." The first thing to be examined is, what is meant by the πολιτεία τοῦ 'Ισραήλ. The *conversatio* (referring, it may be, to citizen-life) of the Vulgate, Jerome, Theophylact, Vatablus, and Estius, is not to be thought of. As Israel was the theocratic appellation of the people, the πολιτεία is so far defined in its meaning. It does not signify mere political right, as Grotius and Rosenmüller secularize it; nor does it denote citizenship, or the right of citizenship, as Luther, Erasmus, Bullinger, Beza, and Michaelis understand it. Though Aristotle defines the word—τῶν τὴν πόλιν οἰκούντων τάξις τις, yet it often denotes the state or commonwealth itself, especially when followed, as here, by a possessive or synonymous genitive containing the people's name. *Polit.* iii. 1; Xenophon, *Memorabilia*, ii. 1, 13; 2 Macc. iv. 11, viii. 17, etc. "The commonwealth of Israel" is that government framed by God, in which religion and polity were so conjoined, that piety and loyalty were synonymous, and to fear God and honour the king were the same obligation. The nation was, at the same time, the only church of God, and the archives of the country were also the records of its faith. Civil and sacred were not distinguished; municipal immunity was identical with religious privilege; and a spiritual meaning was attached to dress and diet, as well as to altar and temple. And this entire arrangement had its origin and its form in the grand national characteristic—the promise of Messiah. The Gentiles had not the Messiah, and therefore were not included in such a commonwealth. This negation is expressed by the strong term ἀπηλλοτριωμένοι. Eph. iv. 18; Col. i. 21; Ezek. xiv. 7; Hos. ix. 10; Homberg, *Parerga*, p. 291; Krebs, *Observat*. p. 326. The contrast is συμπολῖται in the 19th verse. The verb itself is used by Josephus to denote a sentence of expatriation or outlawry. *Antiq*. xi. 4. May not the term imply a previous condition or privilege, from which there has been subsequent exclusion? Harless and Stier, led by Bengel in his note on iv. 18, hold this view. Historically, this interpretation cannot be maintained indeed, as the Gentiles never were united with the actual theocracy. But if the term πολιτεία be used in an ideal sense, as Rückert thinks, meaning *eine wahrhaft göttliche Regierung*—"a true Divine government"—then the exegesis may be adopted. Olshausen finds this notion in the form of the word itself, for the heathen are not simply ἀλλότριοι but ἀπηλλοτριωμένοι—men who had been excluded from the Hebrew commonwealth. Chrysostom notices the word, and ascribes to it πολλὴ ἔμφασις. National distinction did not, indeed, exist in patriarchal times, but by the formation of the theocracy the other races of men were formally abalienated from Israel, and no doubt their own vices and idolatry justified their exclusion. And therefore they were destitute of religious privilege, knowledge of God, modes of accepted worship, enjoyment of Divine patronage and protection, oracle and prophet, priest and sacrifice. And still more awful—

καὶ ξένοι τῶν διαθηκῶν τῆς ἐπαγγελίας—"and strangers from the covenants of the promise"—covenants having the promise as their distinctive possession, and characterized by it. The collocation of the words forbids the exegesis of Anselm, Ambrosiaster, a-Lapide, Estius, Wetstein, and Granville Penn,[1] who join the two last terms to the following clause —"having no hope of the promise." The term διαθῆκαι is used in the plural, not to show that there were distinct covenants, but to indicate covenants often renewed with the chosen people—the Mosaic covenant being a re-ratification of the

[1] *Annotations to the Books of the New Covenant, in loc.*

Abrahamic. Rom. ix. 4. It is erroneous, then, either to say, with Elsner and Wolf, that the plural merely stands for the singular; or to affirm that the two tables of the law are referred to; or to suppose, with Harless and Olshausen, that the covenant made with the Jewish people by Moses is alone the point of allusion. The covenant founded with Abraham, their great progenitor, and repeated to his children and their offspring, was at length solemnly confirmed at Mount Sinai. That νομοθεσία succeeds διαθῆκαι in Rom. ix. 4, is no argument against the idea that there was a covenant in the Mosaic law. Stier restricts the covenants to those made with the fathers, and denies that the transactions at Mount Sinai were of the nature of a covenant. But the covenant was bound up in the Sinaitic code, and ratified by the blood of sacrifice, when Moses formally sprinkled "the book and all the people." The covenant was made with Abraham, Gen. xii. 3, xxii. 18; with Isaac, Gen. xxvi. 3; with Jacob, Gen. xxviii. 13; with the people, Ex. xxiv. 8; and with David, 2 Sam. vii. 12. See also Jer. xxxi. 31-34; Mal. iii. 1; Rom. xi. 27. The use of the plural was common. Sirach xliv. 11; Wisd. xviii. 22; 2 Macc. viii. 15. And when we look to this covenant in its numerous repetitions, we are at no loss to understand what is meant by "the promise"—the article being prefixed. The central promise here marked out by the article was the Messiah, and blessing by Him. That promise gave to these covenants all their beauty, appropriateness, and power. "Covenants of the promise" are therefore covenants containing that signal and specific announcement of an incarnate and triumphant Redeemer. To such covenants the heathen were strangers—ξένοι. This adjective is followed by a genitive, not as one of quality, but as one of negative possession. Bernhardy, p. 171. Or see Matthiae, § 337; Scheuerlein, § 18, 3, α. Thus Sophocles, Œdip. Tyr. 219— ξένος τοῦ λόγου. This second clause represents the effect of the condition noted in the former clause—not only gives a more special view of it, as Harless too restrictedly says, but it also depicts the result. Being aliens from the theocracy, they were, *eo ipso*, strangers to its glorious covenants and their unique promise. The various readings in the MSS. are futile efforts to solve apparent difficulties. Another feature was—

ἐλπίδα μὴ ἔχοντες—"not having hope." The subjective negative particle μή, so often employed with a participle, shows the dependence of this clause on those preceding it. Winer, § 55, 5;[1] Kühner, § 715; Hartung, vol. ii. pp. 105-130; Gayler. It is an erroneous and excessive restriction to confine this hope to that of the resurrection, as is done by Theophylact, from a slight resemblance to 1 Thess. iv. 13. Neither can we limit it to eternal blessing, with Bullinger, Grotius, and Meier; nor to promised good, with Estius; nor to the redemption, with Harless. Ἐλπίς, having the emphasis from its position and without the article, has the wide and usual significance which belongs to it in the Pauline epistles. Thus Wycliffe—"not having hope of biheest." The Ephesians had no hope of any blessing which cheers and comforts, no hope of any good either to satisfy them here, or to yield them eternal happiness. They had hope of nothing a sinner should hope for, of nothing a fallen and guilty spirit writhes to get a glimpse of, of nothing which the "Israel of God" so confidently expected. Their future was a night without a star.

καὶ ἄθεοι—" and without God"—not "atheists" in the modern sense of the term, for they held some belief in a superior power; nor yet antitheists, for many were "feeling after the Lord," and their religion, even in its polytheism, was proof of an instinctive devotion. The word is indeed used of such as denied the gods of the state, by Cicero and by Plato —*De Nat. Deor.* i. 23; *Opera*, vol. ii. p. 311, ed. Bekker, Lond.; but it is also employed by the Greek tragedians as an epithet of impious, or, as we might say, "godless" men. It occurs also in the sense "without God's help," as in Sophocles, *Œdipus Tyrannus*, 661:

> Ἐπεὶ ἄθεος ἄφιλος ὅ, τι πύματον
> Ὀλοίμαν . . .
> "Since I wish to die godless, friendless," etc.

Perhaps the apostle uses the term in this last sense—not so much without belief in God, as without any help from Him. Though the apostle has proved the grovelling absurdity of polytheism and idolatry, and that the Gentiles sacrificed to demons and not to God, he never brands such blind worshippers as

[1] Moulton, p. 606.

atheists. Acts xvii. 23; Rom. i. 20–25; 1 Cor. x. 20. Theodoret understands by the phrase ἔρημοι θεογνωσίας—" devoid of the knowledge of God;" and the apostle himself uses the phrase οὐκ εἰδότες Θεόν, Gal. iv. 8. Compare 1 Thess. iv. 5; 2 John 9. The Gentile world were without God to counsel, befriend, guide, bless, and save them. In this sense they were godless, having no one to cry to, to trust in, to love, praise, and serve; whereas Jehovah, in His glory, unity, spirituality, condescension, wisdom, power, and grace, was ever present to the thinking mind and the pious heart in the Israelitish theocracy, and the idea of God combined itself with daily duty as well as with solemn and Sabbatic service.

ἐν τῷ κόσμῳ—" in the world." The connection of this clause has been variously understood. Koppe refers it to the entire verse; and the view of Calovius is similar. Such an interpretation is a mere nihility, and utters no additional idea. Storr (*Opuscula Academica*, iii. p. 304) paraphrases —*In his terris versabamini;* and Flatt renders—"Ye were occupied with earthly things, and had mere earthly hopes." Œcumenius, Matthies, and Meier understand the clause—of an ungodly life. Olshausen and Stier explain—" in this wicked world in which we have so pressing need of a sure hope, and of a firm hold on the living God." Rückert wanders far away in his ingenuity—" In the world, of which the earth is a part, and which is under God's government, ye lived without God, separated from God." Bloomfield takes the phrase as an aggravation of their offence—" to live in a world made by God, and yet not to know Him." But we are inclined to take ἐν τῷ κόσμῳ as a separate epithet, and we would· not regard it simply as—*inter cæteros homines pravos.* According to Stier and Passavant, these terms crown the description with the blackness of darkness—"the sin of sins, death in death," and they regard it as in apposition with ἐν σαρκί. Schutze intensifies it by his translation—*in perditorum hominum sentinâ.* With Harless and Calovius, we regard ἐν τῷ κόσμῳ as standing in contrast to the πολιτεία. The κόσμος is the entire region beyond the πολιτεία, and, as such, is dark, hostile, and under Satan's dominion, and, as the next verse mentions, it is "far off." The phrase then may not qualify the clause immediately before it, but refer to the whole description, and mark out the sad position of ancient Heathendom, ii. 2. And all their misery sprang from their being "without Christ." Being Christless, they are described in regular gradation as being churchless, hopeless, godless, and homeless.

(Ver. 13.) Νυνὶ δὲ, ἐν Χριστῷ 'Ιησοῦ—" But now, in Christ Jesus." The apostle now reverses the picture, and exhibits a fresh and glowing contrast. Νυνί is in contrast to ἐν τῷ καιρῷ ἐκείνῳ. The present stands in opposition to the past—δέ. 'Εν Χριστῷ 'Ιησοῦ is also the joyous contrast to the previous dark and melancholy χωρὶς Χριστοῦ. Once apart from Messiah, from the very idea and hope of Him, they were now in Him—in Him, not only as Messiah, but as Messiah embodied in the *actual Jesus* of Nazareth. And the phrase stands to this entire verse as χωρὶς Χριστοῦ does to the verse in which it occurs. It states adverbially the prime ground or reason of the subsequent declaration. But "now in Christ Jesus," that is, ye being in Christ Jesus; though there is no reason to espouse the opinion of Luther, Calvin, Harless, and Stier, and supply ὄντες to supplement the construction. We understand the apostle thus: But now—through your union to Christ Jesus—

ὑμεῖς οἵ ποτε ὄντες μακρὰν, ἐγγὺς ἐγενήθητε—" ye, who sometime were far off, became nigh." Lachmann reads—ἐγενήθητε ἐγγύς, but without sufficient authority. The adverbs, μακράν and ἐγγύς, had a literal and geographical meaning under the old dispensation. Isa. lvii. 19; Dan. ix. 7; Acts ii. 39. The presence of Jehovah was enjoyed in His temple, and that temple was in the heart of Judæa, but the extra-Palestinian nations were "far off" from it, and this actual measurement of space naturally became the symbol of moral distance.[1] Israel was near, but non-Israel was remote, and would have remained so but for Jesus. His advent and death changed the scene, and destroyed the wide interval, as the apostle shows in the subsequent verses. They who had been

---

[1] Wetstein (*in loco*) and Schoettgen (p. 761) have illustrated by a variety of examples the modes of Jewish speech on this subject. The Jewish religionists speak of themselves as *near*, and of the heathen as *remote*, and when a man was made a proselyte he was said "to be brought near;" thus, *propinquum facere* equivalent to *proselytum facere*.

"aliens from the commonwealth of Israel," were now incorporated into the spiritual community, were partakers of " a better covenant established on better promises," were filled with " good hope through grace," knew God, or rather " were known of God," and were no longer " in the world," but of the " household of God." The Gentile Christians enjoyed spiritually all that was characteristic of the Hebrew theocracy. As the " true circumcision," they were " near," spiritually as near as the Israelites whom a few steps brought to the temple, altar, and Shechinah. The apostle, having described the position of the Ephesian converts as being in Christ Jesus, next alludes to the means by which this nearness was secured, and the previous distance changed into blessed propinquity—

ἐν τῷ αἵματι τοῦ Χριστοῦ—" in the blood of Christ." Compare i. 7, where διά is employed with a difference of view. The proper name, more emphatic than the simple pronoun, is repeated. The preposition ἐν is sometimes used instrumentally. Winer, § 48, a, d. Still, in such a usage, the power to produce the effect is supposed to dwell in the cause. That power which has changed farness into nearness, resides in the blood of Christ, or as Alford says, but not very precisely— " the blood is the symbol of a faith in which your nearness to God consists." Their being in Jesus was, moreover, the reason why the blood of Christ had produced such an effect on them. How it does so is explained in the next verses. The apostle's object is to show that by the death of Christ the exclusiveness of the theocracy was abolished, that Jew and Gentile, by the abrogation of the Mosaic law, are placed on the same level, and that both, in the blood of Christ, are reconciled to God.

The following passage is magnificent in style as well as idea. No wonder that the pious taste of Bengel has written —*Ipso verborum tenore et quasi rhythmo canticum imitatur:*—

(Ver. 14.) Αὐτὸς γάρ ἐστιν ἡ εἰρήνη ἡμῶν—" For He is our peace." Γάρ introduces the reason of the previous statement. There is peculiar force in the αὐτός. It is not simply " He," but " He Himself "—" He truly," or " He and none other." Winer, § 22, 4, b. The ἡμῶν cannot, as Locke supposes, refer to converted Gentiles, but to Jew and Gentile alike. In its widest sense, as this paragraph teaches, " Christ is the peace," and not merely the peacemaker; the Author of it, for He "makes both one," and "reconciles them to God;" the Basis of it, for He has "abolished the enmity in His flesh," and "by His cross;" the Medium of it, for "through Him we both have access to the Father;" and the Proclaimer of it, for "He came and preached peace." For such reasons Paul may have used the abstract personified form—εἰρήνη. "He Himself," says Olshausen, followed by Stier, "in His essence is peace." Yet we question if this be the apostolic idea, for the apostle illustrates in the following verses, not the essence, but the operations of Christ. This peace is now stated by the inspired writer to be peace between Jew and Gentile viewed as antagonist races, and peace between them both united and God. The first receives fullest illustration, as it fell more immediately within the scope of the apostle's design. Gentiles are no longer formally excluded from religious privilege and blessing, and Jewish monopoly is for ever overthrown. And it is Christ—

ὁ ποιήσας τὰ ἀμφότερα ἕν—"who made both one." The participle is modal in sense, and τὰ ἀμφότερα are clearly the two races, Jew and Gentile, and not, as Stier and others maintain, man and God also. The words are the abstract neuter (Winer, § 27, 5), and in keeping also is the following adjective ἕν. Jew and Gentile are not changed in race, nor amalgamated in blood, but they are "one" in point of privilege and position toward God. The figure employed by Chrysostom is very striking:—"He does not mean that He has elevated us to that high dignity of theirs, but He has raised both us and them to one still higher. . . . I will give you an illustration. Let us imagine that there are two statues, one of silver and the other of lead, and then that both shall be melted down, and the two shall come out gold. So thus He has made the two one." And this harmony is effected in the following way—

καὶ τὸ μεσότοιχον τοῦ φραγμοῦ λύσας—"and broke down the middle wall of partition"—*paries intergerinus.* Καί is explanatory of the foregoing clause, and precedes a description of the mode in which "both were made one." Winer, § 53, 3, *obs.*[1] We see no reason to take the genitive—τοῦ

[1] Moulton, p. 544.

φραγμοῦ—as that of apposition; nor could we, with Piscator, change the clause into τὸν φραγμὸν τοῦ μεσοτοίχου. It is, as de Wette calls it, the genitive of subject or possession—the middle wall which belonged to the fence or was an essential part of it. Donaldson, 454, aa. Φραγμός does not, however, signify "partition;" it rather denotes inclosure. The Mosaic law was often named by the Rabbins a hedge—מְיָג. Buxtorf, *Lex. Talmud. sub voce.* What allusion the apostle had in μεσότοιχον has been much disputed. Dismissing the opinion of Wagenseil, that it refers to the vail hung up before a royal or a bridal chamber; and that of Gronovius, that it signifies such partitions as in a large city, inhabited by persons of different nations, divide their respective boundaries, very much as the Jewish Ghetto is walled off in European capitals—we may mention the popular view of many interpreters, that the allusion is to the wall or parapet which in Herod's temple severed the court of the Jews from that of the Gentiles. The Jewish historian records that on this wall was inscribed the prohibition—μὴ δεῖν ἀλλόφυλον ἐντὸς τοῦ ἁγίου παρεῖναι. Joseph. *Antiq.* xv. 11; *Bellum Jud.* v. 2. Such is the idea of Anselm, Wetstein, Holzhausen, Bengel, and Olshausen. Tyndale translates—"The wall that was a stop bitwene vs." The notion is quite plausible, but nothing more; for, 1. There is no proof that such a wall ever received this appellation. 2. That wall described by Josephus was an unauthorized fence or separation. There was another wall that separated even the Jewish worshippers from the court of the priests. 3. Nor could the heathen party in the Ephesian church be supposed to be conversant with the plan of the sacred fane in Jerusalem. 4. And the allusion must have been very inapposite, because at the time the epistle was written, that wall was still standing, and was not broken down till eight years afterwards. So that, with many expositors, we are inclined to think that the apostle used a graphic and intelligible figure, without special allusion to any part of the architecture of the temple, unless perhaps to the vail. But such a primary allusion to the vail as Alford supposes is not in harmony at all with the course of thought, for it was not a bar between Jew and Gentile, but equally one between them both and God, and could not be identified with the enmity of race the enmity, moreover, was not confined to the Jews; it was not all on their side.[1] Nor can we, with Theodoret, Œcumenius, Theophylact, Luther, Calvin, Beza, Estius, Rückert, and Matthies, join the phrase to λύσας, as it is more natural, and in better harmony with the course of thought, to annex them to καταργήσας, as explanatory of the means or manner of the abolition. This last opinion is that of Harless, Olshausen, Meier, Meyer, and de Wette. Σάρξ is Christ's humanity, but not that humanity specially in its Jewish blood and lineage, as Hofmann contends—as if because He died as a Jew, His death secured that participation in His kingdom did not depend on Israelitism. Καταργήσας means "having made void"—"having superseded." Rom. iii. 31.

The phrase τὸν νόμον τῶν ἐντολῶν ἐν δόγμασι is a graphic description of the ceremonial law. But the meaning and connection of ἐν δόγμασι have been disputed:—I. It has been regarded as the means by which the law has been abolished, to wit, "by doctrines"—Christian doctrines or precepts. Such is the reading of the Arabic and Vulgate, the Syriac being doubtful; and such is the view of Chrysostom, Theodoret, Theophylact, Estius, Zeger, a-Lapide, Bengel, Holzhausen, Scholz, and Fritzsche—*Disser. ad 2 Cor.* p. 168. Winer in his third edition proposed this view, but renounced it in the fourth. Thus Chrysostom says—δόγματα γὰρ καλεῖ τὴν πίστιν. Theodoret and Theophylact as usual follow him, while Œcumenius vindicates the use of the word as applied to Christ's teaching, by quoting from the Sermon on the Mount such phrases as "I say unto you," these being proofs of authoritative diction, and warranting the truth propounded to be called δόγμα. To this theory there are insuperable objections—1. The participle in this case would have two connected words introduced alike by ἐν. 2. The sense given to δόγμα is wholly unbiblical. Δόγμα is equivalent to the participial form—τὸ δεδογμένον, and has

---

[1] Horace sneers at them, too :—

"Hodie tricesima sabbata, vin' tu
Curtis Judæis opperdere."   (*Satir.* Lib. I. ix. 70.)

Diodorus Siculus speaks of their institutions as—τὰ μισάνθρωπα καὶ παράνομα ἔθη. (Lib. xxxiv.) Shakespeare's "Shylock" was the universal picture of a Jew in times not very far distant from our own, and still, alas! the Jew is a "hissing and a proverb."

its apparent origin in the common phrase which prefaced a proclamation or statute—ἔδοξε τῷ λαῷ καὶ τῇ βουλῇ. In the New Testament it signifies decree, and is applied, Luke ii. 1, to the edict of Cæsar, and in Acts xvii. 7 it occurs with a similar reference. But not only does it signify imperial statute, it is also the name given to the decrees of the ecclesiastical council in Jerusalem. Acts xvi. 4. It is found, too, in the parallel passage in Col. ii. 14. In the Septuagint its meaning is the same; and in the sense first quoted, that of royal mandate, it is frequently used in the book of Daniel. To give the term here the meaning of Christian doctrine or precept, is to annex a signification which it did not bear till long after the age of the apostles. It is finical and out of place on the part of Grotius to suppose that Paul used a philosophical term to describe the tuition of the great Teacher, because he might be writing to persons skilled in the idiom of philosophical speech. 3. It is not the testimony of Scripture that Jesus by His teaching abolished the ceremonial law, but the uniform declaration is, that the shadowy economy was abrogated in His death. 4. The phrase ἐν δόγμασι is too general to have in itself such a direct meaning, and αὐτοῦ, or some distinctive appendage, must have been added, did the words bear the sense we are attempting to refute.

II. Harless, Olshausen, and von Gerlach connect ἐν δόγμασι with καταργήσας, but in a different way. They understand ἐν δόγμασι as describing one peculiar phase of the Mosaic law, in which phase Jesus abolished it. The phrase is supposed by them to represent the commanding aspect of the law, and so far as these δόγματα are concerned, the law has been abrogated. "Having abolished as to its ordinances—*Satzungen*— the law of commandments," that is, the law of commandments is still in force, but its δόγματα are set aside. In this view those scholars were preceded by Crellius—*non de tota lege sed ejus parte quæ dogmata continebat*. Von Gerlach understands the "condemning power" of the law to be abolished. But it is rather of the Levitical than of the moral law that the apostle is speaking. But, surely, to show us that δόγματα is a part of the νόμος, the article τοῖς should have been prefixed, or an adjective should have been added. Besides, the spirit of the apostle's doctrine is, that the entire law is abrogated, which sprang from the ceremonial law, as described in the next verse. Any social usage, national peculiarity, or religious exclusiveness, which hedges round one race and shuts out all others from its fellowship, may be called a "middle wall of partition;" and such was the Mosaic law. $\Lambda \acute{v}\sigma as$—"Having pulled down," is a term quite in unison with the figure. John ii. 19. Having pulled down—

(Ver. 15.) $T\grave{\eta}\nu\ \check{\epsilon}\chi\theta\rho a\nu$—"To wit, the enmity." These words might be governed by $\lambda\acute{v}\sigma as$ without incongruity, as Wetstein has abundantly shown. And perhaps we may say with Stier, they are so; for if they be taken as governed by $\kappa a\tau a\rho\gamma\acute{\eta}\sigma as$, as in our version and that of Luther, the sentence is intricate and confused. $T\grave{\eta}\nu\ \check{\epsilon}\chi\theta\rho a\nu$—"the enmity," proverbial and well known, is in apposition to $\mu\epsilon\sigma\acute{o}\tau o\iota\chi o\nu$; "having broken down what formed the wall of separation, to wit, the hatred." This $\check{\epsilon}\chi\theta\rho a$ is not in any direct or prominent sense hatred toward God, as Chrysostom, Theophylact, Œcumenius, and Harless suppose, for it is not the apostle's present design to speak of this enmity. His object is to show first how Jew and Gentile are reconciled. Some again, like Photius and Cocceius, imagine that hatred between Jew and Gentile, and also hatred of man to God, are contained in the word. This hypothesis only complicates the apostle's argument, which is marked by precision and simplicity. The arguments advanced by Ellicott in defence of this hypothesis are not satisfactory; for the phrases—"who hath made both one," "wall of partition," "law of commandments," or Mosaic code—plainly refer to the position of Jew and Gentile, and reconciliation with God is afterwards and formally introduced. At the same time, the idea of enmity towards God could not be absent from the apostle's mind, for this enmity of race had its origin and tincture from enmity towards God. Nor can we accede to the interpretation of Theodoret, Calvin, Bucer, Grotius, Meier, Holzhausen, Olshausen, and Conybeare, who understand by the $\check{\epsilon}\chi\theta\rho a$ the ceremonial law, as the ground of the enmity between Jew and Gentile. The objection of Stier, however, that to represent law as the cause of enmity is saying too much, as it leaves nothing for the other factor the flesh—is, as Turner says, not very forcible. We prefer, with Erasmus, Vatablus, Estius, Rückert, and Meyer, to take the term in its plain significance, as the contrast of εἰρήνη, and as denoting the actual, existing enmity of Israel and non-Israel— an enmity of which the ceremonial law was the virtual but innocent occasion. It was this hatred which rose like a party wall, and kept both races at a distance. Deep hostility lay in their bosoms; the Jew looked down with supercilious contempt upon the Gentile, and the Gentile reciprocated and scowled upon the Jew as a haughty and heartless bigot. Ample evidence is afforded of this mutual alienation. Insolent scorn of the Gentiles breaks out in many parts of the New Testament (Acts xi. 3, xxii. 22; 1 Thess. ii. 15), while the pages of classic literature show how fully the feeling was repaid.[1] This rancour formed of necessity a middle wall of partition, but Jesus, who is our peace, hath broken it down. The next sentence gives the requisite explanation—

ἐν τῇ σαρκὶ αὐτοῦ τὸν νόμον τῶν ἐντολῶν ἐν δόγμασιν καταργήσας—" having abolished in His flesh the law of commandments in ordinances." The course of thought runs thus: Christ is our peace. Then there follows first a statement of the fact, Jew and Gentile are made one; the mode of operation is next described, for He has quenched their mutual hatred, and He has done this in the only effectual way, by removing its cause—the Mosaic law. The words—ἐν τῇ σαρκὶ αὐτοῦ cannot refer to ἔχθρα, as the clause is pointed by Lachmann, as Chrysostom and Ambrose quote, and as Bugenhagen and Schulthess argue, giving σάρξ the sense of kinsfolk—hatred existing among his own people; or as Cocceius, who adopts that view of the connection, renders—*donec appareret in carne*. Such a construction would require the insertion of the article τήν. Σάρξ cannot bear such a meaning here, and

---

[1] When Haman wished to destroy the Jews, he impeached them as a strange people whose "laws are diverse from all people." (Esth. iii. 8.) Tacitus says:—
"Moyses, quo sibi in posterum gentem firmaret, novos ritus contrariosque ceteris mortalibus indidit. Profana illic omnia quæ apud nos sacra. . . . Cetera instituta sinistra, fœda, pravitate valuere. . . . Apud ipsos fides obstinata, misericordia in promptu, sed adversus omnes alios odium. . . . Projectissima ad libidinem gens, alienarum concubitu abstinent, inter se nihil illicitum. . . . Judæorum mos absurdus sordidusque." (*Histor.* v. 4, 5.)

And Juvenal sings :—
"Nil præter nubes, et cœli numen adorant
Nec distare putant humana carne suillam," etc.

and not a mere section of it. The whole Mosaic institute was fulfilled in the death of Jesus. Hofmann's idea, somewhat similar—that Christ has put an end to δόγματα, statutes, *Satzungen*—is, as Meyer says, contradicted by many parts of the New Testament. Rom. iii. 27 ; Gal. vi. 2. Nay, out of it might be developed an antinomian theory. Gal. iii. 18 ; Col. ii. 14.

III. The correct junction of the phrase ἐν δόγμασι is with νόμον τῶν ἐντολῶν. Had it referred to νόμος alone, one would have expected the article to be repeated—νόμον τῶν ἐντολῶν τὸν ἐν δόγμασι. This is in general the view of Erasmus, Calvin, Beza, Rollock, Bodius, Crocius, and Zanchius in former times, and in more recent times of Theile, Tholuck, Rückert, Meier, de Wette, Meyer, Baumgarten-Crusius, and Matthies. Winer, § 31, 10, note 1.[1] The ceremonial institute is named νόμος, as it was a code sanctioned by supreme legislative authority. But, as a code, it comprised a prodigious number of minute, varied, and formal regulations or prescriptions—ἐντολαί, the genitive being that of contents; while the phrase ἐν δόγμασι defines the nature of these ἐντολαί, for they were δόγματα— issued under Divine sanction, and resting on the immediate will of God ; and they had constant reference to health, business, and pleasure, as well as to Divine service. They were *ordonnances*—proclamations in the name of God. In an especial sense, the ceremonial institute seemed good to God— δοκεῖ, and it became a δόγμα. It was not a moral law, having its origin and basis in the Divine nature, and therefore unchanged and unchangeable, binding the loftiest creatures and most distant worlds ; but a positive law, having its foundation simply in the Divine will, established for a period among one people, and then, its purpose being served among them, to be set aside. Viewed as an organic whole, the Mosaic institute was νόμος—a law ; analyzed and looked upon in its separate constituents, it was νόμος ἐντολῶν ; and when these ἐντολαί are inspected in their essence and authority, they are found to be δόγματα—to be obeyed, because the Divine Dictator was pleased to enjoin them. The article, therefore, is not prefixed to δόγμασι, which is descriptive of the form and authority of those statutory regulations, the phrase representing one

[1] Moulton, p. 275.

connected idea. Winer, § 20, 2. The ἐν is not to be taken for σύν, as Heinsius and Flatt take it, nor can it signify *propter*, as Morus renders it. Now, this legal apparatus was abolished "in His flesh," that is, in His incarnate state, especially by the death which in that state He endured. The language of Ambrosiaster is appropriate—*legem quæ data erat Judæis in circumcisione et in neomeniis et in escis et in sacrificiis et in sabbatis evacuavit*. By the abrogation of the Mosaic institute, the ἔχθρα was destroyed, and the party wall, which separated Palestine from the great outfield of the world, laid low. Difference of race no longer exists, and Abrahamic distinction is lost in the wider and earlier Adamic descent.

The apostle now states more fully the purpose of the abrogation of the old law—

ἵνα τοὺς δύο κτίσῃ ἐν ἑαυτῷ εἰς ἕνα καινὸν ἄνθρωπον— "that He might create the two in Himself into one new man." This clause is no mere repetition of the preceding declaration—"Who hath made both one." It is more special and distinctive in its description. The two races are personified, and they are formed not into one man, but into *one new man*. Καινὸς ἄνθρωπος is found elsewhere as an epithet descriptive of spiritual change, as in iv. 24; 2 Cor. v. 17; Gal. vi. 15; Col. iii. 10. The phrase is very different from the *novus homo* of the Latins, and therefore Wetstein's learned array of quotations from Roman authors is wholly useless. And the idea of moral renovation is not to be so wholly excluded here as some critics argue. One *new* man—both races being now enabled to realize the true end of humanity; Gentile and Jew not so joined that old privilege is merely divided among them. The Gentile is not elevated to the position of the Jew—a position which he might have obtained by becoming a proselyte under the law; but Jew and Gentile together are both raised to a higher platform than the circumcision ever enjoyed. The Jew profits by the repeal of the law, as well as the Gentile. Now he needs to provide no sacrifice, for the One victim has bled; the fires of the altar may be smothered, for the Lamb of God has been offered; the priest, throwing off his sacred vestments, may retire to weep over a torn vail and shattered temple, for Jesus has passed through the heaven "into the presence of God for us;" the water of the "brazen sea" may be poured out, for believers enjoy the washing of regeneration; and the lamps of the golden candelabrum have flickered and died, for the church enjoys the enlightening influences of the Holy Spirit. Spiritual blessing in itself, and not merely pictured in type, is possessed by the Jew as well as the Gentile. The Jew gains by the abolition of a law that so restricted him to time, place, and typical ceremony in the worship of God. As unity of privilege distinguishes both races, and that alike, they are formed into *one man*, and as that unity and privilege are to both a novelty, they are shaped into *one new man*. And this metamorphosis is effected ἐν ἑαυτῷ (A, B, F have αὐτῷ)—not δι' ἑαυτόν, as Œcumenius has it; nor *per doctrinam suam*, as Grotius paraphrases it; nor is the phrase synonymous with "in His flesh." It signifies in union with Himself, or, as Chrysostom illustrates—"laying one hand on the Jew and the other on the Gentile, and Himself being in the midst." This harmony of race is effected by the union of both with Christ; that is to say, the unconverted Jew and the unbelieving Gentile may be, and are, at enmity still, but when they are united to Christ, they both feel the high and novel place which His abrogation of the law has secured for them. Both are elevated to loftier and purer privilege than the old theocracy could ever have conferred.

ποιῶν εἰρήνην—"making peace." This εἰρήνη must be the peace described—peace with Jew and Gentile; not, as Harless holds, "peace with God," nor, as Chrysostom takes it, with Alford and Ellicott, "peace with God and with one another" —πρὸς τὸν θεὸν καὶ πρὸς ἀλλήλους, for peace with God is in the order of thought, the formal theme of the next verse, although both results spring together from the same work of Christ. The present participle, referring back to αὐτός, is used, because it does not, like the aorist in the next clause, express a reason for the result contained in the κτίσῃ, but it is contemporaneous with it. The participle covers the entire process—abolition of enmity, abrogation of law, and creation of the new person; for in the whole of it Jesus is "making peace." Scheuerlein, § 31, 2, *a*. There is yet a higher aim—

(Ver. 16.) Καὶ ἀποκαταλλάξῃ τοὺς ἀμφοτέρους ἐν ἑνὶ σώματι τῷ Θεῷ—"And that He might reconcile the twain in one body to God." This verse indicates another and separate purpose of the annulment of the law. Not only are Jew and Gentile to be incorporated, but both are to be united to God. This idea is not, as Olshausen intimates, virtually identical with that of the preceding clause. It is a thought specifically different, and yet closely united. Indeed, the idea of the preceding clause to some extent presupposes it. The two acts, mutual union and Divine reconciliation, are contemporaneous.

The principal difference of opinion regards the phrase— ἐν ἑνὶ σώματι; viz. whether it refer to united Jew and Gentile, or to the one humanity of Christ. The latter opinion is held by Chrysostom, Theodoret, Beza, Crocius, Bengel, Rückert, Harless, Matthies, and Hofmann, *Schriftb.* ii. 379; but it is untenable. For, 1. The order of the words would indicate another meaning—τοὺς ἀμφοτέρους ἐν ἑνὶ σώματι—"the two in one body," the very truth which the apostle had been illustrating and enforcing. He views the union as effected— does not now say τοὺς δύο, but names the united races—*the twain in one body.* The εἰς καινὸς ἄνθρωπος is viewed as ἓν σῶμα. Photius explains it—διὰ μὲν τοῦ ἐν ἑνὶ σώματι, τὴν πρὸς ἀλλήλους ἐμφαίνει καταλλαγήν. 2. If the phrase refer to Christ's humanity, then the words must be understood of that humanity offered as an oblation. The meaning would be much the same as that of διὰ τοῦ σταυροῦ, and the same idea would be again and again repeated in the paragraph. But, 3. Why should Christ's body be called His one body? why attach such an epithet to His single humanity? and we should have expected an αὐτοῦ to have specified the possessor of the body, even though the idea should be—" one body "— they in Him enjoying fellowship with God. It appears better, then, to adopt the other exegesis, and to take the phrase as meaning Jew and Gentile *incorporated.* Such is the view of Œcumenius, Pelagius, Anselm, Erasmus, Calvin, Estius, Meier, Meyer, Olshausen, de Wette, and Baumgarten-Crusius. Besides what we have said in its favour, this idea is in harmony with the context, and with what is advanced in the next chapter. 1 Cor. xii. 12, 20, 27; Col. iii. 15. In the apostle's idiom the phrase is confined to the church; for the church in the preceding chapter is affirmed to be His body. In that body there is no schism, and though it is made up of two different races, it is yet but one body. So that the ἐν ἑνὶ σώματι of this verse is in agreement with ἐν ἑνὶ πνεύματι of the 18th verse.

The action is defined by the verb ἀποκαταλλάξῃ. The double compound is found only in Col. i. 20, 21. The ἀπό in composition with the verb may either signify "again," as Passow, Harless, Olshausen, and Ellicott affirm, which is perhaps doubtful; or it may strengthen the original signification, as seen in such words as ἀπεργάζομαι, ἀποθνήσκω, ἀπέχω. Much has been written on the difference between διαλλάσσω and καταλλάσσω. Verbs compounded with διά have often a mutuality of signification, but they cease in many instances to bear such a distinction. Καταλλάσσω is not practically different from διαλλάσσω, and so Passow holds (*sub voce*) that καταλλάσσω in the middle voice signifies—*sich unter einander versöhnen*—" to effect a mutual reconciliation "[1] The radical idea is to cause enmity to cease—to make up friendship again; but the mode, time, and form of reconciliation must be learned from the context. The meaning of the apostle is not that Jew and Gentile have been reconciled *into* one body by the cross. Such, indeed, is the view of Œcumenius, Photius, Anselm, Calvin, a-Lapide, and Grotius, but it gives the ἐν the sense of εἰς, and takes away the full force of the dative—τῷ Θεῷ, making it mean—*ut Deo serviant*. But τῷ Θεῷ, as in other passages where the words occur, defines the person with

[1] Tittmann has entered at length into the discussion in his book on the Synonyms of the New Testament. According to him, διαλλάσσω refers to the cessation of mutual enmity, and καταλλάσσω is employed in cases where the enmity has existed only on one side. The passage which he refers to in Matthew will not bear out such a distinction as he enforces. Matt. v. 23, 24: "If thou bring thy gift to the altar, and there rememberest that *thy brother hath ought against thee*, leave there thy gift before the altar, and go thy way; first be reconciled to thy brother"—διαλλάγηθι τῷ ἀδελφῷ. But "be reconciled to thy brother" is plainly not—Cease to be at enmity with him, as if you had hated him, and need your own ill-will also to be quenched; for the supposition is not "Thou hast ought against thy brother," but it is "If thy brother has ought against thee." Be reconciled to him, that is, induce *him* to lay aside *his* quarrel against thee. At the same time, while such a philological argument may be maintained, it is not the less true that mutual agreement is the result. The phrase—"Thy brother hath ought against thee," implies that something had been done justly to offend him, and that, upon explanation or apology, his good-will was to be restored. Tholuck (*Bergpredigt*, p. 192) has well exposed the futility of Tittmann's subtle distinction. Usteri, *Lehrb*. p. 102; Fritzsche, *Ad Rom*. i. p. 276.

whom the reconciliation has been secured, while ἐν ἑνὶ σώματι describes the result of a contemporaneous but minor unity between the two races. Winer, § 50, 5. It is probable, however, that ἐν and εἰς were originally one—ἑνς, like μείς—μέν. Donaldson's *New Cratylus*, § 170.

Reconciliation to God is not the removal in the first instance of man's enmity toward God, but Jesus reconciles us to God by turning away the Divine anger from us. As, in 1 Sam. xxix. 4, David was supposed to "reconcile himself" to his master by doing some feat to secure his favour, so Jesus reconciles us to God by the propitiation which He presented to God, and through which He is enabled even as a righteous God to justify the ungodly. This statement is proved by the phrase—διὰ τοῦ σταυροῦ—for the cross has reconciliation to God for its immediate object. Restoration to the Divine favour is the primary and peculiar work of the great High Priest, "who offered Himself without spot to God." A sacrifice had always reference to the guilt of the offerer, and it averted that penalty which a righteous governor might justly inflict. Another proof of our position is found in ver. 18, in which the result of this peace is declared to be "access to the Father," which has been created by the blood of the atonement. True, indeed, God is love, but the provision of an atonement is the glorious expression of it. And His government must be upheld in its majesty; for the pardon, without any peculiar provision, of all who break a law, is tantamount to its repeal. The fact of an atonement seems to prove its own necessity. God has shown infinite love to the sinner, and infinite hatred to his sin, in the sufferings of the cross, so that we tremble at His severity, while we are in the arms of His mercy. The justice of the great Lawgiver is of unchanging claim and perpetuity. The reader will find in Dr. Owen's dissertation on "Divine Justice"[1] many striking remarks on the theory that sin might be pardoned by a mere act of grace on God's part, apart from any satisfaction to His justice—a theory vindicated even by Samuel Rutherford and Mr. Prolocutor Twisse. Jew and Gentile are thus reconciled to God, and the same act which gives them social unity, confers upon them oneness with God, for the abrogation of the ceremonial law was in itself the glorification of the moral law,

---

[1] *Works*, vol. x. p. 495. Edin. 1853.

in the presentation of a perfect obedience to it, and in the endurance of its penalty.

ἀποκτείνας τὴν ἔχθραν ἐν αὐτῷ—" having slain the enmity in it." The enmity referred to has been variously understood. But ἔχθρα cannot exist on God's part, for what He feels toward sin is ὀργή. That it signifies human enmity towards God, is the opinion of many, while others connect with this idea also hatred between Jew and Gentile. But if our view of the nature of reconciliation be correct, and we agree with Meyer, Olshausen, and de Wette, this last can hardly be meant. It is not of man's hatred the apostle speaks, but of God propitiated. Besides, the participle ἀποκτείνας describes an action which precedes that of its verb ἀποκαταλλάξῃ—" and that, having slain the enmity, He might reconcile both in one body to God." Bernhardy, p. 382. The occurrence of the word ἔχθρα here is one of Alford's principal arguments for giving it the extended sense of enmity toward God, as well as enmity between the two races. But the argument will not hold, for — 1. The slaying of the enmity being an act prior to the reconciliation, refers to the sentiments of the preceding verses—the enmity between Jew and Gentile. 2. The word ἔχθρα has special reference to the phrase—ἐν ἑνὶ σώματι—" and having slain the enmity between them, He might reconcile them both in one body unto God." 3. The stress lies on τοὺς ἀμφοτέρους ἐν ἑνὶ σώματι—the twain are in one body as they are in the act of being reconciled—the previous enmity between them being subdued. 4. The idea of union between the races fills the apostle's mind, as is plain from the first half of the following chapter—that is, by the abrogation of the Levitical law the Gentiles come into a new relationship and new privileges. These the apostle dwells on and glories in.

The Vulgate renders ἐν αὐτῷ—*in semet ipso*, and Luther —*in sich selbst*, with which the reading ἐν ἑαυτῷ coincides, and which is naturally vindicated by such exegetes as Bengel, Semler, Hofmann, and others, who refer to σώματι as the antecedent, and understand by σῶμα Christ's humanity. But the more natural interpretation is to refer the pronoun to τοῦ σταυροῦ. The Syriac reads—" and by His cross has slain the enmity." The word ἀποκτείνας, as Grotius suggests, seems to have been employed because the cross referred to was an instrument of death. The cross which slew Jesus slew this hostility; His death was the death of that animosity which rose up between Israel and non-Israel like a wall of separation.

(Ver. 17.) Καὶ ἐλθὼν εὐαγγελίσατο εἰρήνην—" And having come He preached peace." " Peace," in this clause, is to be taken in its widest acceptation; that peace which had just been described—peace between Jew and Gentile, and peace between both and God. It is an error in Chrysostom to restrict it to peace with God, and in Meyer, de Wette, and Olshausen apparently, to confine it to peace between the two races. The clause plainly carries us back to ver. 14—"for He Himself is our peace," and the apostle then proceeds to explain the two kinds of peace. The following verse also proves our view. " For," says the apostle, "we both have access to the Father." And that peace was good tidings, as the verb implies. The middle voice was used also by the earlier writers. Phrynichus, ed. Lobeck, p. 266. Καί does not simply indicate that this clause follows in idea the announcement—αὐτὸς γάρ ἐστιν ἡ εἰρήνη ἡμῶν, as if the intervening verses were parenthetical in their nature. For these intermediate verses expound the starting proposition, and the verse before us continues the illustration. Peace was first secured, and then peace was proclaimed. The publication of the peace is ascribed to Jesus equally with its procurement—καὶ ἐλθών. The notion of Raphelius, Grotius, Koppe, and others, that these words are superfluous, is altogether an inaccurate and negligent exegesis. The " coming " referred to is plainly not to be restricted to His personal manifestation in flesh, as Chrysostom, Anselm, Estius, Holzhausen, Matthies, and Harless argue, for here it is an event posterior to the crucifixion; as it is a coming to proclaim what the death on the cross had secured. Nor can we, with Rückert and Bengel, restrict the coming to the resurrection of Jesus. As little can we hold the sense realized in our Lord's personal preaching, as is the hypothesis of Beza and Calovius, for " Jesus Christ was a minister of the circumcision only." He illustrated this truth to the Syrophenician woman, and His instructions during His life to His apostles were— " Go not into the way of the Gentiles." We would not confine the "coming," with Olshausen and Meyer, to His advent by the Spirit; nor, with Calvin, identify it wholly with the mission of the apostles, for both these are included. Christ brought peace to the Ephesian Christians by means of this Spirit in the apostles—*qui facit per alium, facit per se*. The preaching of the apostles having the truth of Christ for its theme, the commission of Christ for its authority, and the Spirit of Christ for its seal and crowning distinction, may surely in its doctrines and triumphs be ascribed to the exalted Lord and King of the church, the one origin and sole dispenser of "PEACE." The apostle felt that his gifts and graces were of Christ's bestowment—that all his opportunities and successes were the results of Christ's presence and power—that his whole message was from Christ and about Him—that not only was the peace which he announced secured in Christ's mediation and death, but that also his very journeys to proclaim it were prompted and shaped by Him; and therefore all being Christ's, from the inspiration that moved his heart to the secret and irresistible influence that prescribed his missionary tours; his whole work in its every element being so truly identified with Christ—he humbly retired into the shade, that Christ might have all the glory: and therefore he writes—"and He came and preached peace to you." This interpretation appears to us more direct and harmonious than that of Harless, who regards this verse as a parallel to ver. 14, as if the meaning were—"Christ is peace 'in deed' (ver. 14), and also 'in word'" (ver. 17). This would be an anti-climax, for surely the creation of peace was a greater work than its disclosure. And then the two ideas are not parallel. In the former case, Jesus personally and immediately secured peace; in the latter case it was only mediately, and by others, that he proclaimed it. Harless, indeed, regards ἐλθών generally as denoting Christ's appearance upon earth, as in John i. 9, 11, iii. 19, etc. Our objection to such a view is, that Christ's appearance on earth was as necessary to the making of peace as to its proclamation, and more so, as is implied in the phrases—"in His flesh," and "by the cross," nay, "those who were nigh," or those who heard Christ in person, are placed last in the enumeration. Jesus, too, had left the earth ere this peace was formally published by His heralds. Moreover, the coming is plainly marked as posterior to the effecting of peace. As the preaching to the Ephesians is here as distinctly ascribed to Jesus as the coming, both must be understood in a similar way. Similar phraseology is found in Acts xxvi. 23 ; John x. 16. And the peace was preached—

ὑμῖν τοῖς μακρὰν καὶ εἰρήνην τοῖς ἐγγύς—" to you who were far off, and peace to them who were nigh." The dative is governed by the previous verb, and the second εἰρήνην has, on the authority of A, B, E, F, G, and of several versions and fathers, been received by Lachmann and Tischendorf into the text. Isa. lvii. 19. The repetition is emphatic. Rom. iii. 31, viii. 15 ; 2 Cor. ii. 16. The idea contained in μακράν has been already explained under ver. 13. The Gentiles are here placed first; the apostle of the Gentiles magnified his office. Though those "who were nigh" were the first who heard the proclamation based on the commission—" beginning at Jerusalem," yet those " who were afar off" are mentioned first, as they had so deep an interest in the tidings, and as the invitation of Gentiles into the church—a theme the apostle delighted in, proving, as it did, the abolition of class privileges, and the commencement of an unrestricted economy—was the result and proof of the truths illustrated in this paragraph.

(Ver. 18.) "Ὅτι δι᾿ αὐτοῦ ἔχομεν τὴν προσαγωγὴν οἱ ἀμφότεροι—" For by Him we both have access"—access specially theirs, as the article intimates. The ὅτι does not mark the contents of the message of peace, as Morus, Baumgarten, Koppe, and Flatt imagine ; nor yet its essence, as Rückert maintains : but it points out its proof and result. Peace has been made, and has also been proclaimed, for, as the effect of it, and as the demonstration of its reality—" by Him we both have access." Calvin well explains it—*probatio est ab effectu.* Προσαγωγή, formed with the Attic reduplication from ἄγω, is " introduction," entrance into the Divine presence—an allusion, according to some, to approach into the presence of a king by the medium of a προσαγωγεύς—*sequester* (Bos, *Observat.* p. 149) ; according to others, to the entrance of the priest into the presence of God. Herodotus, ii. 58. Rom. v. 2 ; and see under iii. 12. Whichever of these allusions be adopted, or whether the word be used in its proper signification, the meaning is apparent, the word being used probably in its original and transitive sense—not access secured, but introduction enjoyed, and which we are having, that is, have and keep. It is something more than θύρα, John x. 9. Free approach to God is the result of reconciliation. 1 Pet. iii. 18. Those who were "far off" can now draw "nigh." The Divine Being is not clothed in thunder—no barrier stands between Him and us, for all legal obstacles are removed; so that the soul which feels peace with God can come into His sacred presence without shrinking or tremor. It approaches by Christ—δι' αὐτοῦ; and the emphasis from their position lies on these words. Our frail humanity realizes His humanity, and by Him enters into the presence of Jehovah. John xiv. 6. Thus Chrysostom says—οὐκ εἶπεν πρόσοδον ἀλλὰ προσαγωγήν, οὐ γὰρ ἀφ' ἑαυτῶν προσήλθομεν, ἀλλ' ὑπ' αὐτοῦ προσήχθημεν. And this access is—

πρὸς τὸν Πατέρα—"unto the Father;" πρός—into His presence. Christians do not approach some dark and spectral phantom, nor a grim and terrible avenger. It is not Jehovah in the awful attitude of Judge and Governor, but Jehovah as Father—who has a father's heart to compassionate and a father's hand to bestow. And His paternity is no abstraction. He is Christ's Father and our Father. Nay more, and especially, this privilege is enjoyed by Jew and Gentile alike: οἱ ἀμφότεροι—the twain have it. It belonged to the theocracy in one form of it, when the high priest, the representative of the people, passed beyond the vail and sprinkled the mercy-seat. But now the most distant Gentile who is in Christ really and continuously enjoys that august spiritual privilege, which the one man of the one family of the one tribe of the one nation, on the one day of the year, only typically and periodically possessed. We have seen the οἱ ἀμφότεροι forming ἓν σῶμα (ver. 16)—now they are having access to the Father—

ἐν ἑνὶ πνεύματι—"in one Spirit." The collocation οἱ ἀμφότεροι—ἐν ἑνὶ πνεύματι again brings out solemnly and emphatically the leading thought in the passage. The ἐν is not to be identified with διά, as Chrysostom and Theophylact hint; as if the apostle meant to say, by Him and by the Spirit we approach. The πνεῦμα is not "disposition," nor is ἓν πνεῦμα only "unanimity," and so synonymous with ὁμοθυμαδόν, as is the baseless view of Anselm, Homberg, Zachariae, Meier, and Baumgarten-Crusius. That the words refer to the Holy Spirit, is the correct opinion of Œcumenius, Cocceius, Bodius, Meyer, Harless, de Wette, and Stier. The Spirit that dwells in the one body is the one Divine Spirit (iv. 4)—" one and the self-same Spirit." 1 Cor. xii. 11. The one Holy Ghost inhabits the church, and in Him and by Christ believers have access to God. He prompts them to approach, "helpeth their infirmities," deepens their consciousness of sonship as they come to the Father, nay, "makes intercession for them," imparts such intenseness to their aspirations that they cannot be formed into language, but escape from the surcharged bosom in unutterable groanings— στεναγμοῖς ἀλαλήτοις. Rom. viii. 26. As again and again in previous sections, the Triune relation is brought out: we are having access—πρός—unto the Father, whom we worship as we gaze upon His tenderness and majesty; and this—διά —by Jesus, through whom we approach in confidence His Father and our Father; but also—ἐν—in the Spirit, who fills and lifts the heart, and is closely united with Father and Son.

The need of a προσαγωγεύς has been extensively felt by our sinful race. And yet, after the Man-God has been revealed—He of the double nature—whom the Divine Sovereign appointed and man confides in, there are philosophers who deify themselves, and depose the one Mediator. M. Cousin, in the preface to his *Fragm. Philos.*, says, for example, in eulogizing the reason as a higher power than the understanding:—*La raison est le médiateur nécessaire entre Dieu et l'homme, ce λόγος de Pythagore et de Platon, ce Verbe fait chair qui sert d'interprète à Dieu et de précepteur de l'homme.* But we have a Mediator, not our own "reason" even absolute and transcendental; for it strays and wavers and quakes, as Moses on Sinai, and cannot reassure itself; and we have a Λόγος, not *la raison*, but One "in whom are hid all the treasures of wisdom and knowledge"—One who reveals God unerringly, for He lay in His Father's bosom—One who instructs men perfectly, for "grace has been poured into His lips," as He stoops to the senses and speaks to the heart of humanity.

(Ver. 19.) Ἄρα οὖν οὐκέτι ἐστὲ ξένοι καὶ πάροικοι—"Now

therefore, ye are no longer strangers and sojourners." The first two words are a favourite idiom of the apostle. Rom. v. 18, vii. 3, 25, viii. 12, etc.; Gal. vi. 10 ; 1 Thess. v. 6. The formula ἄρα οὖν is not used in Attic Greek, save in the case of the interrogative ἆρα. Hermann, *Vigerus*, 292. The particle ἄρα marks progress in the argument, as if equivalent to καὶ ἀπ' ἐκείνου. Thucyd. vi. 89 ; Donaldson's *New Cratylus*, § 192. The particle οὖν—allied to the substantive verb, and not to αὐτός as Hartung wrongly supposes—has a stronger ratiocinative force than ἄρα (Klotz-Devar. ii. 717), and occurs far more frequently ; and the combined use of both introduces a conclusion based on previous reasoning, equivalent to "these things being so," or the well-known Ciceronian formula—*quæ cum ita sint.* A double image is, or two pairs of figures are, employed by the writer—the one referring to civil franchise, and the other to domestic privilege. Ξένοι—" strangers "— they had been so while the old theocracy stood, the Jews being the children, but they miserable outcasts. Once, too, they were πάροικοι, literally "by-dwellers," men who sojourn in a house without the rights of the resident family. This is the only instance in which the apostle uses the term, but it occurs Acts vii. 6, 29 ; also in many places in the Septuagint, as the representative of the Hebrew גֵּר, and also of תּוֹשָׁב. The two words are found together many times, as in Lev. xxv., etc. It is natural here to view the οἰκεῖοι of the last clause as the contrast of πάροικοι, so that the significations of the word usually given are too vague to sustain this antithesis. In Lev. xxii. 10, the noun denotes an inmate of the family, but without its domestic rights ; πάροικος ἱερέως there signifies a guest with the priest, and stands along with ἢ μισθωτός—or a hired servant. Sirach xxix. 26. The priest's guest, though living in his house, was not to eat the holy things. May not the word bear such a meaning in this place, especially as we are pointed to it by the spiritual antagonism of οἰκεῖοι ? De Wette will not allow it, and says that Koppe, Bengel, Flatt, Harless, and Olshausen *unrichtig erklären.* His idea is, that the two terms ξένοι and πάροικοι express generally the thought *nicht-bürger*—" non-citizens." Ellicott and Alford hold a similar view, regarding πάροικος as the same with μέτοικος, its classic equivalent—a form which occurs only once in the Septuagint. But it is natural to suppose that the apostle used it in the Septuagint sense—that most familiar to him. The pair of terms in the two clauses suggests also a double contrast. That there is any allusion in the epithet πάροικοι to the equivocal relation of proselytes, such as is contended for by Anselm, Whitby, Calixtus, Baumgarten, and Baumgarten-Crusius, is out of the question; for if the proselytes feared God, they could not be described as are those Ephesian Gentiles in the context. The theocracy excluded all but Israel from its pale—the world beyond it were foreigners. Under the idea of its being God's house, it arrogated to itself a spiritual supremacy over all the nations, and so the heathen were regarded as simple sojourners on God's world. But this character of tolerated aliens no longer marked out the Gentile converts in Ephesus. No longer were they strangers to be frowned on, or foreigners to be excluded from domestic privileges; they were now naturalized—

ἀλλ' ἐστὲ συνπολῖται τῶν ἁγίων—" but fellow-citizens with the saints." The spelling συνπολῖται, instead of συμπολῖται, has the authority of A, B[1], C, D, E, F, G. Instead of the simple ἀλλά of the Received Text, the best MSS., such as A, B, C, D[1], G, warrant the reading ἀλλ' ἐστε, which has been adopted by the editors Hahn, Lachmann, and Tischendorf. It gives a vivid solemnity to the contrast: the mind of the apostle dwells on the blessed and present reality of their spiritual state, which he is about to depict. Συνπολίτης, a word occurring both in Ælian, *Var. Hist.* 3, 44, and Josephus, *Antiq.* 19, 2, 2, belongs chiefly, however, like other similar compound words, to the later and inferior Greek. Phrynichus, ed. Lobeck, p. 172, says, with characteristic affectation— πολίτης λέγε, μὴ συμπολίτης. In the declining period of a language, when its first freshness is gone, and its simple terms are not felt in their original power, compound words are brought into use without any proportionate increase of sense. These ἅγιοι are God's people; and there is no occasion to add, with Calvin—*et cum ipsis angelis*. The reader may turn to the first verse of the epistle for the meaning of ἅγιος.[1] The

---

[1] "In what an awful state is the Protestant church, when there are so many thousands, nay, tens, hundreds of thousands belonging to it, who, in their blindness and ignorance, take the very name of God's servants—the very name

"saints" are not the Jews as a race, as is supposed by Vorstius, Hammond, Morus, Bengel, and Adam Clarke; nor yet only contemporary Christians, as Harless and Meyer argue; nor yet simply saints of the Old Testament, as Œcumenius and Theodoret describe the alliance. Chrysostom exclaims— Ὁρᾶς ὅτι οὐχ ἁπλῶς τῶν Ἰουδαιῶν ἀλλὰ τῶν ἁγίων καὶ μεγάλων ἐκείνων ἀνδρῶν τῶν περὶ Ἀβραὰμ καὶ Μωϋσῆν καὶ Ἠλίαν εἰς τὴν αὐτὴν πόλιν ἀπεγράφημεν. These ἅγιοι are viewed as forming a πόλις—a spiritual organization. It was so under the old law—it is so still; for the theocracy is only fully realized under Christianity. To take an illustration from Athenian citizenship—they live no longer, as foreigners did in many Greek states, in the πανδοκεῖον, nor as the μέτοικοι at Athens are they degraded by the symbolical ὑδριοφορία, but they possess the coveted ἰσοτέλεια. With all, then, who belong to this πολιτεία, Christians are now fellow-citizens. They are under that form of government which specially belongs to the saints. These are, therefore, not saints of any time or any class, but saints of all times and all lands, of which the community then existing was the living representative; and in this commonwealth they were now enfranchised. Their names are engraven on the same civic roll with all whom "the Lord shall count, when He writeth up the people." It is as if they who had dwelt "in the waste and howling wilderness," scattered, defenceless, and in melancholy isolation, had been transplanted not only into Palestine, but had been appointed to domiciles on Mount Zion, and were located in the metropolis not to admire its architecture, or gaze upon its battlements, or envy the tribes who had come up to worship in the city which is "compact together;" but to claim its municipal immunities, experience its protection, obey its laws, live and love in its happy society, and hold communion with its glorious Founder and Guardian.

καὶ οἰκεῖοι τοῦ Θεοῦ—"and of the household of God." The church is often likened to a family or house. Num.

of those, of whom some serve Him here on earth, and some surround the Throne of His glory—to be fellow-citizens with whom is the highest privilege of man—and make it a nickname to mock at—'SAINTS!!' The very term with multitudes is a name of scorn."—M'Ghee's *Lectures on Ephesians*, vol. i. p. 323; London, 1848.

xii. 7 ; Hos. viii. 1 ; 1 Tim. iii. 15 ; Heb. iii. 2, 5, 6 ; 1 Pet. iv. 17. When Harless thinks that Christians receive this designation, because they are stones in the house, the conclusion is not only a needless anticipation of the figure in the following verse, but is also contrary to the usual meaning of the term, and destructive of the contrast between the terms οἰκεῖοι and πάροικοι. True, as Ellicott says under Gal. vi. 10, οἰκεῖος is often used with abstract nouns, as οἰκεῖοι φιλοσοφίας, etc., and in such cases the idea proper of family is dropped. But the contrasts in this paragraph are too vivid to allow any dilution of the term. These οἰκεῖοι τοῦ Θεοῦ are God's family ; they form His household. They are not guests —here to-day and away to-morrow; treated with courtesy, but still kept without the hallowed circle of domestic sociality, and strangers as well to the paternal protection as to the brotherly harmony which the family enjoys. The members of that "house which is the church of the living God," can call the οἰκοδεσπότης their father ; for they are "begotten of God," and they have access to Him, enjoy His love, and hold daily and delightful fellowship not only with Him, but with one another—as "heirs of God, and joint heirs with Christ."

(Ver. 20.) Ἐποικοδομηθέντες ἐπὶ τῷ θεμελίῳ τῶν ἀποστόλων καὶ προφητῶν—" built up upon the foundation of the apostles and prophets." The preposition ἐπί in composition is not, as Koppe affirms, without additional meaning, nor can it, as in Theophylact's exegesis, have the sense of "again;" but it gives prominence to the idea of the foundation *on* which the structure rests. Not the form or purpose, but the basis of the building, was the special thought in the writer's mind— *superædificati*, as in the Vulgate. 1 Cor. iii. 10, 12, 14 ; Col. ii. 7. This architectural allusion is a change of figure, or rather, it is the employment of a term in a double meaning. "House" has a similar twofold signification with us, as the "House of Bourbon" or "House of Stuart"—phrases in which the word is employed in a secondary and emphatic signification. We speak too of such houses being "built up" by the wisdom or valour of their founders. In such cases, as Alford says, there is a transition from a political and social to a material image. Having described the believers as οἰκεῖοι, the apostle enlarges the metaphor, by explaining on what the οἶκος rests, what its symmetry is, and what its glorious purpose. That "house" is composed of the οἰκεῖοι, and each of them is a living stone, resting on the one foundation.

What the writer means by ἀποστόλων is plain; but what is meant by the subjoined προφητῶν? With every wish, arising from the usage of quotation, to refer the term to the inspired messengers of the Old Testament, we feel that the force of evidence precludes us. The Greek fathers and critics, along with Erasmus, Calvin, Beza, Calovius, Estius, Baumgarten, Michaelis, Rückert, Bisping, and Barnes, hold the view which we are obliged to abandon. Ambrosiaster also explains—*hoc est, supra Novum et Vetus Testamentum collocati*. Tertullian says that Marcion, believing the reference to be to prophets of the Old Testament, expunged the words *et prophetarum*. *Contra Marc.* v. 17; *Opera*, vol. ii. p. 326, ed. Oehler. The apostle often refers to the prophets of the Old Testament; but in such places as Rom. i. 2 the reference is at once recognized. We prefer, then, with the great body of interpreters, to understand "the prophets" of the New Testament. Our reasons are these—

1. The apostles are placed before the prophets, whereas, in point of time and position, the prime place should be assigned to the prophets.[1] Estius says that the two classes are ranged *dignitatis habita ratione*, as the apostles had seen and heard Christ, enjoyed more endowments than the old prophets, and were immediately instrumental in founding these early churches. Did the phrase occur nowhere else, these ingenious arguments might be of some weight; though still, if the church be regarded as an edifice, the prophets laid the foundation earlier than the apostles, and should have been mentioned first in order. The dignity of Moses, Samuel, David, and Isaiah, under the old dispensation, was not behind that of the

---

[1] My four Scottish predecessors have here shown somewhat of our national "canniness." They do not recognize any difficulty at all, or at least they quietly relieve themselves of it, by the simple and apparently unconscious reversal of the order of the terms. Fergusson and Dickson briefly pass it over in this way, but Principal Rollock no less than six times quotes the phrase as if Paul had written "prophets and apostles." Principal Boyd (Bodius) in his *Comment.* exhibits the same transparent ingenuity, as well as in hosts of subsequent references, nay, even in his Latin notation of the inspired original, he reads—*fundamento prophetarum et apostolorum*.

apostolical college. The ruddy tints of the morning, ere the sun rises, are as fresh and glowing as the softened splendours of the evening, after he has set. And the argument that the apostles are named first because they personally founded the churches, is precisely the reason why we believe that prophets of an earlier time, and living under a different economy, are not meant at all.

2. Other portions of this epistle are explanatory of the apostle's meaning. In iii. 5 he speaks of a mystery, "which was in other ages not made known to the sons of men, as it is now revealed unto His holy apostles and prophets by the Spirit"—$\tau o \hat{i} s$ $\dot{a} \gamma i o i s$ $\dot{a} \pi o \sigma \tau \acute{o} \lambda o i s$ $a \dot{v} \tau o \hat{v}$ $\kappa a \grave{i}$ $\pi \rho o \phi \acute{\eta} \tau a i s$. In this declaration, the prophets are plainly perceived to be the inspired contemporaries of the apostles, enjoying similar revelations of truth from the same Spirit. What more natural than to suppose, that the apostle means the same persons by the very same names in a previous section! This opinion is the more likely, when we consider that the mystery declared to "apostles and prophets" is the union of Jew and Gentile. Again, iv. 11, "And He gave some apostles, and some prophets"—$\tau o \grave{v} s$ $\mu \grave{\epsilon} \nu$ $\dot{a} \pi o \sigma \tau \acute{o} \lambda o v s$, $\tau o \grave{v} s$ $\delta \grave{\epsilon}$ $\pi \rho o \phi \acute{\eta} \tau a s$. So that the prophets are a special class of functionaries, and rank next to the apostles, personally instrumental as they were in founding and building up the churches. Why may not the allusion be to them in this verse, as they are twice named in combination by the writer in the same epistle? The presumption is, that in the three places the same high office-bearers are described.

3. We deny not the relation of the prophets of the Old Testament to the church of the New Testament. They preceded, the apostles followed, and Jesus was in the midst. But in writing to persons who had been Gentiles, who were strangers to the Hebrew oracles, and had enjoyed none of their prophetic intimations—persons whose faith in Christ rested not on old prediction realized in Him, but on apostolic proclamation of His obedience and death—a reference to the seers of the Hebrew nation would not have been very intelligible and appropriate. To Jews with whom the apostle had "reasoned out of the Scripture," and whom he thus had convinced that Jesus was the Christ, the reference would have been natural

and stirring; but not so in an address to the Gentile portion of a church situated in the city of Diana.

The prophets of the New Testament were a class of sufficient importance and rank to be designated along with the apostles. The passages quoted from this epistle show this. And there are many other references. Acts xix. 6; Rom. xii. 6; 1 Cor. xii. 10, xiii. 8; the greater portion of the 14th chapter; and 1 Thess. v. 20. These passages prove that the office was next in order and dignity to the apostolate. The prophets spoke from immediate revelation—" with demonstration of the Spirit and with power;" and prior to the completion of the canon they stood to those early churches in such a relation as the written oracles stand to us. They were the oral law and testimony, and their work was not simply a disclosure of future events. (For illustration of the office of New Testament prophets, see under iv. 11.)

4. Had the apostle meant to distinguish the prophets of the Old Testament as a separate class, the article would probably have preceded the noun. Winer, § 19, 4; Kühner, § 493, 9; Matthiae, § 268, Anm. i.; Middleton, p. 65, ed. Rose. Comp. Matt. iii. 7, xv. 1; Luke xiv. 3, in which places different classes of men, but leagued together, are described. See also Col. ii. 19; 2 Thess. iii. 2; Tit. i. 15; Heb. iii. 1. Not that, as Harless, Rückert, Hofmann (*Schriftb.* vol. ii. p. 103), and Stier seem to say, apostles and prophets are identical—or that apostles were also prophets, as being men inspired. The want of the article clearly shows that both classes of office-bearers are viewed in one category as one in duty and object—one incorporated band. This combination of function and labour shows, that these "prophets" were those of the church of the New Testament.

The relation in which apostles and prophets stood to the church is defined by the words ἐπὶ τῷ θεμελίῳ. The preposition describes the building as resting on the foundation with the idea of close proximity. Kühner, 612, 1, *a, β*; Bernhardy, p. 249—the dative signifying "absolute superposition." Donaldson, *Gr. Gram.* § 483, *b*. The stones are represented not as in the act of being brought, but as already laid, and so the dative is employed rather than the accusative, which occurs in 1 Cor. iii. 12.

But what is the exact relation indicated by the genitive—
τῶν ἀποστόλων καὶ προφητῶν? It has been supposed to
mean, 1. The foundation on which the apostles themselves
have built — the apostles' and prophets' foundation—the
genitive being that of possession. Such is the view of Anselm,
Bucer, Aretius, Cocceius, Piscator, Alford, and Beza, the last
of whom thus paraphrases it—*Supra Christum qui est apostolicæ et propheticæ structuræ fundamentum.* But the object of
the apostle is not to show the identity of the foundation on
which the Ephesian church rested with that of prophets and
apostles, and Christ is here represented, not as the foundation,
but as the chief corner-stone. Thus, as Ellicott says, this
exegesis tacitly mixes up θεμέλιος and the ἀκρογωνιαῖος.

2. In the phrase—"foundation of the apostles and prophets"—the genitive has been thought to be that of apposition, that is, these apostles and prophets are themselves the
foundation. Winer, § 59, 8, *a*. Such is the opinion of
Chrysostom and his imitators, Theophylact and Œcumenius,
of a-Lapide, Estius, Zanchius, Morus, de Wette, Baumgarten-Crusius, Meier, von Gerlach, Turner, Hofmann, and
Olshausen. Θεμέλιος ὑποκείνται, says Theophylact, οἱ προφῆται καὶ οἱ ἀπόστολοι, ὑμεῖς δὲ τὴν λοιπὴν οἰκοδομὴν
ἀναπληρώσατε. This view is supposed to be confirmed by a
passage in the Apocalypse (xxi. 14)—"The wall of the city
had twelve foundations, and in them the names of the twelve
apostles of the Lamb." But these foundations belong to a
wall, a symbol of defence, not to the great Christian temple;
and unless Judas be regarded as deposed, and Matthias as
prematurely chosen and never divinely sanctioned, Paul, the
founder of the Ephesian church, cannot be reckoned among
these twelve. It does not matter for the interpretation
whether θεμελίῳ be masculine or neuter, nor is the argument
of Hofmann (*Schriftb.* vol. ii. sec. part, p. 101) of any avail,
that as the last clause has a personal reference this must have
the same. In one sense the apostles, in their personal teaching
and labours, may be reckoned the foundation; but should such
a sense be adopted here, Christ would be brought into comparison with them. Hofmann (*l.c.*) gets out of this objection
by taking the following αὐτοῦ as referring to θεμελίῳ—"Jesus
Christ being its chief corner-stone"—that is, if He is the

corner-stone of the foundation, the language prevents Him being regarded as *primus inter pares.* But, as we shall see, the exegesis is not tenable. The whole passage, however, gives Jesus peculiar prominence, and the apostle never wearies of extolling His dignity and glory. Still, there is nothing doctrinally wrong in this interpretation, for, personally, prophets and apostles are but living stones in the temple, the next tier above the "corner-stone;" but officially they were not the foundation—they rather laid it. And therefore—

3. The phrase—"foundation of the apostles and prophets," means the foundation laid by them, the genitive being subjective, or that of originating agency—*der thätigen Person oder Kraft.* Scheuerlein, § 17, 1; Winer, § 30, 1; Hartung, *Casus*, p. 12. Such is the exegesis of Ambrosiaster, Bullinger, Bodius, Calvin, Calovius, Piscator, Calixtus, Wolf, Baumgarten, Musculus, Röell, Zanchius, Grotius, Bengel, Koppe, Flatt, Rückert, Harless, Matthies, Meyer, Holzhausen, and Ellicott. The apostles and prophets laid the foundation broad and deep in their official labours. In speaking of the foundation in other epistles, the apostle never conceives of himself as being that foundation, but only as laying it. He stands, in his own idea, as external to it. Referring to his masonic operations, he designates himself "a wise master-builder," and adds—"Other foundation can no man lay, than that is laid, which is Jesus Christ." Similar phraseology occurs in Rom. xv. 20. In this laying of the foundation, apostles and prophets were alike employed, when they preached Jesus and organized into communities such as received their message. The foundation alluded to here is $εἰρήνη$—not so much Christ in person, as Christ "our peace"—a gospel, therefore, having no restrictive peculiarity of blood or lineage, and by accepting which men come into union with God. And no other foundation can suffice. When philosophical speculation or critical erudition, political affinity or human enactment, supplants it, the structure topples and is about to fall. The opinions of Luther, Calvin, Cranmer, Wesley, Knox, or Erskine (and these were all "pillars"), are not the foundation; nor are the edicts and creeds of Trent, Augsburg, Dort, or Westminster Such writings may originate sectional distinctions, and give peculiar shape to column or portico, shaft or capital, on the

great edifice, but they can never be substituted for the one foundation. Yea and further—

ὄντος ἀκρογωνιαίου αὐτοῦ Ἰησοῦ Χριστοῦ—" Jesus Christ Himself being the chief corner-stone." A and B, with the Vulgate, Gothic, and Coptic, reverse the position of the proper names, and their authority is followed by Lachmann, Tischendorf, and Alford; but the majority of uncial MSS. are in favour of the present reading. The pronoun is, by Bengel, Cramer, Koppe, and Holzhausen, referred to the preceding θεμέλιον—" Jesus Christ being its chief corner-stone." That the translation of our English version may be maintained, it is not necessary, as these critics affirm, that the article should precede the proper name. Fritzsche, *Comment.* in Matt. iii. 4; Luke x. 42; John iv. 44. It is, besides, not of the foundation, but of the temple that He is the chief corner-stone. The αὐτοῦ contrasts Christ with apostles and prophets. They lay the foundation, but Jesus Himself in person is the chief corner-stone—ὄντος, " being all the while "—ἀκρογωνιαίου— *scilicet*—λίθου. The reference in the apostle's mind seems to be to Ps. cxviii. 22; Isa. xxviii. 16; Jer. li. 26. These passages suggested the figure which occurs also in Matt. xxi. 42; Acts iv. 11; 1 Pet. ii. 4–6. There are two different Hebrew phrases—ראשׁ פִּנָּה[1]—κεφαλὴ τῆς γωνίας (Ps. cxviii. 22), whereas in Isa. xxviii. 16 the words are אֶבֶן פִּנָּה, rendered by the Seventy —λίθον ἀκρογωνιαῖον. The first expression certainly denotes not the copestone, nor yet the head or point where two walls meet, but the most prominent stone in the corner. In the latter phrase the reference is to a stone specially employed at the angle or junction of two walls, to connect them, as well as to bear their weight. In the first formula, allusion is made more to the position than to the purpose of the block. In Jer. li. 26, the corner-stone and the foundations seem to be distinguished. The corner-stone, placed at the angle of the building, seems to have been reckoned in Oriental architecture of more importance than the foundation-stone. The foundation-stones, θεμέλιοι—plural, were first laid, and indicated the plan of the structure; but the corner-stone,—that is, the foundation-stone placed at the corner—required peculiar size and strength. In short, the " chief corner-stone " is that principal

[1] Gesenius, *Thesaurus, sub voce.*

foundation which was carefully laid at the angle of the building, and on which the connected walls rested. From its position and design it was styled "the head of the corner." While the apostles and prophets generally placed the foundation, the primary stone—on which, in Hebrew idea or image, the structure mainly rests, and by which its unity is upheld —was Jesus Christ. Without this its walls would not have been connected, but there must have been a fissure. As Theodoret, Menochius, Estius, and Holzhausen think, there may be a reference to Jew and Gentile united on the one rock. The laying of the foundation prepares for the setting down of the corner-stone, which connects and concentrates upon itself the weight of the building. That man, "Jesus," who was "Christ," the divinely-appointed, qualified, and accepted Saviour, unites and sustains the church. Saving knowledge is the apprehension of that truth about Him which Himself has announced—saving faith is dependence on the atoning work which He has done—hope rests in His intercession— the sanctifying Spirit is His gift—the unity of the church has its spiritual centre in Him—its government is from Him as its King—and its safety is in Him its exalted Protector. Whether, therefore, we regard creed or practice, worship or discipline, faith or government, union or extension, is He not in His truth, His blood, His power, His legislation, and His presence to His church, "Himself the chief corner-stone"? In short, He is "the Alpha and the Omega," and combined at the same time with every evangelical theme. Should we describe the glories of creation, He is Creator; or enlarge on the wisdom and benignity of Providence, He is Preserver and Ruler. Is the Divine Law the theme of exposition?—He not only enacted it, but exemplified its precepts and endured its penalty. Are we summoned to speak of death?—He has "abolished it;" or if we wander among the tombs, He lay in the sepulchre and rose from it "the first-fruits of them that sleep." If ministers preach, Christ crucified is their text; and if churches "grow in grace," such holiness is conformity to the life of their Lord. He is, moreover, "all in all" in the entire circuit of the operations of the Spirit, who applies His truth to the mind, sprinkles His blood on the heart, and seals the inner man with His blessed image.

(Ver. 21.) 'Ἐν ᾧ πᾶσα οἰκοδομὴ συναρμολογουμένη αὔξει— "In whom the whole building, being fitly framed together, is growing." The relative agrees with the nearest substantive, 'Ἰησοῦ Χριστοῦ—not with τῷ θεμελίῳ, as is the opinion of Holzhausen; nor with ἀκρογωνιαίου, and meaning "on which," as is asserted by Theophylact, Luther, Beza, Koppe, and Scholz. Nor can the words signify "through whom," as is held by Castalio, Vatablus, Menochius, Morus, and Flatt. "In whom," that is, in Christ Jesus; the building being fitly framed together in Him. Its unity and symmetry are originated and maintained in Him. The article ἡ before πᾶσα in A and C, and in the Textus Receptus, appears to be spurious; it is not found in B, D, E, F, G, I, K, and is rejected by the latest editors, Lachmann and Tischendorf. Middleton and Trollope, for mere grammatical reasons, affirm that πᾶσα ἡ is the right reading. Reiche says—*Paulum scripsisse* πᾶσα ἡ οἰκοδομή *cum articulo nullus dubito*, and he ascribes the omission to the homoioteleuton—οἰκοδομή ἡ. *Comment. Crit.* p. 149; Gotting. 1859. Hofmann, *l.c.*, renders, "all which is built"—*was gebaut wird*. Must, then, πᾶσα οἰκοδομή be rendered "every building," as is the opinion of Chrysostom, Beza, Zanchius, and Meyer, or as Wycliffe renders—"eche bildynge," and Tyndale—"every bildynge"? We think not:—For, 1. The object of the apostle is to describe the one temple, which has its foundation laid by apostles and prophets. It is of this one structure, so founded, so united, so raised, and consisting of such materials—for in it the Ephesians were inbuilt—that he speaks. 2. In the later Greek as in the earlier, πᾶς, without the article, sometimes bore the sense of "whole." Bernhardy, p. 323; Gersdorf, p. 376; Scott and Liddell, Pape, Passow, *sub voce*. So in the New Testament, Matt. ii. 3; Luke iv. 13; Acts vii. 22; or Acts ii. 36—Πᾶς οἶκος 'Ἰσραήλ—phraseology based upon the usage of the Septuagint, 1 Sam. vii. 2, 3; Neh. iv. 16; Col. i. 15. If, as Ellicott says, these examples are not in point, as being proper names or abstract substantives, they at least show the transition from an earlier and stricter to a laxer and later use, in which other nouns besides proper names and very familiar or monadic terms may dispense with the articles. Winer, § 18, 4, § 19. So in Josephus, *Antiq.* iv. 5, 1—Ποταμὸς διὰ πάσης ἐρήμου ῥέων—"a river flowing through the whole desert;" Thucydides, ii. 43—πᾶσα γῆ and also in 38—ἐκ πάσης γῆς; *Iliad*, xxiv. 407—πᾶσαν ἀληθείην; Hesiod, *Op. et Dies*, 510—πᾶσα ὕλη; *Theog.* 874—χθὼν πᾶσα. Also—διὰ πάσης νυκτός; Passow, *sub voce*; Thiersch, *De Penta. versione Alexandrina*, p. 121, in which are some examples, though perhaps not all of them strictly analogous. The Syriac has : ܟܠܗ ܒܢܝܢܐ—"the whole building."

Οἰκοδομή, a term of the later Greek, as is shown by Lobeck in his Parerga to the Eclogæ of Phrynichus, signifies properly "the art or process of building," and is originally equivalent to οἰκοδόμησις, but has also the same meaning as οἰκοδόμημα—pp. 421, 487, 490. The structure named has not yet been completed, and πᾶσα οἰκοδομή signifies the entire structure—the structure in every part of it. The edifice in course of erection, being fitly framed together in all its parts, groweth into a holy temple. Such is the opinion of Chrysostom, which Harless sets aside without sufficient evidence. For of what is the "growth" specified? Is the structure complete, and is the growth supposed to be not of it as an edifice in itself, but of its purpose—" into a holy temple"? Does the edifice wax in size, or only grow in destination and object? If you suppose the latter, then you also suppose that the living stones are placed in the temple before its design is realized; or that these stones are themselves changed after they are laid in their places. The growth, therefore, belongs to the edifice itself. It increases in size and height. Even in its unfinished state, the purpose of the fabric may be detected; and when it is completed, that purpose, apparent at every stage of its progress, shall be manifest, fully and for ever—"a holy temple in the Lord."

The present participle συναρμολογουμένη, is a rare term occurring only once more, in iv. 16—συναρμόζειν being the classic form—and denotes "being jointed together," or composed of parts fitted closely to each other. The whole structure is compact and firm; not loose and ill-arranged masonry, which is as unstable in itself as it is offensive to the eye. But every stone is in its place, and fits its place. In this mutual adaptation there is no useless projection, no unsightly chasm. Neither excrescence nor defect mars the beauty of the structure—"in Christ" it is fitly framed together. There is no superfluous doctrine, and no forgotten precept; grace does not clash with statute or service; promises "are yea and amen in Him;" pardon, peace, purity, and hope are linked into one another, because they are closely united to Him; and the members of the true church are so firmly allied, that the gifts and graces of one are supplementary to the gifts and graces of another. No qualification is lost, and none can be dispensed with. One's ingenuity devises what another's activity works out. While conquests are made in distant climes, "she that tarries at home divides the spoil." The huge walls built round the Peiræus by the Athenians under Themistocles, are described by the historian[1] as composed of large stones, square-hewn, and built together, being fixed to one another, on the outside, with iron and lead. But such cumbrous ligatures do not disfigure those spiritual walls; for that magnetic influence which binds all the living stones to the chief Corner-stone, cements them, at the same time and by the same power, to one another in cordial sympathy and reciprocal coherence and support. As Fergusson says—"By taking band with Christ the foundation, they are fastened one to another."

Αὔξει is for the more usual αὐξάνει. It occurs Col. ii. 19, and also in the Greek poets. The present marks actual growth certainly, and may describe normal condition. Even in its immature state, and with so much that is undeveloped, one may admire its beauty of outline, and its graceful form and proportions. Vast augmentations may be certainly anticipated; but its increase does not destroy its adaptations, for it grows as "being fitly framed together." A structure not firm and compact, is in the greater danger of falling the higher it is carried; and "if it topple on our heads, what matters it whether we are crushed by a Corinthian or a Doric ruin?" But this fabric, with walls of more than Cyclopean or Pelasgian strength and vastness, secures its own continuous and illimitable elevation and increase. The design of the edifice is next stated—

---

[1] Δύο γὰρ ἅμαξαι ἐναντίαι ἀλλήλαις τοὺς λίθους ἐπῆγον. Ἐντὸς δὲ οὔτε χάλιξ οὔτε πηλὸς ἦν, ἀλλὰ ξυνῳκοδομημένοι μεγάλοι λίθοι καὶ ἐν τομῇ ἐγγώνιοι σιδήρῳ πρὸς ἀλλήλους τὰ ἔξωθεν καὶ μολύβδῳ δεδεμένοι—Thucydides, i. 93.

εἰς ναὸν ἅγιον ἐν Κυρίῳ—groweth—" into a holy temple in the Lord." It was a temple—a sacred edifice. The words ἐν Κυρίῳ belong to ἅγιον, or rather to ναὸν ἅγιον; not, as Œcumenius, Grotius, Baumgarten, Zachariae, Wolf, and Meyer suppose, to αὔξει; for these critics, with the exception of the last, give ἐν the sense of διά—it groweth " by means of" the Lord. Nor does Κύριος refer to God, as Michaelis, Koppe, Rosenmüller, and Baumgarten-Crusius suppose, but, as in Pauline usage, to Christ. (See chap. i. 2, 3.) Neither are we, with Beza, Koppe, Macknight, and others, to rob the ἐν of its own significance, making the phrase ἐν Κυρίῳ equivalent to a dative, and joining it with ναόν; nor, with Drusius and a-Lapide, to give it the meaning of a genitive. These are rash and ungrammatical modes of interpretation. It has no holiness but from the Lord, neither is it a temple but from its connection with Him. For the meaning of ἅγιος, see i. 1. The signification of the simple dative—" a temple dedicated to the Lord,"[1] cannot be admitted for another reason—that Jesus is represented as the chief corner-stone, and cannot be also depicted as the God of the temple, or its officiating priest. But the chief corner-stone, solid and massive, gives firmness and sanctity to the structure. The term ναός is apparently used of individual believers (1 Cor. iii. 16, 17, vi. 19; 2 Cor.

---

[1] The vivacious fancy of a Frenchman is seen in the following description :—
" Quelle sagesse encore ne remarque-t-on point dans la diverse dispensation des graces que l'Eglise reçoit de Dieu ? Ici il employe l'or brilliant d'une foi extraordinairement éclairée ; là l'argent secourable d'une charité liberale ; là le fer dur et ferme d'une patience invincible ; là le cèdre incorruptible d'une vie pure, et éloignée des corruptions du monde ; là la hauteur des colonnes qui paroissent de loin, pour mettre la verité dans une belle vuë ; là la force des soubassemens qui la soutiennent et l'affermissent ; afin que par ce moyen son Eglise soit un édifice bien ajusté et bien assorti, à qui rien ne manque pour sa subsistance. Il se sert même de la contrarieté des humeurs et des esprits, pour rendre cet ajustement plus parfait. Car par la promptitude et la véhémence des uns, il excite la lenteur des autres : et par la lenteur de ceux-ci il modéré et retient la promptitude de ceux-là. Par les lumières des clairvoyans il instruit les simples, et par la sainte simplicité des idiots, il sanctifie les lumières des clairvoyans. Si tous étoient bouillans dans leur humeur, il y auroit de l'emportement ; si to s étoient froids, il y auroit de la negligence : mais par la violence des uns il échauffe la froideur de tempérament des autres ; et par la froideur des derniers il tempéré la trop grande ardeur des premiers ; faisant et entretenant ainsi un heureux ajustement, et une salutaire harmonie dans son Eglise."—*Sermons sur l'Epître de St. Paul aux Ephesiens*, par feu M. Du Bosc, tome iii. pp. 299, 300. 1699.

vi. 16. Compare 1 Pet. ii. 3, 4), and its peculiar and specific meaning is given in the next clause, by the words κατοικητήριον τοῦ Θεοῦ—" habitation of God;" for ναός, from ναίω, like the Latin *aedes*, is the dwelling of the Divinity. Ex. xxv. 8, 22; 1 Kings vi. 12, 13; 1 Cor. vi. 19. The illustration of the word is naturally postponed to the following verse.

(Ver. 22.) Ἐν ᾧ καὶ ὑμεῖς συνοικοδομεῖσθε—"In which also you are built together." To translate καὶ ὑμεῖς by "you even" may be too broad, but some comparison is involved. Some refer ἐν ᾧ to Κυρίῳ, "in whom." Such is the opinion of Olshausen, Harless, de Wette, Meyer, Stier, Alford, and Ellicott. Others, like Zanchius, Grotius, and Koppe, go back with needless travel to ἀκρογωνιαίου for an antecedent. We prefer, with Calixtus, Rosenmüller, Baumgarten, and Matthies, taking ναὸν ἅγιον ἐν Κυρίῳ as the antecedent. If it be said, on the one hand, that ἐν ᾧ usually in such connections refers to Christ, then it may be said, on the other hand, that to be built *in* or *into* a temple keeps the figure homogeneous. The entire structure compacted in Jesus groweth into a temple, "in which ye also are built" as living stones. The ὑμεῖς may specially refer to the Gentile Christians, as they are peculiarly addressed and reminded of their privileges, for this verse is the conclusion of the paragraph which began with the congratulation—" Ye are no more strangers and foreigners."

The intense signification of *magis magisque* which Bucer gives to the συν- in composition with the συνοικοδομεῖσθε, is wholly unwarranted, save by this implication, that the placing of those stones from the Ephesian quarry on the rising structure added considerably to its size. Nor can we, with Calvin and Meier, look upon the verb as an imperative; for the entire previous context is a recital of privilege, and the same form of syntactic connection is maintained throughout. The idea that seems to be entertained by Harless and Grotius is—As the whole building fitly framed together groweth into a holy temple in the Lord, so ye, individually or socially, are built up in like manner for a habitation of God in the Spirit. This opinion destroys as well the unity of the figure as the connection of the verses. It is one temple which the apostle describes, and he concludes his delineation by telling the Ephesians that they formed part of its living materials and masonry. In

1 Esdr. v. 68, συνοικοδομήσομεν ὑμῖν means—"we will build along with you." The dative is, however, in that clause formally expressed, while in the passage before us no other party is referred to. The ὑμεῖς of this verse are the ὑμεῖς of ver. 19. The συν- may not, therefore, expressly denote "along with others," but rather—"Ye are built together in mutual contact or union among yourselves, or rather with all built in along with you." The verb is thus of similar reference with συναρμολογουμένη. The stones of that building are not thrown together without choice or order, but they adhere with a happy and unchanging union. Christians who have personal knowledge of one another have a closer intimacy, and so they are not wantonly separated in this structure, but, like the Ephesian church, are "built together."

εἰς κατοικητήριον τοῦ Θεοῦ ἐν Πνεύματι—"for an habitation of God in the Spirit." We regard these words as explanatory of the ναὸς ἅγιος of the preceding verse, to the explanation of which the reader may turn. We cannot, with Harless, refer them to individual Christians, for such an idea mars the unity and completeness of the figure. As Stier remarks, too, all the nouns are in the singular, and refer to one structure. The purpose of the holy temple is defined. It is, as we have seen from several portions of the Old Testament, the dwelling of God.[1] "This is my rest"—"here will I stay." Now Jehovah dwelt in His temple for two purposes:—1. To instruct His people by His oracles and cheer them with His presence. "God is in the midst of her"—"Shine forth, Thou that dwellest between the cherubim"—"I will meet thee, and I will commune with thee." Moses brought the causes of the people "before the Lord." God inhabits this spiritual fane for spiritual ends—to teach and prompt, to guide and bless, to lead and comfort. His presence diffuses a light and joy, of which the lustre of the Shechinah was only a faint reflection and emblem. 2. Jehovah dwelt in the temple to accept the services of His people. The offerings were presented in the courts of the house to the God of the house. "Spiritual

---

[1] Josephus records among the omens which preceded the fall of Jerusalem, that a mysterious voice was heard in the temple to utter the awful words—"Let us go hence," as if its Divine inhabitant had been bidding it farewell, and leaving it to its fate.

sacrifices" are still laid on the altar to God, and the odour of such oblations is a "sweet savour," rising with fresh and undispersed perfume to Him who is enshrined in His sanctuary.

Three interpretations have been proposed of the concluding words—ἐν Πνεύματι. 1. Some, such as Chrysostom, Rückert, Olshausen, and Holzhausen, as also Erasmus, Homberg, Koppe, Flatt, and others, give the words an adjectival sense, as if they merely meant "spiritually," and characterized this edifice, in contrast with the Jewish temple "made with hands." But such an exposition is baseless. There is no contrast intended between a material and a spiritual temple, nor is there anything implying it. Nor could the two words, placed as they are by the apostle, naturally bear such a signification. That the article is not necessary to give the words a personal reference, as some, such as Rückert, affirm, is plain from many similar passages, as may be seen in our remarks on i. 17, and in the following paragraph.

2. Some join ἐν Πνεύματι to the verb συνοικοδομεῖσθε, and then the words denote—"built together by means of the Spirit." This is the view of Theophylact, Œcumenius, Meyer, and Hodge. Calvin combines both this and the preceding interpretation. To such an exegesis we might object, with Harless, that it is strange that words of such importance, denoting the medium of erection, should be found in the paragraph as a species of afterthought. Harless indeed adds, that Πνεῦμα, denoting the Spirit objectively, should have the article. But surely the article is not required any more than with the ἐν Κυρίῳ of the preceding verse. The reader may turn for proof to this epistle, iii. 5, vi. 18; and Matt. xxii. 43; Rom. viii. 4; 1 Cor. xiv. 2; Gal. iv. 29, v. 5; in all which places the Holy Ghost is referred to, and the noun wants the article. See under i. 17. Where the Holy Spirit in distinct and external personality is spoken of, or His influences are regarded as coming from without, the noun has the article; but in many places where He is conceived of in His subjective operations, the article is either inserted or omitted. It is omitted Matt. i. 18–20, iii. 11, and inserted Luke ii. 27, iv. 1, 14. Perhaps the idea of Divine power exerted *ab extra* is intended in these last passages. When the epithet ἅγιον is employed, the article is sometimes used and sometimes not, though the cases of

omission are rather more frequent. But no possible difference of meaning can in many places be detected. Harless instances 1 Cor. ii. 4, 13, compared with ver. 10, in which last verse the Spirit is conceived of as God's, and has the article. In the phrases in which the Spirit's relation to the Father is kept in view, the article is used. But revelation is as clearly ascribed to the Spirit in this epistle, iii. 5, as in 1 Cor. ii. 10, and yet in the former place it has no article. The article, without difference of view, is employed and rejected in contiguous verses. Acts viii. 17, 18, 19, xix. 2, 6 ; John iii. 5, 6. The cases of insertion in these quotations may be accounted for on other and mere grammatical principles. Fritzsche, *ad Rom.* viii. 4.

3. The third interpretation is that supported virtually by Stier, de Wette, and Matthies. God dwells in this temple, as in individual believers, " by or in His Spirit." Christians are the temple of God, because the Spirit of God dwelleth in them. 1 Cor. iii. 16. What is true of them separately is also true of them collectively—they are the residence of God in the Spirit. Ἐν Πνεύματι defines the mode of inhabitation. That temple, from its connection with the Spirit—inasmuch as the Spirit has fashioned, quickened, and laid its living stones, and dwells within them—is "a habitation of God." The God who resides in the church is the enlightening, purifying, elevating, comforting Spirit. The apostle's own definition of the formula is—" Ye are ἐν Πνεύματι—in the Spirit, if so be that the Spirit of God dwell in you." Rom. viii. 9. And thus again, as often before, the Trinity or the triune relation of God to His people is brought out. The Father dwells in the Spirit in that temple of which the Son is the chief corner-stone. The church is one, holy and Divine ; it rests on Christ—is possessed by God—filled with the Spirit—and is ever increasing.

## CHAPTER III

HAVING illustrated with such cordial satisfaction and impressive imagery the high privileges of the Gentile converts, the apostle, as his manner is, resolves to present a prayer for them. But other thoughts rush into his mind, suggested by his own personal condition.[1] He was a prisoner; and as he was now writing to Gentiles, at least was at that moment addressing the Gentile portion of the Ephesian church, an allusion to his bonds was natural, and seems to have been introduced at once as a proof of the honesty of his congratulations, and as a circumstance that must have prepared his readers to enter into the spirit of the earnest and comprehensive supplication to be offered on their behalf. But the impressive theme on which he had been dilating with such ecstasy still vibrated in his heart, and the mention of his imprisonment, originating in his attachment to the Gentiles, suggested a reference to his special functions as the apostle of heathendom. These ideas came upon him with such force, and brought with them such associations, that he could not easily pass from them. The clank of his chain at length awakens him to present reality, and he concludes the parenthesis with a request that his readers would not mope and despond over his sufferings, endured for a cause in which they had so tender and blessed interest. The 1st and 13th verses are thus in close connection, and the apostle, as if describing a circle, comes round at length to the point from which he originally started. The connection is — " For this cause, I Paul, the prisoner of Jesus Christ for you Gentiles "—" bow my knees unto the Father of our Lord Jesus Christ."

(Ver. 1.) *Τούτου χάριν*—" For this cause ; " the reference

[1] The accusers of the apostle had not yet come to Rome, and he might therefore be detained for an indefinite period. This law was afterwards altered, and the suspension of a process for a year was held to be tantamount to its abandonment.

being not to any special element in the previous illustration, but to the whole of it—inasmuch as Gentile believers are raised along with believing Jews to those high privileges and honours now common to both of them. The remarks we have made will show that we regard the construction as broken by a long parenthesis, and resumed in ver. 14, not at ver. 8, as Œcumenius and Grotius suppose, nor yet at ver. 13, as Zanchius, Cramer, and Holzhausen maintain. In the former hypothesis, the connection thus stands—" I Paul, the prisoner of Jesus Christ for you Gentiles"—"even to me, less than the least of all saints, is this grace given." But here there is no natural contact of ideas, and the change of case from the nominative to the dative, though vindicated by Œcumenius from examples in Thucydides and Demosthenes, is, as Origen affirms, a solecism, and is fatal to the hypothesis. Catena *in loc.* ed. Cramer. Oxford, 1842. The 8th verse is inseparably connected also with the 6th and 7th verses. The other opinion, that the course of thought is resumed in ver. 13, is proved to be untenable as well by the occurrence of the simple διό in that verse, as by the fact that the repeated τούτου χάριν of the following verse has no foundation in the sentiment of the 13th. The idea expressed in the 13th verse is a subordinate and natural conclusion of the digression. Erasmus, Schmid, Michaelis, and Hammond would consider the whole chapter a parenthesis, but such an opinion makes the digression altogether too long, and overlooks the connecting link in ver. 14. The majority of expositors adopt the view we have given, to wit, that ver. 14 resumes the interrupted sentiment. Theodoret says—ταῦτα πάντα (vers. 1–13) ἐν μέσῳ τεθεικὼς ἀναλαμβάνει τὸν περὶ προσευχῆς λόγον. This opinion plainly harmonizes with the scope and construction of the chapter. Winer, § 62, 4.

But there are some commentators who deny that any parenthesis or digression occurs, and for this purpose various supplements have been proposed for the 1st verse. Many supply the verb εἰμί—" For this cause I Paul *am* the prisoner of Jesus Christ." This conjecture has for its authority the Peschito, which is followed by Chrysostom, Theophylact, Anselm, Erasmus, Aretius, Cajetan, Beza, with a large host of modern critics, the version of Tyndale, and Geneva. The paraphrase of Chrysostom is—διὰ τοῦτο καὶ ἐγὼ δέδεμαι; and he adds in explanation of the phrase—"if my Master was crucified for you, much more am I bound." But our objection is, first, that δέσμιος has the article—I am the prisoner, whereas Paul may be supposed to say, "I am a prisoner." It is alleged by Beza, Rollock, and Meyer, that the notoriety of Paul as a prisoner might have prompted him to use the article. But such a supposition is not in harmony with the apostle's character. Under such an exegesis also, as has been often remarked, τούτου χάριν and ὑπὲρ ὑμῶν would form a tautology. The apostle does not mean to magnify the fact of his imprisonment: he merely hints in passing that it originated in the proclamation of those very truths which he had been discussing. Middleton *on Greek Article,* p. 358. Others, again, such as the Codices D, E, supply πρεσβεύω — a spurious insertion borrowed from vi. 20, and adopted by Ambrosiaster and Castalio, as well as by Calvin in his Latin rendering—*legatione fungor.* Another MS. has the verb κεκαύχημαι, taken from Phil. ii. 16. Jerome supplies—*cognovi mysterium,* and Camerarius gives us—*hoc scribo.* Meyer's rendering is peculiar—*deshalb*—that you may be built—*zu diesem Behufe bin Ich Paulus, der Gefesselte Christi Jesu um euret, der Heiden willen.* But the plain supposition of a long parenthesis renders all such supplements superfluous.

Ἐγὼ Παῦλος—" I Paul," his own name being inserted to give distinctness, personality, and authority to the statement, as in 1 Cor. i. 12, 13, iii. 4, 5, 22; 2 Cor. x. 1; Gal. v. 2; Col. i. 23; 1 Thess. ii. 18; Philem. 9. That name was venerated in those churches, and its formal mention must have struck a deep and tender chord in their bosom. Once Saul, the synonym of antichristian intolerance, it was now Paul, not merely a disciple or a servant, but—

ὁ δέσμιος τοῦ Χριστοῦ Ἰησοῦ—"the prisoner of Christ Jesus." 2 Tim. i. 8; Philem. 9. The genitive, as that of originating cause, signifies not merely "a prisoner belonging to Christ," but one whom Christ, that is, Christ's cause, and not Cæsar, had imprisoned. Winer, § 30, 2, β; Acts xxiii. 11. His loss of liberty arose from no violation of law on his part: it was solely in prosecuting his mission that he was apprehended and confined; for he was in fetters—

ὑπὲρ ὑμῶν τῶν ἐθνῶν—"on behalf of you Gentiles," a common sense of the preposition, which is repeated in ver. 12. It was his office as apostle of the Gentiles which exposed him to persecution, and led to his present incarceration. Acts xxi. 22, xxv. 11, xxviii. 16. His vindication of such truths as formed the last paragraph of the preceding chapter, roused Jewish jealousy and indignation. Nay, in writing to the Ephesians he could not forget that the suspicion of his having taken an Ephesian named Trophimus into the temple with him, created the popular disturbance that led to his capture and his final appeal to Cæsar, his journey to Rome, and his imprisonment in the imperial city. The apostle proceeds to explain more fully the meaning of this clause—

(Ver. 2.) Εἴγε ἠκούσατε τὴν οἰκονομίαν—"If indeed ye have heard of the dispensation." As the translation—"if ye have heard"—seems to imply that Paul was a stranger to the Ephesian church, various attempts have been made to give the words another rendering. (See Introduction.) That εἴγε may bear the meaning "since," is undeniable (iv. 21; Col. i. 23); or, "if indeed, as I take for granted, ye have heard;" or, as Estius and Wiggers translate—"if, as is indeed the case, ye have heard." Hermann, *ad Viger.* p. 834. The particle γε is used in suppletive sentences (Hartung, *Partik.* i. 391), and may be rendered *und zwar*—"and indeed." Harless is inclined to take the words as hypothetical,[1] as indicating want of personal acquaintance with his readers; but Hartung (ii. 212) lays it down, that in cases where the contents of the sentence are adduced as proof of a preceding statement, the meaning of εἴγε approaches that of ὅτι and ἐπεί. Hoogeveen also states the same canon.[2] The apostle says—I am a prisoner for you Gentiles; and he now gives the reason of his assertion—Ye must surely have heard of the dispensation committed to me—a dispensation whose prominent and distinctive element it is to preach among the Gentiles.

Reckless efforts have been made upon the verb ἠκούσατε— as when Pelagius renders it *firmiter tenetis.* So Anselm, Grotius, and Rinck, *Sendschreib. des Korinth.* p. 56. See under i. 15. The apostle has been supposed by Musculus, Crocius, Flatt,

[1] *Stud. und Kritik.* 1841, p. 432.
[2] *Doctrina Particularum*, etc., p. 158, ed. Schütz; Klotz-Devar, p. 308.

and de Wette, to mean "hearing by report of others." There is no proof of this in the language, nor of the other version—"hearing, and also attending and understanding." The writer may refer to his own sermons, for we cannot say with Calvin —*credibile est, quum ageret Ephesi, eum tacuisse de his rebus.* The apostle may, in this quiet form, stir up their memory of the truth, that mission to the heathen was his special work—not his work by accident, but by fixed Divine arrangement. He preached in Ephesus to both Jew and Gentile; and his precise vocation, as the apostle of the Gentiles, might not have been very fully or formally discussed. Still it was a theme which could not have been kept in abeyance. They surely had heard it from his lips; and this εἴγε, rather than ὅτι, is the expression of a gentle hope that they had not forgotten the lesson. Yet there is no reprehension in the phrase, as is supposed by Vitringa and Holzhausen.

The term οἰκονομία does not signify the apostolical office, as is the opinion of Luther, Musculus, Rollock, Aretius, Crocius, Wieseler, and others, for it is explained by the apostle himself in the following verse; and it cannot denote *dispensatio doctrinæ*, as Pelagius translates it; not *officium dispensandæ gratiæ Dei*, as Anselm explains it. See under i. 10. Its meaning is arrangement or plan; and the apostle employs it to describe the mode in which he had been selected and qualified to preach faith and privilege to the Gentiles. Chrysostom identifies the οἰκονομία with the ἀποκάλυψις of the following verse—"As much as to say, I learned it not from man." How came it that a person like Paul—a staunch Pharisee, a scholar of Gamaliel, attached to rabbinical studies, and a zealot in defence of the law—how came it that he, with antecedents so notorious in their contrast, should be the man to preach, as his special mission, the entrance of Gentiles into Christian privilege? The method of his initiation was of God; and that "economy" is described as being—

τῆς χάριτος τοῦ Θεοῦ τῆς δοθείσης μοι εἰς ὑμᾶς—"of the grace of God which is given me to you-ward." This χάρις is not, as Grotius and Rückert imagine, the apostolical office, but the source or contents of it. We see no ground to identify χάρις with the following μυστήριον, though it includes it. The idea is either that the οἰκονομία had its origin in that χάρις, or rather that the χάρις was its characteristic element. Winer, § 30, 2. That grace was given him, not that he might enjoy it as a private luxury, but that he by its assistance might impart it to others—εἰς ὑμᾶς—" to you," not *inter vos*, as Storr makes it. Gal. i. 15, ii. 9 ; Acts xxii. 21. There may, as Stier suggests, be an allusion in the οἰκονομία to the οἰκοδομή of ver. 21 in the previous chapter. In the house-arrangement and distribution of offices, the building of the Gentile portion of the structure was Paul's special function. The apostle now becomes more special in his description—

(Ver. 3.)"Ὅτι κατὰ ἀποκάλυψιν ἐγνωρίσθη μοι τὸ μυστήριον —" How that by revelation was the mystery made known to me." Ἐγνώρισε is the reading of the Received Text, on the authority of D$^{111}$, E, J, K, and many minuscules, and is received by Knapp and Tittmann; but ἐγνωρίσθη has the preponderant authority of A, B, C, D$^1$, F, G, etc., the Syriac and Vulgate, and is adopted by Lachmann, Hahn, and Tischendorf. The "relative particle ὅτι, as the correlative of τί, introduces an objective sentence." Donaldson, *Greek Gram*. § 584. It leads to further explanation, and the clause is a supplementary accusative connected with the previous verb. The mystery itself is unfolded in ver. 6 ; for, as we have seen under i. 9, "mystery" is not something in itself incomprehensible, but merely something unknown till God please to reveal it— something undiscoverable by man, and to the knowledge of which he comes by Divine disclosure—κατὰ ἀποκάλυψιν, the emphasis lying on the phrase, as is indicated by its position. Gal. ii. 2. In Gal. i. 12, the genitive with διά is employed. Grammarians, as Bernhardy (p. 241) and Winer (§ 51), show that κατά, with the accusative, has sometimes an adverbial signification; so Meyer renders *offenbarungsweise*. The difference is not material; but δι' ἀποκαλύψεως would refer to the means or method of disclosure, whereas κατὰ ἀποκάλυψιν may describe the shape which it assumed. The general spirit of the statement is, that his mission to the Gentiles was not created by the expansive philanthropy of his own bosom, nor was it any sourness of temper against his countrymen that prompted him to select, as his favourite sphere of labour, the outfield of heathendom. He might have been a believer, but still, like many thousands of the Jews—" zealous of the law."

It was by special instruction that he comprehended the world-wide adaptations of the gospel, and gave himself to the work of evangelizing the heathen—the mystery being their admission to church fellowship equally with the Jews. He alludes, not perhaps so much to the first instructions of the Divine will at his conversion (Acts ix. 15), as to subsequent revelations. Acts xxii. 21; Gal. i. 16. And he adds—

καθὼς προέγραψα ἐν ὀλίγῳ—" as I have just written in brief;" or, as Tyndale renders—" as I wrote above, in feawe wordes;" i. 9, ii. 13. The parenthetical marking of some editors commencing with this clause, and extending to the end of ver. 4, is useless; and the relative ὅ in ver. 5 belongs to the antecedent μυστήριον in ver. 4. There is no occasion, with Hunnius, Marloratus, Chrysostom, and Calvin, to make the reference in the verb to some earlier epistle. Theodoret says well—οὐχ ὡς τινές ὑπέλαβον, ὅτι ἑτέραν ἐπιστολὴν γέγραφεν. See under i. 12. Such is the view of the great body of interpreters. The apostle refers to what he had now written in the preceding paragraph—from ver. 13 to the end of the second chapter—and apparently not, as Alford says, to i. 9; nor, as Ellicott says, to the fact contained in the immediately preceding clause.

And he had written ἐν ὀλίγῳ—*in brevi* (Vulgate), " in brief" —in a few words. See Kypke, *Observat.* ii. p. 293, in which examples are given from Herodotus, Thucydides, and Aristotle. Theodoret—followed by Erasmus, Camerarius, Calvin, Grotius, Estius, Koppe, Baumgarten-Crusius, and many others—proposes that ἐν ὀλίγῳ should be taken as explanatory of the προ- in προέγραψα, and that the phrase signifies νῦν, or *paulo ante*. Bodius conveniently combines both views. But such a construction cannot be admitted; to express such an idea πρὸ ὀλίγου would have been employed. And the apostle has not intimated simply that such a mystery was disclosed to him, but that he has also noted down the results or contents of the disclosure, and for this purpose—

(Ver. 4.) Πρὸς ὅ. Πρὸς ὅ cannot be identified, as Theophylact does, with ἐξ ὧν. It may mean, as Harless and de Wette translate, "in consequence of which;" or, as in our version, " whereby." We question, however, whether this meaning can be sustained. It may be the ultimate, but it is not the immediate sense. Its more usual signification—" in reference to which"—is as appropriate. Winer, § 49, h. Such is also the rendering of Peile—" referring to which." Herodot. iii. 52; Jelf, § 638; Matthiae, § 591; Bernhardy, p. 265; Vigerus, *De Idiotismis*, ii. p. 694, London, 1824. The reference is subjective—"as I have already written in brief, in reference to which portion—' *tanquam ad specimen*,' when ye read it, ye may understand my knowledge." In the phrase πρὸς ὅ, the apostle quietly claims their special attention to the passage on which such notoriety is bestowed, and adds—

δύνασθε ἀναγινώσκοντες νοῆσαι τὴν σύνεσίν μου ἐν τῷ μυστηρίῳ τοῦ Χριστοῦ—"you can while reading perceive my insight in the mystery of Christ." When this epistle reached them it was presumed that they would read it;[1] and as they read it, they would feel their competence. The present participle expresses contemporaneous action—the reading being parallel in time to the perception; though the latter is expressed by the aorist infinitive, which form, according to Donaldson, "describes a single act either as the completion or as the commencement of a continuity." *Greek Gram.* § 427, d. If this be supposed to be too refined, it may be added that several verbs, as δύναμαι, are in Greek idiom followed by the aorist rather than the present. Winer, § 44, 7. The verb νοῆσαι means to perceive—come to the knowledge of—to mark; whereas σύνεσις is intelligence or insight, and does not require the repetition of the article before ἐν τῷ μυστηρίῳ, as one idea is conveyed. Josh. i. 7; 2 Chron. xxxiv. 12; Dan. i. 17; 3 Esdr. i. 3. Winer, § 20, 2; Tittmann's *Synon.* p. 191. If ye read what I have written, ye shall perceive what grasp I have of the mystery; and my knowledge of it is based on immediate revelation. True, the apostle had written but briefly, yet these hints were the index of a fuller familiarity with the theme. The genitive, τοῦ Χριστοῦ, is probably that of object. Ellicott, following Stier, inclines to make it that of material or identity, which appears too refined and strained—Col. i. 27 not being exactly parallel, but being a subjective

---

[1] "Here he confuteth the papists on account of their cursed practice in taking away the key of knowledge—the reading of the Scriptures; in which fact they are like the Philistines putting out the eyes of Samson, and taking away the smiths, not leaving a weapon in Israel."—Bayne, *on Eph. in loc.* Lond. 1643.

phase of the same great truth. But why should the apostle solemnly profess such knowledge of the mystery? We can scarcely suppose, with Olshausen, Harless, and de Wette, that Paul had in his eye other persons who were strangers to him, or who were hostile to his claims; nor can we imagine, with Wiggers, that he wrote to the Ephesians as representatives of the heathen world. *Stud. und Kritik.* p. 433; 1841. It could be no vulgar self-assertion that prompted the reference. Possibly he was afraid of coming evils from Judaizing teachers and haughty zealots, and therefore, having illustrated the equality of Gentile privilege, he next vindicates it by the solemn interposition of his apostolical authority.

(Ver. 5.) "Ὃ ἑτέραις γενεαῖς οὐκ ἐγνωρίσθη τοῖς υἱοῖς τῶν ἀνθρώπων—" Which in other ages was not made known to the sons of men." The antecedent to ὅ is μυστήριον, the relative forming a frequent link of connection. The ἐν which is found in the Received Text is condemned by the evidence of MSS., such as A, C, D, E, F, G, I, K. The dative as a designation of the time in which an action took place may stand by itself without a preposition, as in ii. 12, though in poetry the preposition is frequently prefixed. Kühner, § 569; Stuart, § 106; Winer, § 31, 9. According to some, γενεαῖς is a species of ablative, with an ellipse of the preposition, and, as usually happens in such a case, MSS. vary in their readings. Bos, *Ellipses Græcæ*, ed. Schæfer, p. 437. Γενεά, corresponding to the Hebrew דּוֹר, signifies here the time occupied by a generation—an age measured by the average length of human life. Acts xiv. 16, xv. 21; Col. i. 26. There is no reason to adopt the opinion of Meyer and Hodge, and take the term to signify men, having, in epexegetical apposition with it, the phrase τοῖς υἱοῖς τῶν ἀνθρώπων. Such a construction is clumsy, and it is far better to give the two datives a differential signification. The formula ἕτεραι γενεαί, so used with the past tense, refers to past ages, and stands in contrast with νῦν.

That the phrase "sons of men" should, as Bengel supposes, mean the prophets of the Old Testament, is wholly out of the question. Ezekiel was often named בֶּן־אָדָם—"son of man," but the prophets never as a body received the cognomen "sons of men." We can scarcely say, with Harless, Matthies, and

Stier, that there is studied emphasis in the words, as if to bring out the need which such generations had of this knowledge, since they were men sprung of men, and were in want of that Spirit so plentifully conferred in these recent times. Mark iii. 28, compared with Matt. xii. 31. The words so familiar to a Hebrew ear, seem to have been suggested by the γενεά to the apostolic mind. As age after age passed away, successive generations of mortal men appeared. Sons succeeded fathers, and their sons succeeded them; so that by "sons of men" is signified the successive band of contemporaries whose lives measured these fleeting γενεαί. The meaning of the apostle, however, is not that the mystery was unknown to all men, for it was known to a few; but he intends to say, that in the minds of men generally it did not possess that prominence and clearness which it did in apostolic times. And he fills up the contrast, thus—

ὡς νῦν ἀπεκαλύφθη τοῖς ἁγίοις ἀποστόλοις αὐτοῦ—" as it has been now revealed to His holy apostles." The aorist is connected with νῦν—a connection possible in Greek, but impossible in English. Revelation is the mode by which the apostles gained an insight into the mystery which in previous ages had not been divulged. Bengel says—*notificatio per revelationem est fons notificationis per præconium*. The points of comparison introduced by ὡς are various:—1. In point of time—νῦν. Only since the advent of Jesus has the shadow been dispelled. 2. In breadth of communication. The apostle speaks of the general intimation which the ancient world had of the mystery, and compares it with those full and exact conceptions of it which these recent revelations by the Spirit had imparted. 3. In medium and object. The "sons of men" are opposed to holy apostles and prophets. The apostle's meaning fully brought out is—As it has been now revealed unto His holy apostles and prophets by the Spirit, and by them made known to the present age. If the mystery needed to be revealed by the Spirit, and to minds of such preparation and susceptibility as those of apostles and prophets; if its disclosure required such supernatural influence and such a selected class of recipients—then it is plain that very inadequate and glimmering notions of it must have been entertained by past generations. The "prophets" have been described under ii. 20, and "apostles and prophets" will be more fully illustrated under iv. 11. The epithet ἅγιοι is unusual in this application, though it is given to the old prophets. 2 Kings iv. 9; Luke i. 70; 2 Pet. i. 21. The term has been explained under i. 1, and in this place its sense is brought out by the following αὐτοῦ. They were His in a special sense, selected, endowed, commissioned, inspired, sustained, and acknowledged by Him, and so they were "holy." Not only were they so officially, but their character was in harmony with their awful functions. They were not indeed holier than others; no such comparison is intended. The Ephesian church was "holy" as well as the apostles; but they are called holy in this special sense and in their collective capacity, from the nearness and peculiarity of their relation to God. The Jewish people were a "holy nation," but on the "forefront of the mitre" of the high priest, of him who stood within the vail and before the mercy-seat, there was a golden plate with the significant inscription—"HOLINESS TO JEHOVAH."

καὶ προφήταις ἐν Πνεύματι—" and prophets in the Spirit." Lachmann, followed by Bisping, places a comma after ἁγίοις, and regards the next words as in apposition. Πνεῦμα has not the article. See under i. 17; see also under ii. 22. Ambrosiaster and Erasmus connect ἐν Πνεύματι with the following verse, a supposition which the structure of the succeeding sentence forbids; and Meier joins the same phrase to ἁγίοις, as if ἐν Πνεύματι explained the term—a hypothesis which is also set aside by the order of the words. The majority of expositors, from Jerome and Anselm to Stier and Conybeare, join the words to the previous verb—"revealed in" or "by the Spirit." The clause will certainly bear this interpretation, and the sense is apparent. Winer, § 20, 4. But the phraseology is peculiar. Peile translates—"apostles and inspired interpreters," but he erroneously thinks that prophets and apostles are the same. See under ii. 20. It might be said that the pronoun seems to qualify ἀποστόλοις—τοῖς ἁγίοις ἀποστόλοις αὐτοῦ—to His holy apostles, while the prophets have no distinctive character given them, unless it be by the words ἐν Πνεύματι, for they were prophets, and had become so, or had a right to the title, ἐν Πνεύματι. 2 Pet. i. 21. This interpretation was before the mind of Chrysostom, though he did not adopt it, and Koppe and Holzhausen have formally maintained it. The construction would then resemble that of the same formula in the last verse of the preceding chapter. Similar construction is found Rom. viii. 9, xiv. 17; 1 Cor. xii. 3; Col. i. 8; Rev. i. 10. The epithet is not superfluous, as these men became prophets only "in the Spirit." The apostles themselves stand in the room of the Old Testament prophets, and their possession of the Spirit was a prominent and functional distinction. But the prophets so called under the New Testament were not to be undervalued; they, too, were "in the Spirit." De Wette objects that such an epithet for the prophets would be too distinctive. But why so? The apostles were God's—$a\mathring{v}\tau o\hat{v}$—in a special sense, and they were $\mathring{a}\gamma\iota o\iota$ in consequence. But Paul does not give the "prophets" either one or other of these lofty designations. The apostles had high office and prerogatives, but the possession of the Spirit was the solitary distinction of the prophets, and by it the sacred writer seems to characterize them. At the same time, the ordinary construction of ἐν Πνεύματι with the verb gives so good a meaning, that we could not justify ourselves in departing from it.

The general sense of the verse is evident. The apostle does not seem to deny all knowledge of the mystery to the ancient world, but he only compares their knowledge of it, which at best was a species of perplexed *clairvoyance*, with the fuller revelation of its terms and contents given to modern apostles and prophets; or as Theodoret contrasts it—οὐ γὰρ τὰ πράγματα εἶδον, ἀλλὰ τοὺς περὶ τῶν πραγμάτων προέγραψαν λόγους. *In Vetere Testamento Novum latet, et in Novo Vetus patet*. The scholium in Matthiæ—"that the men of old knew that the Gentiles should be called, but not that they should be fellow-heirs," contains a distinction too acute and refined. The intimations in the Old Testament of the calling of the Gentiles are frequent, but not full; disclosing the fact, but keeping the method in shade. The apostle James refers to this in Acts xv. 14. But after the death of Christ, which, by its repeal of the ceremonial code, was the grand means of Judæo-Gentile union, a church, without reference to race, was fully organized. The salvation of guilty men of all races became a distinctive feature of the gospel, and therefore the incorporation of non-Israel into the church, revealed to Peter and Paul by the Spirit, was more clearly understood from the results of daily experience and the fruits of missionary enterprise. Acts xi. 17, 18, xv. 7, 13.

(Ver. 6.) This verse explains the mystery. The infinitive εἶναι contains the idea of design if viewed from one point, and of fact if viewed from another—the purpose seen or realized in the purport or contents. It does not depend upon the last verse, but unfolds the unimagined contents of the revelation—

εἶναι τὰ ἔθνη συγκληρονόμα—"that the Gentiles are fellow-heirs." Rom. viii. 17. Remarks have been made on the κληρονομία, under i. 14, 18. The Gentiles were to be co-heirs with the believing Jews, without modification or diminution of privilege. Their heirship was based on the same charter, and referred to the same inheritance. Nor, though that heirship was very recent in date, were they only residuary legatees, bound to be content with any contingent remainder that satiated Israel might happen to leave. No; they inherited equally with the earlier sons. Theirs was neither an uncertain nor a minor portion. And not only were they joint-heirs, but even—

καὶ σύνσωμα—"and of the same body,"—concorporales— a more intimate union still. The form of spelling σύνσωμα is found in A, B$^1$, D, E, F, G. The Gentiles were of the same body—not attached like an excrescence, not incorporated like a foreign substance, but concorporated so that the additional were not to be distinguished from the original members in such a perfect amalgamation. The body is the one church under the one Head, and believing Jew and Gentile form that one body, without schism or the detection of national variety or of previous condition. Thus Theophylact—ἐν γὰρ σῶμα γεγόνασιν οἱ ἐθνικοὶ πρὸς τοὺς Ἰσραηλίτας μιᾷ κεφαλῇ ἐν Χριστῷ συγκρατούμενοι. Comp. ii. 16. Still further—

καὶ συμμέτοχα τῆς ἐπαγγελίας—"and fellow-partakers of the promise." The pronoun αὐτοῦ of the Received Text is not found in the more important MSS. and versions, and is rejected by Lachmann and Tischendorf, though it occurs in D$^2$, D$^3$, E, F, G, K, L. The spelling συνμέτοχα is found in A, B$^1$, C, D$^1$, F, G. It has been thought by many to be too narrow a view to restrict the promise to the Holy

Spirit. But many things favour such an opinion. He is the prominent gift or promise of the new covenant, as Paul hints in his comprehensive question, Gal. iii. 2; while again, in ver. 14 of the same chapter, he adds, as descriptive of the blessing of Abraham coming on the Gentiles—" that we might receive the promise of the Spirit through faith." Joel ii. 28, 29. Peter, vindicating his mission to Cornelius, refers also as a conclusive demonstration of its heavenly origin to the fact, that "the Holy Ghost fell on them as on us." He repeats the same evidence on another occasion. Acts xv. 8. The promise is here singled out by the article; and in the mind of the apostle, who had already referred to the Holy Ghost under a similar designation and in connection with the inheritance (i. 13), the one grand distinctive and dispensational promise was that of the Spirit. And if the αὐτοῦ be spurious, the naked emphasis laid on the term itself shows that to Paul it had a simple, well-known, and unmistakeable meaning. Ellicott says that this view is scarcely consonant with συγκληρονόμα—fellow-heirs. But the theology of the apostle shows the perfect consonance. Rom. viii. 14–17. They alone are heirs who are sons, and they alone are sons who are led by the Spirit of God. Then is added—

ἐν Χριστῷ Ἰησοῦ—in Christ Jesus—as A, B, C, followed by the Coptic and Vulgate, read. We would not, with Vatablus, Koppe, Meier, Holzhausen, and Baumgarten-Crusius, restrict ἐν Χριστῷ Ἰησοῦ to the preceding noun ἐπαγγελία— "promise in Christ"—for then we might have expected a repetition of the article; but, with the majority of critics, we regard it as a qualifying the whole three adjectives, as the inner sphere of union, while the medium or instrumental cause is next stated—

διὰ τοῦ εὐαγγελίου—not, as Locke translates, "in the time of the gospel;" but "by means of the gospel." The prepositions ἐν and διά stand in a similar relation, as in i. 7. "In Christ," were the Gentiles co-heirs, co-incorporated, and co-partakers of the promise with believing Israel, enjoying union in Him, "through that gospel" which was preached to them; for its object was to proclaim Christ—" our peace."

How, then, do the three epithets stand connected? There seems to be no climax, as Jerome, Pelagius, and Baumgarten-

Crusius suppose; nor an anticlimax, as is the opinion of Zanchius: yet we cannot adopt the idea of Valpy and others, that the series of terms is loosely thrown together without discrimination.[1] We apprehend that the apostle employs the three terms, in the fulness of his heart, at once to magnify the mystery, and to prevent mistake. The συν- is thrice repeated, and σύνσωμα and συνμέτοχα, are terms coined for the occasion, though the verb συμμετέχω occurs in classic Greek, as in Euripides, *Supp.* 648—συμμετασχόντες; Xenophon, *Anabasis,* vii. 8, 17; Plat. *Theæt., Opera,* vol. iii. p. 495, ed. Bekker. The Gentiles are fellow-heirs. But such a fellowship might be external to a great extent—Esau might inherit though he severed himself from Jacob's society. The apostle intensifies his meaning, and declares that they are not only fellow-heirs, but of the same body—the closest union; not like Abraham's sons by Keturah, each of whom received his portion and his dismissal in the same act. But while they might be co-heirs, and embodied in one personality, might there not be a difference in the amount of blessing enjoyed and promised? Or with sameness of right, might there not be diversity of gift? Will the Israelite have no higher donation as a memento of his descent, and a tribute of honour to his ancestral glories? No; the Gentiles are also fellow-partakers of that one promise. By this means the apostle shows the amount of Gentile privilege which comes to them in Christ, not by submission to the law, as so many had fondly imagined, but by the gospel. The next verse shows his relation to that gospel—

(Ver. 7.) Οὗ ἐγενήθην διάκονος—" of which I became a minister." Col. i. 23; 2 Cor. iii. 6. This reading is supported by A, B, D¹, F, G; while ἐγενόμην is used in C, D³, E, K, L. The use of the passive might show that he had no concurrence in the act. But Buttmann says that ἐγενήθην is used in Doric for ἐγενόμην, γίγνεσθαι being in that dialect a deponent

---

[1] Jerome affirms on this place, and in apology for the barbarous Latin in which the translation of the three terms was couched—*et singuli sermones, apices, puncta, in Divinis Scripturis plena sunt sensibus.* Stier, as is his wont, and according to the artificial view which he has formed of the epistle and its various sections, finds his three favourite ideas of *Grund, Weg, und Ziel*—basis, manner, and end, with a correspondent reference to Father, Son, and Holy Ghost.

passive. Phryn. ed. Lobeck, pp. 108, 109. Διάκονος (not, as often said, from διά and κόνις—"one covered with dust," but from an old root—διάκω—signifying "I hasten") is a servant in a general sense, and in relation to a master, as in 2 Cor. vi. 4, xi. 23; 1 Tim. iv. 6. Buttmann has shown that the preposition διά cannot enter into the composition of διάκονος, as the *a* is long. The *a* in διά may, from the necessities of metre, be sometimes long in poetry, but never in prose; while the Ionic form of the word under review is διήκονος. *Lexilogus, sub voce* διάκτορος. As an apostle he did not merely enjoy the dignity of office, or the admiration created by the display of miraculous gifts. He busied himself; he served with eager cordiality and unwearied zeal—

κατὰ τὴν δωρεὰν τῆς χάριτος τοῦ Θεοῦ τὴν δοθεῖσάν μοι— "according to the gift of the grace of God which was given to me." Δωρεά is the gift, and χάρις is that of which the gift is composed (ii. 8), the genitive being that of apposition Instead of τὴν δοθεῖσαν in the next clause of the Received Text, some modern editors read—τῆς δοθείσης, which has the authority of the old MSS. A, B, C, D¹, F, G, but which may be borrowed from ver. 2. The Syriac and the Greek fathers are in favour of the first reading, which is retained by Tischendorf, being found in D³, E, K, L. The sense is not affected —"The gift made up of this grace is given, or the grace of which the gift consists is given." The χάρις is not the gift of tongues, as Grotius dreams; nor specially the Holy Ghost, as a-Lapide imagines. The term, resembling that of the Latin *munus*, refers not to the apostolical office conferred out of the pure and sovereign favour of God, as in ver. 2 of this chapter, but it refers here to that office in its characteristic function of preaching the gospel to the Gentiles. It was given—

κατὰ τὴν ἐνέργειαν τῆς δυνάμεως αὐτοῦ—"according to the working of His power." Κατά refers us to δοθεῖσαν. The gift of grace is conferred in accordance with the working of His power. See i. 19. Ἐνέργεια and δύναμις are explained under i. 19. Whitby unnecessarily and falsely restricts this power to that of miraculous agency conferred upon the apostle. But he refers in this place to the "grace" which originated his apostleship, wrought mightily in him when the office of the apostle of heathendom, with all its varied qualifications, was conferred upon him. Unworthy of it he was; and had not the gift been accompanied by a striking manifestation of God's power, he could not have enjoyed it. And he served in harmony with his office—κατὰ τὴν δωρεάν; and that office was conferred upon him in unison with—κατὰ τὴν ἐνέργειαν—such a spiritual change, induced by the Divine might, as changed a Jew into a Christian, a blasphemer into a saint, a Pharisee into an apostle, and a persecutor into a missionary. Calvin remarks—*hæc est potentiæ ejus efficacia ex nihilo grande aliquid efficere.* Chrysostom says truly—"The gift would not have been enough, if it had not implanted within him the power." That grace was bestowed very freely —ἡ δωρεὰ τῆς χάριτος; and that power wrought very effectually—ἡ ἐνέργεια τῆς δυνάμεως. Gal. ii. 8. The apostle becomes more minute—

(Ver. 8.) Ἐμοὶ τῷ ἐλαχιστοτέρῳ πάντων ἁγίων—"To me, who am less than the least of all saints." There is no good reason adduced by Harless for making the first clause of this verse a parenthesis, and joining ἐν τοῖς ἔθνεσιν to the δωρεάν of the preceding verse. The apostle prolongs the thought, and dwells upon it. He was a minister of the gospel through the gracious power of God. This reflection ever produced within him profound wonder and humility; and though in one sense he was greater than the greatest of all saints, yet the consciousness of his own demerit stood out in such striking contrast with the high function to which he had been called, that he exclaims—"To me, who am less than the least of all saints"[1]—ἐμοί being emphatic from its position. Ἐλαχισ-

[1] The following note describes with peculiar terseness and pungency a feeling which is the very opposite of the apostle's humility. It is taken from Baxter's *Reformed Pastor*, a work which, from its honest exposures, many imagined should have been written in Latin. But the author makes this quaint and telling apology: "If the ministers of England had sinned only in Latin, I would have made shift to admonish them in Latin, or else have said nothing to them. But if they will sin in English, they must hear of it in English." The vice of pride in ministers is thus described and scorned: "One of our most heinous and palpable sins is *pride*—a sin that hath too much interest in the best, but is more hateful and inexcusable in us than in any men. Yet is it so prevalent in some of us, that it inditeth our discourses for us; it chooseth us our company, it formeth our countenances, it putteth the accents and emphasis upon our words: when we reason, it is the determiner and exciter of our cogitations; it fills some men's minds with aspiring desires and designs; it possesseth them with envious and bitter thoughts against those that stand in their light, or by

τοτέρῳ is a comparative, founded on the superlative ἐλάχιστος —"less than the least;" a form designed to express the deepest self-abasement. Similar anomalous forms occur in the later Greek, and even occasionally in the earlier, especially among the poets. 3 John 4; Phryn. ed. Lobeck, p. 135. Wetstein has collected a few examples. Ἐλαχιστότατος is found in *Sextus Empir.* ix. p. 627. The English term "lesser" is akin. Matthiæ, § 136; Winer, § 11, 2; Buttmann, § 69, note 3. Πάντες ἅγιοι are not the apostles and prophets merely, but saints generally. Theophylact says justly—καλεῖ οὐ τῶν ἀποστόλων, ἀλλὰ πάντων τῶν ἁγίων, τουτέστι τῶν πιστῶν. In 1 Cor. xv. 9, where he says, "I am the least of the apostles," he brings himself into direct contrast with his ministerial colleagues. 1 Tim. i. 13; Phil. iii. 6. To him— ἐδόθη ἡ χάρις αὕτη—"was this grace given." Χάρις, in this aspect, has been already explained both under verses 2 and 7. That special branch of the apostolate which was entrusted to Paul had the following end in view—

any means do eclipse their glory, or hinder the progress of their idolized reputation. . . . How often doth it choose our subject, and more often choose our words and ornaments! God biddeth us be as plain as we can, for the informing of the ignorant, and as convincing and serious as we are able, for the melting and changing of unchanged hearts; but pride stands by and contradicteth all; and sometimes it puts in toys and trifles, and polluteth rather than polisheth, and under pretence of laudable ornaments, it dishonoureth our sermons with childish gauds: as if a prince were to be decked in the habit of a stage-player or a painted fool. It persuadeth us to paint the window that it may dim the light; and to speak to our people that which they cannot understand, to acquaint them that we are able to speak unprofitably. It taketh off the edge, and dulls the life of all our teachings, under the pretence of filing off the roughness, unevenness, and superfluity. If we have a plain and cutting passage, it throws it away as too rustical and ungrateful. . . . And when pride hath made the sermon, it goes with them into the pulpit; it formeth their tone, it animateth them in the delivery, it takes them off from that which may be displeasing, how necessary soever, and setteth them in a pursuit of vain applause; and the sum of all this is, that it maketh men, both in studying and preaching, to seek themselves and deny God, when they should seek God's glory and deny themselves. When they should ask, 'What should I say, and how should I say it, to please God best, and do most good?' it makes them ask, 'What shall I say, and how shall I deliver it, to be thought a learned, able preacher, and to be applauded by all that hear me?' When the sermon is done, pride goeth home with them, and maketh them more eager to know whether they were applauded, than whether they did prevail for the saving change of souls! They could find in their hearts, but for shame, to ask folks how they liked them, and to draw out their commendation."—*The Reformed Pastor*, etc., pp. 154, 155, Baxter's Works, vol. xiv.; London, 1830.

ἐν τοῖς ἔθνεσιν εὐαγγελίσασθαι—" to preach among the Gentiles." Lachmann omits ἐν, following A, B, C, and so does Alford. But the majority of MSS., and the Syriac, Vulgate, and Gothic versions have the preposition. The phrase ἐν τοῖς ἔθνεσιν, emphatic from its position, describes the special or characteristic sphere of the apostle's labours. The apostle, however, never forgot his own countrymen. His love to his nation was not interdicted by his special vocation as a missionary to the heathen world. And the staple of that good news which he proclaimed was—

τὸ ἀνεξιχνίαστον πλοῦτος τοῦ Χριστοῦ—" the unsearchable riches of Christ." Πλοῦτος is rightly read in the neuter. See under i. 7 and ii. 7. The adjective occurs in Rom. xi. 33, and has its origin in the Septuagint, where it represents the Hebrew formula—אֵין חֵקֶר, in Job v. 9, ix. 10—and לֹא־חֵקֶר, in Job xxxiv. 24. The riches of Christ are not simply "riches of grace"—"riches of glory"—"riches of inheritance," as Pelagius, Grotius, and Koppe are inclined to restrict them, but that treasury of spiritual blessing which is Christ's—so vast that the comprehension of its limits and the exhaustion of its contents are alike impossible. What the apostle wishes to characterize as grand in itself, or in its abundance, adaptation, and substantial permanence, he terms "riches." The riches of Christ are the true wealth of men and nations. And those riches are "unsearchable." Even the value of the portion already possessed cannot be told by any symbols of numeration, for such riches can have no adequate exponent or representative. Their source was in eternity, and in a love whose fervour and origin are above our ken, and whose duration shall be for ages of ages beyond compute. Their extent is boundless, and the mode in which they have been wrought out reveals a spiritual process whose results astonish and satisfy us, but whose inner springs and movements lie beyond our keenest inspection. And our appropriation of those riches, though it be a matter of consciousness, shrouds itself from our scrutiny, for it indicates the presence of the Divine Spirit in His power—a power exerted upon man, beyond resistance, but without compulsion; and in its mighty and gracious operation neither wounding his moral freedom nor impinging on his perfect and undeniable responsibility. The latest periods of time shall find these riches unimpaired, and eternity shall behold the same wealth neither worn by use nor dimmed by age, nor yet diminished by the myriads of its happy participants. Still further—

(Ver. 9.) Καὶ φωτίσαι πάντας—"And to make all men see." Lachmann has assigned no valid reason for throwing suspicion upon πάντας. To restrict the meaning of the adjective to the heathen, as Meyer and Baumgarten-Crusius do, is without any warrant, though πάντας is not emphatic in position. We lay no stress on the fact that πάντας and ἔθνη do not agree in gender, for such a form of concord is not uncommon, and a separate idea is also introduced. The apostle preached to the Gentiles "the unsearchable riches of Christ," but in his discharge of this duty he taught not Gentiles only, but all—Jew and Gentile alike—what is the dispensation of the mystery. The verb φωτίζω, followed by the accusative of the thing, denotes to bring it into light; but followed by the accusative of the person, it signifies to throw light upon him—not only to teach, διδάξαι, but to enlighten inwardly—to give spiritual apprehension—φωτίσαι. See under i. 18. If one gaze upon a landscape as the rising sun strikes successive points, and brings them into view in every variety of tint and shade, both subjective and objective illumination is enjoyed. No wonder that in so many languages light is the emblem of knowledge. That mystery which was now placed in clear light was not discerned by the Jew, and could not have been perceived by the Gentile for the shadow which lay both on him and it. But the result of Paul's mission was, that the Jew at once saw it, and the Gentile plainly understood its scope. They were enlightened—were enabled to make a sudden discovery by the lucid and full demonstration set before them. The point on which they were instructed was this—

τίς ἡ οἰκονομία τοῦ μυστηρίου—"what is the economy of the mystery." That οἰκονομία should supersede the gloss κοινωνία of the Elzevir text is established by the concurrent authority of A, B, C, D, E, F, G, J, supported by a host of the Fathers and by the early versions. The preaching of Paul enabled all to see "what is the arrangement or organization of that mystery which, from the beginning of the world, had been hid in God." The terms οἰκονομία and μυστήριον have been already explained i. 9, 10, and iii. 2, 3. The mystery must be the same as that described in ver. 6, for the same course of thought is still pursued, and varied only by the repetition. That mystery now so open had been long sealed—

τοῦ ἀποκεκρυμμένου ἀπὸ τῶν αἰώνων ἐν τῷ Θεῷ—"which from of old has been hid in God." Col. i. 26; 1 Cor. ii. 7; Rom. xvi. 25. Ἀπὸ τῶν αἰώνων—"from the ages in a temporal sense;" not concealed from the ages, in the sense of Macknight, but hid from of old; not, perhaps, strictly from before all time, but since the commencement of time up to the period of the apostle's commission. During this interval of four thousand years God's purpose to found a religion of universal offer, adaptation, and enjoyment, lay unrevealed in His own bosom. Glimpses of that sublime purpose might be occasionally caught, but no open or formal organization of it was made. There were hints and pre-intimations, oracles that spoke sometimes in cautious, and sometimes in bolder phrase; but till the death of Jesus, the means were not provided by which Judaism should be superseded and a world-wide system introduced. Then the Divine Hierophant disclosed the mystery, after His Son had offered an atonement whose saving value had no national restrictions, and acknowledged no ethnographical impediment, and when He poured out His Spirit on believing Gentiles, and commissioned Saul of Tarsus to go far from Palestine and reclaim the heathen outcasts. In God—

τῷ τὰ πάντα κτίσαντι—"who created all things." The additional words διὰ Ἰησοῦ Χριστοῦ of the Received Text are at least doubtful, and are omitted by recent editors. They are not found in the Codices A, B, C, D¹, F, G, nor in the Syriac, Vulgate, and Coptic versions, nor in the quotations of the Latin fathers. They occur, however, in the Greek fathers, such as Chrysostom, Theophylact, and Œcumenius. The emphasis lies on τὰ πάντα, but the meaning of κτίσαντι has been much disputed:—1. Chrysostom, guided by the words which he admitted into the text, διὰ Ἰησοῦ Χριστοῦ—explains thus—"He who created all things by Him, revealeth also this by Him." But if the phrase διὰ Ἰησοῦ Χριστοῦ be spurious, this interpretation, if it can be called one, is at once set aside. 2. Olshausen says, that the term is employed to show that the institution of redemption is a creative act of God, and could proceed from Him alone who created all things. The view of von Gerlach is similar. *Argumentum est*, says Zanchius, *a creatione ad recreationem.* Bengel suggests this idea—*Rerum omnium creatio fundamentum est omnis reliquæ œconomiæ.* But this exposition is not in harmony with the course of thought. It is of the concealment of a mystery in God the universal Creator that Paul speaks, not of the actual provision of salvation for men. 3. Many understand the reference to be to the spiritual creation, such as Calvin, Zanchius, Calixtus, Grotius, Usteri, Meier, and Baumgarten-Crusius. The deletion of the words "by Jesus Christ," and the want of some other qualifying term, militates against this view. In ii. 10, 15, and in iv. 24, there are accompanying phrases which leave no doubt as to the meaning. But the aorist, and the occurrence of the term here without any explanatory adjunct, seem to prove that it must bear its most usual and simple signification. 4. Beza, Piscator, Flatt, and others, refer τὰ πάντα to men, abridging by this tame exegesis the limitless meaning of the terms.

The real question is, What is meant by this allusion to the creation—what is the relation between the creative work of God and the concealment of this mystery in Himself? Had the apostle said—hid in God who arranges all things, or foresees all things, the meaning would have been apparent. But it is not so easy to perceive the connection between creation and the seclusion of a mystery. The fact that God created all things cannot, as in Rückert's suggestion, afford any reason why he concealed a portion of his plan; nor can we discover, with others, that the additional clause is meant to show the sovereign freeness and power of God in such concealment. Our own view may be thus expressed: The period during which the mystery was hid dates from the ages commencing with creation, for creation built up the platform on which the strange mystery of redemption was disclosed. God, as Creator of the universe, has of necessity a plan according to which all arrangements take place, for creation implies providence or government—the gradual evolution of counsels which had lain folded up with unfathomable secrecy. But those counsels are not disclosed with simultaneous and confusing haste: the Almighty Mind retains them in itself till the fitting period when they may be unveiled. Now, the mystery of the inbringing of the Gentiles was secreted in the Divine bosom for four thousand years, that is, from the epoch of the creation—the origin of time. And it has not come to light by accident, but by a prearranged determination. When God created the world, it was a portion of His plan as its Creator that the Gentile nations, after the call of Abraham, should be without the pale of His visible church; but that after His Son died, and the gospel with universal adaptations was established, they should be admitted into covenant. At the fittest time, not prematurely, but with leisurely exactness, were created both the human materials on which redemption was to work, and that peculiar and varied mechanism by which its designs were to be accomplished. And one grand purpose is declared to be—

(Ver. 10.) *"Ἵνα γνωρισθῇ νῦν*—" In order that there might now be made known." *"Ἵνα γνωρισθῇ* stands connected as a climax with εὐαγγελίσασθαι of ver. 8, and φωτίσαι of ver. 9. *Νῦν* is opposed to ἀπὸ τῶν αἰώνων. We cannot here regard ἵνα as ecbatic in sense, though this signification has been accepted by Bodius, Estius, Meier, Holzhausen, and Thomas Aquinas, who takes the particle—*consecutive, non causaliter*. We prefer to give ἵνα its usual sense—"in order that." It indicates a final purpose; not the grand object, but still an important though minor design. We cannot, however, accede to the opinion of Harless, who connects this verse solely with the clause immediately preceding it. His idea is, that God created all things for the purpose of showing by the church His wisdom to the angelic hosts. We regard such an exegesis as limiting the reference of the apostle. This verse, commencing with ἵνα, winds up, as we think, the entire preceding paragraph, and discloses a grand reason for God's method of procedure. Nor is the notion of Harless tenable on other grounds; because the wisdom of God in creation is made known to the heavenly hierarchy, apart altogether from the church, and has been revealed to them, not simply now and for the first time, but ever since "the morning stars sang together and all the sons of God shouted for joy." Why then, too, should the church be selected as the medium of manifestation? And why should wisdom be singled out as the only attribute which creation exhibits by the church to the higher intelligences? But when we look at the contents of the paragraph, the meaning is apparent. The apostle speaks of a mystery—a mystery long hid, and at length disclosed—a mystery connected with the enlargement and glory of the church—and he adds, this long concealment from other ages, yea, from the beginning of the world, and this present revelation, have for their object to instruct the celestial ranks in God's multiform wisdom. It is the attribute of wisdom which binds itself up with the hiding and the opening of a mystery, and as that wisdom concerns the organization and extension of the church, the church naturally becomes the scene of instruction to celestial spectators. On the connection of Divine wisdom with the disclosure of a mystery, some remarks may be seen under i. 8, 9—" God in all wisdom and prudence made known to us the mystery of His will." That mystery being now disclosed, the princedoms and powers were instructed. In itself, in its concealment, and in the time, place, method, and results of its disclosure, it now exhibited the Divine wisdom in a novel and striking light—

ταῖς ἀρχαῖς καὶ ταῖς ἐξουσίαις ἐν τοῖς ἐπουρανίοις—" to the principalities and the powers in heavenly places "—the article being prefixed to each noun, and giving prominence to each in the statement. These terms have been explained under i. 21, and the following phrase—ἐν τοῖς ἐπουρανίοις, which designates abode or locality, has been considered under i. 3, 20, ii. 6. The following hypotheses are the whimsical devices of erratic ingenuity, viz.: that such principalities and powers are, as is the opinion of Zornius, Locke, and Schoettgen, the leaders and chiefs of the Jewish nation; or, as Van Til imagined, heathen magistrates; or, as Zegerus dreamed, worldly dignities; or, as is held by Pelagius, the rulers of the Christian church. Nor can these principalities and powers be good and bad angels alike, as Bengel, Olshausen, and Hofmann (*Schriftb.* i. pp. 360–362) hold: nor can they be wholly impure fiends, as is supposed by Ambrosiaster and Vatablus. As little can we say, with Matthies, that these principalities "dwell on the earth, and disport on it in an invisible spiritual form, and are taught by the foundation and extension of the church their own weakness." Nor can we agree with the opinion of Van Til, Knatchbull, and Baumgarten, that the words ἐν τοῖς ἐπουρανίοις signify "in heavenly things," and are to be connected with γνωρισθῇ, so as to mean, that the principalities and powers are instructed by the church in celestial themes. And the lesson is given—

διὰ τῆς ἐκκλησίας—"by the church"—the community of the faithful in Christ being the instructress of angels in heaven. That lesson is—

ἡ πολυποίκιλος σοφία τοῦ Θεοῦ—"the manifold wisdom of God." The adjective, one of the very numerous compounds of πολύς, occurs nowhere else in the New Testament. But it occurs in a fragment of Eubulus, *Athen.* xv. 7, applied to the manifold hues of a garland of flowers—στέφανον πολυποίκιλον ἀνθέων; and in Euripides, *Iphig. Taur.* 1149, it describes the variegated colours of a robe—πολυποίκιλα φάρεα; while in a figurative sense it is joined in the Orphic Hymns to the nouns τελετή and λόγος, v. 11, lx. 4. The term, as Chrysostom notes, is not simply "varied," but "much varied." The wisdom described by the remarkable epithet is not merely deep or great wisdom, but wisdom illustrious for its very numerous forms, and for the strange diversity yet perfect harmony of its myriads of aspects and methods of operation.

Such is generally the meaning of the verse, but its specific reference is not so easily ascertained. What peculiar manifestation of Divine wisdom is referred to? We cannot vaguely say that it is God's wisdom in the general plan of redemption, or, as Olshausen remarks, "the marvellous procedure of God in the pardon of the sinner, and the settlement in him of the antagonism between righteousness and grace." Such an idea is scarcely in keeping with the context, which speaks not of the general scheme of mercy, but of one of its distinctive and modern aspects. Nor is the view of some of the Greek fathers more in unison with the spirit of the paragraph. Gregory of Nyssa, whose opinion has been preserved by Theophylact and Œcumenius, thus illustrates—"That the angels prior to the incarnation had seen the Divine wisdom in a simple form without variation; but now they see it in a composite form, working by contraries, educing life from death, glory from shame, trophies from the cross, and God-becoming things from all that was vile and ignoble."[1] The leading idea in this opinion does not fully develop the apostle's meaning as contained in the paragraph; nor could wisdom, acting simply and uniformly in this method, be denominated "manifold wisdom," though it might be deep, benignant, and powerful skill. The idea brought out in the interpretations of Cocceius, Zanchius, Grotius, and Harless, to wit, that reference is had to the modes and series of past Divine revelations, approximates the truth, and Meyer and Calvin are right in attempting to find the meaning within the bounds of the preceding section. The wisdom is connected with the mystery and its opening, and that mystery is the introduction of the Gentiles into the kingdom of God. Once the world at large was in enjoyment of oracle and sacrifice without distinction and tribe, and Melchisedec, a Hamite prince, was "priest of the most high God." Then one nation was selected, and continued in that solitary enjoyment for two thousand years. But now again the human race, without discrimination, have been reinstated in religious privilege. This last and liberal offer of mercy was a mystery long hid, and it might be cause of wonder why infinite love tarried so long in its schemes. But wisdom is conspicuous in the whole arrangement. Not till Jesus died and ceremonial distinctions were laid aside, was such an unconditional salvation presented to the world. The glory of unrestricted dissemination was postponed till the Redeemer's victory had been won, and His heralds were enabled to proclaim, not the gorgeous symbols of a coming, but the blessed realities of an accomplished redemption; not the types and ceremonial apparatus of Moses, but "the unsearchable riches of Christ." There was indeed slow progress, but sure development; occasional interruption, but steady advancement. Divine wisdom was manifold, for it never put forth any tentative process, nor was it ever affronted by any abandoned experiment.

[1] Πρὸ τῶν τῆς ἐνανθρωπήσεως τοῦ σωτῆρος ἡμῶν χρόνων ἁπλῆν ἐγίνωσκον αἱ οὐράνιαι δυνάμεις τὴν σοφίαν τοῦ θεοῦ ἐκ μόνου τοῦ δυνατοῦ κατορθουμένων. Νῦν δέ γε διὰ τῆς εἰς τὴν ἐκκλησίαν καὶ τὸ ἀνθρώπινον γένος οἰκονομίας οὐκέτι μόνον ἁπλῆ ἀλλὰ καὶ πολυποίκιλος ἐγνώσθη ἡ σοφία τοῦ θεοῦ διὰ τῶν ἐναντίων τὰ ἐναντία κατορθοῦσα· διὰ θανάτου ζωὴν, δι' ἀτιμίας δόξαν, διὰ σταυροῦ τρόπαιον, διὰ παντῶν τῶν εὐτελῶν τὰ διοτριπῆ. See also Aquinas, *Summ. Theol.* p. 1; *Quæst.* 57, art. 5.

It was under no necessity of repeating its plans, for it is not feebly confined to a uniform method, while in its omniscient forecast a solitary agency often surrounds itself with various, opposite, and multiplied effects; temporary antagonism issuing in ultimate combination, and apparent intricacy of movement securing final simplicity of result; antecedent improbability changing into felicitous certainty, and feeble instruments standing out in impressive contrast with the gigantic exploits which they have achieved. Every occurrence is laid under tribute, and hostile influence bows at length in auxiliary homage. "Out of the eater came forth meat, and out of the strong came forth sweetness." Times of forbidding aspect have brightened into propitious opportunities, and "the foolishness of preaching" has proved itself to be the means of the world's regeneration. And the mystery was published not by angels, but by men; not by the prudent and powerful of the world, by those who wore a coronet or had studied in the Portico or the Academy, but by one "whose bodily presence was weak and his speech contemptible"—a stranger to "the enticing words of man's wisdom." The initiation of the Gentile world was by the preaching of the cross — that instrument of lingering and unspeakable torture; while He that hung upon it, born of a village maiden, and apprenticed as a Galilean mechanic, was condemned to a public execution as the penalty of alleged treason and blasphemy. The church, which is the scene of these preplexing wonders, teaches the angelic hosts. They have seen much of God's working—many a sun lighted up, and many a world launched into its orbit. They have been delighted with the solution of many a problem, and the development of many a mystery. But in the proclamation of the Gospel to the Gentiles, with its strange preparations, various agencies, and stupendous effects—involving the origination and extinction of Judaism, the incarnation and the atonement, the manger and the cross, the spread of the Greek language and the triumph of the Roman arms—"these principalities and powers in heavenly places" beheld with rapture other and brighter phases of a wisdom which had often dazzled them by its brilliant and profuse versatility, and surprised and entranced them by the infinite fulness of the love which prompts it, and of the power which itself directs and controls. The events that have transpired in the church on earth are the means of augmenting the information of those pure and exalted beings who encircle the throne of God. 1 Tim. iii. 16; 1 Pet. i. 12. The entire drama is at length laid bare before them—

"Like some bright river, that from fall to fall
In many a maze descending, bright through all,
Finds some fair region, where, each labyrinth past,
In one full lake of light it rests at last."

Καὶ πῶς κηρύττεις, εἴπερ ὁ πλοῦτος ἀνεξιχνίαστος? asks Theodoret, τοῦτο γὰρ αὐτό, φησι, κηρύττω ὅτι ἀνεξιχνίαστος.

The whole has been arranged—

(Ver. 11.) Κατὰ πρόθεσιν τῶν αἰώνων—"according to the eternal purpose." The connection of these words is not with the adjective or substantive of the preceding clause: neither with πολυποίκιλος, as is supposed by Anselm and Holzhausen, nor with σοφία, as Koppe conjectures; but with γνωρισθῇ. This revelation of God's multifarious wisdom now and by the church has happened according to His eternal purpose—the purpose of ages, or the purpose of those periods which are so distant, as to be to us identical with eternity. Theodoret thus explains it—πρὸ τῶν αἰώνων προέθετο. 1 Cor. ii. 7; 2 Tim. i. 9. On the other hand, Anselm, a-Lapide, Estius, Baumgarten, Schoettgen, and Holzhausen, take the genitive as that of object, and render the clause —"purpose about the ages." Such is virtually the view of Chandler and Macknight, who make the word "ages" signify the religious dispensations, and regard πρόθεσις as meaning fore-arrangement. The simplest view, and that most in accordance with grammatical usage, is, as we have said, to take the genitive as one of quality—as equivalent to its own adjective αἰώνιος—or of possession, with Ellicott; and such is the opinion of Harless, Olshausen, and Meyer. Winer, § 30, 2. So in Hebrew, צוּר עוֹלָמִים—everlasting strength, Isa. xxvi. 4. See also Dan. ix. 24. It was a purpose—

ἣν ἐποίησεν ἐν τῷ Χριστῷ Ἰησοῦ τῷ κυρίῳ ἡμῶν—"which He wrought in Christ Jesus our Lord. The article before Χριστῷ is doubtful, though Tischendorf inserts it. The antecedent to ἣν is not σοφία, as Theophylact, Jerome, and Luther construe, but πρόθεσις. Two classes of meanings have been attached to ἐποίησεν :—

1. According to Calvin, Beza, Estius, Bengel, Rückert, Meier, Harless, and Baumgarten-Crusius, its meaning is, "Which He made," that is, "formed in Christ." The verb is so used Mark iii. 6, xv. 1, and the idea is scriptural. See i. 3. See for one view of the relation of Christ to the Father in such an expression, Hofmann, *Schriftb.* vol. i. p. 230 ; and for another, Thomasius, *Christi Person*, vol. i. p. 453.

2. But in the view of Theodoret, Vatablus, Grotius, Koppe, Matthies, Olshausen, Scholz, Meyer, de Wette, Stier, and Conybeare, it denotes, "Which He executed or fulfilled in Christ Jesus." This last interpretation is on the whole preferable, for ποιεῖν may bear such a sense, as in ii. 3 ; Matt. xxi. 31 ; John vi. 38 ; 1 Thess. v. 24. Olshausen suggests that Jesus Christ is the historical name, so that the verb refers to the realization of God's decree in Him, and not to the inner act of the Divine will. The words ἐν Χριστῷ Ἰησοῦ signify not "on account of," nor "by," but "in" Christ Jesus, as the sphere or element in which the action of the verb takes effect. The meaning of the three names has been given under i. 2, etc. The lessons of manifold wisdom given to principalities and powers, in connection with the introduction of the Gentiles into the church, are not an accidental denouement, nor an undesigned betrayal of a Divine secret on the part of the church. Nor was the disclosure of the mystery forced on God by the power of circumstances, or the pressure of unforeseen necessities, for, in its period and instruments, it was in unison with His own eternal plan, which has been wrought out in Christ—in His incarnation and death, His ascension and glorification. The lesson to the principalities was intended for them ; they have not profanely intruded into the sacred precincts, and stolen away the guarded science. In all this procedure, which reveals to princedoms and powers God's manifold wisdom, the Divine eternal plan is consistently and systematically developed in Christ. And, as their own experience tells them, He is the same Christ—

(Ver. 12.) Ἐν ᾧ ἔχομεν τὴν παρρησίαν καὶ τὴν προσαγωγὴν —" In whom we have boldness and access"—the ἐν again connected with Christ as the sphere. Lachmann, following

A and B, omits the second article, and there are other but minor variations. Παρρησία is originally "free speech"—the speaking of all. There is no ground for the opinion of Cardinal Hugo and Peter Lombard, that it means *spes*—hope. Its secondary and usual signification is boldness—that self-possession which such liberty implies. It cannot mean free-spokenness towards the world, as is erroneously supposed by Olshausen, for such an idea is totally foreign to the train of thought. This boldness is toward God generally, but especially in prayer, as is indicated by the following term προσαγωγή. Heb. iii. 6, x. 19, 35; 1 John ii. 28, iii. 21, 22, iv. 17, v. 14, 15. In Christ we are ever having this blessing —boldness and access at all times and in every emergency. 1 John ii. 28, iv. 17. That tremor, doubt, and oppression of spirit which sin produces, are absent from believers when they enjoy access to God. Heb. iii. 6; 1 John ii. 28. Προσαγωγή has been already explained under ii. 18. The use of the article before both nouns signalizes them both as the elements of a distinctive and a possessed privilege. And all this—

ἐν πεποιθήσει—"in confidence." 2 Cor. i. 15, iii. 4, viii. 22, x. 2; Phil. iii. 4. This summing up is similar to the previous summing up in ii. 18, as boldness and access in prayer are the highest and conclusive proof—the richest and noblest elements—of spiritual experience. This is a word of the later Greek, and in the New Testament is only used by Paul. Phrynichus, ed. Lobeck, p. 294; Thom. Mag. p. 273. It seems to point out the manner or frame of soul in which the προσαγωγή is enjoyed, and it is involved in the very idea of παρρησία. This is no timorous approach. It is not the access of a distracted or indifferent spirit, but one filled with the assurance that it will not be repulsed, or dismissed with unanswered petition, for though unworthy it is not unwelcome. This state has faith for its medium—

διὰ τῆς πίστεως αὐτοῦ—"by the faith of Him;" the genitive being that of object. The genitive is similarly employed, Rom. iii. 22, 26; Gal. ii. 16, 20; Phil. iii. 9; Jas. ii. 1; Rev. ii. 13, xiv. 12. This clause belongs to the entire verse, and not merely, as some suppose, to πεποίθησις. Faith in Him is the instrument, and ἐν and διά are connected as in i. 7. The means by which our union to Christ secures those privileges is faith. That faith whose object is Jesus is the means to all who are Christ's, first, of "boldness," for their belief in the Divine Mediator gives them courage; secondly, of "access," for their realization of His glorified humanity warrants and enables them to approach the throne of grace; and, thirdly, these blessings are possessed "in confidence," for they feel that for Christ's sake their persons and services will be accepted by the Father.

(Ver. 13.) Διὸ αἰτοῦμαι μὴ ἐγκακεῖν—" Wherefore I entreat you that ye faint not." Διό—" wherefore," since these things are so, referring us back to the sentiments of the five preceding verses. Lachmann and Tischendorf, after A, B, D¹, E, prefer ἐγκακεῖν to the common reading ἐκκακεῖν, which has in its favour C, D³, F, G, I, K. It is doubtful, indeed, whether there be such a word. With all its apparent simplicity of style and construction, this verse is open to various interpretations. And, first, as to the accusative, which must be supplied before the infinitive, some prefer ἐμέ and others ὑμᾶς. In the former case the meaning is, "Wherefore I desire God that I faint not," and in the latter case it is, "Wherefore I entreat you that you lose not heart." The first is that adopted by the Syriac version, by Theodoret, Jerome, Bengel, Vater, Rückert, Harless, Olshausen, and Baumgarten-Crusius. Our objection to such an exposition is, that there is in the clause no formal or implied reference to God; that it is awkward to interpose a new subject, or make the object of the verb and the subject of the infinitive different—2 Cor. v. 20, vi. 1, x. 2; Heb. xiii. 19; and that the apostle possessed little indeed of that faint-heartedness against which he is supposed to guard himself by prayer. Turner's objection to this last statement is only a misconception of it. Besides, as the last clause of the verse is plainly an argument to sustain the request, the connection is destroyed if the apostle be imagined to make petition for himself; while the meaning is clear and pertinent if the request be for them— "Let not my sufferings for you distress you; they are your glory." The proposal of Harless to join ὑπὲρ ὑμῶν to αἰτοῦμαι —" I pray on your account," has little to recommend it. Our view is that of Chrysostom and the majority of interpreters. "That ye faint not"—

ἐν ταῖς θλίψεσίν μου ὑπὲρ ὑμῶν—" in my tribulations for you." No article is needed before ὑπέρ. 2 Cor. i. 6. 'Ἐν is not properly " on account of," as many render it, but it rather represents the close and sympathizing relation in which Paul and his readers stood. His afflictions had become theirs; they were in them as really as he was. Their sympathy with him had made his afflictions their own, and he implored them not to be dispirited or cowardly under such a pressure, and for this reason—

ἥτις ἐστὶ δόξα ὑμῶν—" which is your glory." "Ἥτις is used by attraction with the following predicate δόξα, and signifies " inasmuch as they are," *utpote quæ*. Winer, § 24, 3. But what is its antecedent? Theodoret, Zanchius, Harless, and Olshausen suppose it to be the thought contained in μὴ ἐγκακεῖν, as if the apostle's self-support in such sufferings were their glory. This exegesis proceeds upon an opinion which we have already gainsaid, viz., that Paul offers here a prayer for himself. Rückert exhales the meanings of the clause by finding in it only the vague indistinctness of oratorical declamation. The general opinion appears to be the correct one, that these sufferings of Paul, which came on him simply because he was the apostle of the Gentiles, were the "glory" of the Gentile believers, and not their disgrace, inasmuch as such persecutions not only proved the success of his ministerial labours, but were at the same time collateral evidence of the lofty and unfettered privileges which believing heathendom now possessed and retained, and which, by the apostle's firmness, were at length placed beyond the reach of Jewish fanaticism to annul or even to curtail. As you may measure the pyramid by its shadow, so these afflictions of Paul afforded a similar means of arriving at a relative or antithetical estimate of the spiritual liberty and prerogative of the Gentile churches. The apostle began the chapter by an allusion to the fact that he was a prisoner for the Gentiles, and he now concludes the digression by this natural admonition. His tribulations, the evidence of his official dignity and of their unconditioned exemption from ceremonial bondage, were their glory, and therefore they were not to sink into faintness and lassitude, as if by his "chain" they had been affronted and their apostle disgraced.

The apostle now resumes the thought broken off in ver. 1, and we are carried back at once to the magnificent imagery of a spiritual temple in the concluding section of the second chapter. The prayer must be regarded as immediately following that section, and its architectural terms and allusions will thus be more clearly understood. This connection with the closing paragraph of the former chapter, we take as affording the key to the correct exegesis of the following supplication.

(Ver. 14.) Τούτου χάριν κάμπτω τὰ γόνατά μου—"For this cause I bow my knees." The attitude, which Kant has ventured to call *einen knechtischen* (servile) *Orientalismus*, is described instead of the act, or, as Calvin says—*a signo rem denotat*. The phrase is followed here by πρός—but by a simple dative in Rom. xi. 4; while γονυπετεῖν has an accusative in Matt. xvii. 14; Mark i. 40, x. 17. This compound and γονυκλινεῖν represent in the Septuagint the Hebrew בָּרַע. The posture is the instinctive expression of homage, humility, and petition: the suppliant offers his worship and entreaty on bended knee. 2 Chron. vi. 13; Ps. xcv. 6; Luke xxii. 41; Acts vii. 60, ix. 40, xx. 36, xxi. 5. See Suicer's *Thesaurus*, *sub voce* γονυκλισία. He does not simply say, "I pray," adds Chrysostom—ἀλλὰ τὴν κατανενυγμένην δέησιν ἐδήλωσεν. Τούτου χάριν is repeated from ver. 1, "Because ye are inbuilt in the spiritual temple." I bow my knees—

πρὸς τὸν πατέρα—"toward the Father." Winer, § 49, h. The genitives, τοῦ Κυρίου ἡμῶν Ἰησοῦ Χριστοῦ, of the common text are pronounced by many critics to be spurious. That there was an early variation of reading is evident from Jerome's note—*non ut in Latinis codicibus additum est, ad Patrem Domini nostri Jesu Christi, sed simpliciter ad Patrem, legendum*. The words are wanting in A, B, C, and some of the Patristic citations, are omitted by Lachmann and Tischendorf, and rejected by Rückert, Harless, Olshausen, Meyer, Stier, Ellicott, and Alford. In this opinion we are now inclined to concur. Still the words are found in other Codices, and those of no mean authority, such as D, E, F, G, I, K, etc. They occur, too, in the Syriac and Vulgate, are not disowned by the Greek fathers Chrysostom and Theodoret, and they are retained by Knapp, Scholz, Tittmann, and Hahn, and vindicated by de

Wette. The evidence for them is strong, but not conclusive. They may have been interpolated from the common formula, and their insertion weakens the rhythmical connection between πατέρα and the following πατριά. The question is yet somewhat doubtful. The object of Paul's prayer is the Father—the universal Father—

(Ver. 15.) Ἐξ οὗ πᾶσα πατριὰ ἐν οὐρανοῖς καὶ ἐπὶ γῆς ὀνομάζεται—"Of whom every family in heaven and on earth is named." Calvin, Beza, Musculus, Zanchius, and Reiche refer to Christ as the antecedent. But even if the former clause be genuine, this interpretation cannot be sustained. It is the relation of the πατριά to the πατήρ which the apostle evidently characterizes, and not the relation of the family to its elder brother. The classes of beings referred to by the apostle have become each a Πατριά, from their relation to the Πατήρ. These words admit of a variety of interpretations. Πατριά, it is plain, cannot be equivalent to πατρότης, and denote fatherhood—*paternitas*, as Jerome translates. Yet this view is held by Theodoret, Theophylact, Œcumenius, Anselm, a-Lapide, Allioli, and Nitzsch, *Prakt. Theologie*, i. 269. The Syriac also translates—ܐܒܗܘܬܐ—"paternity," the Gothic version has—*all fadreinis*—*omne paternitatis*, and Wycliffe—*eche fadirheid*. Such a sense the word does not bear, and no tolerable exegesis could be extracted from it. The Greek fathers are even obliged to admit that among the celestial orders no proper fatherhood can exist. Ἐπεί, as Theophylact confesses, ἐκεῖ οὐδεὶς ἐξ οὐδενὸς γεννᾶται; or, as Theodoret adds—οὐρανίους πατέρας τοὺς πνευματικοὺς καλεῖ. Jerome is also obliged to say—*ita puto et angelos ceterasque virtutes habere principes sui generis quos patres gaudeant appellare*. Yet Stier would find no difficulty in defending such phraseology. Giving πατριά the sense of fatherhood, this meaning might be extracted—all paternity has the origin of its name in God the Father of all. Fatherhood takes its name from Father-God—*alle Vaterschaft hat ihres Namens Grund in Vatergott*. Somewhat similar is the opinion of Athanasius—"God, as Father of the Son, is the only true Father, and all created paternity is a shadow of the true." *Orat. in Arian.* i. 24. But an idea of this abstract nature is foreign to the apostle's modes of thought.

Πατριά, while it denotes sometimes lineage by the father's side, signifies also a family, or the individuals that claim a common father and a common descent—what may be called a house or clan. *Herodot.* ii. 143, iii. 75, i. 200; Luke ii. 4; Acts iii. 25. The Seventy represent by it the common Hebrew phrase—בֵּית אָבוֹת. We cannot acquiesce in the view of Estius, Grotius, Wetstein, and Holzhausen, who look upon the clause as a Jewish mode of expressing the idea that God has two families, that of angels in heaven and men upon earth. Schoettgen, *Horæ Heb.* p. 1237; Buxtorf, *Lex. Tal.* p. 1750; Wetstein, *in loc.* Some, again, such as Chrysostom, Bucer, Calvin, Zanchius, Estius, Michaelis, Küttner, and Peile, find a polemical allusion in the term to the union of Jew and Gentile; and a view somewhat similar is taken by Hunnius, Crocius, Calovius, and Wolf, who regard it as synonymous with *tota ecclesia*. Reiche needlessly supposes the allusion to be to the Gnostic æons in some prevalent false philosophy. Bodius shows peculiar keenness in excluding any reference to angels, the allusion under the phrase "family in heaven" being, as he contends, only to the church triumphant. Hodge follows him, and Theodore of Mópsuestia generalizes away the sense when he renders it ὃν ἅπαν σύστημα.

The verb ὀνομάζεται "is named," that is, involves the name, of πατριά. But Bullinger, Bucer, Estius, Rückert, Matthies, and Holzhausen take the verb in the sense of "exists." Καλέω in its passive voice may sometimes indirectly bear such a meaning, but the verb before us never has such a signification. It signifies to bear the—ὄνομα. Ἐξ οὗ— "from whom," or, as we say, "after whom" every family in heaven and earth is named. Homer, *Iliad*, x. 68; Xenophon, *Mem.* iv. 5, 12; Sophocles, *Œdip. Tyr.* 1036. The meaning seems to be: every circle of holy and intelligent creatures having the name of πατριά takes that name from God as Πατήρ. The reference is certainly not to the physical creation, or creation as a whole and in all its parts, as is the groundless opinion of Theophylact, Œcumenius, Estius, Rückert, Matthies, and Bretschneider. The apostle speaks of classes of intelligent creatures, each named πατριά simply after God, for He is Πατήρ. It follows as a natural consequence, though Meyer and de Wette object to such a conclusion, that if angels and "spirits of just men" in heaven, and holy men on earth, receive the name of πατριά from the Divine Father, then they are His children, as is contended for by many interpreters, from Beza and Piscator down to Olshausen. They lose the cold and official name of subjects in the familiar and endearing appellation of sons, and they are united to one another not dimly and unconsciously, as different products of the same Divine workmanship, but they merge into one family—"all they are brethren." Every πατριά must surely possess unbounded confidence in the benignity and protection of the Πατήρ, and to Him, therefore, the prayer of the apostle is directed—

(Ver. 16.) "Ἵνα δῴη ὑμῖν κατὰ τὸ πλοῦτος τῆς δόξης αὐτοῦ —"That He would give you according to the riches of His glory." A, B, C, F, G, read δῷ, and the reading has been adopted by Lachmann, Rückert, and Meyer. Others prefer the reading of the Textus Receptus, which is sustained by D, E, K, L, and most MSS., δῷ being regarded as a grammatical emendation. For the connection of ἵνα with the optative, the reader may turn to the remarks made under i. 17. In this case there is no word signifying "to ask or supplicate," for the phrase "I bow my knees" is a pregnant ellipse —the understood posture and symbol of earnest entreaty. The neuter form, πλοῦτος, is preferred to the masculine on the incontestable authority of A, B, C, D[1], E, F, G, etc. The masculine has but D[3], I, K, etc., in its favour. See under i. 7, ii. 7, iii. 8, where both the form of the word and its meaning have been referred to. The phrase is connected not with κραταιωθῆναι, but with δῴη, and it illustrates the proportion or measurement of the gift, nay, of all the gifts that are comprehended in the apostle's prayer. And it is no exaggeration, for He gives like Himself, not grudgingly or in tiny portions, as if He were afraid to exhaust His riches, or even suspected them to be limited in their contents. There is no fastidious scrupulosity or anxious frugality on the part of the Divine Benefactor. His bounty proclaims His conscious possession of immeasurable resources. He bestows according to the riches of His glory—His own infinite fulness. "That He would give you"—

δυνάμει κραταιωθῆναι διὰ τοῦ Πνεύματος αὐτοῦ εἰς τὸν ἔσω

ἄνθρωπον—" to be strengthened with might by His Spirit in the inner man." We need not, with Beza, Rückert, Olshausen, Matthies, Robinson, and others, regard the substantive δυνάμει as an adverb, nor, with Koppe, identify it with δυνατῶς. Rather, with Meyer, would we take it as the dative of instrument, by which the action of the verb is communicated. Winer, § 31, 7. It is by the infusion of power into the man within, that the process described by κραταιωθῆναι is secured. The verb κραταιόω belongs to the later and especially the Hellenistic Greek; κρατύνω being the earlier form. Meyer supposes a reference to the ἐγκακεῖν of a former clause, but such a supposition can hardly be admitted, for the "fainting" referred to by the apostle was connected solely with his own personal wrongs, while this prayer for strength is of a wider and deeper nature. Nor can we assume, with the Greek commentators, that the reference is merely to "temptations," to surmount which the apostle craves upon them the bestowment of might. We conceive the form of expression to be in unison with the figure which the apostle had introduced into the conclusion of the second chapter. He had likened the Ephesian Christians to a temple, and in harmony with such a thought he prays that the living stones in that fabric may be strengthened, so that the building may be compact and solid.

διὰ τοῦ Πνεύματος αὐτοῦ—" by His Spirit." The Spirit of God is the agent in this process of invigoration. That Spirit is God's, as He bears God's commission and does His work. He has free access to man's spirit to move it as He may, and it is His peculiar function in the scheme of mercy to apply to the heart the spiritual blessings provided by Christ. The direction of the gift is declared to be—

εἰς τὸν ἔσω ἄνθρωπον—" into the inner man." Εἰς cannot be said to stand for ἐν, but it marks out the destination of the gift. Winer, § 49, a; Kühner, § 603. It is not simply "in reference to," as Winer and de Wette render, nor "for," as Green translates it (*Greek Gram.* p. 292); but it denotes or implies that the δύναμις comes from an external source, and enters into the inner man. The phrase ὁ ἔσω ἄνθρωπος is identical with the parallel expression—ὁ κρυπτὸς τῆς καρδίας ἄνθρωπος, which the Apostle Peter, without sexual distinction, applies to women. 1 Pet. iii. 4. The formula occurs in Rom. vii. 22, and with some variation in 2 Cor. iv. 16. The "inner man" is that portion of our nature which is not cognizable by the senses, and does not consist of nerve, muscle, and organic form, as does the outer man. In the physiology of the seventh chapter of the Epistle to the Romans, it is not the soul—$\psi v \chi \eta$—in its special aspect of vital consciousness, but it is more connected with mind—$\nu o \hat{v} s$, and stands in contrast not exactly to $\sigma \acute{a} \rho \xi$, as representing generally depraved humanity, but to that sensuous nature which has action and reaction in and from the members—$\mu \acute{\epsilon} \lambda \eta$. Delitzsch, *System der Bib. Psychol.* p. 331; Reuss, *Théol. Chrét.* vol. ii. p. 56. But "the inner man" is not identical with "the new man"—$\acute{o}$ $\kappa a \iota \nu \grave{o} s$ $\mathring{a} \nu \theta \rho \omega \pi o s$; it is rather the sphere in which such renewal takes effect—our intellectual and spiritual nature personified. We cannot agree with Grotius, Wetstein, Fritzsche, and Meyer in supposing that there is any imitation of Platonic phrase in this peculiar diction. The sage of the Athenian academy did indeed use similar phraseology, for he speaks of the mind as $\acute{o}$ $\grave{\epsilon} \nu \tau \grave{o} s$ $\mathring{a} \nu \theta \rho \omega \pi o s$, and Plotinus and Philo adopted a like idiom. In some of the Jewish books occur also modes of expression not unlike. But the phrase is indeed a natural one—one that is not the coinage of any system of psychology, but which occurs at once to any one who wishes to distinguish easily and broadly between what is corporeal and external, and what is mental and internal, in his own constitution. Still, its theological meaning in the apostle's writings is different from its philosophical uses and applications. And this strength is imparted to the "inner man" by the Spirit's application of those truths which have a special tendency to cheer and sustain. He impresses the mind with the idea of the changeless love of Christ, and the indissoluble union of the believing soul to Him; with the necessity of decision, consistency, and perseverance; with the assurance that all grace needed will be fully and cheerfully afforded; and with the hope that the victory shall be ultimately obtained. Rom. xv. 13; 2 Tim. i. 7. This operation of the Spirit imparts such courage and energy as appear like a species of spiritual omnipotence.

The Syriac version, the Greek fathers, with the Latin commentators Ambrosiaster and Pelagius, join this last clause—

εἰς τὸν ἔσω ἄνθρωπον, with the following verse, and with the verb κατοικῆσαι — " In order that Christ may inhabit the inner man by the faith which is in your hearts." It has been rightly objected by Harless and others, that διὰ τῆς πίστεως cannot well be joined to ἐν ταῖς καρδίαις, and that there would be a glaring pleonasm in the occurrence in the same verse of ὁ ἔσω ἄνθρωπος and ἡ καρδία ὑμῶν. The ordinary division is a natural one, and we accordingly follow it.

(Ver. 17.) Κατοικῆσαι τὸν Χριστόν—" That Christ may dwell." The first point of inquiry is the connection of this infinitive with the previous sentence. Does it depend on δῴη, and is the meaning—" that he would grant that Christ may dwell in your hearts"? or is it dependent on κραταιωθῆναι, and is the meaning—" that he would grant you to be strengthened in the inner man, so that, being thus strengthened, Christ may dwell in your hearts"? The first view is held by Theophylact, Zanchius, Grotius, Estius, Bengel, Flatt, Koppe, Rückert, Holzhausen, Stier, and Baumgarten-Crusius. The connection, however, has been explained differently. Some, as Theophylact and Zanchius, regard the clause as a new petition giving speciality to the first, or, as the Greek father characterizes it,—καὶ τὸ μεῖζον καὶ περισσότερον. Meier adopts the view of Calvin,—*declarat, quale sit interioris hominis robur.* A similar exegesis is maintained by Harless and Matthies, while Olshausen looks upon the clause as a subordinate definition of the phrase "to be strengthened." He maintains that Paul could not pray that Christ would dwell in their hearts, for He already dwelt there. As well might he argue that Paul could not pray for spiritual invigoration, since they already possessed it. When believers pray for a gift in general terms, they emphatically supplicate an enlargement of what of it is already in their possession. Would Olshausen apply his criterion to the prayer contained in the 1st chapter, and affirm that the fact of such gifts being asked for implied the total want of them on the part of the Ephesian church? De Wette takes κατοικῆσαι as an infinitive of purpose or design, and regards the clause as describing the completion of " the strengthening." Bernhardy, p. 365. See on Col. i. 11. We now look upon it as pointing out rather the result of the process of invigoration prayed for. The inspired petitioner solicited spiritual strength for them securing this result—that Christ might dwell in their hearts. The infinitive is connected with the more distant δῷη, and more closely with the preceding infinitive; Winer, § 44, 1. There is little doubt that in the verb κατοικῆσαι, emphatic in its position, the reference is to the last clause of the 2nd chapter— κατοικητήριον τοῦ Θεοῦ—" a dwelling of God." The apostle applies in this prayer the architectural allusion directly to the believing Ephesians themselves, and therefore the figure is not preserved in its rhetorical integrity. Ye are built on the foundation of the apostles and prophets, Christ being the Head-stone of the corner; that spiritual building fitly framed together groweth unto a holy temple, for a habitation of God: and the prayer now is, that compactness and solidity may be granted to them by the Spirit, so as that in them the primary design of such a temple may be realized, and "Christ may dwell in their hearts"—Christ by His Spirit, and not as Fritzsche coldly and tastelessly describes it—*mens quam Christus postulat.* Κράτος, not δύναμις, may be applied to the qualities of physical objects, and so with propriety its derivative verb is here employed. In a temple that was crazy, or was built of loose and incongruous materials, the Divine guest could not be expected to dwell.

The κατοικῆσαι of this verse has, as we have said, its origin in the κατοικητήριον of ii. 22. The language is of common usage, and has its basis in the Old Testament, and in the employment of שָׁכַן and kindred words to describe Jehovah's relation to His house. And as the design of a temple is that its god may inhabit it, so Christ dwells in the heart. This inhabitation is not to be explained away as a mere reception of Christian doctrine, nor is it to be regarded as a mystical exaggeration.[1] Col. i. 27; John xiv. 23; Rom. viii. 9, 11; Gal. ii. 20; Jas. iv. 5. The meaning of His dwelling is—

διὰ τῆς πίστεως—" by faith "—your faith. Faith induces and also realizes His presence. And His abode is in no outer vestibule, but—

ἐν ταῖς καρδίαις ὑμῶν—" in your hearts." The heart, as

[1] When Ignatius was asked, on his trial, by the emperor what was the meaning of his name—Theophorus—he promptly replied, "He who has Christ in his breast."

centre of the spiritual life, is His temple—the inner shrine of emotion and power—*Centrum des sittlichen Lebens.* Delitzsch, *System der Bib. Psychol.* p. 206; Beck, *Seelenlehre,* p. 69. Christ dwells there not as a sojourner, or "as a wayfaring man that turneth aside to tarry for a night," but as a permanent resident. The intercessor continues—

(Ver. 18.) Ἐν ἀγάπῃ ἐρριζωμένοι καὶ τεθεμελιωμένοι ἵνα— "Ye having been rooted and grounded in love, in order that." Some solve the difficulty felt about the connection of this clause by proposing to transfer ἵνα to its commencement. This metathesis was suggested by Photius, and has been followed by Beza, Heinsius, Grotius, Crocius, and the Authorized Version. There is no necessity for such a change, even though the clause be joined, as by Knapp and Lachmann, to that which begins with ἵνα; and the passages usually adduced to justify such an alteration are not precisely parallel, as is acutely shown by Piscator. John xiii. 39; Acts xix. 4; Gal. ii. 10. The clause is, however, connected by some with the preceding one. Theophylact makes it the condition of Christ's dwelling in their hearts. The exegesis of Chrysostom is similar—"He dwelleth only in hearts rooted in His love"— ταῖς καρδίαις ταῖς πισταῖς, ταῖς ἐρριζομέναις. This connection is also advocated by many, including Erasmus, Luther, Harless, Olshausen, and de Wette. But the change of construction is not so easily accounted for, if this view of the connection be adopted. Harless says, indeed, that as the predicate applies both to καρδίαις and to ὑμῶν, it could not with propriety be joined exclusively to any of them. Such a view of grammatical propriety was, however, based on a foregone conclusion, for either the genitive or dative could have been used with equal correctness. On the other hand, the change of syntax indicates a change of connection, and the use of the irregular nominative makes the transition easy to the form adopted with ἵνα. Krüger, § 56, 9, 4; Winer, § 63, 2. Harless adopts the view of Chrysostom and Theophylact, and regards the clause as a condition—"Christ dwells in their heart, since they had been rooted in love." But the clause, so changed, becomes a species of independent proposition, giving a marked prominence to the sense, and connected at once with the preceding context as its result, and with the following context as its starting idea—the perfect being used with propriety, and not the present. Christ dwelling in their hearts—they are supposed, as the effect of this inhabitation, to have been now rooted and grounded in love; and as the design of this confirmation in love—they are then and thus qualified to comprehend with all saints, etc. "Having thus become rooted and grounded in love, in order that ye may be able to comprehend."

The two participles ἐρριζομένοι and τεθεμελιωμένοι, are usually said to express the same idea by different figures—the one borrowed from botany and the other from architecture. But it is more natural to refer both words to the same general symbol, and indeed, the former term is applied to a building. Thus, Herodot. i. 64—Πεισίστρατος ἐρρίζωσε τὴν τυραννίδα; Plutarch, De Fortun. Rom.—ῥιζῶσαι καὶ καταστῆσαι τὴν πόλιν; Sophocles, Œdip. Col. 1591, ὁδὸν γῆθεν ἐρριζωμένον; also Plutarch, De Lib. Educ. 9, etc. The verb is thus used in a general sense, and coupled with τεθεμελιωμένοι may have no specific reference to plantation. The allusion is again to the solid basement of the spiritual temple described in chap. ii.

But to what do the words ἐν ἀγάπῃ describing the foundation refer? Some understand the love of Christ or God to us. Such is the view of Chrysostom and Theophylact, of Beza, Calovius, Aretius, Wolf, Bengel, Storr, Koppe, and Flatt. We cannot lay any stress on the dictum of Harless, that the omission of the article before the substantive proves it to be used in a subjective sense, and to signify our love to Christ. Winer, § 19, 1.[1] Nor can we say, with Meyer, that the substantive standing without the article has almost the force of a participle—"in amando." But the entire context proves that the love referred to is the grace of love. One would have expected a genitive of possession, if ἀγάπη were not predicated of the persons themselves—if it were not a feeling in their hearts. It is a clumsy and equivocal exegesis to comprise under the term both Christ's love to us and our love to Him, as is done by Bucer, Anselm, Zanchius, Crocius, Matthies, and Stier. Nor can we accede to Meyer, who seems to restrict it to brother-love; for if it be the grace of love which is here specified, then it is love to Christ, and to every creature that

[1] Moulton, p. 148.

bears His image. Col. iii. 14; 1 Cor. xiii. Now, as the apostle intimates, this love is the root and foundation of Christian character, as all advancement is connected with its existence and exercise. "He prayeth well who loveth well." Love is the fundamental grace. As love keeps its object enshrined in the imagination, and allows it never to be absent from the thoughts; so love to Jesus gives Him such a cheerful and continued presence in the mind, that as it gazes ever upon the image, it is changed into its likeness, for it strives to realize the life of Christ. It deepens also that consecration to the Lord which is essential to spiritual progress, for it sways all the motives, and moves and guides the inner man by its hallowed and powerful instincts. And it gives life and symmetry to all the other graces, for confidence and hope in a being to whom you are indifferent, cannot have such vigour and permanence as they have in one to whom the spirit is intelligently and engrossingly attached. When the lawgiver is loved, his statutes are obeyed with promptitude and uniformity. Thus resemblance to Jesus, devotion to Him, and growth in grace, as the elements and means of spiritual advancement, are intimately connected with love as their living basis. The entire structure of the holy fane is fitly framed and firmly held together, for it is "rooted and grounded in love."

(Ver. 18.) Ἵνα ἐξισχύσητε καταλαβέσθαι σὺν πᾶσι τοῖς ἁγίοις—"That ye may be able to comprehend with all the saints." The conjunction expresses the design which these previous petitions had in view. Their being strengthened, their being inhabited by Christ, and their "having been rooted and grounded in love," not only prepared them for this special study, but had made it their grand object. By a prior invigoration they were disciplined to it, and braced up for it—"that ye may be fully able"—fully matched to the enterprise.

On ἅγιος, see i. 2. The verb καταλαβέσθαι, used in the middle voice, has in the New Testament the meaning of "to comprehend," or to make a mental seizure. Such a middle voice—according to Krüger, § 52, 8, 4—differs from the active only in so far as it exhibits the idea—*des geschäftlichen oder geistigen Kraftaufwandes*—of earnest or spiritual energy.

The aorist expresses the rapid passing of the act. Winer, § 44, 7, b. In the only other passages where it occurs, as in Acts iv. 13, x. 34, xxv. 25, the verb signifies to come to a decided conclusion from facts vividly presented to the attention. And they were to engage in this study along with the universal church of Christ—not angels, or glorified spirits, or office-bearers in the church exclusively, as some have maintained. The design is to comprehend—

τί τὸ πλάτος καὶ μῆκος καὶ βάθος καὶ ὕψος—" what is the breadth, and length, and depth, and height." This order of the last two nouns is supported by A, K, L, or J, and the Received Text reversing it is apparently a correction intended to give the more natural order, and has in its favour B, C, D, E, F, G, with the Vulgate, Gothic, and Coptic. But to what do these terms of measurement apply? Many endeavours have been made to supplement the clause with a genitive, and it is certain that "many wits run riot in their geometrical and moral discourse upon these dimensions." *Assembly's Annotations, in loc.*

1. We may allude in passing to the supposition of Kypke, that the verb may signify to occupy or fill, and that τι may be used with change of accent in an indefinite sense—" that ye may be able in the company of all saints to occupy the breadth, whatever it is," etc. This exegesis is both violent and unnatural, puts an unusual sense upon καταλαβέσθαι, and treats τί τὸ πλάτος as if it were τὸ πλάτος τι.

2. Nor need we be detained by the opinion of Schrader, who regards the words τί τὸ πλάτος, etc., as only the paraphrastic complement of the verb καταλαβέσθαι, and as indicating the depth and thoroughness of the comprehension.

3. Nor can we suppose, with Beza and Grotius, that there is any allusion in these terms to the quarters of the heavens pointed to in the priestly gestures that gave name to the heave-offering and wave-offering. Ex. xxix. 27.

4. Some of the Fathers referred these four words to the mystery of the cross—τοῦ σταυροῦ φύσις, as Severianus calls it. This view was held by Gregory of Nyssa, Jerome, and Augustine, and has been adopted by Anselm, Thomas Aquinas, and Estius. This quadriform mystery—*sacramentum crucis*— was explained by Augustine as signifying love in its breadth,

hope in its height, patience in its length, and humility in its depth. Ep. cxii.; *De Videndo Deo*, cap. 14; Ep. cxx. cap. 26. Well does Calvin add—*hæc subtilitate sua placent, sed quid ad Pauli mentem?* Estius is more full and precise. He explains how the terms can be applied to the shape and beams of a cross, and adds—*longitudo, temporum est, latitudo locorum, altitudo gloriæ, profunditas discretionis*, etc.—the reference being to the *signum* T *in frontibus inscriptum*. So remote from the train of thought is this recondite mysticism, that it needs and merits no formal refutation.

5. Some refer the nouns—*sacra illa Pauli mathematica*, as Glassius calls them—to the Divine plan of redemption—the mystery of grace. Such is the view of Chrysostom, who calls it—τὸ μυστήριον τὸ ὑπὲρ ἡμῶν οἰκονομηθέν, and Theodoret, who describes it as—τῆς οἰκονομίας τὸ μέγεθος. It is also the view of Theophylact and Œcumenius, followed by Beza, Bullinger, Piscator, Zanchius, Crocius, Crellius, Calovius, Rückert, Meier, Harless, Baumgarten-Crusius, and Olshausen. The supplement in this case appears to be far-fetched, and there is no allusion in the context to any such theme; the mystery referred to in verses 4–10 being the admission of the Gentiles into the church, and not the scheme of grace in its wide and glorious aspects. As little ground is there to go back to ver. 8, to "the unsearchable riches of Christ," and refer such terms to them. Whatever the allusion is, it must be something immediately present to his own mind, and something that he supposed very present to the mind of his readers, the dimensions of which are thus characterized.

6. We might almost pass over the fancy of those who suppose the apostle to take a survey of the Divine nature. Such is the opinion of Ambrosiaster, who believes the apostle to describe a sphere or cube equal in length, breadth, and thickness, and imagines that such a figure represents the perfection and all including infinity of God.[1] Matthies holds the same

[1] "Ut sicut in sphæra tanta longitudo est, quanta latitudo, et tanta altitudo, quantum et profundum; ita et in Deo omnia æqualia sunt immensitate infinitatis. Sphæra enim definito modo concluditur: Deus autem non solum implet omnia, sed et excedit; nec enim clauditur, sed omnia intra se habet, ut solus ineffabilis et infinitus habeatur: et gratiæ huic insufficienter agantur, quia cum tantus sit, dignatus est per Christum hominem visitare peccatis et morti subjectum."—Ambrosius, *Opera*, tom. vii. pp. 280, 281, Venetiis, 1781.

allusion, but refers it to the moral perfections of God. What has led to this view seems to be the similarity of this verse to a passage in Job xi. 8, in which the unfathomable mystery of the Divine nature is described—"It is high as heaven," etc. But there is nothing to warrant such an allusion here, or even to give it a mere probability.

7. That the terms indicate the measurement of God's love to men, is the view advocated partly by Chrysostom, and by Erasmus, Bodius, Vatablus, Grotius, Rollock, Dickson, Baumgarten, Flatt, and von Gerlach. "God's love," as is noted in the paraphrase of Erasmus, "reaches in its height to the angels, and in its depth into hell, and stretches in its length and breadth to all the climates of the world." Or, as Grotius explains it—"The Divine goodness in its breadth affects all men, and in its length endures through all ages; in its depth it reaches to man's lowest depression, and in its height it carries him to highest glory." But this explanation, too, the context abjures, unless such were the sense of the previous ἀγάπη, which, however, means love possessed by us.

8. With greater plausibility, Christ's love to us is supposed to be the theme of allusion, by Calvin, Calixtus, Zanchius Aretius, Semler, Zachariae, Storr, Bisping, Meyer, Holzhausen, Hodge, Peile, and Ellicott. Neither, however, can this opinion be sustained. The previous ἀγάπη could not suggest the thought, for there it is subjective. We apprehend that this exegesis has been borrowed from the following clause—"and to know the love of Christ," which Ellicott says is practically the genitive. But that clause is not epexegetical of the preceding, as is manifest in the use of τε instead of καί, for this particle does not conjoin dependent sentences—it only adjoins collateral or independent propositions. Besides, the phrases "length and breadth" are unusual measurements of love.

9. De Wette, looking to Col. ii. and comparing this phraseology with the second and third verses of that chapter, imagines the apostle to refer to the Divine wisdom. There may be in Job xi. 8 a reference to the Divine wisdom, but the language specially affirms the mystery of the Divine nature. Schlichting also refers to Col. ii. 2—to "the mystery of God the Father and of Christ," as if that were the allusion here.

Such a view is quite as capricious as any of the preceding, for the wisdom of God is not a prominent topic either in this prayer or in the preceding context, where it is only once, though vividly, introduced. Alford somewhat similarly supposes that the genitive is left indefinite—"every dimension of all that God has revealed or done in or for us." This is certainly better than any of the previous explanations.

10. Heinsius, Homberg, Wolf, Michaelis, Cramer, Röell, Bengel, Koppe, Stier, Burton, Trollope, and Dr. Featley in the *Assembly's Annotations*, suppose the allusion to be to the Christian temple; not to the fane of the Ephesian Artemis, as is maintained by Chandler and Macknight. This appears to us to be the most probable exegesis, the genitive being still before the apostle's mind from the end of the previous chapter. We have seen how the previous language of the prayer is moulded by such an allusion; that the invigoration of the inner man, the indwelling of Christ, and the substructure in love, have all distinct reference to the glorious spiritual edifice. This idea was present, and so present to the apostle's imagination, that he feels no need to make formal mention of it. Besides, these architectural terms lead us to the same conclusion, as they are so applicable to a building. The magnificent fabric is described in the end of chap. ii., and the intervening verses which precede the prayer are, as already stated, a parenthesis. That figure of a temple still loomed before the writer's fancy, and naturally supplied the distinctive imagery of the prayer. For this reason, too, he does not insert a genitive, as the substantive is so remote, nor did he reckon it necessary to repeat the noun itself. Yet, to sustain the point and emphasis, he repeats the article before each of the substantives. In explaining these terms of mensuration we would not say with an old commentator quoted by Wolf —"The church has length, that is, it stretches from east to west; and it has breadth, that is, it reaches from the equator to the poles. In its depth it descends to Christ, its cornerstone and basis, and in its height it is exalted to heaven." There is a measurement of area—breadth and length, and a measurement of altitude—height and depth. May not the former refer to its size and growing vastness, embracing, as it will do, so many myriads of so many nations, and spanning

the globe? And may not the latter depict its glory? for the plan, structure, and materials alike illustrate the fame and character of its Divine Builder and Occupant, while its lofty turrets are bathed and hidden from view in the radiant splendour of heaven. And with what reed shall we measure this stately building? How shall we grasp its breadth, compute its length, explore its depth, and scan its height? Only by the discipline described in the previous context—by being strengthened by the Spirit, by having Christ within us, and by being thus "rooted and grounded in love." This ability to measure the church needs the assistance of the Divine Spirit—of Him who forms this "habitation of God"—so that we may understand its nature, feel its self-expansion, and believe the "glorious things spoken" of it. It requires also the indwelling of Jesus—of Him in whom the whole building groweth unto a holy temple, in order to appreciate its connection with Him as its chief corner-stone, the source of its stability and symmetry. And they who feel themselves "rooted and grounded in love" need no incitement to this survey and measurement, for He whom they love is its foundation, while His Father dwells in it, and His Spirit builds it up with generation after generation of believers. None have either the disposition or the skill to comprehend the vastness and glory of the spiritual temple, save they who are in it themselves, and who, being individual and separate shrines, can reason from their own enjoyment to the dignity and splendour of the universal edifice. And not only so, but the apostle also prayed for ability—

(Ver. 19.) Γνῶναί τε τὴν ὑπερβάλλουσαν τῆς γνώσεως ἀγάπην τοῦ Χριστοῦ—"And to know the knowledge-surpassing love of Christ." Γνῶναι is not dependent on καταλαβέσθαι, but is in unison with, or rather parallel to it, being also a similar exercise of mind. The particle τε, not unlike the Latin *que*, does not couple; it rather annexes or adds a clause which is not necessarily dependent on the preceding. Kühner, § 722; Hartung, i. p. 105; Hand, *Tursellinus seu de Particulis Latinis Commentarii*, lib. ii. p. 467. Winer remarks, that in the clause adjoined by τε the more prominent idea of the sentence may be found. § 53, 2.[1] In the phrase

---
[1] Moulton, p. 542.

—ἀγάπην τοῦ Χριστοῦ, Χριστοῦ is the genitive of possession or subject—the love of Christ to us. The genitive γνώσεως is governed by the participle ὑπερβάλλουσαν, and not by the substantive ἀγάπην,—the last a misconstruction, which may have originated the reading of Codex A and of Jerome—*scientiæ caritatem;* a reading adopted also by Grotius and Homberg. The participle, from its comparative sense, governs the genitive. Kühner, § 539; Bernhardy, p. 169; Vigerus, *de Idiotismis,* ii. p. 667, Londini, 1824. Two different meanings have been ascribed to the participle—

1. That adopted by Luther[1] in one version—" the love of Christ, which is more excellent than knowledge." Similar is the view of Wetstein and Wilke. Lexicon, *sub voce.* Such a rendering appears to stultify itself. If the apostle prayed them to know a love which was better than knowledge, the verb, it is plain, is used with a different signification from its cognate substantive. To know such a love must in that case signify to possess or feel it, and there is no occasion to take γνῶσις in any technical and inferior sense. Nor can we suppose the apostle to use such a truism in the form of a contrast, and to say, " I pray that you may know that love to Christ is better than mere knowledge about Him "—a position which nobody could dispute. Nor did there need a request for spiritual strength to enable them to come to the conclusion which Augustine gathers from the clause—*scientia subdita caritati. De Gratia et Lib. Arbit.* cap. 19. Far more point and consistency are found in the second form of exegesis, which—

2. Supposes the apostle to say, that the love of Christ—the love which He bears to us — transcends knowledge, or goes beyond our fullest conceptions. "I pray that you may be able to know the love of Christ, which yet in itself is above knowledge." This figure of speech, which rhetoricians call an oxymoron or a paradox, consists in the statement of an apparent inconsistency, and is one which occurs elsewhere in the writings of the apostle. Rom. i. 20; 1 Cor. i. 21–25; 2 Cor. viii. 2; Gal. ii. 19; 1 Tim. v. 6. The apostle does not mean that Christ's love is in every sense incompre-

---

[1] His first translation was *die Liebe Christi, die doch alle Erkentniss übertrifft*, but in the year 1545 he rendered—*dass Christum lieb haben viel besser ist, denn alles Wissen.*

hensible, nor does he pray that his readers may come to know the fact that His love is unknowable in its essence. This latter view, which is that of Harless and Olshausen, limits the inspired prayer, and is not warranted by the language employed. But in this verse the position of the participle between the article and its substantive, proves it to be only an epithet—"to know the knowledge-surpassing love of Christ." Winer, § 45, 4, note. The incomprehensibility of the love of Christ is not that special element of it which the apostle prayed that the Ephesians might come to the knowledge of, but he asks that they might be strengthened to cherish enlarged conceptions of a love which yet, in its higher aspect and properties, was beyond knowledge. So write Œcumenius and Theophylact,—τὴν ἀγάπην τὴν ὑπερέχουσαν πάσης γνώσεως. The apostle wishes them to possess a relative acquaintance with the love of Christ, while he felt that the absolute understanding of it was far beyond their reach. To know it to be the fact, that it is a love which passeth knowledge, is different from saying—to know it experimentally, though it be a love which in the highest sense passeth knowledge. Thus Theodore of Mopsuestia says—τὸ γνῶναι ἀντὶ τοῦ ἀπολαῦσαι λέγει. It may be known in some features and to some extent, but at the same time it stretches away into infinitude, far beyond the ken of human discovery and analysis. As a fact manifested in time and embodied in the incarnation, life, teaching, and death of the Son of God, it may be understood, for it assumed a nature of clay, bled on the cross, and lay prostrate in the tomb; but in its unbeginning existence as an eternal passion, antedating alike the Creation and the Fall, it "passeth knowledge." In the blessings which it confers—the pardon, grace, and glory which it provides—it may be seen in palpable exhibition, and experienced in happy consciousness; but in its limitless power and endless resources it baffles thought and description. In the terrible sufferings and death to which it led, and in the self-denial and sacrifices which it involved, it may be known so far by the application of human instincts and analogies; but the fathomless fervour of a Divine affection surpasses the measurements of created intellect. As the attachment of a man, it may be gauged; but as the love of a God, who can by searching find it out? Uncaused itself, it originated salvation; unresponded to amidst the "contradiction of sinners," it neither pined nor collapsed. It led from Divine immortality to human agonies and dissolution, for the victim was bound to the cross not by the nails of the military executioner, but by the "cords of love." It loved repulsive unloveliness, and, unnourished by reciprocated attachment, its ardour was unquenched, nay, is unquenchable, for it is changeless as the bosom in which it dwells. Thus it may be known, while yet it "passeth knowledge;" thus it may be experimentally known, while still in its origin and glory it surpassses comprehension, and presents new and newer phases to the loving and inquiring spirit. For one may drink of the spring and be refreshed, and his eye may take in at one view its extent and circuit, while he may be able neither to fathom the depth nor mete out the volume of the ocean whence it has its origin.

This prayer, that the Ephesians might know the love of Christ, is parallel to the preceding one, and was suggested by it. That temple of such glory and vastness which has Christ for its corner-stone, suggests the love of its illustrious Founder. While the apostle prayed that his converts in Ephesus might comprehend the stability and magnificence of the one, he could not but add that they might also know the intensity and tenderness of the other—might understand in its history and results a love that defied their familiar cognizance and penetration in its essence and circuit. From what the church is, and is to be, you infer the love of Christ. And the being "rooted and grounded in love" is the one preparative to know the love of Christ, for love appreciates love, and responds in cordial pulsation. And all this for the ultimate end—

ἵνα πληρωθῆτε εἰς πᾶν τὸ πλήρωμα τοῦ Θεοῦ—" that ye may be filled up to all the fulness of God." This clause depicts the grand purpose and result. "Ἵνα—" in order that," is connected with the preceding clauses of the prayer, and is the third instance of its use in the paragraph—ἵνα δῴη—ἵνα ἐξισ-χύσητε—ἵνα πληρωθῆτε—this last being climactic, or the great end of the whole supplication. (For the meaning of πλήρωμα, the reader may turn to i. 10, 23.) Τοῦ Θεοῦ is in the genitive of subject or possession. "All the fulness of God" is all the fulness which God possesses, or by which He is characterized. Chrysostom is right in the main when he paraphrases it,—

πληροῦσθαι πάσης ἀρετῆς ἧς πλήρης ἐστίν ὁ Θεός. Some, like Harless, refer the fulness to the Divine δόξα; others, like Holzhausen, Baumgarten, and Michaelis, think the allusion is to a temple inhabited or filled with Divinity, or the Shechinah; and others, again, as Vatablus and Schoettgen, dilate the meaning into a full knowledge of God or of Divine doctrine. Many commentators, including Calovius, Zachariae, Wolf, Beza, Estius, Grotius, and Meyer, break down the term by a rash analysis, and make it refer to this or that species of spiritual gifts. Bodius and Olshausen keep the word in its undivided significance, but Conybeare inserts an unwarranted supplement when he renders — "filleth therewith" (with Christ's love) "even to the measure of the fulness of God." Koppe, adopting the idea of Aretius and Küttner, and most unwarrantably referring it to the church, supposes the clause to be adduced as a proof of the preceding statement, that Christ's love surpasses knowledge, and this is seen "in the fact of your admission to the church,"— thus diluting the words into ἐν τῷ πληρωθῆναι ὑμᾶς. Schleusner has a similar view. Codex B reads—ἵνα πληρωθῇ πᾶν τὸ πλήρωμα, an exegetical variation. The πλήρωμα—that with which He is filled—appears to be the entire moral excellence of God—the fulness and lustre of His spiritual perfections. Such is the climax of the prayer. It is plainly contrary to fact and experience to understand the term of the uncreated essence of God, for such an idea would involve us in a species of pantheism.

The preposition εἰς is used with special caution. The simple dative is not employed, nor does εἰς stand for ἐν, as Grotius, Estius, and Whitby imagine, and as it is rendered in the Syriac and English versions. It does not denote "with," but "for" or "into"—filled up to or unto "an end quantitatively considered." The whole fulness of God can never contract itself so as to lodge in any created heart. But the smaller vessel may have its own fulness poured into it from one of larger dimensions. The communicable fulness of God will in every element of it impart itself to the capacious and exalted bosom, for Christ dwells in their hearts. The difference between God and the saint will be not in kind, but in degree and extent. His fulness is infinite; theirs is limited by the essential conditions of a created nature.

Theirs is the correspondence of a miniature to the full face and form which it represents. Stier's version is, " Until you be what as the body of Christ you can and should be, the whole fulness of God." But this proceeds on a wrong idea of πλήρωμα — as if it here signified the church as divinely filled. (See the illustrations of πλήρωμα under i. 23.) The apostle prays for strength, for the indwelling of Jesus, for unmoveable foundation in love, for a comprehension of the size and vastness of the spiritual temple, and for a knowledge of the love of Christ; and when such blessings are conferred and enjoyed, they are the means of bringing into the heart this Divine fulness. CoL ii. 19. There seems to be a close concatenation of thought. The "strength" prayed for is needed to qualify "the inner man" to bear and retain that "fulness." The implored inhabitation of Him in whom "dwells all the fulness of the Godhead bodily," is this fulness in its formal aspect; and that love which founds and confirms the Christian character, and instinctively enables it to comprehend the vast designs of God in His church, and to know the unimaginable love of Christ, is of the same fulness an index and accompaniment. This blessed result may not be completely realized on earth, where so many disturbing influences are in constant operation, but it shall be reached in heaven, where the spirit shall be sated with "all the fulness of God."

(Ver. 20.) Τῷ δὲ δυναμένῳ ὑπὲρ πάντα ποιῆσαι ὑπερεκπερισσοῦ ὧν αἰτούμεθα ἢ νοοῦμεν—" Now to Him who is able to do beyond all things superabundantly beyond what we ask or think." The apostle supposes his prayer to be answered, and all its requests conferred. The Divine Giver of such munificent donations is surely worthy of all homage, and especially worthy of all homage in the character of the answerer of prayer. By δέ he passes to a different subject— from recipients to the Giver. Praise succeeds prayer—the anthem is its fitting conclusion.

The construction is idiomatic, as if the apostle's mind laboured for terms of sufficient intensity. Words compounded with ὑπέρ are often employed by the full mind of the apostle, and are the favourite characteristics of his style, i. 21, iv. 10; Rom. v. 20, viii. 37; 2 Cor. vii. 4, xi. 5, 23; Phil. ii. 9;

1 Thess. iii. 10; 2 Thess. i. 3; 1 Tim. i. 14. Compare Fritzsche, *ad Roman.* vol. i. 351. The general idea is—God's infinite ability to grant spiritual blessing. Ὑπέρ is twice expressed; before πάντα, and in the double compound term ὑπερεκπερισσοῦ. Mark vii. 37; 1 Thess. iii. 10, v. 13. This repetition shows the ardour of the apostle's soul, and his anxiety to body forth the idea of the incomparable power of God to answer petition. The first train of thought seems to have been—ὑπὲρ πάντα ποιῆσαι ἃ αἰτούμεθα—"to do beyond what we ask or think." But this description did not exhaust the apostle's conception, and so he inserts—ὑπερεκπερισσοῦ ὧν αἰτούμεθα—"more than abundantly," or abundantly far beyond what we ask or think. Nor is there any tautology. Ὑπὲρ πάντα ποιῆσαι expresses merely the fact of God's superabundant power, but the subjoined ὑπερεκπερισσοῦ defines the mode in which this illimitable power displays itself, and that is, by conferring spiritual gifts in superabundance—in much more than simple abundance. Harless places the two clauses in apposition, but their union appears to be closer, as our exegesis intimates. Πάντα is closely connected with ὧν, which is governed in the genitive by the ὑπέρ in ὑπερεκπερισσοῦ. Bernhardy, p. 139. And we do not say with Harless that there is any hyperbole, for omnipotence has never exhausted its resources. While omniscience is the actual knowledge of all, omnipotence is the ability to do all, and all that it can do has never been achieved.

God is able to do far "above what we ask," for our asking is limited and feeble. John xvi. 24. But there may be thoughts too sweeping for expression, there may be unutterable groanings prompted by the Spirit (Rom. viii. 26); yet above and beyond our widest conceptions and most daring expectations is God "able to do." God's ability to answer prayer transcends not only our spoken petitions, but far surpasses even such thoughts as are too big for words, and too deep for utterance. And still those desires which are dumb from their very vastness, and amazing from their very boldness, are insignificant requests compared with the power of God. For we know so little of His promises, and so weak is our faith in them, that we ask not, as we should, for their universal fulfilment; and though we did understand their depth and power, our loftiest imaginations of possible blessing would come infinitely short of the power and resources of the Hearer of prayer. *Beati qui esuriunt*, says Bernard, *et sitiunt justitiam, quoniam ipsi saturabuntur. Qui esurit, esuriat amplius, et qui desiderat, abundantius adhuc desideret, quoniam quantumcunque desiderare potuerit, tantum est accepturus:*—

κατὰ τὴν δύναμιν τὴν ἐνεργουμένην ἐν ἡμῖν—" according to the power which worketh in us." These words are not to be joined to νοοῦμεν, as if they qualified it, and as if the apostle meant to say, that God can do more for us than we can think, even when our thoughts are excited and enlarged by His own "power putting itself forth in us." This participle is here, as in many other places, in the middle voice, the active voice being used by Paul in reference to a personal agent, and the middle employed when, as in this case, the idea of personality is sunk. "According to His power that proves or shows itself at work in us." Winer, § 38, 6. That power has been again and again referred to in itself and in its results by the apostle. (i. 19, iii. 16.) From our own blissful experience of what it has already achieved in us, we may gather that its Divine possessor and wielder can do for us "far beyond what we ask or think." That might being God's, can achieve in us results which the boldest have not ventured to anticipate. So that, as is meet—

(Ver. 21.) Αὐτῷ ἡ δόξα ἐν τῇ ἐκκλησίᾳ ἐν Χριστῷ Ἰησοῦ— "To Him be glory in the church in Christ Jesus." Such a pronoun, emphatic in position and from repetition, occurs in common Hebrew usage—a usage, however, not wholly Hebraistic, but often found in classic Greek, and very often in the Septuagint. Bernhardy, p. 290; Winer, § 22, 4. Δόξα may, as an abstract noun, have the article prefixed; or the article may be used in what Bernhardy calls its "*rhetorische form*," signifying the glory which is His especially, and due to Him confessedly, p. 315. The difference of reading is not of essential moment. Some MSS., such as A, B, and C, with the Coptic and Vulgate, supply καί before ἐν X. I., and this reading is preferred by Lachmann, Rückert, and Matthies, but refused by Tischendorf, while D¹, F, G, with Ambrosiaster, reverse the order of the clauses, and read—ἐν Χριστῷ Ἰησοῦ καὶ τῇ ἐκκλησίᾳ. Koppe, on the authority of one MS., 46, is inclined to reject as spurious the whole clause—$\dot{\epsilon}\nu\ \tau\hat{\eta}\ \dot{\epsilon}\kappa\kappa\lambda\eta\sigma\dot{\iota}\alpha$. Harless and Olshausen show that these various readings have their sources in dogmatic views. It could not be borne by some that the church should stand before Christ, and the $\kappa\alpha\dot{\iota}$, without which there would be an asyndeton, was inserted in consequence of certain opinions as to the connection and meaning of the clause which follows it. Hofmann, *Schriftb.* vol. ii. part 2, p. 108, pleads for $\kappa\alpha\dot{\iota}$, and connects $\dot{\epsilon}\nu\ X\rho\iota\sigma\tau\hat{\omega}$ $\prime I\eta\sigma o\hat{v}$ with the following words, $\epsilon\dot{\iota}\varsigma\ \pi\dot{\alpha}\sigma\alpha\varsigma\ \tau\dot{\alpha}\varsigma\ \gamma\epsilon\nu\epsilon\dot{\alpha}\varsigma$, etc. The relation of the two clauses—$\dot{\epsilon}\nu\ \tau\hat{\eta}\ \dot{\epsilon}\kappa\kappa\lambda\eta\sigma\dot{\iota}\alpha$ and $\dot{\epsilon}\nu\ X\rho\iota\sigma\tau\hat{\omega}$ $\prime I\eta\sigma o\hat{v}$—has been variously understood:—

1. Luther, Michaelis, Koppe, Rosenmüller, Flatt, Meier, Holzhausen, Olshausen, and Stier, connect the words thus—" In the church which is in Christ Jesus." Not to say that a second $\tau\hat{\eta}$ is wanting (Gal. i. 22),—which, however, in such a connection is not always repeated,—the meaning does not appear to be appropriate. The second clause has no immediate union with the one before it, but bears a relation to $\delta\dot{o}\xi\alpha$.

2. Some render $\dot{\epsilon}\nu\ X\rho\iota\sigma\tau\hat{\omega}$ by the words "through Christ" —$\delta\iota\dot{\alpha}$, as in the interpretation of Theophylact; $\sigma\dot{\upsilon}\nu$, as in that of Œcumenius; *per Christum*, as in the paraphrase of Grotius, and the exegesis of Calvin and Beza, Rollock and Rückert. Such a translation is not in accordance with the usual meaning of the preposition. The passages adduced by Turner in denial of this are no proof, for in them $\dot{\epsilon}\nu$, though instrumental, retains its distinctive meaning, and is not to be superficially confounded with $\delta\iota\dot{\alpha}$.

3. The words seem to define the inner sphere or spirit in which the glory is presented to God. It is offered in the church, but it is, at the same time, offered "in Christ Jesus," or presented by the members of the sacred community in the consciousness of union with Him, and by consequence in a spirit of dependence on Him. So generally Harless, Meyer, de Wette, Alford, and Ellicott. The place of doxology is the church, and the glory is hymned by its members, but the spirit of the song is inspired by oneness with Jesus. $\varDelta\dot{o}\xi\alpha$ is the splendour of moral excellence, and in what place should such glory be ascribed but in the church, which has witnessed so much of it, and whose origination, life, blessings, and hopes are so many samples and outbursts of it? Ebrard,

*Dog.* § 467. And how should it be presented? Not apart from Christ, or simply for His sake, but in Him—in thrilling fellowship with Him; for no other consciousness can inspire us with the sacred impulse, and praise of no other origin and character can be accepted by that God who is Himself in Christ. The glory is to be offered—

εἰς πάσας τὰς γενεὰς τοῦ αἰῶνος τῶν αἰώνων. Ἀμήν—

"to all the generations of the ages of the ages. Amen." This remarkable accumulation of terms is an intensive formula denoting eternity. The apostle combines two phrases, both of which are used in the New Testament. Εἰς γενεὰς γενεῶν—Luke i. 50—is phraseology based upon the Hebrew דּוֹר דּוֹרִים. Ps. lxxii. 5, cii. 24. The other portion of the phrase occurs as in Gal. i. 5—εἰς τοὺς αἰῶνας τῶν αἰώνων (1 Pet. i. 25), εἰς τὸν αἰῶνα. Heb. v. 6, vi. 20. We have also εἰς τοὺς αἰῶνας in many places; and in the Septuagint, εἰς γενεὰν καὶ γενεάν, ἕως γενεᾶς καὶ γενεᾶς, ἐκ γενεᾶς εἰς γενεάν, εἰς γενεὰς γενεῶν. So ἕως αἰῶνος τῶν αἰώνων stands in Dan. vii. 18 for the Chaldee עַד עָלְמָא וְעַד עָלַם עָלְמַיָּא. This language, borrowed from the changes and succession of time, is employed to picture out eternity. It is a period of successive generations filling up the age, which again is an age of ages—or made up of a series of ages—a period composed of many periods; and through the cycles of such a period of periods, glory is to be ascribed to God. It is needless, with Meyer, to take γενεαί in a literal sense, or in reference to successive generations of living believers, for γενεά often simply means a period of time measured by the average life of man. Acts xiv. 16, xv. 21. The entire phrase is a temporal image of eternity. One wonders at de Wette's question—"Was the apostle warranted to expect such a long duration for the church?" For is not the church to be gathered into the heavens?

The obligation to glorify God lasts through eternity, and the glorified church will ever delight in rendering praise, "as is most due." Eternal perfection will sustain an eternal anthem. The Trinity is here again brought out to view. The power within us is that of the Spirit, and glory in Christ is presented to the Father who answers prayer through the Son, and by the Spirit; and, therefore, to the Father, in the Son, and by the Spirit, is offered this glorious minstrelsy—" as it was in the beginning, is now, and ever shall be, world without end. Amen."

> " To Father, Son, and Holy Ghost,
>   The God whom heaven's triumphant host
>   And saints on earth adore,
> Be glory as in ages past,
> As now it is, and so shall last
>   When time shall be no more."

## CHAPTER IV

THE practical portion of the Epistle now commences, or as Theodoret says—ἐπὶ τὰ εἴδη προτρέπει τῆς ἀρετῆς. But doctrine has been expounded ere duty is enforced. Instructions as to change of spiritual relation precede exhortations as to change of life. It is in vain to tell the dead man to rise and walk, till the principle of animation be restored. One must be a child of God before he can be a servant of God. Pardon and purity, faith and holiness, are indissolubly united. Ethics therefore follow theology. And now the apostle first proceeds to enjoin the possession of such graces as promote and sustain the unity of the church, the members of which are "rooted and grounded in love"—a unity which, as he is anxious to show, is quite compatible with variety of gift, office, and station. Then he dwells on the nature, design, and results of the ministerial functions belonging to the church, points out its special and divine organization, and goes on to the reprobation of certain vices, and the inculcation of opposite graces.

(Ver. 1.) Παρακαλῶ οὖν ὑμᾶς ἐγὼ ὁ δέσμιος ἐν Κυρίῳ— "I exhort you then, I the prisoner in the Lord." The retrospective οὖν refers us to the preceding paragraph— Christian privilege or calling being so rich and full, and his prayer for them being so fervent and extensive. The personality of the writer is distinctly brought out—"I the prisoner," ἐγώ. iii. 1. The phrase ἐν Κυρίῳ is closely connected with ὁ δέσμιος, as the want of the article between the words also shows. Some, indeed, prefer to join it to the verb παρακαλῶ —"I exhort you in the Lord." Such was the view of Semler, and Koppe does not express a decided opinion. But the position of the words is plainly against such a construction. Winer, § 20, 2. The verb παρακαλῶ is not used in its original sense, but signifies "I exhort," as if equivalent to προτρέπω.

It has, however, various shades of meaning in the Pauline writing. See Knapp's *Scrip. Var.* p. 125 et seq. Nor can ἐν Κυρίῳ signify "for Christ's sake," as is the opinion of Chrysostom, Theophylact, Koppe, and Flatt. When we turn to similar expressions, such as τοὺς ὄντας ἐν Κυρίῳ (Rom. xvi. 11)—ἀγαπητὸν ἐν Κυρίῳ (Philem. 16)—γαμηθῆναι, μόνον ἐν Κυρίῳ (1 Cor. vii. 39)—τὸν ἀγαπητόν μου ἐν Κυρίῳ (Rom. xvi. 8)—the meaning of the idiom cannot be doubted. It characterizes Paul as a Christian prisoner—one who not only was imprisoned for Christ's sake, but who was and still is in union with the Lord, as a servant and sufferer. See on Κύριος, ch. i. 2, 3. The apostle in iii. 1 uses the genitive which indicates one aspect of relationship—that of possession; but here he employs the dative as denoting that his incarceration has its element or characteristic, perhaps origin too, from his union with Christ. But why again allude to his bondage in these terms? Not simply to excite sympathy, and claim a hearing for his counsels, nor solely, as Olshausen and Harless maintain, to represent his absolute obedience to the Lord as an example to his readers. All these ideas might be in his mind, but none of them engrossingly, else some more distinctive allusion might be expected in his language. Nor can we accede to Meyer and the Greek fathers, that there is in the phrase any high exultation in the glory of a confessor or a martyr—as if, as Theodoret says, he gloried more in his chains, ἢ βασιλεὺς διαδήματι. But his writing to them while he was in chains proved the deep interest he took in them and in their spiritual welfare—showed them that his faith in Jesus, and his love to His cause, were not shaken by persecution—that the iron which lay upon his limb had not entered into his soul—and that his apostolical prerogative was as intact, his pastoral anxiety as powerful, and his relation to the Lord as close and tender as when on his visit to them he disputed in the school of Tyrannus, or uttered his solemn and pathetic valediction to their elders at Miletus. Letters inspired by love in a dungeon might also have a greater charm than his oral address. Compare Gal. vi. 17. "I exhort you"—

ἀξίως περιπατῆσαι τῆς κλήσεως ἧς ἐκλήθητε—"that ye walk worthy of the calling with which ye were called."

Κλῆσις is the Christian vocation—the summons "to glory and virtue." See under i. 18; Rom. xi. 29; Phil. iii. 14; 2 Tim. i. 9; Heb. iii. 1, etc. In ἧς ἐκλήθητε is a common idiom—ἧς being probably by attraction or assimilation, as Krüger, § 51, 10, prefers to call it, for ᾗ, but perhaps for ἥν (Arrian, Epict. p. 122), and the verb being used with its cognate noun. Winer, § 24, 1; 2 Tim. i. 9; 1 Cor. vii. 20. See also under i. 8, 19, 20, ii. 4. Ἄξιος in the sense of "in harmony with," is often thus used. Matt. iii. 8; Phil. i. 27; Col. i. 10; 1 Thess. ii. 12; 2 Thess. i. 11. On the peculiar meaning of περιπατέω see under ii. 2, 10. It is a stroke of very miserable wit which Adam Clarke ascribes to the apostle, when he represents him as saying, "Ye have your liberty and *may walk*, I am deprived of mine and cannot." Their calling, so high, so holy, and so authoritative, and which had come to them in such power, was to be honoured by a walk in perfect correspondence with its origin and spirit, its claims and destiny. See also under ver. 4.

The apostle now enforces the cultivation of those graces, the possession of which is indispensable to the harmony of the church: for the opposite vices — pride, irascibility, impatient querulousness—all tend to strife and disruption. On union the apostle had already dwelt in the second chapter as a matter of doctrine—here he introduces it as one of practice.

(Ver. 2.) Μετὰ πάσης ταπεινοφροσύνης καὶ πραΰτητος, μετὰ μακροθυμίας, ἀνεχόμενοι ἀλλήλων ἐν ἀγάπῃ—" With all lowliness and meekness, with long-suffering, forbearing one another in love." Col. iii. 12. Μετά is with—accompanied with—visible manifestation. Winer, § 47, h. On πάσης see i. 8. Some suppose the various nouns in the verse to be connected with ἀνεχόμενοι, but such a connection mars the harmony and development of thought, as it rises from general to special counsel.

Ταπεινοφροσύνη is lowliness of mind, opposed to τὰ ὑψηλὰ φρονοῦντες. Rom. xii. 16. It is that profound humility which stands at the extremest distance from haughtiness, arrogance, and conceit, and which is produced by a right view of ourselves, and of our relation to Christ and to that glory to which we are called. It is ascribed by the apostle to himself in Acts xx. 19. It is not any one's making himself small—ὅταν τις μέγας ὤν—as Chrysostom supposes, for such would be mere simulation. Every blessing we possess or hope to enjoy is from God. Nothing is self-procured, and therefore no room is left for self-importance. This modesty of mind, says Chrysostom, is the foundation of all virtue—πάσης ἀρετῆς ὑπόθεσις, Trench, *Synon.* § 43; Tittmann, *De Syn.* p. 140.

Πραΰτης is meekness of spirit in all relations, both toward God and toward man—which never rises in insubordination against God nor in resentment against man. It is a grace ascribed by the Saviour to Himself (Matt. xi. 29), and ascribed to him by the apostle. 2 Cor. x. 1; Gal. v. 23. It is not merely that meekness which is not provoked and angered by the reception of injury, but that entire subduedness of temperament which strives to be in harmony with God's will, be it what it may, and, in reference to men, thinks with candour, suffers in self-composure, and speaks in the "soft answer" which "turneth away wrath." For some differences in spelling the word, see Passow, *sub voce*, and Lobeck, *ad Phrynich.* p. 403. The form adopted is found only in B and E, but it seems supported by the analogy of the Alexandrian spelling.

The preposition μετά is repeated before the next noun, μακροθυμίας, and this repetition has led Estius, Rückert, Harless, Olshausen, and Stier to connect it with ἀνεχόμενοι in the following clause. We see no good ground for this construction. On the contrary, ἀνεχόμενοι has ἐν ἀγάπῃ to qualify it, and needs not μετὰ μακροθυμίας, which, from its position, would then be emphatic. Some, like Lachmann and Olshausen, feeling this, join ἐν ἀγάπῃ as unwarrantably to the following verse. The first two nouns are governed by one preposition, for they are closely associated in meaning, the "meekness" being after all only a phrase of the "lowliness of mind," and resting on it. But the third noun is introduced with the preposition repeated, as it is a special and distinct virtue—a peculiar result of the former two—and so much, at the same time, before the mind of the apostle, that he explains it in the following clause.

Μακροθυμία—"long-suffering," is opposed to irritability, or to what we familiarly name shortness of temper (Jas. i. 19), and is that patient self-possession which enables a man to bear with those who oppose him, or who in any way do him injustice. He can afford to wait till better judgment and feeling on their part prevail. 2 Cor. vi. 6; Gal. v. 22; 1 Tim. i. 16; 2 Tim. iv. 2. In its high sense of bearing with evil, and postponing the punishment of it, it is ascribed to God, Rom. ii. 4, ix. 22. The participle ἀνεχόμενοι is in the nominative, and the anacolouthon is easily explained from the connection with the first verse. An example of a similar change is found in iii. 18. Winer, § 63, 2. It is useless, with Heinsius and Homberg, to attempt to supply the imperative mood of the verb of existence—"Be ye forbearing one another." Ἀνέχομαι, in the middle voice, is to have patience with, that is, "to hold oneself up" till the provocation is past. Col. iii. 13. Verbs of its class govern the genitive. Kühner, § 539. Ἐν ἀγάπῃ describes the spirit in which such forbearance was to be exercised. Retaliation was not to be allowed; all occasionally needed forbearance, and all were uniformly to exercise it. No acerbity of temper, sharp retort, or satirical reply was to be admitted. As it is the second word which really begins the strife, so, where mutual forbearance is exercised, even the first angry word would never be spoken. And this mutual forbearance must not be affected coolness or studied courtesy; it must have its origin, sphere, and nutriment "in love"—in the genuine attachment that ought to prevail among Christian disciples. Œcumenius justly observes —ἔνθα γὰρ ἐστιν ἀγάπη, πάντα ἐστιν ἀνεκτά.

(Ver. 3.) Σπουδάζοντες τηρεῖν τὴν ἑνότητα τοῦ Πνεύματος —"endeavouring to keep the unity of the Spirit." This clause is parallel to the preceding, and indicates not so much, as Meyer says, the inward feelings by which the ἀνέχεσθαι is to be characterized, as rather the motive to it, and the accompanying or simultaneous effort. Πνεῦμα cannot surely mean the mere human spirit, as the following verse plainly proves. Yet such is the view of Ambrosiaster, Anselm, Erasmus, Calvin, Estius, Rückert, Baumgarten-Crusius, and Bloomfield. Calvin also says—*Ego simplicius interpretor de animorum concordia;* and Ambrosiaster quietly changes the terms, and renders—*unitatis spiritum.* Others, again, take the phrase to denote that unity of which the Spirit is the bond. Chrysostom says—διὰ γὰρ τοῦτο τὸ πνεῦμα ἐδόθη, ἵνα τοὺς γένει καὶ τρόποις διαφόροις διεστηκότας ἐνώσῃ. This view is perhaps not sufficiently distinctive. The reference is to the Spirit of God, but, as the next verse shows, to that Spirit as inhabiting the church—"one body", and "one Spirit." The "unity of the Spirit" is not, as Grotius says, *unitas ecclesiæ, quæ est corpus spirituale*, but it is the unity which dwells within the church, and which results from the one Spirit—the originating cause being in the genitive. Hartung, *Casus*, p. 12. The apostle has in view what he afterwards advances about different functions and offices in the church in verses 7 and 11. Separate communities are not to rally round special gifts and offices, as if each gift proceeded from, and was organized by, a separate and rival Spirit. 1 Cor. xii. 4, etc. And this unity of the Spirit was not so completely in their possession, that its existence depended wholly on their guardianship. For it exists independently of human vigilance or fidelity,[1] but its manifestations may be thwarted and checked. They were therefore to keep it safe from all disturbance and infraction. And in this duty they were to be earnest and forward—σπου-δάζοντες, using diligence, "bisie to kepe," as Wycliffe renders; for if they cherished humility, meekness, and universal tolerance in love, as the apostle hath enjoined them, it would be no difficult task to preserve the "unity of the Spirit." And that unity is to be kept—

ἐν τῷ συνδέσμῳ τῆς εἰρήνης — "in the bond of peace." Some understand the apostle to affirm that the unity is kept by that which forms the bond of peace, viz. love. Such an opinion has advocates in Theophylact, Calovius, Bengel, Rückert, Meier, Harless, Stier, and Winzer,[2] who take the genitive as that of object. Such an idea may be implied, but it is not the immediate statement of the apostle. The declaration here is different from that in Col. iii. 14, where love is termed "a bond." See on the place. Εἰρήνης appears to be the genitive of apposition, as Flatt, Meyer, Matthies, Olshausen, Alford, and Ellicott take it. Winer, § 59, 8 ; Acts viii. 23. "The bond of peace" is that bond which is peace. Ἐν does not denote that the unity of the Spirit springs from "the bond of peace," as if unity were the product of peace, or

---

[1] "Einigkeit im Geist dürfen und können wir nicht machen, sondern nur darüber halten."—Rieger, quoted by Stier.

[2] *Commentat.* in Eph. iv. 1-6. Lipsiæ, 1836.

simply consisted of peace, but that the unity is preserved and manifested in the bond of peace as its element. Winer, § 48, a. "Peace" is that tranquillity which ought to reign in the church, and by the maintenance of which its essential spiritual unity is developed and "bodied forth." This unity is something far higher than peace; but it is by the preservation of peace as a bond among church members that such unity is realized and made perceptible to the world. John xvii. The outer becomes the symbol and expression of the inner— union is the visible sign of unity. When believers universally and mutually recognize the image of Christ in one another, and, loving one another instinctively and in spite of minor differences, feel themselves composing the one church of Christ, then do they endeavour to keep "the unity of the Spirit in the bond of peace." The meaning of the English verb "endeavour" has been somewhat attenuated in the course of its descent to us. Trench on *Authorized Version*, p. 17. Unity and peace are therefore surely more than mere alliance between Jew and Gentile, though the apostle's previous illustrations of that truth may have suggested this argument.

(Ver. 4.) Ἐν σῶμα καὶ ἓν Πνεῦμα—"One body and one Spirit." The connection is not, as is indicated in the Syriac version—Keeping the unity of the Spirit in the bond of peace, in order that you may be in one body and one spirit. Others construe as if the verse formed part of an exhortation —"Be ye, or ye ought to be, one body," or keeping the unity of the Spirit as being one body, etc. But such a supplement is too great, and the simple explanation of the ellipsis is preferable. Conybeare indeed renders—"You are one body," but the common and correct supplement is the verb ἐστι. Kühner, indeed (§ 760, c), says that such an asyndeton as this frequently happens in classic Greek, when such a particle as γάρ is understood. Bernhardy, p. 448. But the verse abruptly introduces an assertatory illustration of the previous statement, and in the fervent style of the apostle any connecting particle is omitted. "One body there is, and one Spirit." And after all that Ellicott and Alford have said, the assertatory (*rein assertorisch*, Meyer) clause logically contains an argument—though grammatically the resolution by γάρ be really superfluous. Ellicott, after Hofmann, gives it as

"Remember there is one body," which is an argument surely to maintain the unity of the Spirit. The idea contained in σῶμα—the body or the church—has been already introduced and explained (i. 23, ii. 16), to the explanations of which the reader may turn. The church is described in the second chapter as one body and one Spirit—ἐν ἑνὶ σώματι—ἐν ἑνὶ Πνεύματι; and the apostle here implies that this unity ought to be guarded. Rom. xii. 5; 1 Cor. xii. 3; Col. i. 24. The church or body is one, though its members are οἱ πανταχοῦ τῆς οἰκουμένης πιστοί. (Chrysostom.) There are not two rival communities. The body with its many members, and complex array of organs of very different position, functions, and honour, is yet one. The church, no matter where it is situated, or in what age of the world it exists—no matter of what race, blood, or colour are its members, or how various the tongues in which its services are presented—is one, and remains so, unaffected by distance or time, or physical, intellectual, and social distinctions. And as in the body there is only one spirit, one living principle—no double consciousness, no dualism of intelligence, motive, and action—so the one Spirit of God dwells in the one church, and there are therefore neither rivalry of administration nor conflicting claims. And whatever the gifts and graces conferred, whatever variety of aspect they may assume, all possess a delicate self-adaptation to times and circumstances, for they are all from the "one Spirit," having oneness of origin, design, and result. (See on ver. 16.) The apostle now adds an appeal to their own experience—

καθὼς καὶ ἐκλήθητε ἐν μιᾷ ἐλπίδι τῆς κλήσεως ὑμῶν—"even as also ye were called in one hope of your calling." Καθὼς καί introduces illustrative proof of the statement just made. The meaning of this clause depends very much on the sense assigned to ἐν. Some, as Meyer, would make it instrumental, and render it "by;" others, as Grotius, Flatt, Rückert, and Valpy, would give it the meaning of εἰς, and Chrysostom that of ἐπί. Harless adopts the view expressed by Bengel on 1 Thess. iv. 7, and thinks that it signifies an element—*indoles* —of the calling. We prefer to regard it as bearing its common signification—as pointing to the element in which their calling took place—*in una spe*, as the Vulgate. 1 Cor. vii. 15;

1 Thess. iv. 7; Winer, § 50, 5. Sometimes the verb is simply used, both in the present and aorist (Rom. viii. 30, ix. 11; Gal. v. 8), and often with various prepositions. While ἐν represents the element in which the calling takes effect, ἐν εἰρήνῃ, 1 Cor. vii. 15; ἐν χάριτι, Gal. i. 6; ἐν ἁγιασμῷ, 1 Thess. iv. 7: ἐπί represents the proximate end, ἐπ' ἐλευθερίᾳ, Gal. v. 13; οὐκ, ἐπὶ ἀκαθαρσίᾳ, 1 Thess. iv. 7: εἰς depicts another aspect, εἰς κοινωνίαν, 1 Cor. i. 9; εἰρήνη— εἰς ἥν, Col. iii. 15; εἰς τὸ θαυμαστὸν αὐτοῦ φῶς, 1 Pet. ii. 9— and apparently also the ultimate purpose, εἰς περιποίησιν δόξης, 2 Thess. ii. 14; εἰς βασιλείαν καὶ δόξαν, 1 Thess. ii. 12; τῆς αἰωνίου ζωῆς εἰς ἥν, 1 Tim. vi. 12; εἰς τὴν αἰώνιον αὐτοῦ δόξαν, 1 Pet. v. 10; other forms being εἰς τοῦτο, 1 Pet. ii. 21; εἰς τοῦτο ἵνα, 1 Pet. iii. 9—while the instrumental cause is given by διά; the inner, διὰ χάριτος, Gal. i. 15; and the outer, διὰ τοῦ εὐαγγελίου, 2 Thess. ii. 14. The following genitive, κλήσεως, is that of possession—"in one hope belonging to your calling." See under i. 18, on similar phraseology. The genitive of originating cause preferred by Ellicott is not so appropriate, on account of the preceding verb ἐκλήθητε, the genitive of the correlative noun suggesting what belongs to the call and characterized it, when they received it. The "hope" is "one," for it has one object, and that is glory; one foundation, and that is Christ. Their call—ἡ ἄνω κλῆσις (Phil. iii. 14), had brought them into the possession of this hope. See Nitzsch, *System.* § 210; Reuss, *Théol. Chrét.* vol. ii. p. 219. "There is one body and one Spirit," and the Ephesian converts had experience of this unity, for the hope which they possessed as their calling was also "one," and in connection with—

(Ver. 5.) Εἷς Κύριος, μία πίστις, ἓν βάπτισμα—"One Lord, one faith, one baptism." Further and conclusive argument. For the meaning of Κύριος in its reference to Christ, the reader may turn to i. 2. Had Irenæus attended to the common, if not invariable Pauline usage, he would not have said that the father only is to be called Lord—*Patrem tantum Deum et Dominum. Opera,* tom. i. 443, ed. Stieren, Lipsiæ,1849-50. There is only one supreme Governor over the church. He is the one Head of the one body, and the Giver of its one Spirit. This being the case, there can therefore be only—

"One faith." Faith does not signify creed, or truth believed, but it signifies confidence in the one Lord—faith, the subjective oneness of which is created and sustained by the unity of its object. Usteri, *Paulin. Lehrb.* p. 300. The one faith may be embodied in an objective profession. There being only one faith, there can be only—

"One baptism." Baptism is consecration to Christ—one dedication to the one Lord. Acts xix. 5; Rom. vi. 3; Gal. iii. 27. "One baptism" is the result and expression of the "one faith" in the "one Lord," and, at the same time, the one mode of initiation by the "one Spirit" into the "one body." Tertullian argues from this expression against the repetition of baptism—*felix aqua quod semel affluit. De Bap.* xv. Among the many reasons given for the omission of the Lord's Supper in this catalogue of unity, this perhaps is the most conclusive—that the Lord's Supper is only the demonstration of a recognized unity in the church, whereas faith and baptism are the initial and essential elements of it. These last are also individually possessed, whereas the Lord's Supper is a social observance on the part of those who, in oneness of faith and fellowship, honour the "one Lord." Still farther and deeper—

(Ver. 6.) Εἷς Θεὸς καὶ Πατὴρ πάντων—"One God and Father of all"—ultimate, highest, and truest unity. Seven times does he use the epithet "One." The church is one body, having one Spirit in it, and one Lord over it; then its inner relations and outer ordinances are one too; its calling has attached to it one hope; its means of union to Him is one faith; its dedication is one baptism: and all this unity is but the impress of the great primal unity—one God. His unity stamps an image of itself on that scheme which originated in Him, and issues in His glory. Christians serve one God, are not distracted by a multiplicity of divinities, and need not fear the revenge of one while they are doing homage to his rival. Oneness of spirit ought to characterize their worship. "One God and Father of all," that is, all Christians, for the reference is not to the wide universe, or to all men, as Holzhausen, with Musculus and Matthies, argue—but to the church. Jew and Gentile forming the one church have one God and father. (An illustration of the filial relationship of believers to God will be found under i. 5.) The three following clauses mark a peculiarity of the apostle's style, viz. his manner of indicating different relations of the same word by connecting it with various prepositions. Gal. i. 1; Rom. iii. 22, xi. 36; Col. i. 16; Winer, § 50, 6. It is altogether a vicious and feeble exegesis on the part of Koppe to say that these three clauses are synonymous—*sententia videtur una, tantum variis formulis synonymis expressa.* A triple relationship of the one God to the "all" is now pointed out, and the first is thus expressed—

ὁ ἐπὶ πάντων—"who is over all." These adjectives, πάντων and πᾶσι, are clearly to be taken in the masculine gender, as the epithet πατήρ would also suggest. Erasmus, Michaelis, Morus, and Baumgarten-Crusius take them in ἐπὶ πάντων and διὰ πάντων as neuter, while the Vulgate, Zachariae, and Koppe accept the neuter only in the second phrase. Ὁ ἐπὶ πάντων is rendered by Chrysostom—ὁ ἐπάνω πάντων. The great God is high over all, robed in unsurpassable glory. There is, and can be, no superior—no co-ordinate sovereignty. The universe, no less than the church, lies beneath, and far beneath, His throne, and the jurisdiction of that throne, "high and lifted up," is paramount and unchallenged.

καὶ διὰ πάντων—"and through all." The strange interpretation of Thomas Aquinas has found some supporters. He explains the first clause of God the Father, who is over all—*fontale principium divinitatis;* and the clause before us he refers to the Son—*per quem omnia facta sunt.* But this exegesis, which is adopted by Estius and Olshausen, reverses the idea of the apostle. It is one thing to say, All things are through God, and quite another to say, God is through all things. The latter, and not the former, is the express thought of the inspired writer. Jerome also refers the phrase to the Son—*quia per filium creata sunt omnia;* while Calvin understands by it the third Person of the Trinity—*Deus Spiritu sanctificationis diffusus per omnia ecclesiæ membra.* Meyer holds a similar view. Chrysostom and his patristic followers, along with Beza, Zanchius, Crocius, and Grotius, refer it to God providing for all, and ordering all—τῇ προνοίᾳ καὶ διοικήσει. Bengel, Flatt, and Winer understand it as signifying "through all acting." Winer, § 50, 6. Harless explains it as meaning "works through all, as the head through the members." It is plain that some of these views do not make any real distinction between the διά of this clause and the ἐν of the following. The idea of simple diffusion "through all," is not far from the idea of "in all." But the notion of providence, if taken in a general sense, comes nearer the truth. The thought seems to be that of a pervading, and thus a sustaining and working presence. Though He is "over all," yet He lives not in remote splendour and indifference, for He is "through all;" His influence being everywhere felt in its upholding energies.

καὶ ἐν πᾶσιν—"and in all." The Elzevir Text adds ὑμῖν, as Chrysostom does in his commentary. Others have adopted ἡμῖν, on the authority of D, E, F, G, K, L, the Syriac and Vulgate, Theodóret, Pelagius, and Ambrosiaster—a reading admitted by Griesbach, Knapp, Scholz, and Hahn. But the higher witness of A, B, C, the Coptic and Æthiopic, and the text of Ignatius, Eusebius, Cyril, Epiphanius, Gregory, Chrysostom, and Jerome, exclude such a pronoun altogether, and leave us simply ἐν πᾶσιν. Accordingly, Lachmann and Tischendorf strike out the word as an evident gloss. The pronoun would modify the universality predicated in the two preceding clauses. He is "in all," dwelling in them, filling them with the light and love of His gracious presence. The idea conveyed by διά is more external and general in its nature—acting through or sustaining; while that expressed by ἐν is intimate and special union and inhabitation. Very different is such a conception from either ancient or modern pantheism; from that of Zeno or that of Hegel, or the poetical mysticism of Pope—

> "All are but parts of one stupendous whole—
> Whose body nature is, and God the soul."

Whether there be any reference to the Trinity in this remarkable declaration, it is impossible to affirm with certainty. While Theophylact seems to deny it, because heretical notions were based upon it, Jerome on the other hand maintains it, and it was held by Irenæus and Hippolytus, the former of whom explains the first clause of the Father—*caput Christi;*

the second of the Son—*caput ecclesiæ*; and the third of the Holy Spirit in us—*aqua viva*. Harless, Olshausen, Stier, de Wette, von Gerlach, Ellicott, and Alford are of the same opinion. It has been said in proof, that most certainly in the third clause—" in all "—the reference is to the Holy Ghost, by whom alone God dwells in believers; so that in the second clause, and in the words "through all," there may be an allusion to Him who is now on the throne of the universe, and " by whom all things consist;"[1] and in the first clause to the Eternal Father. In previous portions of the Epistle, triune relation has been distinctly brought out; only here the representation is different, for unity is the idea dwelt on, and it is the One God and Father Himself who works through all and dwells in all.

All these elements of oneness enumerated in verses 4, 5, and 6, are really inducements for Christians to be forward to preserve the unity of the Spirit in the bond of peace. It is plainly of the one holy catholic church that the apostle has been speaking; not of the visible church, which has in it a mixed company, many whom Augustine characterizes as being in fellowship *cum ecclesia*—" with the church," but who are not *in ecclesia*—" in the church." "All are not Israel who are of Israel." But the real spiritual church of the Redeemer is one body. All the members of that church partake of the same grace, adhere to the same faith, are washed in the same blood, are filled with the same hopes, and shall dwell at length in the same blessed inheritance. Heretics and ungodly men may find their way into the church, but they remain really separated from its "invisible conjunction of charity." There may be variations in "lesser matters of ceremony or discipline," and yet this essential unity is preserved. Clement of Alexandria compares the church so constituted to the various chords of a musical instrument, " for in the midst of apparent schisms there is substantial unity." Barrow again remarks, that the apostle says—" one Lord, one faith, one baptism; not one monarch, or one senate or sanhedrim."

---

[1] The suspicious and fantastic extremes to which the idea of Jehovah's triune being and operations may be carried, will be seen in such a work as that of the Danish theologian Martensen, *Die Christliche Dogmatik*, 2 vols., Kiel, 1850. Compare also Marheineke, *Christl. Dogm.* § 426; Schleiermacher, *Christl. Glaube*, ii. § 170, 3rd ed., Berlin, 1835.

He does not insist on unity "under one singular, visible government or polity."[1] How sad to think that the passions of even sanctified men have often produced feuds and alienations, and led them to forget the apostolic mandate! Christ's claim for the preservation of unity is upon all the churches—a unity of present connection and actual enjoyment—not a truce, but an alliance, with one livery and cognizance—not a compromise, but a veritable incorporation among "all who in every place call upon the name of Jesus Christ our Lord, both their Lord and ours."[2] "I will give them one heart and one way"—a promise the realization of which is surely not to be deferred till the whole church assemble in that world where there can be no misunderstanding. The great father of the western church tersely says— *Contra rationem, nemo sobrius; contra Scripturas nemo Christianus; contra Ecclesiam nemo pacificus senserit.*

(Ver. 7.) Ἐνὶ δὲ ἑκάστῳ ἡμῶν ἐδόθη ἡ χάρις—" But to each of us was given grace." Unity is not uniformity, for it is quite consistent with variety of gifts and offices in the church. The δέ marks a transitional contrast, as the writer passes on to individual varieties. Still along with this unity there is variety of gifts. In the addition of ἑνί to ἑκάστῳ, the idea of distribution is expressed more distinctly than by the simple term. Luke iv. 40; Acts ii. 3, xx. 31. B, D¹, F, G, L, omit the article ἡ before χάρις, but there is no valid reason to reject it; the preceding η of ἐδόθη may have led to its omission. This χάρις is gift, not merely in connection with personal privilege or labour, but, as the sequel shows, gift in connection with official rank and function. Ἐδόθη in this verse is explained by ἔδωκε in verse 8. While grace has been given

---

[1] Möhler, in his *Symbolik*, § 48, one of the ablest defences of Romanism, contrasts Lutheranism and Catholicism thus—"The latter teaches that there is first the visible church, and then comes the invisible, whereas Protestantism affirms that out of the invisible comes the visible church, and the first is the ground of the last." Sixth ed., Mainz, 1843.

[2] It is one of the many instances in which Rothe sets himself to overthrow established modes of thought and expression, when he attacks the phrase "visible church," as being deceptive and unphilosophical. His objection, however, compelled Hagenbach to coin a new phrase to express the popular idea, and with the facility of the Teutonic language for compounds, he gives us the untranslatable epithets—*historisch-empirisch, heraustretende, körperliche.*— Lehrbuch der Dogmengeschichte, § 71.

to every individual, and no one is omitted, that grace differs in form, amount, and aspect in every instance of its bestowment; and as a peculiar sample and illustration of such variety in unity, the apostle appeals to the offices and dignities in the church. For this grace is described as being conferred—

κατὰ τὸ μέτρον τῆς δωρεᾶς τοῦ Χριστοῦ—"according to the measure of the gift of Christ." The first genitive is subjective, and the second that of possession or of agent. The gift is measured; and while each individual receives, he receives according to the will of the sovereign Distributor. And whether the measure be great or small, whether its contents be of more brilliant endowment or of humbler and unnoticed talent, all is equally Christ's gift, and of Christ's adjustment; all is equally indispensable to the union and edification of that body in which there is "no schism," and forms an argument why each one gifted with such grace should keep the unity of the Spirit. The law of the church is essential unity in the midst of circumstantial variety. Differences of faculty or temperament, education or susceptibility, are not superseded. Each gift in its own place completes the unity. What one devises another may plead for, while a third may act out the scheme; so that sagacity, eloquence, and enterprise form a "threefold cord, not easily broken." It is so in the material creation—the little is as essential to symmetry as the great—the star as well as the sun—the rain-drop equally with the ocean, and the hyssop no less than the cedar. The pebble has its place as fittingly as the mountain, and colossal forms of life are surrounded by the tiny insect whose term of existence is limited to a summer's twilight. Why should the possession of this grace lead to self-inflation? It is simply Christ's gift to each one, and its amount and character as possessed by others ought surely to create no uneasiness nor jealousy, for it is of Christ's measurement as well as of His bestowment, and every form and quantity of it, as it descends from the one source, is indispensable to the harmony of the church. No one is overlooked, and the one Lord will not bestow conflicting graces, nor mar nor disturb, by the repulsive antipathy of His gifts, that unity the preservation of which here and in this way is enjoined on all the members of His church.

(Ver. 8.) Διὸ λέγει—"Wherefore He saith." This quotation is no parenthesis, as many take it, nor is it any offshoot from the main body of thought, but a direct proof of previous assertion. And it proves those truths—that the ascended Lord confers gifts—various gifts—that men are the recipients, and that these facts had been presented to the faith and hope of the ancient Jewish church. The apostle, too, must have felt that the Jewish portion of the Ephesian church would acknowledge his quotation as referring to Jesus. If they disputed the sense or reference of the quotation, then the proof contained in it could not affect them. The citation is taken from the 18th verse of the 68th Psalm. It is vain to allege, with Storr and Flatt, that the apostle refers to some Christian hymn in use at Ephesus—*quod ab Ephesiis cantitari sciret*. *Opuscula*, iii. 309. The formula λέγει is not uncommon—a pregnant verb, containing in itself its own nominative, though ἡ γραφή often occurs, as in Rom. iv. 3, ix. 17, x. 11; Gal. iv. 30; Surenhusius, *Bibl. Katall.* 9. There are two points which require discussion — first, the difference of reading between the apostle's citation and the original Hebrew and the Septuagint version; and, secondly, the meaning and reference of the quotation itself.

The change of person from the second to the third needs scarcely be noticed. The principal difference is in the last clause. The Hebrew reads — עָלִיתָ לַמָּרוֹם שָׁבִיתָ שֶּׁבִי לָקַחְתָּ מַתָּנוֹת בָּאָדָם, and the Septuagint has in the last clause—ἔλαβες δόματα ἐν ἀνθρώπῳ, or—ἀνθρώποις; but the apostle's quotation reads— καὶ ἔδωκεν δόματα τοῖς ἀνθρώποις—"and He gave gifts to men." Various attempts have been made to explain this remarkable variation, none of them perhaps beyond all doubt. It may be generally said that the inspired apostle gives the quotation in substance, and as it bore upon his argument. Whiston maintained, indeed, that Paul's reading was correct, and that the Hebrew and Seventy had both been corrupted. Carpzovius, *Crit. Sacr.* p. 3. On the other hand, Jarchi, one of the Targums, the Syriac, and Arabic, have—"Thou hast given gifts to the sons of men." Jerome, followed by Erasmus, relieves himself of the difficulty by alleging that, as the work of Christ was not over in the Psalmist's time, these gifts were only promised as future, and He may be said to have taken them or received them. But the giving and taking were alike future on the part of the Messiah in the age of David. More acute than this figment of his Eastern contemporary is the remark of Augustine, that the Psalmist uses the word "*received*," inasmuch as Christ in His members receives the gifts, whereas Paul employs the term "*gave*," because He, along with the Father, divides the gifts. The idea is too subtle to be the right one. Some, again, identify the two verbs, and declare them to have the same significance. Such is the view of Ambrosiaster, Beza, Zanchius, Piscator, Hammond, Bengel, and a host of others. "The one word," says Chrysostom, "is the same as the other." His Greek followers held generally the same view. Theodore of Mopsuestia simply says, "that to suit the connection the apostle has altered the terms," and the opinion of Harless is much the same. Theodoret says—λαμβάνων γὰρ τὴν πίστιν ἀντιδίδωσι τὴν χάριν, a mere *Spielerei* as Harless terms it. We agree with Meyer, that the Hebrew word לקח has often a proleptic signification. "The giving," says Hengstenberg, "presupposes the taking; the taking is succeeded by the giving as its consequence." The verb seems often to have the peculiar meaning of *danda sumere*—Gen. xv. 9—"Take for me," that is, take and give to me; xviii. 5—"And I will take you a morsel of bread," *i.e.* take and give it you; xxvii. 13—"Go, take them," *i.e.* take them and give me them; xlii. 16—"Let him take your brother," *i.e.* let him take and bring him; Ex. xxvii. 20— "That they take thee pure oil," *i.e.* take and present it to thee; so Lev. xxiv. 2; 1 Kings xvii. 10—"Take me a little water," *i.e.* take and offer it me; 2 Kings ii. 20; Hos. xiv. 2; and so in other places; Glassius, *Philol. Sacra*, p. 185; Buxtorf, *Catalecta Philol.-Theol.* p. 39. This interpretation is, therefore, not so capricious as de Wette affirms. Such is the idiomatic usage of the verb, and the apostle, as it especially suited his purpose, seizes on the latter portion of the sense, and renders—ἔδωκε. The phraseology of Acts ii. 33 is corroborative of our view—"Being exalted to the right hand of God, and having received—λαβών—from the Father the promise of the Holy Ghost, He hath shed forth this"—bestowed upon the church such gifts of the Spirit. It is of the gifts of the Spirit, especially in the administration of the church, that the apostle speaks in this paragraph; and Peter, in the style of the Psalmist, describes Messiah as receiving them ere He distributes them. The Mediator wins them by His blood, receives them from the Father who has appointed and accepted the sacrifice, and holds them for the very purpose of conferring them on His church. The Psalmist looks on the gifts in Christ's possession as *taken* and held by Him for men; but the time of bestowment had fully come, what was so held had now been communicated, and so the apostle from his own point of view says—"He *gave* gifts to man." Still, in the original psalm the taking appears to be taking by force of spoil from the conquered foes. But the martial figure of the Hebrew psalmist is not to be strained.

Our attention must now be turned to the general meaning of the quotation. The 68th Psalm is evidently a hymn of victory. The inspired bard praises God for deliverance vouchsafed—deliverance resulting from battle and triumph. This is also the view of Delitzsch in his *Commentar über den Psalter*, published last year (1859). The image of a procession also appears in some parts of the ode. Very many expositors, among them Stier and Hofmann, have adopted the view that it was composed on occasion of the removal of the ark to Mount Zion, and the view of Alford is the same in substance. But the frequent introduction of martial imagery forbids such a hypothesis. What the campaign was at the issue of which this pæan was composed, we cannot ascertain. Hitzig refers it to the campaign of Joram and Jehoshaphat against the Moabites (2 Kings iii.), and von Lengerke refers it to some period of Pharaoh Necho's reign. Hengstenberg thinks the occasion was the termination of the Ammonitic wars, and the capture of Rabbah. 2 Sam. xii. 26. One of his arguments is at best only a probability. He says, there is reference to the ark twice in Ps. lxviii. in verses 1 and 24, and that the ark was with the army during the warfare with Ammon. But the words in verses 1 and 24 of the psalm do not necessarily contain a reference to the ark, and the language of Joab to David, in 2 Sam. xi. 11, does not affirm the presence of the ark in the Israelitish camp, but may be explained by the words of 2 Sam. vii. 2. That the psalm is one of David's times and composition may be proved, against Ewald, de Wette, and Hupfeld, from its style and diction. The last writer, in his recent commentary (*Die Psalmen*, Dritter Band, Gotha, 1860), refers it to the return from Babylon, and supposes that it is perhaps the composition of the so-called pseudo-Isaiah, that is, the author of the latter half of Isaiah's prophecies. Reuss, in a treatise full of "persiflage," as Hupfeld says, and which Delitzsch truly calls a "Pasquill"—a "Harlekinanzug"—brings the psalm down to the period between Alexander the Great and the Maccabees. One of the Targums refers the passage to Moses and the giving of the law.[1] Its pervading idea—probably without reference to any special campaign, but combining what had happened many times when the Lord had shown Himself "mighty in battle"—is, that He, as of old, had come down for His people's deliverance, and had achieved it; had vanquished their foes, and given them a signal victory, and that, the combat being over, and captivity led captive, He had left the camp and gone up again to heaven. This portion of the psalm seems to have been chanted as the procession wound its way up Mount Zion to surround the symbols of the Divine majesty.

"Thou hast ascended on high." The word לַמָּרוֹם—"on high"—in such a connection refers to heaven, in contrast with earth, where the victory had been won. Ps. xviii. 16; Isa. xxiv. 18, xl. 26; Jer. xxv. 30.

"Thou hast led captivity captive"—$ᾐχμαλώτευσας\ αἰχμαλωσίαν$. The meaning of this idiom seems simply to be—Thou hast mustered or reviewed Thy captives. Judg. v. 12; Gesenius, *sub voce*. The allusion is to a triumphal procession in which marched the persons taken in war.

"Thou hast received gifts for men." There is no need, with de Wette and others, to translate ב *in*, and to regard this

---

[1] The following note is translated from the Rabbinical Commentary of Mendelssohn :—"As he mentions (v. 8, 18) the consecration of Sinai, he adds the act by which it was inaugurated, and says, 'Thou hast ascended and sat on high, after giving Thy law, and there Thou hast led captives, viz., the hearts of the men who said, We shall act and be obedient; Thou hast taken gifts from amongst men; Thou hast taken and chosen some of them as a present, viz., Thy people, whom Thou hast purchased with Thy mighty hand, who are given to Thee and are obedient. Though they are at times disobedient, still hast Thou taken them to dwell amongst them, to forgive their sins.'"

as the meaning—"Thou hast received gifts in men," that is, men constituted the gifts, the vanquished vassals or proselytes formed the acquisition of the conqueror. *Commentar über die Psalmen*, p. 412; Boettcher, *Proben*, etc. § 62; Schnurrer, *Dissertat.* p. 303. The preposition ב often signifies "for" or "on account of." Gen. xviii. 28, xxix. 18; 2 Kings xiv. 6; Jonah i. 14; Lam. ii. 11; Ezek. iv. 17, etc.; Noldius, *Concord. Part. Heb.* p. 158. Hafniæ, 1679. "Thou hast received gifts on account of men" to benefit and bless them; or the preposition may signify "among," as in 2 Sam. xxiii. 3; Prov. xxiii. 28; Jer. xlix. 15; Ewald, *Gram. der Heb. Sprache*, § 521, and Delitzsch. These gifts are the results of His victory, and they are conferred by Him after He has gone up from the battle-field. To obtain such a sense, however, it is out of the question, on the part of Bloomfield, to disturb the Septuagint reading and change the ἐν into ἐπί. But how can ἐν ἀνθρώπῳ denote "after the fashion of a man," and how can בָּאָדָם in this connection mean, as Adam Clarke and Wordsworth conjecture, "in man"—that is, by virtue of His incarnation as the head of redeemed humanity?

In what sense, then, are those words applicable to the ascended Redeemer? They are not introduced simply as an illustration, for the apostle reasons from them in the following verses. This bare idea of accommodation, vindicated by such exegetes as Morus and even by Doddridge, can therefore have no place here. Nor can we agree with Calvin, that Paul has somewhat twisted the words from their original meaning—"*nonnihil a genuino sensu hoc testimonium detorsit Paulus*"— an opinion which wins suspicious praise from Rückert. The argument of the next verse would in that case be without solid foundation. Nor does Olshausen, in our apprehension, fix upon the prominent point of illustration. That point is in his view not the proof that Christ dispenses gifts, but that men receive them, so that Gentiles, as partakers of humanity, have equal right to them with Jews. While the statement in the latter part is true, it seems to be only a subordinate inference, not the main matter of argument. That men had the gift was a palpable fact; but the questions were—Who gave them? and does their diversity interfere with the oneness of the church? Besides, it is the term ἀναβάς on which the apostle comments. Nor can we bring ourselves to the notion of a typical allusion, or "emblem" as Barnes terms it, as if the ark carried up to Zion was typical of Christ's ascent to heaven; for we cannot convince ourselves that the ark is, so formally at least, referred to in the psalm at all. Nor will it do merely to say, with Harless, that the psalm is applicable to Christ, because one and the same God is the revealer both of the Old and New Testaments. Still wider from the tenor of the apostle's argument is one portion of the notion of Locke, that Paul's object is to prove to unconverted Jews out of their own scriptures that Jesus must die and be buried. Our position is, that the same God is revealed as Redeemer both under the Old and New Testament, that the Jehovah of the one is the Jesus of the other, that Ps. lxviii. is filled with imagery which was naturally based on incidents in Jewish history, and that the inspired poet, while describing the interposition of Jehovah, has used language which was fully realized only in the victory and exaltation of Christ. Not that there is a double sense, but the Jehovah of the theocracy was He who, in the fulness of the time, assumed humanity, and what He did among His people prior to the incarnation was anticipative of nobler achievements in the nature of man. John xii. 41; Rom. xiv 10, 11; 1 Cor. x. 4; Heb. i. 10. The Psalmist felt this, and under the influence of such emotions, rapt into future times, and beholding salvation completed, enemies defeated, and gifts conferred, thus addressed the laurelled Conqueror—"Thou hast ascended on high." Such a quotation was therefore to the apostle's purpose. There are gifts in the church—not one donation but many—gifts the result of warfare and victory—gifts the number and variety of which are not inconsistent with unity. Such blessings are no novelty; they are in accordance with the earnest expectations of ancient ages; for it was predicted that Jesus should ascend on high, lead captivity captive, and give gifts to men. But those gifts, whatever their character and extent, are bestowed according to Christ's measurement; for it was He who then and now ennobles men with these spiritual endowments. Nor has there been any change of administration. Gifts and graces have descended from the same Lord. Under the old theocracy, which had a civil organization, these gifts

might be sometimes temporal in their nature; still, no matter what was their character, they came from the one Divine Dispenser, who is still the Supreme and Sovereign Benefactor. The apostle says—
ἀναβὰς εἰς ὕψος ᾐχμαλώτευσεν αἰχμαλωσίαν—" having ascended on high, He led captivity captive." The reference in the aorist participle is to our Lord's ascension, an act preceding that of the finite verb. Winer, § 45, 6; Krüger, § 56, 10; Acts i. 9. The meaning of the Hebrew phrase corresponding to the last two words has been already given. Such a use of a verb with its cognate substantive is, as we have seen again and again, a common occurrence. Lobeck, *Paralipomena*, Dissert. viii., *De figura etymologica*, p. 499, has given many examples from the classics. The verb, as well as the kindred form αἰχμαλωτίζω, belongs to the later Greek—*extrema Grœciœ senectus novum palmitem promisit.* Lobeck, *ad Phrynichus*, p. 442. The noun seems to be used as the abstract for the concrete. Kühner, ii. § 406; Jelf, § 353; Diodorus Siculus, xvii. 76; Num. xxxi. 12; Judg. v. 12; 2 Chron. xxviii. 11–13; Amos i. 6; 1 Macc. ix. 70, 72, xiv. 7. The prisoners plainly belong to the enemy whom He had defeated, and by whom His people had long been subjugated. This is the natural order of ideas—having beaten His foes, He makes captives of them. The earlier fathers viewed the captives as persons who had been enslaved by Satan—as Satan's prisoners, whom Jesus restored to liberty. Such is the view of Justin Martyr,[1] of Theodoret and Œcumenius in the Greek church, of Jerome and Pelagius in the Latin church, of Thomas Aquinas in mediæval times, of Erasmus, and in later days, of Meier, Harless, and Olshausen. But such an idea is not in harmony with the imagery employed, nor can it be defended by any philological instances or analogies. On the contrary, Christ's subjugation of His enemies has a peculiar prominence in the Messianic oracles; Ps. cx. 1; Isa. liii. 12; 1 Cor. xv. 25; Col. ii. 15; and in many other places.

What, then, are the enemies of Messiah? Not simply as in the miserable rationalism of Grotius, the vices and idolatries

[1] *Dial. cum Tryph.* p. 129, ed. Otto, Jenæ, 1843. The genuineness of this Dialogue has, however, been disputed.

of heathendom, nor yet as in the equally shallow opinion of Flatt, the hindrances to the spread and propagation of the gospel. Quite peculiar is the strange notion of Pierce, that the "captives" were the good angels, who, prior to Christ's advent, had been local presidents in every part of the world, but who were now deprived of this delegated power at Christ's resurrection, and led in triumph by Him as He ascended to glory. *Notes on Colossians*, appendix. The enemies of Messiah are Satan and his allies—every hostile power which Satan originates, controls, and directs against Jesus and His kingdom. The captives, therefore, are not merely Satan, as Vorstius and Bodius imagine; nor simply death, as is the view of Anselm; nor the devil and sin, as is the opinion of Beza, Bullinger, and Vatablus; but, as Chrysostom, Calvin, Calixtus, Theophylact, Bengel, Meyer, and Stier show, they include Satan, sin, and death. "He took the tyrant captive, the devil I mean, and death, and the curse, and sin"—such is the language of Chrysostom. The psalm was fulfilled, says Calvin—*quum Christus, devicto peccato, subacta morte, Satanâ profligato, in cœlum magnifice sublatus est.* Christ's work on earth was a combat—a terrible struggle with the hosts of darkness whose fiercest onsets were in the garden and on the cross—when hell and death combined against Him those efforts which repeated failures had roused into desperation. And in dying He conquered, and at length ascended in victory, no enemy daring to dispute His right or challenge His march; nay, He exhibited His foes in open triumph. He bruised the head of the Serpent, though His own heel was bruised in the conflict. As the conqueror returning to his capital makes a show of his beaten foes, so Jesus having gone up to glory exposed His vanquished antagonists whom He had defeated in His agony and death.

[καὶ] ἔδωκεν δόματα τοῖς ἀνθρώποις—"and He" (that is, the exalted Saviour) "gave gifts to men." Acts ii. 33. There is no καί in the Septuagint, and it is omitted by A, C², D¹, E, F, G, the Vulgate, and other authorities; while it is found in B, C¹ (C³), D³, I, K, L, and a host of others. Lachmann omits it; Tischendorf omitted it in his second edition, but inserts it in his seventh; Alford inserts and Ellicott rejects it. The Septuagint has ἐν ἀνθώρπῳ, which Peile would harshly render—"after the fashion of a man."[1] In their exegesis upon their translation of the Hebrew text, Harless, Olshausen, and von Gerlach understand these gifts to be men set apart to God as sacred offerings. "Thou hast taken to Thyself gifts among men—that is, Thou hast chosen to Thyself the redeemed for sacrifices," so says Olshausen with especial reference to the Gentiles. According to Harless, the apostle alters the form of the clause from the original to bring out the idea—"that the captives are the redeemed, who by the grace of God are made what they are." But men are the receivers of the gift—not the gift itself. *Comment. in Vet. Test.* vol. iii. p. 178. Lipsiæ, 1838; *Uebersetz. und Ausleg. der Psalmen*, p. 305. Hofmann understands it thus—that the conquered won by Him get gifts from Him to make them capable of service, and so to do Him honour. *Schriftb.* ii. part 1, p. 488. See also his *Weissagung und Erfüllung*, i. 168, ii. 199. Stier says rightly, that these δόματα are the gifts of the Holy Spirit — *die Geistes-gaben Christi*. These gifts are plainly defined by the context, and by the following καὶ αὐτὸς ἔδωκεν. Whatever they are—a "free Spirit," a perfect salvation, and a completed Bible—it is plain that the office of the Christian ministry is here prominent among them. The apostle has now proved that Jesus dispenses gifts, and has made good his assertion that grace is conferred "according to the measure of the gift of Christ."

(Ver. 9.) Τὸ δὲ, ἀνέβη, τί ἐστιν—"Now that he ascended, what is it?" Now this predicate, ἀνέβη, what does it mean or imply? The particle δέ introduces a transitional explanation or inference. The apostle does not repeat the participle, but takes the idea as expressed by the verb and as placed in contrast with κατέβη—

εἰ μὴ ὅτι καὶ κατέβη εἰς τὰ κατώτερα [μέρη] τῆς γῆς;— "unless that He also descended to the lower parts of the earth." The word πρῶτον found in the Textus Receptus before εἰς has no great authority, but Reiche vindicates it (*Com. Crit.* p. 173); and μέρη is not found in D, E, F, G. Tischendorf rejects it, but Scholz, Lachmann, Tittmann, Hahn, and Reiche retain it, as it has A, B, C, D³, K, L, and

---

[1] Bloomfield has well remarked, that Peile's ingenious reading of this clause in the Septuagint virtually amounts to a re-writing of it.

the Vulgate in its favour. The Divinity and heavenly abode of Christ are clearly presupposed. His ascension implies a previous descent. He could never be said to go up unless He had formerly come down. If He go up after the victory, we infer that he had already come down to win it. But how does this bear upon the apostle's argument? We can scarcely agree with Chrysostom, Olshausen, Hofmann, and Stier, that the condescension of Christ is here proposed as an example of those virtues inculcated in the first verse, though such a lesson may be inferred. Nor can we take it as being the apostle's formal proof, that the psalm is a Messianic one —as if the argument were, descent and ascent cannot be predicated of God the Omnipresent; therefore the sacred ode can refer only to Christ who came down to earth and again ascended to glory. But the ascension described implies such a descent, warfare, and victory, as belong only to the incarnate Redeemer.

εἰς τὰ κατώτερα τῆς γῆς—" to the lower parts of the earth." Compare in Septuagint such places as Deut. xxxii. 22; Neh. iv. 13; Ps. lxiii. 9, 10, lxxxvi. 13, cxxxix. 15; Lam. iii. 55, and the prayer of Manasseh in the Apocrypha. The phrase represents the Hebrew formula—תַּחְתִּיּוֹת הָאָרֶץ, the superlative being commonly employed—κατώτατος. The rabbins called the earth sometimes generally הַתַּחְתּוֹנִים. Bartolocci, *Bib. Rab.* i. p. 320.

1. Some suppose the reference to be to the conception of Jesus, basing their opinion on Ps. cxxxix. 15, where the psalmist describes his substance as not hid from God, when he was "made in secret," and "curiously wrought in the lower parts of the earth." Such is the opinion of scholars no less distinguished than Colomesius, *Observat. Sacræ*, p. 36, Cameron, *Myrothecium Evang.* p. 251, Witsius, Piscator, and Calixtus. But the mere poetical figure in the psalm denoting secret and undiscoverable operation, can scarcely be placed in contrast to the highest heaven.

2. Chrysostom, with Theophylact and Œcumenius, Bullinger, Phavorinus, and Macknight, refer it to the death of Christ; while Vorstius, Baumgarten, Drusius, Cocceius, Whitby, Wilke, and Crellius, see a special reference to the grave. But there is no proof that the words can bear such

a meaning. Certainly the descent described in the psalm quoted from did not involve such humiliation.

3. Many refer the phrase to our Lord's so-called descent into hell—*descensus ad inferos*. Such was the view of Tertullian, Irenæus, Jerome, Pelagius, and Ambrosiaster among the Fathers; of Erasmus, Estius, and the majority of Popish expositors; of Calovius, Bengel, Rückert, Bretschneider, Olshausen, Stier, Turner, Meyer in his third edition, Alford, and Ellicott. See also Lechler, *das Apost. Zeit.* p. 84, 2nd ed. 1857; *Acta Thomæ*, xvi. p. 199, ed. Tischendorf, 1851. Thus Tertullian says, that Jesus did not ascend *in sublimiora cœlorum*, until He went down *in inferiora terrarum, ut illic patriarchas et prophetas compotes Sui faceret*. *De Anima*, 55; *Opera*, vol. ii. p. 642, ed. Œhler. Catholic writers propose a special errand to our Lord in His descent into hell, viz., to liberate the old dead from torment—or a peculiar custody in the *limbus patrum*, or Abraham's bosom. *Catechismus Roman.* § 104. These doctrines are, however, superinduced upon this passage, and in many parts are contrary to Scripture. Pearson *on the Creed*, p. 292, ed. 1847. Stier admits that Christ could suffer no agony in Hades. Olshausen's tamer idea is, that Jesus went down to Sheol, not to liberate souls confined in it, but that this descent is the natural consequence of His death. The author shrinks from the results of his theory, and at length attenuates his opinion to this—"That in His descent Jesus partook of the misery of those fettered by sin even unto death, that is, even unto the depths of Hades." Such is also the view of Robinson (*sub voce*).[1] But the language of the apostle, taken by itself, will not warrant those hypotheses. For, 1. Whatever the view taken of the "descent into hell," or of the language in 1 Pet. iii. 19, the natural interpretation of which seems to imply it, it may be said, that though the superlative κατώτατος may be the epithet of Sheol in the Old Testament, why should the comparative in the New Testament

[1] In Pott's *Excursus*, in connection with his interpretation of 1 Pet. iii. 18, 19, will be found a good account of the various opinions on the "descent into hell," as also in Dittelmeier, *Historia Dogmatis de Descensu C.*, etc., Altorf, 1761. But a more complete treatise on the same dogma in its various aspects is the more recent one of Güder—*Die Lehre von der Erscheinung Jesu Christi unter den Todten*, etc., 1853.

be thought to have the same reference? Is it in accordance with Scripture to call Hades, in this special sense, a lower portion of the earth, and is the expression analogous to Phil. ii. 10; Matt. xii. 40? 2. The ascension of Jesus, moreover, as has been remarked, is always represented as being not from Hades but from the earth. John iii. 13, xvi. 28, etc. 3. Nor is there any force in Ellicott's remark, that the use of the specific term ᾅδης "would have marred the antithesis," for we find the same antithesis virtually in Isa. xiv. 13, 15, and expressly in Matt. xi. 23, while ὑπεράνω and κατώτερα are in sharp contrast on our hypothesis. But heaven and earth are the usual contrast. John viii. 23; Acts ii. 19. And the phrase, "that He might fill all things," depends not on the descent, but on the ascension and its character. 4. Those who suppose the captives to be human spirits emancipated from thraldom by Jesus, may hold the view that Christ went to hell to free them, but we have seen that the captives are enemies made prisoners on the field of battle. 5. Nor can it be alleged, that if Satan and his fiends are the captives, Jesus went down to his dark domain and conquered him; for the great struggle was upon the cross, and on it "through death He destroyed him that had the power of death, that is, the devil." When He cried, "It is finished," the combat was over. He commended His spirit into the hands of His Father, and promised that the thief should be with Himself in paradise—certainly not the scene of contention and turmoil. But if we adopt Hebrew imagery, and consider the region of death as a vast ideal underworld, into which Jesus like every dead man descends, there would then be less objection to the hypothesis under review. 6. If we suppose the apostle to have had any reference to the Septuagint in his mind, then, had he desired to express the idea of Christ's descent into Hades, there were two phrases, any of which he might have imitated—ἐξ ᾅδου κατωτάτου (Ps. lxxxvi. 13); or more pointed still, ἕως ᾅδου κατωτάτου. Deut. xxxii. 22. See Trom. *Concord.* Why not use ᾅδης, when it had been so markedly employed before, had he wished to give it prominence? Unmistakeable phraseology was provided for him, and sanctioned by previous usage. But the apostle employs γῆ with the comparative, and it is therefore to be questioned whether he had the Alexandrian version in his mind at all. And if he had, it is hard to think how he could attach the meaning of Hades to the words ἐν τοῖς κατωτάτω τῆς γῆς; for in the one place where they occur (Ps. cxxxix. 15), they describe the scene of the formation of the human embryo, and in the only other place where they are used (Ps. lxiii. 9), they mark out the disastrous fate of David's enemies, —a fate delineated in the following verse as death by the sword, while the unburied corpses were exposed to the ravages of the jackal. Delitzsch *in loc.* Nor is there even sure ground for supposing that in such places as Isa. xliv. 23, Ezek. xxvi. 20, xxxii. 18-24, the similar Hebrew phrase which occurs, but which is not rendered ᾅδης in the Septuagint, means Sheol or Hades. In Isa. xliv. 23, it is as here, earth in contrast with heaven, and perhaps the foundations of the globe are meant, as Ewald, the Chaldee, and the Septuagint understand the formula. In Ezek. xxvi. 20 "the low parts of the earth" are "places desolate of old;" and in Ezek. xxxii. 18-24 the "nether parts of the earth" are associated with the "pit," and "graves set in the sides of the pit"—scenes of desolation and massacre. The phrase may be a poetical figure for a dark and awful destiny. It is very doubtful whether Manasseh in the prayer referred to deprecates punishment in the other world, for he was in a dungeon and afraid of execution, and, according to theocratic principles, might hope to gain life and liberty by his penitence; for, should such deliverance be vouchsafed, he adds, "I will praise Thee for ever, all the days of my life." It is to be borne in mind, too, that in all these places of the Old Testament, the phraseology occurs in poetical compositions, and as a portion of Oriental imagery. But in the verse before us, the words are a simple statement of facts in connection with an argument, which shows that Jesus must have come down to earth before it could be said of Him that He had gone up to heaven.

4. So that we agree with the majority of expositors who understand the words as simply denoting the earth. Such is the view of Thomas Aquinas, Beza,[1] Aretius, Bodius, Rollock, Calvin, Cajetan, Piscator, Crocius, Grotius, Marloratus, Schoett-

---

[1] Beza refers his reader with a query to the first opinion we have noted. Nor

gen, Michaelis, Bengel, Loesner, Vitringa, Cramer, Storr, Holzhausen, Meier, Matthies, Harless, Wahl, Baumgarten-Crusius, Scholz, de Wette, Raebiger, Bisping, Hofmann, Chandler, Hodge, and Winer, § 59, 8, a. A word in apposition is sometimes placed in the genitive, as 2 Cor. v. 5, τὸν ἀρραβῶνα τοῦ πνεύματος—the earnest of the Spirit—the Spirit which is the earnest; Rom. viii. 23, iv. 11, σημεῖον περιτομῆς—the sign of circumcision, that is, the sign, to wit, circumcision. Acts iv. 22; 1 Pet. iii. 7; Col. iii. 24; Rom. viii. 21, etc. The same mode of expression occurs in Hebrew—Stuart's *Heb. Gram.* § 422; Nordheimer's do. § 815. So, too, we have in Latin—*Urbs Romæ*—the city of Rome; *fluvius Euphratis*—or as we say in English, "the Frith of Clyde," or "Frith of Forth." Thus, in the phrase before us, "the lower parts of the earth" mean those lower parts which the earth forms or presents in contrast with heaven, as we often say—heaven above and earth beneath. The ὕψος of the former verse plainly suggested the κατώτερα in this verse, and ὑπεράνω stands also in correspondence with it. So the world is called ἡ γῆ κάτω. Acts ii. 19. When our Lord speaks Himself of His descent and ascension, heaven and earth are uniformly the termini of comparison. Thus in John iii. 13, and no less than seven times in the sixth chapter of the same gospel. *Comparantur*, says Calvin, *non una pars terræ cum altera, sed tota terra cum cœlo*. Reiche takes the genitive, as signifying *terra tanquam universi pars inferior*. Christ's ascension to heaven plainly implies a previous descent to this nether world. And it is truly a nether or lower world when compared with high heaven. May not the use of the comparative indicate that the descent of Christ was not simply to ἡ γῆ κάτω, but εἰς τὰ κατώτερα? Not that with Zanchius, Bochart (*Opera*, i. 985, ed. Villemandy, 1692), Fesselius (*Apud Wolf., in loc.*), Küttner, Barnes, and others, we regard the phrase as signifying, in general, lowliness or humiliation—*status exinanitionis*. Theologically, the use of the comparative is suggestive. He was born into the world, and that in a low condition; born not under fretted roofs and amidst marble halls, but He drew His first breath in a stable, and enjoyed His first sleep in a

are we sure whether by "terra" he does not mean the grave, when he defines it as—*pars mundi infima.*

manger. As a man, He earned His bread by the sweat of His brow, at a manual occupation with hammer and hatchet, "going forth to His work and to His labour until the evening." The creatures He had formed had their house and haunt after their kind, but the Heir of all things had no domicile by legal right; for "the foxes have holes, and the birds of the air have nests, but the Son of man hath not where to lay His head." Reproach, and scorn, and contumely followed Him as a dark shadow. Persecution at length apprehended Him, accused Him, calumniated Him, scourged Him, mocked Him, and doomed the "man of sorrows" to an ignominious torture and a felon's death. His funeral was extemporized and hasty; nay, the grave He lay in was a borrowed one. He came truly "to the lower parts of the earth."

(Ver. 10.) Ὁ καταβὰς, αὐτός ἐστιν καὶ ὁ ἀναβὰς ὑπεράνω πάντων τῶν οὐρανῶν—" He that descended, He it is also who ascended high above all the heavens." Ὁ καταβάς is emphatic, and αὐτός is He and none other. Winer, § 22, 4, note. Οὐ γὰρ ἄλλος κατελήλυθε, says Theodoret, καὶ ἄλλος ἀνελήλυθεν. The identity of His person is not to be disputed. Change of position has not transmuted His humanity. It may be refined and clothed in lustre, but the manhood is unaltered. That Jesus—

"Who laid His great dominion by,
On a poor virgin's breast to lie;"

who, to escape assassination, was snatched in His infancy into Egypt—who passed through childhood into maturity, growing in wisdom and stature—who spoke those tender and impressive parables, for He had "compassion on the ignorant, and on them that were out of the way"—who fed the hungry, relieved the afflicted, calmed the demoniac, touched the leper, raised the dead, and wept by the sepulchre, for to Him no form of human misery ever appealed in vain—He who in hunger hasted to gather from a fig-tree—who lay weary and wayworn on the well of Jacob—who, with burning lips, upon the cross exclaimed "I thirst"—He whose filial affection in the hour of death commended his widowed mother to the care of His beloved disciple—HE it is who has gone up. No wonder that a heart which proved itself to be so rich with every tender, noble, and sympathetic impulse, should rejoice in expending its spiritual treasures, and giving gifts to men. Nay, more, He who provided spiritual gifts in His death, is He who bestows them in His ascension on each one, and all of them are essential to the unity of His church. But as His descent was to a point so deep, His ascent is to a point as high, for He rose—

ὑπεράνω πάντων τῶν οὐρανῶν—"above all the heavens." John iii. 13 ; Heb. vii. 26. See under i. 21. Οἱ οὐρανοί are those regions above us through which Jesus passed to the heaven of heavens—to the right hand of God. The apostle himself speaks of the third heaven. 2 Cor. xii. 2. It is needless to argue whether the apostle refers to the third heaven, as Harless supposes, or to the seventh heaven, as Wetstein and Meyer argue. There was an ἀήρ, an αἰθήρ, and τρίτος οὐρανός (Schoettgen, 773 ; Wetstein under 2 Cor. xii. 2); but the apostle seems to employ the general language of the Old Testament, as in Deut. x. 14, 1 Kings viii. 27, where we have "the heaven, and the heaven of heavens;" or Ps. lxviii. 33, cxlviii. 4, in which the phrase occurs—"heavens of heavens." We find the apostle in Heb. iv. 14 saying of Jesus—διεληλυθότα τοὺς οὐρανούς—that He has "passed through the heavens," not "into the heavens," as our version renders it. Whatever regions are termed heavens, Jesus is exalted far above them, yea, to the heaven of heavens. The loftiest exaltation is predicated of Him. As His humiliation was so low, His exaltation is proportionately high. Theophylact says— He descended into the lowest parts—μεθ' ἃ οὐκ ἔστιν ἕτερόν τι, and He ascended above all—ὑπὲρ ἃ οὐκ ἔστιν ἕτερα. His position is the highest in the universe, being "far above all heavens"—all things are under His feet. See under i. 20, 21, 22. And He is there—

ἵνα πληρώσῃ τὰ πάντα—"that He might fill all things." The subjunctive with ἵνα, and after the aorist participle, represents an act which still endures. Klotz-Devarius, ii. p. 618. The ascension is past, but this purpose of it still remains, or is still a present result. The translation of Anselm, Koppe, and others, "that He might fulfil all things," that is, all the prophecies, is as remote from the truth as the exegesis of Matthies and Rückert, "that He might complete the work of redemption." Nor is the view of Zanchius more tenable, "that he might discharge all his functions." The versions of Tyndale and Cranmer, and that of Geneva, use the term "fulfil," but Wickliffe rightly renders, "that he schulde fill alle thingis." Jer. xxiii. 24. The bearing of this clause on the meaning of the term $\pi\lambda\acute{\eta}\rho\omega\mu a$, the connection of Christ's fulness with the church and the universe, and the relation of the passage to the Lutheran dogma of the ubiquity of the Redeemer, will be found in our exegesis of the last verse of the first chapter, and need not therefore be repeated here. We are not inclined to limit $\tau\grave{a}$ $\pi\acute{a}\nu\tau a$ to the church, as is done by Beza, Grotius, and Meier, for reasons assigned under the last clause of the first chapter. The church filled by Him becomes "His fulness," but that fulness is not limited by such a boundary. The explanation of Calvin, that Jesus fills all, *Spiritus sui virtute;* and of Harless, *mit seiner Gnadengegenwart*—appears to be too limited. Chrysostom's view is better — $\tau\hat{\eta}\varsigma$ $\dot{\epsilon}\nu\epsilon\rho\gamma\epsilon\acute{\iota}a\varsigma$ $a\dot{\upsilon}\tau o\hat{\upsilon}$ $\kappa a\grave{\iota}$ $\tau\hat{\eta}\varsigma$ $\delta\epsilon\sigma\pi o\tau\epsilon\acute{\iota}a\varsigma$. Stier compares the phrase with the last clause of the verse quoted from Ps. lxviii., that "God the Lord might dwell among them," to which corresponds the meaning given by Bengel—*Se Ipso.*

(Ver. 11.) The apostle resumes the thought that seems to have been ripe for utterance at the conclusion of ver. 7.

$K a\grave{\iota}$ $a\dot{\upsilon}\tau\grave{o}\varsigma$ $\ddot{\epsilon}\delta\omega\kappa\epsilon$—"And Himself gave"—$a\dot{\upsilon}\tau\acute{o}\varsigma$ emphatic, and connected with the $a\dot{\upsilon}\tau\acute{o}\varsigma$ of the preceding verse, while at the same time the apostle recurs to the aorist. This Jesus who ascended—this, and none other, is the sovereign donor. The provider and bestower are one and the same; and such gifts, though they vary, cannot therefore mar the blessed unity of the spiritual society. There is no reason, with Theophylact, Harless, Meier, Baumgarten-Crusius, and Bisping, to call $\ddot{\epsilon}\delta\omega\kappa\epsilon$ a Hebraism, as if it were equivalent to $\ddot{\epsilon}\theta\epsilon\tau o$—the term which is used in 1 Cor. xii. 28; Acts xx. 28. See under chap. i. 22. $"E\delta\omega\kappa\epsilon$ is evidently in unison with $\dot{\epsilon}\delta\acute{o}\theta\eta$ and $\delta\omega\rho\epsilon\acute{a}$ in ver. 7, and with $\ddot{\epsilon}\delta\omega\kappa\epsilon$ $\delta\acute{o}\mu a\tau a$ in ver. 8. The object of the apostle, in harmony with the quotation which he has introduced, is not simply to affirm the fact that there are various offices in the church, or that they are of divine institution; but also to show that they exist in the form of donations, and are among the peculiar and distinctive gifts which the exalted Lord has bequeathed. The writer wishes his readers to contemplate them more as gifts than as functions. Had they sprung up in the church by a process of natural development, they might perchance have clashed with one another; but being the gifts of the one Lord and Benefactor, they must possess a mutual harmony in virtue of their origin and object. He gave—

τοὺς μὲν ἀποστόλους—" some as, or to be, apostles." On the particle μέν, which cannot well be rendered into English, and on its connection with μία—see Donaldson's *New Cratylus*, § 154, and his *Greek Grammar*, § 548, 24, and § 559. The official gifts conferred upon the church are viewed not in the abstract, but as personal embodiments or appellations. Instead of saying—" He founded the apostolate," he says— " He gave some to be apostles." The idea is, that the men who filled the office, no less than the office itself, were a Divine gift.

The apostles were the first and highest order of office-bearers—those "twelve whom also He named apostles." Luke vi. 13. Judas fell; Matthias was appointed his successor and substitute (if a human appointment, and one prior to Pentecost, be valid); and Saul of Tarsus was afterwards added to the number. The essential elements of the apostolate were—

1. That the apostles should receive their commission immediately from the living lips of Christ. Matt. x. 5; Mark vi. 7; Gal. i. 1. In the highest sense, they held a charge as "ambassadors for Christ;" they spoke "in Christ's stead." Matt. xxviii. 19; John xx. 21, 23; Hase, *Leben Jesu*, § 64.

2. That having seen the Saviour after He rose again, they should be qualified to attest the truth of His resurrection. So Peter defines it, Acts i. 21, 22; so Paul asserts his claim, 1 Cor. ix. 1, 5, 8; so Peter states it, Acts ii. 32; and so the historian records, Acts iv. 33. The assertion of this crowning fact was fittingly assumed as the work of those "chosen witnesses to whom He showed Himself alive after His passion, by many infallible proofs."

3. They enjoyed a special inspiration. Such was the promise, John xiv. 26, xvi. 13; and such was the possession,

1 Cor. ii. 10; Gal. i. 11, 12; 1 Thess. ii. 13. Infallible exposition of Divine truth was their work; and their qualification lay in their possession of the inspiring influences of the Holy Ghost.

4. Their authority was therefore supreme. The church was under their unrestricted administration. Their word was law, and their directions and precepts are of permanent obligation. Matt. xviii. 18, 20; John xx. 22, 23; 1 Cor. v. 3–6; 2 Cor. x. 8.

5. In proof of their commission and inspiration, they were furnished with ample credentials. They enjoyed the power of working miracles. It was pledged to them, Mark xvi. 15; and they wielded it, Acts ii. 43, v. 15; and 2 Cor. xii. 12. Paul calls these manifestations "the signs of an apostle;" and again in Heb. ii. 4, he signalizes the process as that of "God also bearing them witness." They had the gift of tongues themselves, and they had also the power of imparting spiritual gifts to others. Rom. i. 11; Acts viii. 17, xix. 6.

6. And lastly, their commission to preach and found churches was universal, and in no sense limited. 2 Cor. xi. 28.

This is not the place to discuss other points in reference to the office. The title seems to be applied to Barnabas, Acts xiv. 4, 14, as being in company with Paul; and in an inferior sense to ecclesiastical delegates. Rom. xvi. 7; 2 Cor. viii. 23; Phil. ii. 25; Winer, *Real-Wörterbuch*, art. Apostel; Kitto's *Bib. Cycl.* do.; M'Lean's *Apostolical Commission*, Works, i. p. 8; Spanhemius, *de Apostolatu*, etc., Leyden, 1679.

τοὺς δὲ προφήτας—" and some to be prophets." Δέ looks back to μέν and introduces a different class. We have already had occasion to refer especially to this office under ii. 20 and iii. 5. The prophets ranked next in order to the apostles, but wanted some of their peculiar qualifications. They spoke under the influence of the Spirit; and as their instructions were infallible, so the church was built on their foundation as well as that of the apostles; ii. 20. Prophecy is marked out as one of the special endowments of the Holy Ghost (1 Cor. xii. 10), where it stands after the apostolic prerogative of working miracles. The revelation enjoyed by apostles was communicated also to prophets, iii. 5. The name has its origin in the peculiar usages of the Old Testament. The Hebrew term נָבִיא has reference, in its etymology, to the excitement and rhapsody which were so visible under the Divine afflatus; and the cognate verb is therefore used in the niphal and hithpael conjugations. Gesenius, *sub voce;* Knobel, *Prophetismus,* i. 127. The furor was sometimes so vehement that, in imitation of it, the frantic ravings of insanity received a similar appellation. 1 Sam. xviii. 10; 1 Kings xviii. 29. As the prophet's impulse came from God, and denoted close alliance with Him, so any man who enjoyed special and repeated Divine communications was called a prophet, as Abraham, Gen. xx. 7. Because the prophet was God's messenger, and spoke in God's name, this idea was sometimes seized on, and a common internuncius was dignified with the title. Ex. vii. 1. This is the radical signification of προφήτης—one who speaks —πρό—for, or in name of another. In the Old Testament, prophecy in its strict sense is therefore not identical with prediction; but it often denotes the delivery of a Divine message. Ezra v. 1. Prediction was a strange and sublime province of the prophet's labour; but he was historian and bard as well as seer. Again, as the office of a prophet was sacred, and was held in connection with the Divine service, lyric effusions and musical accompaniments are termed prophesying, as in the case of Miriam (Ex. xv. 20), and of the sons of the prophets, 1 Sam. x. 5. So it is too in Num. xi. 26; Tit. i. 12. In 1 Chron. xxv. 1, similar language occurs—the orchestra " prophesied with a harp to give thanks and to praise the Lord." Koppe, *Excursus* iii. *ad Comment. in Epist. ad Ephesios.* Thus, besides the special and technical sense of the word, prophesying in a wider and looser signification means to pour forth rapturous praises, in measured tone and cadence, to the accompaniment of wild and stirring music. Similar is the usage of the New Testament in reference to Anna in Luke ii. 36, and to the ebullition of Zachariah in Luke i. 67. While in the New Testament προφήτης is sometimes used in its rigid sense of the prophets of the Old Testament, it is often employed in the general meaning of one acting under a Divine commission. Foundation is thus laid for the appellation before us. Once, indeed (Acts xi. 28), prediction is ascribed to a prophet; but instruction of a peculiar nature—so sudden and thrilling, so lofty and penetrating—merits and receives the generic term of prophecy. Females sometimes had the gift, but they were not allowed to exercise it in the church. This subordinate office differed from that of the Old Testament prophets, who were highest in station in their church, and many of whose inspired writings have been preserved as of canonical authority. But no utterances of the prophets under the New Testament have been so highly honoured.

Thus the prophets of the New Testament were men who were peculiarly susceptible of Divine influence, and on whom that afflatus powerfully rested. Chrysostom, on 1 Cor. xii. 28, says of them—ὁ μὲν προφητεύων πάντα ἀπὸ τοῦ πνεύματος φθέγγεται. They were inspired *improvisatori* in the Christian assemblies—who, in animated style and under irresistible impulse, taught the church, and supplemented the lessons of the apostles, who, in their constant itinerations, could not remain long in one locality. Apostles planted and prophets watered; the germs engrafted by the one were nurtured and matured by the other. What the churches gain now by the spiritual study of Scripture, they obtained in those days by such prophetical expositions of apostolical truth. The work of these prophets was in the church, and principally with such as had the *semina* of apostolical teaching; for the apostle says —"He that prophesieth speaketh unto men, to edification, and exhortation, and comfort" (1 Cor. xiv. 3); and again, "prophesying serveth not for them that believe not, but for them that believe," though not for unbelievers wholly useless, as the sudden and vivid revelation of their spiritual wants and belongings often produced a mighty and irresistible impression. 1 Cor. xiv. 22, 24, 25; Neander, *Geschichte der Pflanzung der Christl. K.* p. 234, 4th ed. Though the man who spake with tongues might be thrown out of self-control, this ecstasy did not fall so impetuously upon the prophets; they resembled not the Greek μάντις, for "the spirits of the prophets are subject to the prophets." One would be apt to infer from the description of the effect of prophecy on the mind of an unbeliever, in laying bare the secrets of his heart, that the prophets concerned themselves specially with the subjective side of Christianity—with its power and adaptations;

that they appealed to the consciousness, and that they showed the higher bearings and relations of those great facts which had already been learned on apostolical authority. 1 Cor. xiv. 25. This gift had an intimate connection with that of tongues (Acts xix. 6), but is declared by the apostle to be superior to it. Though these important functions were superseded when a written revelation became the instrument of the Spirit's operation upon the heart, yet the prophets, having so much in common with the apostles, are placed next to them, and are subordinate to them only in dignity and position. Rom. xii. 6. Whether all the churches enjoyed the ministrations of these prophets we know not. They were found in Corinth, Rome, Antioch, Ephesus, and Thessalonica. If our account, drawn from the general statements of Scripture, be correct, then it is wrong on the part of Noesselt, Rückert, and Baumgarten-Crusius to compare this office with that of modern preaching; and it is too narrow a view of it to restrict it to prediction; or to the interpretation of Old Testament vaticinations, like Macknight; or to suppose, with Mr. M'Leod, that it had its special field of labour in composing and conducting the psalmody of the primitive church. *Divine Inspiration*, by E. Henderson, D.D., p. 207: London, 1836; *A View of Inspiration*, etc., by Alexander M'Leod, p. 133: Glasgow, 1831. Most improbable of all is the conjecture of Schrader, that the apostle here refers to the prophets of the Old Testament.

τοὺς δὲ εὐαγγελιστάς—" and some to be evangelists." That those evangelists were the composers of our historical gospels is an untenable opinion, which Chrysostom deemed possible, and which Œcumenius stoutly asserts. On the other hand, Theodoret is more correct in his description—περιϊόντες ἐκήρυττον—" going about they preached." Eusebius, *Historia Eccles.* iii. 37. The word is used only thrice in the New Testament—as the designation of Philip in Acts xxi. 8, and as descriptive of one element of the vocation of Timothy. 2 Tim. iv. 5. In one sense apostles and prophets were evangelists, for they all preached the same holy evangel. 1 Cor. i. 17. But this official title implies something special in their function, inasmuch as they are distinguished also from "teachers." These gospellers may have been auxiliaries of the apostles, not endowed as they were, but furnished with clear perceptions of saving truth, and possessed of wondrous power in recommending it to others. Inasmuch as they itinerated, they might thus differ from stationary teachers. Neander, *Geschichte der Pflanzung*, etc., 259, 4th ed. While the prophets spoke only as occasion required, and their language was an excited outpouring of brilliant and piercing thoughts, the evangelists might be more calm and continuous in their work. Passing from place to place with the wondrous story of salvation and the cross, they pressed Christ on men's acceptance, their hands being freed all the while from matters of detail in reference to organization, ritual, and discipline. The prophet had an ἀποκάλυψις as the immediate basis of his oracle, and the evangelist had "the word of knowledge" as the ultimate foundation of his lesson. Were not the seventy sent forth by our Lord a species of evangelists, and might not Mark, Luke, Silas, Apollos, Tychicus, and Trophimus merit such a designation? The evangelist Timothy was commended by Paul to the church in Corinth. 1 Cor. iv. 17, xvi. 10. Mr. M'Leod's notions of the work of an evangelist are clearly wrong, as he mistakes addresses given to Timothy as a pastor for charges laid upon him in the character of an evangelist. *A View of Inspiration*, p. 481. The command to "do the work of an evangelist," if not used in a generic sense, is something distinct from the surrounding admonitions, and characterizes a special sphere of labour.

τοὺς δὲ ποιμίνας καὶ διδασκάλους—" and some to be pastors and teachers." Critical authorities are divided on the question as to whether these two terms point out two different classes of office-bearers, or merely describe one class by two combined characteristics. The former opinion is held by Theophylact, Ambrose, Pelagius, Calvin, Beza, Zanchius, Calixtus, Crocius, Grotius, Meier, Matthies, de Wette, Neander, and Stier; and the latter by Augustine, Jerome, Œcumenius, Erasmus, Piscator, Musculus, Bengel, Rückert, Harless, Olshausen, Meyer, and Davidson. *Ecclesiastical Polity*, p. 156.

Those who make a distinction between pastors and teachers vary greatly in their definitions. Thus Theodoret, followed by Bloomfield and Stier, notices the difference, as if it were only local—τοὺς κατὰ πόλιν καὶ κώμην—" town and country clergy." Theophylact understands by "pastors" bishops and presbyters, and deacons by "teachers," while Ambrosiaster identifies the same teachers with exorcists. According to Calixtus, with whom Meier seems to agree, the "pastors" were the working class of spiritual guides, and the "teachers" were a species of superintendents and professors of theology, or, according to Grotius, metropolitans. Neander's view is, that the "pastors" were rulers, and the "teachers" persons possessed of special edifying gifts, which were exerted for the instruction of the church. The Westminster Divines also made a distinction—"The teacher or doctor is also a minister of the Word as well as the pastor;" "He that doth more excel in exposition of Scripture, in teaching sound doctrine, and in convincing gainsayers, than he doth in application, and is accordingly employed therein, may be called a teacher or doctor;" "A teacher or doctor is of most excellent use in schools and universities," etc. Stier remarks that "each pastor should, to a certain extent at least, be a teacher, but every teacher is not therefore a pastor." By some reference is made for illustration to the school of divinity in Alexandria, over which such men as Didymus, Clement, and Origen presided.[1] None of these distinctions can be scripturally and historically sustained.

We agree with those who hold that one office is described by the two terms. Jerome says—*Non enim ait; alios autem pastores et alios magistros, sed alios pastores et magistros, ut qui pastor est, esse debeat et magister;* and again—*Nemo pastoris sibi nomen assumere debet, nisi possit docere quos pascit.* The view of Bengel is similar. The language indicates this, for the recurring τοὺς δέ is omitted before διδασκάλους, and a simple καί connects it with ποιμένας. The two offices seem to have had this in common, that they were stationary— περὶ ἕνα τόπον ἠσχολημένοι, as Chrysostom describes them. Grotius, de Wette, and others, refer us to the functional vocabulary of the Jewish synagogue, in which a certain class of officers were styled פרנסים, after which Christian pastors were named ἐπίσκοποι and πρεσβύτεροι. Vitringa, *De*

---

[1] But Bodius compares "teachers" to titular doctors of divinity, a title, he adds, which is not without its value—*si absit hinc quidem omnis ambitus, et vanus titulorum hujusmodi affectus.*

*Synagog. Vet.* p. 621; Selden, *De Synedriis Vet. Heb.* lib. i. cap. 14.

The idea contained in ποιμήν is common in the Old Testament. The image of a shepherd with his flock, picturing out the relation of a spiritual ruler and those committed to his charge, often occurs. Ps. xxiii. 1, lxxx. 1; Jer. ii. 8, iii. 15, and in many other places; Isa. lvi. 11; Ezek. xxxiv. 2, xxxvii. 24; Zech. x. 3; John x. 14, xxi. 15; Acts xx. 28; 1 Pet. v. 2. Such pastors and guides rule as well as feed the flock, for the keeping or tending is essential to the successful feeding. The prominent idea in Ps. xxiii. is protection and guidance in order to pasture. The same notion is involved in the Homeric and classic usage of ποιμήν as governor and captain. "The idea of administration is," Olshausen remarks, "prominent in this term." It implies careful, tender, vigilant superintendence and government, being the function of an overseer or elder. The official name ἐπίσκοπος is used by the apostle in addressing churches formed principally out of the heathen world—as at Ephesus, Philippi, and the island of Crete (Acts xx. 28; Phil. i. 1; 1 Tim. iii. 2; Tit. i. 7); while πρεσβύτερος, the term of honour, is more Jewish in its tinge, as may be found in many portions of the Acts of the Apostles, and in the writings of James, Peter, and John. Speaking to Timothy and Titus, the apostle styles them elders (and so does the compiler of the Acts, in referring to spiritual rulers); but describing the duties of the office itself, he calls the holder of it ἐπίσκοπος. See under Phil. i. 1.

The διδάσκαλοι, placed in the third rank by the apostle in 1 Cor. xii. 28, were persons whose peculiar function it was to expound the truths of Christianity. While teaching was the main characteristic of this office, yet, from the mode of discharging it, it might be called a pastorate. The διδάσκαλος in teaching, did the duty of a ποιμήν, for he fed with knowledge; and the ποιμήν in guiding and governing, prepared the flock for the nutriment of the διδάσκαλος. It is declared in 1 Tim. iii. 2 that a Christian overseer or pastor must be "apt to teach"—διδακτικός; and in Tit. i. 9 it is said that, in virtue of his office, he must be able "by sound doctrine both to exhort and convince the gainsayers." Again, in Heb.

xiii. 7, those who had governed the church are further characterized thus—οἵτινες ἐλάλησαν ὑμῖν τὸν λόγον τοῦ Θεοῦ. The one office is thus honoured appropriately with the two appellations. It comprised government and instruction, and the former being subordinate to the latter, διδάσκαλοι are alone mentioned in the Epistle to the Romans, but there the evangelists are formally omitted; while the apostle by a sudden change uses the abstract, and the "helps" and "governments" then referred to are, like "healing" and "tongues," not distinct offices possessed by various individuals, but associated with those previously named. The evangelists and deacons were indeed helps, but government devolved upon the teachers and elders. See Henderson, *Divine Inspiration*, Lect. iv. p. 184; Rückert, 2nd Beilage—*Komment. über Corinth-B.*; Davidson, *Ecclesiastical Polity*, 178. We are ignorant to a very great extent of the government of the primitive church, and much that has been written upon it is but surmise and conjecture. The church represented in the Acts was only in process of development, and there seem to have been differences of organization in various Christian communities, as may be seen by comparing the portion of the epistle before us with allusions in the three letters to Rome, Corinth, and Philippi. Offices seem to be mentioned in one which are not referred to in others. It would appear, in fine, that this last office of government and instruction was distinct in two elements from those previously enumerated; inasmuch as it was the special privilege of each Christian community—not a *ministerium vagum*, and was designed also to be a perpetual institute in the church of Christ. The apostle says nothing of the modes of human appointment or ordination to these various offices. He descends not to law, order, or form, but his great thought is, that though the ascended Lord gave such gifts to men, yet their variety and number interfere not with the unity of the church, as he also conclusively argues in the twelfth chapter of his first epistle to the church in Corinth.[1]

---

[1] How a learned Irvingite of the Continent labours to find in such a passage the kind of intricate hierarchy which his so-called apostolic church delights in, may be seen in the work of Thiersch—*Die Kirche in dem Apostolischen Zeitalter*, etc. Frankfurt, 1852.

(Ver. 12.) Πρὸς τὸν καταρτισμὸν τῶν ἁγίων, εἰς ἔργον διακονίας, εἰς οἰκοδομὴν τοῦ σώματος τοῦ Χριστοῦ—"In order to the perfecting of the saints, for the work of the ministry, for the edifying of the body of Christ." The meaning of this verse depends upon its punctuation. There are three clauses, and the question is—how are they connected?

1. Some regard the three clauses as parallel or co-ordinate. He gave all these gifts "for the perfecting of the saints, for the work of the ministry, for the edifying of the body of Christ." Such is the rendering of the English version, as if each clause contained a distinct purpose, and each of the three purposes related with equal independence to the divine gift of the Christian ministry. This mode of interpretation claims the authority of Chrysostom, Zanchius, Bengel, von Gerlach, Holzhausen, and Baumgarten - Crusius. But the apostle changes the preposition, using πρός before the first clause, while εἰς stands before the other two members of the verse, so that, if they are all co-ordinate, a different relation at least is indicated.

2. A meaning is invented by Grotius, Calovius, Rollock, Michaelis, Koppe, and Cramer, through the violent and unwarranted transposition of the clauses, as if Paul had written—"for the work of the ministry, in order to the perfecting of the saints, in order to the edifying of the body of Christ." Similarly Tyndale—"that the sainctes might have all things necessarie to work and minister withall."

3. Harless and Olshausen suppose the prime object to be described in the first clause which begins with πρός, and the other clauses, each commencing with εἰς, to be subdivisions of the main idea, and dependent upon it, as if the meaning were—the saints are prepared some of them to teach, and others, or the great body of the church, to be edified. Our objection to such an exegesis is, that it introduces a division where the apostle himself gives no hint, and which the language cannot warrant. For all the ἅγιοι are described as enjoying the "perfecting," and they are identical with "the body of Christ" which is to be edified. The opinion of Zachariae is not very different, as he makes the second εἰς depend upon the first—"For the work of the ministry instituted in order to the edifying of the body of Christ."

4. Meier, Schott, Rückert, and Erasmus also regard the two clauses introduced by εἰς as dependent upon that beginning with πρός. Their opinion is—that the apostle meant to say, "for the perfecting of the saints unto all that variety of service which is essential unto the edification of the church." This interpretation we preferred in our first edition. But Meyer argues that διακονία, in such a connection, never signifies service in general, but official service; and his objection therefore is, that the saints, as a body, are not invested with official prerogative.

5. Meyer's own view is, that the two last clauses are co-ordinate, and that both depend on ἔδωκε, while the first clause contains the ultimate reason for which Christ gave teachers. He has given teachers—εἰς—" for the work of the ministry, and—εἰς—for the edifying of His body—πρός—in order to the perfecting of His saints." Ellicott and Alford follow Meyer, and we incline now to concur in this opinion, though the order of thought appears somewhat inverted. Jelf, § 625, 3. It is amusing to notice the critical manœuvre of Piscator— εἰς ἔργον, says he, stands for ἐν ἔργῳ, and that again means δι' ἔργου—the perfecting of the saints by means of the work of the ministry.

The verbal noun καταρτισμός is not, as Pelagius and Vatablus take it, the filling up of the number of the elect, but as Theodoret paraphrases the participle—τέλειος ἐν πᾶσι πράγμασι. The verb καταρτίζειν—to put in order again—is used materially in the classics, as to refit a ship (Polyb. i. 24, 4; Diodorus Sic. xiii. 70) or reset a bone (Galen); also in Matt. iv. 21; Mark i. 19; Heb. x. 5, xi. 3. In its ethical sense it is used properly, Gal. vi. 1; and in its secondary sense of completing, perfecting, it is found in the other passages where it occurs, as here. Luke vi. 40; 2 Cor. xiii. 11. The meaning of ἅγιος has been explained under i. 1. The Christian ministry is designed to mature the saints, to bring them nearer the Divine law in obedience, and the Lord's example in conformity.

εἰς ἔργον διακονίας—" for work of service." For the etymology of the second term, see under iii. 7. These various office-bearers have been given for, or their destination is, the work of service. Ἔργον is not superfluous; as Koppe says, it is that work in which the διακονία busies itself. Winer,

§ 65, 7 ; Acts vi. 4, xi. 29 ; 1 Cor. xvi. 15 ; 2 Cor. ix. 12, 13, xi. 8 ; 2 Tim. iv. 5, iv. 11. Neither noun has the article; for διακονίας being indefinite, the governing noun becomes also anarthrous. Middleton, *Gr. Art.* p. 48.

εἰς οἰκοδομὴν τοῦ σώματος τοῦ Χριστοῦ—"for the building up of the body of Christ." This second parallel clause is a more specific way of describing the business or use of the Christian ministry—a second purpose to which the office-bearers are given. In ii. 21, οἰκοδομή signified the edifice —here it denotes the process of erection. The ideas involved in this term have been illustrated under ii. 22, and those in σῶμα Χριστοῦ have been given under i. 23. The spiritual advancement of the church is the ultimate design of the Christian pastorate. It labours to increase the members of the church, and to prompt and confirm their spiritual progress. The ministry preaches and rules to secure this, which is at the same time the purpose of Him who appointed and who blesses it. So that the more the knowledge of the saints grows and their piety ripens; the more vigorous their faith, the more ardent their love, and the more serene and heavenly their temperament; the more of such perfecting they gather to them and enjoy under the ordinances of grace—then the more do they contribute in their personal holiness and influence to the extension and revival of the church of Christ.

(Ver. 13.) Μέχρι καταντήσωμεν οἱ πάντες—"Until we all come." Μέχρι measures the time during which this arrangement and ministry are to last, and it is here used, without ἄν,[1] with a subjunctive, a usage common in the later writers and in the New Testament. Winer, § 41, 3, b ; Stallbaum, *Plato, Philebus,* p. 61 ; Schmalfeld on "Ἕως, § 128. Kühner, § 808, 2. This formula occurs only in this place ; ἄχρις οὗ being the apostle's common expression. The insertion of the particle ἄν would have given such an idea as this, "till we come (if ever we come)." Hartung, ii. p. 291 ; Bernhardy, p. 400. The subjunctive is employed not merely to express a future aim, as Harless says, but it also connects this futurity with the principal verb—ἔδωκε—as its expected purpose. Jelf, § 842, 2 ; Scheuerlein, § 36, 1. "We all,"

---

[1] On ἄχρι and μέχρι, see Tittmann, *de Synon.* p. 33 ; and on the various forms of the words, Phrynichus, ed. Lobeck, p. 14 ; Fritzsche, *ad Rom.* i. p. 308.

the apostle includes himself among all Christians, for he stood not apart from the church, but in it, the article specifying them as one class. Καταντάω needs not to be taken in any such sense as to intimate that believers of different nations meet together; nor can πάντες denote all men, as Jerome, Morus, and Allioli understand it, but only all the saints—ἅγιοι. The meaning is, that not only is there a blessed point in spiritual advancement set before the church, and that till such a point be gained the Christian ministry will be continued, but also and primarily, that the grand purpose of a continued pastorate in the church is to enable the church to gain a climax which it will certainly reach; for that climax is neither indefinite in its nature nor contingent in its futurity. And the apostle now characterizes it by a triple description, each member beginning with εἰς—

εἰς τὴν ἑνότητα τῆς πίστεως καὶ τῆς ἐπιγνώσεως τοῦ υἱοῦ τοῦ Θεοῦ—" to the unity of the faith and the knowledge of the Son of God." Καταντάω is followed by εἰς in a literal sense, as often in Acts, and here also in a tropical sense. See under Phil. iii. 11. Very different is the sense from that involved in the view of Pelagius—*ejus plenitudinem imitari*. Every noun in the clause has the article prefixed. We take the genitive τοῦ υἱοῦ τοῦ Θεοῦ as that of object, and as governed both by πίστεως and ἐπιγνώσεως—" the faith of the Son of God, and the knowledge of the Son of God." Winer, § 30. But we cannot adopt the view of Calvin, Calovius, Bullinger, and Crocius, that τῆς ἐπιγνώσεως is epexegetical of τῆς πίστεως, for it expresses a different idea. Nor can we with Grotius regard εἰς as meaning ἐν—the rendering also of the English version, while Chandler gives it the sense of " by means of," and Wycliffe renders " into unyte of faith." The preposition marks the *terminus ad quem*. The apostle has already in this chapter introduced the idea of unity, and has shown that difference of gifts and office is not incompatible with it; and now he shows that the variety of offices in the church of Christ is intended to secure it. For the meaning of the term Son, the reader may go back to what is said under i. 3. The apostle uses this high appellation here, for Jesus as God's Son—a Divine Saviour, is the central object of faith. Christians are all to attain to oneness of faith, that is, all of them shall be filled with the same ennobling and vivifying confidence in this Divine Redeemer—not some leaning more to His humanity, and others showing an equally partial and defective preference for His divinity—not some regarding Him rather as an instructor and example, and others drawn to Him more as an atonement—not some fixing an exclusive gaze on Christ without them, and others cherishing an intense and one-sided aspiration for Christ within them—but all reposing a united confidence in Him—"the Son of God." It would be too much to say that subjectively all shall have the same faith so far as vigour is concerned, but a unity in essence and permanence, as well as in object, is an attainable blessing.

Unity of knowledge is also specified by the apostle. $\mathring{E}\pi\acute{\iota}\gamma\nu\omega\sigma\iota\varsigma$ is a term we have considered under i. 17. Christians are not to be, as in times past, some fully informed in one section of truth, but erring through defective information on other points concerning the Saviour—some with a superior knowledge of the merits of His death, and others with a quicker perception of the beauties of His life; His glory the theme of correct meditation with one, and His condescension the subject of lucid reflection with another—but they are to be characterized by the completeness and harmony of their ideas of the power, the work, the history, the love, and the glory of the "Son of God." Olshausen thinks that the unity to which the apostle refers, is a unity subsisting between faith and knowledge, or, as Bisping technically words it—*fides implicita* developing into *fides explicita*. This idea does not appear to be the prominent one, but it is virtually implied, since knowledge and faith are so closely associated—faith not only embracing all that is known about the Saviour, and its circuit enlarging with the extent of information, but also being itself a source of knowledge. The hypothesis of Stier is at once mystical and peculiar. The phrase $\tau o \hat{v}\ v \acute{\iota} o \hat{v}\ \tau o \hat{v}\ \Theta \epsilon o \hat{v}$ is, he says, "the genitive of subject or possession;" and the meaning then is, till we possess that oneness of faith and knowledge which the Son of God Himself possessed in His incarnate state, till the whole community become a son of God in such respects. Now, one great aim of preaching and ecclesiastical organization, is to bring about such a unity. There is no doubt, therefore, that it is attainable; but whether here or hereafter has perplexed many commentators. The opinion of Theodoret—τῆς δὲ τελειότητος ἐν τῷ μέλλοντι βίῳ τευξόμεθα —has been adopted by Calvin, Zanchius, Koppe, and Holzhausen. On the other hand, the belief that such perfection is attainable here, is a view held by Chrysostom, Theophylact, and Œcumenius, by Jerome and Ambrosiaster, by Thomas Aquinas and Estius, by Luther, Calovius, Crocius, and Cameron, and by the more modern expositors, Rückert, Meier, Matthies, de Wette, Meyer, Delitzsch, and Stier. Perfection, indeed, in an absolute sense, cannot be enjoyed on earth, either personally or socially. But the apostle speaks of the results of the Christian ministry as exercised in the church below; for that faith to which Christians are to come exists not in its present phase in heaven, but is swallowed up in vision. Had faith been described only as a means, the heavenly state might have been formally referred to. Still the terms employed indicate a state of perfection that has never been realized, either by the apostolic or by any other church. Phil. iii. 13. Our own view is not materially different from that of Harless, viz., that the apostle places this destiny of the church on earth, but does not say whether on earth that destiny is to be realized. Olshausen says, that Paul did not in his own mind conceive any antithesis between this world and that to come, and he gives the true reason, that "the church was to the apostle one and only one." For the church on earth gradually passes into the church in heaven, and when it reaches perfection, the Christian ministry, which remains till we come to this unity, will be superseded. In such sketches the apostle holds up an ideal which, by the aim and labour of the Christian pastorate, is partially realized on earth, and ought to be more vividly manifested; but which will be fully developed in heaven, when, the effect being secured, the instrumentality may be dispensed with.

εἰς ἄνδρα τέλειον—" to a perfect man."[1] This expressive figure was perhaps suggested by the previous σῶμα

---

[1] Augustine says, *Nonnulli propter hoc quod dictum est—donec occurramus omnes in virum perfectum, nec in sexu femineo resurrecturas feminas credunt— sed in virili.—De Civitate*, xxvii. 16. See also Aquinas and Anselm.

Χριστοῦ. The singular appears to be employed as the concrete representative of that unity of which the apostle has been speaking. Ἀνὴρ τέλειος is opposed to νήπιος in the following verse, which probably it also suggested, and is used in such a sense by the classics. Τέλειος is tropically contrasted with νήπιος in 1 Cor. ii. 6 and iii. 1, and it stands opposed to τὸ ἐκ μέρους. 1 Cor. xiii. 10. Other examples may be seen from Arrianus and Polybius in Raphelius, *Annotat. Sac.* ii. p. 477. Xenophon, *Cyrop.* viii. 7, 6. Hofmann, *Schriftb.* ii. part 2, p. 111, proposes to begin a new period with this clause, connecting it with αὐξήσωμεν of the 15th verse, thus separating it from any connection with the previous ἵνα, and giving it the sense of "let us grow." Such a construction is needlessly involved, and mars the rapid simplicity of the passage. The Christian church is not full-grown, but it is advancing to perfect age. What the apostle means by a perfect manhood, he explains by a parallel expression—

εἰς μέτρον ἡλικίας τοῦ πληρώματος τοῦ Χριστοῦ—"to the measure of the stature of the fulness of Christ." The important term ἡλικία is rendered "full age"—*œtas virilis*—by Morus, Koppe, Flatt, Meier, Matthies, Holzhausen, and Harless. "It is," says Harless, "the ripeness of years in contrast with the minority of youth." Meyer takes it simply as age—age defined by the following words. Chrysostom says, "by stature here he means perfect knowledge." It may signify age, John ix. 21, or stature, Luke xix. 3. The last is the view of Erasmus, Beza, Grotius, Bengel, Rückert, Stier, Ellicott, Alford, and the Syriac version. And to this view we are inclined, first, because ἀνὴρ τέλειος is literally a full-grown man—a man of mature stature; and, secondly, because the apostle gives the idea of growth, and not of age, very peculiar prominence in the subsequent illustrations, and particularly in the sixteenth verse. Though μέτρον, as in the well-known phrase, ἥβης μέτρον (Homer, *Od.* xviii. 217), bears a general signification, there is no reason why it should not have its original meaning in the clause before us, for the literal sense is homogeneous—"measure of stature." Lucian, *Imag.* p. 8, *Opera*, vol. vi. ed. Bipont. The words are but an appropriate and striking image of spiritual advancement. The stature referred to is characterized as that of "the fulness of Christ." This phrase, which has occurred already in the epistle, has been here most capriciously interpreted even by some of those who give ἡλικία the sense of stature. Luther, Calvin, Beza, Morus, and others, take πλήρωμα as an adjective—ἡλικία πεπληρωμένη or ἡλικία πληρωθέντος Χριστοῦ. Luther renders *in der masse des vollkommenen Alters Christi* —"the measure of the full age of Christ." Calvin gives it, *ætas justa vel matura;* Beza has it, *ad mensuram staturæ adulti Christi.* Such an exegesis does violence to the language, and is not in accordance with the usual meaning of πλήρωμα. It is completely out of place on the part of Storr, Koppe, and Baumgarten-Crusius, to understand πλήρωμα of the church, for the phrase qualifies ἡλικία, and is not in simple apposition. Nor is the attempt of Œcumenius and Grotius at all more successful, to resolve πλήρωμα into the knowledge of Christ. For πλήρωμα see under i. 10, 23. Χριστοῦ is the genitive of subject, and πληρώματος that of possession; the connection of so many genitives indicating a varied but linked relationship characterizing the apostle's style. Winer, § 30, 3, *Obs.* i.; Eph. i. 6, 19. The church, as we have seen, is Christ's fulness as filled up by Him, and so this "stature" is of His "fulness"—filled up by Him, and deriving from this imparted fulness all its height and symmetry. Such is the general view of Harless, Olshausen, Meyer, Meier, and Holzhausen, save that they do not take ἡλικία in the sense of stature. But this translation of "stature" appears, as we have said, more in harmony with the imagery employed, for he says, "we grow up" "and the whole body maketh increase of the body." This stature grows just as it receives of Christ's fulness; and when that fulness is wholly enjoyed, it will be that of a "perfect man." The idea conveyed by the figure cannot be misunderstood. The Christian ministry is appointed to labour for the perfection of the church of Christ, a perfection which is no romantic anticipation, but which consists of the communicated fulness of Christ. We need scarcely notice the hallucinations of some of the Fathers —that man shall rise from the grave in the perfect age of Christ—that is, each man's constitution shall have the form and aspect of thirty-three years of age, the age of Christ at

His death. Augustine, *De Civit.* lib. xxii. cap. 15. Another purpose is—

(Ver. 14.) *"Ἵνα μηκέτι ὦμεν νήπιοι*—" In order that we may be no longer children." This and the following verse are illustrative of the preceding one, and show the peculiar weakness and dangers to which believers in an imperfect state are exposed. *Ἵνα* points to a negative and intermediate purpose resulting from that of the preceding verses, but not as if that were taken as realized, for he immediately adds *αὐξήσωμεν*— implying that *τελειότης* has not been attained. The period of maturity is, indeed, future; but meantime, in the hope of it, and with the assistance of the Christian ministry, believers are to be " no longer children;" ceasing to be children is meanwhile our duty. The ministry is instituted, and this glorious destiny is portrayed, in order that in the meantime we may be no longer children. *Νήπιος* is opposed to *ἀνὴρ τέλειος*. Polybius, *Hist.* v. 29, 2. *Μηκέτι* is employed after *ἵνα*. Gayler, *Part. Grœc. Neg.*, cap. vii. A, 1–β, p. 168. We have been children long enough—let us " put away childish things."

The apostle now refers to two characteristics of childhood —its fickleness, and its liability to be imposed upon. Childhood has a peculiar facility of impression—

*κλυδωνιζόμενοι καὶ περιφερόμενοι παντὶ ἀνέμῳ τῆς διδασκαλίας* — " tossed and driven about with every wind of teaching." *Κλυδωνιζόμενοι*—tossed about as a surge; *κλυδωνιζόμενοι* is passive; instances may be found in Krebs and Wetstein. Heb. xiii. 9; Jas. i. 6. The billow does not swell and fall on the same spot, but it is carried about by the wind, driven hither and thither before it—the sport of the tempest. The term *ἀνέμῳ*, dative of cause (Krüger, § 48, 15), is applied to *διδασκαλία*—not to show its emptiness, as Matthies explains it by *windig-leere Einfälle*, but to describe its impulsive power. The article *τῆς* before *διδασκαλίας* gives definitive prominence to " the teaching," which, as a high function respected and implicitly obeyed, was very capable of seducing, since whatever false phases it assumed, it might find and secure followers. Such wind, not from this or that direction only, but blowing from any or " every " quarter, causes the imperfect and inexperienced to surge about in fruitless commotion. The moral phenomenon is common. Some men have just enough of Christian intelligence to unsettle them, and make them the prey of every idle suggestion, the sport of every religious novelty. How many go the round of all sects, parties, and creeds, and never receive satisfaction! If in the pride of reason they fall into rationalism, then if they recover they rebound into mysticism. From the one extreme of legalism they recoil to the farthest verge of antinomianism, having travelled at easy stages all the intermediate distances. Men like Priestley and Channing have gradually descended from Calvinism to Unitarianism; others, like Schlegel and the Countess Ida Hahn-Hahn, make a swift transition from Protestant nihilism to Popish pietism and superstition. Decision and firmness are indispensable to spiritual improvement. Only one form of teaching is beneficial, and all deviations are pernicious. More pointedly—

ἐν τῇ κυβείᾳ τῶν ἀνθρώπων—"in the sleight of men." Κυβεία from κύβος—a cube, or one of the dice—signifies gambling, and then by an easy and well-known process, the common accompaniment and result of gambling—fraud and imposition. Suicer, *sub voce*. The rabbins have the word also in the form of קוּבְיָא. Schoettgen, *Horæ Heb.* p. 775; Buxtorf, *Lex. Tal.* p. 1984. Salmasius renders the term *actio temeraria;* Beza, *variæ et ineptæ subtilitates;* and Matthies, *gewinnsüchtiges Spiel*—"play for the greed of winning." These meanings are inferior to the ordinary translation of *fallacia* by Jerome, the *nequitia* of the Vulgate, and "sleight" of the English version. Theodoret renders the noun by πανουργία. The opinion of Meyer and de Wette, that ἐν denotes the instrumental cause, is scarce to be preferred to that of Harless, Matthies, Olshausen, and Ellicott, who suppose that the preposition signifies the element in which the false doctrine works. The apostle shows how the false teaching wields its peculiar power—acting like a wary and dexterous gambler, and winning by dishonesty without being suspected of it. Οἱ ἄνθρωποι are men, in contrast not with Christ's office-bearers, but with the "Son of God." The next clause is parallel and explanative—

ἐν πανουργίᾳ πρὸς τὴν μεθοδείαν τῆς πλάνης—"in craft

with a view to a system of error." Codex A adds τοῦ διαβόλου. "Craft" is the meaning which is uniformly attached to the first noun in the New Testament. 1 Cor. iii. 19; 2 Cor. iv. 2, xi. 3. Πρός indicates the purpose of the πανουργία which is not followed by any article. The craft is exercised in order to carry out the tricks of error; πλάνης being genitive of subject and defined by the article. Μεθοδεία is rendered by Hesychius τέχνη, and by Theodoret μηχανή, plan or settled system. Aquila renders צָדָה, "to lie in wait" (Ex. xxi. 13), by μεθόδευσε. The Greek verb originally had a good meaning, "to pursue a settled plan," but the bad meaning soon came—its history and use, as in the case of such English words as "prevent" and "resent," showing man's evil nature. This false teaching, ἡ πλάνη, has a systematic process of deception peculiar to itself— ἡ μεθοδεία; and that this mechanism may not fail or scare away its victims by unguarded revelations of its nature and purpose, it is wrought with special manœuvre—πανουργία. There is, however, no distinct declaration that such seduction and mischievous errors were actually in the church at Ephesus, though the language before us seems to imply it, and the apostle's valedictory address plainly anticipated it. Acts xx. 29. We may allude, in fine, to the strange remark of Rückert, that this severe language of Paul against false teachers, sprang from a dogmatical defiance, and was the weak side in him as in many other great characters. But the apostle's attachment to the truth originated in his experience of its saving power, and he knew that its adulteration often robbed it of its healing virtue. Love to men, fidelity to Christ, and zeal for the purity and glory of the church, demanded of him this severe condemnation of errorists and heresiarchs. The spiritual vehemence and truth-love of such a heart are not to be estimated by a common criterion, and when such puerile estimates of Paul's profound nature are formed, we are inclined to ascribe it to moral incompetence of judgment, and to say to Herr Rückert—"Sir, thou hast nothing to draw with, and the well is deep."

(Ver. 15.) Ἀληθεύοντες δὲ, ἐν ἀγάπῃ αὐξήσωμεν εἰς αὐτὸν τὰ πάντα—"But imbued with truth, that in love we should grow up to or into Him in all things." The construction still depends upon ἵνα in ver. 14, δέ placing the following positive clauses in opposition to the preceding negative ones. We must hold, against Meyer, that the context requires ἀληθεύων to be understood as meaning not "speaking the truth," which it often or usually means, but "having and holding the truth,"—"truthing it;" for it is plainly opposed to such vacillation, error, and impositions as are sketched in the preceding verse. Had the false teachers been referred to, speaking truth would have been the virtue enjoined on them; but as their victims, real or possible, are addressed, holding the truth is naturally inculcated on them. We cannot say with Pelagius and others, that it is truth in general to which the apostle refers; but we agree with Theophylact, that the allusion is to ψευδῆ δόγματα, though we cannot accede to his additional statement, that it specially regards and inculcates sincerity of life. Nor can we adopt the translation of the Syriac ܫܪܝܪܝܢ ܒܚܘܒܐ—being "confirmed in love." The Gothic renders *sunja taujandans*—"doing truth," and the Vulgate—*veritatem facientes*. Many of the professed interpretations of the words are, therefore, inferential rather than exegetical. So far from being children tossed, wandering, and deluded with error, let us be possessing and professing the truth.

Many expositors join ἐν ἀγάπῃ to the participle, and impute very various meanings to the phrase. Perhaps the majority understand it as signifying "striving after the truth in love" —and such is in general the view of Erasmus, Calvin, Koppe, Flatt, Rückert, de Wette, and Alford. Some refer it to *studium mutuæ communicationis;* others regard it as meaning a species of indulgence to the weaker and the erring brethren; while others, such as Luther, Bucer, and Grotius, take the participle as pointing out the sincerity and truthful quality of this ἀγάπη—*sincere alios diligentes.* Conybeare's version is very bald—"living in truth and love." But while it is evident that truth and love are radically connected, and that there can be no truth that lives not in love, and no love that has not its birth in truth, still we prefer, with Harless, Meyer, Passavant, Olshausen, and Baumgarten-Crusius, to join ἐν ἀγάπῃ to the verb αὐξήσωμεν—for the words in the conclusion of the following verse have plainly such a connection. Besides, in Pauline style, though Alford denies it, qualifying clauses may precede the verb. See under i. 4. The chief element of spiritual growth is love—ἐν ἀγάπῃ being repeated.

Αὐξήσωμεν is used not in an active, but in an intransitive sense, as Œcumenius, Theophylact, and Jerome understood it. The verb has reference at once to the condition of the νήπιοι —children immature and ungrown, and to the μέτρον ἡλικίας —the full stature of perfect manhood. Our growth should be ever advancing—spiritual dwarfhood is a misshapen and shameful state. Besides, as believers grow, their spiritual power developes, and their spiritual senses are exercised, so that they are more able to repel the seductions of false and crafty teachers.

Harless connects εἰς αὐτόν with ἐν ἀγάπῃ—"in love to Him." But the position of the words forbids such a connection; and though the hyperbaton were allowable, the idea brought ought by such an exegesis is wholly out of harmony with the train of thought. Kühner, § 865. The idea of Harless is, that the spiritual growth here referred to, is growth toward the unity of the faith and knowledge of the Son of God, and that this depends on love to Christ. Now, we know that love to Christ rules and governs the believing spirit, and that it contributes to spiritual advancement; but in the passage before us such a connection would limit the operation of this grace, for here, as in the following verse, it stands absolutely. Ἐν ἀγάπῃ describes the sphere of growth, and the meaning is, not that we are to grow in love, as if love were the virtue in which progress was to be made, but that in love we are to grow in reference to all things—all the elements essential to perfection; love being the means and the sphere of our advancement. The phrase εἰς αὐτόν does not mean "in Him," according to the erroneous rendering of Jerome, Pelagius, Grotius, and Rückert; nor yet "like Him," as is the paraphrase of Zanchius; but "to Him," to Him as the end or aim of this growth, as is held by Crocius, Estius, Holzhausen, Meyer, Olshausen, and de Wette; or "into Him," into closer union with Him, as the centre and support of life and growth. Buttmann, *Neutest. Sprach.* p. 287.

It is almost superfluous to remark, that the syntax of

Wahl, Holzhausen, Koppe, and Schrader, in making τὰ πάντα equivalent to οἱ πάντες, cannot be received. The words mean "as to all"—κατά being the supplement, if one were needed; but such an accusative denoting "contents or compass" often follows verbs which cannot govern the accusative of object. Madvig, § 25. And the phrase is not simply πάντα, but τὰ πάντα. We cannot acquiesce in the view of Harless, who restricts the words to the ἑνότης of ver. 13. Stier, giving the article the same retrospective reference, includes faith, knowledge, truth, and love. That τὰ πάντα has often a special contextual reference, the passages adduced by Harless are sufficient proof. But it is often used in an absolute sense (Rom. xi. 36 ; 1 Cor. viii. 6); or if these, from their peculiarity of meaning, be not reckoned apposite references, we have in addition 1 Cor. xv. 28 ; Mark iv. 11 ; Acts xvii. 25 ; Rom. viii. 32. Besides, "the unity of the faith and of the knowledge of the Son of God," is the end to which Christians are to come, and cannot therefore be well reckoned also among the elements of growth. Meyer's idea is, that τὰ πάντα denotes " all in which we grow," and he supposes the apostle to mean, that all things in which we grow should have reference to Christ. Luther, Beza, Rückert, and Matthies, render *pro omnia*, or *prorsus*. The article gives πάντα an emphatic sense—"the whole ;" and as the reference of the apostle is to a growing body, τὰ πάντα may signify all that properly belongs to it; or, as Olshausen phrases it, "we are to grow in all those things in which the Christian must advance." The apostle first lays down the primary and permanent means of growth, holding the truth—ἀληθεύοντες ; then he describes the peculiar temperament in which this growth is secured and accelerated—ἐν ἀγάπῃ ; then he specifies its aim and end—εἰς αὐτόν ; and, lastly, he marks its amount and harmony—τὰ πάντα. The body becomes monstrous by the undue development of any part or organ, and the portion that does not grow is both unsightly and weak, and not fitted to honour or serve the head. The apostle thus inculcates the duty of symmetrical growth, each grace advancing in its own place, and in perfect unison with all around it. That character is nearest perfection in which the excessive prominence of no grace throws such a withering shadow upon the rest, as to signalize or perpetuate their defect, but in which all is healthfully balanced in just and delicate adaptation. Into Him—

ὅς ἐστιν ἡ κεφαλή, Χριστός—"who is the head—Christ." D, E, F, G, K, L, prefix the article to Χριστός, but A, B, and C, with other authorities, read Χριστός without the article, perhaps rightly. The article in the New Testament is oftener omitted than inserted. When Alford warns against our former rendering—"the Christ"—he evidently puts a polemic meaning into the phrase—which is not necessarily in it. The meaning of κεφαλή in such a connection has been already explained; i. 22. That Head is Christ—Χριστός being placed with solemn emphasis at the end of the verse—being in the nominative and in assimilation with the preceding relative. Stallbaum, *Plato Apol.* p. 41; Winer, § 59, 7. The Head is Christ—one set apart, commissioned, and qualified as Redeemer, and who by His glorious and successful interposition has won for Himself this illustrious pre-eminence.

(Ver. 16.) We would not say with Chrysostom, that "the apostle expresses himself here with great obscurity, from his wish to utter all at once—τῷ πάντα ὁμοῦ θελῆσαι εἰπεῖν;" but we may say that the language of this verse is as compacted as the body which it describes.

ἐξ οὗ—"from whom," that is, from Christ as the Head. This phrase does not and cannot mean "to whom," as Koppe gives it, nor "by whom," as Morus, Holzhausen, and Flatt maintain. The preposition ἐκ marks the source. "From whom," as its source of growth, "the body maketh increase." The body without the head is but a lifeless trunk. It was εἰς αὐτόν in the previous verse, and now it is ἐξ οὗ. The growth is to Him, and the growth is from Him—Himself its origin and Himself its end. The life that springs from Him as the source of its existence, is ever seeking and flowing back to Him as the source of its enjoyment. The anatomical figure is as follows—

πᾶν τὸ σῶμα συναρμολογούμενον καὶ συμβιβαζόμενον—"all the body being fitly framed together and put together." The verb connected with σῶμα as its nominative is ποιεῖται. The first participle occurs at ii. 21, and is there explained. It denotes—"being composed of parts fitted closely to each other." The second participle is used in a tropical sense in the New Testament (Acts ix. 22, xvi. 10; 1 Cor. ii. 16), but here it has its original signification—"brought and held together." The two participles express the idea that the body is of many parts, which have such mutual adaptation in position and function, that it is a firm and solid structure—

διὰ πάσης ἁφῆς τῆς ἐπιχορηγίας—"by means of every joint of the supply." This clause has originated no little difference of opinion. We take it as closely connected by διά with the two preceding participles, and as expressing the instrumentality by which this symmetry and compactness are secured. Meyer, Stier, and Alford, following Bengel, and contrary to its position, join the phrase to the verb ποιεῖται. The Greek fathers, followed by Meyer, render ἁφή by αἴσθησις—touch, sense of touch; *tactum subministrationis* is found in Augustine, *De Civ. Dei*, xxii. 18, and similarly Wycliffe—"bi eche joynture of undir seruynge." But, with the majority of expositors, we take the word as explained by the parallel passage in Col. ii. 19, and as the Vulgate renders it—*junctura*. Ἐπιχορηγία denotes aid or assistance, and is taken by Flatt, Rückert, Harless, and Olshausen, as the genitive of apposition, and as referring to the Holy Spirit. The Greek fathers, and Meyer, render—"through our feeling of divine assistance." Chrysostom says—"that spirit which is supplied to the members from the head, touches, or communicates itself to each single member, and thus actuates it." Their idea is, through the joint or bond of union, which is the supply or aid of the Holy Spirit. We prefer taking ἐπιχορηγίας as the genitive of use—compacted together by every joint which serves for supply. John v. 29; Heb. ix. 21; Winer, § 30, 2 β. Ἐπιχορηγία is thus the assistance which the joints give in compacting and organizing the body. So in Col. ii. 19—διὰ τῶν ἁφῶν καὶ συνδέσμων ἐπιχορηγούμενον. Such is also the general view of Grotius, Zanchius, Calvin, Matthies, Baumgarten-Crusius, and Ellicott. We understand it thus—From whom all the body, mutually adapted in all its parts, and closely compacted by means of every joint whose function it is to afford such aid—

κατ' ἐνέργειαν ἐν μέτρῳ ἑνὸς ἑκάστου μέρους—"according to energy in the measure of each individual part." The MSS.

A and C, with others of less note, along with the Vulgate, Coptic, and Syriac versions, and Chrysostom, Jerome, and Pelagius, read μέλους, which fits the passage so well as an explanation of μέρους, that we can easily conceive how it was introduced. Rückert and Bretschneider take κατ' ἐνέργειαν as an adverbial phrase, but without any real ground. The noun has been explained under i. 19, iii. 7. It signifies "inworking"—effectual influence or operation, and is a modal explanation attached to the following verb. No article is between it and the following noun indicating unity of conception. 'Εν μέτρῳ—"in the measure of every one part," a plain reference to ver. 7. Bernhardy, p. 211. The connection has been variously supposed:—1. Harless takes the phrase in connection with the participle συμβιβαζόμενον. Such a connection is, we think, fallacious, for the compactness and the union of the body depend upon the functional assistance of the joints, not merely on the energy which pervades each part of the body, and which to each part is apportioned. But the growth depends on this ἐνέργεια, or distributed vital power, and so we prefer to connect the clause with the following verb—"maketh increase." And it puzzles us to discover any reason why Harless should understand by the "parts" of the body, the pastors and teachers mentioned in ver. 11. Such an idea wholly mars the unity of the figure. 2. Others, among whom are Stier, Flatt, and Matthies, join the phrase to ἐπιχορηγίας, as if the assistance given by the joints were according to this energy. To this we have similar objection, and we would naturally have expected the repetition of the article, though it is not indispensable. "Energy," "measure," "part," belong rather to the idea of growth than to stability. This energy is supposed by some, such as Theophylact, Grotius, and Beza, to be that of Christ, and Zanchius takes along with this the reflex operation of grace among the members of the church. The whole body—

τὴν αὔξησιν τοῦ σώματος ποιεῖται—"carries on the increase of the body." Col. ii. 19. Though σῶμα was the nominative, σώματος is repeated in the genitive—the body maketh increase of the body, even of itself. Luke iii. 19; John ix. 5; Winer, § 22, 2; Bornemann, *Scholia in Luc.* xxx. p. 5. The sentence being so long, the noun is repeated, especially as ἑαυτοῦ occurs in the subsequent clause. The use of the middle voice indicates either that the growth is of internal origin, and is especially its own—it makes growth "for itself," or a special intensity of idea is intended. See under, iii. 18; Krüger, § 52, 8, 4. The middle voice in this verb often seems to have little more than the active signification (Passow, *sub voce*), but the proper sense of the middle is here to be acknowledged, signifying either that the growth is produced from vital power within the body, or denoting the spiritual energy with which the process is carried on. Winer, § 38, 5, note. The body, so organized and compacted, developes the body's growth according to the vital energy which is measured out to each one of its parts. The purpose of this growth is now stated—

εἰς οἰκοδομὴν ἑαυτοῦ ἐν ἀγάπῃ—"for the building up of itself in love." The phrase ἐν ἀγάπῃ, however, plainly connects this verse with the preceding one. Meyer errs in connecting ἐν ἀγάπῃ with the verb or the whole clause. The words are the solemn close, and the verb has been twice conditioned already. Love is regarded still as the element in which growth is made. And it is not to be taken here in any restricted aspect, for it is the Christian grace viewed in its widest relations—the fulfilment of the law. Such we conceive to be the general meaning of the verse.

The figure is a striking one. The body derives its vitality and power of development from the head. See under i. 22, 23. The church has a living connection with its living Head, and were such a union dissolved, spiritual death would be the immediate result. The body is fitly framed together and compacted by the functional assistance of the joints. Its various members are not in mere juxtaposition, like the several pieces of a marble statue. No portion is superfluous; each is in its fittest place, and the position and relations of none could be altered without positive injury. "Fearfully and wonderfully made," it has its hard framework of bone so formed as to protect its vital organs in the thorax and skull, and yet so united by "curiously wrought" joints, as to possess freedom of motion both in its vertebral column and limbs. But it is no ghastly and repulsive skeleton, for it is clothed with flesh and fibre, which are fed from ubiquitous vessels, and interpenetrated with nerves—the Spirit's own sensational agents and messengers. It is a mechanism in which all is so finely adjusted, that every part helps and is helped, strengthens and is strengthened, the invisible action of the pores being as indispensable as the mass of the brain and the pulsations of the heart. When the commissioned nerve moves the muscle, the hand and foot need the vision to guide them, and the eye, therefore, occupies the elevated position of a sentinel. How this figure is applicable to the church may be seen under a different image at ii. 21. The church enjoys a similar compacted organization—all about her, in doctrine, discipline, ordinance, and enterprise, possessing mutual adaptation, and showing harmony of structure and power of increase.

"The body maketh increase of the body" according to the energy which is distributed to every part in its own proportion. Corporeal growth is not effected by additions from without. The body itself elaborates the materials of its own development. Its stomach digests the food, and the numerous absorbents extract and assimilate its nourishment. It grows, each part according to its nature and uses. The head does not swell into the dimensions of the trunk, nor does the "little finger" become "thicker than the loins." Each has the size that adapts it to its uses, and brings it into symmetry with the entire living organism. And every part grows. The sculptor works upon a portion only of the block at a time, and, with laborious effort, brings out in slow succession the likeness of a feature or a limb, till the statue assumes its intended aspect and attitude. But the plastic energy of nature presents no such graduated forms of operation, and needs no supplement of previous defects. Even in the embryo the organization is perfect, though it is in miniature, and harmonious growth only is required. For the "energy" is in every part at once, but in every part in due apportionment. So the church universal has in it a Divine energy, and that in all its parts, by which its spiritual development is secured. In pastors and people, in missionaries and catechists, in instructors of youth and in the youth themselves, this Divine principle has diffused itself, and produces everywhere proportionate advancement. And no ordinance or member is superfluous. Blessing is invoked on the word preached, and the eucharist is the complement of baptism. Praise is the result of prayer, and the "keys" are made alike to open and to shut. Of old the princes and heroes went to the field, and "wise-hearted women did spin." While Joshua fought, Moses prayed. The snuffers and trays were as necessary as the magnificent lamp-stand. The rustic style of Amos the herdsman has its place in Scripture, as well as the polished paragraphs of the royal preacher. The widow's mite was commended by Him who sat over against the treasury. Solomon built a temple. Joseph provided a tomb. Mary the mother gave birth to the child, and the other Maries wrapt the corpse in spices. Lydia entertained the apostle, and Phœbe carried an epistle. A basket was as necessary for Paul's safety at one time as his burgess ticket and a troop of cavalry at another. And the result is, that the church is built up, for love is the element of spiritual progress. That love fills the renewed nature, and possesses peculiar facilities of action in "edifying" the mystical body of Christ. And, lastly, the figure is intimately connected with the leading idea of the preceding paragraph, and presents a final argument on behalf of the unity of the church. The apostle speaks of but one body—$\pi\hat{a}\nu$ $\tau\grave{o}$ $\sigma\hat{\omega}\mu a$. Whatever parts it may have, whatever their form, uses, and position, whatever the amount of energy resident in them, still, from their connection with the one living Head, and from their own compacted union and mutual adjustment, they compose but one growing structure "in love:"—

> "I'm apt to think, the man
> That could surround the sum of things, and spy
> The heart of God and secrets of His empire,
> Would speak but love. With him the bright result
> Would change the hue of intermediate scenes,
> And make one thing of all theology."

(Ver. 17.) $To\hat{v}\tau o$ $o\hat{v}\nu$ $\lambda\acute{e}\gamma\omega$—"This, then, I say." The apostle now recurs to the inculcation of many special and important duties, or as Theodoret writes—$\pi\acute{a}\lambda\iota\nu$ $\dot{a}\nu\grave{e}\lambda a\beta\epsilon$; and he begins with the statement of some general principles. The singular $\tauo\hat{v}\tau o$ gives a species of unity and emphasis to the following admonitions, for it here refers to succeeding statements, as in 1 Cor. vii. 29; 1 Thess. iv. 15. Other examples may be seen in Winer, § 23, 5. Οὖν is not merely resumptive of the ethical tuition begun in ver. 1 (Donaldson, § 548, 31), but it has reference also to the previous paragraph from vers. 4 to 16, which, thrown out as a digression from ver. 3, runs at length into an argument for the exhortations which follow. Granting, as Ellicott contends, that grammatically οὖν is only resumptive, it may be admitted that such a resumption is modified by the sentiment of the intervening verses. The apostle in resuming cannot forget the statements just made by him—the destined perfection of the church, its present advancement, with truth for its nutriment and love for its sphere, and its close and living connection with its glorified Head. How emphatic is his warning to forsake the sins and sensualities of surrounding heathendom! Rom. xii. 3.

λέγω καὶ μαρτύρομαι ἐν Κυρίῳ—" I say and testify in the Lord." Rom. ix. 1; 1 Thess. iv. 1; 1 Tim. v. 21; 2 Tim. ii. 14, iv. 1. The apostle does not mean to call the Lord to witness, as if ἐν Κυρίῳ could mean "by the Lord," as Theodoret and some of his imitators render it; but he solemnly charges "in the Lord"—the Lord being the element in which the charge is delivered—

μηκέτι ὑμᾶς περιπατεῖν καθὼς καὶ τὰ λοιπὰ ἔθνη περιπατεῖ —"that ye walk no longer as also the other Gentiles walk." 1 Pet. iv. 3. It is to the Gentile portion of the church that the apostle addresses himself. The adverb μηκέτι, "no longer," is here used with the infinitive, though often with ἵνα and the subjunctive. The infinitive, which grammatically is the object of λέγω, expresses not so much what is, as what ought to be. Bernhardy, p. 371; Phryn. ed. Lobeck, p. 371; Winer, § 44, 3, b; Donaldson, § 584. They once walked as Gentiles, but they were to walk so no longer. The verb περιπατεῖν, in its reference to habits of life, has been explained under ii. 2. The καί after καθώς means "also." Hartung, i. p. 126. In some such cases καί occurs twice, as in Rom. i. 13, on which see the remarks of Fritzsche in his *Comment*. A, B, D¹, F, G, the Coptic, the Vulgate, and most of the Latin fathers omit λοιπά. But the great majority of MSS. retain it, such as D², D³, E, K, L, and the Greek fathers, with the old Syriac version. We therefore prefer, with Tischendorf, to keep it, and we

can easily imagine a finical reason for its being left out by early copyists, as the Ephesian Christians seem by λοιπά to be reckoned among Gentiles yet. But being Gentiles by extraction, they are exhorted not to walk as the rest of the Gentiles —such as still remain unconverted or are in the state in which they always have been. Just as a modern missionary might say to his congregation in Southern Africa, Walk not as the other Kaffirs around you. The other Gentiles walked—
ἐν ματαιότητι τοῦ νοὸς αὐτῶν—" in the vanity of their mind." The sphere in which they walk is described by ἐν. Rom. i. 21. Νοῦς is not intellect simply, but in the case of believers it signifies that portion of the spiritual nature whose function is to comprehend and relish Divine truth. Usteri, *Lehrb.* p. 35. It is the region of thought, will, and susceptibility—the mind with its emotional capabilities. Beck, *Seelenl.* p. 49, etc.; Delitzsch, *Psych.* p. 244. In the Hebrew psychology the intellect and heart were felt to act and react on one another, so that we have such phrases as "an understanding heart," 1 Kings iii. 9; "hid their heart from understanding," Job xvii. 4; "the desires of the mind," Eph. ii. 3, etc. That mind was characterized by "vanity." Its ideas and impulses were perverse and fruitless. We do not, with some exegetes, restrict this vanity to the Hebrew sense of idolatry— הֶבֶל—or as Theodoret thus defines it—τὰ μὴ ὄντα θεοποιοῦντα. The meaning seems to be, that all the efforts and operations of their spiritual nature ended in dreams and disappointment. Speculation on the great First Cause, issued in atheism, polytheism, and pantheism; and discussions on the supreme good failed to elicit either correct views of man's intellectual nature in its structure, or to train its moral nature to a right perception of its capabilities, obligations, and destiny; while the future was either denied in a hopeless grave without a resurrection, or was pictured out as the dreary circuit of an eternal series of transmigrations, or had its locality in a shadowy elysium, which, though a scene of classical retirement, was "earthly, sensual, devilish"—the passions unsubdued, and the heart unsanctified. The ethical and religious element of their life was unsatisfactory and cheerless, alike in worship and in practice, the same as to present happiness as to future prospect, for they knew not "man's chief end."

(Ver. 18.) 'Εσκοτισμένοι τῇ διανοίᾳ, ὄντες ἀπηλλοτριωμένοι τῆς ζωῆς τοῦ Θεοῦ—"Darkened in their understanding, and being alienated from the life of God." Critics have differed as to which of the two leading perfect participles the participle ὄντες should be joined. Many attach it to the first of them, such as Clement (*Protrept.* ix. p. 69), Theodoret, Bengel, Harless, Meyer, Stier, de Wette, and the editors Knapp, Lachmann, and Tischendorf. In the New Testament, when any part of the verb εἰμί is joined to a participle, it usually precedes that participle. Besides, in the twin epistle (Col. i. 21) the very expression occurs, the second participle being regarded as a species of adjective. Nor by such a connection is the force of the sentence broken, as Alford contends. For the first participle, ἐσκοτισμένοι, assigns a reason for the previous clause—"darkened, inasmuch as they are darkened;" and the second, ἀπηλλοτριωμένοι, parallel to the first, adjoins another reason and yet more emphatically—ὄντες—being alienated and remaining so. Winer, § 45, 5. The gender is changed to the masculine, agreeing in meaning but not in form with τὰ λοιπὰ ἔθνη, and the entire sense is often said to be a species of parallelism, which might be thus arranged—

> Having been darkened in their understanding,
> By the ignorance that is in them,
> Forasmuch as they have been alienated from the life of God,
> By the hardness of their hearts.

Bengel and Olshausen arrange the verse thus, and Jebb calls it an "alternate quatrain." *Sacred Literature,* p. 192, ed. London, 1831. Forbes, *Symmetrical Structure of Scripture,* p. 21. But such an artificial construction, though it may happen in Hebrew poetry, can scarcely be expected to be found in a letter. Nor does it, as Meyer well argues, yield a good sense. According to such a construction, "the ignorance that is in them" must be regarded as the cause or instrument of their being darkened in their understanding. But this reverses the process described by the apostle, for ignorance is the effect, and not the cause, of the obscuration. Shadow results from darkening or the interception of light. De Wette tries to escape the difficulty by saying that ἄγνοια is rather theoretic ignorance, while the first clause has closer reference to what is practical; but it is impossible to establish such a distinction on sufficient authority. We therefore take the clauses as the apostle has placed them. Διανοίᾳ, explained under ii. 3 and i. 18, is the dative expressive of sphere. Winer, § 31, 3. The word here, both from the figurative term joined with it, and from the language of the following clause, seems to refer more to man's intellectual nature, and is so far distinguished from νοῦς before it and καρδία coming after it. See Rom. i. 21, and xi. 10. Other instances of similar usage among the classics may be seen in the lexicons. Deep shadow lay upon the Gentile mind, unrelieved save by some fitful gleams which genius occasionally threw across it, and which were succeeded only by profounder darkness. A child in the lowest form of a Sunday school, will answer questions with which the greatest minds of the old heathen world grappled in vain.

And that darkness of mind was associated with spiritual apostasy. The participle ἀπηλλοτριωμένοι has been explained in our remarks on ii. 12, and there it occurs also in a description of Gentile condition. Ζωὴ τοῦ Θεοῦ is not a life according to God—ἡ κατὰ Θεὸν ζωή, or a virtuous life, as Theodoret, Theophylact, and others describe it; nor is it merely "a life which God approves," as is held by Koppe, Wahl, Morus, Scholz, Whitby, and Chandler. The term does not refer to course or tenor of conduct—βίος—but to the element or principle of Divine life within us. Vömel, *Synon. Wörterb.* p. 168. Nor has the opinion of Erasmus any warrant, that the genitive is in apposition—*vera vita, qui est Deus.* The genitive Θεοῦ is *genitivus auctoris*—that of origin, as is rightly held by Meyer, de Wette, Harless, Rückert, and Olshausen. It is that life from God which existed in unfallen man, and re-exists in all believers who are in fellowship with God—the life which results from the operation and indwelling of the Holy Ghost. Compare ii. 1-5; Trench, *Syn.* § xxviii. Harless will not admit any allusion to regeneration in this life, but refers us to the Logos in whom is "the life of men." Granted; but that light only penetrates, and that life only pulsates, through the applying energies of the Holy Ghost. The Gentile world having severed itself from this life was spiritually dead, and therefore a sepulchral pall was thrown over its intellect. There could be no light in their mind, because there was no life in their hearts, for the life in the Logos is the light of men. The heart reacts on the intellect. And the apostle now gives the reason—

διὰ τὴν ἄγνοιαν τὴν οὖσαν ἐν αὐτοῖς, διὰ τὴν πώρωσιν τῆς καρδίας αὐτῶν—"through the ignorance which is in them, through the hardness of their hearts." These clauses assign the reason for their alienation from the Divine life—first, ignorance of God, His character, and dispensations; this ignorance being "in them"—τὴν οὖσαν (ὄντες being already employed)—as a deep-seated element of their moral condition. In reference to immortality, for example, how sad their ignorance! Thus Moschus sighs—

"One rest we keep,
One long, eternal, unawakened sleep."

*Nox est perpetua, una, dormienda*, sobs Catullus. The second clause commencing with διά assigns a co-ordinate and explanatory second reason for their alienation from the life of God—the hardness of their hearts. Πώρωσις—obtuseness or callousness, not blindness, as if from πωρός (Fritzsche, *ad Rom.* xi. 7), is a very significant term—their πώρωσις having, as Theodoret says, no feeling—διὰ τὸ παντελῶς νενεκρῶσθαι. The unsusceptibility of an indurated heart was the ultimate cause of their lifeless and ignorant state. The disease began in the callous heart. It hardened itself against impression and warning, left the mind uninformed and indifferent, alienated itself from the life of God, and was at last shrouded in the shadow of death. Surely the Ephesians were not to walk as the other Gentiles placed in this hapless and degraded state. This view of the Gentile world differs from that given in chap. ii. This has more reference to inner condition, while that in the preceding chapter characterizes principally the want of external privilege with its sad results.

(Ver. 19.) Οἵτινες ἀπηλγηκότες ἑαυτοὺς παρέδωκαν τῇ ἀσελγείᾳ—"Who as being past feeling have given themselves over to uncleanness." For ἀπηλγηκότες, the Codices D, E read ἀπηλπικότες, and F, G ἀφηλπικότες; the Vulgate with its *desperantes*, and the Syriac with its ܘܣܒܪܗܘܢ

follow such a reading. But the preponderance of evidence is on the side of the Textus Receptus, which is also vindicated by Jerome, who, following out the etymology of the word, defines it in the following terms—*hi sunt, qui, postquam peccaverint, non dolent*. The heathen sinners are described as being a class—οἵτινες—beyond shame, or the sensation of regret. Kühner, § 781, 4, 5. The apathy which characterized them only induced a deeper recklessness, for they abandoned themselves to lasciviousness; ἑαυτούς being placed, as Meyer says, *mit abschreckendem Nachdruck*—with terrific emphasis. Subjection to this species of vice is represented as a Divine punishment in the first chapter of the Epistle to the Romans —" God gave them up to it." But here their own conscious self-abandonment is brought out—they gave themselves up to lasciviousness. Self-abandonment to deeper sin is the Divine judicial penalty of sin. 'Ασελγεία is insolence (Joseph. *Antiq.* iv. 612, xviii. 13, 1; Plutarch, *Alcibiades*, viii.), and then lust, open and unrestrained. Trench, *Syn.* § xvi. Lobeck, *ad Phryn.* p. 184. This form of vice was predominant in the old heathen world, and was indulged in without scruple or reserve. Rom. i. 24, xiii. 13; 2 Cor. xii. 21; Gal. v. 19. The apostle introduces it here as a special instance of that degraded spiritual state which he had just described in the former verse.

εἰς ἐργασίαν ἀκαθαρσίας πάσης—"to the working of all uncleanness." Εἰς denotes purpose, "in order to"—πάσης being placed after the noun, and not, as more usually, before it. 'Εργασία is not a trade, as in Acts xix. 25, nor the gain of traffic, but as in Septuagint, Ex. xxvi. 1; 1 Chron. vi. 49. 'Ακαθαρσία in Matt. xxiii. 27 signifies the loathsome impurity of a sepulchre; but otherwise in the New Testament, and the instances are numerous, it usually denotes the special sin of lewdness or unchastity. The vice generally is named lasciviousness, but there were many shapes of it, and they wrought it in all its forms. Even its most brutal modes were famous among them, as the apostle has elsewhere indicated. The refinements of art too often ministered to such grovelling pursuits. The naked statues of the goddesses were not exempted from rape (Lucian, *Amores*, 15, p. 272, vol. v. ed. Bipont), and many pictures of their divinities were but the excitements of sensual gratifications. The most honoured symbols in their possessions and worship were the obscenest, and thus it was in India, Asia Minor, Greece, Egypt, and Etruria. There was a brisk female trade in potions to induce sterility or barrenness. In fact, one dares not describe the forms, and scenes, and temptations of impurity, or even translate what classical poets and historians have revealed without a blush. The relics preserved from Herculaneum and Pompeii tell a similar tale, and are so gross that they cannot meet the public eye. The reader will see some awful revelations in Tholuck's *Tract on Heathenism*, published in Neander's *Denkwürdigkeiten*, and translated in the 2nd vol. of the *American Bib. Repository*. Who can forget the sixth satire of Juvenal?

Ἐν πλεονεξίᾳ—" in greediness "—the spirit in which they gave themselves up to wantonness. The explanation of this word is attended with difficulty:—1. Many refer the term to the greed of gain derived from prostitution, and both sexes were guilty of this abomination. Such is the view of Grotius, Bengel, Koppe, Chandler, Stolz, Flatt, Meier, and Bähr. 2. The Greek commentators educe the sense of ἀμετρία—insatiableness; and also Jerome, Erasmus, Calvin, Estius, Röell, Crocius, Harless, Stier, Baumgarten-Crusius, Bisping, and Trench, *Syn.* xxiv. Suicer, in his *Thesaurus*, says, "that such a meaning was no uncommon one among the Greek fathers," but they seem to have got it from the earlier interpretations of this very verse. The meaning assigned it by the Greek fathers cannot be sustained by the scriptural usage to which appeal is made, as 1 Cor. v. 10, Eph. v. 3—as in the first instance it is disjoined by ἤ from πόρνος, but joined by καί to the following ἅρπαξιν according to preponderant authority. In this epistle, v. 2, πορνεία and ἀκαθαρσία are joined by καί, but dissociated from πλεονεξία by ἤ—and in v. 5, πλεονέκτης is termed an idolater. See under Col. iii. 5. See Ellicott. 3. Olshausen takes it as meaning "physical avidity, pampering oneself with meat and drink, or that luxury and high feeding by which lust is provoked." This last meaning suits well, and embodies a terrible and disgusting truth, but it takes πλεονεξία in a sense which cannot be borne out. Beza and Aretius render it *certatim*, as if the heathen outvied one another in impurity. 4. We prefer the common meaning of the noun—"greediness." This spirit of covetous extortion was an accompaniment of their sensual indulgences. Self was the prevailing power—the gathering in of all possible objects and enjoyments on oneself was the absorbing occupation. This accompaniment of sensualism sprang from the same root with itself, and was but another form of its development. The heathen world manifested the intensest spirit of acquisition. It showed itself in its unbounded licentiousness, and its irrepressible thirst of gold. There might be reckless and profligate expenditure on wantonness and debauchery, but it was combined with insatiable cupidity. Its sensuality was equalled by its sordid greed —πλέον, more; that point gained, πλέον—more still. Self in everything, God in nothing.

(Ver. 20.) Ὑμεῖς δὲ οὐχ οὕτως ἐμάθετε τὸν Χριστόν—" But ye did not thus learn Christ." Δέ is adversative, and ὑμεῖς is placed emphatically. Χριστός is not simply the doctrine or religion of Christ, as is the view of Crellius and Schlichting, nor is it merely ἀρετή—virtue, as Origen conceives it (*Catena*, ed. Cramer, Oxford, 1842), but Christ Himself. Col. ii. 6. See also Phil. iii. 10. Harless even, Rückert, Meier, and Matthies, take the verb μανθάνω in the sense of "to learn to know"—" ye have not thus learned to know Christ." But this would elevate a mere result or reference to be part of the translation. The knowledge of Christ is the effect of learning Christ; but it is of the process, not of its effect, that the apostle here speaks. Christ was preached, and Christ was learned by the audience—οὕτως. The manner of their learning is indicated—" Ye have not learned Christ so as to walk any more like the rest of the Gentiles." Your lessons have not been of such a character—they have been given in a very different form, and accompanied with a very different result. Once dark, dead, dissolute, and apathetic, they had learned Christ as the light and the life—as the purifier and perfecter of His pupils. The following division of this clause is a vain attempt—ὑμεῖς δὲ οὐχ οὕτως [ἐστέ]—" but ye are not so;"— ye have learned Christ. Yet such an exegesis has the great names of Beza and Gataker in its support. *Adversaria Sacra*, p. 158.

(Ver. 21.) Εἴγε αὐτὸν ἠκούσατε—" If indeed Him ye have

heard;" not in living person, but embodied and presented in the apostolical preaching. 1 Cor. i. 23. The particle εἴγε does not directly assert, but rather takes for granted that what is assumed is true. See under iii. 2.

καὶ ἐν αὐτῷ ἐδιδάχθητε—" and in Him were taught." Ἐν αὐτῷ signifies, as in other previous portions of the epistle— "in Him," that is, "in union with Him;" i. 7, etc. It does not mean "by Him," as is the rendering of the English version, and of Castalio, who translates—*ab eo*, and of Beza, one of whose versions is—*per eum*. Still less can the words bear the translation—about Him. It denotes, as is proved by Harless, Olshausen, and Matthies, preceded by Bucer—"in Him." Winer, § 48, a. It is the spiritual sphere or condition in which they were taught. They had not received a mere theoretic tuition. The hearing is so far only external, but being "in Him," they were effectually taught. One with Him in spirit, they were fitted to become one with Him in mind. The interpretation of Olshausen gives the words a doctrinal emphasis and esoterism of meaning which they cannot by any means bear. The hearing Christ and in Him being taught, are equivalent to learning Christ, in the previous verse—are rather the two stages of instruction.

The connection of this clause with the next clause, and with the following verse, has originated a great variety of criticisms. The most probable interpretation is that of Beza, Koppe, Flatt, Harless, Olshausen, de Wette, and Winer, and may be thus expressed: "If indeed ye heard Him, and in Him were taught, as there is truth in Jesus—taught that ye put off the old man." This appears to be the simplest and most natural construction. The apostle had been describing the gloom, death, and impurity of surrounding heathenism. His counsel is, that the Ephesian converts were not to walk in such a sphere; and his argument is, they had been better tutored, for they learned Christ, had heard Him, and in Him had been taught that they should cast off the old man, the governing principle in the period of their irregeneracy, when they did walk as the other Gentiles walked. Meyer and Baumgarten-Crusius, preceded by Anselm, Vatablus, and Bullinger, however, connect ἀποθέσθαι in the following verse with ἀλήθεια—it is "the truth in Jesus, that ye put off the

old man;" thus making it the subject of the sentence. The instances adduced by Raphelius of such a construction in Herodotus are scarcely to the point, and presuppose that ἀλήθεια has the same signification as the term νόμος employed by the historian. Meyer lays stress on the ὑμᾶς, but it is added to mark the antithesis between their present and former state. It is certainly more natural to connect it with the preceding verb, but we cannot accede to the view of Bengel, a-Lapide, Stier, and Zachariae, who join it with μαρτύρομαι in ver. 17, for in that case there would be a long and awkward species of parenthesis. "Taught"—
καθώς ἐστιν ἀλήθεια ἐν τῷ Ἰησοῦ—"as there is truth in Jesus." We cannot but regard the opinion of de Wette, Harless, and Olshausen as defective, in so far as it restricts the meaning of ἀλήθεια too much to moral truth or holiness. "What in Jesus," says Olshausen, "is truth and not semblance, is to become truth also in believers." The idea of Harless is, "As there is truth in Jesus, so on your part put off the old man;" implying a peculiar comparison between Jesus and the Ephesian believers addressed. This is not very different from the paraphrase of Jerome—*Quomodo est veritas in Jesu sic erit et in vobis qui didicistis Christum;* nor is the paraphrase of Estius greatly dissimilar. The notions of the Greek fathers are narrower still. Œcumenius makes it the same as δικαιοσύνη. It means τὸ ὀρθῶς βιοῦν, says Chrysostom; and the same view, with some unessential variety, is expressed by Luther, Camerarius, Raphelius, Wolf, Storr, Flatt, Rückert, Meier, and Holzhausen. But the noun ἀλήθεια does not usually bear such a meaning in the New Testament, nor does the context necessarily restrict it here. It is directly in contrast not only with ἀπάτης in the next verse, but with ἐν ματαιότητι—ἐσκοτισμένοι—ἄγνοια in vers. 17, 18. Nor can the word bear the meaning assigned to it by those who make ἀποθέσθαι depend upon it—their rendering being, "If indeed ye heard Him, and in Him were taught, as it is truth in Jesus for you to put off the old man." The meaning held by Meyer is, that unless the old man is laid off, there is no true fellowship in Jesus. But this notion elevates an inference to the rank of a fully expressed idea. We take ἀλήθεια in its common meaning of spiritual truth,

that truth which the mediatorial scheme embodies—truth in all its own fulness and circuit; that truth especially which lodged in the man Jesus—ἀλήθεια and ἐν τῷ 'Ιησοῦ being one conception. The words ἐν τῷ 'Ιησοῦ express the relation of the truth to Christ, not in any sense the fellowship of believers with Him. The historical name of the Saviour is employed, as if to show that this truth had dwelt with humanity, and in Him whom, as Christ, the apostles preached, and whom these Ephesians had heard and learned. We find the apostle commencing his hideous portraiture of the heathen world by an assertion that they were the victims of mental vanity, that they had darkened intellects, and that there was ignorance in them. But those believers, who had been brought over from among them into the fold of Christ, were enlightened by the truth as well as guided by it, and must have felt the power and presence of that truth in the illumination of their minds as well as in the renewal of their hearts and the direction of their lives. Why, then, should this same ἀλήθεια be taken here in a limited and merely ethical sense? It wants the article, indeed, but still it may bear the meaning we have assigned it. The article is in F, G, but with no authority.

The phrase, καθώς ἐστιν ἀλήθεια ἐν τῷ 'Ιησοῦ, points out the mode of tuition which they had enjoyed. The meaning of καθώς may be seen under i. 4, and here it is a predicate of manner attached to the preceding verb. It stands in contrast to οὐχ οὕτως in ver. 20—"ye have not so learned"—ye have not learned Him in such a way—οὐχ οὕτως—as to feel a licence to walk like the other Gentiles, but ye heard Him, and in Him were taught in this way—καθώς—as there is truth in Him. It tells the kind of teaching which they had enjoyed, and the next verse contains its substance. Their teaching was not according to falsehood, nor according to human invention, but according to truth, brought down to men, fitted to men, and communicated to men, by its being lodged in the man Jesus. They were in Him—the Christ—and so came into living contact with that truth which was and is in Jesus. This appears on the whole to be a natural and harmonious interpretation, and greatly preferable to that of Calixtus, Vatablus, Piscator, Wolf, and others, who give καθώς the sense of "that"

—*quod;* ye have been taught that there is truth in Jesus, or what the truth in Jesus really is. Such a version breaks up the continuity both of thought and syntax, and is not equal to that of Flatt and Rückert, who give the καθώς an argumentative sense—"And ye in Him have been taught, for there is truth in Him." Calvin, Rollock, Zanchius, Macknight, Rosenmüller, and others, falsely suppose the apostle to refer in this verse to two kinds of religious knowledge—one vain and allied still to carnality, and the other genuine and sanctifying in its nature. Credner's opinion is yet wider of the mark, for he supposes that the apostle refers to the notion of an ideal Messiah, and shows its nullity by naming him Jesus. "Taught"—

(Ver. 22.) 'Αποθέσθαι ὑμᾶς—"That you put off." The infinitive, denoting the substance of what they had been thus taught (Donaldson, § 584; Winer, 44, 3), is falsely rendered as a formal imperative by Luther, Zeger, and the Vulgate. Bernhardy, p. 358. Our previous version, "have put," is not, as Alford says of it, "inconsistent with the context, as in ver. 25," for perfect change is not inconsistent with imperfect development. But as Madvig, to whom Ellicott refers, says, § 171, *b*—the aorist infinitive in such a case "differs from the present only as denoting a single transient action." See on Phil. iii. 16. It is contrary alike to sense and syntax on the part of Storr and Flatt, to take ὑμᾶς as governed by ἀποθέσθαι—"that you put off yourselves!" and it is a dilution of the meaning to supply δεῖν, with Piscator. 'Αποθέσθαι and ἐνδύσασθαι are figurative terms placed in vivid contrast. 'Αποθέσθαι is to put off, as one puts off clothes. Rom. xiii. 12–14; Col. iii. 8; Jas. i. 21. Wetstein adduces examples of similar imagery from the classics, and the Hebrew has an analogous usage. The figure has its origin in daily life, and not, as some fanciful critics allege, in any special instances of change of raiment at baptism, the racecourse, or the initiation of proselytes. Selden, *de Jure Gentium*, etc., lib. ii. 5; Vitringa, *Observat. Sac.* 139. "That you put off"—

κατὰ τὴν προτέραν ἀναστροφὴν τὸν παλαιὸν ἄνθρωπον—"as regards your former conversation, the old man." It is contrary to the ordinary laws of language to translate these words as if the apostle had written—τὸν παλαιὸν ἄνθρωπον τὸν κατὰ προτέραν ἀναστροφήν. Yet this has been done by Jerome and Œcumenius, Grotius and Estius, Koppe, Rosenmüller, and Bloomfield. Ἀναστρέφω occurs under ii. 3. Gal. i. 13 ; 1 Tim. iv. 12 ; Suicer, *sub voce*. This former conversation is plainly their previous heathen or unconverted state. The apostle says, they were not now to live like the rest of heathendom, for they had been instructed to put off as regards their manner of life, " the old man "—τὸν παλαιὸν ἄνθρωπον. Rom. vi. 6 ; Col. iii. 9. The meaning of a somewhat similar idiom—ὁ ἔσω ἄνθρωπος—may be seen under iii. 16. Rom. vii. 22. It is needless to seek the origin of this peculiar phrase in any recondite or metaphysical conceptions. It has its foundation in our own consciousness, and in our own attempts to describe or contrast its different states, and is similar to our current usage, as when we speak of our " former self " and our " present self," or when we speak of a man's being " beside himself " or coming " to himself." It does not surprise us to find similar language in the Talmud, such as— " the old Adam," etc. Schoettgen, *Hor. Heb.* 516 ; Tr. Jovamoth, 62. Phraseology not unlike occurs also among the classics. Diogenes Laertius, 9, 66. The words are, therefore, a bold and vivid personification of the old nature we inherit from Adam, the source and seat of original and actual transgression. The exegesis of many of the older commentators does not come up to the full idea. This " self " or man is " old," not simply old in sin, as Jerome and Photius imagine— ἐν ταῖς ἁμαρτίαις παλαιωθείς—but as existing prior to our converted state, and as Athanasius says—τὸν ἀπὸ τῆς πτώσεως τοῦ Ἀδὰμ γεγεννημένον—yet not simply original sin. This old man within us is a usurper, and is to be expelled. As the Greek scholiast says, the old man is not φύσις in its essential meaning, but—τῆς ἁμαρτίας ἐνέργεια. With all his instincts and principles, he is to be cast off, for he is described as—

τὸν φθειρόμενον κατὰ τὰς ἐπιθυμίας τῆς ἀπάτης—"being corrupt according to the lusts of deceit." Κατὰ τὰς ἐπιθυμίας stands in contrast with κατὰ Θεόν in ver. 24, and τῆς ἀπάτης with τῆς ἀληθείας of the same verse. The old man is growing corrupt, and this being his constant condition and characteristic, the present tense is employed—the corruption is becoming more corrupt. And this corruption does not describe merely the unhappy state of the old man, for, as Olshausen remarks, this opinion of Harless is superficial. The old man is "corrupt," filled with that sin which contains in it the elements of its own punishment, and he is unfitted by this condition for serving God, possessing the Divine life, or enjoying happiness. That corruption is described in some of its features in vers. 17 and 18. But the apostle adds more specifically—"according to the lusts of deceit." The preposition κατά does not seem to have a causal significance. Harless indeed ascribes to it a causal relation, but it seems to have simply its common meaning of "according to" or "in accordance with." Winer, § 49, d. Ἐπιθυμία is irregular and excessive desire. Olshausen is wrong in confining the term to sensual excesses, for he is obliged to modify the apostle's statement, and say, that "from such forms of sin individual Gentiles were free, and so were the mass of the Jewish nation." But ἐπιθυμία is not necessarily sensual desire. Where it has such a meaning—as in Rom. i. 24, 1 Thess. iv. 5—the signification is determined by the context. The "lusts of the flesh" are not restricted to fleshly longings. Gal. v. 16, 24. The term is a general one, and signifies those strong and self-willed desires and appetites which distinguish unrenewed humanity. Rom. vi. 12, vii. 7; 1 Tim. vi. 9; Tit. iii. 3. The genitive—τῆς ἀπάτης—may be, as Meyer takes it, the genitive of subject, ἀπάτη being personified. Though it is a noun of quality, it is not to be looked on as the mere genitive of quality. These lusts are all connected with that deceit which is characteristic of sin; a deceit which it has lodged in man's fallen nature—the offspring of that first and fatal lie which

"Brought death into the world and all our woe."

Heb. iii. 13; 2 Cor. xi. 3. This "deceit" which tyrannizes over the old man, as the truth guides and governs the new man (ver. 24), is something deeper than the erroneous and seductive teaching of heathen priests and philosophers. These "lusts of deceit" seduce and ensnare under false pretensions. There is the lust of gain, sinking into avarice; of power swelling into ruthless and cruel tyranny; of pleasure falling into beastly sensualism. Nay, every strong passion that fills the spirit to the exclusion of God is a "lust." Alas! this deceit is not simply error. It has assumed many guises. It gives a refined name to grossness, calls sensualism gallantry, and it hails drunkenness as good cheer. It promises fame and renown to one class, wealth and power to another, and tempts a third onward by the prospect of brilliant discovery. But genuine satisfaction is never gained, for God is forgotten, and these desires and pursuits leave their victim in disappointment and chagrin. "Vanity of vanities," cried Solomon in vexation, after all his experiments on the *summum bonum*. "I will pull down my barns, and build greater," said another in the idea that he had "much goods laid up for many years;" and yet, in the very night of his fond imaginings, "his soul was required of him." Belshazzar drank wine with his grandees, and perished in his revelry. The prodigal son, who for pleasure and independence had left his father's house, sank into penury and degradation, and he, a child of Abraham, fed swine to a heathen master.

(Ver. 23.) Ἀνανεοῦσθαι δὲ τῷ πνεύματι τοῦ νοὸς ὑμῶν—"And be renewing in the spirit of your mind." This passive (not middle) infinitive present still depends on ἐδιδάχθητε—δέ being adversative, as the apostle passes from the negative to the positive aspect. As Olshausen has observed, all attempts to distinguish between ἀνανεοῦσθαι and ἀνακαινοῦσθαι are needless for the interpretation of this verse. See Trench, *Syn.* xviii.; Col. iii. 10; Tittmann, p. 60. The ἀνα, in composition, denotes "again" or "back"—restoration to some previous state—renovation. See on following verse. Such moral renovation had its special seat "in the spirit of their mind." This very peculiar phrase has been in various ways misunderstood. Œcumenius, Theophylact, Hyperius, Bull, and Ellicott understand πνεῦμα of the Holy Ghost, the Spirit renewing the mind by dwelling within it διὰ τοῦ πνεύματος τοῦ ἐν τῷ νοὶ ἡμῶν κατοικοῦντος. See Fritzsche, *ad Rom.* vol. ii. p. 2. But, 1. The πνεῦμα belongs to ourselves—is a portion of us—language that can scarcely in such terms be applied to the Spirit of God. 2. Nor does Ellicott remove the objection by saying that πνεῦμα is not "the Holy Spirit exclusively, or *per se*, but as in a gracious union with the human spirit." This idea is in certain aspects theologically correct, but is not conveyed by these words—πνεῦμα in such a case cannot mean God's Spirit, for it is called τοῦ νοὸς ὑμῶν; it is only man's spirit though it be filled with God's. In Rom. viii. 6, the apostle makes a formal distinction. 3. There is no analogous expression. None of the genitives following πνεῦμα are like this, but often denote possession or character as Spirit of God—Spirit of holiness—Spirit of adoption. 4. Nor can we give it the meaning which Robinson has assigned it, of "disposition or temper." Quite like himself is the notion of Gfrörer, that πνεῦμα is but the rabbinical figment of a נְשָׁמָה, founded on a misinterpretation of Gen. ii. 7, and denoting a kind of Divine "breathing" or gift conferred on man about his twentieth year. *Urchrist*. ii. p. 257. 5. Augustine, failing in his usual acuteness, identifies πνεῦμα and νοῦς — *quia omnis mens spiritus est, non autem omnis spiritus mens est, spiritum mentis dicere voluit eum spiritum, quæ mens vocatur. De Trinitate*, lib. xiv. cap. 16. Estius follows the Latin father. Grotius and Crellius hold a similar view, joined by Koppe and Küttner, who idly make the unusual combination a mere periphrasis. 6. Πνεῦμα is not loosely, as Rückert and Baumgarten-Crusius take it, the better part of the mind, or νοῦς; nor can we by any means agree with Olshausen, who puts forth the following opinion with a peculiar consciousness of its originality and appropriateness—" that πνεῦμα is the substance and νοῦς the power of the substance." Such a notion is not supported by the biblical psychology. 7. Πνεῦμα is the highest part of that inner nature, which, in its aspect of thought and emotion, is termed νοῦς. So the apostle speaks of "soul" and "spirit" —ψυχή often standing to σῶμα as πνεῦμα to νοῦς. It is not merely the inmost principle, or as Chrysostom phrases it, "the spirit which is in the mind," but it is the governing principle, as Theodoret explains it—τὴν ὁρμὴν τοῦ νοὸς πνευματικὴν εἴρηκε. This generally is the idea of Röell, Harless, de Wette, Meier, and Turner. Meyer in his last edition retracts his opinion in the second, and says that the usual interpretation is correct, according to which—*das πνεῦμα das menschliche ist*—that πνεῦμα being—*das Höhere Lebensprincip*.

Delitzsch, *Bib. Psych.* p. 144. The renewal takes place not simply in the mind, but in the spirit of it. The dative points out the special seat of renewal. Winer, § 31, 6, a; Matt. xi. 29; Acts vii. 51; 1 Cor. xiv. 20. The mind remains as before, both in its intellectual and emotional structure—in its memory and judgment, imagination and perception. These powers do not in themselves need renewal, and regeneration brings no new faculties. The organism of the mind survives as it was, but the spirit, its highest part, the possession of which distinguishes man from the inferior animals, and fits him for receiving the Spirit of God, is being renovated. The memory, for example, still exercises its former functions, but on a very different class of subjects; the judgment still discharging its old office, is occupied among a new set of themes and ideas; and love, retaining all its ardour, attaches itself to objects quite in contrast with those of its earlier preference and pursuit. The change is not in mind psychologically, either in its essence or in its operation; neither is it in mind, as if it were a superficial change of opinion, either on points of doctrine or of practice; but it is "in the spirit of the mind," in that which gives mind both its bent and its materials of thought. It is not simply in the spirit, as if it lay there in dim and mystic quietude; but it is "in the spirit of the mind," in the power which, when changed itself, radically alters the entire sphere and business of the inner mechanism.

(Ver. 24.) Καὶ ἐνδύσασθαι τὸν καινὸν ἄνθρωπον—"And put on the new man." Col. iii. 10. The renewal, as Meyer remarks, was expressed in the present tense, as if the moment of its completion were realized in the putting on of the new man, expressed by the aorist. The verb also is middle, denoting a reflexive act. Trollope and Burton discover, we know not by what divination, a reference in this phraseology to baptism. The putting on of the new man presupposes the laying off of the old man, and is the result or accompaniment of this renewal; nay, it is but another representation of it. This renewal in the spirit, and this on-putting of the new man, may thus stand to each other as in our systems of theology regeneration stands to sanctification. The "new man" is καινός, not νέος—recent. The apostle, in Col. iii. 10, says τὸν νέον τὸν ἀνακαινούμενον; here he joins ἀνανεοῦσθαι with τὸν καινὸν ἄνθρωπον. In the other epistle the verbal term from καινός is preceded by νέος; in the place before us the verbal term from νέος is followed by καινός. Νέος generally is recent—οἶνον νέον, wine recently made, opposed to παλαιόν, made long ago; ἀσκοὺς καινούς—fresh skins—opposed to παλαιούς, which had long been in use. Matt. ix. 17. So καινὴ διαθήκη is opposed to the economy so long in existence (Heb. viii. 8), but once it is termed νέα (Heb. xii. 24) as being of recent origin. Compare Rom. xii. 2 ; 2 Cor. iv. 16, v. 15, 17; Gal. vi. 15. Hence also, John xix. 41, μνημεῖον καινόν—not a tomb of recent excavation, but one unused, and thus explained, ἐν ᾧ οὐδέπω οὐδεὶς ἐτέθη. Pillon, *Syn. Grecs.* 332. The "new man" is in contrast with the "old man," and represents that new assemblage of holy principles and desires which have a unity of origin, and a common result of operation. The "new man" is not, therefore, Christ Himself, as is the fancy of Jerome, Ambrosiaster, and Hilary, *De Trinitate*, lib. xii. The origin of the "new man" is next shown—

τὸν κατὰ Θεὸν κτισθέντα—" who was created after God." Winer, § 49, d. What the apostle affirms is not that creation is God's work and prerogative and His alone, but that as the first man bore His image, so does the new man, for he is created κατὰ Θεόν, "according to God," or in the likeness of God; or, as the apostle writes in Col. iii. 10, κατ' εἰκόνα τοῦ κτίσαντος αὐτόν. Hofmann's exegesis is feeble and incorrect—*von dem göttlicher Weise geschaffenen Menschen.* The allusion is to Gen. i. 27. What God created, man assumes. The newness of this man is no absolute novelty, for it is the recovery of original holiness. As the Creator stamps an image of Himself on all His workmanship, so the first man was made in His similitude, and this new man, the result also of His plastic energy, bears upon him the same test and token of his Divine origin; for the moral image of God reproduces itself in him. It is no part of our present task to inquire what were the features of that Divine image which Adam enjoyed. See under Col. iii. 10 ; Müller, *Lehre von der Sünde*, vol. ii. p. 482, 3rd ed. The apostle characterizes the new man as being created—

ἐν δικαιοσύνῃ καὶ ὁσιότητι τῆς ἀληθείας—" in the righteousness and holiness of the truth"—the elements in which this creation manifests itself. Morus and Flatt, on the one hand, are in error when they regard ἐν as instrumental, for the preposition points to the manifestation or development of the new man; and Koppe and Beza blunder also in supposing that ἐν may stand for εἰς, and denote the result of the new creation. In Col. iii. 10, as Olshausen remarks, "the intellectual aspect of the Divine image is described, whereas in the passage before us prominence is given to its ethical aspect." In Wisdom ii. 23, the physical aspect is sketched. Δικαιοσύνη is that moral rectitude which guides the new man in all relationships. It is not bare equity or probity, but it leads its possessor to be what he ought to be to every other creature in the universe. The vices reprobated by the apostle in the following verses, are manifest violations of this righteousness. It follows what is right, and does what is right, in all given circumstances. See under v. 9. Ὁσιότης, on the other hand, is piety or holiness—Τὰ πρὸς τοὺς ἀνθρώπους δίκαια καὶ τὰ πρὸς τοὺς θεοὺς ὅσια. Scholium, *Hecuba*, v. 788. The two terms occur in inverted order in Luke i. 75, and the adverbs are found in 1 Thess. ii. 10; Tit. i. 8. The new man has affinities not only with created beings, but he has a primary relationship to the God who made him, and who surely has the first claim on his affection and duty. Whatever feelings arise out of the relation which a redeemed creature bears to Jehovah, this piety leads him to possess—such as veneration, confidence, and purity. Both righteousness and holiness are—

τῆς ἀληθείας—"of the truth." John i. 17; Rom i. 25, iii. 7. This subjective genitive is not to be resolved into an adjective, after the example of Luther, Calvin, Beza, Bodius, Grotius, Holzhausen, and the English version, as if the meaning were—true righteousness and holiness; nor can it be regarded as joining to the list a distinct and additional virtue —an opinion advanced by Pelagius, and found in the reading of D[1], F, G—καὶ ἀληθείᾳ. Those critics referred to who give the genitive the simple sense of an adjective, think the meaning to be "true," in opposition to what is assumed or counterfeit; while the Greek fathers imagine the epithet to be opposed to the typical holiness of the ancient Israel. The exegesis of Witsius, that the phrase means such a desire to please as is in harmony with truth (*De Œconomia Fœderum*, p. 15), is as truly against all philology as that of Cocceius, that it denotes the studious pursuit of truth. Ἡ ἀλήθεια in connection with the new man, stands opposed to ἡ ἀπάτη in connection with the old man, and is truth in Jesus. While this spiritual creation is God's peculiar work—for He who creates can alone re-create—this truth in Jesus has a living influence upon the heart, producing, fostering, and sustaining such rectitude and piety.

The question of natural and moral ability does not come fairly within the compass of discussion in this place. The apostle only says, they had been taught the doctrine of a decided and profound spiritual change, which had developed its breadth and power in a corresponding alteration of character. He merely states the fact that the Ephesians had been so taught, but how they had been taught the doctrine, in what connections, and with what appliances and arguments, he says not. Its connection with the doctrine of spiritual influence is not insisted on. "Whatever," says Dr. Owen, "God worketh in us in a way of grace, He presenteth unto us in a way of duty, and that, because although He do it in us, yet He also doth it by us, so as that the same work is an act of His Spirit, and of our own will as acted thereby." *On the Holy Spirit*, Works, iii. p. 432; Edinburgh, 1852. See under ii. 1.

The apostle descends now from general remarks to special sins, such sins as were common in the Gentile world, and to which Christian converts were, from the force of habit and surrounding temptation, most easily and powerfully seduced.

(Ver. 25.) Διὸ ἀποθέμενοι τὸ ψεῦδος—"Wherefore, having put away lying." By διό—"wherefore"—he passes to a deduction in the form of an application. See under ii. 11. Since the old man and all his lusts are to be abandoned, and the new man assumed who is created in the righteousness and holiness of the truth—ἀλήθεια; the vice and habit of falsehood—ψεῦδος—are to be dropt. Col. iii. 9. It might be a crime palliated among their neighbours in the world, but it was to have no place in the church, being utterly inconsistent with spiritual renovation. The counsel then is—

λαλεῖτε ἀλήθειαν, ἕκαστος μετὰ τοῦ πλησίον αὐτοῦ—"speak

ye truth every one with his neighbour." The clause is found in Zech. viii. 16, with this variation, that the apostle uses μετά for the πρός of the Septuagint which represents the particle in אֶת־רֵעֵהוּ. The "neighbour," as the following clause shows, is not men generally, as Jerome, Augustine, Estius, and Grotius suppose, but specially Christian brethren. Christians are to speak the whole truth, without distortion, diminution, or exaggeration. No promise is to be falsified—no mutual understanding violated. The word of a Christian ought to be as his bond, every syllable being but the expression of " truth in the inward parts." The sacred majesty of truth is ever to characterize and hallow all his communications. It is of course to wilful falsehood that the apostle refers—for a man may be imposed upon himself, and unconsciously deceive others—to what Augustine defines as *falsa significatio cum voluntate fallendi.* As may be seen from the quotations made by Whitby and other expositors, some of the heathen philosophers were not very scrupulous in adherence to truth, and the vice of falsehood was not branded with the stigma which it merited. And the apostle adds as a cogent reason— ὅτι ἐσμὲν ἀλλήλων μέλη—" for we are members one of another." Rom. xii. 5; 1 Cor. xii. 12–27. Christians are bound up together by reciprocal ties and obligations as members of the one body of which Christ is the one Head—the apostle glancing back to the image of the 16th verse. Their being members one of another springs from their living union with Christ. Trusting in one God, they should therefore not create distrust of one another; seeking to be saved by one faith, they should not prove faithless to their fellows; and professing to be freed by the truth, they ought not to attempt to enslave their brethren by falsehood. Truthfulness is an essential and primary virtue. Chrysostom, taking the figure in its mere application to the body, draws out a long and striking analogy—" Let not the eye lie to the foot, nor the foot to the eye. If there be a deep pit, and its mouth covered with reeds shall present to the eye the appearance of solid ground, will not the eye use the foot to ascertain whether it is hollow underneath, or whether it is firm and resists? Will the foot tell a lie, and not the truth as it is? And what again if the eye were to spy a serpent or a wild beast, will it lie to the foot?" etc.

(Ver. 26.) Ὀργίζεσθε καὶ μὴ ἁμαρτάνετε—" Be ye angry and sin not." This language is the same as the Septuagint translation of Ps. iv. 4. The verb רִגְזוּ may bear such a sense, as Hengstenberg maintains,—Prov. xxix. 9; Isa. xxviii. 21; Ezek. xvi. 43,—though Gesenius, Hupfeld, Ewald, and Phillips maintain that the meaning is "tremble," or "stand in awe," as in the English version. Delitzsch also renders *Bebet*—"quake," Tholuck, *Erzittert*, and J. Olshausen, *Zittert*. The Hebrew verb is of the same stock with the Greek ὀργή and the Saxon "rage," and denotes strong emotion. The peculiar idiom has been variously understood: 1. Some understand it thus—" If ye should be angry, see that ye do not sin." Such is the view of Chrysostom, Theophylact, Œcumenius, Piscator, Wolf, Koppe, Flatt, Rückert, Olshausen, Holzhausen, Meier, and Bishop Butler; while Harless supposes the meaning to be—*zürnet in der rechten Weise*—be angry in the right way. Hitzig renders it *grollet, aber verfehlt euch nicht*. 2. Beza, Grotius, Clarius, and Zeltner take the first verb in an interrogative sense—Are ye angry? It is plain that the simple construction of the second clause forbids such a supposition. The opinion of the Greek fathers has been defended by a reference to Hebrew syntax, in which, when two imperatives are joined, the first expresses a condition, and the second a result. Gesenius, § 127, 2; Nordheimer, § 1008. This clause does not, however, come under such a category, for its fair interpretation under such a law would be—" Be angry, and so ye shall not sin," or, as in the common phrase —*divide et impera*—"divide, and thou shalt conquer." The second imperative does not express result, but contemporaneous feeling. 3. Nor do we see any good grounds for adopting the notion of a permissive imperative, as is argued for by Winer, § 43, 2 [1]—" Be angry "—(I cannot prevent it). 1 Cor. vii. 13. As Meyer has remarked, there is no reason why the one imperative should be permissive and the other jussive, when both are connected by the simple καί. 4. The phrase is idiomatic—" Be angry "—(when occasion requires), "but sin not;" the main force being on the second imperative with μή. It is objected to this view by Olshausen and others, that anger is forbidden in the 31st verse. But the anger there repro-

[1] Moulton, p. 392.

bated is associated with dark malevolence, and regarded as the offspring of it. Anger is not wholly forbidden, as Olshausen imagines it is. It is an instinctive principle—a species of thorny hedge encircling our birthright. But in the indulgence of it, men are very apt to sin, and therefore they are cautioned against it. If a mere trifle put them into a storm of fury—if they are so excitable as to fall into frequent fits of ungovernable passion, and lose control of speech or action—if urged by an irascible temper they are ever resenting fancied affronts and injuries, then do they sin. Matt. v. 21, 22. But specially do they sin, and herein lies the danger, if they indulge anger for an improper length of time :—

ὁ ἥλιος μὴ ἐπιδυέτω ἐπὶ τῷ παροργισμῷ ὑμῶν—"let not the sun go down upon your indignation." Similar phraseology occurs in Deut. xxiv. 15; in Philo, and in Plutarch. See Wetstein, *in loc.* Παροργισμός, a term peculiar to biblical Greek, is a fit of indignation or exasperation; παρά —referring to the cause or occasion; while the ὀργή, to be put away from Christians, is the habitual indulgence of anger. 1 Kings xv. 30; 2 Kings xxiii. 26; Neh. ix. 18. Παροργισμός is not in this clause absolutely forbidden, as Trench wrongly supposes (*Synon.* p. 141), but it is to cease by sunset. The day of anger should be the day of reconciliation. It is to be but a brief emotion, slowly excited and very soon dismissed. If it be allowed to lie in the mind, it degenerates into enmity, hatred, or revenge, all of which are positively and in all circumstances sinful. To harbour ill-will; to feed a grudge, and keep it rankling in the bosom; or to wait a fitting opportunity for successful retaliation, is inconsistent with Christian discipleship—" Let not the sun go down upon your wrath." Augustine understands by sun, "the Sun of righteousness" (on Ps. xxv.; *Op.* vol. iv. p. 15, ed. Paris), and Anselm "the sun of reason." Theodoret well says—μέτρον ἔδωκε τῷ θυμῷ τῆς ἡμέρας τὸ μέτρον. The Pythagorean disciple was to be placated, and to shake hands with his foe —πρὶν ἢ τὸν ἥλιον δῦναι. Plutarch, *de Am. Frat.* 488, b.[1]

---

[1] The exegesis of the witty Thomas Fuller may be subjoined: "St. Paul saith —'Let not the sun go down upon your wrath;' to carry news to the antipodes in another world of thy revengeful nature. Yet let us take the apostle's meaning rather than his words—with all possible speed to depose our passion;

(Ver. 27.) Μηδὲ δίδοτε τόπον τῷ διαβόλῳ—"Also give no place to the devil." Μηδέ, not μήτε, is the true reading, upon preponderant authority, and closely connects this clause with the preceding exhortation, not certainly logically or as a developed thought, but numerically as an allied injunction, more closely than what Klotz calls *fortuitus concursus*. *Ad Devar.* ii. p. 6. Hartung, i. 210; Buttmann, § 149; Winer, § 55, 6; Fritzsche, *ad Marc.* p. 157. Ὁ διάβολος is plainly the Evil One, not viewed simply in his being, but in some special element of his character. It is wrong to render it here—the accuser or calumniator, though the Syriac version, Luther, Er. Schmid, Baumgarten-Crusius, and others, have so rendered it. The notion of Harless appears to be too restricted, namely, that the reference is to Satan as endangering the life and peace of the Christian church, not as gaining the ascendency over individuals. To "give place to," is to yield room for, *dare locum*. Luke xiv. 9; Rom. xii. 19; Cicero, *de Natura Deorum*, ii. 33. See also Wetstein, *in loc.* The idea indicated by the connection is, that anger nursed in the heart affords opportunity to Satan. Satan has sympathy with a spiteful and malignant spirit, it is so like his own. Envy, cunning, and malice are the pre-eminent feelings of the devil, and if wrath gain the empire of the heart, it lays it open to him, and to those fiendish passions which are identified with his presence and operations. Christians are not, by the indulgence of angry feeling, to give place to him; for if he have any place, how soon may he have all place! Give him "place" but in a point, and he may speedily cover the whole platform of the soul.

(Ver. 28.) Ὁ κλέπτων μηκέτι κλεπτέτω—"Let the stealer steal no more." We cannot say that the present participle is here used for the past, as is done by the Vulgate in its *qui furabatur*, by Luther, Erasmus, Grotius, Cramer, and others. Even some MSS. have ὁ κλέψας. Ὁ κλέπτων is the thief,

not understanding him so literally that we may take leave to be angry till sunset: then might our wrath lengthen with the days; and men in Greenland, where days last above a quarter of a year, have plentiful scope of revenge. And as the English, by command from William the Conqueror, always raked up their fire and put out their candles when the curfew-bell was rung, let us then also quench all sparks of anger and heat of passion." *Holy and Profane State*, p. 161; London, 1841.

one given to the vice of thieving, or, as Peile renders it, "the thievish person." Winer, § 45, 7; Bernhardy, p. 318; Gal. i. 23. It is something, as Stier says, between κλέψας and κλέπτης. Some, again, shocked at the idea that any connected with the Ephesian church should be committing such a sin, have attempted to attenuate the meaning of the term. Jerome set the example, and he has been followed by Calvin, Bullinger, Estius, Zanchius, Holzhausen, and partially by Hodge. But the apostle condemns theft in every form, and in all probability he alludes to some peculiar aspect of it practised by a section of the idle population of Ephesus. According to the testimony of Eusebius, in the tenth chapter of the sixth book of his *Præparatio Evangelica*, throughout the Eastern world few persons were much affronted by being convicted of theft— ὁ λοιδορούμενος ὡς κλέπτης οὐ πάνυ ἀγανακτεῖ. See 1 Cor. v. 1, and 2 Cor. xii. 21, for another class of sinners in the early church. The apostle's immediate remedy for the vice is honourable industry, with a view to generosity—

μᾶλλον δὲ κοπιάτω ἐργαζόμενος ταῖς ἰδίαις χερσὶν τὸ ἀγαθόν

—"but rather let him labour, working with his own hands that which is good." The differences of reading are numerous in this brief clause. In some MSS. ταῖς χερσίν is omitted, and in others τὸ ἀγαθόν. Clement reads simply τὸ ἀγαθόν, and Tertullian only ταῖς χερσίν. Some insert ἰδίαις before χερσίν, and others affix αὐτοῦ after it. Several important MSS., such as A, D¹, E F, G; the Vulgate, Gothic, Coptic, and Ethiopic Armenian; Basil, Gregory Nazianzen, Epiphanius, Jerome, Augustine, and Pelagius—read ταῖς ἰδίαις χερσὶν τὸ ἀγαθόν. Lachmann adopts this reading; K inverts this order, τὸ ἀγαθὸν ταῖς ἰδίαις χερσίν; but Tischendorf, Hahn, and Alford read τὸ ἀγαθὸν ταῖς χερσίν, with L and the great majority of mss., Chrysostom, Theophylact, Œcumenius, and the Received Version. B has ταῖς χερσὶν τὸ ἀγαθόν. We agree with Stier in saying that Harless and Olshausen overlook the proof, when at once they prefer the shortest reading, and treat τὸ ἀγαθόν as an interpolation taken from Gal. vi. 10. Μᾶλλον δέ—but "rather or in preference" let him work, and with his own hands, ταῖς ἰδίαις χερσίν. Ἴδιος, like *proprius* in Latin instead of *suus* or *ejus*, is here used with distinct force. Matt. xxv. 15; John x. 3; Rom. viii. 32;

Winer, § 22, 7. Manual employment was the most common in these times. Acts xx. 34; 1 Thess. iv. 11. Τὸ ἀγαθόν is something useful and profitable. His hands had done what was evil, and now these same were to be employed in what was good. If a man have no industrious calling, if he cannot dig, and if to beg he is ashamed, his resort is to plunder for self-support:

> "Now goes the nightly thief, prowling abroad
> For plunder; much solicitous how best
> He may compensate for a day of sloth
> By works of darkness and nocturnal wrong."

But if a man be active and thrifty, then he may have not only enough for himself, but even enjoy a surplus out of which he may relieve the wants of his destitute brethren—
ἵνα ἔχῃ μεταδιδόναι τῷ χρείαν ἔχοντι—"that he may have to give to him who hath need." This is a higher motive than mere self-support, and is, as Olshausen remarks, a specifically Christian object. Not only is the thief to work for his own maintenance, but Christian sympathy will cheer him in his manual toil, for the benefit of others. Already in the days of his indolence had he stolen from others, and now others were to share in the fruits of his honest labour—truest restitution. "It is more blessed to give than to receive."

(Ver. 29.) Πᾶς λόγος σαπρὸς ἐκ τοῦ στόματος ὑμῶν μὴ ἐκπορευέσθω—"Let no filthy word come out of your mouth." This strong negation contained in the use of πᾶς with μή, is a species of Hebraism. Winer, § 26, 1; Ewald, *Heb. Gram.* § 576. The general meaning of σαπρός is foul, rotten, useless, though sometimes, from the idea of decay—old, obsolete, ugly, or worthless. Phrynich. ed. Lobeck, p. 337. In Matt. vii. 17, 18, xii. 33, and in Luke vi. 43, the epithet characterizes trees and their fruit, and in the Vulgate is rendered simply *malus*. In Matt. xiii. 48, it is applied to fishes. In all these places the contrasted adjective is ἀγαθός. Locke in his paraphrase has, "no misbecoming word." The term is of course used here in a tropical sense, but its meaning is not to be restricted, as Grotius advocates, to unchaste or obscene conversation, which is afterwards and specially forbidden. It signifies what is noxious, offensive, or useless, and refers to language which, so far from yielding "grace" or benefit, has a tendency to corrupt the hearer. 1 Cor. xv. 33; Col. iv. 6. Chrysostom, deriving his idea from the contrast of the following clause, defines the term thus—ὃ μὴ τὴν ἰδίαν χρείαν πληροῖ; and several vices of the tongue are also named by him, with evident reference to Col. iii. 8. Meier narrows its meaning, when he regards it as equivalent to ἀργός in Matt. xii. 36. May there not be reference to sins already condemned? All falsehoods and equivocations; all spiteful epithets and vituperation; all envious and vengeful detraction; all phrases which form a cover for fraud and chicanery —are filthy speech, and with such language a Christian's mouth ought never to be defiled. "Nothing"—

ἀλλ' εἴ τις ἀγαθὸς πρὸς οἰκοδομὴν τῆς χρείας—"but that which is good for edification of the need." Instead of χρείας, some MSS., as $D^1$, $E^1$, F, G, and some of the Latin fathers, read πίστεως, which is evidently an emendation, as Jerome has hinted. Ἀγαθός, followed by πρός, signifies "good," in the sense of "suitable," or rather serviceable for, examples of which may be found in Kypke, *Observat.* ii. 298; Passow, *sub voce;* Rom. xv. 2. Our version, following Beza, inverts the order and connection of the two nouns, and renders, "for the use of edifying," whereas Paul says, "for edification of the need." Χρείας, as the genitive of object, is almost personified. To make it the genitive of "point of view," with Ellicott, is a needless refinement. The paraphrase of Erasmus, *quâ sit opus*— and that of Casaubon, *quoties opus est,* are defective, inasmuch as they suppose the need to be only incidental or occasional, whereas the apostle regards it as a pressing and continuous fact. The precious hour should never be polluted with corrupt speech, nor should it be wasted in idle and frivolous dialogue. We are not indeed to "give that which is holy to dogs "—a due and delicate appreciation of time and circumstance must govern the tongue. *Juxta,* says Jerome, *juxta opportunitatem loci, temporis, et personœ œdificare audientes.* Conversation should always exercise a salutary influence, regulated by the special need. Words so spoken may fall like winged seeds upon a neglected soil, and there may be future germination and fruit. Trench on *Authorized Version,* p. 120.

ἵνα δῷ χάριν τοῖς ἀκούουσιν—"that it may give grace to the hearers." Χάρις is taken by some to signify what is agreeable or acceptable. Theodoret thus explains it—ἵνα φανῇ δεκτὸς τοῖς ἀκούουσι—"that it may seem pleasant to the hearer;" and the same view has been held by Luther, Rückert, Meier, Matthies, Burton, and the lexicographers Robinson, Bretschneider, Wilke, Wahl, and Schleusner. One of the opinions of Chrysostom is not dissimilar, since he compares such speech to the grateful effect of ointment or perfume on the person. That χάρις may bear such a meaning is well known, but does it bear such a sense in such a phrase as χάριν διδόναι? In Plut. *Agis*. c. 18—δεδωκότα χάριν; Euripides, *Medea*, v. 702—τήνδε σοι δοῦναι χάριν; Sophocles, *Ajax*, 1354—μέμνησ' ὁποίῳ φωτὶ τὴν χάριν δίδως; and in other quotations adduced by Harless, χάριν δοῦναι is "to confer a favour—to bestow a gift." Ast, *Lex Platon. sub voce*. So we have the phrase in Jas. iv. 6; 1 Pet. v. 5; and it is found also in the Septuagint, Ex. iii. 21; Ps. lxxxiv. 12. And such is the view of Olshausen, Harless, Meyer, de Wette, and in former times of Bullinger, Zanchius, and virtually of Beza, Grotius, Elsner, and Calvin. Speech good to the edification of need brings spiritual benefit to the hearer; it may excite, or deter, or counsel—stir him to reflection or afford materials of thought. "A word spoken in season, how good is it!—like apples of gold in pictures of silver." Prov. xxv. 11.

Ver. 30. Καὶ μὴ λυπεῖτε τὸ Πνεῦμα τὸ ἅγιον τοῦ Θεοῦ— "And grieve not the Holy Spirit of God." The term πνεῦμα, and the epithet ἅγιον, have been already explained under i. 13, and solemnly and emphatically is the article repeated. He is called the Spirit of God, and the Holy Spirit of God, each term having a distinct and suggestive significance. This sentence is plainly connected with the previous exhortations, and specially by καί, with the preceding counsel. And the connection appears to be this:—Obey those injunctions as to abstinence from falsehood, malice, dishonesty, and especially corrupt speech, and grieve not the Holy Spirit of God. True, indeed, the Godhead is unruffled in its calm, yet there are feelings in it so analogous to those excited in men, that they are named after such human emotions. The Holy Spirit represents Himself as susceptible of affront and of sorrow. Παροξύνειν is used in a similar passage in Isa. lxiii. 10

by the Seventy, but it is not a perfect representation of the original Hebrew—עצב. We regard it as wrong to dilute the meaning of the apostle, explaining it either with Bengel—*contristatur Spiritus Sanctus non in se sed in nobis;* or rashly affirming with Baumgarten-Crusius, that the personality of the Holy Spirit is only a form of representation, and no proof of what Harless calls objective reality; or still further declaring with Rieger, that the term Spirit may be referred to—*des Menschen neugeschaffenen Geist*—"the renewed spirit of man;" or, in fine, so attenuating the meaning with de Wette as to say, that by the Holy Spirit is to be understood moral sentiment, as depicted from the Christian point of view. It is the Holy Spirit of God within us (not in others, as Thomas Aquinas imagines), that believers grieve—not the Father, nor the Son, but the blessed Spirit, who, as the applier of salvation, dwells in believers, and consecrates their very bodies as His temple. Eph. ii. 22; 1 Cor. vi. 19; Rom. viii. 26, 27. According to our view, the verse is a summation of the argument—the climax of appeal. If Christians shall persist in falsehood and deviation from the truth—if they shall indulge in fitful rage or cherish sullen and malignant dislikes—if they shall be characterized by dishonesty, or idle and corrupt language—then, though they may not grieve man, do they grieve the Holy Spirit of God, for all this perverse insubordination is in utter antagonism to the essence and operations of Him who is the Spirit of truth, and inspires the love of it; who assumed, as a fitting symbol, the form of a dove, and creates meekness and forbearance; and who as the Spirit of holiness, leads to the appreciation of all that is just in action, noble in sentiment, and healthful and edifying in speech. What can be more grieving to the Holy Ghost than our thwarting the very purpose for which He dwells within us, and contravening all the promptings and suggestions with which He warns and instructs us? Since it is His special function to renew the heart, to train it to the abandonment of sin, and to the cultivation of holiness—and since for this purpose He has infleshed Himself and dwells in us as a tender, watchful, and earnest guardian, is He not grieved with the contumacy and rebellion so often manifested against Him? Nay more—

ἐν ᾧ ἐσφραγίσθητε εἰς ἡμέραν ἀπολυτρώσεως—" in whom ye were sealed for the day of redemption." Εἰς is " for "— reserved for, implying the idea of "until;" the genitive being a designation of time by its characteristic event. Winer, § 30, 2, a. For the meaning of the verb ἐσφραγίσθητε, the explanation already given under i. 14 may be consulted. It is a grave error of Chandler and Le Clerc to refer this sealing to the extraordinary gifts of the Spirit; for surely these were not possessed by all the members of the church, nor could we limit the sin of grieving the Spirit to the abuse of the gift of prophecy, which the second of these expositors supposes to be specially intended in the preceding verse. In i. 14, the apostle speaks of the redemption of the purchased possession, and that period is here named "the day of redemption." The noun ἀπολύτρωσις has already occupied us under i. 14, and the comment needs not be repeated. This clause is evidently an argument, or the motive why believers should not grieve the Holy Spirit. If He seal you, and so confirm your faith, and preserve you to eternal glory—if your hope of glory, your preparation for it, and especially your security as to its possession, be the work of God's blessed Spirit, why will you thus grieve Him? There is no formal mention made of the possibility of apostasy, or of the departure of the Spirit. Nor does it seem to be implied, as the verb "sealed" intimates. They who are sealed are preserved—the seal is not to be shivered or effaced. A security that may be broken at any time, or the value of which depends on man's own fidelity and guardianship, is no security at all. Not only does the Socinian Slichtingius hold that the seal may be broken, but we find even the Calvinist Zanchius speaking of the possibility of so losing the seal as to lose salvation: and in such an opinion some of the divines of the Reformation, such an Aretius, join him. The Fathers held a similar view. Theophylact warns—μὴ λύσῃς τὴν σφραγῖδα. See also the *Shepherd of Hermas*, ii. 10, where the phrase occurs —μήποτε ἐντεύξηται τῷ θεῷ καὶ ἀποστῇ ἀπὸ σοῦ. Ambrosiaster says—*Quia deserit nos, eo quod læserimus eum.* Harless admits that the phrase may teach the possibility of the loss of the seal; while Stier displays peculiar keenness against those who held the opposite doctrine, or what he calls—*prædestina-*

*tionisches Missverständniss.* Were the apostle speaking of the striving of the Spirit, or of His ordinary influences, the possibility of His departure might be thus admitted. Gen. vi. 3 ; Isa. lxiii. 10 ; Acts vii. 51. Or if he had said—grieve not the Holy Spirit, by whom men are sealed, or whose function it is to seal men, the hypothesis of Stier would not be denied. But the inspired writer says—"by whom ye were sealed." They had been sealed, set apart, and secured, for perseverance is the crowning blessing and prerogative of the saints ; not to say, with Meyer, that if the view of Harless were correct—παροξύνετε would have been the more natural expression. The apostle appeals not to their fears, lest the Spirit should leave them; but he appeals to their sense of gratitude, and entreats them not to wound this tender, continuous, and resident Benefactor. 2 Cor. i. 21. It may be said to a prodigal son—grieve not your father lest he cast you off; or grieve not your mother lest you break her heart. Which of the twain is the stronger appeal? and this is the question we put as our reply to Alford and Turner. In fine, the patristic and popish phraseology, in which this seal is applied to the imposition of hands, to baptism, or the sacrament of confirmation, is wholly foreign from the sense and purpose of the passage before us, though its clauses have been often adduced in proof. *Catechismus Roman.* § 311 ; Suicer, *sub voce* σφραγίς.

Ver. 31. Πᾶσα πικρία, καὶ θυμὸς, καὶ ὀργὴ, καὶ κραυγὴ, καὶ βλασφημία, ἀρθήτω ἀφ' ὑμῶν, σὺν πάσῃ κακίᾳ—"Let all bitterness, and wrath, and anger, and clamour, and evil-speaking be put away from you, with all malice;"—all feelings inconsistent with love—all emotions opposed to the benign influence and presence of the Divine Spirit—were to be abandoned.

Πικρία—"bitterness"—is a figurative term denoting that fretted and irritable state of mind that keeps a man in perpetual animosity—that inclines him to harsh and uncharitable opinions of men and things—that makes him sour, crabbed, and repulsive in his general demeanour—that brings a scowl over his face, and infuses venom into the words of his tongue. Rom. iii. 14 ; Jas. iiii. 14. Wetstein, under Rom. iii. 14, has adduced several examples of the similar use of πικρία from the classical writers. Aristotle justly says—οἱ δὲ πικροὶ δυσδιάλυτοι, καὶ πολὺν χρόνον ὀργίζονται, κατέχουσι γὰρ τὸν θυμόν. Loesner has also brought some apposite instances from Philo, *Observat. ad N. T.* p. 345. Θυμός is that mental excitement to which such bitterness gives rise—the commotion or tempest that heaves and infuriates within. Donaldson, *New Cratylus*, § 476. 'Οργή (Deut. ix. 19) is resentment, settled and dark hostility, and is therefore condemned. See under iv. 26. Ὁ θυμὸς γεννητικός ἐστι τῆς ὀργῆς—is the remark of Œcumenius. See Trench, *Synon.* § 37; Tittmann, *de Synon.* p. 132; Donaldson, *New Cratylus*, § 477. Κραυγή —"clamour," is the expression of this anger—hoarse reproach, the high language of scorn and scolding, the yelling tones, the loud and boisterous recrimination, and the fierce and impetuous invective that mark a man in a towering rage. *Ira furor brevis est.* "Let women," adds Chrysostom, "especially attend to this, as they on every occasion cry out and brawl. There is but one thing in which it is needful to cry aloud, and that is in teaching and preaching." Βλασφημία—signifies what is hurtful to the reputation of others, and sometimes is applied to the sin of impious speech toward God. It is the result or one phase of the clamour implied in κραυγή, for anger leads not only to vituperation, but to calumny and scandal. In the intensity of passion, hot and hasty rebuke easily and frequently passes into foulest slander. The wrathful denouncer exhausts his rage by becoming a reviler. Col. iii. 8; 1 Tim. vi. 4. All these vicious emotions are to be put away. Κακία is a generic term, and seems to signify what we sometimes call in common speech bad-heartedness, the root of all those vices. 1 Pet. ii. 1. Let all these vices be abandoned, with every form and aspect of that condition of mind in which they have their origin, and of that residuum which the indulgence of them leaves behind it. The word is in contrast with the epithet, "tender-hearted," in the following verse. Now this verse contains not only a catalogue, but a melancholy genealogy of bad passions—acerbity of temper exciting passion—that passion heated into indignation—that indignation throwing itself off in indecent brawling, and that brawling darkening into libel and abuse—a malicious element lying all the while at the basis of these enormities. And such unamiable feeling and language are not to be allowed any apology or indulgence. The adjective πᾶσα belongs to the five sins first mentioned, and πάσῃ to the last. Indeed, the Coptic version formally prefixes to all the nouns the adjective ⲛⲓⲃⲉⲛ—"all." They are to be put away in every kind and degree—in germ as well as maturity—without reserve and without compromise.[1]

(Ver. 32.) Γίνεσθε δὲ εἰς ἀλλήλους χρηστοί—"But become ye kind to one another." The δέ has been excluded by Lachmann, on the authority of B, but rightly retained by Tischendorf. Δέ—"But"—passing to the contrast in his exhortation, he says—"become ye kind to one another"—χρηστοί—full of benign courtesy, distinguished by mutual attachment, the bland and generous interchange of good deeds, and the earnest desire to confer reciprocal obligations. Col. iii. 12. Rudeness

---

[1] Wetstein on Rom. iii. 14. We cannot but quote, from Jeremy Taylor, the following paragraph, unequalled in its imagery and magnificence:—" Anger sets the house on fire, and all the spirits are busy upon trouble, and intend propulsion, defence, displeasure, or revenge; it is a short madness, and an eternal enemy to discourse, and sober counsels, and fair conversation; it intends its own object with all the earnestness of perception, or activity of design, and a quicker motion of a too warm and distempered blood; it is a fever in the heart, and a calenture in the head, and a fire in the face, and a sword in the hand, and a fury all over; and therefore can never suffer a man to be in a disposition to pray. . . . Anger is a perfect alienation of the mind from prayer, and therefore is contrary to that attention which presents our prayers in a right line to God. For so have I seen a lark rising from his bed of grass, and soaring upwards, singing as he rises, and hopes to get to heaven, and climb above the clouds; but the poor bird was beaten back with the loud sighings of an eastern wind, and his motion made irregular and inconstant, descending more at every breath of the tempest, than it could recover by the libration and frequent weighing of his wings; till the little creature was forced to sit down and pant, and stay till the storm was over; and then it made a prosperous flight, and did rise and sing, as if it had learned music and motion from an angel, as he passed sometimes through the air about his ministries here below. So is the prayer of a good man; when his affairs have required business, and his business was matter of discipline, and his discipline was to pass upon a shining person, or had a design of charity, his duty met with infirmities of a man, and anger was its instrument, and the instrument became stronger than the prime agent, and raised a tempest, and overruled the man; and then his prayer was broken, and his thoughts were troubled, and his words went up towards a cloud, and his thoughts pulled them back again, and made them without intention; and the good man sighs for his infirmity, but must be content to lose the prayer, and he must recover it when his anger is removed, and his spirit is becalmed, made even as the brow of Jesus and smooth like the heart of God; and then it ascends to heaven upon the wings of the holy dove, and dwells with God, till it returns, like the useful bee, loaden with a blessing and the dew of heaven."—Works, *The Return of Prayers*, vol. v. pp. 67, 70. London, 1822.

and censoriousness are opposed to this plain injunction. That there should be any allusion in χρηστός to the sacred name Χριστός, is wholly incredible.

Εὔσπλαγχνοι—(1 Pet. iii. 8; Col. iii. 12)—"tender-hearted" —the word being based upon the common and similar use of רַחֲמִים in the Old Testament. The epithet is found, as in Hippocrates, with a literal sense. See Kypke. So far from being churlish or waspish, Christians are to be noted for their tenderness of heart. They are to be full of deep and mellow affection, in opposition to that wrath and anger which they are summoned to abandon. A rich and genial sympathy should ever characterize all their intercourse—

χαριζόμενοι ἑαυτοῖς—"forgiving one another." Ἑαυτοῖς is used for ἀλλήλοις. This use of the reflexive for the reciprocal pronoun has sometimes an emphatic significance— forgiving one another, you forgive yourselves—and occurs in Mark x. 26; John xii. 19; Col. iii. 13, 16; and also among classical writers. Kühner, § 628, 3; Jelf, § 654, 3; Bernhardy, p. 273; Matthiæ, § 489, 6. May not the use of ἑαυτοῖς also point, as Stier says, to that peculiar unity which subsists among Christ's disciples? The meaning of the participle, which is contemporaneous with the previous verb, is plainly determined by the following clause. It does not mean being gracious or agreeable, as Bretschneider thinks, nor yet does it signify, as the Vulgate reads—*donantes*, but *condonantes*. Luke vii. 42, 43; 2 Cor. ii. 10; Col. ii. 13, iii. 13. Instead of resentment and retaliation, railing and vindictive objurgation, Christians are to pardon offences—to forgive one another in reciprocal generosity. Faults will be committed and offences must come, but believers are to forgive them, are not to exaggerate them, but to cover them up from view, by throwing over them the mantle of universal charity. And the rule, measure, and motive of this universal forgiveness are stated in the last clause—

καθὼς καὶ ὁ Θεὸς ἐν Χριστῷ ἐχαρίσατο ὑμῖν—"as also God in Christ forgave you." Some MSS., as B², D, E, K, L, the Syriac, and Theodoret read ἡμῖν; others, as A, F, G, I, and Chrysostom in his text, read ὑμῖν. The latter appears the better reading, while the other may have been suggested by v. 2. Καθὼς καί—"as also"—an example with an implied comparison. Klotz, *ad Devar.* ii. 635. But the presentation of the example contains an argument. It is an example which Christians are bound to imitate. They were to forgive because God had forgiven them, and they were to forgive in resemblance of His procedure. In the exercise of Christian forgiveness, His authority was their rule, and His example their model. They were to obey and also to imitate, nay, their obedience consisted in imitation. 'Ἐν Χριστῷ is "in Christ" as the element or sphere, and signifies not " on account of, or by means of Christ," but ὁ Θεὸς ἐν Χριστῷ is God revealed in Christ, acting in Him, speaking in Him, and fulfilling His gracious purposes by Him as the one Mediator. 2 Cor. v. 19. For the pardon of human guilt is no summary act of paternal regard, but sin was punished, government vindicated, and the moral interests of the universe were guarded by the atonement which Christ presented. The nature of that forgiveness which God in Christ confers on sinners, has been already illustrated under i. 7. That pardon is full and free and irreversible—all sin forgiven; forgiven, not because we deserve it; forgiven every day of our lives; and, when once forgiven, never again to rise up and condemn us. Now, because God has pardoned us, we should be ready to pardon others. His example at once enjoins imitation, and furnishes the pattern. God is presented, as Theophylact says—εἰς ὑπόδειγμα. And thus the offences of others are to be pardoned by us fully, without retaining a grudge; and freely, without any exorbitant equivalent; forgiven not only seven times, but seventy and seven times; and when pardoned, they are not to be raked out of oblivion, and again made the theme of collision and quarrel. According to the imagery of our Lord's parable, our sins toward God are weighty as talents, nay, weighty and numerous as ten thousand talents; while the offences of our fellows toward ourselves are trivial as pence, nay, as trivial and as few as a hundred pence. If the master forgive such an immense amount to the servant so far beneath Him, will not the forgiven servant be prompted, by the generous example, to absolve his own fellow-servant and equal from his smaller debt? Matt. xviii. 23–35.

## CHAPTER V

(Ver. 1.) Γίνεσθε οὖν μιμηταὶ τοῦ Θεοῦ—"Do ye then become followers of God." The collective οὖν connects this verse with the preceding exhortation, and its γίνεσθε δέ— indeed μιμητής is usually accompanied with γίνομαι. The example of God's forgiving generosity is set before them, and they are solicited to copy it. God for Christ's sake has forgiven you; "become ye then imitators of God," and cherish a forgiving spirit towards one another. God's example has an authoritative power. The imitation of God is here limited to this peculiar duty, and cannot, as Stier thinks, have connection with the long paragraph which precedes, especially as the verb περιπατεῖτε, which is so commonly employed, need not be taken as resumptive of περιπατῆσαι in iv. 1. The words μιμηταὶ τοῦ Θεοῦ are peculiar, and occur only in this place, though the terms, in an ethical sense, and with reference to a human model, are to be found in 1 Cor. iv. 16, xi. 1; 1 Thess. i. 6, ii. 14; Heb. vi. 12. Ye should forgive, as God forgives, and thus be imitators of Him, or, as Theodoret says —ζηλώσατε τὴν συγγένειαν. And they are enjoined to study and perfect this moral resemblance by the blessed thought that, in doing so, they feel and act—

ὡς τέκνα ἀγαπητά—" as children beloved;" as children who, in their adoption, have enjoyed so much of a father's affection. They cannot be imitators of God as Creator. They may resemble Him as the God of Providence, in feeding and clothing the indigent; but especially can they copy Him in His highest character as Redeemer, when, like Him, they pardon offenders, and so imitate His royal and lofty prerogative. Disinterested love is a high element of perfection, as described by the great Teacher Himself. Matt. v. 45-48. Tholuck, *Bergpredigt*, Matt. v. 45. This duty of imitation on the part of God's children is well expressed by Photius—

"To institute an action against one who has injured us is human; not to take revenge on him is the part of a philosopher: but to compensate him with benefit is Divine, and shows men of earth to be followers of the Father who is in heaven."[1]

(Ver. 2.) Καὶ περιπατεῖτε ἐν ἀγάπῃ—"And walk in love." The same admonition under another and closer aspect is continued in this verse. The love in which we are to walk is such a love in kind as Christ displayed in dying for us. The apostle had just spoken of "God in Christ" forgiving men, and now, and very naturally, that Christ in the plenitude and glory of His love is also introduced—

καθὼς καὶ ὁ Χριστὸς ἠγάπησεν ἡμᾶς—"as also, or even as, Christ loved us." Tischendorf, after A and B, reads ὑμᾶς, and on the authority of B reads also ὑμῶν in the following clause; but the ordinary reading is preferable, as the direct form of address may have suggested the emendation. The immeasurable fervour of Christ's love is beyond description. See under iii. 19. That love which is set before us was noble, ardent, and self-sacrificing; eternal, boundless, and unchanging as its possessor—more to Him than the possession of visible equality with God, for He veiled the splendours of divinity; more to Him than heaven, for He left it; more to Him than the conscious enjoyment of His Father's countenance, for on the cross He suffered the horrors of a spiritual eclipse, and cried, "Why hast Thou forsaken me?" more to Him, in fine, than His life, for He freely surrendered it. That love was embodied in Christ as He walked on earth, and especially as He bled on the cross; for He loved us—

καὶ παρέδωκεν ἑαυτὸν ὑπὲρ ἡμῶν—"and gave Himself for us"—in proof and manifestation of His love—καί being exegetical. The verb implies full surrender, and the preposition ὑπέρ points out those over whom or in room of whom such self-tradition is made. Usteri, *Lehrb*. p. 117; Meyer on Rom. v. 6; Ellicott on Gal. iii. 13. John xv. 13; Rom. v. 8; Gal. ii. 20. The general idea is, that Christ's love led

---

[1] Τὸ μὲν δίκην ἀπαιτεῖν τὸν ἠδικηκότα, ἀνθρώπινον, τὸ δὲ μὴ ἀμύνεσθαι, φιλόσοφον, τὸ δὲ καὶ εὐεργεσίαις ἀμείβεσθαι λοιπὸν ἤδη θεῖον καὶ μιμητὰς τοῦ ἐν οὐρανοῖς Πατρὸς τοὺς γηγενεῖς ἀποφαῖνον—Ep. 193. See also the Epistle to Diognetus, cap. 10; Justin Martyr, *Opera*, vol. ii. p. 496; ed. Otto, Jenæ, 1843.

to His self-surrender as a sacrifice. He was no passive victim of circumstances, but in active and spontaneous attachment He gave up Himself to death, and for such as we are—His poor, guilty, and ungrateful murderers. The context and not simply ὑπέρ shows that this is the meaning. The manner of His self-sacrifice is defined in the next words—

προσφορὰν καὶ θυσίαν—"an offering and a sacrifice"—*oblationem et hostiam.* Vulgate. The words are in the accusative, and in apposition with ἑαυτόν, forming its predicate nouns. Madvig, § 24. A similar combination of terms occurs in Heb. x. 5, 8, while δῶρα, a noun of kindred meaning, is used with θυσία in Heb. v. 1, viii. 3, ix. 9. Δῶρον usually represents in Leviticus and Numbers the Hebrew קָרְבָּן, and is not in sense different from προσφορά. Deyling, *Observ.* i. 352. The first substantive, προσφορά, represents only the Hebrew מִנְחָה, once in the Septuagint, though oftener in the Apocrypha. It may mean a bloodless oblation, though sometimes in a wider signification it denotes an oblation of any kind, and even one of slain victims. Acts xxi. 26; Heb. x. 10, 18. Θυσία, as its derivation imports, is the slaying of a victim—the shedding of its blood, and the burning of its carcase, and frequently represents זֶבַח in the Septuagint; Ex. xxxiv. 15; Lev. ii. and iii. *passim*, vii. 29; Deut. xii. 6, 27; 1 Sam. ii. 14; Matt. ix. 13; Mark xii. 33; Luke ii. 24, xiii. 1; Acts vii. 41, 42; 1 Cor. x. 18; Heb. vii. 27, ix. 23, 26, x. 12. It sometimes in the Septuagint represents חַטָּאת, sin-offering, and often in representing מִנְחָה it means a victim. See Tromm. *Concord.* We do not apprehend that the apostle, in the use of these terms, meant to express any such precise distinction as that now described. We cannot say with Harless, "that Jesus, in reference to Himself and His own free-will, was an offering, but in reference to others was a sacrifice." On the other hand, "the last term," says Meyer, "is a nearer definition of the former." We prefer the opinion, that both terms convey, and are meant to convey, the full idea of a sacrifice. It is a gift, and the gift is a victim; or the victim slain is laid on the altar an offering to God. Not only is the animal slain, but it is presented to God. Sacrifice is the offering of a victim. The idea contained in προσφορά covers the whole transaction, while that contained in θυσία is a distinct and characteristic portion of the process. Jesus gave Himself as a sacrifice in its completest sense—a holy victim, whose blood was poured out in His presentation to God. In the meantime it may be remarked, that the suffering involved in sacrifice, such unparalleled suffering as Christ endured as our sacrifice, proves the depth and fervour of His affection, and brightens that example of love which the apostle sets before the Ephesian church.

τῷ Θεῷ εἰς ὀσμὴν εὐωδίας—" to God for the savour of a sweet smell "—the genitive being that of characterizing quality. Winer, § 30, 2; Scheuerlein, § 16, 3. Some, such as Meyer and Holzhausen, join τῷ Θεῷ to the verb παρέδωκεν, but the majority connect them with the following phrase:—
1. They may stand in close connection with the nouns προσφορὰν καὶ θυσίαν, with which they may be joined as an ethical dative. Harless says indeed, that εἰς θάνατον is the proper supplement after παρέδωκε, but θυσία here implies it. Εἰς θάνατον may be implied in such places as Rom. iv. 25, viii. 32, but here we have the same preposition in the phrase εἰς ὀσμήν. The preposition εἰς occurring with the verb denotes the purpose, as in Matt. xxiv. 9; Acts xiii. 2. Winer, § 49; Bernhardy, p. 218. In those portions of the Septuagint where the phraseology occurs, κυρίῳ follows εὐωδίας, so that the connection cannot be mistaken. 2. Or the words τῷ Θεῷ may occupy their present position because of their close connection with ὀσμή, and we may read—" He gave Himself an offering and a sacrifice to God for a sweet-smelling savour." It is not easy to say which is preferable, τῷ Θεῷ being peculiarly placed in reference both to the beginning and the end of the verse. The phrase is based on the peculiar sacrificial idiom of the Old Testament—רֵיחַ־נִיחוֹחַ. Gen. viii. 21; Lev. i. 9, 13, 17, ii. 9, 12, iii. 5. It is used tropically in 2 Cor. ii. 14, and is explained and expanded in Phil. iv. 18—" a sacrifice acceptable, well-pleasing to God." The burning of spices or incense, so fragrant to the Oriental senses, is figuratively applied to God. Not that He has pleasure in suffering for its own sake. Nor can we say, with Olshausen, that the Divine pleasure arises wholly from the love and obedience which Jesus exhibited in His sufferings and death. This idea of Olshausen is to some extent similar to that of several recent

writers, who do not give its own prominence to the vicarious suffering of our Lord, but, as we think, lay undue stress on several minor concomitants.

Now the radical idea of sacrifice is violent and vicarious suffering and death. But the theory referred to seems to place the value of Christ's sufferings not in their substitutionary nature, but in the moral excellence of Him who endured them. This is a onesided view. That Jehovah rejoiced in the devoted and self-sacrificing spirit of His Son —in His meekness, heroism, and love, is most surely believed by us. And we maintain, that the sufferings of Christ gave occasion for the exhibition of those qualities and graces, and that without such sufferings as a dark setting, they could never have been so brilliantly displayed. The sacrifice must be voluntary, for forced suffering can have no merit, and an unwilling death no expiatory virtue. But we cannot say with Dr. Halley—" that the sufferings, indirectly, as giving occasion to these acts, feelings, and thoughts of the holy Sufferer, procured our redemption." *Congregational Lecture— The Sacraments*, part ii. p. 271, Lond. 1852. The virtues of the holy Sufferer are subordinate, although indispensable elements in the work of atonement, which consisted in His obedience unto the death. That death was an act of obedience beyond parallel; yet it was also, and in itself—not simply, as Grotius held, a great penal example—but a propitiatory oblation. The endurance of the law by our Surety is as necessary to us as His perfect submission to its statutes. The sufferings of the Son of God, viewed as a vicarious endurance of the penalty we had incurred, were therefore the direct means of our redemption. In insisting on the necessity of Christ's obedience, the equal necessity of His expiatory death must not be overlooked. That Jesus did suffer and die in our room is the fact of atonement; and the mode in which He bore those sufferings is the proof of His holy obedience, which was made "perfect through suffering." But if the manifestation of Christ's personal virtues, and not the satisfaction of law, is said to be the prime end of those sufferings, then do we reckon such an opinion subversive of the great doctrine of our Lord's propitiation, and in direct antagonism to the theology taught us in the inspired oracles. " It pleased the Lord to bruise him"—"Worthy is the Lamb that was slain"—"He suffered once for sins," etc. The uniform testimony of the word of God is, that the sufferings of Jesus were expiatory—that is, so borne in the room of guilty men, that they might not suffer themselves—and that this expiatory merit lies in the sufferings themselves, and is not merely or mainly dependent on those personal virtues of love, faith, and submission, which such anguish evoked and glorified. True, indeed, the victim must be sinless—pure as the fire from heaven by which it is consumed; but its atoning virtue is not to be referred to the bright display of innocence and love in the agonies of immolation, as if all the purposes of sacrifice had been to exhibit unoffending goodness, and bring out affection in bold relief. No; in the sufferings of the "Holy One," God was glorified, the law magnified, the curse borne away, and salvation secured to believers.

Nor do we deem it correct on the part of Abelard and Peter Lombard in the olden time, or of Maurice recently,[1] to regard the love of Christ alone as the redeeming element of the atonement, overlooking the merit of all that spontaneous and indescribable anguish to which it conducted. Such a hypothesis places the motive in the room of the act. It is true, as Maurice remarks, that we usually turn the mind of sinners to the love of Christ, and that this truth comforts and sustains the heart of the afflicted and dying; but he forgets that this love evolved its ardour in suffering for human transgressors, and derives all its charm from the thought that the agony which it sustained was the endurance of a penalty which a guilty world has righteously incurred. The love on which sinners lean is a love that not only did not shrink from assuming their nature, but that feared not to die for them. The justice of God in exacting a satisfaction is not our first consolation, but the fact, that what justice deemed indispensable, love nobly presented. If love alone was needed to save, why should death have been endured? or would a love that fainted not in a mere martyrdom and tragedy be a stay for a convicted spirit? No; it is atoning love that soothes and blesses, and the objective or legal aspect of the work of Christ is not to be merged in any subjective or moral phases

[1] *Theological Essays*, p. 128. Cambridge, 1853.

of it; for both are presented and illustrated in the inspired pages. Even in the first ages of the church this cardinal doctrine was damaged by the place assigned in it to the devil, and the notion of a price or a ransom was carried often to absurd extremes, as it has also been in some theories of Protestant theology, in which absolute goodness and absolute justice appear to neutralize one another.[1] But still, to warrant the application of the term "sacrifice" to the death of Christ, it must have been something more than the natural, fitting, and graceful conclusion of a self-denied life—it must have been a violent and vicarious decease and a voluntary presentation. Many questions as to the kind and amount of suffering, its necessity, its merits as *satisfactio vicaria*, and its connection with salvation, come not within our province.

Harless and Meyer have well shown the nullity of the Socinian view first propounded by Slichting, and advocated by Usteri (*Paulin. Lehrbegriff,* p. 112) and Rückert, that the language of this verse does not represent the death of Christ as a sin-offering. But the Pauline theology always holds out that death as a sacrifice. He died for our sins—ὑπέρ—1 Cor. xv. 3; died for us—ὑπέρ—1 Thess. v. 10; gave Himself for our sins—περί—Gal. i. 4; died for the ungodly—ὑπὲρ ἀσεβῶν—Rom. v. 6; died for all—ὑπὲρ πάντων—2 Cor. v. 14; and a brother is one on whose behalf Christ died—δι' ὃν Χριστὸς ἀπέθανεν—1 Cor. viii. 11. His death is an offering for sin—προσφορὰ περί—Heb. x. 18; one sacrifice for sin— μίαν ὑπὲρ ἁμαρτιῶν θυσίαν—Heb. x. 12; the blood of Him who offered Himself—τὸ αἷμα, ὃς ἑαυτὸν προσήνεγκεν—Heb. ix. 14; the offering of His body once for all—διὰ τῆς προσφορᾶς τοῦ σώματος ἐφάπαξ—Heb. x. 10. His death makes expiation —εἰς τὸ ἱλάσκεσθαι—Heb. ii. 17; there is propitiation in His blood—ἱλαστήριον—Rom. iii. 25; we are justified in His blood—δικαιωθέντες ἐν τῷ αἵματι αὐτοῦ—Rom. v. 9; and we are reconciled by His death—κατηλλάγημεν—Rom. v. 10. He gave Himself a ransom—ἀντίλυτρον—1 Tim. ii. 6; He redeemed us from the curse of the law, being made a curse for us—γενόμενος ὑπὲρ ἡμῶν κατάρα—Gal. iii. 13; Christ our

---

[1] Baur, *Geschichte der Versöhnungslehre*, p. 30. Compare, too, some expressions of Gregory of Nyssa with those of Athanasius and Augustine, and Gregory the Great.

passover was sacrificed for us—ὑπὲρ ἡμῶν ἐτύθη—1 Cor. v. 7. So too in Matt. xx. 28; 1 Pet. i. 18, 19. The view of Hofmann, which is not that commonly received as orthodox, is defended at length by him against Ebrard and Philippi in his *Schriftb.* ii. 329. See Ebrard, *Lehre von der stellvertretenden Genugthuung*, Königsberg, 1857, or a note in his Commentary on 1 John i. 9, in which some important points in the previous treatise are condensed; Thomasius, *Christi Person und Werk*, § 57, *dritter Theil*; and Bodemeyer, *Zur Lehre von der Versöhnung und Rechtfertigung, mit Beziehung auf den Hofmann-Philippischen Streit über die Versöhnungs-lehre*, Göttingen, 1859; Lechler, *das Apost. Zeit.* p. 77. The death of Christ was a sacrifice which had in it all the elements of acceptance, as the death of one who had assumed the sinning nature, and was yet possessed of Divinity—who could therefore place Himself in man's room, and assume his legal liabilities—who voluntarily obeyed and suffered in our stead, in unison with God's will and in furtherance of His gracious purposes. What love on Christ's part! And what an inducement to obey the injunction—" walk in love "—in that love the possession of which the apostle inculcates and commends by the example of Christ! And, first, their love must be like their Lord's love, ardent in its nature and unconquerable in its attachment; no cool and transient friendship which but evaporates in words, and only fawns upon and fondles the creatures of its capricious selection; but a genuine, vehement, and universal emotion. Secondly, it must be a self-sacrificing love, in imitation of Christ's, that is, in its own place and on its own limited scale, denying itself to secure benefits to others; stooping and suffering in order to convey spiritual blessing to the objects of its affection. Matt. xx. 26-28. Such a love is at once the proof of discipleship, and the test and fruit of a spiritual change. John xiii. 35; 1 John iii. 14.

In a word, we can see no ground at all for adopting the exegesis of Stier, that the last clause of the verse stands in close connection with the first, as if the apostle had said—"Walk in love, that ye may be an odour of a sweet smell to God." Such an exegesis is violent, though the idea is virtually implied, for Christian love in the act of self-devotion is pleasing to God.

(Ver. 3.) Πορνεία δὲ, καὶ πᾶσα ἀκαθαρσία, ἢ πλεονεξία—
"But fornication, and all uncleanness, or covetousness." Again the apostle recurs by δέ, which is not without a distinct adversative force, to vices prevalent in the heathen world. Πορνεία—"fornication," a sin which had eaten deep into the Gentile world (Acts xv. 20, 29)—καὶ ἀκαθαρσία—"and uncleanness"—πᾶσα—in every form and aspect of it. Πλεονεξία is not insatiable lust, as many maintain, but "covetousness." See iv. 19. The word was the matter of a sharp encounter between Heinsius (*Exercitat. Sac.* 467) and Salmasius (*De Fœnere Trapezitico*, 121), the latter inflicting on the former a castigation of characteristic severity, because he held that πλεονεξία denoted inordinate concupiscence. The apostle uses the noun in Col. iii. 5, and in all other passages it denotes avaricious greed. Luke xii. 15; Rom. i. 29; 2 Cor. ix. 5. And it is joined to these preceding words, as it springs from the same selfishness, and is but a different form of development from the same unholy root. It is a dreadful scourge —*sæva cupido*, as the Latin satirist names it. More and more yet, as the word denotes; more may be possessed, but more is still desired, without limit or termination. Yet Conybeare affirms that πλεονεξία in the meaning of covetousness "yields no intelligible sense." But, as de Wette and Meyer remark, the disjunctive ἢ shows it to belong to a different class of vices from those just mentioned. It is greed, avarice, unconquerable love of appropriation, morbid lust of acquisition, carrying in itself a violation of almost every precept of the decalogue. See Harris' *Mammon*. As for each of those sins—

μηδὲ ὀνομαζέσθω ἐν ὑμῖν—"let it not be named even among you." Μηδέ—"not even." Mark ii. 2; 1 Cor. v. 11; Herodotus, i. 138—ποιέειν οὐκ ἔξεστι, ταῦτα οὐδὲ λέγειν ἔξεστιν. Not only were these sins to be avoided in fact, but to be shunned in their very name. Their absence should be so universal, that there should be no occasion to refer to them, or make any mention of them. Indelicate allusion to such sins should not soil Christian lips. For the apostle assigns a reason—

καθὼς πρέπει ἁγίοις—"as becometh saints." Were the apostle to say, Let despondency be banished, he might add, as becometh believers, or, Let enmity be suppressed, he might subjoin, as becometh brethren; but he pointedly says in this place, "as becometh saints." "Saints" are not a higher class of Christians who possess a rare and transcendental morality —all genuine believers are "saints." See under i. 1. The inconsistency is marked and degrading between the purity and self-consecration of the Christian life and indulgence in or the naming of those sensual and selfish gratifications. "Let their memorial perish with them."

(Ver. 4.) Καὶ αἰσχρότης—"And filthiness"—*immunditia*, Vulgate. Some MSS., such as A, D¹, E¹, F, G, read ἢ αἰσχρότης, and there are other variations which need not be noted. Tischendorf retains the Textus Receptus, on the authority of B, D³, E², K, L, and almost all mss. Some, such as Œcumenius, imitated by Olshausen, Rückert, Meier, and Baumgarten-Crusius, regard, without foundation, αἰσχρότης as equivalent to αἰσχρολογία. Col. iii. 8. Αἰσχρότητος γέμουσαν τὴν ψυχὴν εἶδεν—Plato, *Gorg.*; *Op.* vol. ii. p. 366, ed. Bekker. The noun denotes indecency, obscenity, or wantonness; whatever, not merely in speech but in anything, is opposed to purity.

καὶ μωρολογία—"and foolish talking." The MSS. just quoted insert ἢ before this noun too, but καί is found in the majority, and in those already named. Not mere gossip or tattle, but speech wretched in itself and offensive to Christian decency and sobriety is condemned. The noun occurs only here, but we have not only the Latin compound *stultiloquium* in Plautus (*Miles Gloriosus*, ii. 3, 25, the scene of which drama is laid at Ephesus), but also the Latin form *morologus* in the same dramatist. *Persa*, i. 1, 50. The Emperor Hadrian, in his well-known address to his departing spirit, ends the melancholy ode with these words—

"Nec, ut soles, dabis jocos."

The term may look back to iv. 29, and is, as Trench says, the talk of fools, which is folly and sin together. *Synon.* § 34.

ἡ εὐτραπελία — "or jesting" — the disjunctive being employed. This noun is a ἅπαξ λεγόμενον as well as the preceding. It denotes urbanity — *urbanitas* — and as its derivation implies, dexterity of *turning* a discourse—παρὰ τὸ εὖ τρέπεσθαι τὸν λόγον; then wit or humour; and lastly deceptive speech, so formed that the speaker easily contrives to wriggle out of its meaning or engagements. Josephus, *Antiq.* xii. 4, 3; Thucyd. ii. 41; Plato, *Pol.* viii. 563; Arist. *Ethic. Nicom.* iv. 8; Pindar, *Pythia, Carmen* i. 176, iv. 186; Cicero, *Ep. ad Div.* vii. 32, *Opera*, p. 716, ed. Nobbe, 1850. It is defined in the Etymologicon Magnum—ἡ μωρολογία, κουφότης, ἀπαιδευσία —levity, or grossness. Chrysostom's amplified definition is—ὁ ποικίλος, ὁ παντοδαπός, ὁ ἄστακτος, ὁ εὔκολος, ὁ πάντα γινόμενος—" the man called εὐτράπελος is the man who is versatile, of all complexions, the restless one, the fickle one, the man who is everything or anything." Jerome also says of it—*vel urbana verba, vel rustica, vel turpia, vel faceta.* It is here used evidently in a bad sense, almost equivalent to βωμόλοχος, from which Aristotle distinguishes it, and denotes that ribaldry, studied artifice, and polite equivoque, which are worse in many cases than open foulness of tongue. The distinction which Jerome makes between μωρολογία and εὐτραπελία is indicated by the Latin terms, *stultiloquium* and *scurrilitas*. Pleasantry of every sort is not condemned by the apostle. He seems to refer to wit in connection with lewdness—*double entendre.* See Trench on the history of the word. *Synon.* § 34. The vices here mentioned are severely reprobated by Clement in the sixth chapter of the second book of his Παιδαγωγός. Allusions to such "jestings" are not unfrequent in the classics. Even the author of the "*Ars Amoris*" pleads with Augustus, that his writings are not so bad as others referred to—

" Quid si scripsissem Mimos obscœna jocantes,
Qui vetiti semper crimen amoris habent," etc.

τὰ οὐκ ἀνήκοντα—" which are not becoming things"— in opposition to the concluding clause in the previous verse. Another reading—ἃ οὐκ ἀνῆκεν—is supported by A, B, and C, while Chrysostom and Theodoret, following the reading in Rom. i. 28, read τὰ μὴ καθήκοντα—but wrongly; for here the apostle refers to an objective reality. Winer, § 55, 5. Buttmann, *Gram. des Neutest. Sprach.* § 148, 7. Suidas defines ἀνῆκον by πρέπον. The Vulgate confines the connection of this clause to the term immediately preceding —*scurrilitas quæ ad rem non pertinet*. All the three vices

—but certainly, from the contrast in the following clause, the two previous ones — may be included. Such sins of the tongue are to be superseded by thanksgiving[1]—

ἀλλὰ μᾶλλον εὐχαριστία, "but rather giving of thanks." There is a meaning which may attach to εὐχαριστία, which is plausible, but appears to be wholly contrary to Pauline usage. It signifies, in the opinion of some, pleasant and grateful discourse, as opposed to that foolish and indecorous levity which the apostle condemns. Jerome says—*Forsitan igitur gratiarum actio in hoc loco non ista nominata juxta quam gratias agimus Deo, sed juxta quam grati, sive gratiosi et salsi apud homines appellamur.* So Clement of Alexandria — χαριεντιστέον τε οὐ γελωτοποιητέον. This opinion has been followed by Calvin, Cajetan, Heinsius, Salmasius, Hammond, Semler, Michaelis, Meier, and by Wahl, Wilke, and Bretschneider. However consonant to the context this interpretation may appear, it cannot be sustained by any analogies. Such examples as γυνὴ χάριτος or γυνὴ εὐχάριστος belong not to New Testament usage. We therefore prefer the ordinary signification, "thanksgiving," and it is contrary to sound hermeneutical discipline on the part of Bullinger, Musculus,

[1] Fergusson says, "honest and sometimes piercing ironies were used by holy men in Scripture." One of the best descriptions of wit ever written is that of Barrow, in his sermon on this text. "It is," he says, "indeed a thing so versatile and multiform, appearing in so many shapes, so many postures, so many garbs, so variously apprehended by several eyes and judgments, that it seemeth no less hard to settle a clear and certain notion thereof, than to make a portrait of Proteus, or to define the figure of the fleeting air. Sometimes it lieth in pat allusion to a known story, or in seasonable application of a trivial saying, or in forging an apposite tale : sometimes it playeth in words and phrases, taking advantage from the ambiguity of their sense, or the affinity of their sound : sometimes it is wrapped in a dress of humorous expression : sometimes it lurketh under an odd similitude ; sometimes it is lodged in a sly question, in a smart answer, in a quirkish reason, in a shrewd intimation, in cunningly diverting or cleverly retorting an objection : sometimes it is couched in a bold scheme of speech, in a tart irony, in a lusty hyperbole, in a startling metaphor, in a plausible reconciling of contradictions, or in acute nonsense : sometimes a scenical representation of persons or things, a counterfeit speech, a mimical look or gesture passeth for it : sometimes an affected simplicity, sometimes a presumptuous bluntness giveth it being : sometimes it riseth from a lucky hitting upon what is strange, sometimes from a crafty wresting obvious matter to the purpose : often it consisteth in one knows not what, and springeth up one can hardly tell how. Its ways are unaccountable and inexplicable, being answerable to the numberless rovings of fancy and windings of language."— Works, vol. i. p. 131, Edin. 1841.

and Zanchius, to take the term in both acceptations. The verb usually supplied is ἔστω—"but let there be rather thanksgiving." Examples of such brachylogy are numerous. Kühner, § 852, i.; Jelf, § 895; Winer, § 66, 1, 2. But why may not ὀνομαζέσθω still guide the construction? "Rather let thanksgiving be named"—let there be vocal expression to your grateful emotions. Bengel, justified by Stier, supplies ἀνήκει, which is not a probable supplement. For the apostolic idea of the duty of thanksgiving, the reader may compare v. 20; Col. ii. 7, iv. 2; 1 Thess. v. 18. The Christian life is one of continuous reception, which should prompt to continuous praise. Were this the ruling emotion, an effectual check should be given to such sins of the tongue as are here condemned.

(Ver. 5.) Τοῦτο γὰρ ἴστε γινώσκοντες, "For this ye know—being as you are aware." Winer, § 45, 8. Γάρ states a reason, and an awful and solemn one it is. For the ἐστε of the Textus Receptus, found in D³, E, H, L, and the Syriac, ἴστε is now generally acknowledged to be the genuine reading, as having the preponderance of authority, as A, B, D¹, F, G, the Vulgate (*scitote intelligentes*), Coptic, and several of the Fathers. Ἴστε γινώσκοντες is a peculiar construction, and is not wholly identical with the Hebrew usage of connecting two parts of the same Hebrew verb together, or with the similar usage in Greek. Kühner, 675, 3; Jelf, § 708, 3. The instances adduced from the Septuagint, Gen. xv. 13—γινώσκων γνώσῃ, and Jer. xlii. 19¹—γνόντες γνώσεσθε, are therefore not in point, as ἴστε is the second person plural of οἶδα. We take the phrase to be in the indicative—as is done by Calvin, Harless, Meyer, and de Wette, for the appeal in the participle is to a matter of fact—and not in the imperative, as is found in the Vulgate, and is thought by Estius, Bengel, Rückert, Matthies, and Stier. Wickliffe renders—"Wite ye this and vndirstonde" (see under verse 3). Ye know—

ὅτι πᾶς πόρνος, ἢ ἀκάθαρτος, ἢ πλεονέκτης, ὅς ἐστιν εἰδωλολάτρης—"that every whoremonger or unclean person, or covetous man who is an idolater." Col. iii. 5. Πλεονέκτης is explained under the preceding verse. See under iv. 19. The differences of reading are these:—Griesbach, Lach-

---

[1] In Jer. xlii. 19, Theodotion reads—ἴστι γινώσκοντις.

mann, and Alford read ὅ after B and Jerome who has *quod*. Other MSS., such as F, G, have εἰδωλολατρεία, which reading is found in the Vulgate, Cyprian, and Ambrosiaster. The first reading, found in A, D, E, K, L, the Syriac, and Coptic, seems to be the correct one—the others are merely emendations. Harless, Meier, von Gerlach, and Stier, suppose the relative to refer to the three antecedents. Harless can adduce no reason for this opinion save his own view of the meaning of πλεονεξία. As in Col. iii. 5, the apostle particularizes covetousness as idolatry. Wetstein and Schoettgen adduce rabbinical citations in proof that some sins were named by the Jews idolatry, but to little purpose in the present instance. The covetous man makes a god of his possessions, and offers to them the entire homage of his heart. That world of which the love and worship fill his nature, is his god, for whose sake he rises up early and sits up late. The phrase is not to be diluted into this—"who is as bad as an heathen," as in the loose paraphrase of Barlee—but it means, that the covetous man deifying the world rejects the true Jehovah. Job viii. 13; Matt. vi. 24. Every one of them—

οὐκ ἔχει κληρονομίαν—"has no inheritance," and shall or can have none; the present stating a fact, or law unalterably determined. Winer, § 40, 2. Πᾶς ... οὐκ. Winer, § 26; see under iv. 29—and for κληρονομία, see under i. 11, iii. 6. And the very name of the inheritance vindicates this exclusion; for it is—

ἐν τῇ βασιλείᾳ τοῦ Χριστοῦ καὶ Θεοῦ—"in the kingdom of Christ and God." Phil. iii. 19. F and G read εἰς τὴν βασιλείαν τοῦ Θεοῦ καὶ Χριστοῦ—an evident emendation. The genitive Χριστοῦ has its analogy in the expressions used Matt. xvi. 28; 2 Tim. iv. 1, 18. βασιλεία and ἐκκλησία have been sometimes distinguished, as if the first referred to the church in heaven, and the other to the church on earth, while others reverse this opinion. Usteri, *Paulin. Lehrbeg.* 352; Koppe, *Excursus I. ad Thessalon.* But such a distinction cannot be sustained. βασιλεία is used with perfect propriety here; ἐκκλησία is the church called and collected together, into which one of these bad characters may intrude himself; but βασιλεία is the kingdom under the special jurisdiction of its King, and no one can or dare enter without His sanction;

for it is, as Origen calls it, πόλις εὐνομουμένη. That kingdom which begins here, but is fully developed in the heavens, is that of Christ and God, the second noun wanting the article. Winer, § 19, 4. We do not apprehend that the apostle means to identify Christ and God, though the latter noun wants the article. Though Christ is possessed of Divinity, yet He is distinct from God. Jerome, indeed, says—*ipsum Deum et Christum intelligamus . . . ubi autem Deus est, tam Pater quam Filius intelligi potest.* Such is the general view of Beza, Zanchius, Glassius, Bengel, Rückert, Harless, Hodge, and Middleton. Others, such as Meyer, Stier, Olshausen, and Ellicott, suppose the apostle to mean that the kingdom of Christ is also the kingdom God—"in the kingdom which is Christ's and God's." Θεός often wants the article, and the use of it here would have seemed to deny the real Divinity of Christ. Christ is called God in other places of Paul's writings; but the idea here is, that the inheritance is common to Christ and God. The identity of the kingdom is the principal thought, and the apostle does not formally say—καὶ τῇ τοῦ Θεοῦ, as such phraseology might imply that there were two kingdoms; nor, as Stier remarks, does he even say—τοῦ Θεοῦ, as he wishes to show the close connection, or place both nouns in a single conception. Bishop Middleton's canon does not therefore apply, whatever may be thought of its application to such passages as Tit. ii. 13, 2 Pet. i. 1, Jude 4, in all of which the pronoun ἡμῶν is inserted, while in two of them σωτήρ is an attributive, and in one of them δεσπότης has a similar meaning. Θεοῦ appears to be added, not merely to exhibit the authority by which the exclusion of selfish and covetous men is warranted, but principally to show the righteous doom of the idolater who has chosen a different deity. It is baseless to say, with Grotius, Vatablus, Gerhardt, Moldenhauer, and Baumgarten, that Christ's kingdom exists on earth and God's in heaven. The kingdom is named Christ's inasmuch as He secures it, prepares it, holds it for us, and at length conveys us to it; and it is God's as it is His originally, and would have remained His though Christ had never come; for He is in Christ, and Christ's mediation is only the working out of His gracious purposes—God having committed the administration of this kingdom into His hands. Into Christ's kingdom the fornicator and sensualist cannot come; for, unsanctified and unprepared, they are not susceptible of its spiritual enjoyments, and are filled with antipathy to its unfleshly occupations; and specially into God's kingdom "the covetous man, who is an idolater," cannot come, for that God is not his god, and disowning the God of the kingdom, he is self-excluded. As his treasure is not there, so neither there could his heart find satisfaction and repose.

(Ver. 6.) Μηδεὶς ὑμᾶς ἀπατάτω κενοῖς λόγοις—" Let no one deceive you with vain words." Whatever apologies were made for such sensual indulgences were vain words, or sophistry —words without truth, pernicious in their tendency, and tending to mislead. See examples from Kypke, *in loc.*; Septuagint—Ex. v. 9; Hos. xii. 1. The Gothic reads—*uslusto, concupiscat*. It is a refinement on the part of Olshausen to refer such opinions to antinomian teachers, and on that of Meier to confine them to heathen philosophers. Harless admits that the precise class of persons referred to by the apostle cannot now be defined; but we agree with Meyer in the idea, that they appear to be their heathen neighbours; for they were not to associate with them (ver. 7), and they were to remember that their present profession placed them in a state of perfect separation from old habits and confederates (ver. 8). Such vices have not wanted apologists in every age. The language of Bullinger, quoted also by Harless, has a peculiar power and terseness—*Erant apud Ephesios homines corrupti, ut hodie apud nos plurimi sunt, qui hæc salutaria Dei præcepta cachinno excipientes obstrepunt: humanum esse quod faciant amatores, utile quod fœneratores, facetum quod joculatores, et iccirco Deum non usque adeo graviter animadvertere in istiusmodi lapsus.*[1] They were to be on their guard—

---

[1] Whitby says too—"That the Ephesians stood in need of these instructions we learn from Democritus Ephesius, who, speaking of the temple of the Ephesian Diana, hath much περὶ τῆς χλιδῆς αὐτῶν—'of the softness and luxury of the Ephesians;' and from Euacles in his book *de Ephesiacis*, who saith—ἐν Ἐφέσῳ ἱερὰ ἱδρύσασθαι ἑταίρᾳ Ἀφροδίτῃ—'In Ephesus they built temples to Venus, the mistress of the whores;' and from Strabo, who informs us that 'in their ancient temples there were old images, but in their new, σκολιὰ ἔργα—vile works were done.' (Lib. xiv. p. 640.) Among the heathens, simple fornication was held a thing indifferent; the laws allowed and provided for it in many nations; whence the grave Epictetus counsels his scholars, 'only to whore—ὡς νόμιμον

διὰ ταῦτα γὰρ ἔρχεται ἡ ὀργὴ τοῦ Θεοῦ ἐπὶ τοὺς υἱοὺς τῆς ἀπειθείας—" for because of these things cometh the wrath of God on the sons of disobedience." The phrase διὰ ταῦτα, emphatic in position, refers not to the " vain words," but more naturally to the vices specified—" on account of these sins." Col. iii. 6. The Greek commentators, followed by Stier, combine both opinions, but without any necessity. The noun stands between two warnings against certain classes of sins and sinners, and naturally refers to them by ταῦτα. 'Οργή has been illustrated, and so has υἱοὶ ἀπειθείας, under ii. 2, 3. Suicer, *sub voce*. Many, such as Meyer, restrict the manifestation of the Divine anger to the other world. His argument is, that ὀργὴ Θεοῦ is in contrast with βασιλεία Θεοῦ. Granted, but we find the verb ἔχει in the present tense, as indicating a present exclusion—an exclusion which, though specially to be felt in the future, was yet ordained when the apostle wrote. So this anger, though it is to be signally poured out at the Second Coming, is descending at this very time—ἔρχεται. It is thus, on the other hand, too narrow a view of Calvin, Meier, and Baumgarten-Crusius, to confine this ὀργή to the present life. It begins here—the dark cloud pours out a few drops, but does not discharge all its terrible contents. Such sins especially incur it, and such sinners

ἔστι—according to law ;' and in all places they connived at it. 'He that blames young men for their meretricious amours,' saith Cicero, 'does what is repugnant to the customs and concessions of our ancestors, for when was not this done? when was it not permitted?' This was suitable both to the principles and practices of many of their grave philosophers, especially of the Stoics, who held it 'lawful for others to use whores, and for them to get their living by such practices.' Hence even in the church of Corinth some had taught this doctrine."

"Prenons garde surtout à *l'avarice*. Elle ne s'annonce pas sous des dehors aussi dégoûtants que l'impudicité et la fornication ; on la déguise sous de beaux noms, tels que ceux d'économie sévère, d'esprit d'ordre, de prévoyance ou de sagesse, et, par ce moyen, elle établit plus facilement son empire sur le cœur des hommes. Mais considérons attentivement la qualification que lui donne ici saint Paul. Il déclare qu'elle est *une idolâtrie*. Qu'importe, en effet, qu'on n'adore pas des idoles d'or et d'argent, comme les païens, si l'on adore l'or et l'argent eux-mêmes, si ce sont eux que l'on recherche pardessus tout, si l'on met son bonheur à les posséder et si c'est en eux que l'on espère ? Hélas ! la grande idole du siècle est encore la statue d'or, comme du temps de Nébucadnézar ; c'est vers sa figure éblouissante que se tournent les regards et les cœurs des peuples, et c'est d'elle que l'on attend la joie et la délivrance."—Gauthey, *Méditations sur l'Epître de S. Paul aux Ephésiens*, p. 124. Paris, 1852.

receive in themselves "that recompense of their error which is meet." Rom. i. 27. The wrath of God is also poured out on impenitent offenders in the other world. Rev. xxi. 8.

(Ver. 7.) Μὴ οὖν γίνεσθε συμμέτοχοι αὐτῶν—" Become not then partakers with them." The spelling συνμέτοχοι has the authority of A, B¹, D¹, F, G; see also under iii. 6. The meaning is not, as Koppe paraphrases, "Take care lest their fate befall you," but, " become not partakers with them in their sins;" ver. 11. Do not through any temptation fall into their wicked courses. Οὖν is collective: because they are addicted to those sins on which Divine judgment now falls, and continued indulgence in which bars a man out of heaven —become not ye their associates.

(Ver. 8.) Ἦτε γὰρ ποτὲ σκότος—" For ye were once darkness." As Chrysostom says, he reminds them τῆς προτέρας κακίας. Γάρ introduces a special reason for an entire separation between the Church and the Gentile world. Their past and present state were in perfect contrast—ἦτε ποτὲ σκότος— " ye were once darkness—ἦτε—emphatic;" and deeds of darkness were in harmony with such a state. Σκότος is the abstract—darkness itself—employed to intensify the idea expressed. See iv. 18. Darkness is the emblem and region of ignorance and depravity, and in such a miserable condition they were " once." But that state was over—" the dayspring from on high" had visited them—

νῦν δὲ φῶς ἐν Κυρίῳ—" but now ye are light in the Lord." No μέν precedes, as the first clause is of an absolute nature. Klotz, ad Devarius, vol. ii. p. 356. Δέ is adversative, " now " being opposed to " once." Chrysostom says, ἐννοήσαντες τι ἦτέ ποτε ὑμεῖς καὶ τι γεγόνατε νῦν. Φῶς, an abstract noun also, is the image of knowledge and purity. See under i. 18. Their condition being so thoroughly changed, their conduct was to be in harmony with such a transformation. Ἐν Κυρίῳ —" in fellowship with the Lord;" and light can be enjoyed in no other element. The phrase is never to be diluted as is done by Fritzsche in his allusion to similar phrases. *Comment. ad Roman.* viii. 4; 1 John i. 5, 6, 7. For Κύριος as applied to Christ, see i. 2, 3. Such being the case, there follows the imperative injunction—

ὡς τέκνα φωτὸς περιπατεῖτε—" walk as children of light."

There needs no formal οὖν to introduce the inference, it makes itself so apparent, and is all the more forcible from the want of the particle. 2 Cor. vi. 14, 16. Υἱός is often used in a similar connection. See τέκνον under ii. 3. The genitive is one of source, and neither noun has the article. Middleton, *Gr. Art.* p. 49. Luke x. 6, xvi. 8; John xii. 36; 1 Thess. iv. 5. Negatively they were not to be partakers; but neutrality is not sufficient—positively they were to walk as children of the light. "As children of light," they were to show by their conduct that they loved it, enjoyed it, and reflected its lustre. Their course of conduct ought to prove that they hated the previous darkness, that they were content with no ambiguous twilight, but lived and acted in the full splendour of the Sun of Righteousness, hating the secret and unfruitful deeds of darkness referred to in the following context. Περιπατεῖτε, under ii. 2. First, the apostle has referred to love as an element of Christian walk, vers. 1 and 2; and now he refers to light as an element of the same walk; different aspects of the same spiritual purity; love, and not angry and vengeful passions; light, and not dark and unnameable deeds.

(Ver. 9.) This verse is a parenthesis, illustrative and confirmatory of the previous clause.

Ὁ γὰρ καρπὸς τοῦ φωτός—"For the fruit of the light." Instead of φωτός the Textus Receptus has Πνεύματος. For φωτός we have the authority of A, B, D, E[1], F, G, and the Vulgate; while the Stephanic text is found in D[3], E[2], K, L, the majority of mss., in the Syriac too, and in two of the Greek commentators. Internal evidence here can have but little weight. One may say that φωτός was inserted in room of Πνεύματος, to give correspondence with the φῶς of the preceding verse; or one may say, on the other hand, that Πνεύματος supplanted φωτός from a reminiscence of Gal. v. 22. The particle γάρ is used here, as often, to introduce a parenthetic confirmation. The verse not only explains what is meant by walking as children of light, but really holds out an inducement to the duty. "The fruit is"—

ἐν πάσῃ ἀγαθωσύνῃ—"in all goodness." We cannot say, with so many expositors, that ἐστι being supplied, the meaning is—the fruit of the Spirit is in, that is—*ponitur*—consists in, all goodness, etc. In that case, the simple nominative might have been employed. We understand the apostle to mean, that the fruit is always associated with goodness as its element or sphere. Winer, § 48 (3) *a*. These qualities uniformly characterize its fruits. No one will assent to the unscholarly remark of Küttner, that the three following nouns are merely synonymous. Ἀγαθωσύνη does not signify beneficence, properly so called, but that moral excellence which springs from religious principle (Gal. v. 22; Rom. xv. 14), and leads to kindness, generosity, or goodness. It here may stand opposed to the dark and malignant passions which the apostle has been reprobating—κακία.

καὶ δικαιοσύνῃ—"and righteousness." This is integrity or moral rectitude (Rom. vi. 13; 1 Tim. vi. 11), and is in contrast not only with the theft and covetousness already condemned, but with all defective sense of obligation, for it rules itself by the Divine law, and in every relation of life strives to be as it ought to be—and is opposed to ἀδικία. For the spelling of this and the preceding noun, see *Etymol. Mag. sub voce δίκαιος*. See under iv. 24.

καὶ ἀληθείᾳ—"and truth." Truth stands opposed to insincerity and dissimulation—ψεῦδος. These three ethical terms characterize Christian duty. We cannot agree with Baumgarten-Crusius, who thus distinguishes the three nouns: the first as alluding to what is internal, the second as pertaining to human relations, and the third as having reference to God. For the good, the right, and the true, distinguish that fruit which is produced out of, or belongs to, the condition which is called "light in the Lord," and are always distinctive elements of the virtues which adorn Christianity.

(Ver. 10.) Δοκιμάζοντες τί ἐστιν εὐάρεστον τῷ Κυρίῳ— "Proving what is well-pleasing to the Lord." Rom. xii. 2; Phil. i. 10; 1 Thess. v. 21. The participle agrees with the previous verb περιπατεῖτε, as a predicate of mode, and so used in its ordinary sense—trying—proving. Phil. i. 10. As they walked, they were to be examining or distinguishing what is pleasing to the Lord. Εὐάρεστον—"well-pleasing" —what the Lord has enjoined and therefore approves. The obedience of Christians is not prompted by traditionary or unthinking acquiescence, but is founded on clear and discriminative perception of the law and the will of Christ. And that obedience is accepted not because it pleases them to offer it, but because the Lord hath exacted it. The believer is not to prove and discover what suits himself, but what pleases his Divine Master. The one point of his ethical investigation is, Is it pleasing to the Lord, or in harmony with His law and example? This faculty belongs, as Theophylact says, to the perfect—τῶν τελείων ἐστὶ τῶν κρίνειν δυναμένων.

(Ver. 11.) Καὶ μὴ συνκοινωνεῖτε τοῖς ἔργοις τοῖς ἀκάρποις τοῦ σκότους—" And have no fellowship with the unfruitful works of darkness." The spelling συνκοινωνεῖτε is found in A, B¹, D¹, F, G, L, and the reason for preferring it is given by Tischendorf, with many examples, in his *Prolegomena*, page xlvii. Καί connects this clause with περιπατεῖτε. Phil. iv. 14; Rev. xviii. 4. Ἄκαρπος is plainly in contrast with καρπός in ver. 9. These ἔργα have no good fruits—their only fruit, as Theophylact says, is death and shame. See the contrast between ἔργα and καρπός in Gal. v. 19, 22. Σκότος has been explained under the 8th verse. This admonition is much the same as that contained in the 7th verse. Rom. vi. 21, viii. 12; Gal. vi. 8. A line of broad demarcation was to separate the church from the world; and not only was there to be no participation and no connivance, but there was in addition to be rebuke—

μᾶλλον δὲ καὶ ἐλέγχετε. *Μᾶλλον δὲ καί*—" Yea, much more "—or better, " but rather even "—a formula which gives special intensity to the antithesis. Fritzsche, *ad Rom*. viii. 34; Hartung, i. 134; Gal. iv. 9. It was a duty to have nothing to do with the deeds of darkness; but it was a far higher obligation to reprimand them. There was to be not simply negative separation, but positive rebuke—not by the contrast of their own purity, but by formal and solemn reproof. 1 Cor. xiv. 24; 2 Tim. iv. 2; Xen. *Symp*. viii. 43.

(Ver. 12.) Τὰ γὰρ κρυφῇ γινόμενα ὑπ' αὐτῶν αἰσχρόν ἐστιν καὶ λέγειν—" for the things in secret done by them it is shameful even to speak of." Such a use of καί discursive is explained in Hartung, vol. i. 136, and more fully by Klotz, *ad Devarius*, vol. ii. 633, etc. The adverb κρυφῇ occurs only here, and according to some should be written κρυφῆ, with iota subscribed. Ellendt, *Lex. Soph. sub voce;* Passow, *sub voce*. Deut. xxviii. 57; Wisdom xviii. 9. The connection of

this verse with the preceding has led to no little dispute :—
1. Baumgarten-Crusius regards it as a hyperbole of indignation, and easily evades the difficulty. 2. Koppe and Rückert give γάρ the sense of "although," as if the apostle meant to say—Rebuke these sins, even though you should blush to mention them. But γάρ cannot bear such a meaning. 3. Von Gerlach fills in such a supplement as this—It is a shame even to speak of their secret sins, yet that should not keep us from exposing and rebuking them. 4. On the other hand, Bengel, Baumgarten, and Matthies, preceded, it would seem, by Œcumenius, take the clause as giving a reason why the deeds of darkness are not specified like the fruit of the light : "Have no fellowship with the unfruitful works of darkness ; I pause not to name them—it is a shame to mention them." But such sentimental qualms did not trouble the apostle, as may be seen from many portions of his writings. Rom. i. 24–32 ; 1 Cor. vi. 9, 10 ; Gal. v. 19–21 ; 1 Tim. i. 9, 10. This opinion also identifies "deeds of darkness" with "the things done of them in secret." Now such an opinion cannot be sustained, as it changes the meaning of σκότος from a moral into a material sense. It is used in a moral sense in ver. 8, and we know that many of the sins of this darkness were not committed in secret, but were open and public vices. 5. The opinions of Meier and Holzhausen are somewhat allied. Meier's notion is, that λέγειν means to speak in a loose and indecorous way, and he supposes the apostle to say, "Rebuke these sins openly, for it is a shame to make mention of them in any other way than that of reproof;" or as Alford says— "Your connection with them must only be that which the act of ἔλεγξις necessitates." 6. Holzhausen imagines that in the phrase τὰ κρυφῇ γινόμενα there is reference to the heathen mysteries, and that the apostle warns Christians not to unveil even in speech their hideous sensualities. But both interpretations give an emphatic and unwonted meaning to the clause. Nor is there the remotest proof that the so-called mysteries are referred to. 7. Stier's idea, which is that of Photius, Theophylact, and Erasmus, is, that ἐλέγχειν cannot mean verbal reproof, for this verse would forbid it—it being a shame to speak of those secret sins—but that it signifies reproof conveyed in the form of a consistent life of light.

Matt. v. 16; Phil. ii. 15. "The only rebuke you can give must be in the holy contrast of your own conduct, for to speak of their secret vices is a shame." Such is virtually also the exegesis of Bloomfield and Peile. But that ἐλέγχω signifies other than verbal rebuke, cannot be proved. Where the verb may be rendered "convince"—as in 1 Cor. xiv. 24, Jas. ii. 9 — language is supposed to be the medium of conviction. The word, in John iii. 20, has the sense of —"exposed," but such a sense would not well suit the exegesis of Stier. This exposition thus requires more supplementary ideas than sound interpretation will warrant. 8. Anselm, Piscator, Zanchius, Flatt, and Harless take the verse not in connection with ἐλέγχετε, but with συγκοινωνεῖτε, that is—"Have no fellowship with such deeds, for it is a shame even to speak of them, surely much more to do them." This opinion identifies too strongly ἔργα σκότους with τὰ κρυφῇ γινόμενα—the latter being a special class of the former. Lastly, Musculus, de Wette, Meyer, and Olshausen, connect the verse immediately with μᾶλλον δὲ καὶ ἐλέγχετε—the meaning being, "By all means reprove them, and there is the more need of it, for it is a shame even to speak of their secret sins." This connection is on the whole the simplest, and follows, we think, most naturally the order of thought and earnest admonition. That these "things done in secret" have any reference to the foul orgies of the heathen mysteries, is a position that cannot be proved, though it has been advanced by Grotius, Elsner, Wolf, Michaelis, Holzhausen, Macknight, and Whitby. But there were in heathendom forms of sins so base and bestial, that they shunned the light and courted secrecy.

(Ver. 13.) Τὰ δὲ πάντα ἐλεγχόμενα, ὑπὸ τοῦ φωτὸς φανεροῦται—"But all those things being reproved, are by the light made manifest." This verse shows why Christians should engage in the work of reproof—it is so salutary: for it exhibits such vices in all their odious debasement, and proves its own purity and lustre in the very exposure. Many and varied have been the interpretations of this statement. Olshausen remarks, that the words have *gnomenartige Kürze*. We take τὰ δὲ πάντα as referring to the τὰ κρυφῇ γινόμενα, and not, as Rückert does—in a general sense, or all things generally. Jerome thus understands it—*haud dubie quin ea quæ occulte fiunt*. Δέ has its adversative force—they are done in secret, but they may and ought to be exposed. The apostle bids them reprove those sins, and he here states the result. Reprove them, and the effect is, "all these sins being so reproved, are made manifest by the light." Storr in his *Dissertationes Exegeticæ*, and Kuinoel—in a paper on this verse printed in the third volume of the *Commentationes Theologicæ* of Velthusen, Kuinoel, and Ruperti—needlessly argue that the neuter here stands for the masculine. Kuinoel's view is, "all who are reproved and amended ought to be reproved and amended by a man who is a genuine and consistent Christian. He who engages in this work of instruction is light—is a son of the light—is a true Christian." Such a violent interpretation cannot be received.

But with which of the terms should ὑπὸ τοῦ φωτός be associated? 1. De Wette, Crocius, Bloomfield, and Peile, join them to the participle ἐλεγχόμενα—all "these reproved by the light." Our objection to this connection is, that φῶς agrees more naturally with φανεροῦται—the idea being homogeneous, for light is the agent which reveals. De Wette's objection, that rebuke is not uniformly followed by such manifestation, proceeds on the assumption that rebuke is all but identical with conversion. 2. On the other hand, Stephens and Mill place a comma after ἐλεγχόμενα, and the connection of φῶς with the verb is advocated by Bengel, Meier, Harless, Olshausen, Meyer, and Stier. All those sins done in secret, if they are reproved, are brought into open view by the light. Φῶς is used, as in a previous verse, to denote the gospel as a source of light. When such sins are reproved, they are exposed, they are unveiled in their hideousness by the light let in upon them. Being deeds of darkness, they need the light of Christianity to make them manifest, for other boasted lights only flickered and failed to reveal them. Philosophy was only "darkness visible" around them.

πᾶν γὰρ τὸ φανερούμενον φῶς ἐστιν. Πᾶν τό. Winer, § 18, 4. The meaning depends greatly on this—whether φανερούμενον be taken in a middle or passive sense. Many prefer the passive sense, which is certainly the prevailing one in the New Testament, and occurs in the previous clause. The exposition of Olshausen, Stier, Ellicott, and Alford is—"whatever is made manifest is light"—"all things illuminated by the light are themselves light." Well may Olshausen add—"this idea has somewhat strange in it," for he is compelled to admit "that light does not always exercise this transforming influence, for the devil and all the wicked are reproved by the light, without becoming themselves light." Alford calls this objection "null," as being a misapprehension of φῶς ἐστι, but φῶς in his exegesis changes its meaning from the previous verse. This opinion of Olshausen is virtually that of the Greek patristic expositors, who are followed by Peter Lombard. Theophylact says—ἐπειδὰν δὲ φανερωθῇ, γίνεται φῶς. Harless renders, "what has been revealed is no longer a hidden work of darkness: it is light." The view of Röell, Robinson, and Wilke is not dissimilar. Thus also Ellicott—"becomes light, as of the nature of light." A dark object suddenly illumined may indeed be said to be all light, because it is surrounded with light, and this is the notion of Bretschneider. But if this be the view, it seems to make the apostle use a tautology, "whatever is revealed, is enlightened;" unless you understand the apostle to say, that by such a process they themselves who were once darkness become light. De Wette's explanation of the same rendering is—without φῶς there is no φανερούμενον, and where there is φανερούμενον there is light. But the apostle does not utter such a truism —where everything is manifested there is light. Piscator's hypothesis is equally baseless—"whatever is manifested is light, that is, is manifested by the light." The passive meaning may be adopted, with the proviso that the apostle does not say whether the light be for conversion or condemnation. But while this view may thus be grammatically defended, still we feel as if the context led us to take the last clause as a reason of the statement contained in the first. Thus, some prefer, with Beza, Calvin, Vatablus, Grotius, Rollock, Zanchius, Morus, Wahl, Turner, and the Peschito, to give the participle a reflexive or medial signification. Meyer affirms that φανεροῦμαι is always passive, but the passive may have a medial signification, as it seems to have sometimes in the New Testament. Mark xvi. 12; John i. 31, ix. 3; 2 Cor. iv. 10, 11; Jelf, § 367, 2. Olshausen takes up the exegesis of Grotius, which is also that of Bodius and Dickson—"for the light is the element that makes all clear," and then argues grammatically against such a rendering. But according to the accurate position of subject and predicate, the meaning is—"whatever makes manifest or renders apparent, is light." Such manifestation is the nature and function of light. These clandestine sins, when reproved, are disclosed by the light so cast upon them, for it belongs to light to make such disclosures. The apostle urges his readers to reprove such sins, which, though done in secret, will and must be exposed; yea, all of them being reproved, are shone upon by the light—that light which radiates from Christianity. And this power of unveiling in Christianity is properly called "light," for whatever causes such things to disclose themselves is of the essence of light. Such is a natural and simple view of the verse. See Lücke—*Commentar*, John iii. 21, vol. i. p. 550, 3rd ed.

And that this rebuke is a duty, the discharge of which is attended with the most salutary results, is now shown by a reference to the ancient inspired oracles.

Ver. 14. Διὸ λέγει—" Wherefore He saith." See under iv. 8; διό, ii. 11. It would be quite contrary to Pauline usage to suppose that this formula introduced any citation but one from the Old Testament. But the quotation is not found literally in any portion of the Hebrew oracles. Grotius and Elsner propose to make φῶς the nominative to λέγει—" wherefore a man of light—one of these reprovers says;" an opinion not very remote from Seiler's version—*die Erleuchteten sollen sprechen*—those who are light themselves should speak to the children of darkness in the following terms—"Awake, thou that sleepest, and arise from the dead." An early opinion, reported by Theodoret as belonging to τινὲς τῶν ἑρμηνευτῶν, has been adopted by Heumann, *Pœcile*, ii. p. 396; Michaelis; Döpke, *Hermeneutik*, p. 275, Leipzig, 1829; Storr, Stolz, Flatt, and Bleek, *Stud. und Krit.* 1853, p. 331. It is that the quotation is taken from one of the hymns of the early Christian church. Michaelis regards it, indeed, as an excerpt from some baptismal formula. Of such a supposition there is no proof; and the reference to 1 Cor. xiv. 26 is certainly no argument in its favour. In a similar spirit Barnes says—"I see no evidence that Paul meant to make a quotation at all." The idea of Stier is, that the apostle quotes some *Geisteswort*—some saying given to the church by its inspired prophets, and based upon Isa. lx., and therefore warranting the διὸ λέγει, as truly as any clause of canonical writ. But the language of the apostle gives no hint of such a source of quotation, nor have we any parallel example. Others have recourse to the hypothesis that Paul has quoted from some apocryphal composition. Such an opinion has been mentioned by Jerome as a *simplex responsio*, while he adds the saving clause—*non quod apocrypha comprobaret;* by Epiphanius, *Contra Hæreses*, p. 42, who refers to the prophecy of Elias; by Euthalius, and George Syncellus (*Chronolog.* p. 21), who appeal to the apocryphal treatise named Jeremiah; while Codex G gives the citation to the book of Enoch, and Morus holds generally by the hypothesis, which is also espoused by Schrader, that the clause is borrowed from some lost Jewish oracle. Rhenferd contends that reference is made here, as in Acts xx. 35, to one of Christ's unwritten sayings. Nor is the difficulty removed by adopting the clumsy theory to which Jerome has also alluded, and which Bugenhagen and Calixtus have adopted, that the nominative to λέγει is a subjective influence—the Spirit, or Christ within Paul himself, an imitation of the older idiom—" thus saith the Lord." Nor is the solution proposed by Bornemann at all more tenable, viz. that λέγει is impersonal, and that the clause may be rendered—" wherefore it may be said "—or " one may say." *Scholia in Lucam*, p. 48. But the active form is not used impersonally, though the passive is, and φησί is the common term. Pape, and Passow, *sub vocibus;* Bernhardy, p. 419. Rückert confesses that the subject lies in impenetrable darkness; but the most extraordinary of all the solutions is the explanation of Meyer, and by those who believe in a plenary inspiration it will be rebuked—not refuted. His words are —" The διὸ λέγει shows that Paul intended to quote from a canonical writing, but as the citation is not from any canonical book, he adduced, through lapse of memory, an apocryphal passage, which he, citing from memory, took to be canonical. But out of what apocryphal writing the quotation is taken we know not."

Assuming that the quotation is made from the Old Testament, as the uniform use of διὸ λέγει implies, the question still remains—what place is cited ? Various verses and clauses have been fixed upon by critics, the majority of whom, from Thomas Aquinas down to Olshausen, refer to Isa. lx. 1, though some, such as Beza, Meier, and others, prefer Isa. xxvi. 19. Isa. ix. 2 is combined, by Baumgarten, Holzhausen, and Klausen, with lx. 1 (*Hermeneutik*, p. 416, Leipzig, 1841). Other combinations have been proposed. The matter is involved in difficulty, and none of these places is wholly similar to the verse before us. Harless and Olshausen make it plausible that the reference is to Isa. lx. 1—קוּמִי אוֹרִי כִּי־בָא אוֹרֵךְ וּכְבוֹד יְהוָה עָלַיִךְ זָרָח—" Arise, shine ; for thy light is come, and the glory of the Lord is risen upon thee." The imperative is there used with the verb " arise ;" and if we turn back to lix. 10, the figure of darkness is employed by the prophet, as well as in the 2nd ver. of chap. lx. The words of the apostle may, therefore, be viewed as the quintessence of the prophet's exclamation—" Arise." That idea suggested to the apostle's mind the previous condition of those to whom this trumpet-note was addressed, and he describes it thus— " Awake, thou that sleepest ;" and as that species of slumber was a lethargy of death, he adds—" arise from the dead." " Arise, be light," says the prophet, " for thy light is come, and the glory of Jehovah has risen upon thee ;"[1]—but the apostle resolves the prophecy into a more prosaic description of its fulfilment—" and Christ shall give thee light." The use of the name Christ shows us, as Alford insists, that the apostle meant to make no direct or verbal quotation. But the entire subject of New Testament quotation is not without its difficulties. Gouge, *New Testament Quotations*, London, 1855 ; Davidson, *Hermeneutics*, p. 334. We find that similar examples of quotation, according to spirit, are found in the New Testament, as in Jas. iv. 5 ; 2 Cor. vi. 16, 17 ; Matt. ii. 23. The prophecy is primarily addressed to Zion, as the symbol of the church. Nor do we apprehend that the application is different in the quotation before us, as the words are addressed still to the church—as one that had been asleep and dead, but the Divine appeal had startled it. It

---

[1] See the respective commentaries of Vitringa, Gesenius, Henderson, Hitzig, and Alexander on the passage.

had realized the blessed change of awakening and resurrection, and had also rejoiced in the light poured upon it by Christ. Nay, though it was "some time darkness, it was now light in the Lord;" and its light was not to be hidden—it was to break in upon the dark and secret places around it, that they too might be illuminated. In the formation and extension of any church the prophecy is always realized in spirit; for it shows of whom a church is composed, what was the first condition of its members, by what means they have been transformed, and what is one primary duty of their organization.

ἔγειρε ὁ καθεύδων—"awake, thou that sleepest." For the case, see Winer, § 29, 2. Lachmann reads ἔγειραι after the Textus Receptus, but the majority of critics adopt the spelling ἔγειρε. It is used not as the active for the middle, but, as Fritzsche suggests, it was the form apparently employed in common speech. *Comm. ad Marc.* ii. 9. That sleep was profound, but there had been a summons to awake. To awake is man's duty, for he is commanded to obey, and he does obey under the influence of the Divine Spirit.

καὶ ἀνάστα ἐκ τῶν νεκρῶν—"and arise from the dead." The meaning of νεκρός so used may be seen under ii. 1. Bornemann, *in Luc.* p. 97. 'Ἀνάστα is a later form for ἀνάστηθι. Winer, § 14, 1, h. The command is similar to that given by our Lord to the man with the withered hand—"Stretch it forth." The man might have objected and said, "Could I obey thee in this, I would not have troubled thee. Why mock me with my infirmity, and bid me do the very thing I cannot?" But the man did not so perplex himself; and Christ, in exciting the desire to obey, imparted the power to obey. See under ii. 2, v. 6.

καὶ ἐπιφαύσει σοι ὁ Χριστός—"and Christ shall enlighten thee." The various spellings of the verb, and the change of φ into ψ, have arisen from inadvertence. On the different forms of this verb, see Fritzsche on Mark ii. 11; Winer, § 15. This variation is as old as the days of Chrysostom, for he notices it, and decides for the common reading. The verb itself occurs nowhere else in the New Testament, though it is once found in the "Acts of Thomas"—ἐπέφαυσε γάρ μοι— § 34. This light Christ flashes upon the dead, and startles them into life. And the apostle continues—

(Ver. 15.) βλέπετε, οὖν, ἀκριβῶς περιπατεῖτε. "Take heed then how ye walk correctly." Calvin has been felicitous in his view of the connection—*si aliorum discutere tenebras fideles debent fulgore suo: quanto minus cœcutire ipsi debent in proprio vitæ instituto?* In this view οὖν is closely joined to the verse immediately preceding, and such is the view of Harless. De Wette and Alford, however, connect it with ver. 8—a connection which reduces unwarrantably all the preceding verses to a parenthesis; while Meyer quite arbitrarily joins it to the last clause of the 11th verse. The truth is, that the whole train of thought from the 8th verse to the 14th is so similar, that the apostle follows it all up with the injunction before us. Οὖν is retrospective, indeed (Klotz, *ad Devarius,* ii. 718), but the last verse is present specially to the apostle's mind. The indicative, and not the subjunctive, is used, the meaning being, how you walk, not how you should walk. Winer, § 41, *b*, 1, b; or *videte igitur . . . quomodo illud efficiatis ut provide vivatis.* Fritzschiorum, *Opuscula,* pp. 208, 209, note. The necessity of personal holiness in themselves, and the special duty of reproof and enlightenment which lay on them toward their unbelieving fellows, taught them this accuracy of walk. Πῶς is different in aspect from ἵνα as in 1 Cor. xvi. 10, and it stands after βλεπέτω in 1 Cor. iii. 10. The verb is followed by ἀπό in Mark viii. 15, and by a simple accusative in Phil. iii. 2; Col. iv. 17. Such passages show that it would be finical to suppose that this verb of *vision* was used from its connection with the term *light* in the former verse. To ἀκριβῶς, which qualifies not βλέπετε but περιπατεῖτε, some give the meaning of "accurately," or as Bengel renders it—*pünktlich,* a rendering in which Harless and Stier acquiesce; while others follow Luther, who translates *vorsichtig,* of which the "circumspectly" of our version is an imitation. Col. iv. 5 adds — πρὸς τοὺς ἔξω, a phrase which Olshausen supposes should be understood here. 1 Thess. iv. 1. The first meaning is more in accordance with the prevailing usage of the word in all other places of the New Testament. Matt. ii. 8; Luke i. 3; Acts xviii. 25; 1 Thess. v. 2. Still the second meaning is virtually involved in the first, for this accuracy or perfection of walk has a special reference to observers. They were to see to it that they were walking—

μὴ ὡς ἄσοφοι, ἀλλ' ὡς σοφοί—"not as unwise, but as wise men;" first a negative, and secondly a positive aspect. Kypke, p. 350; Winer, § 65, 5. The subjective μή connects the clause with περιπατεῖτε. If the Ephesian Christians walked without taking heed to their ways, then they walked as fools do, who stumble and fall or miss the path. Wisdom, not in theory, but in practice—wisdom, and not mere intelligence — was to characterize them; that wisdom which preserves in rectitude, guides amidst temptations, and affords a lesson of consistency to surrounding spectators. And if there be any allusion to verse 11, then the inferential meaning is—it would be the height of folly to rebuke that sin which the reprover is openly committing; to condemn profane swearing, and barb the reprimand with an oath; or exemplify the vices of wrath and clamour in anathematizing such as may be guilty of them. It is strange infatuation to be obliged, in pointing others to heaven, to point over one's shoulder. And one peculiar proof and specimen of wisdom is now given—

(Ver. 16.) 'Εξαγοραζόμενοι τὸν καιρόν—"Redeeming the time." Col. iv. 5. The participle has been variously understood. The translation of Luther—"suit yourselves to the time," is plainly without foundation—*schicket euch in die Zeit*. The paraphrase of Ambrosiaster is similar—*scire quemadmodum unicunque respondeat*. The verb denotes to buy out of —ἐκ; and the middle voice intimates that the purchase is for oneself—for one's own personal benefit. Καιρός, probably allied to κείρω, is not χρόνος, simply time, but opportunity.[1] Tittmann, *De Synon.* p. 39; Donaldson, *New Cratylus*, p. 320; see, however, Benfey, *Wurzellex.* vol. ii. p. 288. This opportunity is supposed to be in some other's possession, and you buy it. You make it your own by purchase, by giving in exchange those pleasures or that indolence, the indulgence of which would have made you forego such a bargain. The

---

[1] "Mitylena oriundus Pittacus sum Lesbius,
Γίγνωσκε καιρὸν qui dixi sententiam.
Sed iste καιρὸς, tempus ut noris, monet :
Et esse καιρὸν, tempestivum quod vocant.
Romana sic est vox, VENITO IN TEMPORE."
—Ausonius, *Opera*, p. 145, Biponti, 1785.

meaning is, then—making the most of every opportunity. Such is at least a signification that neither the words themselves nor the context disprove. We are not on the one hand to say with Meyer, that ἐκ is merely intensive, for it points to that out of which, or out of whose power, the purchase is to be made; still, we are not anxiously, on the other hand, to find out and specify from whom or what the time is to be redeemed, and to call it "bad men," with Jerome and Bengel, or "the devil," with Calvin. Such is too hard a pressure upon the figure. Neither are we curiously to ask, what is the price given in exchange? Such is the gratuitous minuteness of Chrysostom, Theophylact, and Œcumenius, who refer us to "opponents bribed off," and of Augustine, Calvin, Estius, Zanchius, Rückert, and Stier, who understand by the alleged price the offering of all earthly hindrance and pleasure. Beza's better illustration is that of a merchant whose foresight enables him to use all things for his own purposes; and Olshausen remarks that such a lesson is taught in the parable recorded in Luke xvi. 1–16. The exegesis of Harless is by far too restricted, for he confines the phrase to this meaning—"to know the right point of time when the light of reproof should be let in on the darkness of sin." Still farther removed from the right conception is the interpretation of Grotius, as if the command were addressed to Christians, to avoid danger and so prolong their life; or that of Wilke, Macknight, and Bretschneider, which is—"seize every opportunity to shun danger." It is thought by some that the phrase is founded on the Greek version of Dan. ii. 8, where Nebuchadnezzar said to the Magi of Babylon—דִּי עִדָּנָא אַנְתּוּן זָבְנִין, rendered — ὅτι καιρὸν ὑμεῖς ἐξαγοράζετε. Even though we were obliged to agree with Dathe, Rosenmüller, Gesenius, Maurer, and Hitzig, that the phrase meant there, to buy up or to prolong the time, or seek delay, yet here the article prefixed by the apostle gives the noun a definite speciality. *Sese (id quod difficillimum fuerit) tempus ipsum emisse judicii sui.* Cicero *in Verrem,* iii. p. 240; *Opera,* ed. Nobbe, Lipsiæ, 1850. The "unwise" allow the propitious moment to pass, and it cannot be recalled. They may eulogize it, but they have missed it. The "wise," on the other hand, who walk correctly, recognize it, appreciate it, take hold of it, make it at whatever sacrifice their own, and thriftily turn it to the best advantage. They redeem it, as Severianus says—ὥστε καταχρήσασθαι αὐτῷ πρὸς εὐσέβειαν. The apostle adds a weighty reason—

ὅτι αἱ ἡμέραι πονηραί εἰσιν—"because the days are evil." The apostle, as Olshausen remarks, does not adduce the fewness of the days to inculcate in general the diligent use of time, but he insists on the evil of the days for the purpose of urging Christians to seize on every opportunity to counteract that evil. Beza, Grotius, Rückert, Robinson, Wilke, and Wahl, take the adjective in the sense of—"sorrowful, calamitous, or dangerous." But we prefer the ordinary meaning—"evil," morally evil, and it furnishes a strong argument. Their days were evil. All days have indeed been evil, for sin abounds in the world. But the days of that period were characterized by many enormities, and the refining power of Christianity was only partially and unequally felt. If these days so evil afforded any opportunities of doing good, it was all the more incumbent on Christians to win them and seize them. The very abundance of the evil was a powerful argument to redeem the time, and the apostle writing that letter in a prison was a living example of his own counsel. It is wholly foreign to the context, on the part of Holzhausen, to refer these evil days to the period of the mystery of iniquity. 2 Thess. ii. 4; 1 Tim. iv. 1. The Greek fathers are careful to remark that the apostle calls the days evil, not in themselves—τὴν οὐσίαν—as they are creatures of God; but on account of the events with which they are connected.

(Ver. 17.) Διὰ τοῦτο μὴ γίνεσθε ἄφρονες — "On this account become not senseless." On this account—not because the days are evil—ἐπειδὴ ἡ πονηρία ἀνθεῖ—as is supposed by Œcumenius, Menochius, Zanchius, Estius, Rückert, and de Wette; but because we are summoned to walk wisely, redeeming the time, the days being evil, therefore we are to possess a high amount of Christian intelligence. The epithet ἄφρων characterizes a man who does not use his rational powers. Ast, *Lex. Plat. sub voce*. It differs from ἄσοφος, which has reference more to folly in action and daily work; whereas it, as this verse intimates, signifies a non-comprehension of the principles on which that walk is to be regulated. Tittmann, *De Synon.* 143.

ἀλλὰ συνιέντες τί τὸ θέλημα τοῦ Κυρίου—"but understanding what the will of the Lord is." The participle is variously read. A and B read in the imperative, συνίετε, which Jerome follows, a reading also approved by Lachmann and Rückert, though it is probably an emendation conforming to the other imperatives; while συνιόντες is the reading of $D^1$, F, G, and is preferred by Harless, Alford, and Meyer; while $D^3$, E, K, L, and almost all MSS. read as the Textus Receptus — συνιέντες. We have no objection to the common reading, which is retained by Tischendorf. The participle signifies knowing intelligently, and means more than γινώσκειν. Luke xii. 47. That will which it is their duty to understand is the authoritative expression of the mind of Christ, who embodied in His own example the purity and benignity of all His precepts. Codex B adds ἡμῶν, and Codex A has Θεοῦ—both evidently without authority. The Ephesian Christians, in order to enable themselves to redeem the time, were not to be thoughtless, but to possess a perfect understanding of the Master's will. They would then form just conceptions of daily duty, and would not lose time through the perplexity of conflicting obligations. For θέλημα see under i. 5, 9, 11, and for Κύριος, under i. 2, 3.

(Ver. 18.) Καὶ μὴ μεθύσκεσθε οἴνῳ—"And be not made drunk with wine." Prov. xx. 1, xxiii. 20; 1 Thess. v. 7. Again, there is first the negative, and then the positive injunction. By καί transition is made from a general counsel to a particular instance, and the injunction thus becomes climactic. The dative οἴνῳ is like the Latin ablative of instrument. Winer, § 31, 7. There is no proof in the context for the opinion held, and reckoned possible by de Wette, Koppe, and Holzhausen, that the apostle alludes, as in 1 Cor. xi., to any abuse of the old love-feasts, or of the Lord's Supper. Οἶνος (with the digamma—*vinum,* Wein), as the common drink of the times, is specified by the apostle as the means of intoxication. And he adds—

ἐν ᾧ ἐστὶν ἀσωτία—"in which is dissoluteness," or. profligacy—*Luxuria;* Vulgate. Tittmann, *De Synon.* p. 152; Trench, *Synon.* § 16. Prov. xxviii. 7; Tit. i. 6; 1 Pet. iv. 4.

The antecedent to ᾧ is not οἶνος, but the entire previous clause. The Syriac borrows simply—ܐܣܘܛܘܣ The term ἄσωτος, from a privative and σώζω, is the picture of a sad and very common result. It is sometimes used by the classics to signify one who is, as we say, "past redemption"—παρὰ τὸ σώζω (*Etymolog. Mag.*); oftener one *qui servare nequit*. The adverb ἀσώτως is used of the conduct of the prodigal son in the far country in Luke xv. 13. See Tit. i. 6; 1 Pet. iv. 4; Sept. Prov. xxviii. 7; 2 Macc. iv. 6. Aristotle, in his *Ethics*, iv., virtually defines the term thus—τὸ φθείρειν τὴν οὐσίαν,—or again, ἀσωτία ἐστιν ὑπερβολὴ περὶ χρήματα—or again, τοὺς ἀκρατεῖς καὶ εἰς ἀκολασίαν δαπανηροὺς ἀσώτους καλοῦμεν. Cicero (*De Finibus*) says—*nolim mihi fingere asotus, ut soletis, qui in mensam vomant*, p. 1006, *Opera*, ed. Nobbe. Theophylact, alluding to the etymology, says—οὐ σώζει ἀλλ' ἀπόλλυσιν οὐ τὸ σῶμα μόνον ἀλλὰ καὶ τὴν ψυχήν; and the drunkard's progress, described by Clement in the first chapter of the second book of his *Pædagogue*, is a series of tableaux without veil or reserve. Referring to the origin which he assigns to the term, he also says—Ἀσώτους τε αὐτοὺς οἱ καλέσαντες εὖ μοι δοκοῦσιν αἰνίττεσθαι τὸ τέλος αὐτῶν, ἀσώστους αὐτούς, κατὰ ἔκθλιψιν τοῦ σ στοιχείου νενοηκότες.

There is in the vice of intemperance that kind of dissoluteness which brooks no restraint, which defies all efforts to reform it, and which sinks lower and lower into hopeless and helpless ruin. It is erroneous, therefore, on the part of Schoettgen,[1] to restrict the term to lasciviousness, though intemperance be, as Varro called it, *Veneris suscitabulum*; as Jerome too, *venter mero aestuans facile despumat in libidinem*. The connection between the two vices is notorious; but

[1] Bammidbar rabba, sect. 10, fol. 206, 3. כל מקום שיש יין יש ערות. Ubicunque est vinum, nimirum quod abundanter bibitur, ibi est immunditia, scortatio, et adulterium.

Ibidem, fol. 208, 3. Si homo unum poculum bibit, nempe רביעית, quarta pars rationis ab ipso recedit. Si duos bibit, duæ partes rationis abeunt. Si tres, totidem partes rationis abeunt, et cor ipsius conturbatum est, et statim ejusmodi verba loquitur, quæ nulli rei quadrant. Si vero quatuor bibit, tunc omnis ratio abscedit, et renes ejus (in quibus ex mente Judæorum etiam pars quædam rationis resident) perturbantur, et cor diripitur, et lingua officium non facit, vult quidem aliquid proferre, sed non potest.

Post pauca ibid. אין טוב יוצא מן היין. Non egreditur bonum quid e vino.

libidinous indulgence is only one element of the ἀσωτία. This tremendous sin of intemperance is all the more to be shunned as its hold is so great on its victims, for with periodical remorse there is periodical inebriety; the fatal cup is again coveted and drained; while character, fortune, and life are risked and lost in the gratification of an appetite of all others the most brutal in form and brutifying in result. There are few vices out of which there is less hope of recovery—its haunts are so numerous and its hold is so tremendous. As Ephesus was a commercial town and busy seaport, its wealth led to excessive luxury, and Bacchus was the rival of Diana. The women of Ephesus, as the priestesses of Bacchus, danced round Mark Antony's chariot on his entrance into the city. Drunkenness was indeed an epidemic in those times and lands. Alexander the Great, who died a sacrifice to Bacchus and not to Mars, offered a prize to him who could drink most wine, and thirty of the rivals died in the act of competition. Plato boasts of the immense quantities of liquor which Socrates could swill uninjured; and the philosopher Xenocrates got a golden crown from Dionysius for swallowing a gallon at a draught. Cato often lost his senses over his choice Falernian. The "excess" or dissoluteness attendant on drunkenness and the other vices referred to in the previous context, is also illustrated by many passages in the *Miles Gloriosus* of Plautus, the Latin version of an older Greek drama. The "braggart captain," a citizen of Ephesus, is described in the prologue by his own servant as "a vain, impudent, foul fellow, brimful of lying and lasciviousness."[1] Another character of the piece thus boasts—"Either the merry banterer likewise, or the agreeable boon companion will I be; no interrupter of another am I at a feast. I bear in mind how properly to keep myself from proving disagreeable to my fellow-guest," etc. . . . "In fine, at Ephesus was I born, not among the Apulians, not at Animula"[2]—(there being in this last term a difference of reading).

[1] "Hoc oppidum Ephesu'st : inde Miles meus herus,
   Qui hinc ad forum abiit, gloriosus, impudens,
   Stercoreus, plenus perjurii atque adulterii."—Act ii. Sc. 1.

[2] "Et ego amoris aliquantulum habeo, humorisque meo etiam in corpore :
   Neque dum exarui ex amœnis rebus et voluptariis,
   Vel cavillator facetus, vel conviva commodus

ἀλλὰ πληροῦσθε ἐν Πνεύματι—" but be filled with the Spirit." The terms οἶνος and πνεῦμα are not contrasted simply, as is pleaded by Harless, but the two clauses are in antithesis. The verb is in the passive voice, and is followed by the instrumental ἐν—an unusual construction. It has after it sometimes the genitive and sometimes the dative or accusative, with different meanings. Winer, § 31, 7. 'Ἐν, therefore, may denote the element, as frequently, and not the instrument; the Spirit, as Matthies says, being represented not merely als Mittel und Inhalt. Col. ii. 10, iv. 12. Not only were they to possess the Spirit, but they were to be filled in the Spirit, as vessels filled to overflowing with the Holy Ghost. Men are intoxicated with wine, and they attempt to "fill" themselves with it; but they cannot. The exhilaration which they covet can only be felt periodically, and again and again must they drain the wine cup to relieve themselves of despondency. But Christians are "filled" in or with the Spirit, whose influences are not only powerful, but replete with satisfaction to the heart of man. Ps. xxxvi. 8; Acts ii. 15, 16. It is a sensation of want—a desire to fly from himself, a craving after something which is felt to be out of reach, eager and restless thirst to enjoy, if at all possible, some happiness and enlargement of heart— that usually leads to intemperance. But the Spirit fills Christians, and gives them all the elements of cheerfulness and peace; genuine elevation and mental freedom; superiority to all depressing influences; and refined and permanent enjoyment. Of course, if they are so filled with the Spirit, they feel no appetite for debasing and material stimulants.

(Ver. 19.) Λαλοῦντες ἑαυτοῖς—" Speaking to one another." Under the relaxing influence of wine the tongue is loosened, and the unrestrained conversation too often passes into that

Item ero: neque ego unquam oblocutor sum alteri in convivio.
Incommoditate abstinere me apud convivas commode
Commemini, et meæ orationis justam partem persequi;
Et meam partem itidem tacere, cum aliena est oratio.
Neque ego unquam alienum scortum subigito in convivio,
Neque præripio pulpamentum, neque prævorto poculum,
Neque per vinum unquam ex me exoritur dissidium in convivio.
Si quis ibi est odiosus, abeo domum, segrego,
Venerem, amorem, amœnitatemque accubans exerceo.
Minime sputator, screator sum, itidem minime muccidus.
Post Ephesi sum natus; non in Apulis, non sum in Umbria."—Act iii. Sc. 1.

species of language, the infamy of which the apostle has already exposed. The participle is connected in syntax with πληροῦσθε, for this "speaking" is the result of spiritual fulness. Ἑαυτοῖς is for ἀλλήλοις, as in iv. 32, and cannot signify, as Morus and Michaelis would render it—"with yourselves," or "within you," but "among yourselves," or "in concert." The verb λαλεῖν has the general signification of "using the voice," and is specifically different from εἰπεῖν and λέγειν, for it is used of the sounds of animals and musical instruments. See the Lexicons, and Tittmann, *De Synon.* pp. 79, 80. Each was not to repeat a psalm to his neighbour, for in such a case confusion and jargon would be the result; but the meaning of the clause seems to be this—" Giving expression among yourselves, or in concert, to your joyous emotions in psalms and hymns and spiritual songs." Λαλοῦντες ἑαυτοῖς, different from λέγοντες πρὸς ἑαυτούς, may, perhaps, signify "in responsive chorus," or *dicere secum invicem*, as Pliny's letter describes it. We know that ancient sacred song was of this antiphonal nature; nay, Nicephorus Callistus in his *History*, xiii. 8, says, that such a practice was handed down from the apostles—τὴν τῶν ἀντιφώνων συνήθειαν ἄνωθεν ἀποστόλων ἡ ἐκκλησία παρέλαβε. Theodoret traces the same custom to the church at Antioch (*Hist. Eccles.* ii. 24), while Socrates ascribes the origin of it to Ignatius. *Hist.* vi. 8. Augustine, however, carries such *responsoria* no higher than the episcopate of Ambrose at Milan. But indeed many of the psalms were composed so as to be sung by a chorus and semichorus, as is plainly marked in the 2nd and in the 24th.

The apostle refers certainly to social intercourse, and in all probability also, and at the same time, to meetings for Divine service. The heathen festivals were noted for intemperate revelry and song, but the Christian congregation was to set an example of hallowed exhilaration and rapture. The pages of Clement of Alexandria throw some light on such ancient practices. *Pædagog.* lib. ii. cap. 4. We cannot say, with Le Clerc and Rückert, that the three following terms are synonymous repetitions, and that the apostle does not characterize different kinds of sacred poetry:—

ψαλμοῖς—" in psalms"—the dative being what Winer calls "the simple dative of direction." § 31, 4. This term, from ψάλλειν—to strike the lyre, is, according to its derivation, a sacred song chanted to the accompaniment of instrumental music. So Basil rightly defines it—ὁ ψαλμὸς, λόγος ἐστὶ μουσικὸς, ὅταν εὐρύθμως κατὰ τοὺς ἁρμονικοὺς λόγους πρὸς τὸ ὄργανον κρούηται. On Ps. xxix. The definition of Gregory of Nyssa is similar—ψαλμός ἐστιν ἡ διὰ τοῦ ὀργάνου τοῦ μουσικοῦ μελῳδία. This specific idea was lost in course of time, and the word retained only the general sense of a sacred poetical composition, and corresponds to the Hebrew מִזְמוֹר. It denotes sometimes the Book of Psalms (Luke xx. 42; Acts i. 20, xiii. 33); and in one place it signifies the improvised effusion of one who possessed some of the charismata, or gifts of the early church. 1 Cor. xiv. 26.

καὶ ὕμνοις—" and hymns." These are also sacred poetical compositions, the primary purpose of which is to praise, as may be seen in those instances in which the verb occurs, Acts xvi. 25; Heb. ii. 12. The term corresponds to the Hebrew words שִׁיר and תְּהִלָּה. Deyling, *Observat. Sacr.* vol. iii. 430; Le Moyne, *Notæ in Varia Sacra*, p. 970. The hymn was more elaborate and solemn in its structure than the ode. The idea of Grotius appears to be quite baseless, that hymns were *extemporales Dei laudes*. The idea of *improvisation* is not necessarily implied in the word, but belongs rather to the following term. The hymn is thus defined by Phavorinus— ὕμνος, ἡ πρὸς Θεὸν ᾠδή; and by Gregory of Nyssa—ὕμνος, ἡ τῷ Θεῷ εὐφημία. The same meaning of the term is found in Arrian—ὕμνοι μὲν ἐς τοὺς θεοὺς ποιοῦνται, etc.—" hymns are composed for the gods, but eulogies for men "—ἔπαινοι δὲ ἐς ἀνθρώπους. *Exped. Alex.* 4. Augustine on Ps. lxxxii. says— *si sit laus, et nisi sit Dei, non est hymnus ; si sit laus, et Dei laus, et non cantetur, non est hymnus. Oportet ergo, ut si sit hymnus, habeat hæc tria, et laudem, et Dei, et canticum.* The Coptic version translates the noun by— ⲈⲨⲤⲘⲞⲨ —"doxologies."

καὶ ᾠδαῖς πνευματικαῖς—" and spiritual songs." Πνευματικαῖς is put within brackets by Lachmann and Alford, on the authority of B and a few authorities. The ode is a general term, and denotes the natural outburst of an excited bosom— the language of the sudden impulses of an Oriental temperament. Such odes as were allowed to Christians are termed "spiritual," that is, prompted by the Spirit which filled them.

But the psalms and hymns are already marked out as consecrated, and needed no such additional epithet. For the prevailing meaning of the adjective, see under i. 3. Odes of this nature are found in Scripture, as that of Hannah at her boy's consecration, that of the Virgin at the Annunciation, and that of Zechariah on the birth of his son. It is plain that the hymn and the ode might pass into one another, but we cannot agree with Harless, in regarding the "songs" as simply a more general designation; or with Meyer, in supposing, whatever the general meaning and the usage elsewhere, that here and in such a connection they are the genus of which psalms and hymns are the species, and that the clause is one of the apostle's common cumulations. As a considerable portion of the church at Ephesus was composed of Jews, these psalms in the idiom of a Jew might be the Psalms of the Old Testament, and not merely sacred poems thus named by them, as is the opinion of Harless; and the hymns might be compositions of praise specially adapted to the Gentile mind, though not inapposite to the Jew. The imagery, allusions, and typical references of the Psalms could not be fully appreciated by the Gentile sections of the churches. And these "spiritual odes," perhaps of a more glowing and individual nature, taking the shape both of psalms and hymns, might be recited or chanted in their assemblies or churches, as the Spirit gave utterance. Acts x. 46. Tertullian says in his *Apology—ut quisquis de Scripturis Sanctis, vel de proprio ingenio potest, provocatur in medium Deo canere.* Many hymns which were originally private and personal, have thus become incorporated with the psalmody of our churches. Stier, who does not coincide with all we have said on this subject, yet gives this definition "biblical, ecclesiastical, and private poems;" and his idea is far better than that of Baumgarten-Crusius, who understands the terms as denoting "songs of thanks, of praise, and lyrics." Jerome says—Hymni *sunt qui fortitudinem et majestatem prædicant Dei, et ejusdem semper vel beneficia vel facta mirantur. Quod omnes* psalmi *continent, quibus Alleluja vel præpositum, vel subjectum est, Psalmi autem proprie ad ethicum locum pertinent, ut per organum corporis, quid faciendum et quid vitandum sit, noverimus. Qui vero de superioribus disputat et concentum mundi omniumque creaturarum ordinem atque concordiam sub-*

*tilis disputator edisserit, iste* spirituale canticum *canit.* The service of song enjoyed peculiar prominence in the ancient church. The Fathers often eulogize the Psalms of David. An exuberant encomium of Basil's may be found in his commentary on the first Psalm. Hooker has some beautiful remarks on the same theme in the fifth book of his *Ecclesiastical Polity*, and the tender and exquisite preface of Bishop Horne must be fresh in the memory of every reader. Eusebius testifies, that besides the Psalms, other compositions were sung in the churches. They were to be—

ᾄδοντες καὶ ψάλλοντες ἐν τῇ καρδίᾳ ὑμῶν—" singing and making melody in your heart." Some MSS., such as A, D, E, F, G, read καρδίαις, but they are counterbalanced by Codices B, K, L, the Syriac version, and the Greek fathers. The previous λαλοῦντες is defined by ᾄδοντες as being co-ordinate with it. The second participle may denote an additional exercise. Their speech was to be song, or they were to be singing as well as speaking. Ψάλλειν, originally " to strike the lyre," came to signify " to strike up a tune," and it denotes the prime accompaniment of these songs, to wit, the symphony of the soul. This is indeed secret and inaudible melody, but it is indispensable to the acceptance of the service—

" Non vox, sed votum, non chordula musica, sed cor;
Non clamans, sed amans, cantat in aure Dei."

Rückert, Harless, Baumgarten-Crusius, Olshausen, and Meyer understand the apostle to inculcate a species of silent warbling, totally distinct from the common practice of song, and which was to be felt as the result of this fulness of the Spirit. But it seems to be to the open and audible expression of Christian feeling that the apostle refers in the phrase λαλοῦντες—καὶ ᾄδοντες; while coupled with this, he adds with emphasis— " playing in your hearts." The words, indeed, denote secret melody, but may not the secret and inner melody form an accompaniment to the uttered song ? The phrase, as Harless says, does not mean heartily, or ἐκ καρδίας would have been employed. Compare Rom. i. 9—ἐν τῷ πνεύματί μου. Theodoret comes nearer our view when he says—" He sings with his heart who not only moves his tongue, but also excites his mind to the understanding of the sentiments repeated,"—

ἀλλὰ καὶ τὸν νοῦν εἰς τὴν τῶν λεγομένων κατανόησιν διεγείρων. Now this silent playing in the heart will be that sincere and genuine emotion, which ought to accompany sacred song. The heart pulsates in unison with the melody. Mere music is but an empty sound; for compass of voice, graceful execution, and thrilling notes are a vain offering in themselves. The Fathers complained sometimes that the mere melody of the church service took away attention from the spirit and meaning of the exercise. Thus Jerome says justly on this passage—"Let young men hear this: let those hear it who have the office of singing in the church, that they sing not with their voice, but with their heart, to the Lord; not like tragedians physically preparing their throat and mouth, that they may sing after the fashion of the theatre in the church. He that has but an ill voice, if he has good works, is a sweet singer before God."[1] . . . "Let the servant of Christ so order his singing, that the words which are read may please more than the voice of the singer; that the spirit which was in Saul may be cast out of them who are possessed with it, and not find admittance in those who have turned the house of God into a stage and theatre of the people."[2] Cowper, with a delicate stroke of satire, says of some in his day—

> "Ten thousand sit
> Patiently present at a sacred song
> . . . . . . . . Content to hear
> (O wonderful effect of music's powers!)
> Messiah's eulogies, for Handel's sake."

τῷ Κυρίῳ—" to the Lord," or as Pliny reported—*Christo quasi Deo*. To Him who loved the church, and died for it— to Him, the Lord of all, who sends down that Spirit which fills the heart and prompts it to melody—such praise is to be

---

[1] "Audiant hæc adolescentuli : audiant hi quibus psallendi in ecclesia officium est, Deo non voce, sed corde cantandum : nec in tragœdorum modum guttur et fauces dulci medicamine colliniendas, ut in ecclesia theatrales moduli audiantur et cantica, sed in timore, in opere, in scientia Scripturarum. Quamvis sit aliquis, ut solent illi appellare κακόφωνος, si bona opera habuerit, dulcis apud Deum cantus est."

[2] "Sic cantet servus Christi, ut non vox canentis, sed verba placeant quæ leguntur : ut spiritus malus, qui erat in Saule, ejiciatur ab his, qui similiter ab eo possidentur, et non introducatur in eos, qui de domo scenam fecere populorum."

rendered. And the early church, in obedience to the apostle's mandate, acknowledged His Divinity, and sang praise to Him as its God. The hymnology of the primitive church leaves not a doubt of its belief in Christ's supreme Divinity. Pye Smith's *Scripture Testimony*, vol. ii. p. 460, ed. 1859; August., *Christl. Archäol.* vol. ii. p. 113 ; Bingham, *Antiquities*, vol. iv. p. 380. One of these very old and venerable relics, the Morning Hymn preserved in the Liturgy of the Church of England, is subjoined as a specimen, not only in its spirit and theology, but in its antiphonal structure—

"Glory be to God on high, and in earth peace, good will towards men. We praise Thee, we bless Thee, we worship Thee, we glorify Thee, we give thanks to Thee for Thy great glory, O Lord God, heavenly King, God the Father Almighty.

"O Lord, the only-begotten Son Jesu Christ ; O Lord God, Lamb of God, Son of the Father, that takest away the sins of the world, have mercy upon us. Thou that takest away the sins of the world, have mercy upon us. Thou that takest away the sins of the world, receive our prayer. Thou that sittest at the right hand of God the Father, have mercy upon us.

"For Thou only art holy ; Thou only art the Lord ; Thou only, O Christ, with the Holy Ghost, art most high in the glory of God the Father. *Amen*."

(Ver. 20.) Εὐχαριστοῦντες πάντοτε ὑπὲρ πάντων—" Giving thanks always for all things." Many collocations as πάντοτε —πάντων are given by Lobeck, *Paralip.* vol. i. pp. 56, 57. This clause is still connected with πληροῦσθε ἐν Πνεύματι, and is further descriptive of one of its results and accompaniments. The heart becomes so susceptible in the possession of this fulness of the Spirit, that grateful emotions predominate, for its own unworthiness is contrasted with God's gifts poured down upon it in crowded succession. 1 Thess. v. 18. And this thanksgiving, from its very nature and causes, is continuous— πάντοτε ὑπὲρ πάντων. Thanksgiving cannot be always formally rendered, but the adverb has the same popular intensive meaning in 1 Thess. v. 18. Some, such as Theodoret, take πάντων in the masculine, which is against the context ; for it is of duty toward God the apostle speaks, not duty toward man, nor can we, with Meyer and others, limit the "all things" to blessings. We take it in a more extended and absolute sense, with Chrysostom, Jerome, and others. Chrysostom, indeed, says—"we are to thank God for hell"—ὑπὲρ τῆς γεέννης αὐτῆς. Whether this extreme sentiment be just or not, it is foreign to the context, for the apostle speaks of "all things" now possessed by us, or sent upon us—οὐχ ὑπὲρ τῶν ἀγαθῶν μόνον, says Theophylact; *etiam in iis quæ adversa putantur*, says Jerome. It is an easy thing to thank God for blessings enjoyed, but not so easy to bless Him in seasons of suffering; yet when men are filled with the Spirit, their modes of thought are so refined and exalted, and their confidence in the Divine benignity is so unhesitating, that they feel even adversity and affliction to be grounds of thanksgiving, for—

"Behind a frowning providence,
He hides a smiling face."

So many and so salutary are the lessons imparted by chastisement—so much mercy is mingled in all their trials—so many proofs are experienced of God's staying "His rough wind in the day of His east wind," that the saints will not hang their harps on the willows, but engage in earnest and blessed minstrelsy. And such eucharistic service is to be presented—

ἐν ὀνόματι τοῦ Κυρίου ἡμῶν Ἰησοῦ Χριστοῦ—" in the name of our Lord Jesus Christ." These thanks are rendered not to "the honour of His name," for the phrase is not εἰς τὸ ὄνομα. To do anything "to the name of," and to do it "in the name" of another, are widely different. The former implies honour and homage; the latter authority and warrant. Compare εἰς τὸ ὄνομα, Matt. xxviii. 19; Acts xix. 5; 1 Cor. i. 13, 15; but ἐν τῷ ὀνόματι has a very different meaning, as may be seen in John xiv. 13; Acts iv. 12, x. 48; Col. iii. 17; 2 Thess. iii. 6; 1 Pet. iv. 14. His name is the one element in which thanks are to be rendered—that is, by His warrant thanks are offered, and for His sake they are accepted. The phrase occurs in many connections, of which Harless has given only a sample. Thus in His name miracles are done, Luke x. 17, Acts iii. 6, iv. 10, xvi. 18, Jas. v. 14; ordinances are dispensed, Acts x. 48, 1 Cor. v. 4; devotional service is offered and prayer answered, John xiv. 13, xvi. 23, 26, Phil. ii. 10; claim of Divine commission is made, Mark xi. 9, Luke xix. 38; blessing is enjoyed, Acts iv. 12, 1 Cor. vi. 11; the spiritual rule of life is enjoined, Col. iii. 17; a solemn charge is made, 2 Thess. iii. 6; reproach is borne,

1 Pet. iv. 14; or certain states of mind are possessed, Acts ix. 27, 28. Whatever the varieties of relation, or act, or state, the same generic idea underlies them all—as Bengel says, *ut perinde sit ac si Christus faciat.* Giving thanks—
τῷ Θεῷ καὶ Πατρί—"to God and the Father." The article, as in similar places, is not repeated before the second noun, for it is but another epithet of Him who is named under the first term. Winer, § 19, 3, note. See under i. 3. As to the relation of Πατήρ, Erasmus, Estius, Harless, Meyer, and Baumgarten-Crusius refer it to Christ; but others, as Zanchius, Rückert, and Matthies, refer it to believers. The word, however, appears to have been employed in a general sense, for the paternal character of God has relation as well to His own Son, as to all His adopted human children.

(Ver. 21.) Ὑποτασσόμενοι ἀλλήλοις ἐν φόβῳ Χριστοῦ— 'Submitting yourselves to one another in the fear of Christ." Rom. xiii. 1; 1 Pet. ii. 13, v. 5. The authority for Θεοῦ is so slight, that it need not be recounted. This additional participial clause, which concludes the paragraph, forms also a link between it and the next. Indeed, it commences a new section in Knapp's edition, and Olshausen inclines to the same opinion, but the participial form ὑποτασσόμενοι forbids such a supposition. Chrysostom joins the clause to the former verses, and his arrangement is followed by Rückert, Meier, Estius, Meyer, Harless. Winer, § 45, 6. Olshausen mistakes the connection when he wonders how an advice to subordination can be introduced as a sequel to spiritual joy. But the participle ὑποτασσόμενοι is joined to πληροῦσθε, and has no necessary or explanatory connection with the other dependent participles preceding it. It introduces a new train of thought, and is so far connected with the previous verb, as to indicate that this reciprocal deference has its root and origin in the fulness of the Spirit. It would perhaps be going too far to say, that as the phrase, "be not drunk with wine," is related to the clause, "be filled with the Spirit," so this connected verse stands opposed, at the same time, to that self-willed perversity and that fond and foolish egotism which inebriety so often creates. It is out of all rule, on the part of Calvin, Zanchius, Koppe, Flatt, and Matthies, to take the participle as an imperative. The words ἐν φόβῳ Χριστοῦ describe the element of this submission. It is reverential submission to Christ. Acts ix. 31 ; 2 Cor. v. 11, vii. 1 ; 1 Pet. iii. 2. Φόβος here is not terror or slavish apprehension, but that solemn awe which the authority of Christ inspires. In this the mutual deference and submission commanded by the apostle must have their seat. This Christian virtue is not cringing obsequiousness ; and while it stands opposed to rude and dictatorial insolence, and to that selfish preference for our own opinion and position which amounts to a claim of infallibility, it is not inconsistent with that honest independence of disposition and sentiment which every rational and responsible being must exercise. It lays the foundation also, as is seen in the following context, for the discharge of relative duty, as in the three instances of wives, children, and servants, nor is it without room for exhibition in the case of husbands, parents, and masters; in short, it should be seen to develop itself in all the relations of domestic life.

(Ver. 22.) With regard to the following admonition it is to be borne in mind, that in those days wives, when converted and elevated from comparative servitude, might be tempted, in the novel consciousness of freedom, to encroach a little—as if to put to the test the extent of their recent liberty and enlargement. The case was also no uncommon one for Christian wives to have unbelieving husbands, and the wife might imagine that there was for her an opportunity to manifest the superiority of a new and happy creed. 1 Pet. iii. 1–6. And those Ephesian wives had little of the literary and none of the religious education enjoyed by the daughters of modern Christian households. Even under the Mosaic law, women and wives had few legal rights, and they too, when baptized, needed the injunction of the apostle—

αἱ γυναῖκες τοῖς ἰδίοις ἀνδράσιν, ὡς τῷ Κυρίῳ—" wives, submit yourselves to your own husbands, as to the Lord." The sentence has no verb, and it afforded, therefore, a fair opportunity for the ingenuity of the early copyists. Some MSS., such as D, E, F, G, add ὑποτάσσεσθε after γυναῖκες. Scholz and Hahn place the same word after ἀνδράσιν, while A and some minusculi add ὑποτασσέσθωσαν—a reading followed by Lachmann. There are other variations in the form of attempted supplement. Jerome proves that there was nothing in the Greek Codices to correspond to the *subditæ sint* of the Latin version. The continuity of the apostle's style did not require any verbal supplement, and though the gender differs, every tyro will acquiesce in the reason given by Jerome —ἐκ κοινοῦ *resonat*. Jelf, § 391. The idea conveyed in the participle of the previous verse guides the sense. Wives, in the spirit of this submission, are to be directed in their duty to their husbands. The noun ἀνήρ often signifies a husband, as "man" does in vernacular Scotch. Matt. i. 16; John iv. 16–18; Homer, *Od*. xxiv. 195; Herod. i. 140. So also איש in Hebrew, Deut. xxii. 23. The precise meaning of ἰδίοις in this connection has been disputed. There are two extremes; that indicated by Valla, Bullinger, Bengel, Steiger, and Meyer, as if the apostle meant to say, Your own husbands—not other and stranger men; and that maintained by de Wette, Harless, and Olshausen, that ἰδίοις merely stands for the common possessive pronoun. But in all such injunctions in which ἰδίοις is used, as in 1 Cor. vii. 2, Col. iii. 18, 1 Pet. iii. 1, the word seems to indicate peculiar closeness of possession and relation, though indeed in later Greek its meaning is somewhat relaxed. John v. 18; Rom. viii. 32; 1 Cor. xiv. 35, etc. Winer, § 22, 7; Phrynich. ed. Lobeck, 441. The duty of submission is plainly based on that tenderness, speciality, or exclusiveness of relationship which ἰδίοις implies. But that submission is not servitude, for the wife is not a mere vassal. The sentiment of Paul is not that of the heathen poet—

Πᾶσα γὰρ δούλη πέφυκεν ἀνδρὸς ἡ σώφρων γυνή,[1]
ἡ δὲ μὴ σώφρων ἀνοίᾳ τὸν ξυνόνθ' ὑπερφρονεῖ.

The insubordination of wives has always been a fertile source of satire; and yet Christian ladies in early times drew forth this compliment from Libanius, the "last glory of expiring paganism"—*proh, quales feminas habent Christiani!* The essence of this submission is explained by the important words—

ὡς τῷ Κυρίῳ—" as to the Lord." Pelagius, Thomas Aquinas, and Semler capriciously regard this noun as standing for the plural κυρίοις, and render it "as to your masters," referring to their husbands. Rückert, Harless, Olshausen, Meyer, and

[1] Euripides, *Œdip. Fragm. Opera, curâ Dindorf*, ii. p. 923.

Matthies take it to mean, that ye render this submission to your husbands as if it were rendered to Christ who enjoins it; or, as Chrysostom more lucidly explains it—ὡς εἰδυῖαι ὅτι τῷ Κυρίῳ δουλεύετε. The adverb ὡς denotes the character of the obedience enjoined, and such seems to be the grammatical meaning of the clause. The context, however, might suggest another phase of meaning. "Women," says Olshausen, "are to be in submission, not to their husbands as such, but to the ordinance of God in the institution of marriage." And so de Wette, preceded by Erasmus, observes that the clause is explained by the following verse. The husband stands to the wife in the same relation as Christ stands to the church, and the meaning then is, not as if she were doing a religious duty, but "in like manner as to the Lord"—the duties of the church to Him being the same in Spirit as those of a wife to her husband. In either case, the submission of a wife is a religious obligation. She may be in many things man's superior—in sympathy, in delicacy of sentiment, warmth of devotion, in moral heroism, and in power and patience of self-denial. Still the obedience inculcated by the apostle sits gracefully upon her, and is in harmony with all that is fair and feminine in her position and temperament:

> "For contemplation he and valour formed—
> For softness she and sweet attractive grace:
> He for God only, she for God and him."

(Ver. 23.) "Ὅτι ἀνήρ ἐστιν κεφαλὴ τῆς γυναικὸς, ὡς καὶ ὁ Χριστὸς κεφαλὴ τῆς ἐκκλησίας—"For the husband is head of the wife, as also Christ is Head of the church." The preponderance of authority is against the article ὁ before ἀνήρ, which appears in the Received Text. It does not need the article (Winer, § 19), though the article would not alter the meaning. It stands here as a species of monadic noun; or it may be rendered as a general proposition—"as a husband is the head of the wife"—the article before γυναικός pointing out the special relation—"his wife." Ὅτι introduces the reason why wives should be submissive—"as to the Lord." In the phrase ὡς καί—"as also"—καί is not superfluous, though it occurs only in the second clause and marks the sameness of relation in κεφαλή. Klotz, Devar. vol. ii. 635. The meaning of the sentiment, Christ is the Head of the church, has been already explained under i. 22, and again under iv. 15, 16. The reader may turn to these explanations. As Christ is Head of the church, so the husband is head of the wife. Authority and government are lodged in him; the household has its unity and centre in him; from him the wife receives her cherished help; his views and feelings are naturally adopted and acted out by her; and to him she looks up for instruction and defence. Severed from him she becomes a widow, desolate and cheerless; the ivy which clasped itself so lovingly round the oak, pines and withers when its tree has fallen. And there is only one head; dualism would be perpetual antagonism. This marital headship is man's prerogative in virtue of his prior creation, for he was first formed in sole and original dignity. 1 Tim. ii. 13. "Neither was the man created for the woman, but the woman for the man," so that he is in position the superior. "The man is not of the woman, but the woman of the man"—a portion of himself—his other self; taken out from near his heart; and, therefore, though his equal in personality and fellowship, being of him and for him and after him, she is second to him. Nay, more, "Adam was not deceived; but the woman, being deceived, was in the transgression;" and to her the Lord God said, "Thy desire shall be to thy husband, and he shall rule over thee," though the gospel lightens this portion of the curse which has been so terribly felt in all non-Christian lands. Each sex is indeed imperfect by itself, and the truest unity is conjugal duality. Still, though the woman was originally of the man, yet now "the man is by the woman"—"the mother of all living." Finally, the apostle illustrates this headship by the striking declaration, that the woman is the "glory of the man," but "the man is the image and glory of God." 1 Cor. xi. 3-12; 1 Tim. ii. 14.

αὐτὸς σωτὴρ τοῦ σώματος—"Himself Saviour of the body." The words καί and ἐστι in the Received Text are found in $D^2$, $D^3$, $E^2$, K, L, in the majority of MSS., and in the Syriac and Gothic versions. Tittmann and Reiche also hold by the longer reading, but the words are wanting in A, B, $D^1$, $E^1$, F, G, while Codex A reads ὁ σωτήρ. Αὐτός is emphatic, and can refer only to Χριστός. "Christ is Head of the church—Himself, and none other, Saviour of the body." Winer,

§ 59, 7, note. Some refer it to ἀνήρ. Chrysostom's exposition would seem to imply such a reference, and Holzhausen formally adopts it. But it is of Christ the apostle is speaking, and the independent and emphatic clause, thrown off without any connecting particle, gives a reason why He is head of the church, to wit—" Himself Saviour of the body." The reader may turn to the meaning of σῶμα under i. 23, iv. 15, 16. The paronomasia is imitated by Clement, *ad Corinth.* xxxviii. —σωζέσθω οὖν ἡμῶν ὅλον τὸ σῶμα ἐν Χριστῷ Ἰησοῦ. Christ is the Saviour of His body the church—not only its Redeemer by an act of atonement, but its continued Deliverer, Preserver, and Benefactor, and so is deservedly its Head. This Headship originated in the benefits which His church has enjoyed, and is based on His saving work; while the conscious enjoyment of that salvation brings the church gladly to acknowledge His sole supremacy. Some, indeed, suppose that in this clause there is an implied comparison, and that the husband is a species of σωτήρ to his wife. Bucer, Bullinger,[1] Musculus, Aretius, Zanchius, Erasmus, Grotius, Beza, Schrader, Rückert, Baumgarten-Crusius, Meier, Matthies, de Wette, and Peile are of this mind. But the clause is peculiar, αὐτός separating it from what is said before. There is a comparison in κεφαλή, that is, in the point of position and authority, but none in σωτήρ; for the love and protection which a husband may afford a wife can never be called σωτηρία, and has no resemblance to Christ's salvation. Some even suppose that the wife is here called σῶμα, basing their opinion on the language of ver. 28. There is no warrant for supposing that in the apostle's mind there was any etymological affinity between σωτήρ and σῶμα, which in Homer signifies a dead body. See Stier, *in loc.*; Benfey, *Wurzellex.* i. p. 412; and the two derivations in Plato, *Cratylus,* § 38, p. 233; *Op.* vol. iv. ed. Bekker.

(Ver. 24.) Ἀλλ' ὡς ἡ ἐκκλησία ὑποτάσσεται τῷ Χριστῷ— " But as the church is subject to Christ." The reading ὥσπερ has no decided authority. The commencement of this clause occasions some difficulty. The hypothesis of Harless—not unlike that of Rückert, that ἀλλά is used to resume the main discourse—has been ably refuted by Olshausen. It is true

[1] Bullinger says—*maritus uxoris saluti, consulat, erudiat, defendat, nutriat.*

that ἀλλά does often follow a digression, but there is none here; and even if the words were a digression, they form but a single clause, and did not surely necessitate a formal ἀλλά. To give this particle, with Zanchius and others, the meaning of "now" or "wherefore," cannot be allowed, however such a meaning may seem to suit the reasoning. 'Ἀλλά, says Olshausen, simply introduces the proof drawn from what precedes. The husband is head of the wife, as Christ is Head of the church, and the apostle argues—"but as the church is subject to Christ, so ought wives to be to their husbands." Winer, § 53, 7, $a$,[1] says that ἀλλά concludes the demonstration. De Wette's view is similar—"the clause exhibits the other aspect of the relation, as if he said—*aber daraus folgt auch.*" Hofmann understands the antithesis thus—"but where the husband is not to his wife what he should be, in imitation of Christ, still subordination on her part remains a duty." *Schriftb.* vol. ii. 2, p. 116. Robinson says that ἀλλά is used in an antithetic clause to express something additional, and may be rendered "but," "but now," "but further." In the instances adduced by him there is marked antithesis; but though this passage is placed among them, there is in it no expressed contrast. Baumgarten-Crusius smiles at such as find any difficulty in ἀλλά, for it means, he says, *dennoch aber*—though the husband has his obligation as saviour of the body, the wife, yet the wife has hers too, and should be obedient. This interpretation creates an antithesis by giving the clause "He is Saviour of the body" a meaning it cannot bear. See Bretschneider's *Lexicon, sub voce.* Meyer and Stier follow an alternative explanation of Calvin, making the antithesis of the following nature—"Christ has this as a special characteristic, that He is Saviour of His church; nevertheless, let wives know, that their husbands are over them after the example of Christ." Meyer's improved representation of this idea is—"He Himself, and none other, is the Saviour of the body, yet this relation, which belongs to Him exclusively, does not supersede the obligation of obedience on the part of wives towards their husband; but as the church is subject to Christ, so ought wives to submit to their husbands." The same antithesis is more lucidly phrased by Bengel—"though

---

[1] Moulton, pp. 551-2.

Christ and not the husband is the Saviour, and though the husband can have no such claim on his wife, yet the wife is to obey him as the church obeys Christ." Similarly Hodge, Ellicott, and Alford. The sense is good, but sounds like a truism. "Himself is Saviour of the body—that certainly man is not and cannot be, nevertheless as," etc.—you are to obey your husbands, who can never have claims on you like Christ. The choice is between this and giving ἀλλά an antithetic reference. It is very often used after an implied negative, especially after questions which imply a negative answer. Luke vii. 7; John vii. 49; Acts xix. 2. See also Rom. iii. 31, viii. 37; 1 Cor. vi. 8, ix. 12. And without a question, such usage, implying a suppressed negative answer, is prevalent. Compare Luke xxiii. 15; 2 Cor. viii. 7, xiii. 4; Gal. ii. 3; Phil. i. 18, ii. 17; 1 Tim. i. 15, 16; Vigerus, *De Idiotismis*, cap. viii. § 1. A singularly acute paper on οὐκ ἀλλά will be found in the appendix to the Commentary of Fritzsche on Mark. If we apply such an idiom to the passage before us, the sense will then be this: The man is head of the woman, as Christ is Head of the church—Himself Saviour of the body—do not disallow the marital headship, for it is a Divine institution—ἀλλά—but as the church is subject to Christ—

οὕτως καὶ αἱ γυναῖκες τοῖς ἀνδράσιν ἐν παντί (ὑποτασσέσ-θωσαν)—"so let the wives be subject to their husbands in everything." Ἰδίοις, which in the Received Text stands before ἀνδράσιν, is properly rejected from the text. The words ἐν παντί mean in everything within the proper circuit of conjugal obligation. If the husband trespass beyond this sphere he usurps, and cannot insist upon the obedience implied in the matrimonial contract. Obedience on the part of a wife is not a superinduced obligation. It springs from the affection and softness of her very nature, which is not fitted for robust and masculine independence, but feels the necessity of reliance and protection. It is made to confide, not to govern. In the domestic economy, though government and obedience certainly exist, they are not felt in painful or even formal contrast; and, in fact, they are so blended in affectionate adjustment, that the line which severs them cannot be distinguished. The law of marital government is a νόμος ἄγραφος. Even the heathen poets, as may be seen in the following quotations from

Menander, Philemon, and Euripides, acknowledged such a law, though they could not treat the subject with the tenderness, beauty, and propriety of the apostle. Their notions are harder—

'Αγαθῆς γυναικός ἐστιν, . . . .
Μὴ κρεῖττον εἶναι τ' ἀνδρὸς, ἀλλ' ὑπήκοον.

Their images are humiliating—

Τὰ δευτερεῖα τὴν γυναῖκα δεῖ λέγειν,

and the feminine consciousness both of weakness and degradation occasionally breaks out—

'Αλλ' ἐννοεῖν χρὴ τοῦτο μὴν, γυναῖχ' ὅτι
Ἔφυμεν, ὡς πρὸς ἄνδρας οὐ μαχουμένα.

(Ver. 25.) *Οἱ ἄνδρες, ἀγαπᾶτε τὰς γυναῖκας ἑαυτῶν*—" Husbands, love your own wives." The apostle now turns to the duties of husbands. There is some doubt as to the word ἑαυτῶν. Lachmann and Tischendorf reject it; A and B want it; but D, E, K, L, have it. Some MSS., such as F and G, read ὑμῶν instead. But there is not sufficient ground to reject it. As wives are summoned to obedience, so husbands are commanded to cherish love. The apostle dwells upon it. In Eastern countries, where polygamy was so frequent, conjugal love was easily dissipated; and among the Jews, the seclusion of unmarried young women often made it possible that the bridegroom was a stranger not only to the temper and manners of his bride, but even to the features of her face. Disappointment, followed by quarrel and divorce, must have been a frequent result. Therefore the apostle wished Christian husbands to be patterns of domestic virtue, and to love their wives. If love leads to conjugal union, and to the selection of a woman to be a wife, surely the affection which originated such an alliance ought to sustain and cheer it. Surliness, outbursts of temper, passionate remonstrances for mere trifles, are condemned. Husbands are not to be domestic tyrants; but their dominion is to be a reign of love. As the example of the church in her relation to Christ is set before wives, so the example of Christ, in His relation to the church, is set before husbands—

καθὼς καὶ ὁ Χριστὸς ἠγάπησεν τὴν ἐκκλησίαν—" as also Christ loved the church." For καθώς, see i. 4, and καθὼς καί, iv. 32 and v. 2; and for ἐκκλησια, see i. 22. That church was originally impure and sinful—an infant exposed on the day of its birth, " to the loathing of its person;" but the Divine Lover passed by and said to it, " Live," for its "time was the time of love." The exposed foundling was His foster-child before it became His bride. Ezek. xvi. Similar phraseology as to love embodied in atonement has been employed in the 2nd verse of this chapter. What infinite pity and ineffable condescension are found in Christ's love to His church! Every blessing enjoyed by her must be traced upward and backward to the attachment of the Saviour. The church did not crave His love: He bestowed it. It was not excited by any loveliness of aspect on the part of the church, for she was guilty and impure—unworthy of His affection. But His love for her was a fondness tender beyond all conception, and ardent beyond all parallel—

καὶ ἑαυτὸν παρέδωκεν ὑπὲρ αὐτῆς—" and gave Himself for her." This phraseology has also occurred in the 2nd verse of this chapter, and been there considered. Christ's sacrificial death in the room of His church, is the proof and expression of His love. What love to present such a gift! None could be nobler than Himself—the God-man—and so cheerfully conferred! That gift involved a death of inexpressible anguish, rendered still more awful by the endurance of the terrible penalty; and yet He shrank not from it. Who can doubt a love which has proved its strength and glory in such suffering and death? Now the love of the husband towards his wife is to be an image or reflection of Christ's love to the church; like it, ardent and devoted; like it, tender and self-abandoning; and like it, anxious above all things and by any sacrifice to secure the happiness of its object. He gave Himself—

(Ver. 26.) Ἵνα αὐτὴν ἁγιάσῃ, καθαρίσας τῷ λουτρῷ τοῦ ὕδατος ἐν ῥήματι—" In order that He might sanctify her, having cleansed her by the laver of the water in the word." This verse contains the nearer purpose, and the following verse unfolds the ulterior design of the Saviour's love and death, both being introduced by the telic ἵνα. The account given of the term ἅγιος under i. 1, will serve so far to explain the meaning of the allied verb which occurs in this clause. It denotes to consecrate or to set apart, and then to make holy as the result of this consecration. Matt. xxiii. 17; 1 Cor. vii. 14; 1 Thess. v. 23; Heb. ii. 11. Calvin, Beza, Harless, and Meier take the verb in the former sense. Others, such as Piscator, Rückert, Meyer, de Wette, Baumgarten-Crusius, Matthies, and Stier, give the meaning of moral or spiritual purification. The first appears to us to be the prominent idea, but not, certainly, to the exclusion of the last signification. That He might consecrate her, or set her apart to Himself as His own redeemed and peculiar possession—that she should be His and His alone—His by a special tie of tender devotedness—was the object of His death. Rückert objects to this exegesis, that the dative ἑαυτῷ or τῷ Θεῷ is wanting, but the supplement is implied in the verb itself. Wholly out of the question is the interpretation of Koppe, Flatt, and Matthies, that the verb means to make expiation for—to absolve from guilt. It is true that ἁγιάζω is used in the Septuagint for the Hebrew—כִּפֶּר (Ex. xxix. 33, 36), and Stuart (*Commentary on Heb.* ii. 10) maintains that the verb has such a meaning in the Epistle to the Hebrews, but the examples which he has adduced admit of the meaning we have assigned to the word in the passage before us. Heb. x. 10, etc., xiii. 11, 12. See Delitzsch *in loc.*, *Comment. zum B. an die Hebräer*, p. 71, and Bleek *in loc.*, *Der B. an die Hebräer*, who hold our view. Moreover, if καθαρίσας refer, as it does, to spiritual purification, then it can scarcely be thought that the apostle expresses the same idea in the previous verb ἁγιάσῃ. The meaning is, that having purified her He might consecrate her to Himself; this idea being suspended till it is brought out with special emphasis in the following verse. Meyer distinguishes ἁγιάσῃ from καθαρίσας, as if the last were the negative and the first the positive aspect of the idea. The distinction is baseless, for the purifying is as positive as is the sanctification. Harless errs in denying that here, whatever may be the fact elsewhere, the action of the participle precedes that of the verb, and in supposing that they coincide in time—καθαρίσας being a further definition of ἁγιάσῃ. Hofmann, *loc. cit.*, connects καθαρίσας immediately with ἵνα παραστήσῃ, but very needlessly. This exegesis is as baseless as is the Syriac version and our

English translation—"that He might sanctify and cleanse it." The nominative to the verb is contained in the participle. Rückert, Matthies, and Olshausen render it "after that He has purified"—*nachdem*. De Wette, on the other hand, prefers *indem*—"since that." The meaning is not different, if the participle be thus supposed to contain a pre-existent cause.

The idea expressed by καθαρίσας is that of purification, and its nature is to be learned from the following terms expressive of instrumentality. That the phrase τῷ λουτρῷ τοῦ ὕδατος refers to the rite of baptism, is the general and correct opinion, the genitive being that of material, and the dative that of instrument, while the two articles express the recognized prominence as well of the water as of the laver. But as the entire paragraph presents a nuptial image, we see no reason on the part of Harless, Olshausen, and others, for denying all allusion to the peculiar and customary antenuptial lustrations. The church is the bride, "the Lamb's wife;" and described under this appellation, her baptism may be viewed as being at the same time—λουτρὸν νυμφικόν. Bos (*Exercitat.* p. 186), Elsner, Wetstein, Flatt, Bengel, Rückert, Matthies, Holzhausen, and Stier concur in the same representation. The washing of water in baptism was the sacrament expressive of purification. Acts ii. 38, xxii. 16; Heb. x. 22. Baptism is called λουτρὸν παλιγγενεσίας—"the laver of regeneration," a phrase farther explained by the following words—ἀνακαινώσεως πνεύματος ἁγίου—"the renewing of the Holy Ghost." Tit. iii. 5.

But the additional words, ἐν ῥήματι, are not so easily understood. Quite foreign to the thought is the opinion of Hofmann, that as a man declares his will to make a woman his wife by a word or declaration, and so takes her from the unhonour of her maiden condition, so has Christ done to the church. *Schriftb.* vol. ii. 2, 173. Some of the conflicting opinions may be noted:—

I. The Greek fathers, followed by Ambrosiaster, Anselm, Thomas Aquinas, Calovius, Flatt, and de Wette, easily understand the phrase of the baptismal formula. Chrysostom says —ἐν ῥήματι φησί; then he puts the question, ποίῳ? "in what word?" and his ready answer is, "In the name of the

Father, and of the Son, and of the Holy Ghost." But it is not at all probable that ῥῆμα should stand for ὄνομα; and if it did, we should expect, as Harless intimates, to have it emphasized with an article prefixed. Nor has the word such a signification in any other portion of the New Testament.

II. Semler would strike out the words altogether; Michaelis would regard ῥῆμα as a Pauline Cilicism for ῥεῦμα; while Ernesti and Koppe, imitated by Stolz, join the words ἐν ῥήματι ἵνα together, and suppose that they stand for the Hebrew formula—עַל דְּבַר אֲשֶׁר—"in order that." The Seventy, however, never so render the Hebrew idiom, but translate it by ἕνεκεν. Gen. xx. 6, 11; Num. xvi. 49; Ps. xliv. 4.

III. Some join ἐν ῥήματι to the verb ἁγιάσῃ—" that He might sanctify by the word," the intervening clause, " having cleansed by the washing of water," being a parenthesis. This exegesis yields a good meaning, and is contended for by Jerome, Flacius, Baumgarten, Morus, Bisping, Rückert, Meyer, and Winer, § 20, 2 (b.).[1] But the position of ἐν ῥήματι at the very end of the verse, forbids such an exegesis. It is a forced expedient, and the only reason for adopting it is the confessed difficulty of explaining the words in their obvious and natural connection.

IV. By other critics the phrase ἐν ῥήματι is joined to τῷ λουτρῷ τοῦ ὕδατος, as a qualificative or descriptive epithet. Such is the view of Augustine, Sedulius, Luther, Estius, Calvin, Erasmus, Flatt, Storr, Homberg, Holzhausen, and Stier. But though these scholars agree as to the general connection, their opinions vary much as to the special signification. The common argument against this and similar constructions, to wit, that the article should have been repeated before ἐν ῥήματι, has many exceptions, though in such a proposed construction its insertion would appear to be necessary:—

1. Augustine (*Tractatus* lxxx. *in Johannem*), Estius, Bodius, Röell, Crellius, Slichtingius, Flatt, Holzhausen, and the critics generally who are enumerated under No. IV., take ῥῆμα as signifying the gospel. Augustine says—*accedit verbum ad elementum, et fit sacramentum. Sacramento simul et fidei*, says Estius; or again, *aquæ baptismo per verbum evangelii creditum*

[1] Moulton, p. 172.

*ac fide susceptum mundat.* Bodius writes—*verbum ut diploma, sacramentum ut sigillum.* These meanings give ἐν an unwonted sense of "along with, or by means of." Had the apostle meant to say that the efficacy of baptism lies in faith in the word, surely other language would have been employed. The view of Knapp (*Vorlesungen über die Christ. Glaubenslehre,* ii. § 140) is of the same nature, and is liable to similar objections. "The Word," he says, "is the evangelical system in its fullest extent — its precepts and promises." "In baptism," he adds, "the latter are made over, and we pledge ourselves to obey the former. Baptism may be thus called *verbum Dei visibile.*"

2. Others look on ῥῆμα as denotive of Divine agency in baptism. This was Luther's view, as expressed in his *Smaller Catechism*—*verbum Dei quod in et cum aqua est* (*Die Symbolischen Bücher der Evang. Luth. Kirche,* p. 362, ed. Müller). Calvin's view is somewhat similar—*verbo sublato perit tota vis sacramentorum. . . . Porro verbum hic promissionem significat, qua vis et usus signi explicatur. . . In verbo tantum valet atque per verbum.* This notion is imitated also by Rollock. The preposition ἐν may bear such a signification. Still, had the apostle meant to say that baptism derived its efficacy from the word, surely something more than the simple addition ἐν ῥήματι might have been expected. Olshausen looks upon ἐν ῥήματι as equivalent to ἐν Πνεύματι—" as signifying a bath in the word, that is, a bath in which one is born of water and of the Spirit." This strange opinion cuts the knot, but does not untie it. Similar is the view of Stier, and Homberg who paraphrases—*aqua verbalis et spiritualis.* The proposition of Grotius is no less violent, inserting the particle ὡς before τῷ λουτρῷ—washing them by the word "as" in a bath of water.

3. A third party, such as Storr—*Opuscula Academica,* i. 194 —and Peile, give ῥῆμα the sense of mandate—*præscriptum.* "The apostle," says Peile, "declares water-baptism to be the divinely-instituted sign or sacrament whereby men are regenerated." This notion gives ἐν the strange sense of " in conformity to."

V. and lastly. Others, such as Bengel, Matthies, and Harless, join the words ἐν ῥήματι with καθαρίσας. To this opinion we incline; but we cannot agree with Harless in giving the phrase the meaning of *ausspruchsweise, verheissungsweise*. The idea in such an explanation is, that the cleansing is given in the form of a declaration or promise made in the ordinance. But there is no need to depart from the ordinary meaning of ῥῆμα in the New Testament. The Syriac reads—"that he might sanctify and purify her in the laver of water and by the word;" and the Vulgate has—*in verbo vitæ*. But we regard ἐν as denoting the instrument in its internal operation, and so far different from διά; and by ῥῆμα we understand the gospel, the usual meaning of the Greek term. Acts. x. 44, xi. 14; Rom. x. 8, 17; Eph. vi. 17; Heb. vi. 5. It wants the article as if it were used, as Meyer suggests, like a proper name. It is a mere refinement on the part of Baumgarten-Crusius to understand by it "a preached gospel." The church is cleansed "by the laver of the water"—cleansed by "the word." The washing of water symbolizes the pardon of sin and the regeneration of the heart. While this cleansing has its sacramental symbol in the washing of water, it has its special instrument in the word; or τῷ λουτρῷ in the simple dative may denote the instrument (Bernhardy, p. 100), and ἐν ῥήματι the "conditional element," as Alford calls it. The word is the Spirit's element in effecting a blessed and radical change, and in guiding, ruling, and prompting the heart into which the new life has been infused. Men are thus cleansed by baptism in the word. Ps. cxix. 9; 1 Pet. i. 23. Thomasius, *Christi Person und Werk*, § 66, Erlangen, 1859. Christ accomplishes these results through His death, and what is properly done by His Spirit may be ascribed to Himself, who for this other purpose loved the church and gave Himself for it—

(Ver. 27.) *Ἵνα παραστήσῃ αὐτὸς ἑαυτῷ ἔνδοξον τὴν ἐκκλησίαν*—"in order that He might present, Himself to Himself, the church glorious." Αὐτός, supported by the authority of A, B, D¹, F, G, L, and many versions and Fathers, is decidedly to be preferred to the αὐτήν of the Textus Receptus. This verse declares the ultimate purpose of the love and death of Him who is "both Ransom and Redeemer voluntary." Harless errs in regarding the two clauses beginning with ἵνα as co-ordinate. The allusion is still to a nuptial ceremony, and to the presentation of the bride to her husband—αὐτὸς—ἑαυτῷ. The august Bridegroom does not present His spouse to Himself till He can look upon her with complacency. Harless affirms that the presentation described is that of a sacrifice on the altar, because the epithets employed by the apostle are occasionally applied to victims and offerings; but such a view is in conflict with the entire language and imagery on to the end of the chapter. Nay, there is a peculiar beauty in applying sacrificial terms to the fair and immaculate bride, as she is fit, even according to legal prescription, to be presented to her Lord. So Meyer remarks ἑαυτῷ would be out of place in the theory of Harless—Jesus presenting an oblation to Himself! The word παραστήσῃ occurs with a similar meaning in 2 Cor. xi. 2—" that I may present you as a chaste virgin to Christ." Αὐτὸς—ἑαυτῷ—He and none other presents the bride, and HE and none other receives her to HIMSELF. No inferior agency is permitted; a proof in itself, as well as His death, of His love to the church. "Ἔνδοξον—" glorious;" the epithet being a tertiary predicate and emphatic in position. Donaldson, § 489. The same idea occurs in Rev. xix. 7, 8. The term refers originally to external appearance—the combined effect of person and dress. The illustrious epithet is explained by the succeeding clauses—first negative—

μὴ ἔχουσαν σπίλον, ἢ ῥυτίδα, ἤ τι τῶν τοιούτων—" having neither spot, or wrinkle, or any one of such things." Σπῖλος, which ought to be spelled with a simple accent—σπίλος (ἄσπιλος forming a dactyle), is a stain or blemish, and is one of the words of the later Greeks. 2 Pet. ii. 13. Λέγε δὲ κηλίς, as the older Attic term, says Phrynicus (p. 28). Ῥυτίς is a wrinkle or fold on the face, indicative of age or disease. Dioscorides, i. 39; Passow, *sub voce*. Not only are spots and wrinkles excluded, but every similar blemish. The terms are taken from physical beauty, health, and symmetry, to denote spiritual perfection. Cant. iv. 7. The attempts made by some critics, such as Anselm, Estius, and Grotius, to distinguish nicely and formally between the virtues or graces described in these terms respectively, are needless. Thus Augustine takes the first term to mean *deformitas operis*, and the second *duplicitas intentionis*, and the last inclusive phrase to comprehend *reliquiæ peccatorum ut pravæ inclinationis, motus involuntarii et multiplicis ignorantiæ*. Not only negatively but positively—

ἀλλ' ἵνα ᾖ ἁγία καὶ ἄμωμος—"but that she should be holy and without blemish." One might have expected ἀλλ' οὖσαν, but it is as if ἵνα μὴ ἔχῃ σπίλον had stood in the previous clause. The syntax is thus changed, no uncommon occurrence in Greek composition, as may be seen in John viii. 53; Rom. xii. 1, 2. On the *oratio variata*, compare Winer, § 63, 2, 1. The syntactic change here, with the repetition of ἵνα, gives special prominence to the idea which has been expressed, first negatively, but now in this clause with positive affirmation. The meaning of ἁγία has been given already under i. 1, 4; and of ἄμωμος under i. 4, and needs not be repeated here. Such, then, is to be the ultimate perfection and destiny of the church. In her spotless purity the love of Christ finds its extreme and glorious design realized. That love which led Him to die, in order to bestow pardon and to secure holiness, is not contented till its object be robed in unsullied and unchanging purity.

But when is this perfection to be for the first time possessed, and when does this presentation take place? We have already said that the presentation is not contemporary with the consecration, but is posterior to it, and does not finally and formally take place on earth. The "church" we understand in its full significance, as the whole company of the redeemed, personified and represented as a spiritual Spouse. The presentation belongs therefore to the period of the second coming, when the human species shall have completed its cycle of existence on earth; and every one whom the Saviour's all-seeing eye beheld as belonging to His church, and whom, therefore, He loved and died for, and cleansed, has shared in the final redemption. (The reader may turn to what is said upon the phrase—"redemption of the purchased possession," i. 14.) Augustine and Jerome among the Fathers, Primasius, Bernard, and Thomas Aquinas among scholastic divines, along with Estius, Calvin, and Beza, hold to this view as to the epoch of the presentation, in antagonism with Cajetan, Bucer, Wolf, Bengel, and Harless, who regard the glorification of the church as a species of present operation. The loose language of the Greek commentators seems to intimate that they held the same hypothesis. Augustine flagellates the Donatists and Pelagians, who believed in the present sinlessness of the church; for truly such a state can only be such a comparative perfection as John Wesley describes when he says, " Christian perfection does not imply an exemption from ignorance or mistakes, infirmities or temptations." The church as it now is, and as it has always been, has many spots and wrinkles upon it. But perfection is secured by a process of continuous and successful operation, and shall be ultimately enjoyed. "The bride, the Lamb's wife," hath for centuries been making herself ready, and at length Christ, as He looks upon His church, will pronounce her perfect without tinge of sin or trace of any corruption; she will appear "holy and without blemish" in His view whose "eyes are a flame of fire." As He originally loved her in her impurity, how deep and ardent must be His attachment now to her when He sees in her the realization of His own gracious and eternal purpose! The nuptial union is at length consummated amidst the pealing halleluiahs of triumph and congratulation. So fervent, self-sacrificing, and successful is Christ's love to His church; and now He rejoices over her with joy, and His toil and death being amply compensated, "He will rest in His love."

(Ver. 28.) Οὕτως καὶ οἱ ἄνδρες ὀφείλουσιν ἀγαπᾶν τὰς ἑαυτῶν γυναῖκας, ὡς τὰ ἑαυτῶν σώματα—" So also ought husbands to love their own wives, as being their own bodies." The reading adopted has A, D, E, F, G, and the Vulgate, Gothic, and Coptic versions in its favour. The adverb οὕτως carries us back to καθώς, and indicates the bringing home of the argument. It is contrary to the plain current of thought on the part of Estius, Meier, de Wette, Baumgarten-Crusius, and Alford, to make it refer to ὡς in the following clause, as if the apostle said, Ye are to love your wives in the way in which ye love your own bodies. The οὕτως takes up the comparison between the husband and Christ, the wife and the church. "Thus," that is, in imitation of Christ's love, "husbands ought to love their own wives." The instances adduced by Alford and Ellicott against the statement in our first edition are not all of them quite parallel, in the position and use of οὕτως, in reference to *præcedentia*. There is no parenthesis in the two preceding verses, as Zanchius and Harless suppose. It is putting a special pressure upon the words to insist, after the example of Macknight and Barnes, that the husband's love to his wife shall be an imitation of Christ's love, in all those enumerated features of it. When Christ's love is mentioned, the full heart of the apostle dilates upon it, and in its fervour, tenderness, devotedness, and nobility of aim, a husband's love should resemble it. In the phrase "as their own bodies," Harless and Stier, in imitation of Theophylact, Zanchius, and Calovius, suppose that ὡς is used argumentatively, and that the verse contains two comparisons —" As Christ loved the church, so husbands are to love their wives "—" As they love their own bodies, so are they to love their wives." But the introduction of a double comparison only cumbers the argument. The idea is well expressed by Meyer—" So ought husbands to love their wives, as being indeed their own bodies." The language is based on the previous imagery. The apostle calls Christ the Head, and the church the body, that body of which He is Saviour. Christ loved the church as being His body. Now the husband is the head of the wife, and as her head he ought to love her as being his body. And therefore—

ὁ ἀγαπῶν τὴν ἑαυτοῦ γυναῖκα ἑαυτὸν ἀγαπᾷ—"he that loveth his own wife loveth himself." But the phrase, "loveth himself," is not identical with the formula of the preceding clause—" as their own bodies;" it is rather an inference from it. If the husband, as the head of the wife, loves his wife as being his own body, it is a plain inference that he is only loving himself. His love is not misspent: it is not wasted on some foreign object; it is a hallowed phasis of self-love.

(Ver. 29.) Οὐδεὶς γάρ ποτε τὴν ἑαυτοῦ σάρκα ἐμίσησεν— " For nobody ever hated his own flesh " (fools and fanatics excepted). This is a general law of nature. Eccles. vi. 7. Γάρ is argumentative, and σάρξ is used by the apostle rather than σῶμα, because of its occurrence in the words of the first institution of marriage—"they twain shall be one flesh." It has here also its simple original meaning, and not such a sense as it has in ii. 3. It is as if the apostle had said, " It is as unnatural a thing not to love one's wife, as it is not to love oneself." Every one loves his own flesh, and in harmony with the same law of nature he will love his other self—his wife. The commentators have adduced similar phraseology from the classics, such as Curtius, Seneca, and Plutarch.

ἀλλὰ ἐκτρέφει καὶ θάλπει αὐτήν—" but nourisheth and cherisheth it." "Ἕκαστος is understood before the two verbs. Stallbaum, *Plato, De Rep.* ii. p. 366. A man's care over his body, is that of a nursing-mother over a child. The verbs may be distinguished thus, that the former means to supply nutriment—ἐκ—referring to result; and the latter literally to supply warmth, but really and generally to cherish—more than Bengel's—*id spectat amictum.* Deut. xxii. 6; Job xxxix. 14; 1 Thess. ii. 7. More, certainly, than food and clothing is meant by the two verbs. This being a man's instinct towards his own flesh, it would, if freely developed, dictate his duty toward her who is with him "one flesh"—the complement of his being.

καθὼς καὶ ὁ Χριστὸς τὴν ἐκκλησίαν—" as also Christ the church." On the authority of A, B, D,[1] E, F, G, the Syriac, and Vulgate, with Chrysostom and Theodoret, Χριστός is the preferable reading to Κύριος, and is adopted by Lachmann and Tischendorf. Christ nourishes the church, feeds it with His word, fosters it by His Spirit, gives it the means of growth in the plenitude and variety of His gifts, revives and quickens it by His presence, and guards it by His own almighty power from harm and destruction. It is a quaint and formal interpretation of Grotius—" that Jesus *nourishes* the church by his Spirit, and *clothes* it with virtues." Something more, therefore, than food and clothing is demanded from the husband to the wife; he is to give her love and loyalty, honour and support. As Christ nourishes and cherishes His church, and as every man nourishes and cherishes his own flesh; so the bidding of nature and the claim of religious duty should lead the husband to nourish and cherish his wife.

(Ver. 30.) Ὅτι μέλη ἐσμὲν τοῦ σώματος αὐτοῦ, ἐκ τῆς σαρκὸς αὐτοῦ, καὶ ἐκ τῶν ὀστέων αὐτοῦ—" For members we are of His body, of His flesh, and of His bones." The last two clauses beginning with ἐκ are not found in A, B, and other Codices of less note, such as 17 and 67[2]; but they are found in D, E, F, G, K, L, almost all mss., in Chrysostom and

Theodoret, and in the Syriac and Vulgate versions. We cannot, therefore, exclude them with Lachmann and Davidson, *Biblical Criticism*, vol. ii. p. 378. Tischendorf adopts them in his seventh edition. They have been omitted at first, as de Wette suggests, by a ὁμοιοτέλευτον; αὐτοῦ . . . αὐτοῦ, or because they seem to express gross and material ideas. This verse adduces a reason why Christ nourishes and cherishes the church, for it stands in the nearest and dearest relation to Him. We are members of His body, as being members of His church, and, as members of that body, we are nourished and cherished by the Head—ἐκ in both the last clauses pointing to origin. Winer, § 47. See under iv. 15, 16. Bengel, Harless, Olshausen, and Stier understand by σῶμα the actual personal body of Jesus—the body of His glorified humanity. But in what sense are or can we be members—μέλη—of that body ? It has its own organs and members which it took in the Virgin's womb. But the apostle has his thoughts occupied with conjugal duties, and he has, in subordination to this, introduced Christ and His church as bridegroom and bride ; therefore his mind reverts naturally to the imagery and language of the original matrimonial institute, and so he adds—" we are members of His flesh and of His bones." Gen. ii. 23.[1] The argument of Harless against this view, which appears so natural, is lame and inconclusive, and he holds the opinion, that the two clauses are simply a further explanation of the statement—" we are members of His body."

[1] "It is too cold an interpretation, whereby some men expound our being in Christ to import nothing else, but only that the selfsame nature which maketh us to be men, is in Him, and maketh Him man as we are. For what man in the world is there which hath not so far forth communion with Jesus Christ ? It is not this that can sustain the weight of such sentences as can speak of the mystery of our coherence (John xiv. 20, xv. 4) with Jesus Christ. The church is in Christ as Eve was in Adam. Yea, by grace we are every of us in Christ and in His church, as by nature we are in those our first parents. God made Eve of the rib of Adam. And His church He frameth out of the very flesh, the very wounded and bleeding side of the Son of man. His body crucified and His blood shed for the life of the world, are the true elements of that heavenly being which maketh us such as Himself is of whom we come (1 Cor. xv. 48). For which cause the words of Adam may be fitly the words of Christ concerning His church, 'flesh of my flesh, and bone of my bones,' a true native extract out of mine own body. So that in Him even according to His manhood we according to our heavenly being are as branches in that root out of which they grow."—Hooker, *Works*, vol. i. p. 626, ed. Ox. 1841.

What is really meant by the striking phraseology has been a subject of no little dispute.

1. Cajetan, Vatablus, Calovius, Bullinger, Vorstius, Grotius, Zanchius, and Zachariae refer the words to the origin of the church from the flesh and bones of Christ, nailed to the cross, and there presented to God. Such an idea is neither prominent in the words nor latent in the context.

2. Not more satisfactory is the view which is held in part by Theodoret, by Calvin, Beza, and Grotius, who find in the phrase a reference to the Lord's Supper. Kahnis, *Abendmahl*, p. 143. These critics differ in the way in which they understand such a reference, and no wonder; for the communion there enjoyed is only a result of the union which this verse describes. Strange, if there be any allusion to the eucharist, that there is a reference to the bones, but none to the blood of Christ.

3. Not so remote from the real sense is the opinion of Chrysostom, Theophylact, Ambrosiaster, Œcumenius, Bengel, and Matthies, who suppose an allusion in the phraseology to that new birth which is effected by Christ, as if it had been shadowed out by Eve's extraction from Adam's side. Œcumenius says—ἐξ αὐτοῦ δὲ καθὸ ἀπαρχὴ ἡμῶν ἐστι τῆς δευτέρας πλάσεως ὥσπερ ἐκ τοῦ Ἀδὰμ διὰ τὴν πρώτην. It is indeed as renewed men that believers have any fellowship with Christ. But the idea of birth is not naturally nor necessarily implied in the apostle's language, and it is founded upon an incorrect interpretation of our Lord's expression about eating His flesh and drinking His blood. John vi. 53.

4. As plausible is the theory which explains the clauses by a reference to that identity of nature which Christ and His people possess. They are partakers of one humanity. Chrysostom and Theophylact also give this view; Irenæus, Augustine, and Jerome maintain it; and it has been held by Thomas Aquinas, Aretius, Cocceius, and Michaelis. The reply, "that in that case the language must have been, He took upon Him our flesh and bone," has been met by Estius, who says, "the language is just, because in His incarnate state He is the Head and we are only members." But our principal objection is, that this simple community of nature

with Christ is common to all men; whereas it is only of believers, and of a union peculiar to them, that the apostle speaks.

5. We confess our inability to understand the meaning of Bisping, Olshausen, and others. "The words refer," they say, "to Christ's imparting of His glorified humanity to believers through the communion of His flesh and blood. . . . It is by the self-communication of His divine-human (theanthropic) nature that Christ makes us His flesh and bone. He gives to His followers His flesh to eat and His blood to drink." Bisping, a Romanist, says, "In the regeneration through baptism, the glorified body of Christ is communicated to us." That is, as he explains, "the germ of the resurrection of the body is implanted in us at baptism, and this germ is only an outflow from Christ's glorified body." Such an idea could only be consistently based on the Lutheran view of consubstantiation, or some species of pantheism, or what Turner calls Panchristism. But—

6. The apostle has the idea of marriage and its relations before him, and he employs the imagery of the original institute, which first depicted the unity of man and wife, to describe the origin and union of the church and Christ. As the woman was literally, by being taken out of Adam, bone of his bone and flesh of his flesh; as this duality sprung from unity, and was speedily resolved into it: so the church is originated out of Christ, and, united to Him as its Head or Husband, is one with Him. The language is, therefore, a metaphorical expression of this union, borrowed from the graphic diction of Genesis; and this image evidently presented itself to the apostle's mind from its connection with the origin and nature of those conjugal duties which he is inculcating in the paragraph before us. The error of Meyer's exegesis is his restriction of the imagery to the one example of Adam and Eve, whereas it has its verification in every nuptial union, and hence the apostle's use of it. As Eve derived her life and being out of Adam, and was physically of his body, his flesh, and his bones, so believers are really of Christ—of His body, His flesh, and His bones, for they are one with Christ in nature and derive their life from His humanity, nay, are connected with Him, not simply and

generally by a spiritual union, but in some close and derivative way which the apostle calls a mystery, with His body; so that they live as its members, and become with it "one flesh." Besides, in the next verse, the apostle takes his readers to the source of his imagery—

(Ver. 31.) Ἀντὶ τούτου, καταλείψει ἄνθρωπος τὸν πατέρα αὐτοῦ καὶ τὴν μητέρα, καὶ προσκολληθήσεται πρὸς τὴν γυναῖκα αὐτοῦ, καὶ ἔσονται οἱ δύο εἰς σάρκα μίαν. "For this cause shall a man leave his father and mother, and shall be joined unto his wife, and they two shall be one flesh." There are some variations of reading. Some MSS. of superior weight omit the articles τόν and τήν, as well as αὐτοῦ, but the longer reading has A, D³, E, K, L in its favour, with many Codices, and the Syriac and Coptic versions. It is, however, rejected by Lachmann and Tischendorf as a conformation to the Seventy. The critical note of Origen seems to confirm the suspicion. Instead of πρὸς τὴν γυναῖκα found in B, D³, E, K, L, τῇ γυναικί is read in D¹, E¹, F, G, and is introduced by Lachmann. The words are a free quotation from Gen. ii. 24, though the formula of quotation is wanting. This want of such a formula was not unfrequent. Surenhusius, *Bib. Katal.* p. 21. Ἄνθρωπος is without the article (not used for ἀνήρ), but having "its general aphorismatic sense"—an argument in itself against Alford's interpretation. These future verbs indicate prophetically the future impulse and acting of the race which was to spring from Adam and Eve. Winer, § 40, 6. The Septuagint has ἕνεκεν τούτου changed by the apostle into ἀντὶ τούτου, "on this account" (Winer, § 47, *a*; Donaldson, § 474, *a, dd*), and these words are in this place no introduction to the quotation, but simply a portion of it; and therefore Estius, Holzhausen, Meier, and Matthies labour to no purpose in endeavouring to affix a special meaning to them. The quotation is introduced to show the apostle's meaning, and exhibit the source of his imagery. His language was remarkable; but this verse points out its true signification, by showing whence it was taken, and how it was originally employed. From early times, however, the language has been directly applied to Christ. Jerome's interpretation is the following:—*primus homo et primus vates Adam hoc de Christo et ecclesia prophetavit; quod reliquerit*

*Dominus noster atque Salvator patrem suum Deum et matrem suam cœlestem Jerusalem, et venerit ad terras propter suum corpus ecclesiam, et de suo eam latere fabricatus sit et propter illam Verbum caro factum sit.* Such is the view of Heinsius, Balduin, Bengel, Bisping, who explains μητέρα by *die Synagoge*, and even of Grotius. Some of the critics who held this view refer the words so mystically understood to Christ's second coming, when He shall present the bride to Himself in formal wedlock. Such, also, is Meyer's view. His words are, "This, therefore, is the interpretation, Wherefore, that is, because we are members of Christ, of His flesh and bones, shall a man leave (that is, Christ as the second Adam) his Father and his Mother (that is, according to the mystical sense of Paul, He will leave His seat at the right hand of God) and shall be joined to His wife (that is, to the church), and they two shall be one flesh," etc.[1] Such an exegesis, which may be found also in Jeremy Taylor's sermon of *The Marriage Ring*, has nothing to justify it, for there is no hint in this verse that the apostle intends to allegorize. In spite of what Ellicott and Alford have said, we cannot adopt that view, or see the propriety of the language as applied formally to Christ. The allegory is not in this verse, but in the application of nuptial figure and language to Christ and His Church; this verse showing the source and authority. True, as Alford says, "the allegory is the key to the whole," but the apostle does not in this citation allegorize Gen. ii. 24, by applying its language directly to Christ. Nor is it deep thought or research that finds allegories in the interpretation of this place or other places. The process is often of a contrary nature.

Others, again, suppose a reference to Christ and the church only in the last clause, for the sake of which the preceding words of the verse have been introduced. This is the exegesis of Harless and Olshausen, who conceive in the phrase a reference to the Lord's Supper, and Olshausen illustrates his

[1] "*Deshalb*, weil wir Glieder Christi sind, von seinem Fleisch und von seinen Beinen *wird verlassen ein Mensch* (d. i. Christus, bei der Parusie) *seinen Vater und seine Mutter* (d. i. nach der mystischen Deutung Pauli : er wird seinen Sitz zur Rechten Gottes verlassen) *und vereiniget werden mit seinem Weibe* (mit der Gemeinde), *und* (und dann) *werden die Zwei* (der Mann und die Frau, d. i. der herabgestiegene Christus und die Gemeinde) *zu Einem Fleische sein.*"—*Der Brief an die Epheser*, p. 234. Göttingen, 1853.

meaning with an approach to indelicacy. But there is no ground for deeming all the preceding part of the verse superfluous, nor is there any reason for departing from the plain, ordinary, and original meaning of the terms. The words of the quotation, then, are to be understood simply of human marriage, as if to show why language borrowed from it was applied in the preceding verse to depict the union of Christ and His church. The verse in Genesis appears to be not the language of Adam, as if, as in Jerome's description of him, he had been *primus vates*, but is at once a legislative and prophetic comment upon the language of Adam—" This is now bone of my bone, and flesh of my flesh." The love which a son bears to a father and a mother, is at length surmounted by a more powerful attachment. He leaves them in whose love and society he has spent his previous life; so that, while love cements families, love also scatters them. " He is joined to his wife " in a union nearer and more intimate than that which united him to his parents; for his wife and he become " one flesh "—not one in spirit, or in affection, or in pursuit, but in personality, filled with " coequal and homogeneal fire "—

"The only bliss
Of Paradise that has survived the fall."

They are " one flesh," and a junction so characterized supplied the apostle with language to describe the union of Christ and His Church—" we are of His flesh and of His bones."[1] This

[1] "They are one now, and one for ever; he is greater than Omnipotence who can rend that tie; that 'marriage was made in heaven!' Alone—it was in the depths of eternity—stood Christ and His church before the altar of that divine espousal; none was witness but the Father of glory and the Spirit of life, when the vow was plighted and the contract sealed; but all heaven shall yet be witness, when the redeemed church shall vindicate the fidelity of the church's Redeemer; when she shall 'come up from the wilderness' of this barren world, 'leaning on her Beloved,' and by Him be publicly invested with those privileges of her rank which are hers now, but hers in silence, secrecy, and sorrow! Then shall the 'fellowship of one with another,' and of all with God, be indeed complete; and that wondrous prayer be fulfilled, in which (as one who ties and doubles a knot) the Saviour, by returning on His words, seems purposely to have sought to express the infolded closeness of that maze of love in which the 'children of light'—having within them the abiding of the Spirit—are one with the Father and the Son." Archer Butler's *Sermons*, 1st Series, p. 421, 5th ed., Cambridge, 1859.

doctrine of marriage must have excited surprise when divorce was of scandalous frequency by an action of ἀπόλειψις or ἀπόπεμψις in Grecian states, and with less formality under the emperors in the West, by *diffarreatio* and *remancipatio*. See Harless, *Ethik*, § 52, and his *Die Ehescheidungsfrage. Eine erneute Versuch der Neut. Schriftstellen*, 1860.

(Ver. 32.) Τὸ μυστήριον τοῦτο μέγα ἐστίν, ἐγὼ δὲ λέγω εἰς Χριστὸν καὶ εἰς τὴν ἐκκλησίαν—" This mystery is a great one, but I speak concerning Christ and concerning the church." Μυστήριον is rendered in the Vulgate *sacramentum*, and the Popish church regards marriage as one of its sacraments.[1] Cajetan and Estius, however, disavow the Latin translation, on which their own church rests its proof.[2] The Cardinal honestly says, *non habes ex hoc loco, prudens lector, a Paulo conjugium esse sacramentum. Non enim dixit, esse sacramentum, sed mysterium.* Bisping more guardedly says that the sacramental character of marriage cannot be proved directly and immediately. Erasmus is yet more cautious. *Neque nego matrimonium esse sacramentum, sed an ex hoc loco doceri possit proprie dici sacramentum quemadmodum baptismus dicitur, excuti volo.* The phrase סוֹד גָּדוֹל, "a great mystery," is found among the rabbinical formulæ. Those who hold that the previous verse refers to Christ leaving His Father and Mother, and coming down to our earth to woo and win His spiritual bride, find no difficulty in the explanation of the verse before us. Such a representation, couched in such language, might well be named a great mystery, in connection with Christ and the church. But the language of this verse does not prove it, or afford any explanation of it.

The question to be determined is, What is the real or implied antecedent to τοῦτο ? 1. Is the meaning this: Marriage as described in the preceding verse is a great mystery, but I speak of it in its mystical or typical connection with Christ and the church ? Those who, like Harless, Olshausen, and others, take the last clause, "they two shall be one flesh," as referring to Christ and His church, say

---

[1] Council of Trent, Sess. 24.

[2] Yet in an encyclical letter in 1832 occurs the statement—"Marriage is, according to St. Paul's expression, a great sacrament in Christ and in the church."

that the sense is—"the mystery thus described is a great one, but it refers to Christ and the church." But were the meaning of that clause so plain as Harless supposes, then this exegetical note, "I speak concerning Christ and the church," might be dispensed with. 2. Others, such as Baumgarten-Crusius, look upon the word μυστήριον as equivalent to allegory, and suppose the apostle to refer to a well-known Jewish view as to the typical nature of the marriage of Adam and Eve. Schoettgen, *Hor. Heb.* p. 783. The allegory, however, of Philo on the place is of quite a different kind. "Ἕνεκα τῆς αἰσθήσεως ὁ νοῦς, ὅταν αὐτῇ δουλωθῇ, καταλίπῃ καὶ τὸν πατέρα, τὸν ὅλων θεόν, καὶ τὴν μητέρα τῶν συμπάντων, τὴν ἀρετὴν καὶ σοφίαν τοῦ θεοῦ, καὶ προσκολλᾶται καὶ ἐνοῦται τῇ αἰσθήσει, καὶ ἀναλύεται εἰς αἴσθησιν, ἵνα γίνωνται μία σάρξ, καὶ ἓν πάθος, οἱ δύο. "On account of the external sensation, the mind, when it has become enslaved to it, shall leave both its father, the God of the universe, and the mother of all things, namely, the virtue and wisdom of God, and cleaves to and becomes united to the external sensations, and is dissolved into external sensation, so that the two become one flesh and one passion." Allix, in his *Judgment of the Jewish Church*, says the first match between Adam and Eve was a type of that between Christ and His church. A note on this subject may be seen in Whitby's *Commentary*. Such an opinion gives the word μυστήριον the meaning of something spoken, having in it a deep or occult sense; a meaning which Koppe, Morus, de Wette, Meier, and Grotius, and Stier to some extent, without any biblical foundation, attach to the term in this place. 3. The exegesis of Peile is wholly out of the question—" this mystery is of great depth of meaning, and for my part I interpret it as having reference to Christ;" a paraphrase as untenable as that of Grotius — *verba ista explicavi vobis non κατὰ πόδας, sed sensu μυστικωτέρῳ*. But Scripture affords us no warrant for such notions; nor is such allegorization any portion of the apostle's hermeneutics. 4. Hofmann, *loc. cit.*, quite apart from the reasoning and context, understands the apostle to say that the sacred unity of marriage—one flesh—is a great mystery to the heathen. 5. We understand the apostle to refer to the general sentiment of the preceding section, summed up in the last verse, and in the clause, "they two shall be one flesh;" or rather to the special image which that clause illustrates, viz., that Christ and the church stand in the relation of husband and wife. The allowed application of conjugal terms to Christ and the church is "a great mystery;" and lest any one should think that the apostle refers to the "one flesh" of an earthly relationship, he is cautious to add, "I speak concerning Christ and the church." This great truth is a great mystery, understood only by the initiated; for the blessedness of such a union with Christ is known only to those who enjoy it. Somewhat differently from Ellicott, we would say that verses 25–28 introduce the spiritual nuptial relation, that ver. 29 affirms its reality, that ver. 30 gives the deep spiritual ground or origin of it, while the quotation in ver. 31 shows the authorized source of the image, and ver. 32 its ultimate application guarding against mistake. The meaning of μυστήριον the reader will find under i. 9. The word is used in the same sense as here in vi. 19; 1 Tim. iii. 16.

ἐγὼ δὲ λέγω εἰς Χριστὸν, καὶ εἰς τὴν ἐκκλησίαν—" but I am speaking in reference to Christ, and in reference to the church." The pronoun is not without subjective significance. Winer, § 22, 6. The δέ is not simply explicative, but has also an adversative meaning, as if the writer supposed in his mind that the phraseology employed by him might be interpreted in another and different way. Λέγω, introducing an explanation, is followed by the εἰς of reference (*von der Richtung*, Winer, § 49, a, (δ)), as in Acts ii. 25; and ἐλάλησεν has a similar complement in Heb. vii. 14. The interpretation of Zanchius, Bodius, and Cameron, imitated by Macknight, supposes the marriage of Eve with Adam to be a type or a designed emblem of the union of Christ and His church. Macknight dwells at length and with more than usual unction on the theme. But the apostle simply compares Christ and His church to husband and wife, and the comparison helps him to illustrate and enforce conjugal duty. Nay, so close and tender is the union between Christ and His church, that the language of Adam concerning Eve may be applied to it. The nuptial union of our first parents was not a formal type of this spiritual matrimony, nor does the apostle allegorize the record of it, or say that the words contain a deep or mystic sense. But these primitive espousals afforded imagery and language which might aptly and truly be applied to Christ and the church, which is of His "flesh and His bones;" and the application of such imagery and language is indeed a mystery—a truth, the secret glory and felicity of which are known but to those who are wedded to the Lord in a "perpetual covenant." The apostle might have in his eye such passages as Ps. xlv.; Hos. ii. 19–23; the Song of Solomon; Isa. liv. 5, lxi. 10; Ezek. xvi. 8. The same imagery is found in 2 Cor. xi. 2, and in the conclusion of the Apocalypse.

(Ver. 33.) Πλὴν καὶ ὑμεῖς οἱ καθ' ἕνα, ἕκαστος τὴν ἑαυτοῦ γυναῖκα οὕτως ἀγαπάτω ὡς ἑαυτόν—" Nevertheless also as to every one of you, let each love his wife as himself." The word πλήν does not indicate, as Bengel, Harless, and Olshausen wrongly suppose, any return from a digression. The preceding verses are no digression, but an interlinked and extended illustration. As Meyer insists, πλήν means, " yet apart from this;" that is, apart from this illustration of the conjugal relationship of Christ to His church. The term, therefore, does not indicate a return from a formal digression, but rather a return to the starting thought. The καί contains an allusion to the leading idea of the preceding illustration—the love of Christ to His spiritual spouse. As He loves His spouse, do you also, every one of you, love his wife. Οἱ καθ' ἕνα. 1 Cor. xiv. 27–31; Jelf, § 629; Winer, § 49, d. The verb ἀγαπάτω is singular, agreeing with ἕκαστος and not ὑμεῖς— a mode of construction which individualizes and intensifies the injunction.

ὡς ἑαυτόν—" as being himself" one flesh with him. (Verses 31 and 28.) Not that he is to idolize her, as if, among all his other bones, Adam's "extracted rib alone had been of ivory."

ἡ δὲ γυνὴ ἵνα φοβῆται τὸν ἄνδρα—" and the wife that she reverence her husband." The construction of this clause is idiomatic, as in Gal. ii. 10; 2 Cor. viii. 7; Mark v. 23; Winer, § 63, II. 1. In such an idiom γυνή, in effect, is the nominative absolute, though in the resolution of the idiom a verb must be supplied; or as Ellicott, who objects to our statement, admits—it is not so definitely unsyntactic as Acts

vii. 40, and that is all we meant to say. Δέ may be slightly adversative, the conjugal duties being in contrast. The verb to be supplied, and on which, in the mind of the writer, ἵνα depends, is furnished by the context (Meyer on 2 Cor. viii. 7, and Osiander on the same place), as, "I command," or "let her see." In such a case ὅπως is used by the classical writers. Raphelius, *Annotat.* 488. The wife is to reverence her husband—*numquam enim erit voluntaria subjectio nisi præcedat reverentia.* Calvin. One peculiarity in this injunction has been usually overlooked. What is instinctive on either side is not enforced, but what is necessary to direct and hallow such an instinct is inculcated. The woman loves, but to teach her how this fondness should know and fill its appropriate sphere, she is commanded to obey—μὴ δουλοπρεπῶς. *Œcumenius.* The man, on the other hand, feels that his position is to govern; but to show him what should be the essence and means of his government, he is enjoined to love. "He rules her by authority, and she rules him by love: she ought by all means to please him, and he must by no means displease her." *Sermon on the Marriage Ring,* by Jeremy Taylor; Works, vol. xv. When this balance of power is unsettled, happiness is lost, and mutual recriminations ensue. "A masterly wife," as Gataker says, "is as much despised and derided for taking rule over her husband as he for yielding to it."

In fine, the apostle, by the language he has employed in reference to Christ and His church, has given marriage its highest honour. No ascetic condemnation of it occurs in the New Testament. "Single life makes men in one instance to be like angels, but marriage in very many things makes the chaste pair to be like Christ." *Sermon on the Marriage Ring,* by Jeremy Taylor; Works, vol. xv.

## CHAPTER VI

THE apostle, after expounding the duties that spring out of the conjugal relation, as one sphere in which the maxim—submitting yourselves to one another in the fear of Christ—came into operation, naturally turns to another and kindred sphere of domestic life, and addresses himself to children. And he does not speak about them, or tell their parents of them, but he looks them in the face, and lovingly says to them—"children." It is plainly implied that children were supposed by him to be present in the sanctuary when this epistle was read, or to be able to read it for themselves, when it should be transcribed and circulated.

(Ver. 1.) *Τὰ τέκνα, ὑπακούετε τοῖς γονεῦσιν ὑμῶν ἐν Κυρίῳ*—"Children, obey your parents in the Lord"—that is, "in Christ." The words *ἐν Κυρίῳ* are wanting in B, D¹, F, G, and are, on that account, excluded by Lachmann, but they are found in A, D³, E, I, K, the major part of mss., and the Greek fathers. They describe the element or sphere of that obedience which children are to render to their parents, and certainly do not qualify *γονεῦσιν*—as if the reference were to fathers in the faith, in contrast to fathers after the flesh. Not merely natural instinct, but religious motive should prompt children to obedience, and guard them in it. The love which Jesus showed to children, when He took them in His arms and blessed them, should induce them, in a spirit of filial faith and fondness, to obey their parents, and to regard with special sacredness every parental injunction. And that obedience, if prompted, regulated, and bounded by a sense of religious obligation, will be cheerful, and not sullen; prompt, and not dilatory; uniform, and not occasional; universal, and not capricious in its choice of parental precepts.

*τοῦτο γάρ ἐστιν δίκαιον*—"for this is right;" the *νῦ ἐφελκυστικόν* in *ἐστιν*, and other similar verbal forms being a general characteristic in the spelling of ancient MSS. The reference of the clause is not to ἐν Κυρίῳ, but to the injunction itself. Filial obedience is "right," for it is not based on anything accidental or expedient. The meaning is not that obedience is "according to the law of God, or Scripture"—κατὰ τὸν τοῦ Θεοῦ νόμον—as is said by Theodoret and Calvin, and virtually by Harless and Meyer, but that it has its foundation in the very essence of that relation which subsists between parents and children. Nature claims it, while Scripture enjoins it, and the Son of God exemplified it. It is in perfect consistency with all our notions of right and moral obligation— φύσει δίκαιον, as Theophylact rightly adds. For the very names τέκνα and γονεῖς point out the origin and essential reason of that filial duty which the apostle, in Colossians, calls "well-pleasing to the Lord."

(Ver. 2.) Τίμα τὸν πατέρα σου καὶ τὴν μητέρα—" Honour thy father and thy mother "—a quotation from the fifth commandment—כַּבֵּד אֶת־אָבִיךָ וְאֶת־אִמֶּךָ. Ex. xx. 12; Deut. v. 16. This citation does not, as Harless supposes, give the ground of the preceding injunction, for δίκαιον contains a specific reason; but it is another form of the same injunction, based not upon natural right, but upon inspired authority. Honour comprehends in it all that respect, reverence, love, and obedience, which the filial relation so fully implies. Though the Mosaic law did not by any means place man and woman on the same level in respect of conjugal right, yet here, in special and delicate homage to maternal claim, it places the mother in the same high position with the father himself. Marcion, according to Tertullian, left out this quotation in his so-called Epistle to the Laodiceans, because it recognized the authority of the God of the Old Testament, p. 329, vol. ii., *Op.* ed. Oehler.

ἥτις ἐστὶν ἐντολὴ πρώτη ἐν ἐπαγγελίᾳ—" for such is," or " as it is the first command with promise;" ἥτις giving explanation, or expressing reason. Winer, § 24.[1] Some critics give πρῶτος the sense of prime or chief—" which is the chief commandment connected with promise." Such is the view of Wetstein, Koppe, Flatt, Meier, Matthies, Hodge, and Robinson. The adjective may bear this signification; but such cannot be its meaning here, for the fifth commandment

[1] See Moulton, p. 209, n 3.

cannot surely be deemed absolutely the most important which God has ordained with promise. Matt. xxii. 38, 39; Rom. xiii. 9. Stier regards it as a first command, in point of importance, to the children whom Paul directly addresses. Ambrosiaster, Michaelis, von Gerlach, and Holzhausen propose to take πρώτη as meaning first in a certain position; and the last affirms that ἐντολή denotes only the statutes which belong to the second table—duties not of man to God, but of man to man. This is only a philological figment, devised to escape from a theological difficulty. The division of the decalogue into first and second tables has no direct foundation in Scripture; but if it be adopted, we quite agree with Stier that the fifth commandment belongs to the first table. Its position in Lev. xix. 3, and its omission in Rom. xiii. 9, seem to prove this. The second table is comprised in this, "Love thy neighbour as thyself;" but obedience to parents cannot come under such a category. The parent stands in God's place to his child. On the division of the ten commandments separately, and on that into two tables, see Sonntag and Züllig, *Stud. und Kritik.* 1836-37; and Kurtz, *Geschichte des Alten Bundes*, vol. iii. § 10. We are obliged to join πρώτη with ἐν ἐπαγγελίᾳ, and render—"which is the first command with a promise," ἐν pointing to that in which the firstness consists, and the promise being expressed in the following verse. Such is the view of the Greek commentators, of Jerome, of the Reformers, of Bodius, a-Lapide, Aretius, Zanchius, Crocius, and of Harless, de Wette, Meyer, Olshausen, Baumgarten-Crusius, and Winer, § 48, a.[1] It has been remarked by others, that what appears a promise in the second commandment is only a broad declaration of the great principles of the divine government, and that this is really, therefore, the earliest or first of the ten commands with a promise—first, as Chrysostom says, not τῇ τάξει ἀλλὰ τῇ ἐπαγγελίᾳ. It has been objected that there is only one command with a promise in the decalogue, and that the apostle, if he thought of the decalogue alone, would have said, not the "first," but the "only" command with promise. Harless says that "first" refers to what precedes, not to what follows; and Meyer suggests that Paul included in his reckoning, not the decalogue alone, but other

---

[1] Moulton, p. 488.

succeeding injunctions of the Mosaic code. As a "first" implies a second, we should be inclined to adopt the last view, limiting, however, the calculation of the apostle to the first body of commands delivered at Sinai. The fifth is thus the first commandment in point of promise. The article is not needed, for ordinals having a specific power in themselves often want it. Phil. i. 12 ; Middleton *on the Greek Article*, p. 100.

(Ver. 3.) "Ἵνα εὖ σοι γένηται καὶ ἔσῃ μακροχρόνιος ἐπὶ τῆς γῆς—" That it may be well with thee, and that thou be long-lived on the earth." The quotation is from the Septuagint version of Ex. xx. 12, but somewhat varied—לְמַעַן יַאֲרִכוּן יָמֶיךָ עַל הָאֲדָמָה אֲשֶׁר־יְהוָֹה אֱלֹהֶיךָ נֹתֵן לָךְ the words omitted being—τῆς ἀγαθῆς ἧς Κύριος ὁ Θεός σου δίδωσί σοι. Such is the promise. The phrase "that it may be well with thee"—as in Gen. xii. 13, Deut. iv. 40—seems to have been a common mode of expressing interest in another's welfare. In the second clause, the apostle changes the construction of the Septuagint, which reads—καὶ ἵνα μακροχρόνιος γένῃ. It had been affirmed by Erasmus, and has been reasserted by Winer (§ 41, *b*, b, 1)[1] and de Wette, that the apostle drops the construction with ἵνα and uses ἔσῃ in the simple future. We agree with Meyer, that there is no genuine grammatical ground for separating ἔσῃ from ἵνα, since the apostle has in some instances connected ἵνα with the future (1 Cor. ix. 18), and there is a change of construction similar to that which this verse presents, in the Apocalypse, xxii. 14. Klotz-Devarius, vol. ii. 630.[2] The future ἔσῃ stands here in its proper significance, but still connected with ἵνα; and such a use of the future tense may in a climactic form indicate the direct and certain result of the previous subjunctive. Obedience secures well-being, and this being the case, "thou shalt live long on the

---

[1] Moulton, p. 361.

[2] A similar construction with ὅπως occurs in classical Greek. Dawes indeed laid it down as a rule that ὅπως was never joined with the subjunctive of the first aorist, active or middle ; but that in place of them the indicative future is employed, and that therefore the indicative future and the subjunctive are often interchanged. The critic cordially congratulated himself on the discovery of such a usage—*mirum, opinor, quod dicturus sum, plerisque omnibus videbitur ; sed nihilo tamen idcirco minus verum est.* Dawes, *Miscellan. Crit.* p. 418, Lond. 1827. But Kühner (ii. § 777) has shown that the whole is error, as many instances abundantly testify. Gayler, *Part. Neg.* p. 209.

earth." The longevity is the result and development of its being well with thee.

Μακροχρόνιος is "long-lived" or "long-timed," and belongs to the later Greek. What then is the nature of this promise annexed to the fifth commandment? In its original form it had reference to the peculiar constitution of the theocracy, which both promised and secured temporal blessings to the people. The words are, "that thy days may be long in the land which the Lord thy God giveth thee." The promise in its first application has been supposed to mean, that filial obedience being the test and exponent of national religion and morality, would preserve the Hebrew nation from those aberrations and crimes which led to their deportation and their ultimate expulsion. Or if the command be supposed to possess an individualizing directness, then it may mean, that under Jehovah's special guardianship the coveted blessing of longevity would be the sure fruit and noble reward of filial piety. But what is the force of the promise now? The apostle gives it a present meaning and reality, and omits as if on purpose the clause which of old restricted it to the theocracy. It is out of the question on the part of Olshausen, Schrader, and Gauthey, preceded by Estius, to spiritualize the promise, and to suppose that as Canaan was a type of heaven, so the blessing here promised is happiness in a better world. Hints of this view are found in Jerome and Thomas Aquinas. The epithet μακροχρόνιος can never denote immortal duration, and the apostle omits the very words which placed the earthly Canaan in its peculiar position and meaning as a type. On the other hand, Meyer regards this omission as unessential, and pronounces that the words "in the earth or land" refer historically and only to the land of Canaan. Our question then is, Why did the apostle make the quotation? Does it merely record an ancient fact which no longer has any existence? or does that fact suggest lessons to present times? If the former alternative, that of Meyer and Baumgarten-Crusius, be adopted, then the language of the apostle loses its significance and applicability to Christian children. Meyer says that the apostle dropt the last clause of the commandment because he presumed that his readers were well acquainted with it—a presumption we can scarcely admit in reference to the Gentile portion of the church. Rather, as we have said, do we believe, with Calvin, Rückert, and Matthies, that the apostle omitted the last clause just to make the promise bear upon regions out of Palestine, and periods distant from those of the Hebrew commonwealth. Bengel, Rosenmüller, Morus, Flatt, Harless, and Baumgarten-Crusius regard the original promise as applicable not to individuals, but to the mass of the Jewish society. The meaning, says Morus, as applied to our times is simply, *patriam florere diu, ubi liberorum sit erga parentes reverentia*. This comment is certainly better, though it is in a similar strain: as if blessings were promised to the mass, in which the individual shares if he remain a part of it. But such views dilute the apostle's meaning, and proceed in their basis upon a misconception of the Hebrew statute. The command is addressed to individuals, and so is the promise. The language plainly implies it—"that thy days may be long." Our Lord so understands it (Matt. xv. 4–6), and thus in the sermon on the mount He expounds the other statutes. Is it so, then, that long life is promised to obedient children? The special providence of the theocracy could easily secure it in ancient times; nay, disobedient children were by law punished with death. Nor is the hand of the Lord slackened in these days. Under i. 3 the reader will find a reference to the place which temporal blessings occupy under the Christian economy. Godliness has "the promise of the life which now is." Matt. vi. 25, etc.; Mark x. 29, etc. Obedient children sometimes die, as ripe fruit falls first. But the promise of longevity is held out—it is a principle of the Divine administration and the usual course of providence. Not that we can say with Grotius, that man therefore has it somewhat in his power to prolong his days; or with Stier, that the life would be long, *quoad sufficientiam* —for obtaining salvation; or as in the maxim, *sat vixit diu, quem nec pudet vixisse, nec piget mori*. We understand the command, as modified by its Christian and extra-Palestinian aspect, to involve a great principle, and that is, that filial obedience, under God's blessing, prolongs life, for it implies the possession of principles of restraint, sobriety, and industry, which secure a lengthened existence. It is said in Prov. x. 27, "The fear of the Lord prolongeth days, but the years of the wicked shall be shortened;" and in ix. 11, "By me thy days shall be multiplied, and the years of thy life shall be increased;" and again in Ps. lv. 23, "Bloody and deceitful men shall not live out half their days." Not that God shortens their days by an express and formal judgment from heaven, or that all of them without exception drop into a premature grave; but the principle of the Divine government does secure that sin is its own penalty, and that vicious or criminal courses either ruin the constitution, or expose their victim to the punishment of civil law, as in the case of men whose existence is early and suddenly broken off by intemperance, imprisonment, or exile, by the scourge or the gallows. The Greeks had apothegms similar to this of the apostle. Obedient children are guided and guarded by their very veneration for their parents, and prevented from these fatal excesses; whereas the "children of disobedience" are of necessity exposed to all the juvenile temptations which lead to vice and crime. God does not bribe the child to obedience, but holds out this special and blessed result to "tender understandings" as a motive which they can appreciate and enjoy. Œcumenius says—τί γὰρ ἡδύτερον παισὶ τῆς μακροχρονίας?

(Ver. 4.) Καὶ οἱ πατέρες, μὴ παροργίζετε τὰ τέκνα ὑμῶν— "And ye, fathers, provoke not your children to wrath." The καί connects closely this injunction, as one parallel or complementary to the one preceding it. The address of the apostle is to fathers, not to parents, as Flatt, Meier, Baumgarten-Crusius, Robinson, Wahl, and Bretschneider erroneously hold it. Πατέρες can scarcely be supposed to change its signification from that which it bears in the 2nd verse, and why should the apostle not have employed γονεῖς, as in the 1st verse? Fathers are here singled out, not, as Rückert wrongly holds, because mothers were in no high position in the East. Prov. xxxi. 10, etc. Nor is the reference to "fathers" because the father as husband is head of the wife, and this idea of Meyer, Harless, and Stier is too vague, for the advice seems scarcely appropriate to mothers, who so usually err through fondness, if the apostle spoke to them through their husbands. Nor is there any ground for Olshausen's hypothesis, that Paul refers to the education of adolescent children, which, from the nature of the case, belongs to fathers more than mothers. But the training of children is the father's special function; for the duty is devolved upon him to select and put into operation the best means and methods for the culture of his offspring. And especially does the prohibition of this first clause apply to fathers. As Chrysostom remarks, He does not say—love them—τοῦτο γὰρ καὶ ἀκόντων αὐτῶν ἡ φύσις ἐπισπᾶται. Chastisement is within their province, and they are apt to administer castigation in a passion, as if to gratify their ill-humour. The caution does not apply so much to mothers, for they are apt, on the other hand, to spoil the child by indulgence.

The verb παροργίζω signifies to irritate—to throw into a passion. See under iv. 26. In Col. iii. 21 the apostle uses ἐρεθίζετε—" do not rouse or provoke." The paternal reign is not to be one of terror and stern authority, but of love. The rod may be employed, but in reason and moderation, and never from momentary impulse and anger. Children are not to be moved to "wrath" by harsh and unreasonable treatment, or by undue partiality and favouritism. If they be uniformly confronted with paternal frown and menace, then their spirit is broken, and the most powerful motive to obedience—the desire to please—is taken from them. No—

ἀλλὰ ἐκτρέφετε αὐτὰ ἐν παιδείᾳ καὶ νουθεσίᾳ Κυρίου— " but bring them up in the discipline and admonition of the Lord" — *in disciplina et correptione.* Vulgate. The verb refers here to spiritual culture, and not as in v. 29 to physical support. Παιδεία may not signify discipline in itself, but rather the entire circuit of education and upbringing which a παῖς requires, and of which discipline is the necessary and prominent element. The sense of chastisement was taken from the Hebrew מוּסָר, which it represents in the Septuagint. Lev. xxvi. 18; Ps. vi. 1; Isa. liii. 5; 2 Tim. iii. 16. Augustine renders it *per molestias eruditio.* Ast, *Lex. Plat., sub voce.* Chastisement is thus quite consistent with obedience to the previous injunction. Children are not to be provoked, but yet are to be corrected. Νουθεσία (νουθέτησις being the earlier form—Phryn. ed. Lobeck, p. 512), as several expositors have remarked, is one special element or aspect of the παιδεία. It denotes, as the composition of the word indicates, " putting in mind, admonition, or formal instruction." Job

iv. 3; Rom. xv. 14; Col. i. 28; 1 Thess. v. 12; 2 Thess. iii. 15; Plutarch, *De Cohib. Irâ,* 2; Xenophon, *Mem.* i. 2, 21. Jerome says—*admonitionem magis et eruditionem quam austeritatem sonat.* Trench, *Synon.* § 32. Koppe, as usual, makes the two words synonymous. The philological commentators, such as Kypke, adduce some peculiar phraseology from the classical writers, but not with great pertinence, such as from Plutarch—οἱ ῥάβδοι νουθετοῦσι, and from Josephus—μάστιξιν νουθετεῖν. Stier adopts the opinion of Luther, who renders—*mit Werk und Wort,* a translation which has been followed by Grotius, who takes the first term as *pœna,* and the second as *verba.* We have in Prov. xxix. 15—שֵׁבֶט וְתוֹכַחַת—"the rod and reproof." The genitive Κυρίου belongs to both substantives, and refers not to God, but to Christ. See under i. 2. It cannot signify "worthy of the Lord," as Matthies wrongly understands it; nor can it bear the meaning which Luther and Passavant give it—"to the Lord." Neither can we accede to the view of Erasmus, Beza, Estius, Menochius, Semler, Morus, and others, who render "according to the Lord," or in harmony with Christianity—an idea, however, which is implied. Michaelis, Scholz, a-Lapide, Grotius, and Peile give the sense "about Christ"—instruction about Christ, making the genitive that of object. Olshausen, Harless, Stier, and Meyer rightly take it as the genitive of possession—"that nurture and admonition which the Lord prescribes," or which belongs to Him and is administered by Him. Chrysostom refers especially to the Scriptures as one source of this instruction. Such training leads to early piety, and such is ever welcome to Christ and His church. For the sun shining on a shrub, in its green youth, is a more gladsome spectacle than the evening beam falling dimly on the ivy and ruins of an old and solitary tower. Harless, *Christliche Ethik,* § 53, 1860, 5th ed.

The apostle next turns to a numerous and interesting class of the community—the slaves—δοῦλος, which is distinct from μίσθιος or μισθωτός, and is opposed in verse 8 to the ἐλεύθερος. Slavery existed in all the cities of Ionia and Asia Minor, and in many of them slaves were greatly more numerous than freemen.[1] In fact, the larger proportion of

[1] Ample information on this subject may be found in such writers on Greek

artisans and manufacturers, and in general of the industrial classes, were in bondage. There is little doubt that very many of these bondmen embraced the gospel, and became members of the early churches. Indeed, Celsus said, and no doubt with truth, that those who were active proselytizers to Christianity were—ἐριουργοὺς καὶ σκυτοτόμους καὶ κναφεῖς— weavers, cobblers, fullers, illiterate and rustic men. Origen, *Contra Celsum*, lib. iii. p. 144, ed. Spencer, Cantab. 1677. But Christianity did not rudely assault the forms of social life, or seek to force even a justifiable revolution by external appliances. Such an enterprise would have quenched the infant religion in blood. The gospel achieved a nobler feat. It did not stand by in disdain, and refuse to speak to the slave till he gained his freedom, and the shackles fell from his arms, and he stood erect in his native independence. No; but it went down into his degradation, took him by the hand, uttered words of kindness in his ear, and gave him a liberty which fetters could not abridge and tyranny could not suppress. Aristotle had already described him as being simply ἔμψυχον ὄργανον—a tool with a soul in it; and the Roman law had sternly told him he had no rights, *quia nullum caput habet*—because he was not a person. He may have been placed on the πρατὴρ λίθος—" the auction block," and sold like a chattel to the highest bidder; the brand— στίγμα, of his owner might be burned into his forehead, and he might bear the indelible scars of judicial torture—that βάσανος without which a slave's evidence was never received; but the gospel introduced him into the sympathies of a new brotherhood, elevated him to the consciousness of an immortal nature, and to the hope of eternal liberty and glory. Formerly he was taught to look for final liberation only in that world which never gave back a fugitive, and he might anticipate a melancholy release only in the grave, for "there the wicked cease from troubling, and there the weary be at rest; there the prisoners rest together; they hear not the voice of the oppressor; the small and great are there, and the servant is free from his master." Now, not only was he to

antiquities as Wachsmuth, Böckh, and Becker; in Reitermeier's *Geschichte der Sclaverei in Griechenland*, Berlin, 1789; and in *Histoire de l'Esclavage dans l'Antiquité*, par F. Wallon, Paris, 1847.

look beyond the sepulchre to a region of pure and noble enjoyments; but as he could even in his present servitude realize the dignity of a spiritual freeman in Christ, the friction of his chain was unfelt, and he possessed within him springs of exalted cheerfulness and contentment. Yes, as George Herbert sings—

> "Man is God's image, but a poor man is
> Christ's stamp to boot."

At the same time, Christianity lays down great principles by the operation of which slavery would be effectually abolished, and in fact, even in the Roman empire, it was suppressed in the course of three centuries. Other references of the apostle to slavery occur in 1 Cor. vii. 20-24; 1 Tim. vi. 1; Col. iii. 22; Tit. ii. 9; the Apostle Peter also refers to it in 1st Ep. ii. 18.

(Ver. 5.) Οἱ δοῦλοι, ὑπακούετε τοῖς κυρίοις κατὰ σάρκα— "Slaves, be obedient to your masters according to the flesh." The phrase κατὰ σάρκα, though the article be not repeated, qualifies κυρίοις, and so some MSS., such as A, B, read τοῖς κατὰ σάρκα-κυρίοις, imitating Col. iii. 22. Koppe, Olshausen, and Meyer suppose in the phrase a tacit contrast to a—κύριος κατὰ πνεῦμα. Still there is no need for such a supposition, for the contrast belongs, not to such a supposed formula, but pervades the entire paragraph—"the Master," or "the Lord," "the Master in heaven." Various meanings have been attached to the phrase, many of which are inferences rather than explanations. The formula κατὰ σάρκα plainly denotes a corporeal or external relationship. 1 Cor. i. 26; 2 Cor. v. 16, etc. Their master's sway was only over the body and its activities, and the relation was one which was bounded by bodily limits in its sphere and exactions. So that, such being its nature, the inferential exegesis of Chrysostom is plain, that the tyranny endured by the slave was only δεσποτεία πρόσκαιρος καὶ βραχεῖα—"a temporary and brief despotism." The exegesis of Harless is a mere deduction in the form of a truism, "that in the predicate lies this idea, though in one jurisdiction they were free, still they had masters in their earthly relations." Not less an inference is the thought of Calvin, "*mitigat quod potuisset esse nimis asperum in statu servili.*" If the relation of master and slave be only κατὰ σάρκα, then it is also a just deduction on the part of Grotius, Rückert, Matthies, Baumgarten-Crusius, Kistmacher, and others, that such a relation has reference only to external or earthly matters, and leaves spiritual freedom intact. Even Seneca could say—*Servitus non in totum hominem descendit; excipitur animus*. Now, if the slave followed the apostle's advice, he acquired happiness, and commended the new religion; while sullenness and refractory insolence, on pretence of spiritual freedom, would have led to misery, and brought an eclipse on Christianity.

The apostle, in the following clauses, hits upon those peculiar vices which slavery induces, and which are almost inseparable from it. The slave is tempted to indolence and carelessness. When a man feels himself doomed, degraded, and little else than a chattel, driven to work, and liable at any moment to be sent to the market-place and sold as an ox or a horse, what spring of exertion or motive to obedience can really exist within him? The benevolent shrewdness of Seneca (*Ep.* 47) had led him to say—*Arrogantiæ proverbium est, totidem esse hostes quot servos. Non habemus illos hostes, sed facimus.* The apostle urges this obedience to be—

μετὰ φόβου καὶ τρόμου—" with fear and trembling." The words do not mean with abject terror, but with that respect and reverence which their position warranted. The strong language shows, according to some, that this "fear and trembling" are not before "fleischli lordes," but before the one Divine Lord. The words occur 1 Cor. ii. 3, 2 Cor. vii. 15, Phil. ii. 12, and in two of these places they seem to describe sensations produced by mere human relationships. The preposition μετά indicates that such emotions were to be the regular accompaniments of obedience:—

ἐν ἁπλότητι τῆς καρδίας ὑμῶν—" in singleness of your heart." While μετά in the first clause refers to the accompaniment of obedience, ἐν here, as usual, characterizes the internal element. "Singleness of heart" is plainly opposed to duplicity; ἁπλοῦς, *quasi plicis carens*. Tittmann, *De Syn.* p. 28; Beck, *Seelenl.* p. 166; Rom. xii. 8; 2 Cor. viii. 2, ix. 11; Jas. i. 5. The slave is ever tempted to appear to labour while yet he is loitering, to put on the seeming of obedience and obey with a double heart. The counsel of the apostle therefore is, that he should obey in singleness of aim, giving undivided effort and attention to the task in hand, for it was to be done—

ὡς τῷ Χριστῷ—"as to Christ;" the dative governed by the verb ὑπακούετε. Obedience with all these characteristics was to be yielded to earthly masters as to Christ. As common and secular inducements can have but small influence on the mind of a slave, so the apostle brings a religious motive to bear upon him. See under v. 22.

(Ver. 6.) Μὴ κατ' ὀφθαλμοδουλείαν, ὡς ἀνθρωπάρεσκοι— "Not in the way of eye-service, as men-pleasers;" κατά, Winer, § 49, d. The duty is explained, first negatively, and then positively. The two nouns have their meaning indicated sufficiently by their composition. The first of them, which occurs only elsewhere in Col. iii. 22, is an expressive term of the apostle's own coinage. In an allusion to this place the adjective occurs, μὴ ὡς ὀφθαλμόδουλος ἀλλ' ὡς φιλοδέσποτος. Apostol. Const. iv. 12, p. 98, ed. Ultzen, 1853. The second noun belongs to the later Greek. Ps. liii. 5; Lobeck, ad Phryn. p. 621. Eye-service is labour when the master is present, but relaxation and sloth so soon as he is gone, labour only—τῷ σχήματι. Theophylact. Need we add that this is a vice which slavery everywhere creates and exhibits? Hence the necessity for drivers and overseers, whips and collars, treadmills and dungeons. The slave has usually no higher aim than to please him who has in his hands the power of punishment and sale; and whether in deception, or in an ingenious show of obedience, or a cunning feint of attention, this one motive prevails—to prevent his master taking offence at him. But the apostle presents another and deeper inducement, which should lead to punctual and honest industry carried on to please the Lord in heaven. For the slaves were to work not as man's—

ἀλλ' ὡς δοῦλοι Χριστοῦ—"but as the slaves of Christ"— His by peculiar purchase and special proprietorship. The article in the Received Text before Χριστοῦ is struck out on the authority of A, B, D¹, F, G, etc.

ποιοῦντες τὸ θέλημα τοῦ Θεοῦ ἐκ ψυχῆς—"doing the will of God from the soul." Mark xii. 30; Luke x. 27; Col. iii. 23. This clause, according to some, is not to be joined with the one before it—"as the servants of Christ," but with the first clause of the verse—"not with eye-service, as menpleasers, ... doing the will of God." There is no reason to adopt such a view. Though they were slaves to a human master, they were to live and labour in the character of Christ's servants, the characteristic of whose industry is, that they do God's will from the heart. That sphere in which they had been placed was of God's allotment; and when they discharged its duties, they were to labour not to please men, as if simply doing man's bidding, but to please God, and under the idea that they were doing His will. Such an impression must create motives which no secular premiums or penalties could ever have originated.

But the connection of ἐκ ψυχῆς has been disputed. Numerous and eminent authorities join the words to the next verse. So the Syriac reads —"and serve them with all your soul." Chrysostom adopts this disposition of the clauses, with Œcumenius and Jerome, followed by Bengel, Koppe, Harless, de Wette, Stier, and Alford, as well as by the editors Knapp and Lachmann. But we see no reason for following such a connection, as the keeping of the words in union with the preceding clause yields a good and appropriate sense. Col. iii. 23. The phrase ἐκ ψυχῆς signifies "heartily," and stands in contrast with "eye-service." Delitzsch, *Psych.* p. 160. The slave is to do the will of God from the soul—not reluctantly, and as if from mere conviction that it should be done. This cordiality is an essential element of Christian service. The limbs of the slave move with a reluctant tardiness and heartlessness; and such forced or feigned obedience is one of those inevitable results of slavery, against which the apostle is cautioning this class of his readers. But if the words ἐκ ψυχῆς be joined to the next verse, its first clause will then have the aspect of tautology, ἐκ ψυχῆς, μετ' εὐνοίας δουλεύοντες. Had there been a καί connecting the two nouns, this exegesis might have had some probability. Harless distinguishes the two nouns thus, that ἐκ ψυχῆς points out the relation of the servant to his work, and μετ' εὐνοίας characterizes the relation of the servant to his master. See Passow, Liddell and Scott, and Pape, *sub vocibus*; Xenophon, *Œconom.* p. 673; *Cyrop.* iii. p. 54; Elsner, ii. p. 228. But though such a distinction be just, it is no argument for connecting the two terms in one clause. It rather affords to us the best reason for separating them, because the clause to which we attach ἐκ ψυχῆς speaks of work to be done, and that cordially; while the next clause, to which μετ᾽ εὐνοίας belongs, turns attention to the master for whom this labour is to be performed. That master being Christ, goodwill to Him must characterize the performance of it.

(Ver. 7.) Μετ᾽ εὐνοίας δουλεύοντες—" Serving with a well-affected mind," that is, not only cordially, but higher yet—remembering that He whom you really serve is not a tyrant, but a generous master; for your service is done to Christ. It is no goodwill which the slave often bears to his master, his common feeling being the torment of his master's presence and the terror of his lash. Serving—

ὡς τῷ Κυρίῳ, καὶ οὐκ ἀνθρώποις—"as to the Lord, and not to men;" the phrase being in contrast with "men-pleasers." The particle ὡς, not found in the Received Text, is now rightfully inserted, on the authority of A, B, D¹, F, G, and many other concurrent authorities. The spirit of their service was to be Christian. They were to remember Christ the Master, and in serving others were to serve Him—the Master not according to the flesh. In external aspect the service was to men, but in motive and spirit it was to the Lord. It is evident that if the slaves cherished such religious feelings, the hardships of their condition would be greatly lightened. Menander has also said—ἐλευθέρως δούλευε, δοῦλος οὐκ ἔσῃ—" serve freely, and you are no longer a slave." The spirit of this paragraph, as Olshausen remarks, *detractis detrahendis*, should regulate all service. "Whatever ye do in word or in deed, do all in the name of Christ." Or, as Luther says in a quotation by Stier, "when a servant-maid sweeps out a room, she can do a work in God."[1]

(Ver. 8.) Εἰδότες ὅτι ὃ ἐάν τι ἕκαστος ποιήσῃ ἀγαθὸν, τοῦτο κομίσεται παρὰ Κυρίου, εἴτε δοῦλος, εἴτε ἐλεύθερος—"Knowing," or "as ye know that whatsoever good each one shall have done, this shall he receive from the Lord, whether he be bond or free." Lachmann, supported by A, D, E, F, G, etc., reads

---

[1] "Wenn eine Magd die Stube auskehrt, kann sie ein Work in Gott thun;" or, as John Wesley says, "Making every action of common life a sacrifice to God."

ὅτι ἕκαστος ὃ ἐὰν ποιήσῃ, but Tischendorf reads as we have printed it. There are also many other variations which need not be noted, as they have sprung from emendation. The ὅ and τι are separated by a tmesis, and ἐάν stands after the relative for ἄν. Winer, § 42, 6, *Obs*.[1] Instead of κομίσεται, which is supported by A, B, D[1], F, G, the Stephanic text has κομιεῖται, on what appears to be the minor authority of D[4], E, K, L, and the texts of Basil and Chrysostom. The Received Text has the article τοῦ before Κυρίου, but without sufficient evidence. Τοῦτο, "this," and not something else, the verb being in the middle, and really meaning "shall receive back for himself." Col. iii. 24, 25. The object of the apostle is, to encourage the slaves to the cultivation of those virtues which he has described. If they obeyed him, and became diligent and industrious, and served their masters with conscientious fidelity and goodwill, then, though their master might fail either to note or reward their conduct, they were not to be disheartened. For the one Master on high is also the Judge, and He will not fail to confer on them a recompense, not of merit indeed, but of grace. The hope of a future world, in which there would be a gracious recognition of their character and actions, would preserve them from impatience and discontent amidst insults and ingratitude on the part of thankless and "froward" masters. The Christian doctrine of rewards is too often lost sight of or kept in abeyance, as if it were not perfectly consistent with the freest bestowment of heavenly glory.

(Ver. 9.) Καὶ, οἱ κύριοι, τὰ αὐτὰ ποιεῖτε πρὸς αὐτούς— "And, ye masters, do the same things towards them." Καί indicates an immediate connection, for the duties were reciprocal. The master needed instruction as well as his slave, for irresponsible power is above all things apt to be abused. Plato has well said, that treatment of slaves is a test of character, because a man may so easily wrong them with impunity.[2] The apostle had stooped to the slave, and he was not afraid

---

[1] Moulton, p. 390.

[2] Διάδηλος γὰρ ὁ φύσει καὶ μὴ πλαστῶς σίβων τὴν δίκην μισῶν δὲ ὄντως τὸ ἄδικον ἐν τούτοις τῶν ἀνθρώπων ἐν οἷς αὐτῷ ῥᾴδιον ἀδικεῖν.—Plato, *Leges*, lib. vi. Opera, vol. viii. p. 245; ed. Bekker, London, 1826. (Macrobius, *Saturnalia*, i. cap. 11, vol. i. p. 144; ed. Bipont.)

to speak with erect attitude to the master. The masters are summoned to do the same things—τὰ αὐτά—to the slaves, as their slaves are enjoined to do to their masters. The language is general, and expresses what Calvin well calls *jus analogum*. They were to act toward their servants in a general spirit of reciprocal kindness, or as the apostle says in Col. iv. 1, they were to give them "that which is just and right." The duty taught to the slave was earnest, conscientious, and religious service; the corresponding duty taught to the master was earnest, conscientious, and religious government. All the elements of service were to be also those of proprietorship. Such appears to us to be the general sense of the language, and such is the general view of Zanchius, Crocius, and Matthies; while Theodoret, Bengel, Harless, Meier, Olshausen, Rückert, Stier, and Meyer dwell, perhaps, too much on the mere εὔνοια already recommended. Many other commentators confine and enfeeble the meaning, by specifying too minutely the reference of τὰ αὐτά. The Greek commentators refer the words at once to δουλεύοντες in ver. 7, as if the apostle meant to say—" your slaves serve you, you are also to serve them." Chrysostom shrinks, however, from this full form of putting his meaning. "The apostle," he adds, "does not actually say it, but he means it"—ἀλλ' οὐκ εἶπε, δουλεύετε, καίτοι γε εἰπὼν τὰ αὐτὰ τοῦτο ἐδήλωσε. Flatt restricts the reference to doing the will of God, that is, "so demean yourselves towards your slaves, that ye accomplish in reference to them the will of God." De Wette refers to the clause τὸ ἀγαθὸν ποιεῖν in ver. 8, as if there were a paraphrastic allusion to the τὴν ἰσότητα.[1]

---

[1] The following note is comprehensive and eloquent :—

"And with respect to all servants of every denomination, *equity* requires that we treat them with humanity and kindness : that we endeavour to make their service easy, and their condition comfortable ; that we forbear rash and passionate language ; that we overlook accidental errors, and remit trivial faults ; that we impose only such labour as is reasonable in itself and suitable to their capacity ; that our reproofs be calm and our counsels well timed ; that the restraints we lay upon them be prudent and salutary ; that we allow them reasonable time for rest and refreshment, for the culture of their minds, and for attendance on the worship of God ; that we set before them a virtuous example, instil into them useful principles, warn them against wickedness of every kind, especially against the sin which most easily besets them ; that we afford them opportunity for reading and private devotion, and furnish them with the necessary means of ἀνιέντες τὴν ἀπειλήν—"forbearing threatening." Chrysostom, Calvin, Harless, and Baumgarten take these words too vaguely, as if, *sub una specie*, they generally forbade contumelious treatment. The reference is more pointed. Bloomfield, preceded by the Syriac, on the other hand, presses too hard upon the clause when he understands it as signifying "remitting the threatened punishment," and he bases his opinions upon two passages from Xenophon and Plutarch which call a menaced penalty, or the thing threatened, a threatening. The former of these two interpretations is forbidden by the use of the article. But, alas! threatening has always been the special characteristic and weapon of slave-owners. Ἀπειλή is a feature of mastership so well known, that the apostle defines it as ἡ ἀπειλή—that system of threatening which was a prevalent and familiar feature of slavery. Now, however, not only was no unjust and cruel punishment to be inflicted, but even "threatening" was to be spared. The apostle hits upon a vice which specially marks the slave-holder; his prime instrument of instigation to labour is menace. The slave is too often driven on to his toil by truculent looks, and words and acts of threatening; and, by the sight of the scourge and the imitated application of it, he is ever reminded of what awaits him if his task be not accomplished. Masters were not merely to modify this procedure, but they were at once to give it up. The Lex Petronia had already forbidden a master on his own responsibility to throw a slave to the wild beasts, but no statute ever forbade "threatening." *Homines tamen esse memento*—"remember your slaves are men," says Cato; but Lactantius goes further, and adds what Cato's pen would have shrunk from—*eos et habemus et dicimus spiritu fratres religione conservos*. And this is the motive—

εἰδότες ὅτι καὶ αὐτῶν καὶ ὑμῶν ὁ Κύριός ἐστιν ἐν οὐρανοῖς —"knowing, as ye know, that both their and your Master is in heaven." This reading has A, B, D[1], many minuscules, with the Vulgate, Gothic, Coptic, Clement, and Jerome in its favour, while F and G read αὐτῶν ὑμῶν, and L has ὑμῶν καὶ

learning the way of salvation; that we attend to the preservation of their health, and have compassion on them in sickness; and, in a word, that we contribute all proper assistance to render them useful, virtuous, and happy."—Lathrop, *Discourses on the Ephesians*, p. 538, Worcester, U.S., 1810.

αὐτῶν. The readings have arisen from homoioteleuton and other causes. The Master in heaven is your Judge and theirs equally, and you and they are alike responsible to Him. Such an idea and prospect lodged in the mind of a Christian master would have a tendency to curb all capricious and harsh usage, and lead him to feel that really and spiritually he and his serfs were on a level, and that all this difference of social rank belonged but to an external and temporary institution. Could he either threaten or scourge a Christian brother with whom but the day before, and at the Lord's table, he had eaten of the one bread and drunk of the one sacramental cup?

καὶ προσωποληψία οὐκ ἔστι παρ' αὐτῷ—" and there is no respect of persons with Him;" "and the takynge of persouns is not anentis God." *Wyckliffe*. This compound substantive is imitated from the Hebrew idiom—נָשָׂא פָנִים. In the New Testament the word is always used with a bad sense. Matt. xxii. 16; Mark xii. 14; Jas. ii. 1, etc. The Divine Master who bought them with His blood has no partialities. Strictest equity characterizes His judgment. Difference of worldly station has no influence with Him, but bond and free have a perfect parity before Him. The gold ring of the master does not attract His eye, and it is not averted from the iron fetter of the slave. Slaves may be denied justice in earthly courts; the law may, *a priori*, injure the bondman by acting upon the presumption that he is in the wrong, and his evidence may be legally refused as unworthy of credit: but there is a tribunal above, where the servant shall have equal position with his lord, and where the sentence pronounced shall be devoid of all that one-sidedness which has too often disgraced the judicial bench in matters between a master and his slaves.

(Ver. 10.) Τὸ λοιπόν, ἀδελφοί μου—" In conclusion, my brethren "—a reading of far higher authority than τοῦ λοιποῦ, adopted by Lachmann after A and B, and meaning—" henceforward." Madvig, § 66. It is as if he said, What remains for me to tell you but this? The address, ἀδελφοί μου, of the Received Text is omitted by Tischendorf and Lachmann —an omission which the majority of modern expositors approve. The words are not found in B, D, E, and several of the patristic writers. They seem to have been introduced from other passages where they occur in connection with τὸ λοιπόν. 2 Cor. xiii. 11; Phil. iii. 1, iv. 8; 1 Thess. iv. 1; 2 Thess. iii. 1. Olshausen says, that the apostle never in this epistle addresses his reader by such an appellation as ἀδελφοί, though as an epithet it occurs in the 23rd verse of this chapter.

The apostle now represents the church as engaged in an active warfare with the powers and principles of evil. Olshausen suggests that his residence in the Prætorium at Rome, where the equipment and discipline of soldiers were a daily spectacle, may have originated the allegory. Similar allusions are found in Isa. xi. 5, lix. 17; Ps. xviii. and cxliv.; 2 Cor. x. 4; 1 Thess. v. 8. The primary charge to the spiritual militia is—

ἐνδυναμοῦσθε ἐν Κυρίῳ καὶ ἐν τῷ κράτει τῆς ἰσχύος αὐτοῦ—" be strengthened in the Lord and in the power of His might." The verb is passive, not middle, as some suppose. It is a word peculiar to the Alexandrian Greek, and occurs in the Septuagint, Ps. lii. 7, and in Acts ix. 22; Rom. iv. 20; 2 Tim. ii. 1; Heb. xi. 34. "In the Lord," or in union with Him, is this strengthening to be enjoyed. The nouns of the last clause have been explained under i. 19. Comp. Phil. ii. 13, iv. 13. The second clause—καί—further points out or explains the special blessings which result to the Christian warrior from his union with Jesus—he is strengthened in "the power of His might." This command is one of primary necessity. No matter what armour is provided, how finely tempered, how highly polished, or how closely fitted it may be, if there be no strength in the heart—if the man have merely the dress of a soldier, with the spirit of a poltroon. And the valour is spiritual, as is the armour; for physical courage and intellectual prowess are often, alas! allied to spiritual cowardice. Moreover, soldiers have an invincible courage when they have confidence in the skill and bravery of their leader; and the power of His might, in which they are strong, has proved its vigour in routing the same foes which they are summoned to encounter. As the Captain of salvation, "He spoiled principalities and powers, and triumphed over them." The order to the spiritual host is now given, as if with the stirring peal of a trumpet—

(Ver. 11.) Ἐνδύσασθε τὴν πανοπλίαν τοῦ Θεοῦ—"Put on the panoply of God." Stier regards the rest of this clause and that of the preceding verse as identical in inner meaning. The sense cannot indeed be very different, though the image before us is distinct—first, strength or courage, and then preparation in that strength to meet the enemy. Πανοπλία is complete armour, as the name implies. Luke xi. 22. It is also found in the Septuagint (2 Sam. ii. 21 ; Job xxxix. 20), and in 2 Macc. iii. 25 ; Judith xiv. 3. It denotes full armour, and not simply, as some erroneously suppose, "the equipment" of God. The specification of the pieces of armour proves that Paul meant panoply in its literal sense. In fact, as Meyer remarks, on this word lies the emphasis, and not on τοῦ Θεοῦ, as Harless erroneously supposes. Did the emphasis lie on τοῦ Θεοῦ, it might imply that other armour than this might be used in the combat. But the strength of the charge is—Do not enter into battle with such adversaries naked and defenceless, but take to you armour. Do not cover one portion and leave another exposed ; do not assume the cuirass and neglect the helmet ; but put on "the whole armour." Do not resort to any arsenal of your own, for its armour is weak and useless ; but put on the whole armour of God. "And furthermore, we must neuer leaue these armours as long as we be in thys worlde, for we shall alwayis haue batayle." Taverner's *Postils*, p. 495 ; ed. Oxford, 1841. The genitive, Θεοῦ, is that of origination : God provides the armour. Winer, § 30. It cannot mean, as Anselm dreams, such armour as God uses. Each of its pieces—its girdle, breastplate, boots, shield, helmet, and sword—is furnished by Him. It is armour forged on no earthly anvil, and tempered by no human skill. See Winer's *Realwört.;* Kitto's *Cyclopedia ;* Smith's *Dictionary, sub voce.*

πρὸς τὸ δύνασθαι ὑμᾶς στῆναι πρὸς τὰς μεθοδείας τοῦ διαβόλου—"in order that ye may be able to stand against the stratagems of the devil." The reading μεθοδίας has good authority, A, B, D¹, E, G, K, L. Winer, § 5, 4.[1] The first πρός indicates purpose. Winer, § 49, h. But στῆναι πρός is, in military phrase, to stand in front of, with the view of opposing. Kypke (ii. 301) illustrates the phrase from Polybius, iv. 61, and Antoninus, lib. vi. § 41. Lœsner, *Obser-*

[1] Moulton, p. 49, note e.

*vat.* p. 347. Xenophon makes this contrast—οὐκέτι ἵστανται, ἀλλὰ φεύγουσι. *De Expeditione Cyri,* i. 10, 1. The plural μεθοδείας seems to denote instances of the abstract singular— *Ausdruck mannichfaltiger Arten und Fälle*—of which usage Bernhardy gives examples, p. 62. Μεθοδεία has been explained under iv. 14, and διάβολος has been considered under iv. 27. The great enemy of man, a veteran fierce and malignant, has a method of warfare peculiar to himself, for it consists of "wiles." His battles are the rush of a sudden ambuscade. He fights not on a pitched field, but by sudden assault and secret and cunning onslaught. Vigilance, self-possession, and promptitude are therefore indispensable to meet him: and as his aim is to throw his opponents off their guard and then to surprise them, so there is need to be ever clothed in this complete armour of God. His "wiles" are seen in unsettling the mind of Eve by representing God as jealous of the first man and woman; in stirring up the warlike aspirations of David to take a military census and force a conscription as the basis of a standing army; in inflaming the avaricious and sordid spirit of Judas; and in his assaults on our Lord by an appeal to appetite, piety, and ambition.

(Ver. 12.) "Ὅτι οὐκ ἔστιν ἡμῖν ἡ πάλη πρὸς αἷμα καὶ σάρκα —"For our struggle is not against flesh and blood." The reading ὑμῖν, commended by Griesbach, and adopted by Lachmann, Rückert, and Olshausen, has the authority of B, D¹, F, G, but ἡμῖν is supported by the preponderant authority of A, D³, E, K, L, etc., with other concurrent witnesses. Olshausen's argument for ἡμῖν proves the reverse of his position, for the temptation was to alter ἡμῖν to ὑμῖν, since the rest of the paragraph is delivered in the second person. The idea of a necessary combat on the part of man with evil of all kinds around him, is so natural, that we find it under various representations in classical writers. Homer, *Il.* xx. 47, and especially Plato, *De Leg.* x. 906. This latter passage is regarded by some of the Fathers as parallel to the one before us (Clemens Alex. *Strom.* 593; Eusebius, *Evang. Præp.* xi. 26), and as an echo from some old oracle of the Jewish scriptures.

The apostle has just spoken of the wiles of the devil, and he justifies the statement now—ὅτι—"because." The article is prefixed to πάλη, not simply because the contest is already supposed in the preceding verse, but because it is the one contest in which each must engage—a contest of life and death. The noun πάλη occurs only here, and is not used by the Seventy. It signifies a personal encounter, and is rendered *colluctatio* in the Vulgate. The phrase " flesh and blood" denotes humanity, viewed in its palpable characteristics, and as opposed to such spiritual and uncompounded natures as the apostle describes in the following clauses. The terms do not point out humanity in its sinful or fallen state, but only in its ordinary and organized form. Matt. xvi. 17; 1 Cor. xv. 50; Gal. i. 16. The conflict which the apostle describes is no equal one with humanity, no wrestling on equal terms of potsherd with potsherd; and man being placed at this terrible disadvantage, there is therefore all the more need of the panoply of God. The common notion, adopted also by Stier, Passavant, and Burton, that the apostle means to say that we wrestle *not only* with the evil of human corruption, but against superhuman adversaries, cannot be sustained. Yet Bloomfield and Trollope without hesitation supply μόνον. Our struggle is not against flesh and blood—

ἀλλὰ πρὸς τὰς ἀρχάς, πρὸς τὰς ἐξουσίας—" but against principalities, against powers." The combat is with spirits, and those of high rank and position. It has been remarked by Meyer and de Wette, that οὐκ . . . ἀλλά does not mean *non tam, non tantum*, for the apostle excludes flesh and blood from the lists altogether: the combat is only with principalities and with powers. Winer, § 55, 8; Klotz-Devarius, vol. ii. 9. The two substantives are explained under i. 21. The terms there employed to denote the good are here used to denote the evil chiefs. The apostle therefore refers to fallen spirits, who once occupied positions of rank and prerogative in heaven, and may still retain a similar place among the hosts of apostate angels. It is no vulgar herd of fiends we encounter, but such of them as are darkly eminent in place and dignity. For we fight—

πρὸς τοὺς κοσμοκράτορας τοῦ σκότους τούτου—" against the world-rulers of this darkness." The Received Text interposes τοῦ αἰῶνος before τούτου, but without valid proof. The words are wanting in A, B, D[1], F, G, and in many versions and Fathers, though they are found in D[3], E, K, L. It is wrong on the part of Harless to sink the meaning of κόσμος by explaining the compound term as meaning only rulers. When applied to earthly sovereigns, it is always to those of most extensive sway, who were supposed to have the world under control—*munditenentes*. Tertullian. The strong term denotes world-lords, and is so far equivalent to ὁ ἄρχων τοῦ κόσμου τούτου in John xii. 31; xiv. 30, xvi. 11; and ὁ θεὸς τοῦ αἰῶνος τούτου in 2 Cor. iv. 4. The rabbins have also adopted the word—קוֹזְמוֹקְרָטוּר. See also 1 John v. 19. What influence is ascribed in these texts to Satan, is here ascribed to others of his unholy associates or subjects. These evil spirits, who are our wary and vengeful antagonists, have acquired a special dominion on earth, out of which they are loath to be dislodged. "This darkness" is that spiritual obscurity which so painfully environs the church—that zone which surrounds an unbelieving world with an ominous and lowering shadow. The moral obscurity of paganism and impiety is fitly presided over by beings congenial in gloom and guilt. See ii. 2, v. 8; Acts xxvi. 10. The darkness, as Chrysostom says, is not that of the night, but τῆς πονηρίας. It is plain that fallen spirits have a vast and mysterious agency in the world, and that in many ways inscrutable to man they lord it over ungodliness—shaping, deepening, or prolonging the means and methods of spiritual subjugation. Not, says Theophylact, as if they were lords of the creature, but only of the world of sin—of such as voluntarily submit to them—αὐθαιρέτως ὑποδουλωθέντων; not, says Theodoret, as if God gave them such government—οὐχ ὡς παρὰ τοῦ Θεοῦ τὴν ἀρχὴν δεξαμένοις. This dark spirit-world is anxious to possess and maintain supremacy, and therefore Christians must wage incessant warfare with it. The term κοσμοκράτωρ is used by Irenæus as synonymous with the devil—διάβολον, ὃν καὶ κοσμ. καλοῦσι. *Contra Hæreses*, lib. i. cap. v. p. 64; ed. Stieren, Lipsiæ, 1848–52. The same idea pervaded the demonology of the later Judaism, as Schoettgen (*Horæ Hebr.* p. 790), Buxtorf (*Lexicon Talmud.* p. 2006), and Wetstein (*in loc.*) abundantly prove. Elsner has also produced similar language and epithets from the "Testament of Solomon" and Jamblichus "on the Egyptian Mysteries." *Observat.* p. 229. Not that the apostle fancifully adopted either their nomenclature or their notions, but these citations prove that the inspired language was well understood and recognized in the Eastern world.

πρὸς τὰ πνευματικὰ τῆς πονηρίας ἐν τοῖς ἐπουρανίοις— "against the spirits" or "spiritual bands of evil, in heavenly places." Our English version, preceded by Erasmus, Zegerus, and a-Lapide, renders "spiritual wickednesses"—*spirituales nequitiæ*. Adopting such a meaning of the adjective, the sense, as Meyer suggests, would be, the spiritual elements or aspects of evil. But the following genitive shows that the preceding adjective has the form of a substantive, and here of a collective noun. Winer compares πνευματικά with δαιμόνια, which is really an adjective (§ 34, note 3). So we have τὸ ἱππικόν—the cavalry. Rev. ix. 16. Other critics compare τὰ δαιμόνια to the τὰ ληστρικά—band of robbers, Polyænus, *Strat.* v. 14; τὸ πολιτικόν, Herodot. vii. 103; τὰ ναυτικά, etc. Kühner, § 474,, δ, § 479, *b;* Bernhardy, p. 326; Lobeck, ad Phryn. p. 378. The genitive will then be that of character or quality—the spiritual cohorts of evil. Scheuerlein, p. 115. Their nature is evil, their commission is evil, their work is evil. Evil and evil only are they, alike in essence and operation. This interpretation has the concurrence of Harless, Meyer, Olshausen, Meier, Matthies, Stier, Ellicott, and the Greek fathers Œcumenius and Theophylact.

The fivefold repetition of πρός adds intensity to the sentiment, which displays the emphatic vehemence of martial excitement. Not only is πρός repeated, but the usual καί is omitted. The verse is thus a species of asyndeton, in which each clause, as it is dwelt upon and individualized, stands out as a vivid, independent thought. Winer, § 50, 7. To rouse up the Christian soldiery, the apostle brings out into bold relief the terrible foes which they are summoned to encounter. As to their position, they are no subalterns, but foes of mighty rank, the nobility and chieftains of the fallen spirit-world; as to their office, their domain is "this darkness" in which they exercise imperial sway; as to their essence, they are not encumbered with an animal frame, but are "spirits;" and as to their character, they are "evil"—their appetite for evil only exceeds their capacity for producing it.

ἐν τοῖς ἐπουρανίοις—"in the heavenly places." See under

i. 3, 20, ii. 6, iii. 10. It needs scarcely be remarked—
1. That the exegesis which makes τὰ ἐπουράνια signify heavenly things cannot be borne out, but is wholly against the idiom of the epistle. See under i. 3. Yet this false meaning is adhered to in this place by Chrysostom, Theodoret, and Œcumenius, by Cajetan, Heinsius, Glassius, Rosenmüller, and Tyndale, who renders—"against spretuall wickednes for hevenly thinges," giving ἐν an unsustainable signification. 2. We need not stay to refute the notion of those who, like Schoettgen, Wilke, Crellius, Van Til, Brennius, and the editors of the "Improved Version," think the apostle means, in whole or in part, in this verse to describe bad men of station and influence, like the Jewish rabbinical doctors, or provincial Gentile governors. The meaning of the phrase depends on the connection assigned it:—1. The phrase may describe the scene of combat. To sustain this interpretation, there is no necessity either, with Augustine, to join the words to ἡμῖν, or to connect them with πάλη, as is done by Rückert, Matthies, and Baumgarten-Crusius, for perhaps they are too remote in position. Or, 2, τὰ ἐπουράνια may mean the seat of these evil spirits. This view is maintained by no less names than Jerome, who adds—*hæc autem omnium doctorum opinio est;* by Ambrosiaster, Luther, Calvin, Beza, Estius, Grotius, Bengel, Hammond, Meier, Holzhausen, Meyer, Olshausen, Harless, de Wette, Ellicott, and Alford. See Photius, *Quæst. Amphiloch.* p. 94; Petavius, *Dogmata Theol.* lib. iii. c. iv. But Jerome says—*non quo dæmones in cælestibus commorentur, sed quo supra nos aër hoc nomen acceperit.* But the "heavenly places" have been referred to by the apostle as the scenes of divine blessing, of Christ's exaltation, of His people's elevation, and as the region of unfallen and pure intelligences, and how can they be here the seat or abode of impure fiends? The first opinion does not, as Alford hints, stultify itself; for the scene of warfare may be different from the scene of proper residence. His view is, in effect at least, coincident with ours—the place of abode becomes the place of combat. Nor is there any proof that τὰ ἐπουράνια means heaven, in the sense of the air or atmosphere. None of the other clauses in which the phrase occurs can bear such a signification, and yet such is the sense put

upon the words by the majority of those whom we have quoted. Allioli renders—*in der Luft.* Consult what is said under ii. 2, as to the meaning of ἀήρ. Τὰ ἐπουράνια are the celestial spots occupied by the church (i. 3, ii. 6); and in them this combat is to be maintained. Those evil spirits have invaded the church, are attempting to pollute, divide, secularize, and overthrow it; are continually tempting its members to sin and apostasy; are ever warring against goodness and obstructing its progress; and therefore believers must encounter them and fight them "in the heavenly places." Such appears to us to be the plain allusion of the apostle, and the exegesis is not beset either with grammatical or theological difficulty. Still the subject is one of mystery, and we dare not definitely pronounce on the express meaning of the terms employed.

Our translators felt a dilemma here, and shrank from the same right rendering which they had given in the other verses where the phrase occurred. Under the same perplexity, some have proposed to read ὑπουρανίοις, for which unwarranted emendation Erasmus and Beza had a kindly preference; and the version of Luther is—*unter dem Himmel.* The Syriac also renders ܠܬܚܬ ܫܡܝܐ — "under heaven."[1] The perplexity was felt to be so great, that no less a scholar than Daniel Heinsius actually proposes the desperate shift of transposing the words ἐν τοῖς ἐπουρανίοις to the beginning of the verse, and making out this sense—"in heavenly things our contest is not with flesh and blood." *Exercitat. Sac.* p. 472. Neither of the renderings of Storr can be sustained

---

[1] The following is the description of Prudentius, in his *Hamartigenia* :—

> "Non mentem sua membra premunt, nec terrea virtus
> Oppugnat sensus liquidos, bellove lacessit:
> Sed cum spiritibus tenebrosis nocte dieque
> Congredimur, quorum dominatibus humidus iste,
> Et pigris densus nebulis obtemperat aër.
> Scilicet hoc medium, coelum inter et infima terræ,
> Quod patet ac vacuo nubes suspendit hiatu,
> Frena potestatum variarum sustinet, ac sub
> Principe Belial rectoribus horret iniquis.
> His colluctamur prædonibus; ut sacra nobis
> Oris Apostolici testis sententia prodit."
>
> —*Opera,* vol. i. p. 578. Lond. 1824.

—*qui in cœlo fuere*, or *qui cœlestes origine sunt*. *Opuscula*, i. p. 179; *Observat.* p. 174. The opinions of Locke and Doddridge are erroneous. The former renders—" the spiritual managers of the opposition to the kingdom of God ;" and the latter—" spirits who became authors and abettors of wickedness even while they abode in heavenly places." Hofmann generalizes, or as Meyer says, rationalizes the phrase in saying —that it refers not to place—that evil spirits are not confined to this or that locality of this earthly world—*sondern dieselbe überwaltend, wie der Himmel die Erde umspannt. Schriftb.* i. p. 455. Not much different from the view of Doddridge is that of Cocceius and Calovius, who join πονηρίας closely with the phrase—" spirits who do evil in the heavenlies." The exegesis of Peile is as arbitrary as any of these—" wickedness exhibited in spiritual beings who kept not their first estate, their righteous principality in the centre of heaven."

(Ver. 13.) Διὰ τοῦτο ἀναλάβετε τὴν πανοπλίαν τοῦ Θεοῦ— " Wherefore take up the panoply of God." "Wherefore," the foes being so formidable in power, operation, and nature, what need is there not to be fully protected with this complete and divine suit of mail? The charge is repeated from ver. 11, and the words employed are the usual military phraseology, as is shown by the illustrations of Elsner, Kypke, and Wetstein. Thus, Deut. i. 41—ἀναλαβόντες ἕκαστος τὰ σκεύη τὰ πολεμικὰ αὐτοῦ; Jer. xxvi. 3; 2 Macc. x. 21.

ἵνα δυνηθῆτε ἀντιστῆναι ἐν τῇ ἡμέρᾳ τῇ πονηρᾷ—" that ye may be able to withstand in the evil day." The soldier is equipped for the purpose of defending himself and opposing the enemy. The Christian armour is not worn for idle parade, or as holiday attire. The enemy must be encountered. But what is meant by "the evil day"? Similar phraseology is found (Ps. xli. 1, xlix. 5) in the Septuagint version. If we preserve the spirit of the imagery, we should at once be led to conclude that it was the day of battle, or, as Theodoret calls it—τῆς παρατάξεως. That is an evil day; for it may lead to wounds, though it does not destroy life. It is not specially and of necessity the day of death, as Schmid supposes, though it may be, and has often proved so. Nor is it every day of our life, as Chrysostom, Œcumenius, and Jerome understand it—τὸν παρόντα βίον—for there may be many a lull during a campaign, and there may be a long campaign ere a decisive battle be fought. Our view is that of most modern commentators, with the exception of Koppe and Meyer, who suppose Paul to refer to some future and terrible outbreak of Satan before the expected advent of Christ, which the apostle thought to be near at hand. Such is also the view of Usteri. *Paulin. Lehrbeg.* p. 341. But there can be no allusion to such a prospect in the verse before us. The evil day is that of resolute Satanic assault; "evil"—on account of the probability, or even possibility, of the sad consequences which failure or unpreparedness so often involves—damaged reputation, impaired usefulness, and the bitter regrets and memories of subsequent years. To how many has it been an evil day! Did not our Lord bid us pray, " Lead us not into temptation, but deliver us from evil "?

καὶ ἅπαντα κατεργασάμενοι στῆναι—" and having done all to stand." Two distinct interpretations have been given of the deponent middle participle κατεργασάμενοι:—1. Some give it this sense, " having subdued or overcome all," as in the margin of our English Bibles. This is the exegesis of Œcumenius and Theophylact, the former of whom expressly says that κατεργασάμενοι is used for καταπολεμήσαντες. The view of these Greek critics is followed not only by Beza, Grotius, and Wetstein, but also by Harless, Olshausen, Rückert, Conybeare, and de Wette. There is no doubt that the verb does bear such a meaning among the classical writers; but though the word occurs often, there is no instance of such a sense in the New Testament. Raphelius, *in loc.*; Fritzsche, *ad Rom.* i. p. 107. Why then should this place be an exception?

2. Others, therefore, prefer the signification " having done or accomplished all," that is, not simply "having made all necessary preparation," as the Syriac, Morus, and Bengel too narrowly take it; but having done everything which the crisis demanded, in order to quell the foe and maintain their position. This preferable exegesis is supported by Erasmus, Bucer, Meier, Meyer, and Baumgarten-Crusius. Now, not to say that the neuter ἅπαντα is against the former view, and more in accordance with the second, which refers it not to enemies, where we would have expected another gender, but

to the general elements of military duty, we may add, in contradiction of Harless, that the spirit of the context is also in favour of the last exegesis. For, 1. The apostle proceeds to arm the Christian soldier, and it is not natural to suppose that he speaks of victory prior to equipment and battle. 2. The verb στῆναι cannot be supposed to have a different signification from what it has in ver. 11. If the first opinion be adopted, "having vanquished all your enemies, to stand," then στῆναι would denote to stand victorious; or, as Luther has it, *das Feld behalten*—"to keep the field." Now this is changing the meaning of the verse, for it signifies in verses 11 and 14 to stand, not when the combat is over, but to stand with the front to the foe, in the very attitude of resistance and self-defence, or in expectation of immediate assault. 3. The clause appears to be explained by the succeeding verses; "Stand therefore" (ver. 14) with girdle, cuirass, sandals, shield, helmet, and sword, ever praying. The rendering of the Vulgate—*in omnibus perfecti*—is a deviation, probably borrowed from such a reading as Codex A presents—κατειργασμένοι. Jerome has *omnia operati*.

(Ver. 14.) This warlike picture of the apostle is to be taken in its general aspect. It is useless, on the one hand, to seek out the minutiæ of far-fetched resemblances, as is done by some foreign divines, and by Gurnall (*Christian in Complete Armour*, fol., Glasgow, 1763) and Arrowsmith (*Tactica Sacra*, 4to, 1657), and more elaborately learned than either, Lydius in his *Syntagma sacrum de re militari*, ed. Van. Til, 1698, Dordraci. All that we can affirm is, that certain spiritual acquisitions or gifts endow us with peculiar powers of self-protection, and that these graces, in their mode and province of operation, bear some similitude to certain pieces of ancient armour. So that it is an error, on the other hand, to imagine that the apostle selects at random some graces, and compares them to portions of military harness. It is probably to the armour of a Roman soldier that the apostle refers, the fullest account of which may be found in Lipsius (*De Milit. Roman.*, ed. Plant. 1614) and Vegetius (*Epitome Institutorum Rei Militaris*, ed. Schwebel, Bipont. 1806), or in Polybius, lib. vi. 20; Martial, ix. 57. See Smith's *Dictionary of the Bible*, *sub voce* "Arms." The apostle's account, as has been remarked, coincides with the figures sculptured on the Arch of Severus. First, there are three pieces of iron armour—armour fitted on to the body—girdle, breastplate, and shoes; thus—

στῆτε οὖν περιζωσάμενοι τὴν ὀσφὺν ὑμῶν ἐν ἀληθείᾳ—
"stand therefore, having girt about your loins with truth." Isa. xi. 5; Dan. x. 5. The aorist participles precede in point of time the verb. 'Ἐν is instrumental. The allusion is to the ancient military belt or girdle, which was often highly ornamented with laminæ and clasps of gold and silver, and used occasionally, when thrown over the shoulder, to support the sword or quiver. This zone is formed of truth, not objective truth, as Harless believes, for that is declared to be the sword; but, as the article is wanting, of subjective truth—truthfulness. It is not simply integrity or sincerity, but the assured conviction that you believe, and that it is God's truth you believe. Such a sincere persuasion binds tightly the other pieces of armour; and "trussing up his loins" gives the combatant alertness and buoyancy in the battle, enabling him to "endure hardness as a good soldier of Christ." He feels supported and braced by his conscious knowledge and reception of the truth. Harless errs in supposing the baldric to be a mere ornament, for the ungirded soldier had not done all to qualify him for the fight—is not fully prepared for it. Grotius says—*veritas adstringit hominem, mendaciorum magna est laxitas.* 1 Sam. xxv. 13; Ps. xviii. 32, xlv. 4.

καὶ ἐνδυσάμενοι τὸν θώρακα τῆς δικαιοσύνης—" and having put on the breastplate of righteousness." The genitive is that of apposition, and the article before it may be that of correlation, though we incline to give it a more distinctive meaning. Isa. xi. 5, lix. 17. The breastplate, as its name implies, covered and protected the chest. It was sometimes formed of linen or plates of horn, but usually of metallic scales or feathers. Pliny, *Hist. Natur.* xxxiii. 54. Roman soldiers wore chain mail, that is, hauberks or habergeons—

"Loricam consertam hamis, auroque trilicem."

But sometimes the breastplate was made of two pieces of leather or bronze, which fitted to the person, and were united by hinges or fastened by buckles. Smith's *Dictionary of Greek and Roman Antiquities*, p. 576. The righteousness which forms this καρδιοφύλαξ is, according to Meyer, Fergusson, Olshausen, Holzhausen, and Meier, moral rectitude, or, as Ellicott says, "the righteousness which is the result of the renovation of the heart by the Holy Spirit;" and, according to Baumgarten-Crusius, the conscious possession of it. The article before δικαιοσύνη has a special prominence, and we are inclined, with Harless, de Wette, Matthies, and Winzer (*Pfinstprogramm, über Ephes.* vi. 10, 17, Leipz. 1840), to understand it as the righteousness of God, or of faith, or as "justification by the blood of the cross," three scriptural phrases meaning in general one and the same thing. What Christian can boast of entire rectitude, or use as his defence what Turner unhappily calls "his own righteousness"—*nil conscire sibi, nulla pallescere culpa?* But when the justifying righteousness of Christ is assumed as a breastplate by sinners, they can defy the assaults of the tempter. To every insinuation that they are so vile, guilty, worthless, and perverse—so beset with sin and under such wrath that God will repulse them—they oppose the free and perfect righteousness of their Redeemer, which is "upon them." Rom. iii. 22. So that the dart thrown at them only rings against such a cuirass, and falls blunted to the earth.

(Ver. 15.) Καὶ ὑποδησάμενοι τοὺς πόδας ἐν ἑτοιμασίᾳ τοῦ εὐαγγελίου τῆς εἰρήνης—"And having shod your feet with the preparedness of the gospel of peace." Isa. iii. 7. The usage of such an accusative following the verb may be seen in Buttmann (§ 135, 3), though oftener the sandal itself is put in the accusative. The last genitive is that of contents (Bernhardy, p. 16), and the one before it that of source, that is, the preparedness is from the gospel, and that gospel has peace for its substance. The reference is not to greaves, which were a kind of military leggings, but to the— προκνημῖδες—*caligæ* or sandals, which were worn by the ancient warriors, and the soles of which were thickly studded with hobnails. Bynæus, *de Calcibus*, Dordraci, 1715. The military sandal of this spiritual host "is the preparation of the gospel of peace;" Wyckliffe—"in makynge redi." The preposition ἐν is instrumental or quasi-local, and ἑτοιμασία is represented as forming the sandals. So that there is error on the part of Erasmus, who renders — *parati ad evangelium.*

The noun ἑτοιμασία has in the Septuagint an active meaning, as—εἰς ἑτοιμασίαν τροφῆς—Wisdom xiii. 12; also an intransitive meaning—readiness or preparedness—ἵππους εἰς ἑτοιμασίαν ὑμῖν παρέχειν—Josephus, *Antiq.* x. 1, 2; and still in a more spiritual sense, Ps. x. 17—τὴν ἑτοιμασίαν τῆς καρδίας. The term is sometimes employed in the Septuagint as the representative of the Hebrew מָכוֹן, as in Ps. lxxxix. 15, where it is said to mean foundation, and therefore Beza, Wolf, Bengel, Koppe, and Flatt take the word in such a sense here—the firm basis of the gospel of peace. Ezra ii. 68; Dan. xi. 7. The figure is not appropriate; it might apply, indeed, to the road on which they were to march, but not to their boots. The feet were to be shod "with preparedness." The feet in fighting are so protected or cased. The feet, too, are the instruments, and therefore the appropriate symbols of motion. The Christian warrior must move as the battle shifts; his career is indeed but a battle and a march, and march and a battle. And whence is this promptitude to be derived? From "the gospel of peace"—or peace the substance of the gospel, the same gospel which was called i. 13 —the gospel τῆς σωτηρίας. For the possession of peace with God creates blessed serenity of heart, and confers upon the mind peculiar and continuous preparedness of action and movement. There is nothing to disconcert or perplex it, or divide and retard its energies. Consequently it is an error on the part of many expositors, from Chrysostom down to Conybeare, to represent the meaning thus—" preparation to preach or publish the gospel of peace," for it is of defensive armour alone the apostle is now speaking.

(Ver. 16.) Ἐπὶ πᾶσιν ἀναλαβόντες τὸν θυρεὸν τῆς πίστεως —" In addition to all, taking up the shield of faith"—the genitive being that of apposition. Lachmann, almost on the single authority of B, reads ἐν πᾶσιν, which might justify Jerome's rendering—*in omni opere*. Some, such as Luther, Beza, and Bengel, give the words the sense "above all," or "especially," "above all things," as if the most important piece of armour were now to be specified. The Gothic has "*ufar all.*" But the meaning is simply "in addition to all." Luke iii. 20; Winer, § 48, c. And the construction is changed. The pieces of armour already mentioned being fitted on to the body and fastened to it, each by appropriate mechanism, have each its characteristic verb—περιζωσάμενοι, ἐνδυσάμενοι, ὑποδησάμενοι; but shield, helmet, and sword need no such special fastening, for they are simply taken up or assumed, and therefore they are joined to the one general participle, ἀναλαβόντες, and the verb δέξασθε. Θυρεόν— scutum—a word of the later Greek,[1] denotes, as the name implies, a large door-like shield, differing in form and especially in size from the ἀσπίς—clypeus—and was, according to Polybius, two feet and a half broad and four feet long—τὸ πλάτος . . . πένθ' ἡμιποδίων, τὸ δὲ μῆκος, ποδῶν τεττάρων. Polybius, lib. vi. cap. 20, 23. The shield preserved the soldier from being struck, and his armour, too, from being hacked or notched. Such a large and powerful shield is faith—that unwavering confidence in God and His grace which guards the mind from aberration and despondency, and easily wards off such assaults as are made upon it. John v. 4, 5. The special value and purpose of the shield are then described—

ἐν ᾧ δυνήσεσθε πάντα τὰ βέλη τοῦ πονηροῦ τὰ πεπυρωμένα σβέσαι—"in," or, "with which ye shall be able to quench all the fiery darts of the wicked one." The article τά before πεπυρωμένα is not found in B, D₁, F, G, and is rejected by Lachmann, but probably without sufficient authority. It seems to imply that the devil throws other darts besides those so specified. Ὁ πονηρός is "the wicked one," either in proper person or as leader and representative of the foes so vividly described in ver. 12. 2 Thess. iii. 3; Matt. vi. 13; John xvii. 15; 1 John v. 18. In the phrase τὰ βέλη τὰ πεπυρωμένα, there is a reference to a species of missile which was tipped or armed with some combustible material. Ps. vii. 13; Lipsius, de Milit. Roman. p. 106; Alberti, Observat. Philol. in loc. This malleolus resembled a hammer, as its name imports. The inflammatory substances were compressed into its transverse portion or head, and this being ignited, the mallet was thrown among the enemy. References to such weapons are found in Herodotus, lib. viii. 52; Arrian,

---

[1] Phrynichus, ed. Lobeck, p. 366. He quotes Homer, who uses the term for the trong door of a cave, adding, that it means a shield, but not among approved or old authors.

*Alexan. Exped.* ii. 18; Thucydides, ii. 75; Smith's *Dictionary of Greek and Latin Antiquities, sub voce*—Malleolus; Winer, art. "Bogen;" and other ancient writers. Thucydides calls these shafts πυρφόροι ὀϊστοί; and Apollodorus gives them the same name as the apostle. *Bibl.* ii. 4. See also Livy, lib. xii. c. 8; Ammianus Marcellinus, 23, 4. The Coptic version reads ⲉⲟⲩⲟϩ—"filled" with fire. These blazing arrows are shot by the evil one—ὁ πονηρός—who is evil and undiluted evil; the evil one "by merit raised to that bad eminence." In the verb σβέσαι there is an allusion not to any power in the shield to quench the burning darts, as many try to show with learned labour, but to the simple fact, that such a missile caught on, or in, the shield, glances off it, and falling to the earth, is speedily extinguished. It is a misconception of the meaning of the participle πεπυρωμένα on the part of Bodius, Rollock, Hammond, and Bochart, that poisoned darts are meant, and are named "fiery" because of the burning sensation, or fever, which they produce; as if they received this appellation not from their effect, but from their nature. *Hierozoicon*, Opera, tom. iii. p. 425, ed. Leusden, Lugd. Batav. 1692. What they are, it is difficult to say. The Greek fathers, with too great restriction, think that reference is made to such lusts and desires as we sometimes term "burning" lusts and desires. The darts appear to be Satanic assaults, sudden and terrible—such suggestions to evil, such unaccountable impulses to doubt or blaspheme, such horrid insinuations about the Divine character and one's own state, as often distract persons, especially of a nervous temperament. The biographies of Luther and Bunyan afford apposite examples. But the shield of faith must be used to repel such darts, and if brought to intercept them, it preserves the Christian warrior intact. His confidence in God keeps him from being wounded, or from falling a prisoner into the hands of his ruthless enemies. Whatever happens moves him not; his faith saves him from despondency and defeat. The future form of the verb by no means supports Meyer's view as to the period of the evil day.

(Ver. 17.) Καὶ τὴν περικεφαλαίαν τοῦ σωτηρίου δέξασθε—"And take the helmet of salvation." D¹, F, and G omit the verb; δέξασθαι, a glaring emendation, is found, however, in A, D³, K, and L. The adjectival form σωτήριον is found also in Luke ii. 30, iii. 6; Acts xxviii. 28. This use of the finite verb in such a series is a characteristic of Pauline style, as if from the participial construction his mind likes to rest at length on the finite form. The military helmet protected the head. It was a cap usually made of leather, strengthened and ornamented with metallic plates or bosses, and commonly surmounted with a crest or plume. In 1 Thess. v. 8, the apostle says, " For an helmet the hope of salvation"—ἐλπίδα σωτηρίας—and therefore many suppose that the same idea is expressed elliptically here. Such is the view of Calvin, Zanchius, Calovius, Grotius, Estius, Bodius, Meier, and Winzer, but a view which is as unwarranted as that of Theodoret, Bullinger, Cocceius, and Bengel, who refer σωτήριον to the Saviour Himself, because He has received such an appellation in Luke ii. 30. The apostle takes the phrase from the Alexandrian version of Isa. lix. 17, in which the Hebrew כּוֹבַע יְשׁוּעָה is translated περικεφαλαίαν σωτηρίου. Salvation, and not the hope of it, is here represented as forming the helmet; not salvation in an objective sense, but in conscious possession. It is the assurance of being interested in this salvation that guards the head. He who knows that he is safe, who feels that he is pardoned and sanctified, possesses this "helme of helthe," as Wyckliffe renders it, and has his "head covered in the day of battle:"—

καὶ τὴν μάχαιραν τοῦ Πνεύματος, ὅ ἐστιν ῥῆμα Θεοῦ—" and the sword of the Spirit, which is the word of God." The last genitive is that of source, and the relative ὅ is neuter, by attraction or assimilation. This is the only offensive weapon which the Christian soldier is to assume. That sword is described as being the "word of God." By "the word of God" we understand the gospel, or revealed will of God— and to us it is in effect Holy Scripture, not in any restricted sense, as limited either to its commands or its threatenings. Theodore of Mopsuestia says, however, that ῥῆμα Θεοῦ is equivalent to Θεοῦ ἐνέργεια—referring in proof to such phrases as " by the word of the Lord the heavens were made," the meaning of which is easily understood. And this weapon— "the word of God"—is "the sword of the Spirit," for it is the Spirit who supplies it. By the special organic influence of the Spirit, plenary inspiration was enjoyed, and God's ideas became, in the lips and from the pens of apostles and prophets, God's words. The genitive, πνεύματος, thus indicates the relation in which God's word stands to the Spirit. How strange on the part of Harless, Olshausen, Matthies, Stier, and von Gerlach, to make it the genitive of apposition, and to represent the sword as the Spirit Himself! In this erroneous view they had been preceded by Basil, who has adduced this verse as a proof that not only the Son, but the Spirit, is called the Word—the Son being the Word of the Father, and the Spirit the Word of the Son. *Contra Eunom.* lib. v. cap. 11. Such an exposition only darkens the passage, and compels Olshausen himself to ask in perplexity a question which his own false exegesis originates—How can the Word of God be represented as the Spirit? and he answers the insoluble query by a statement no less erroneous and unintelligible, that the Spirit is an operation which the Word of God produces. Harless argues, that as the previous genitives specifying the pieces of armour are those of apposition, so analogy must justify the same syntax in this clause. But the argument is wholly out of place, and that because the apostle subjoins an explanation. Had he simply said "the sword of the Word," then according to the analogy of previous clauses the exegesis of Harless and Olshausen would be the correct one, but he enters into fuller and more precise detail. Away at the other extreme from this exposition is that of Chrysostom in one of his interpretations, of Œcumenius and Theophylact, with Michaelis and Grotius, which makes the clause merely mean—"take the spiritual sword of the Word; and still more remote is the lame exegesis of Morus, Rosenmüller, and de Wette, which understands by "spirit" the human spirit, as if the apostle meant to say—"take your soul's best sword, the word of God."

The word of God is thus the sword of the Spirit, by which the spiritual foe is cloven down. The Captain of salvation set the example, and once and again, and a third time, did He repel the assault of the prince of darkness by three brief and simple citations from Scripture. Diplomacy and argument, truce and armistice, are of no avail—the keen bright sword of the Spirit must be unsheathed and lifted.

(Ver. 18.) Διὰ πάσης προσευχῆς καὶ δεήσεως προσευχόμενοι ἐν παντὶ καιρῷ ἐν Πνεύματι—" With all prayer and supplication praying always in the Spirit." The participle is not, with Conybeare, to be rendered as a simple imperative. We cannot agree with de Wette and others in regarding prayer as a separate weapon, for the apostle now drops the figure. It is indeed an effectual means of repulse, not by itself, but in its connection with all these other graces. So that we understand this verse as describing the spirit or temper in which the armour should be assumed, the position taken, the enemy met, and the combat pursued, that is, as still connected with στῆτε οὖν. We cannot, with Olshausen, restrict it to the previous clause, namely, that prayer must accompany the use of the sword of the Spirit. The order of thought is—make preparation, take the armour, stand, fight, and all the while be praying.

Meyer's effort to make διὰ πάσης προσευχῆς καὶ δεήσεως an independent sentence, at least disconnected with the following participle, is not happy; and his argument as to tautology and the impossibility of "praying always" is without force.[1] The preposition διά expresses the means by, or the condition in or through which, the spiritual exercise implied in προσευχόμενοι developes itself. The two nouns are distinguished not as *imprecatio* and *deprecatio*, as is the opinion of Chrysostom, Theodoret, Grotius, and others; nor can we say, with de Wette, that the first term denotes the form, and the second the contents, of prayer. The two words are conjoined in the Septuagint. 1 Kings viii. 28; 2 Chron. vi. 19; Ps. vi. 9; and in Phil. iv. 6; 1 Tim. ii. 1. We believe with Harless, Meier, Meyer, and others, that προσευχή is prayer in general—the general aspects and attitudes of devotion, in adoration, confession, and thanksgiving; and that δέησις is a special branch of prayer, direct and earnest petition. The adjective πάσης adds the idea of "every kind" of prayer—all the forms, public and private, secret and domestic, oral and

---

[1] "'Praying always'—what does it mean? Being always on our knees? always engaged in the very act of prayer? This I believe to be one of the grossest glosses that Satan casts on that text. He has often given that gloss; monkery, nunnery, abstraction from the world in order to give oneself up to prayer, are but the effects of that false gloss."—Evans, *Sermons on the Ephesians*, p. 393 (British Pulpit), Lond.

unexpressed, formal and ejaculatory, which prayer may assume. And such prayer is not to be restricted to peculiar times, but is to be employed—ἐν παντὶ καιρῷ, at every season. Luke xxi. 36. " Not only the minor officers along the ranks, but the whole hosts are to join in these yearnings."[1] And such continuous and diversified prayer must be—.

ἐν Πνεύματι—" in the Spirit "—as its sphere. It is surely an unhallowed and perverse opinion of Castalio, Crocius, Grotius, Homberg, Koppe, Rosenmüller, and Zanchius even, which gives these words the meaning of ἐκ πνεύματος, and makes them signify " out of the heart, or sincerely." Bloomfield indeed lays down the canon that πνεῦμα, not having the article, cannot mean "the Holy Spirit"—a canon which is contradicted by numerous passages of the New Testament, as already stated under i. 17. The theology of the apostle is, that while the Son pleads for His people in heaven, the Spirit within them makes intercession for them and by them, by giving them an enlarged and appropriating view of the Divine promises, that they may plead them in faith and fervour, and by so deepening their own poignant consciousness of want as to induce them to cry for grace with an agony of earnestness that cannot be fitted into words. Rom. viii. 26. Jude speaks also of "praying in the Holy Ghost" (ver. 20), that is, in His exciting and assisting influence. The soldier needs courage, vigilance, and skill, and therefore he ought, with continued prayer and supplication, to look up to the Lord of hosts, " who teaches his hands to war and his fingers to fight," and who will make him " more than a conqueror ; " so that in due time, the combat being over and his foes defeated, the hand that wielded the sword will carry the palm, and the brow that wore the helmet will be crowned with immortal garlands before the throne. Praying always—

καὶ εἰς αὐτὸ ἀγρυπνοῦντες ἐν πάσῃ προσκαρτερήσει καὶ δεήσει περὶ πάντων τῶν ἁγίων—" and for this watching in all perseverance and supplication for all the saints." Τοῦτο, found in the Stephanic text after αὐτό, is regarded as doubtful on the authority of A, B, and other concurrent testimonies. Εἰς αὐτό—" for this," that is, for the purpose specified in the

---

[1] *The Soldier of the Cross*, by J. Leyburn, D.D., Philadelphia ; a series of popular and discursive sermons on Eph. vi. 10-18. Reprinted, Glasgow, 1853.

clauses preceding, not, as Koppe and Holzhausen argue, for the design expressed in the following verse—ἵνα μοι δοθῇ. To secure this earnest supplication at all times in the Spirit, they were to be ever on their guard against remissness, for many "*impedimenta*" exist in the Christian army. The phrase ἐν πάσῃ προσκαρτερήσει καὶ δεήσει, is one of pregnant emphasis. Acts i. 14; Rom. xii. 12; Col. iv. 2. "Perseverance and prayer," though not properly a hendiadys (the technical order of the words, as they should occur in such a figure, being inverted), practically means perseverance characterized by prayer, the one and the other noun having a distinct, though blended signification. The term ἁγίων has been explained under i. 3. We are inclined to take the two clauses as somewhat parallel, the second clause as containing, at the same time, a specific addition. Thus, first, the apostle exhorts them, by means of "all prayer and supplication," to be praying at all times in the Spirit, the tacit or implied reference being for themselves; and then he adds, but without any formal transition, "and for this watching along with all perseverance and prayer for all saints." The two thoughts are closely connected. To their persistent supplication for themselves, they were to join, not as a separate and distinct duty, prayer for all saints, but rather, as the compact language of the apostle suggests, in praying for themselves they were uniformly to blend petitions for all the saints. "All the saints," in obedience to the same mandate, pray for us, and in a spirit of reciprocity it becomes us to pray for them. They need our prayers; for many of them, at every given moment, must be in trial, temptation, warfare, sickness, or death. And as but a very few of them can ever be known to us, our all-inclusive sympathy with them will prove its vitality by universal and unwearying supplication for them.

(Ver. 19.) Καὶ ὑπὲρ ἐμοῦ—"And for me." When καί knits, as here, a part to a whole, it has an intensive or climactic signification. Winer, § 53, 3; Hartung, i. 45. The apostle lays emphasis on this mention of himself. And we apprehend that the same speciality of request is marked by the change of preposition. When he bids them pray for all saints, he says περὶ πάντων τῶν ἁγίων; but when he points to himself as the object of supplication, he writes ὑπὲρ ἐμοῦ.

Meyer and de Wette, indeed, and Robinson, apparently deny that any change of idea is involved in the change of preposition. Harless admits such a distinction as is between *pro* and *propter*. Certainly, in the later writers περί and ὑπέρ are almost identical in use and sense. They are even found together, as Demosthenes, *Philip.* ii. p. 162, vol. v. Oratores Att., ed. Dobson, Oxon.; Thucyd. vi. 78, 1, p. 152, vol. iii. sect. 2, ed. Poppo. No one denies this, but surely it may be asked, Why should the preposition here be changed? not, perhaps, for mere variety of phrase and style. The preposition περί—" about,"[1] used generally in a tropical sense when it governs the genitive, may be regarded as the vaguer in its reference. They could not know much about all saints, and they were to pray about them. All saints were to be ideally encircled with their supplications. The prayer for the apostle was more direct and personal, and ὑπέρ is employed, while the blessing to be prayed for is also clearly specified. In Rom. viii. 26, 1 Tim. ii. 1, Heb. vii. 25, where ὑπέρ is used, there is marked directness in the supplication, though it be for all men. 1 Pet. iii. 18. In Col. iv. 3, the apostle, in making a similar request, uses περί; but he includes himself with others, and writes ἡμῶν, and so in Heb. xiii. 18. Though such a distinction cannot be uniformly carried out, yet the use of these two different prepositions in two consecutive clauses would seem to indicate that some ideal change of relation is intended. Turner says that the prepositions are changed "for the mere sake of variety," and he instances ἐκ and διά in Rom. iii. 20, which in his opinion "apparently convey precisely the same thought." But the explanation is slovenly; for though there is a kindred meaning, there is a distinct difference of image or relation indicated by the two prepositions. And for what were they to pray?

ἵνα μοι δοθῇ λόγος ἐν ἀνοίξει τοῦ στόματός μου—" that to me may be given speech in the opening of my mouth." The conjunction ἵνα denotes the purpose, which is told by telling the purport of the prayer. The Received Text has δοθείη,

---

[1] Περί, in Sanscrit *pari*, from the root 𐌂, is "round about," differing from ἀμφί, Latin *amb*, German *um*, which means on both sides, while ὑπέρ, Sanscrit *upari*, from the root 𐌽, Latin *super*, Gothic *ufar*, German *über*, English *over*, signifies "upon" or "over."

a more subjective representation, but the principal uncial MSS. are against such a reading. Λόγος here denotes power of speech—utterance—as in 1 Cor. xii. 8; 2 Cor. xi. 6. The connection of the next clause has been much disputed. It appears to us plainest and easiest to join ἐν ἀνοίξει τοῦ στόματός μου to the preceding words—"that utterance may be given unto me in the opening of my mouth." The arguments for this view, and against the opposing hypotheses of Kypke and Koppe, are ably given by Fritzsche, *Dissert.* ii. *ad Cor.* p. 99. Such is the critical opinion of the three Greek fathers, Chrysostom, Œcumenius, and Theophylact, of Luther and Calvin, of Estius, Morus, Rückert, Harless, Olshausen, Matthies, and Meyer. The sense then is, not that the opening of his mouth was in itself regarded also as a Divine gift; but the prayer is, that utterance should be given him when the opportunity of self-vindication or of preaching should be enjoyed. Bullinger, a-Lapide, and Harless give ἄνοιξις an active signification, as if the sense were, that utterance along with the opening of my mouth may be given me, referring to Ps. li. 15, Ezek. iii. 27. We prefer the simple signification—" in the opening of my mouth," that is, when I shall have occasion to open my mouth. Matt. v. 2; Acts viii. 35, x. 34; 2 Cor. vi. 11. Wholly baseless is the translation of Beza and Piscator—*ut aperiam os meum.* That the phrase describes not the simple act of speech, but also specifies its quality as bold or open, is the view of Pelagius, Vatablus, Bodius, Zanchius, Rückert, Meier, and Matthies. See Alford on 2 Cor. vi. 11. But this view gives an emphasis to the simple diction which cannot be proved to belong to it. We believe that its only emphasis lies in its use—prefacing a set discourse of some length, and not merely a brief or conversational remark. That the apostle refers to inspiring influence we have little doubt, whether that influence be regarded as essential to the general preaching of the gospel, or to the apostle's vindication of himself and his mission at the imperial tribunal in Rome; for he was now prosecuting the appeal which he had originated at Cæsarea. Luke xxi. 14; Matt. x. 19, 20; Mark xiii. 11. His pleading for himself involved in it a description and defence of his office, and that he refers to such unpremeditated orations is the view of

Œcumenius. The next clause is explanatory, or gives the result—

ἐν παρρησίᾳ γνωρίσαι τὸ μυστήριον τοῦ εὐαγγελίου—" in boldness to make known the mystery of the gospel." B, F, G, omit τοῦ εὐαγγελίου, but the words have good authority. The genitive may be that of subject or of object, as in i. 9. Ellicott prefers the former. The noun παρρησία has been explained under iii. 12, and does not signify "freely," as Koppe and Grotius take it, that is, in contrast with previous confinement. Wyckliffe has—"with truth to make known." It characterizes the speaking in itself or in quality, as bold and open—without reserve or trepidation. Γνωρίσαι is the infinitive of design. Μυστήριον has been spoken of under i. 9. In the first chapter the apostle calls one special result and purpose of the gospel—to wit, the re-capitulation of all things under Christ—a mystery; and in the third chapter he characterizes the doctrine of the union of Jew and Gentile in one church by a similar appellation. But here he gives the same general name to the gospel. For it is a system which lay hidden till God's time came for revealing it. To know it, there must be a Divine initiator, for its truths are beyond the orbit of all human anticipations. The God-man—a vicarious death—a gratuitous pardon—the influence of the Spirit—are doctrines which man never could have discovered. They are to him a mystery, not indeed something unknowable, but something unknown till it be revealed. This gospel, without mutilation, in its fulness and majesty, and with all its characteristic elements, the apostle wished to proclaim with plain and unfaltering freedom, and for this purpose he asked the prayers of the Ephesian church.

(Ver. 20.) Ὑπὲρ οὗ πρεσβεύω ἐν ἁλύσει—" On behalf of which I am an ambassador in chains." The antecedent to οὗ is not barely εὐαγγελίου—the gospel, but the preceding clause. It was not simply because of the gospel, but because of making known the gospel, that he was imprisoned. This simple sentence has been variously analyzed. Some, as Rückert and Matthies, translate it—" for which doing of the office of ambassador, I am in chains;" while others give it this turn—" for which, even in chains, I am an ambassador." The apostle calls himself an ambassador, but one in chains.

His evangelical embassy—an office peculiar to the apostles—has been described under iv. 11. It is perhaps too much to infer, with Paley, Macknight, and Wieseler, that the singular term ἅλυσις refers to that form of military surveillance in which the prisoner had his arm bound with a chain to that of the "soldier who kept him." Acts xxviii. 16, 20. The singular form may bear a collective signification (Bernhardy, p. 58), yet, as we find the same expression in 2 Tim. i. 16, there is a possibility at least that such may be the reference. Still, we find the apostle, when in military custody at Cæsarea, employing the plural, and saying—τῶν δεσμῶν τούτων. An ambassador in chains was a rare spectacle. Τοὺς πρέσβεις νόμος μηδὲν πάσχειν κακόν, says Theophylact. The person of an ambassador is by international law sacred and inviolable; and yet Paul, a legate from the mightiest Sovereignty, charged with an embassy of unparalleled nobleness and urgency, and bearing with him credentials of unmistakeable authenticity, is detained in captivity. The object of the prayer was—

ἵνα ἐν αὐτῷ παρρησιάσωμαι, ὡς δεῖ με λαλῆσαι—"in order that I may speak boldly in this, as I ought to speak." This clause resumes the object or design of the prayer, and is parallel to the previous ἵνα μοι δοθῇ λόγος. Rom. vii. 13; Gal. iii. 14; 2 Cor. ix. 3. It dwells upon the same thought. The phrase ἐν αὐτῷ refers back to the relative οὗ—"that in this," in making known the gospel—and there is thus no repetition or tautology. It is not the ground, but the sphere of the παρρησία. This meaning of the sentence is lost in the exegesis of Meier, who follows Chrysostom and Bengel, and makes ἵνα and its clause dependent on πρέσβευω ἐν ἁλύσει, the sense then being—"that even my imprisonment may produce its effect." The apostle's earnest wish was, that he might expound his message in a manner that became him and his high commission, that his imprisonment might have no dispiriting effect upon him, and that he might not in his addresses compromise the name and dignity of an ambassador for Christ. The epistle now ends with some personal matters—

(Ver. 21.) Ἵνα δὲ εἰδῆτε καὶ ὑμεῖς τὰ κατ' ἐμέ, τί πράσσω, πάντα ὑμῖν γνωρίσει Τύχικος ὁ ἀγαπητὸς ἀδελφὸς, καὶ πιστὸς διάκονος ἐν Κυρίῳ—"But that ye also may know my state, how I fare, Tychicus, the beloved brother and faithful in the

Lord, shall make known all things to you." The reading, καὶ ὑμεῖς εἰδῆτε, is found in A, D[1], E, F, G. This verse needs almost no exposition. The supposition that in καὶ ὑμεῖς there is a reference by contrast to the Colossians, has been already noticed in the Introduction. The particle δέ is one of transition to another subject—the conclusion of the epistle. The words τὰ κατ' ἐμέ—res meæ—are a very common Greek idiom (Phil. i. 12; Acts xxiv. 22, xxv. 14), and they are further explained by τί πράσσω, a phrase which means "how I fare"—"what" or "how I do"—not what I am employed about in prison, but with the same meaning as in the common salutation—"How do ye do." The apostle was well aware of their anxiety to know many particulars as to his health, spirits, condition, facilities and prospects of labour; and not to burden an inspired composition with such minutiæ, he charged Tychicus with an oral message. Little is known of Tychicus save what is contained in a few allusions, as in Acts xx. 4; Col. iv. 7. In 2 Tim. iv. 12 the apostle says, referring, as some suppose, to this mission—"Tychicus have I sent to Ephesus." There is no ground for supposing, with Estius, that διάκονος refers here to any office in the church. Tychicus, like Mark, was useful for general service. 2 Tim. iv. 11. The words ἐν Κυρίῳ show the spirit and sphere of the labours of Tychicus, that it was Christian service which he rendered to the apostle and their common Lord. We understand πιστός to denote "trusty"—"trewe mynystre." See under i. 1. The previous epithet "brother" implies his profession of faith, but he was selected to this mission, out of many other believers, because of his trustiness, and he was commended to the Ephesians as one on whom they might rely with implicit confidence. And therefore Paul says of him—

(Ver. 22.) Ὃν ἔπεμψα πρὸς ὑμᾶς εἰς αὐτὸ τοῦτο, ἵνα γνῶτε τὰ περὶ ἡμῶν, καὶ παρακαλέσῃ τὰς καρδίας ὑμῶν—"Whom I have sent unto you for this very reason, that ye might know our affairs, and that he might comfort your hearts." The verb might bear the translation, "I send." Phil. ii. 28; Winer, § 40, 5, 2. The phrase τὰ περὶ ἡμῶν is a common idiom, and the apostle includes himself among others who were identified with him and his position in Rome. There is plain reference in the last clause to iii. 13. The different readings in these two verses principally refer to the position and order of some of the words. Now comes the farewell—

(Ver. 23.) Εἰρήνη τοῖς ἀδελφοῖς, καὶ ἀγάπη μετὰ πίστεως— "Peace to the brethren, and love with faith." Εἰρήνη is not concord, as some suppose, and it cannot be so in a parting salutation. The word in such a relation has not a special theological sense, but means, in a Christian mouth, "all that was good for them here and hereafter." See the term explained under i. 2. "Peace be to the brethren"—the Christian brotherhood in Ephesus; and not, as Wieseler restricts it, to the Jewish portion of the church. *Chronol.* p. 444.

καὶ ἀγάπη μετὰ πίστεως—" and love with faith," that is, love in union with faith. "Love" is not God's love to us, but our love to one another; or as the apostle has already called it, "love unto all the saints." And that love is "with faith," as its accompaniment, for "faith worketh by love." The apostle wishes them a more fervent love along with a more powerful faith. He had heard that they possessed these already, but he wished them a larger inheritance of the twin graces. See under i. 15. We could not say, with Robinson, that in this instance, and in some others, μετά is equivalent to καί, for close relation seems always to be indicated.¹ Μετά indicates something which is to be regarded not as an addition, but as an accompaniment. Ἀγάπη καὶ πίστις— "love and faith," might mean love, then faith, as separate or in succession, and σὺν πίστει would have denoted coherence, but "love with faith" denotes love and faith in inseparable combination with it. The reading of Codex A, ἔλεος for ἀγάπη, is an emendation suggested to some old copyists for the very reasons which have led Rückert to adopt it. The concluding salutations in the other epistles are commonly brief, but the sympathy and elevation which reign in this letter stoop not to a curt and common formula. In his fulness of heart the apostle bestows an enlarged benediction on the Christian community at Ephesus—

ἀπὸ Θεοῦ Πατρὸς καὶ Κυρίου Ἰησοῦ Χριστοῦ—"from God the Father and the Lord Jesus Christ." In the 2nd verse of the first chapter, the apostle says, "from God our Father,"

---

¹ Μιτά, in Sanscrit *mithas*, from the root मिथ्, is connected with μίσος, mid, middle, and still contains the germ of its original meaning.

and the Syriac reads here also ܠܢ. Though ἡμῶν be not expressed, the meaning is the same, and the exposition will therefore be found under i. 2.

(Ver. 24.) Ἡ χάρις μετὰ πάντων τῶν ἀγαπώντων τὸν Κύριον ἡμῶν Ἰησοῦν Χριστὸν ἐν ἀφθαρσίᾳ—" Grace be with all them who love our Lord Jesus Christ in incorruption." This is a second and more general benediction. The article is prefixed to χάρις in the valediction. See under i. 2. The words "our Lord Jesus Christ," occurring previously in i. 3, have also been already explained.

The concluding difficulty of the expositor, and it is no slight one, lies in the concluding words of the epistle— ἐν ἀφθαρσίᾳ. Wyckliffe has "vncorrupcioun," Tyndale "puernes," the Genevan "to their immortalitie," and Cranmer "vnfaynedly."

The connection and meaning are alike matter of doubt. —1. Some, such as Drusius, Wilke, and Peile, connect ἐν ἀφθαρσίᾳ with χάρις, as if the meaning were—"grace with immortality," or immortal grace. But this exegesis appears on the face of it contrary to the verbal order of the clause. Piscator, taking ἐν for σύν, regards grace and immortality as two separate gifts. Beza, Musculus, Bengel, Michaelis, Matthies, and Bloomfield (supplemental volume, *in loc.*), give the phrase another turn of meaning, and render—"grace to immortality," or "grace for ever abide with you." The opinion of Harless is similar — ἐν, he says, "marks the element in which this grace reveals itself, and ἀφθαρσία is its indestructible essence." And this is also the view of Baumgarten-Crusius. Such a construction, however, has no philological foundation, for the two nouns are not so homogeneous in meaning as to be used in such a connection. Olshausen resorts to the desperate expedient of an ellipse, saying that the words mean—ἵνα ζωὴν ἔχωσιν ἐν ἀφθαρσίᾳ. This ellipse, as Meyer says, is a pure fiction. 2. As far removed from a natural exegesis is the opinion of Wetstein, Reiners, and Semler, who join ἐν ἀφθαρσίᾳ to Ἰησοῦν Χριστόν, and give this interpretation—"who love the Lord Jesus Christ in His incorruptible or exalted state." We should have expected a very different phraseology if that had been the apostle's meaning, and at least, with the present words, the repetition of the article — Ἰησοῦν Χριστὸν τὸν ἐν ἀφθαρσίᾳ. 3. Whatever difficulty may be involved in the exegesis, we are obliged to take the ἐν ἀφθαρσίᾳ as qualifying ἀγαπώντων. This appears to be the natural connection. But as to the meaning—

1. Chrysostom and Theophylact give an alternative explanation—" on account of those things which are incorruptible." These critics say—τὸ ἐν διά ἐστι, that is, ἐν stands for διά. But such violence to the words cannot be warranted.

2. Some give the meaning—" in sincerity." Such is the view of Chrysostom and Theophylact in another of their interpretations, in which they explain ἐν ἀφθαρσίᾳ by ἐν κοσμιότητι; and they are followed by Pelagius, Erasmus, Calvin, a-Lapide, Estius, and Robinson. At the same time there is some difference of opinion among this class, some giving more prominence to sincerity as an element of the love itself, and others regarding this sincerity as proved by the result and accompaniment of a chaste and holy life.

3. Others give the phrase this meaning—" in perpetuity." Among this party are Œcumenius, who employs as synonyms ἄφθαρτος καὶ ἀμείωτος, and Luther, Zegerus, Wolf, Meyer, Wahl, Bretschneider, and Meier. Rückert and de Wette are undecided, though the latter seems to incline to the first interpretation of the Greek expositors. The Gothic version reads *in unriurein*—" in incorruptibility." It is somewhat difficult to decide. The noun means incorruption, and must define either the sphere or character of this love. If it refer to the sphere, there then may be an allusion to the heavenly places to which believers are elevated—a region of unchanging and undecaying love to Jesus (Rom. i. 23; 1 Cor. ix. 25, xv. 52; 1 Tim. i. 17); or if, as Meyer says, it describe the character of this affection, then it signifies that it possesses an enduring freshness—that it glows for ever. A similar construction is found in Tit. iii. 15. We are inclined to believe that the word characterizes the nature of this love, perpetuity being a necessary element of this incorruption. The term points out that in this love there is no source of decay or change, that it does not contain within itself the seeds of dissolution, and that it is of

such compactness, that its elements cannot one after another fall out and itself gradually perish. Incorruptness is immortality based upon simplicity of essence. And therefore this love to Jesus — filling the entire nature, burning with pure and quenchless fervour, proving itself a holy instinct, unmixed with baser motives and attachments, one and indivisible—is " in incorruption,"—$\dot{\epsilon}\nu$ $\dot{a}\phi\theta a\rho\sigma\dot{\iota}a$. AMEN.

# INDEX OF PRINCIPAL SUBJECTS TREATED OF

ACCESS to the Father by Christ, 186-188, 237
Adoption into the Divine family, 30-35
Anger. which is not sinful, 348; which is sinful, 349; its evil effects (*note*), 359
Apostle, the office of, and its institution, 298, 299
Apostleship, Paul's designation thereto, 1, 2
Armour, spiritual; offensive and defensive, 457, 464, and foll. pp.
Atonement; the doctrine thereanent, 367
Author of this Epistle; his designation, 1, 2, 210; his qualification to be a teacher of the Gentiles, 211-214

BAPTISM, 275
Blessings, spiritual, enjoyed in Christ, 13

CHARITY enjoined, 363
Christ, His Divine Sonship, 11, 12; recapitulation of all in Him, 54; His Headship over the Church, 321; His humiliation, 293 and foll. pp.; His sacrificial death, 369; His exaltation, 99-105; His execution of the plan of redemption, 235; His boundless love, 249-258; He is the believer's inheritance, 58-60; dwells in the believer, 246-247; has received and conferred gifts on men, 281 and foll. pp.; subjugates His enemies, 287
Christians should remember their former condition, 160; which is described, 130-140, 160-167; their present condition described, 169, 170, see also 145, 155, 156; should do all in Christ's name, 405; should be mutually submissive, in order to right discharge of relative duties, 406, 407; should be established in the faith, 315
Church, the; in relation to Christ, 104-116; in relation to the Father,

a family, 241; should glorify God, 262; her subjection to Christ, 411; her presentation to Christ in purity, 420-422
Circumcision, the; who so called, 162
Colosse, the Epistle to; compared with that to Ephesus, xlv-xlviii
Commandments; the first with promise, 438
Commentators on the Ephesians, liii.
Conclusion of the Epistle; refers to personal matters, 481
Conversation (language) to be pure, 352, 371, 372
Converts are to manifest that they are of the light, by proper fruits, 382, 383; must have no fellowship with evil, 382; ought to be wise, 392; ought to redeem the time, 393; ought to be sober, 395
Creation, idea of, used to delineate a spiritual change, 156, 178; ascribed to God, 230

DARKNESS, moral and spiritual, of the Gentile world, 329 and foll. pp.
Death of Christ, sacrificial, 367-373; is an atonement, 369
Depravity inborn in man, 133, 138
Descent into hell of Christ, doctrine of, 291
Devil, the, described as "the prince of the power of the air," 123-128; his activity and its sphere of operation, 128
Domestic duties, 407 and foll. pp. and also 435-440
Doxology, the introductory, 10; concluding a prayer, 260-265
Drunkenness and dissoluteness forbidden, 395

ELECTION, doctrine of, 18; its cause is in God, 18; believers chosen in Christ, 20; believers chosen from eternity, 21; believers chosen to

holiness, 22; general remarks on this doctrine, 23-25
Ephesians, the; their steadfastness in the faith, 73; love to the saints, 75; cause Paul to give thanks, and offer up prayers on their behalf, 76; are built into the temple of the Lord, 204; no longer walk as the Gentiles, 327
Ephesus, and the planting of a Christian church in it, xiii.
Epistle, the; its title and destination, x; its genuineness, xxxiii; its relationship to that to Colosse, xlv; its place and date of composition, xlix; its object and contents, li; works on the Epistle, liii
Epistle to the Ephesians; parties addressed, 2; its fitness to show Paul's insight into Divine truth, 215; practical portion commences, chap. iv. 266
Eternity scripturally expressed, 267
Evangelist, the office of, 302
Evil; question of its origin, 139
Exaltation of believers, 145; is for the manifestation of the Divine excellence, 147
Exaltation of Christ, the, 98-107, 295, and foll. pp.; is eternal, 103

FAINTING under tribulation forbidden, 238
Faith and holiness intimately connected, 6
Faithful, the; its twofold sense, 4-6
Farewell salutation, the, 480
"Father of glory," the, expression analyzed, 80, 81
Fathers; tenderness to their children enjoined, 443; and careful upbringing, 444
Filial duties—obedience and honour, 437; inculcated by nature, 437; and by revelation, 438
Filial piety or dutifulness co-exists with, or is generally accompanied by temporal advantages, 440
Flesh, the; its peculiar Scriptural meaning, 131
Foes, the Christian's spiritual, 458 and foll. pp.
Forgiveness of sin; meaning of phrase, 42
Forgiving spirit required, a, 360
Foundation of the Church and of individual believers, 192; its cornerstone Christ, 198
Fulness of times; meaning of this expression, 51

GENTILES, the; by Christ are fellow-heirs with the Jews, and made partakers of equal privileges, 220 and foll. pp.; their former condition described, 327-334, 379-383
Gifts, diversity of, in the Church, 279
God; riches of His mercy, 140; love to man, 141
Godhead, the; the Father, 241, 276; the Father in His relations to all, 277; "The Father of Glory," phrase analyzed, 80-82; the Son in His relation to the Father, 78, 80
Grace; sense of the word in salutation, 7; its usages in scholastic theology (*note*), 150; the source of salvation, 144, 149
Graces, Christian, inculcated, 268 and foll. pp.

HEADSHIP, Christ's universal, 105; over the Church, 321
Heaven and heavenly places, 15-18
Hierarchy, the celestial, 101-103
Humiliation of Christ, 290-296
Husband's position and duty relative to the wife, 409, 414; the measure of his love to the wife, 415, 423, 435; the reason of it, 424; and the reasonableness of it, 425

IMITATION of God, commanded, 362
Impurity of the Gentile world, 332, (*note*) 377; forbidden to Christians, 370; all such practices exclude from heaven, 377
Intemperance of the Gentile world, 395-397

JEWS despised and disliked by Gentiles (*note*), 175

LABOUR inculcated, 351
Long-suffering inculcated, 268-9
Lord, the title as applied to Christ, 9
Love of God to man; its greatness, 141
Love in the heart; the foundation necessary for comprehending the love of Christ, 249-256
Lowliness inculcated, 268

MANHOOD, Christian, 313-315; necessary for security, 316
Marriage; its reciprocal duties, 435 and foll. pp.; is applied to illustrate Christ's relation to the Church, 425-435, and specially in 428
Masters; their relative duties, 453; solemn warnings to stimulate to their right discharge, 454, 455
Meekness inculcated, 269
Members; their individual efficiency

in perfecting the Christian body, 322–326
Mosaic economy abolished, 175
Mystery ; meaning and application of the term, 49, 215 ; erroneously rendered sacrament, 432 ; of Christ, first fully revealed in apostolic times, 217, 218 ; and God's wisdom thereby manifested, 232

OFFICE-BEARERS of the Church instituted by Christ, 297 and foll. pp. ; ordinary, 303–306 ; extraordinary, 297–301 ; purpose of their institution, 307 ; period of their continuance, 309
Oneness, Christian, 272–281 ; is different from uniformity, 280

PASTOR, office of Christian, 303
Paul, his apostleship, 1 ; his bonds, 210, 480 ; his gospel ministry was according to the measure of grace and strength received, 223 ; his sphere of action, 226 ; his personal humility, 224
Peace ; sense of the word as a salutation, 7, 482 ; inculcated as a grace, 272 ; as a blessing preached by Christ, 185
Perfection, Christian, 313–317 ; is inculcated in order to security, 318
Prayer ; attitude to be assumed therein, 240 ; must be made in the Spirit, 474 ; addressed to the Father, 240 ; should embrace all saints, 475 ; and may be answered beyond our desires, 261 ; examples : Paul's for the Ephesians, 76, 243, and foll. pp.
Predestination, 31 ; is according to God's sovereign will, 33
Predestination, is for the Divine glory, 35, 61 ; is to adoption, 32 ; and to inheritance in Christ, 60
Pride, a besetting sin of ministers ; Baxter's reproof of it (note), 224
Privileges of believers ; access to the Father, 186 ; heavenly citizenship, 190 ; admission to God's household, 191 ; spiritual habitation, 205
Prophets, were such through the Spirit, 218 ; office, etc., under the Old and New Testament dispensations, 299 and foll. pp.
Psalms and hymns of the early Church, 399–404

QUICKENING with Christ ; meaning of phrase, 143–146
Quotations from Jewish Scriptures ; how made by Paul, 281 and foll. pp., 387–392

RECONCILE ; use of the verb and its cognates in New Testament (note), 181
Reconciliation of Jews and Gentiles in Christ, 178
Redemption is by blood, 40 ; the doctrine concerning it, 68–71 ; the plan thereof manifests the Divine wisdom, 232 ; was revealed according to God's eternal purpose, and was executed by Christ, 235
Regeneration in life and character ; how described, 338–347
Resurrection of Christ manifested the Divine power, the, 95
Right hand of God, the ; its signification, 99

SACRIFICE, the, of Christ, 366–369 ; is atoning, 377
Saints, primary and derivate sense of the term, 3
Salutation, the, 7
Salvation is by grace, 145–149 ; through faith, 150 ; not of ourselves, 151 ; nor of works, 153 ; is the gift of God, 153 ; boasting excluded, 154
Seal of the Spirit, the, 64–67
Sensual indulgences not to be excused, 377 ; those who practise them will experience God's wrath, 378 ; they ought to be exposed and reproved, 382
Separation between the Jewish and Gentile world done away with, 169–173 ; by abolition of the Mosaic economy, 173 ; in order to their being united in Christ, 178 ; and made one, 180 ; with equal privileges, 220–222
Slave, the ; his condition described, 445–446 ; his duties and vices, 447 ; his conduct, how influenced by Christian motives, 451
Sojourner, scriptural usage of word, 189
Song ; a service to be rendered to God, 399–405
Spirit, the Holy ; why so named ? 65–66
Spirit, the Holy ; seals believers, 66–68, 356 ; ought not to be grieved, 355 ; his work in the soul, 244–247 ; is the source of revelation, 219
Spiritual, as respects blessings, its signification, 13–15
Stranger, Scriptural usage of word, 189

TEACHER, office of Christian, 303
Temperance, duty of, 395

Temple of the Lord, believers so named, 203
Thanksgiving enjoined, 373
Theft condemned, 350
Tribulations not to be succumbed to, 238 ; but gloried in, 239
Truth, the, gospel so characterised, 63
Truth ; to be strictly practised, 347

UBIQUITY of Christ, Lutheran dogma of, 99, 115, 297
Unbelievers — spiritually dead, 117 ; children of disobedience, 129
Uncharitableness forbidden, 357
Uncircumcision, the, who thereby designated, 162
Union, the mystic, of Christ and His people ; its analogy to the human relation of marriage, 425–435
Unity of knowledge ; a future perfection of the Church, 311–312

Unity of Spirit inculcated, 272–277
Unregenerated, the ; their character and condition, 128–139

VALEDICTION, the, 482 to end.

WARFARE, the Christian's, 457 and foll. pp. ; the scene of the conflict, 462
Wife's, the, subjection to her husband, 407–413 ; the reason and manner of it, 408, 411-413 ; reverence to her husband, 436
Wisdom, Divine, manifested in the plan of redemption, 232
Word of God, the, the Christian weapon, 473
Works, good, the fruit and end of faith, not the cause of it, 157–160

# INDEX OF GREEK TERMS MORE PARTICULARLY REFERRED TO

| | | | | | |
|---|---|---|---|---|---|
| Ἀγαθωσύνη, | . . . v. 9. | | Γενεά, | . . . | iii. 5, 21. |
| ἁγιάζω, | . . . v. 26. | | γυνή, | . . . | . v. 22. |
| ἅγιος, | . i. 1, 4, 15, 18 ; iii. 5. | | δέησις, | . . . | . vi. 18. |
| ἀήρ, | . . . . ii. 2. | | δεξιᾷ, καθίζειν ἐν, | . . | . i. 20. |
| ἄθεος, | . . . . ii. 12. | | διαθήκη, | . . . | . ii. 12. |
| αἰσχρότης, | . . . . v. 4. | | διακονία, | . . . | . iv. 12. |
| αἰχμαλωσία, | . . . . iv. 8. | | διάκονος, | . . . | . iii. 7. |
| αἰχμαλωτεύω, | . . . . iv. 8. | | διάνοια, | . . . | . ii. 3. |
| αἰών, | . i. 22 ; ii. 2, 7 ; iii. 21. | | διδάσκαλος, | . . . | . iv. 11. |
| ἀκαθαρσία, | . . iv. 19 ; v. 3. | | δίδωμι, | . . . | . iv. 8. |
| ἄκαρπος, | . . . . v. 11. | | δικαιοσύνη, | . . | iv. 24; v. 9. |
| ἀκούω, | . . . . i. 15. | | διὸ λέγει, | . . | . v. 14. |
| ἀκροβυστία, | . . . . ii. 11. | | δόγμα, | . . . | . ii. 15. |
| ἀκρογωνιαῖος, | . . . . ii. 20. | | δόμα, | . . | . iv. 8. |
| ἀλλά, | . . . . v. 24. | | δόξα, | . . . | . i. 17. |
| ἁμαρτία, | . . . . ii. 1. | | δύναμις, | . . | . i. 21. |
| ἄμωμος, | . . . . i. 4. | | Ἐγγύς, | . . | . ii. 13, 17. |
| ἀνακεφαλαιόω, | . . . . i. 10. | | εἴγε, | . . | iii. 2; iv. 21 |
| ἀναλαμβάνω, | . . . vi. 13. | | εἰρήνη, | . . | i. 2; ii. 14, 17. |
| ἀνανεόω, | . . . . iv. 23. | | ἐκλέγω, | . . . | . i. 4. |
| ἀναστροφή, | . . . . iv. 22. | | ἐκκλησία, | . . . | . i. 22. |
| ἀνέχομαι, | . . . . iv. 2. | | ἐκτρέφω, | . . . | . v. 29. |
| ἀνήρ, | . . . . v. 22. | | ἐλαχιστότερος, | . . | . iii. 8. |
| ἀνθρωπάρεσκος, | . . . . vi. 6. | | ἥλιος, | . . | . ii. 4. |
| ἀπαλλοτριόω, | . . ii. 12; iv. 1. | | ἐλπίς, | . | . i. 18; ii. 12. |
| ἀπείθεια, | . . . . ii. 2. | | ἐνδείκνυμι, | . . . | . ii. 7. |
| ἀπειλή, | . . . . vi. 9. | | ἐνδυναμόω, | . . . | . vi. 10. |
| ἁπλότης, | . . . . vi. 5. | | ἐνέργεια, | . . . | . i. 20. |
| ἀποκάλυψις, | . . i. 17 ; iii. 3. | | ἐντολή, | . . . | . ii. 15. |
| ἀποκαταλλάσσω, | . . . . ii. 16. | | ἐξαγοράζω, | . . . | . v. 16. |
| ἀπολύτρωσις, | . . . i. 7, 14. | | ἐξουσία, | . . | . i. 21; ii. 2. |
| ἀποτίθημι, | . . . . iv. 22. | | ἐπαγγελία, | . . . | . ii. 12. |
| ἀπόστολος, | . . . i. 1; iv. 11. | | ἐπίγνωσις, | . . | . i. 17; iv. 13. |
| ἀρραβών, | . . . . i. 14. | | ἐπιθυμία, | . . | . ii. 3; iv. 22. |
| ἀρχή, | . . . . i. 21. | | ἐπιφαύω, | . . . | . v. 14. |
| ἀσέλγεια, | . . . . iv. 19. | | ἐπιχορηγία, | . . . | . iv. 16. |
| ἀσωτία, | . . . . v. 18. | | ἐπουράνιος, | . i. 3, 20 ; ii. 6; vi. 12. |
| ἄφεσις, | . . . . i. 7. | | ἐργασία, | . . . | . iv. 19. |
| ἀφθαρσία, | . . . . vi. 24. | | ἔσω ἄνθρωπος, ὁ, | . . | . iii. 16. |
| ἄφρων, | . . . . v. 17. | | ἑτοιμασία, | . . . | . vi. 15. |
| Βέλος, πεπυρωμένον, | . . . vi. 16. | | εὐαγγελιστής, | . . . | . iv. 11. |
| βλασφημία, | . . . . iv. 31. | | εὐάρεστος, | . . . | . v. 11. |
| βουλή, | . . . . i. 11. | | εὐδοκία, | . . . | i. 5, 10. |

| | | |
|---|---|---|
| εὐλογητός, | . . . . i. 3. | Ξίνος, . . . . ii. 12, 19. |
| εὔσπλαγχνος, | . . . iv. 32. | Οἰκεῖος, . . . . . ii. 20. |
| εὐτραπιλία, | . . . . v. 4. | οἰκοδομή, . . . ii. 21; iv. 12. |
| εὐχαριστέω, | . . . . i. 16. | οἰκονομία, . . . i. 10; iii. 2. |
| εὐχαριστία, | . . . . v. 4. | ὄνομα τοῦ Κυρίου, . . v. 20. |
| ἔχθρα, | . . . . ii. 15, 16. | ὀργή, . . . . ii. 3; iv. 31. |
| Ἡλικία, | . . . . iv. 13. | ὀργίζω, . . . . . iv. 26. |
| Θάλπω, | . . . . v. 29. | ὁσιότης, . . . . . iv. 24. |
| θέλημα, | . . . . i. 11. | ὀσμὴ εὐωδίας, . . . . v. 2. |
| θεμέλιος, | . . ii. 20; iii. 18. | ὅστις, . . . . . i. 23. |
| θυμός, | . . . . iv. 31. | οὐρανοῖς, τὰ ἐν τοῖς, . i. 10; iv. 10. |
| θυρεόν, | . . . . vi. 16. | ὀφθαλμοδουλεία, . . . . vi. 6. |
| θυσία, | . . . . v. 2. | Παιδεία, . . . . vi. 4. |
| θώραξ, | . . . . vi. 15. | πανοπλία, . . . . vi. 11. |
| Ἵνα, | . . . . i. 17. | πανουργία, . . . . iv. 14. |
| ἰσχύς, | . . . . i. 20. | παράπτωμα, . . . i. 7; ii. 1. |
| Καθίζω, | . . . . i. 20. | πάροικος, . . . . ii. 19. |
| καθώς, | . . . . i. 4. | παροργίζω, . . iv. 26; vi. 4. |
| καί and μετά, | . . . vi. 23. | παροργισμός, . . . . iv. 26. |
| καινός, | . . . . iv. 24. | παῤῥησία, . . . . iii. 12. |
| καιρός, | . . i. 10; ii. 12; v. 16. | πᾶς, . . . . . ii. 21. |
| κακία, | . . . . iv. 31. | Πατὴρ τῆς δόξης, . . . i. 17. |
| κάμπτω, | . . . . iii. 14. | πατριά, . . . . iii. 15. |
| καταβολή, | . . . . i. 4. | πιστοίδησις, . . . . iii. 12. |
| καταλαμβάνομαι, | . . . iii. 18. | περί and ὑπέρ, . . . . vi. 19. |
| καταντάω, | . . . . iv. 13. | περικεφαλαία, . . . . vi. 17. |
| καταρτισμός, | . . . . iv. 12. | περιπατέω, . . . ii. 2, 10. |
| κατοικητήριον, | . . ii. 22; iii. 17. | περιποίησις, . . . . i. 14. |
| κατώτερα τῆς γῆς, τὰ, | . . iv. 9. | περισσύω, . . . . i. 8. |
| κληρονομία, | . . . . i. 18. | πικρία, . . . . . iv. 31. |
| κληρόω, | . . . . i. 11. | πιστός, . . . . . i. 1. |
| κλῆσις, | . . i. 18; iv. 2. | πλεονεξία, . . . iv. 19; v. 3. |
| κλυδωνίζομαι, | . . . . iv. 14. | πληρόω, . . . i. 23; iv. 10. |
| κόσμος, | . . . . ii. 13. | πλήρωμα, . . . . i. 10, 23. |
| κοσμοκράτωρ, | . . . . vi. 12. | πλοῦτος, . . . i. 7, 18; iii. 8. |
| κράτος, | . . . . i. 20. | πνεῦμα, . . i. 17; ii. 2, 18; iii. 5. |
| κραταιόω, | . . . . iii. 16. | πνεῦμα τοῦ νοός, . . . iv. 23. |
| κραυγή, | . . . . iv. 31. | πνευματικός, . . . . i. 3. |
| κρυφῇ, | . . . . v. 12. | πνευματικόν, τὸ, . . . vi. 12. |
| κτίζω, | . . ii. 10; iii. 9. | ποιμήν, . . . . . iv. 11. |
| κυβεία, | . . . . iv. 14. | πολιτεία, . . . . ii. 12. |
| κύριος, | . . . . i. 2, 15. | πολυποίκιλος, . . . . iii. 10. |
| κυριότης, | . . . . i. 21. | πραΰτης, . . . . . iv. 2. |
| Λόγος, | . . . . vi. 19. | προετοιμάζω, . . . . ii. 10. |
| Μακράν, | . . . ii. 13, 17. | προορίζω, . . . . . i. 5. |
| μακροθυμία, | . . . . iv. 2. | προσαγωγή, . . . ii. 18; iii. 12. |
| μᾶλλον δὲ καί, | . . . . v. 11. | προσευχή, . . . . . vi. 18. |
| μεθοδεία, | . . . . iv. 14. | προσφορά, . . . . . v. 2. |
| μεθύσκω, | . . . . v. 18. | προσωποληψία, . . . . vi. 19. |
| μέν, | . . . . iv. 11. | προφήτης, . . ii. 20; iii. 5; iv. 11. |
| μετά and καί, | . . . . vi. 23. | πώρωσις, . . . . . iv. 18. |
| μεσότοιχον, | . . . . ii. 14. | Ῥυτίς, . . . . . v. 27. |
| μέχρι, | . . . . iv. 13. | Σαπρός, . . . . . iv. 29. |
| μηκέτι, | . . . . iv. 17. | σάρξ, . . ii. 3, 11, 15; v. 29. |
| μιμητής, | . . . . v. 1. | σοφία, . . . . i. 8, 17. |
| μυστήριον, i. 9; iii. 3, 4; v. 32; vi. 19. | | σπίλος, . . . . . v. 27. |
| μωρολογία, | . . . . v. 4. | στῆναι πρός, . . . . vi. 11. |
| Ναός, | . . . . ii. 21. | συζωοποιέω, . . . . ii. 5. |
| νεκρός, | . . . . ii. 1. | συμβιβάζω, . . . . iv. 16. |
| νόμος, | . . . . ii. 15. | συμπολίτης or συνπολίτης, . . ii. 19. |
| νουθεσία, | . . . . vi. 4. | σύνεσις, . . . . . iii. 4. |
| νοῦς, | . . . . iv. 17. | Ταπεινοφροσύνη, . . . iv. 2. |

# INDEX

| | | | |
|---|---|---|---|
| τέλειος, | . iv. 13. | φωτίζω, | .i. 18; iii. 9. |
| Υἱοθεσία, | . i. 5. | Χάρις, | . i. 2, 6; ii. 7, 8. |
| ὕμνος, | . v. 19. | χαρίζομαι, | . iv. 32. |
| ὑπέρ and περί, | . vi. 19. | χαριτόω, | . i. 6. |
| ὑπεράνω, | i. 21; iii. 20; iv. 10. | χρηστός, | . iv. 32. |
| ὑπερβάλλον, | i. 19; ii. 7; iii. 20. | χρηστότης, | . ii. 7. |
| Φανεροῦμαι, | . v. 13. | χωρίς, | . ii. 12. |
| φραγμός, | . ii. 14. | Ψάλλω, | . v. 19. |
| φρόνησις, | . i. 8. | ψαλμός, | . v. 19. |
| φύσις, | . ii. 3. | Ὠιδή, | . v. 19. |

www.ingramcontent.com/pod-product-compliance
Lightning Source LLC
Chambersburg PA
CBHW052012040526
R18239600001BA/R182396PG44108CBX00003BA/5